MW00812608

ENDORSEMENTS

"I have invited Jack to Hawaii several times to speak at our 'How To Walk' conferences and he is always one of the best received presenters. His down-to-earth communication skill's have been transferred to 'The Jesus Chronicles.' An excellent resource for the bible student or to simply curl up with a good book about Jesus on a rainy day."

—Bill Stonebraker
Senior Pastor, Calvary Chapel
Honolulu

"Jack Abeelen's book, *The Jesus Chronicles*, was a real blessing for me to read, and I know it will bless many others. Jack is a great story teller and he tells the story of Jesus with clarity, practical application, and good scholarship, while at the same time communicating with a warmth and comfort that gives the reader an up close and intimate personal contact with Jesus. You can open this book to any page, read for a few, and get to know Jesus a little bit better. I highly recommend this book, as a study resource, or as a devotional tool. You will pick it up again and again."

—Dave Rolph
Senior Pastor, Calvary Chapel Pacific Hills
Radio Bible Teacher, The Balanced Word
General Editor, The Word for Today Bible

"Jack Abeelen shares the love of Jesus Christ in such a way that we get in touch with that One who lived here among us. We can walk with Jesus, watch Him, listen to Him, and reflect on Him. Jack Abeelen takes us on an insightful journey into the greatest life that has ever been lived. He helps us to know Jesus better."

—Carl Westerlund
Assistant pastor, Calvary Chapel of Costa Mesa
Director, Calvary Chapel School of Ministry
Director, Calvary Chapel Bible College Graduate School

"Frankly I was pleasantly surprised with this new book, *The Jesus Chronicles*. It's a fresh look at an age-old dilemma—the chronological layout of the gospel record—but this one is far different than most other tomes. Jack Abeelen doesn't merely harmonize the synoptic accounts and John's gospel to tell the story. He follows the flow of Jesus ministry applicationally, not just chronologically. I love books on the life of Jesus and I have loved seeing Jesus through Jack's clear eyes and ready pen."

—Skip Heitzig
Pastor, Calvary Chapel
Albuquerque, New Mexico

"As you read this book, you will understand why Jack Abeelen is highly sought as a conference speaker and why his congregation is so loyal. At the same time, your understanding of Scripture grows immensely."

—Gayle D. Erwin

"Jack Abeelen is a faithful expositor of God's Word. In this book he provides keen insights into the life and ministry of our Lord and Savior. It will serve as a great guide for those who are wanting to know Jesus better, and as a helpful resource for others who choose to teach God's Word."

—Greg Laurie
Pastor of Harvest Ministries

THE JESUS CHRONICLES

A CHRONOLOGICAL STUDY THROUGH THE GOSPELS

JACK ABEELEN

WinePress **WP** Publishing™

WinePress Publishing (PO Box 428, Enumclaw, WA 98022) functions only as book publisher. As such, the ultimate design, content, editorial accuracy, and views expressed or implied in this work are those of the author.

Unless otherwise indicated, all Scriptures are taken from the Scofield Study Bible, *New King James Version*. C.I. Scofield, D.D. New York: Oxford University Press, Inc, 2002.

ISBN 13: 978-1-57921-988-8
ISBN 10: 1-57921-988-8
Library of Congress Catalog Card Number: 2008935250

Printed in China.

APC-FT6681

And truly Jesus did many other signs in the presence of His disciples, which are not written in this book; but these are written that you may believe that Jesus is the Christ, the Son of God, and that believing you may have life in His name.

—John 20:30–31

And there are also many other things that Jesus did, which if they were written one by one, I suppose that even the world itself could not contain the books that would be written. Amen.

—John 21:25

I dedicate this book to the saints at Morningstar Christian Chapel who allow me the opportunity to study and teach them the marvelous truths of God's Word several times each week. They are a supportive and loving fellowship of which I am blessed to be a part. And most especially I dedicate this work to my wife and best friend, Debbie, without whom I would scarcely be the man I have become. God knew what I needed and He gave me all and more in her. She is God's greatest gift to me next to His Son Jesus.

CONTENTS

Section IV: The Final Week of Ministry

ACKNOWLEDGMENTS

I must express my utmost gratitude and appreciation to the work of Nikki Smith, who while attending our services received a vision from the Lord in her heart to have these studies edited and published for others. Without her transcriptions, rewrites, editing, and tireless dedication to share God's Word, this never would have become a reality.

Additionally, the weekly proofreading by my wife, Debbie, and our secretary Mrs. Brenda Woodard, and the prayerfulness of our staff and support of the publishers at WinePress must not go unnoticed. God is faithful and so were these whom He used so mightily.

Finally, to those I have looked up to and who have meant so much to my own spiritual growth in Christ: Pastor Chuck Smith and Calvary Chapel, where I grew to know the Lord well and heard God call me into ministry. To the excellent teaching of Pastor John McArthur from whom I learned God's Word was enough, and the awesome studies by Kent Hughes that have shaped my view of Scripture and love for Jesus as few others could. May I be allowed to affect others to some degree the way these men have touched my life, ministry and walk with our Lord.

Book Style

Because these studies were first taught as sermons and transcribed from them, the style is such that from time to time, verses that were spoken were paraphrased, though many are referenced in the written manuscript. We have chosen to leave those paraphrased references in the text, however, as they maintain the flavor of the sermon given. Each chapter represents one sermon with the intention of studying through the Gospels chronologically and focusing on the public ministry Jesus undertook as He came to save us from our sins. In reading, you might feel you are listening in on a sermon rather than reading a manuscript someone sat down to write, and you would be right. May God bless you as you study and meditate upon His wonderful word and especially here through the Gospels as we focus on Jesus our Lord.

INTRODUCTION: JESUS OF NAZARETH

Luke 2:39–52

So when they had performed all things according to the law of the Lord, they returned to Galilee, to their own city, Nazareth.

—Luke 2:39

B ecause Luke's focus is on Jesus as the Son of Man, he deals with His humanity more than any of the other Gospel writers. It is Luke who tells us the most about the circumstances of Jesus' birth, Luke who takes us with Mary and Joseph to His dedication, and Luke who records both Anna's and Simeon's prophecies over Him.

Following His dedication, Mary and Joseph stayed in Bethlehem. It was there months later that the wise men found Him. But before a crazed Herod sought to eliminate the competition for the throne by ordering the death of every boy in that area two years of age and under, the Lord had spoken to Joseph in a dream, telling him to take his family to Egypt. Joseph and Mary obediently headed south, even as the prophet Hosea had written so many years earlier that from Egypt the Lord would call forth His Son (Hosea 11:1).

According to Matthew 2, after Herod's death, Mary and Joseph returned to Israel and had plans to stay in Bethlehem, but Herod's son, Archelaus, the tetrarch of the area, was even more wicked than his father. So Joseph and Mary went to Nazareth, where Jesus would grow up.

The thirty years that preceded Jesus' public ministry—which would last but three-and-a-half years—are covered in these last few verses of Luke 2. This is the only place where we read of Jesus' early years, His upbringing, growth, insights and disposition before He came upon the scene publicly. Although there are numerous extra-biblical writings and apocryphal gospels that tell us fanciful stories of the boy Jesus, they are just that, fanciful, not biblical. In John 2, we are told that Jesus' first miracle was at a wedding in Cana. So we'll stick with the Bible's account and not some stories of men.

Joseph's absence in the Gospel record following his return from Egypt suggests that he died at some point before the beginning of Jesus' public ministry. If this is so, Jesus, as the oldest son, would have had to assume full responsibility for the family, run the family business, pay the bills, take care of His mother and siblings, providing for them all. But, as Luke writes, His formative years prepared Him for this:

> And the Child grew and became strong in spirit, filled with wisdom; and the grace of God was upon Him. His parents went to Jerusalem every year at the Feast of the Passover.
>
> —Luke 2:40–41

All good parents take great interest in their children's development: how tall they have grown already, how quickly they learned the alphabet or how far they can throw a baseball. Yet God's assessment of His Son focuses primarily on His spiritual growth—in God's wisdom, by His Spirit, and how even now God's grace was upon His young life. He grew up in a godly home with parents who respected God's Law—and it showed.

How important a responsibility for us parents to place the greatest priority on the spiritual well-being of our children. Many years earlier in the Bible we are given the story of Eli, the high priest, who never taught his sons the Lord's ways (1 Sam. 2–3). "Why don't you speak to your kids? Why don't you tell them that what they're doing is wrong? They're turning people from Me," the Lord asked of Eli. But Eli continued to ignore his responsibility as a father and one day the Lord took from him his place as high priest, in judgment for rarely having confronted his son's wickedness and rebellion. Yet in the interim, his sons were allowed to continue in their sinful ways working in the tabernacle and stumbling many who came to seek and worship God there.

David was another godly man who unfortunately was not a very good father. We read in 1 Kings that he had never "displeased his son" by saying at any time in his life, "What are you doing?" As a parent, I remember that being one of my favorite phrases with the kids! But not David. He didn't so much as challenge his son in all of his son's decisions and ways as he was growing up.

Indeed whatever our children's accomplishments might be in this life (run faster, jump higher, get the best grades . . .) they pale in comparison to who rules in their lives. If they know the Lord, they will be fine; if not, the greatest worldly achievements won't keep them. So we read that Jesus grew up in a home filled with spiritual wisdom and God's grace at work.

> And when He was twelve years old, they went up to Jerusalem according to the custom of the feast.
>
> —Luke 2:42

According to the Mishna, the written interpretation of the Law, at thirteen years of age a child was considered a full member of the synagogue. But the Mishna also taught that a father should bring his son to the synagogue several years earlier so he would become accustomed to the practice and learn the reason for his coming.

We see Jesus here at twelve years of age coming to Jerusalem with Joseph and Mary, along with several hundred thousand others to gather in the city together in obedience to the Law. Some would go to the sheep gate to buy a sacrificial lamb. At the temple all twenty-four courses of the priesthood would be at work that week because of the crowds and the busyness. Jesus would have watched Joseph slay the lamb and bring it to the priest, where the blood was poured out. Then the lamb would have been prepared and brought back to the place the family was staying, where it would have been eaten together in celebration of Passover.

The question asked at dinner would have been, "Why is this night so unique?" And Joseph would have explained to his family how the Lord had brought His people out of Egypt after that final plague of the slaying of the firstborn. Of how God had passed over the homes where the blood of the Lamb had been applied to the door and how they ate that first Passover prepared to leave Egypt and follow the Lord. Here in Jerusalem, the people would have flooded into the streets and, for a week, sang and had great fellowship together for a time of rejoicing over God's provision for them. At age twelve, with the next year being the year He would assume the responsibility Himself, Jesus spent time learning the customs of the feast and worshipping with His family.

> When they had finished the days, as they returned, the Boy Jesus lingered behind in Jerusalem. And Joseph and His mother did not know it; but supposing Him to have been in the company, they went a day's journey, and sought Him among their relatives and acquaintances. So when they did not find Him, they returned to Jerusalem, seeking Him.
>
> —Luke 2:43–45

Lest you think Joseph and Mary were negligent parents, the trip from Jerusalem and the feasts back to the outlying lands in Israel were usually made in caravans, both for safety and fellowship. Entire cities often came and returned together. If they had traveled from the north, they had to pass through antagonistic Samaria on back roads frequented by robbers. Oftentimes the women were sent ahead with guards while the men followed closely behind as added security.

Jesus could have been at the front, at the back, with an uncle, or with friends from down the street that first day of travel. But when everyone stopped for the night, He was nowhere to be found. A day's travel away, and Jesus only twelve years old—you can only imagine Mary and Joseph's worry. He was a twelve-year-old boy who could have been in trouble just about anywhere. So they spent a sleepless night trying to return to Jerusalem, risking the roads and the evening travel, the isolation and the fear, driven no doubt by guilt and fear. It wouldn't be until the third day that they found Him.

> Now so it was that after three days they found him in the temple, sitting in the midst of the teachers, both listening to them and asking him questions. And all who heard him were astonished at His understanding and answers.
>
> —Luke 2:46–47

Did Jesus sin by not returning with His parents? Of course not—the Bible declares He never sinned. But He was absorbed in His learning, in His development and spiritual insight. What a revelation it must have been for Him to realize who He was and God's plan for Him. Because Jesus was fully human, He had to grow. He could have been the wise Child who, at three years old, knew everything. But the Bible says otherwise. He grew in faith.

Scouring the city, retracing their steps, Mary and Joseph (in panic mode I suspect) finally turned the corner at the temple—and there He was. That both Mary and Joseph found Jesus in the temple meant He must have been in the outer porticos because, as a woman, Mary could not have come into the temple areas where men alone could go. They found a twelve-year-old Jesus sitting with a group of men who were older and wiser in the Lord. But Jesus was the One leaving a lasting impression. The questions He asked, the insights He shared, and the zeal He demonstrated amazed these scholars.

Paul would later write to Timothy, "Don't let anyone despise your youth. Be a witness and an example of the believer" (1 Tim. 4:12). Here Jesus as a young man was doing just that. Eighteen years from now, some of these same men would be involved with the plots to kill Him, but for now they sat here amazed by Him.

> So when they saw Him, they were amazed; and His mother said to Him, "Son, why have You done this to us? Look, Your father and I have sought You anxiously."
>
> —Luke 2:48

This seems like a controlled rebuke to me: "You've caused us some anxiety." I would think so! If it were me, I would have said, "Three days. I haven't slept a wink. Look at the bags under my eyes!" But not Mary. She was calm and relieved.

> And He said to them, "Why did you seek Me? Did you not know that I must be about My Father's business?" But they did not understand the statement which He spoke to them.
>
> —Luke 2:49–50

What insight into God's purposes and knowledge Jesus had! At such a young age, who He was and what He had come to do was already beginning to make sense to Him. "I've got to be serving My Father," He said.

> Then He went down with them and came to Nazareth, and was subject to them, but His mother kept all these things in her heart. And Jesus increased in wisdom and stature, and in favor with God and men.
>
> —Luke 2:51–52

What does a twelve-year-old who is "about His Father's business" do? Jesus went home. He took direction from His parents, being subject to them until the Father would tell Him it was time to make Himself known.

The word *wisdom* here speaks of spiritual insight. The word *stature* of physical development. Jesus continued to get stronger and wiser, to grow up and to know God, to become a man in stature and in wisdom.

Jesus grew in the things of God. Unfortunately some Christians never grow up. They get older, but no wiser. Paul wrote to the Corinthians in his first epistle to them in chapter 3: "I want to talk to you like spiritual men, but I can't. You're still babies." The writer to the Hebrews said in chapter 3 that when the time had come that they should now be able to teach others, they would instead have to be re-taught the first things of God.

Jesus continued to grow. He grew in favor with God as His spiritual habits and practice, and understanding of His ways continued to develop. And he continued to grow in His relationship with people, with whom He found favor. As Christians, we too should be drawing nearer to the Lord in our walks and then finding favor with others. The Gospel will offend people—but we should not. There ought to be no better friend than a Christian and no better employee or businessman than a believer. If you bought a table from Jesus, it would have been good—or He would have fixed it.

We aren't told anything further regarding the next eighteen years of Jesus' life except for what we find in these few verses. But they are sufficient for what God would have us to know. Growing up in a godly home, developing godly habits, having an ever-growing understanding of His calling and purpose, growing in favor with God and man, these silent years speak volumes of how God prepares us for what He has prepared for us.

I've heard it said that much of life are dull years interspersed with moments of great anxiety. But look at Jesus. He essentially went home, went to work, mowed the lawn, and shopped for birthday gifts. Waste of time? No. He was growing in favor with God and man. The ordinary and the mundane were not a waste of time but a useful season to prepare for what would come later. Thirty years of silence for little more than three years of public ministry—almost a 10:1 ratio.

Preparation for anything good always takes a lot of time. So God is at work preparing us for what lies ahead. All we have to do is be faithful each day and He will ready us. In fact, much of our lives—the Monday through Friday, the eight to five, the going to work again, the doing the same thing again, the meeting with the same people again—will indeed become a place of growing in favor with God and others as we approach each part heartily serving the Lord.

Many people complain about the routine-ness of life, but if you go through the Bible and look at those God used, invariably you find them spending years in relative anonymity where they proved their faithfulness and discovered His, followed by a time in the place of what we might call "real" accomplishment. John the Baptist spent years in the desert.

Paul was in Arabia before the Lord brought him forth. David was a shepherd without even a family to support him for years—and spent seven more years on the run and living in caves—before he was made king. Yet all of that prepared him for what God was going to do with him.

For these eighteen years, Jesus was faithful at home, for that too fell under the category of being about His Father's business.

It's both a matter of the heart and a matter of diligence. Make sure everyone at your job knows you're a Christian and that the Gospel can be found with you. If they have questions, be certain they know you have answers.

Be a faithful light right where you are. You say, "But I want to go to the mission field in Africa." Try going to work first—then tackle Africa. God will get you there in His time.

Jesus was called "Jesus of Nazareth," but that denoted far more than simply being a reference to His hometown. It speaks to me of the character He developed there. It is in Nazareth that we see Him hunger for the things of God with the spirit of grace upon His life. It is in Nazareth that we see the daily development that seems to take so long but without which one never can go forward—it is in obscurity that we rise to prominence as God prepares us in the silent and not so silent years. What is God preparing you for?

SECTION I

THE FIRST YEAR

Chapter 1

HANDLING TEMPTATION

Luke 4:1–13
(Matthew 4:1–11; Mark 1:12–13)

Jesus' public ministry began with His baptism. He traveled from Nazareth to the Jordan River in the south where, for the first time in their national history, Jews were being baptized. John the Baptist was baptizing Jewish men and women who confessed they were sinful and acknowledged they needed a Savior, a Messiah; the One John assured them was soon to come. Then one day, down by the river, Jesus came to be baptized to identify with us in our sin and need. John was hesitant but obedient, and as Jesus went into the water, God's voice thundered from heaven:

"This is My beloved Son in whom I am well pleased. Hear Him."

Jesus' baptism—a picture of His own death, burial, and resurrection—and ours in Him (Rom. 6) was His introduction to the world publicly. He would die for our sins. We would be redeemed by the price He would pay for us. So it is no small wonder that on the heels of His baptism and identification that the Devil came against Him with all his might. Luke 4:1 begins with the word *then*, which attaches this confrontation directly to Jesus' baptism, the preceding event. After being filled with the Spirit and declared to be the Son of God, Jesus is immediately driven into the wilderness by the Father's will to be tested of the Devil.

Jesus' temptation may cause us to wonder if the Son of God could have sinned. I believe the answer is an emphatic no. He was however, fully tested in every way as you and I are—and He relied upon the Holy Spirit and the Word of God to see Him through as an example to us of what we are to do when tempted. Will we fail? Yes of course. But the key for us is to recognize where our help lies and to know we have a Lord who's been there, who's heard the temptations, and who has had to deal with the enemy coming at Him full force. We have a Savior who knows what we're going through. And He offers the same solution to us that He used when He Himself was tempted. So we read:

> Then Jesus, being filled with the Holy Spirit, returned from the Jordan and was led by the Spirit into the wilderness, being tempted for forty days by the Devil.
> —Luke 4:1–2

I think sometimes we entertain the mistaken idea that if we are truly walking with God, life will get easier. Notice here however that the Spirit of God led Jesus into the wilderness.

1

In other words, He was right where His Father wanted Him to be, here in the desolation facing these trials. The promise of some that coming to Jesus will make life easier is not a biblical truth. Life in some respects was easier when I was totally unaware of my sin or the battle that raged. Yet the end of that road without Him is too horrible to even consider. Being in God's will does not assure us a bed of roses. Jesus warned, "In the world you'll have tribulation, but be of good cheer. I have overcome the world" (John 16:33). There will be trials in this world as we seek to walk with our Lord, but He assures us that in Him we will overcome them all. Yet though we are promised victory, walking with Jesus in this world will mean having to walk a difficult road. We read here that the enemy didn't let up and Jesus was tempted throughout the entire forty days. Our Lord as our example shows us how we must learn through our trials that God's Word and ways are to be trusted.

In 2 Kings 14 and 2 Chronicles 25 we have the story of a young king named Amaziah, a man the Lord introduces as a good king but one who didn't follow Him with his whole heart. When the Edomites came to fight against him, he hired a group of mercenaries to aid him in the fight. God spoke to him at that time telling him he wouldn't be needing them, to send them away for God would give him victory. Instead of rejoicing he argued with God that he had spent a great deal of money that now would be lost. God's response was that it was far "Better you lose the money than lose My help."

Amaziah reluctantly obeyed and God did help as the Edomites were wiped out. Yet Amaziah hardly learned a lesson that day. Rather than worshipping God for all He had done, Amaziah took the idols from the Edomites and set them up in mockery for himself, concluding he had plenty of reasons to be self-confident. He didn't grow spiritually through his trial; instead, his flesh became stronger.

To the north of Judah in Israel was Jehoash, a wicked king indeed. Amaziah decided it was a good time to pick a fight with him thinking *I've taken care of one enemy. I guess I can take care of another.* So he wrote Jehoash a brazen letter containing warnings and threats.

Jehoash wrote back to this young king and said, "You have had one victory. Enjoy it! But don't come messing with me or you will find yourself meddling to your own hurt."

It's hard to teach humility to a young guy who's just had a great victory and even more difficult when that same young man has lost sight of who gave him the victory. Amaziah ignored the counsel of Jehoash and headed north with his army. Jehoash was prepared and came forth, crossing quickly into Judah's territory and the battle took place on Amaziah's turf in a place called Bethshemesh. By the time the fighting was over, Judah had been soundly defeated. Amaziah was captured, hundreds of feet of the wall around Jerusalem had been torn down, many had been carried away and killed, and treasures had been stolen from the city treasury.

What a phrase to remember, "meddling to our own hurt"! It is certainly what we will do if we forget that we need God's help to stand. Amaziah didn't see it that way and learned the hard way. We can't stand against the Devil in our own strength. Yet God will give us victory as we look to Him. When we were born-again, we quickly became aware of the spiritual battle we faced, but also of the solution we have in Jesus Christ.

> And in those days He ate nothing, and afterward, when they had ended, He was hungry.
>
> —Luke 4:2

After thirty years of preparation and immediately following His public introduction at His baptism, Jesus spent nearly six weeks in the wilderness fasting, praying and waiting upon His Father. I am sure He looked ahead to His public ministry: the ridicule, the threats, the disciples, the cross, the resurrection, and the salvation He would provide as He laid down His life for us.

We read here that after a prolonged period of fasting Jesus became hungry once again. When fasting it usually takes about a week to lose your appetite. Yet when it returns you have to eat because at that point your body is starving. So Jesus came to that point of starving and the enemy sought to capitalize on His weakness and come against Him with three demonic temptations.

John wrote in 1 John 2:15–16, "Do not love the world or the things in the world. If anyone loves the world, the love of the Father is not in him. For all that is in the world: the lust of the flesh, the lust of the eyes, and the pride of life is not of the Father but is of the world." Satan's temptations of Jesus fell into these same three categories: lust of the flesh, lust of the eyes and pride of life.

As you read the accounts of Jesus' temptations in the wilderness in Matthew, Mark, and Luke, you quickly conclude that they came to Jesus as they would come to us: attacks from within. There wasn't some red-tailed, pitchfork-holding Devil saying, "All right, Jesus, we're going to have a battle." No, the trials Jesus faced were the same ones we would. The Devil doesn't pop up, but he does pop in—whispering in our ears, making suggestions, and trying to convince us to walk another way or follow another path. I suspect that all of these temptations were not external in nature but internal—the same way we face the enemy.

> And the Devil said to Him, "If You are the Son of God, command this stone to become bread." But Jesus answered him, saying, "It is written, 'Man shall not live by bread alone, but by every word of God.'"
>
> —Luke 4:3–4

The word *if* here is in the subjunctive mood in Greek, which makes this a statement of fact. In other words, you could translate the word *if* as *since*. The Devil did not doubt that Jesus was the Son of God. His first temptation required Him to be God so: "Since You are the Son of God, use Your power and make Yourself a sandwich." Because Jesus is now starving, the temptation is very real and this would only be a temptation if you could do that. If you told me to turn rocks into bread, that wouldn't be much of a temptation for me, because I am unable to do so. Jesus, on the other hand, could have used His power as the Son of God to make a deli sandwich out of a boulder. He had the ability. He had the need. Why is this a temptation?

A couple of things to think about. First, Jesus was led by the Spirit into the wilderness and the will of the Father had brought Him there. But what the Father hadn't seen fit to do yet was feed Him, direct Him to leave, or tell Him to use His power to become a chef. If the Father wanted to send manna from heaven, fine. But if not, Jesus would wait for His direction rather than follow the counsel of the Devil. Jesus' words to the Devil focused on the eternal benefit of knowing and following God's word and its value over temporary pursuits apart from God.

Jesus would later speak to a large group of people who had run around the Sea of Galilee to get to where Jesus would land, because He had fed them previously in the wilderness. "You shouldn't put so much effort into getting food that perishes," He told them. "You should seek food that leads to everlasting life" (John 6:27). Seek the eternal over the temporal.

Additionally, there is the Father's will to be considered. If you're going to serve the Lord and walk with God, the Father's will must be most important to you, for it will keep you from being tempted by the enemy through the lust of the flesh.

How often does the enemy move us on fleshy terms. Skip church. Work overtime. Get that raise. Get the applause. Get the recognition. It all sounds so reasonable. Appeals to our flesh and additionally, temptations in areas of our abilities. For example, you might have the gift of charm where winning people to you is easy and effortless. You can either use that as an opportunity to meet people and share the Gospel and God's love with them—or you can use that gift for yourself to get only what you want.

If you have a great job with tremendous income, you have the privilege to invest in those things that bring God glory, or you can use them to satisfy your temporal desires. One is the Lord's direction, the other comes from the enemy to fulfill the lust of your flesh. If you have a great mind, you can surrender it to the Lord and use your intelligence and insight to communicate that which God has taught—or you can use that mind to seek to lord over others and selfishly serve yourself. In whatever place you find yourself, the grim fact of temptation is that it often hits where you are the strongest and suggests you use what God has given you to serve yourself rather than Him.

It was that approach the serpent took with Eve in the garden. God is holding out, look how beautiful the fruit, eat it and you will be like God. And Eve bought his lies, ate the fruit her eye was attracted to, and died because the lust of her flesh overwhelmed the promises of God.

"Did God really say you can't eat of that tree?" he asked.

"Yes," she answered. "He said we'll die."

"You won't die," the Devil said. "God just doesn't want you to be as smart as He is. Go ahead and eat. You'll be able to know good and evil. It will be great."

I have learned that if God says no, it's because it's not good for you. To circumvent His restrictions and have your own way is to head for disaster.

Here in His hungry condition, weakened in the flesh but strong as ever in the Spirit, our Lord turned to the Word, quoted Scripture in context, and answered from Deuteronomy 8. "The Bible says man shall not live by bread alone but by every word of God." What an example for us to learn from and then follow.

In the book of Deuteronomy, Moses asked the people to be seated and then over 40 days reviewed for them all God had done. Jesus quoted from (Deut. 8) where Moses said, "You remember how the Lord humbled you, allowed you to be hungry in the wilderness, and brought manna to you so that you would know that man does not live by bread alone but by every word that proceeds from the mouth of God?" In other words, "You were stuck in the middle of nowhere with nowhere to turn for food and yet God fed you. Why? To learn you must be dependent upon Him."

There's an even better answer than to get food. It's to get God—because if you get Him, you've got food. You can depend on Him. First things first.

Job was able to say to his accusers, "I have not departed from the commandments of His lips. I've treasured the words of His mouth more than my necessary food" (Job 23:12). It's following God's Word and His will that takes His gifts and makes them useful. But Satan wasn't done yet and now tries again to appeal to the flesh.

> Then the Devil, taking Him up on a high mountain, showed Him all the kingdoms of the world in a moment of time. And the Devil said to Him, "All this authority I will give You, and their glory; for this has been delivered to me, and I give it to whomever I wish. Therefore, if You will worship before me, all will be Yours." And Jesus answered and said to him, "Get behind Me, Satan! For it is written, 'You shall worship the Lord your God, and Him only you shall serve.'"
> —Luke 4:5–8

In a moment of time, the Devil showed Jesus every nation of the world as he said, "This can all be Yours—for a small price. Just bow down and worship me." Could Satan really offer Jesus the kingdoms of the world? He could. Jesus didn't question His ability to do so. When God made Adam and Eve, He gave to them dominion over the earth. But because men are servants to whomever they submit, when Adam and Eve gave in to Satan's temptation they handed dominion of the world to the Devil. That is why he is called the god of this world and the prince of the power of the air.

One day this world will be judged and there will be a new heaven and earth that Satan won't control. But for now, he is the god of this world. Yet most in the blindness of sin serve him without really being aware of him.

The first problem with Satan's offer to Jesus is that his reign is temporary. And to accept it, Jesus would have had to take a different path than God intended. He had come to die for the sins of the world. Satan offered the world to Him without the sacrifice. But it was a shortcut that was nothing more than a lie because had Jesus accepted it, we could not be saved.

The god of this world is good at offering shortcuts that provide immediate gratification but lead nowhere and in which there is no future hope. The very purpose of Jesus' coming was to buy us back from God's judgment, and a shortcut wouldn't do that. The wages of sin is death—a steep price to pay. Yet only the cross of our Lord—Jesus' separation from the Father and His becoming sin for us—would provide for man a way home.

So often the enemy will seek to tempt us with the lust of the eye. "Do you see this? Want that?" he asks. And people sell their souls for the sake of a temporary financial, sexual, or emotional gain. They give all they have for something that won't last, for they have entered the Devil's playing field and the deck is stacked.

"Do as you please. Why wait? It's your life. No one will get hurt. Have it all now. And the cost is so simple: just worship me," he says. According to Isaiah 14, Satan fell from heaven because he wanted to be like the most high God. He wanted to be worshipped. That was his downfall—and it's what he still wants from the people who follow him today.

God however has a different plan. It's a straight path through a narrow gate that calls for obedience to and dependence upon Him. It isn't always the easiest path. It doesn't always seem to have the most immediate reward. Sometimes you might feel like you're getting the short end of the stick. But the promise is that at the end, there awaits for you real life!

Jesus wasn't about to bargain with the father of lies. His Father's way would be through the cross. And that would get Him not only the kingdoms of the world, but eternal life for everyone who would believe on Him. Jesus would continue to please the Father and follow His ways, one day triumphantly sitting down at His right hand. So Jesus again declares God's Word—worship is to be offered only to Almighty God! Satan has one suggestion left.

> Then he brought Him to Jerusalem, set Him on the pinnacle of the temple, and said to Him, "If You are the Son of God, throw Yourself down from here. For it is written: 'He shall give His angels charge over you. To keep you,' and, 'In their hands they shall bear you up, Lest you dash your foot against a stone.'" And Jesus answered and said to him, "It has been said, 'You shall not tempt the Lord your God.'"
>
> —Luke 4:9–12

Finally, in a vision, Satan took Jesus to what was then the portico of Herod's palace on the southern corner of the city wall, high above the Kidron Valley. Even today, this corner of the city wall looms high above the valley beneath.

"Okay, Bible Guy," sneers the Devil. "You're not the only one who can quote the Scriptures. I know it says that the angels will protect You if You fall (Ps. 91:12)—so jump.

You'll have a crowd in no time. The angels will catch You. Your feet will land softly and everyone will know who You are. It'll be great!"

This pride of life temptation is always a bit more subtle, but works on the premise of bringing glory to you so that you might then give glory to God. How often have you heard of people doing the craziest things, supposedly "for the Lord" and then claiming God promised to take care of them? Snake handlers and poison drinkers foolishly seek to attract people to Jesus through sensationalism that only draws men to themselves. All the while, Satan will be helping them along by misquoting and twisting the Scriptures. Jesus called putting yourself in that place of hurt wilfully: tempting God!

We are called to follow the Lord and to be witnesses for Him, but not through strange or irresponsible behavior. We are to be shining lights reaching the world for Jesus, yet not by eccentricity but by walking in His love. More often than not, the way God uses us is by showing how our lives have been changed by His presence. I am able now in Him to forgive those who have hurt me and to love those who persecute me. I put God first. I deny myself. I live to serve Him. My life has been touched by Almighty God.

The Devil's temptation on the other hand is often to enhance your testimony and elevate your status in the eyes of others; to get glory so you can "pass" that glory along. But it's a lie. People come to Jesus by hearing God's Word and seeing the Holy Spirit's testimony in the lives of those He has touched. "By this shall all men know that you are My disciples," Jesus said. By snake handling? No. By love (John 13:35).

Notice that during these trials and temptations, Jesus never had much of a discussion with the Devil. There was no need for argument, no trying to reason with him, no compromise. That sounds good to me. I don't want a discussion with the enemy. I just want to hide behind God's robe and stand in Him.

Jesus filled with the Holy Spirit was brought out into the wilderness to be tempted in every way as we are, and given victory at every step, for the Word of God was firmly attached to His heart and the lust of the flesh, the lust of the eyes, and the pride of life—the Devil's workshop tools—had no place in which to tempt our Lord.

> Now when the Devil had ended every temptation, he departed from Him until an opportune time.
>
> —Luke 4:13

Satan's vacations are short but God's victories are eternal. So the battle is over, but not the war. How do we have victory over the enemy of our souls? By knowing what God declares and following Him. By relying on the power of the Holy Spirit and guarding against the lust of the flesh, the lust of the eyes, or the pride of life. By quoting the Word of God in context as temptation arises and standing upon it. Then, again and again, the Devil will have to depart because he's got nothing he can sell us that we're going to buy. We've already got life.

Chapter 2

INVITED
TO A WEDDING FEAST

John 2:1–11

John wrote in his gospel that his purpose for writing was to make sure the reader understood that Jesus is the Lord and that when one believes in Him, they find eternal life (John 20:31). To that end, he chose eight specific miracles around which to build his case. The first miracle he recorded is this one and took place at a wedding. The last one he chooses will take place at a funeral—seemingly to say that both in the happy times and in the saddest time of all, the Lord wants us to look to Him.

> On the third day there was a wedding in Cana of Galilee, and the mother of Jesus was there. Now both Jesus and His disciples were invited to the wedding. And when they ran out of wine, the mother of Jesus said to Him, "They have no wine."
>
> —John 2:1–3

Cana is a little town a few miles from Nazareth in northern Israel's Galilee. According to verse 12, Jesus had come to this city and the wedding with His disciples, His brothers, His friends, and His family. We can presume it was a family wedding. And Mary's involvement in being responsible for the food and beverages, according to Hebrew wedding practices, suggests this was a close family member.

Jesus had just recently begun His public ministry. He would have only three-and-a-half years to get out His message before laying down His life—and yet, He still found time to attend a wedding.

Wherever you find the Lord, you see Him meeting with and ministering to people the way of life—from Nicodemus, to the wedding guests here, from the woman at the well to the lost around the lake. Wherever He was, He found time to share, for true ministry is more than scheduled events. It is the heart of God reaching to man where he lives, God meeting with us! Later, the Pharisees would come to His disciples and ask why their Master ate with sinners. By then the answer was clear, for them He had come.

I also love the fact that Jesus attends this formal wedding and in so doing puts His stamp of approval on weddings and on the civil act of marriage. There are Christians who think that as long as they are married in the Lord's eyes, they don't have to go to the state. Biblically, that's baloney. A marriage license is not just a piece of paper but a civil commitment before others. The wedding in Cana was just such a ceremony—and the Lord was happy to be there.

Marriage is a lifelong commitment to someone else in the Lord's eyes. It is by far the greatest example that God uses of our corporate relationship to Him. As the church is the Bride of Christ, we are waiting today for our Bridegroom to come. And just as the Lord never will leave us or forsake us, marriage is no temporary relationship.

Whether you like it or not, God refers to a man and woman living together without being married as fornication. Stick with God's Word. Marriage is honorable in God's eyes, and faithfulness is what He is interested in. After all, the first miracle to show the people who Jesus was took place at a wedding where marriage was honored!

In the first century, wedding feasts were interesting because after a yearlong engagement where the bride and groom were legally married but weren't together physically, there was a one-week celebration. Although the party usually would take place at the bridegroom's house, he and the bride were nowhere to be found. They would be spending time together while all of their guests were downstairs or out in the parlor eating and drinking. At the end of the week the bride and groom would join the party.

In our lesson, it was sometime during this feast that the wine ran out. Wine was the staple drink in the culture of that day, and being a good host was of utmost importance. Therefore, to run out of wine at a wedding party would have caused great embarrassment and even disgrace. In Scripture, whenever wine is associated with spiritual things, it always speaks of the joy the Lord gives. But when it comes to physical drink, be careful that you don't use the fact that Jesus made wine to justify drinking.

We first find wine in the Bible in Genesis 9:21 where Noah drank wine and became drunk. From cover to cover, the Bible is filled with warnings about the hazards of drinking alcohol. The facts that it was a staple of the day and that Paul told Timothy to drink wine for his stomach are not justifications for its use in our own day. In fact, throughout Scripture, warnings are given that it will lead to no good. In Leviticus 10, when Aaron's sons showed up drunk at the very first worship service, they were killed by fire. In Romans 14, Paul said it is better that you don't eat or drink if your brother who is weak might be offended. It isn't the directive of the Bible to say, "Go ahead and drink wine," as some would try to make it.

As you look around our culture today, you will not find any benefits from the drinking practices of our people. No one takes his first drink saying, "Today, I'm starting down the road to join the other twenty million American alcoholics." Instead most start drinking because it's the social thing to do. Proverbs 23 talks about looking into the redness of the cup and the destruction that waits there, about hitting your head and not feeling it, and about losing your memory for a time and forgetting what you did. God doesn't want us to stumble in that way. Yet here wine was used as a staple and often safer than water to drink.

So Mary speaks to her eldest Son Jesus about her dilemma.

> Jesus said to her, "Woman, what does your concern have to do with Me? My hour has not yet come."
>
> —John 2:4

In English, Jesus' response may not sound very respectful. But the word *woman*, or *gune* in Greek, is a respectful word. In John 19, Jesus would use it again to direct Mary into the apostle John's care as they both stood at the foot of the cross.

But look again at His answer here. Mary wanted help with the wine, but in His answer Jesus spoke to Mary's intention. I believe that He used His power to miraculously alleviate the problem and make Himself known. "Your problem of not having enough to drink isn't really My problem. My time is not yet come" He replied. Throughout the Gospels, Jesus will often voice this same concern: My hour is not yet come. When the crowd wanted to make Him king, He said, "My hour is not yet come." When the people wanted to follow Him and He had to leave town because the crowds were so great, He said, "My hour is not yet come." But when He rode into town on a donkey on Palm Sunday and the Pharisees protested the people's worship, He said, "My hour is here. If they don't sing, the rocks will."

Put yourself in Mary's shoes for a moment and you will see why she was interested in more than just wine. She had one of the worst reputations in town. In John 8, the Pharisees insinuated that Jesus was born through fornication. For thirty years Mary had hidden things in her heart and loved her Son as any mother would. But as of the wedding, things had started to change. John had identified Jesus as the Messiah. Jesus had spent six weeks in the wilderness. He had a following of disciples. Therefore, I wouldn't be at all surprised to know Mary had said to Jesus, "Half the town is here. This would be a great place to make known who You are." Jesus' answer as well shows He understood her request was for more than help with the wine. Understood the motivation behind it. But His time had not yet come.

So often we want God to work in our time frame rather than seeking His. We tell Him what He should do—we call that prayer—and when He doesn't do it, we wonder why. But the biblical view concerning God's timing is that if He has you wait, there's always a good reason. Days that God doesn't act are days that are to be spent seeking Him, so that when He's ready to move, we will be ready as well, having been prepared.

At age sixteen or so Daniel was carried into captivity from Jerusalem by Nebuchadnezzar and the Babylonians, taken some seven hundred miles away from home. He was part of a large group taken to prepare leadership for many folks that would be deported here eventually. Over time Daniel was promoted as God gave him favor and used him to bring the word of the Lord. Eventually he became second in command. When Daniel turned sixty-five years old however, a new ruler named Belshazzar came to power, and he set

Daniel aside. For the next twenty years or so no one heard from Daniel at all. For twenty years he was the man in the shadows, perhaps himself wondering if God was finished with him. Yet one day the handwriting of God's impending judgment appeared on the wall of the palace. Belshazzar, finding no one to read or interpret the words, appealed to Daniel and his past reputation to hear from God. Daniel came and gave him the grim news that his kingdom had been weighed in the balance and found wanting. That day the entire kingdom of Babylon fell—and Daniel was right back on top, orchestrating, directing, and being God's point man for the return of His people to their land as the Medo-Persians took world dominance. Times of waiting are purposeful as we trust God's timing above our own ideas and plans. Just ask Daniel!

Jesus' hour was coming. But the wedding at Cana was not the time to put on such a display. And it wasn't yet Mary's time to have her reputation restored.

> His mother said to the servants, "Whatever He says to you, do it."
>
> —John 2:5

Mary graciously accepted Jesus' words, sure she would get help—although not in the way she may have wanted to help clear her name. "Whatever He says to you, do it," she said to the servants. These are Mary's last words in the Bible. We will next find her in the Gospels at the cross, watching her Son give His life for the sins of the world. We'll see her for the last time in the Book of Acts, gathered with the 120 disciples in the Upper Room, waiting for the outpouring of the Spirit God had promised. You won't find her mentioned in the early church or in the practices or habits of the church because Jesus is the only Mediator we need. How Mary would grieve to see what some have made of her in light of all Jesus had come to do.

A few years down the road from now, an excited woman in a crowd, after watching Jesus work, will cry out, "Blessed is the womb that bore You and the breasts that nursed You."

But Jesus will say to her, "No, blessed is the man who hears the Word of God and keeps it" (Luke 11:27–28).

Mary looked to Jesus for vindication and she certainly would get it when His hour came. But at this point, the Lord met her need in such a quiet way that, besides the disciples and the servants, no one was probably even aware of the miracle He performed, though John tells us of it here.

> Now there were set there six waterpots of stone, according to the manner of purification of the Jews, containing twenty or thirty gallons apiece. Jesus said to them, "Fill the waterpots with water." And they filled them up to the brim.
>
> —John 2:6–7

These jars were used for ceremonial cleansing and, together, held 180 gallons of wine. This was a big event. Notice that they were empty because religion and ceremony without a heart for God will always run on empty. But Jesus can bring life to empty vessels like us. So He told the servants to fill the waterpots.

These were not the days of the garden hose and ease of access to that much water. This would require carrying water in buckets from a well. A servant would not look forward to this hard labor and even when the pots were two-thirds full, might declare, "That's good enough!" Yet these servants obeyed what Jesus had asked of them, filling each jar to the brim. I can hear them saying, "I think this one could use one more bucket. There, that's full!" They weren't only obedient, they were exuberant and so should we be as we serve Jesus.

I love it when people serve the Lord "to the brim." There are always those who look to see what the minimum requirement is, who ask, "How little can I do and still get into heaven?" Others serve far more enthusiastically. We don't want to serve the Lord with half-hearted efforts, and He is looking for whole-hearted saints. We want to go to the brim, don't we? Sing with joy. Pray with conviction. Pull weeds energetically. "Whatever you do, do it heartily, as to the Lord, and not to men" (Col. 3:23).

"Do whatever Jesus says," Mary told the servants. Jesus said to fill the waterpots. And, boy, did they fill them!

> And He said to them, "Draw some out now, and take it to the master of the feast." And they took it.
>
> —John 2:8

If I were one of these servants, I think I would be a bit nervous to serve well-water to the guy in charge! But these "to the brim" servants didn't hesitate.

> When the master of the feast had tasted the water that was made wine, and did not know where it came from (but the servants who had drawn the water knew), the master of the feast called the bridegroom. And he said to him, "Every man at the beginning sets out the good wine, and when the guests have well drunk, then the inferior. You have kept the good wine until now!"
>
> —John 2:9–10

This water-turned-to-wine that so few knew about is instrumental in teaching us that God can not only take empty religious lives and fill them to the brim, but He can make them extra special. That is why Jesus came, and so His miracles declare.

"What happened to you?" people ask.

"I got saved," we answer.

"Man, you're different. You have love and peace. There's joy in your life."

"That's right. Jesus has filled me to overflowing!"

The guy in charge of the party didn't know what to think, but he could taste it. The empty jars of religious practice had become jars filled with joy, and it showed and left an impression on all around.

> This beginning of signs Jesus did in Cana of Galilee, and manifested His glory; and His disciples believed in Him. After this He went down to Capernaum, He, His mother, His brothers, and His disciples; and they did not stay there many days.
>
> —John 2:11–12

The wedding at Cana is a great story. It speaks of the believer's joyful life, the sanctity of marriage, the need to wait upon God's timing, and to ever be seeking the Lord as we wait so that when our hour comes, we're prepared. The servants—obedient, faithful, enthusiastic—experienced the first miracle, while everyone else except the disciples and Mary missed out on it entirely. We too can see His glory by obeying His word!

Chapter 3

JESUS AND NICODEMUS

John 3:1–36

Through the following accounts of Jesus' encounters with Nicodemus in chapter 3 and the woman at the well and the nobleman in crisis in chapter 4, John wants to convince us of our need for Jesus, no matter where we have come from. Nicodemus, the woman, and the nobleman each came from entirely different backgrounds, but all found hope and life in Jesus. They came with different needs, but received the same direction.

In context, Jesus had been working miracles and preaching the Gospel and had recently cleansed the temple in Jerusalem—He did so both at the beginning and again at the end of His earthly public ministry. It had left an impact upon this man of the temple who now came to Jesus to ask what He knew God and life.

> Now when He was in Jerusalem at the Passover, during the feast, many believed in His name when they saw the signs which He did. But Jesus did not commit Himself to them, because He knew all men, and had no need that anyone should testify of man, for He knew what was in man. There was a man of the Pharisees named Nicodemus, a ruler of the Jews. This man came to Jesus by night and said to Him, "Rabbi, we know that you are a teacher come from God; for no one can do these signs that You do unless God is with him."
>
> —John 2:23–3:2

Our text from John tells us Jesus knows people's hearts. I like that truth. God knows you. He knows your heart, knows what you need, and knows what you're going through. No one else might understand—but He does. Jesus didn't need advice or insight about Nicodemus because he already knew him. But Nicodemus desperately needed to know Jesus.

Nicodemus was a devout man who had spent his entire life in religious service. And yet with all that he knew or thought he knew, he also realized he lacked some basic answers in his heart. He had a prominent, very influential position in life yet lacked peace and assurance in heart. Yet watching Jesus he had seen something else—something he wanted, something he hoped he could gain from Him—intimacy with God.

Nicodemus was after all a very religious man. He was a Pharisee—one of a group who practiced the strictest adherence to the Old Testament Law as they understood it. He was a ruler of the Jews. He had been elected to the Sanhedrin, the Supreme Court of the land.

14

He was a man sought after for his decisions, influence, and opinions. He had a long list of credentials. If credentials were all that were needed, Nicodemus would have made it. Jesus would only have had to say, "Let Me see your list. Oh, I see you're well ahead of the game. You have so much going for you. Soon you will arrive!" Nicodemus' list of accomplishments, however, had not produced rest in him.

In fact, it was that very turmoil in Nicodemus' heart that first brought him to Jesus. An educated, powerful Supreme Court justice of the land came to have a night meeting with a thirty-year-old uneducated carpenter because He had something Nicodemus wanted and had observed in Him without speaking to Him.

Nicodemus came with questions. He didn't come with repentance—that he would have to learn. He didn't come with sorrow over his sin. He saw Jesus as an equal, a peer, and a teacher. But the Lord would fix that for him.

Every time, by the way, that we see Nicodemus in the Scriptures, it's at night. Nic at night. And what a wonderful sense of humor our Lord has, having John write down for us all to read how Nicodemus only came out at night to meet with Jesus. Can't really keep that quiet for long!

Nicodemus might have said, "Rabbi, we've come to the conclusion that the miracles we've seen in Your life and all that we watch You do indicate You must be a man from God." He knew Jesus had something no one else had. What he didn't know was that his religion didn't please God and that his best wasn't nearly good enough. He didn't understand the concept of being dead in sin and the blindness it brought. But for now his lack and Jesus' abundance brought him out to find out.

There are many physical diseases that can render muscles unable to respond to the brain's signals and thus isolate them to uselessness. In a spiritual sense, that is us in sin. God sends out a signal but we can't respond because we're dead in our sins. Nicodemus came this first night in the pride of being a peer and in the hopes of getting some answers for his dissatisfaction. He wasn't yet ready to acknowledge that he was a sinner who needed grace and a new birth—that Jesus would tell him about. All he knew so far was that Jesus had something he did not and that churned within. He was determined to find out what that was. By the end of the Gospels, Nicodemus is a full believer in Jesus Christ.

If you read carefully, you find that, after verse 2, Nicodemus' comments are cut off before he has a chance to ask a question. I don't know what his question would have been. Maybe, "What must I do to get to heaven?" or, "What's the greatest of the commandments?" But it doesn't really matter because Jesus knew what Nicodemus needed and knew His heart was sincere. So He got right to the point and spoke directly to his needs.

In verses 3, 5, and 7, Jesus essentially says the same thing: "Here you are; here's heaven; and here's how you get from here to there."

> Jesus answered and said to him, "Most assuredly, I say to you, unless one is born
> again, he cannot see the kingdom of God." Nicodemus said to Him, "How can a

man be born when he is old? Can he enter a second time into his mother's womb and be born?" Jesus answered, "Most assuredly, I say to you, unless one is born of water and the Spirit, he cannot enter the kingdom of God. That which is born of the flesh is flesh, and that which is born of the Spirit is spirit. Do not marvel that I said to you, 'You must be born again.'"

—John 3:3–7

Nicodemus called Jesus "Teacher," but it was as if Jesus said, "I can't teach you anything yet. I'm going to talk to you as a Savior. I'm not going to teach you how you can live your life. I'm going to tell you how you can find life."

We know biblically that all physical life came from God. Genesis 2:7 tells us God took dirt and breathed life into it and that dirt became a living being. To be spiritually born again requires that same work of God. Verse 3 tells us that unless we're born again, we cannot even see the kingdom of God. Verse 5 adds that unless we're born again, we cannot enter His kingdom.

If we're ever going to fully grasp God's goodness and all that He says, we're going to need this new birth experience. Paul told the Corinthians in the third chapter of his first letter that the natural person cannot receive the things of the Spirit, for they are foolishness to him. That is why Jesus said to Nicodemus, "If you want understanding, you're going to have to be born again. If you want to get into heaven, you're going to have to be born again."

In one sentence, Jesus cut the ground out from under the feet of a religious man who, like most people, hoped he would hear what it took for him to get to heaven on his own. "Give me a list of things I can do. That's what I want"—that's what most people look for. But Jesus said that no breeding, success, friends in high places, or education could gain Nicodemus any spiritual advantage. He had to be born again.

"Yeah, but I'm an old guy who's been around for years. I even have the keys to the temple," Nicodemus could have said. The keys to the temple and the new birth would get him to heaven. But the keys to the temple alone wouldn't get him anywhere.

Nicodemus should teach us that there is no spiritual advantage in what you have or what you have become. The only need you have is the need everyone has: to be saved. When you begin to look at your life, the veneer grows very thin when, like Nicodemus, you realize that what you have doesn't satisfy you and won't satisfy God, for the wages of sin is death. So to Nicodemus and later to Paul, who both felt they had much to talk about in terms of accomplishment, Jesus speaks one word and removes their confidence, so they, and we, might quickly learn that salvation is a work of God by His grace.

Nicodemus' response is proof enough that Jesus' statement is true. He didn't get it. He didn't understand this idea of spiritual birth. He immediately related it to physical birth. His hunger had brought him to Jesus, but now he was stumped. Jesus makes clear that he can indeed start over in the Spirit as a new baby in Christ.

God isn't interested in hiding the truth from us. He wants us to know it. When Nicodemus said, "I don't get it," Jesus said, "Let Me explain it to you." In verses 3, 5, and 11, He uses the phrase "Most assuredly" or "truly." In other words, "If there's anything you can count on, then count on this!"

The words *water* and *of the Spirit* must be taken together because they are the method by which people come to God. The reference to water is a reference to the Word of God's cleansing work that the Spirit uses to convict. Whenever you find the metaphorical use of water in Scripture, it is always to speak of God's Word washing and cleansing us. How do I get saved? How do I become born again? I must be cleansed by the Scriptures and impacted by the Spirit.

When Nicodemus asked how he could be born again when he was an old man, Jesus answered, "You've got to be born of water and the Spirit. The birth I'm talking about is a spiritual birth and, without it, you can't see the kingdom of God. The flesh produces flesh; the Spirit produces spirit. Only God can give this life."

The Bible tells us in Genesis 1 that everything reproduces after its kind. So spiritual birth can only come from God. There's no way to work yourself into a new birth. There's no way to buy it. There isn't any way to inherit it from your family or produce it on your own. You have to be given new life from God.

In his second letter, Peter wrote, "We have been given by God great and exceedingly precious promises that, through them, we might become partakers of the divine nature." To the Corinthians, Paul said that if any man is in Christ, he is a new creation. The new believer doesn't turn over a new leaf, start a new page, or begin a new chapter or write a new book. He becomes a new person.

There's no sense preaching better behavior. That doesn't get a person to heaven. Kinder actions won't get somewhere there either. It's not reformation—it's regeneration. And it takes place when I repent and come to Jesus by the work of God's Word washing me and the Holy Spirit convicting me. As I listen to Jesus' message, I turn to Him by faith, and believing and trusting in Him and His work for me, I am saved.

> "The wind blows where it wishes, and you hear the sound of it, but cannot tell where it comes from and where it goes. So is everyone who is born of the Spirit."
>
> —John 3:8

Maybe a breeze was rustling leaves overhead as Jesus said to Nicodemus, "You don't know where the wind comes from, but you see the result."

That's the way it is with the new birth. The process you have to leave with God, but the evidence is obvious. The wind's presence is betrayed by the moving of leaves just as the Holy Spirit's presence is betrayed by a life that has been changed, having been convicted of sin and self. The fruit of God's presence becomes obvious. When you get saved, it shows for God moves into your heart and the presence of the Holy Spirit will be obvious for all to see producing in us love and peace, rest and hope, kindness and mercy.

The Hebrew word for wind, *ruach*, or *pneuma* in Greek, is the same word for "spirit." Nicodemus was here because the wind of the Holy Spirit had been blowing on his heart. So here he was—out late one night, sneaking around to find life. Not yet ready for anyone to see him or know of his search, but ready to come and ask Jesus for help.

> Nicodemus answered and said to Him, "How can these things be?" Jesus answered and said to him, "Are you the teacher of Israel, and do not know these things? Most assuredly, I say to you, We speak what We know and testify what We have seen, and you do not receive Our witness. If I have told you earthly things and you do not believe, how will you believe if I tell you heavenly things? No one has ascended to heaven but He who came down from heaven, that is, the Son of Man who is in heaven. And as Moses lifted up the serpent in the wilderness, even so must the Son of Man be lifted up, that whoever believes in Him should not perish but have eternal life."
>
> —John 3:9–15

Jesus was surprised that although Nicodemus was a teacher, he didn't know certain things. It was as if He was saying, "Haven't you ever taught Ezekiel 36–37? It says right there that God will give people a new heart and a new spirit. They'll know God's Word in their hearts."

"Most assuredly," Jesus said, "We know what we're talking about." He used the word *we* because it was the Father who sent the Son and the Holy Spirit, who testifies of the Son. One God in three persons and thus the term "we".

The description of faith in verses 13–15 speak of the last of Moses' miracles, recorded in Numbers 21. The Israelites had been murmuring again that God hadn't been good to them and that Moses hadn't taken care of them. The Lord in judgment sent deadly snakes into the camp. As the people began to die from snakebites, they cried out to Moses, saying, "We have sinned. Pray for us that the Lord doesn't destroy all of us and that He would take these serpents away." In answer to his prayer, the Lord told Moses to make a serpent of brass, stick it upon a pole, and hold it up for all to see. Those who looked at the serpent on the pole would live, those who would not look would die. If it sounded like an odd remedy, they only had to wait a little while and watch everyone around them die before they decided to give it a try. I suspect soon all were looking intently at the brass serpent upon the pole, odd remedy or not.

Today, the preaching of the cross seems as much an odd remedy to people as those words of Jesus of the new birth first seemed to Nicodemus, but it's the only way of life. Jesus is the only way and coming to Him by faith will cause you to be born again.

It would take three years of mulling over the truth followed by Jesus' death before Nicodemus would come to publicly proclaim his faith. He missed out on a lot in the process. He could have come that night. You still can.

> "For God so loved the world that He gave His only begotten Son, that whoever believes in Him should not perish but have everlasting life."
>
> —John 3:16

John 3:16 is probably the best-known verse in the Bible. I'll be interested when we get to heaven to see how many saints are there just because of this one verse—twenty-five English words that spell out the Gospel's simplicity, expressing it in very clear terms—God's mind, God's heart, and God's will. His heart: He so loves the world. His mind: He sent His Son to be the solution for our sin. His will: that whoever believes in Him has eternal life. You can't miss the picture, can you? God so loves us that it prompted Him to bring a solution for our sin. God so loved us that He wants to save us from our sin. And although one day we will physically die unless the Lord returns in our lifetime, we will never perish. Instead, we'll be given everlasting life.

The word translated *everlasting* is the Greek word *aionios*. It literally means "age-abiding" and speaks not only of the length of life but of the quality of that life. Notice that Jesus used the present tense to speak of this *aionios*. Whoever believes in Him *has*—not will have, not might have, but *has*—everlasting life presently. God moves in. The world changes. The outlook changes. And then dying is just a change of clothes or a change of position, but not of relationship, for I have to know God, be born again and adopted into His family as His child forevermore.

In both verses 15–16, the issue is believing. A couple of years ago, a national Poll indicated that 80 percent of people who live in America declare they believe in God. I'm not sure that's anything to cheer about. In James 2:19, James said the Devil believes in God and he trembles. But his belief is not what God is looking for. In fact, here in John, this word for belief means "to throw your entire weight upon." I've got to cast my every weight upon Jesus. He's got to be the only One in whom I believe. I have to lean on Him and rely on Him for everything. I have to transfer all my hope to His Word.

According to the Bible, you have to put all your eggs in one basket if you want to be saved. Jesus can't be one face on a Mount Rushmore of hope flanked by many others. You can't "cover all the bases" claiming that is faith, for it is not saving faith. If you want to be saved, there are no bases to cover but one. There is no name given among men but one whereby you can be saved (Acts 4:12). So when Jesus speaks of whoever believes in Him, He's talking about the person who has transferred all of his or her hope to Him—not Jesus plus good works, not Jesus plus baptism, not Jesus plus family background, just Jesus period. That certainly narrows the field and the road, yet that is saving faith!

> "For God did not send His Son into the world to condemn the world, but that the world through Him might be saved."
>
> —John 3:17

Notice the word *world* is repeated several times in verses 16–17. God loves the world and sent Jesus to save the world. I think the very fact that God sent His Son ought to show you His heart. Peter wrote to the saints scattered all over the world, "I want you to know that the Lord isn't slack concerning His promises but He's longsuffering. He's not willing that any should perish. He wants all to come to repentance" (2 Pet. 3:9).

If God seems to be dragging His feet when it comes to His return for us, it's because of His love. Aren't you glad He didn't come back for the church in 1965, 1988, or even three months ago? How many of us would have been left behind?

Religious Nicodemus knew he didn't have what it took. He was told to be born again. How? Turn to Jesus and lay all of our care, trust, and weight upon Him, and believe in Him. Then we won't perish. Instead, we'll get everlasting life.

If you apply the religions of the world's messages to a man sinking in the quicksand of sin and death, you'll find as many different answers but no solution:

Confucius would say, "Man should avoid such situations."

Mohammed would tell him it's the will of Allah.

Buddha would say, "Let this be a lesson to many."

Krishna would say, "Better luck next time."

Only Jesus says, "Look to Me and you won't perish." Everyone else has a diversionary tactic. God sent His Son to save. He's unique. He alone came to seek and to save the lost. He alone can save the soul. So Jesus declares:

> "He who believes in Him is not condemned; but he who does not believe is condemned already, because he has not believed in the name of the only begotten Son of God."
>
> —John 3:18

Because Jesus came, we are all obligated now to respond to His coming and to look to Him because we've been bitten by sin. It isn't that Jesus came to pass judgment. Judgment has already come. Do nothing and you're already condemned, so what can believing do but profit your life, bring you life, and bless your life? Nicodemus was a perfect example of a person who didn't have what it took, although he thought he had tried everything and had done most things to benefit spiritually. He was wrong.

> "And this is the condemnation, that the light has come into the world, and men loved darkness rather than light, because their deeds were evil. For everyone practicing evil hates the light and does not come to the light, lest his deeds

should be exposed. But he who does the truth comes to the light, that his deeds may be clearly seen, that they have been done in God."

—John 3:19–21

With such awesome promises, what then keeps people from Jesus? Intellectual arguments? Absolutely not. In fact, if anyone is honest with himself, he would intellectually have to say, "I'm a sinner. What I want to do sometimes I can't do. What I see in myself sometimes I hate. I'm not where I should be. I'm not what I could be."

Intellectual arguments are not the reason people turn away from Jesus. Neither are philosophical concerns. The old response of: "Well, this is what I've been taught to believe and it's hard to change." That too is an excuse without reason.

What then keeps people from Jesus? The answer from the above verses is they simply refuse to come. When all is said and done, the reason folks don't get saved is because they don't want to get saved. I can't begin to tell you the number of people over the years who, when I've shared the Gospel with them, say, "So if I get saved, do I have to quit drinking? If I get saved, do I have to quit going to nightclubs, watching movies, and running around? I like my life the way it is."

My answer to them is always the same: "If you get saved, you can do whatever you want. But if you get saved, you won't want to do *those* things."

What most keeps people from coming to Jesus is they love the way they live. It doesn't make any difference what they tell you, the truth is they don't want to be confronted with their lives. When folks bring people to church who are very uncomfortable, they fidget and squirm because God shines His light on their lives and it's uncomfortable. It's not a pleasure to realize one day you're going to die and have to answer to God. People would rather just talk football.

Jesus tells us clearly here that men love darkness rather than light. The solution enters the picture and they don't want anything to do with it. They don't want to be changed. They like their sinful ways.

The Lord turns on the light but people prefer darkness. Talk about Jesus to someone who is not saved and sometimes they can't wait to get away from you. The next time someone gives you the intellectual brush-off when you share the Gospel with him or her, you might say, "What sin is it that you don't want to let go of? What part of your life are you unwilling to let God have?"

It is so unlike a man to hide. Man in his sin and pride more often want to be seen and heard and acknowledged. "Look at my accomplishments," he boasts. "Look at what I've become. Look at the money I've made, the house I live in. Look at the car I drive. Look at the influence I have. Just don't look at my sin." People want to put everything on display—except their sin. When the Lord shines the light on that, they want to hide in the corner.

You can see the difference in those who are saved. Their lives tend to be very open, aware of their failures but trusting the Lord. They are quick to admit weakness, quick to share

God's strength and always thankful to Jesus for the grace He has brought. But until I meet Him, the idea of hiding my worst is always at work and the lies of leading a double or triple life (church, home, work find me all different) keep me from coming to His Light.

I don't think there's a more painful moment than the one right before you get saved, because as God's light shines on you, you see yourself for who you really are. I thank the Lord He doesn't show us everything at once. It would kill us. It would have killed me! It's kind of like coming out of the dark movie theater into the sunshine. It takes your eyes a while to adjust. God just takes us a little bit at a time. His Word is a lamp to our feet, a light to our path. The Holy Spirit begins to make us sensitive to sin. But the danger for us is to close our eyes to His convicting light and walk away.

This is the condemnation. One day you're going to stand before the Lord and He's going to say, "Why didn't you believe in My Son? Why didn't you trust in Him? Why didn't you look to Him?" If you want to walk in the light, go to the Lord. Although God clearly sees your sin, you'll be covered by His grace. You'll be born again.

> After these things Jesus and His disciples came into the land of Judea, and there He remained with them and baptized. Now John also was baptizing in Aenon near Salim, because there was much water there. And they came and were baptized. For John had not yet been thrown into prison.
>
> —John 3:22–24

Why was John baptizing at this particular place? Because there was much water there. I like this for it seems to me God's will is often found in the practical. John knew what he had to do. Now he had to find a place where he could do it the best way possible.

Saint Augustine said that if you love God with all of your heart, you can do what you want. If you love the Lord, your life will be in line with His desires for you. You'll know what's right. The hard thing is getting people to love God with all their heart. When they don't do that, they're always wondering about what's right and wrong. They always want to know how far away from the line they can live. But if you love God with all your heart, then you'll never see that line, you will instead be in the center of His will. Delight yourself in the Lord and He'll give you the desires of your heart (Ps. 37:4).

> Then there arose a dispute between some of John's disciples and the Jews about purification. And they came to John and said to him, "Rabbi, He who was with you beyond the Jordan, to whom you have testified—behold, He is baptizing, and all are coming to Him!" John answered and said, "A man can receive nothing unless it has been given to him from heaven. You yourselves bear me witness, that I said, 'I am not the Christ,' but, 'I have been sent before Him.' He who has the bride is the bridegroom; but the friend of the bridegroom, who stands and hears him, rejoices greatly because of the bridegroom's voice. Therefore this joy of mine is fulfilled. He must increase, but I must decrease."
>
> —John 3:25–30

The growing number of people coming to Jesus frustrated some of John's disciples but John had the right outlook. He couldn't have been happier for a couple of reasons. First, he was aware that you don't get anything unless God gives it to you. So even his popularity—his success—had been a gift from God.

Secondly, his job of running before the Lord caused him to know it was the Lord who was supposed to be honored, not him. And like the best man at a wedding, he would soon be done with his work and join the others rejoicing in hearing the bridegroom's voice, speaking of his love for his bride. Within weeks John would be arrested and imprisoned and eventually beheaded by Herod at the behest of his wicked mistress.

> "He who comes from above is above all; he who is of the earth is earthly and speaks of the earth. He who comes from heaven is above all. And what He has seen and heard, that He testifies; and no one receives His testimony. He who has received His testimony has certified that God is true."
>
> —John 3:31–33

It is very difficult in Greek and in the context to determine whether this is John the Baptist continuing his preaching or whether this is John the Apostle's commentary, writing near the end of the first century. The verb tenses suggest John the Apostle.

The point in verse 31 is that Jesus was more than a prophet, more than an angel, and more than a man born upon the earth. He came from heaven and He possessed a quality only God possesses. He knew everything. He could testify to everything. He could say, "As it was in the days of Noah" because He was there. Even though He displayed those attributes, He was rejected by most. Yet those who believed in Him, declared God was true, as were the prophets who spoke of His coming.

According to Luke 7:30, the Pharisees did not receive God's testimony against themselves and so were not baptized by John the Baptist. If you refuse to be born again, you're literally telling God you don't agree with His assessment of your life and of His gracious solution for your sin. But if you go to Jesus and believe in Him, throwing all your weight of hope upon Him by crying out: "I'm a sinner. The snake of sin has bitten me. I need help. I need new life. I need to be born again." Then you agree with God—and you are saved as God intended when He sent His Son.

> "For He whom God has sent speaks the words of God, for God does not give the Spirit by measure."
>
> —John 3:34

Every word out of Jesus' mouth was 100 percent God's Word without flaw or error. Look at the church and you see the Holy Spirit oftentimes grieved by sin or restrained by disobedience or unbelief. That's not the case with Jesus. Everything He said and did was the result of the unrestrained fullness of the Spirit (Col. 2:9).

"The Father loves the Son, and has given all things into His hand. He who believes in the Son has everlasting life; and he who does not believe the Son shall not see life, but the wrath of God abides on him."

—John 3:35–36

If you want to see the kingdom of heaven, you must be born again. John declares that Jesus is our only hope. Refusing to receive Him will be the greatest mistake you will ever make. It will leave you hopeless and without a future, except to wait for judgment and hell.

If you choose to give Jesus your life, however, and if you lay it before Him even with all of the weight of the sin that accompanies it, you will find life in Him our Savior and our Lord.

Chapter 4

IMAGINE MEETING YOU
IN A PLACE LIKE THIS

John 4:1–42

Nicodemus may have seemed an obvious person to come looking for the Lord in Jesus. He was a Jewish ruler and a wealthy, powerful scholar. Outwardly, he was as moral as could be and he did live beside the law of God. Yet following His conversation with Nicodemus, Jesus turned to a woman who had a terrible reputation in a town that the Jews despised, a woman who hated her way of life and hung on to her religion for dear life, though she wasn't sure it was right. She will receive from Jesus the very same counsel and insight into His Person that religious Nicodemus had found. Her reputation however, did not restrain her from immediately telling all of what she had found in Him.

Nicodemus' testimony would eventually be, "You can't do it alone no matter how religiously right you think you are." This woman at the well will testify, "You can't fall so low where God can't reach you by Jesus Christ." He is the answer for both lives and circumstances, as He will be for the nobleman later in our studies.

Although Nicodemus and the woman at the well had dissimilar backgrounds, they had plenty in common. They both had a religion on which they relied and they both were honest enough to say, "It's not working for me." Nicodemus came on his own while Jesus came to reel in this woman more than ready to be reeled in. Both of them came to the conclusion that Jesus was the Christ, the Savior of the world.

> Therefore, when the Lord knew that the Pharisees had heard that Jesus made and baptized more disciples than John (though Jesus Himself did not baptize, but His disciples), He left Judea and departed again to Galilee. But He needed to go through Samaria. So He came to a city of Samaria which is called Sychar, near the plot of ground that Jacob gave to his son Joseph. Now Jacob's well was there. Jesus therefore, being wearied from His journey, sat thus by the well. It was about the sixth hour.
>
> —John 4:1–6

Throughout His first year of ministry, Jesus spent much time in the Jerusalem area. But the opposition was growing. He had become so popular with the people that the religious leaders were beginning to wonder what they could do to turn people away from Him. But for Jesus, it wasn't yet time for confrontation, arrest, or the cross. There were two and a half more years of ministry remaining. We find Him here heading north from Jerusalem, through Samaria and towards the Galilee region.

He would arrive in the north about the time John the Baptist would be arrested, and he would take up where John left off, preaching the same message. For now, however, He was traveling and on the road when He stopped to rest in this area in the middle of the country that we today know as the West Bank. Then it was called Samaria.

The Jews and the Samaritans were at great odds and had despised each other for generations for both religious and racial reasons. In John 9, Jesus' opponents accuse Him of being a Samaritan and equate this with being possessed by the Devil. Their animosity was grounded in years of history and bigotry.

A king named Omri had bought the city of Samaria back in 930 B.C. The most wicked of the northern kings up to that time, he had made Samaria his home. When the ten tribes moved north in revolt of heavy taxation following Solomon's death, they used this town as one of their places of idol worship. In 722 B.C., when the Assyrians came in, they gained control of both the town and countryside of Samaria. The Assyrians' method of handling conquest, however, was not to kill their captives, but instead simply to relocate them to other areas of their dominance. They concluded if they conquered you, the best way they could control you was to move you into an area of the country where you didn't know the language, couldn't follow the customs, didn't like the food, and couldn't organize. So they would split conquered peoples and move them around. That's exactly what happened here in Samaria. Leaving the Jewish poor and handicapped in the land, the Assyrians basically moved everyone else away while importing others here.

The result of this was a religious mixture of truth and error. In 2 Kings 17, we see the transplanted people now placed in Samaria asking what the God of this land required of the people, a question for them based solely on superstition. The people groups over the years that lived here held to some of the truths of Judaism but in time blended them with the cultic beliefs they brought back with them from their various cultures. The end result was a mixture that certainly was far from the truth. For example, they believed only in the Pentateuch—the first five books of the Bible—and rewrote everything they found in it to revolve around Mount Gerizim, the mountain on which their city was built. In other words, Abraham offered his son, Isaac, as a sacrifice on Mount Gerizim. The Garden of Eden was on Mount Gerizim. Noah's ark landed on Mount Gerizim. So a clear religious divide between Jews and Samaritans at this time was clearly established.

In Nehemiah's day, Sanballat, a man who opposed everything God did, built a temple in Samaria on Mount Gerizim. This temple stood until about 108 B.C., when it was leveled in battle. It was to this temple that the woman here at the well would refer. But she, as all of us who come from many different religious backgrounds, can only find life when we turn to Jesus, God in the flesh, the One come to save us and lead us into all truth.

In Jesus' day, the Jewish view concerning the Samaritans was seeing them as half-breeds—unclean peoples from which they separated themselves. So great was the contention, that

Jews leaving Jerusalem for the Sea of Galilee some ninety miles to the north, would rarely take the direct route through Samaria, but instead traveled east, crossing the Jordan and traveling north on the eastern side of the Jordan, and then crossing back over west further north as they got near Galilee, thereby avoiding Samaria altogether. The Samaritans, in turn, fought back by often closing the road that led through town towards Jerusalem.

So here was Jesus, leaving Judea and headed for Galilee. But the Scripture says He *needed* to go through Samaria.

I love that word *needed*. Regardless of how others responded to this area and its people, Jesus violated customs, thumbed His nose at tradition, didn't follow public opinion, and headed for hostile territory because His eyes were on their souls. He didn't have any racial prejudice to deal with or religious prejudice to stop Him. He had to go to Samaria. There were lives to touch. There was much to be done, many to reach—and He was willing to reach them all. He was willing to be the One—the only one, if need be—to reach out to them.

To this end, Jesus and His disciples traveled for two days before arriving at Sychar. In Old Testament times, Sychar was called Shechem. Today, it's called Nablus. There in Nablus to this day is this well, one of the few landmarks in Israel about which there is no disagreement.

It was in the middle of the day, high noon in the desert, when Jesus and the disciples stopped to rest. Notice our Lord fully experienced what it meant to be hot and tired. He sat down at a well, hoping to get some water but lacking a bucket.

He'd come a long way looking for the lost and now, sitting at Jacob's well, He waited for a drink of water. The next time we will hear Him say He's thirsty is on the cross, right before He declares, "It is finished." Here we read:

> A woman of Samaria came to draw water. Jesus said to her, "Give Me a drink."
> For his disciples had gone away into the city to buy food.
>
> —John 4:7, 8

Noon is not a good time in the desert to do your work. In fact, everywhere else in Scripture we see the women coming to the wells early in the morning or late in the afternoon, when the weather is cooler, the conditions more favorable for this hard labor. But this woman came at noon. Why? We will read she had a terrible reputation in town. The other women didn't like her. She'd had five husbands and was living with another man now to whom she was not married. She was a threat to every wife. So she had to come alone to get water for her family. And that's where Jesus sat, waiting for the outcast—for the woman filled with shame, for the rejected one—so He might restore her. How awesome our God, see His heart. He came to get those no one else wanted. He came for us.

> Then the woman of Samaria said to Him, "How is it that You, being a Jew, ask a
> drink from me, a Samaritan woman?" For Jews have no dealings with Samaritans.
> —John 4:9

I love the picture of Jesus sweating and tired while the disciples were out to get some lunch. The Creator of Niagara Falls was thirsty and waiting for the disciples to bring some Chicken McNuggets when He could feed five thousand men plus women and children with just a couple of loaves of bread and a few fish. Jesus never performed a single miracle for Himself however. That was the Devil's temptation in the wilderness—for Him to make Himself food out of rocks. But Jesus didn't take him up on the challenge because miracles were for others to show whom He was. In situations like these where he has physical need, He chose to be as limited as we are. So He sits thirsty with no bucket, hungry with no food. And here came a hated Samaritan woman with a chip on her shoulder big enough to see.

If you read carefully through the Gospels, you will find that Jesus' ministry among the Samaritans in the couple of days He was there left tremendous fruit behind. Who's the hero of the Good Samaritan story in Luke 10? Not a Jewish priest but a Samaritan—a guy who was rejected by everyone else but found by the Lord. Who's the one leper who comes back when the ten are healed in Luke 17? Not a Jew but a Samaritan—a man who was rejected by everyone but feels the Lord's touch and is more grateful than anyone else. When the church is persecuted in Acts and scattered out of Jerusalem, the first place God sends them is to Samaria. "Go to the Samaritans," He says. "Go tell them the good news." God loved the Samaritans indeed!

It's no wonder however that this woman showed up here being so very defensive. She had been burned a lot. She was used to being taken advantage of. She'd had to fight for everything she had gotten in a town that was way too small for her reputation.

> Jesus answered and said to her, "If you knew the gift of God, and who it is who
> says to you, 'Give Me a drink,' you would have asked Him, and He would have
> given you living water."
> —John 4:10

Jesus said, "If you knew Me and the gift of life I could offer, you'd be asking Me for a drink rather than My asking you for one." And in this one sentence, Jesus addressed her need, aroused her curiosity, and declared how life can be had.

To a woman in the heat of the day, thirsty in her heart, Jesus was talking about living water. I love the way the Lord is always so relevant in the examples and illustrations He uses to communicate His truth to man. To a weary and older Nicodemus, Jesus talked about being born again. To the blind, He talked about being the Light of the World. To Peter and John, He said, "I can make you fishers of men." After their brother Lazarus had died, to Mary and Martha He said, "I am the resurrection and the life." And in the heat of the day sitting at a well, He spoke of being Living Water.

> The woman said to Him, "Sir, You have nothing to draw with, and the well is deep. Where then do You get that living water? Are You greater than our father Jacob, who gave us the well, and drank from it himself, as well as his sons and his livestock?"
>
> —John 4:11–12

To the woman, living water meant water that moved. Living water was different than stagnant water that simply sat in a well. This was a deep well, a well fed by underground springs. It had been giving life to people for thousands of years. "Where do You expect to get living water?" she asked. "This is a deep well. It's got living water, but You don't even have a bucket. I suppose You're greater than our father, Jacob, who was just fine drinking this water."

The first problem with this woman's reasoning is that her father wasn't Jacob. She was a Samaritan. But notice how her titles for Jesus changed as she began to melt. She began with, "You're a Jew." Now, she says, "Sir." Soon she will be calling Him her Lord. Even so, at this point I think you and I might have chosen to give up on this caustic woman all together. Jesus, however, would not!

> Jesus answered and said to her, "Whoever drinks of this water will thirst again, but whoever drinks of the water that I shall give him will never thirst. But the water that I shall give him will become in him a fountain of water springing up into everlasting life."
>
> —John 4:13–14

"You're thinking of the water in this well. I'm talking about the Holy Spirit, the eternal life that will spring up in you," Jesus said. Well water only satisfies for a while. The woman at the well knew that all too well. She came every day at noon all by herself. The bucket was heavy, the water heavier still.

"Whoever drinks of Me will never thirst again," Jesus said. I've been a Christian for thirty-one years now. During that time, I've bought and sold and had a lot of things in life—and all of them have just worn out. But my relationship with God hasn't. I'm not tired of it. I'm not tired of going to church, not tired of reading the Bible, not tired of praying. To this day, I look forward to all of it. It's all as fresh and exciting as the first day I was saved. I can't say that about anything else I've ever had in my life.

I love the way the Lord slowly brought this woman from the physical, from the defiance, and from the difficulty, to the spiritual. "I have something you need," He said. "I can give you living water. I can give you eternal life."

> The woman said to him, "Sir, give me this water, that I may not thirst, nor come here to draw."
>
> —John 4:15

She still hadn't taken a spiritual leap, but this woman was beginning to sense that it was more than just well water Jesus was talking about. "If I didn't have to come here every noon, if I didn't have to be hot and tired, oh, that would be wonderful," she said. Remember, she began the conversation by saying, "How are You going to get water?" Now she is saying, "I'd like what You're offering."

Then Jesus brought her to step two, which is essential for salvation, the need to see our sin and confess it. That has to take place for life to be given. Jesus now had her interested so He put His finger on that which was bothering her the most, that to which she could readily admit. He now would help her see her sin.

> Jesus said to her, "Go, call your husband, and come here." The woman answered and said, "I have no husband." Jesus said to her, "You have well said, 'I have no husband,' for you have had five husbands, and the one whom you now have is not your husband; in that you spoke truly."
>
> —John 4:16–18

As the woman was brought face to face with God's knowledge of her life and her failure, her responses to Him suddenly became very short. "I don't have a husband," she said. Her fight was gone. Her sin was obvious. And Jesus did something I hope you don't miss. Both at the beginning and at the end of what He said to her, He complimented her on her honesty. He didn't tear her apart. Sin had done that enough. He didn't drag her over the coals. Instead, He said, "You're absolutely right in what you've said. You've spoken truly." And with great kindness, Jesus brought this woman forward.

When Jude wrote about witnessing, he said in verse 21, "On some have compassion and make a difference." The Lord came with compassion. Yes, he talked to this woman about her failures in her life. But He didn't do anything beyond bringing her to the place of admission. It was all she needed to confess her sin.

Jesus didn't say to her, "You've been married five times. This is going to take some serious counseling. You have issues. You've had five husbands. It couldn't be all their fault. It must be you." Jesus' counseling clinic wouldn't make much money today, as quickly as He fixed people. Here within minutes the past life and sins and waywardness of this woman that He loved were washed away, and she was given new life by Him in its place.

> The woman said to Him, "Sir, I perceive that You are a prophet. Our fathers worshipped on this mountain, and you Jews say that in Jerusalem is the place where one ought to worship."
>
> —John 4:19–20

The woman now adds another moniker to Jesus; first a "Jew" then "sir" and now "prophet." Yet she also did what many do when they go to church, hear the message, and as the Gospel begins to hit too close to home: turn the subject to something else. It can be any religious subject, as long as it's not personal. But Jesus wouldn't let her get away so easily. It was for her heart he had come.

> Jesus said to her, "Woman, believe Me the hour is coming when you will neither on this mountain, nor in Jerusalem, worship the Father. You worship what you do not know; we know what we worship, for salvation is of the Jews.
>
> —John 4:21–22

"If you want to know who's right, the Jews are," Jesus said. "They're the ones who have been entrusted with the Gospel, with the promise of the Messiah to come."

> "But the hour is coming, and now is, when the true worshipers will worship the Father in spirit and truth; for the Father is seeking such to worship Him. God is Spirit, and those who worship Him must worship in spirit and truth."
>
> —John 4:23–24

"You want to know where to worship," Jesus said. "But I want to tell you how to worship. If you want to have a relationship with God, you'll have to come in spirit and in truth. It's not geography—it's the condition of the heart. It's not where—it's why. It all depends on the heart." And because Jesus didn't take the standard Jewish position, the woman softened a bit.

> The woman said to Him, "I know that Messiah is coming" (who is called Christ). "When He comes, He will tell us all things." Jesus said to her, "I who speak to you am He."
>
> —John 4:25–26

The woman by this time really had no way to argue. Unfortunately, at this point, as we see in verse 27, the disciples return with food from town. Whenever God's about to do a great work, doesn't something always interrupt? The cell phone goes off in church at the altar call. That's just the way it is when there's spiritual warfare for people's souls.

> And at this point His disciples came, and they marveled that He talked with a woman; yet no one said, "What do You seek?" or, "Why are You talking with her?" The woman then left her waterpot, went her way into the city, and said to the men, "Come, see a Man who told me all things that I ever did. Could this be the Christ?" Then they went out of the city and came to Him.
>
> —John 4:27–30

The disciples were amazed that Jesus would talk to a woman at all, let alone a Samaritan woman. And although they said nothing, they must have made known their intentions because they interrupted the conversation. The woman didn't get a chance to respond. Her eyes got big. Her waterpot was left behind. I don't know if she left it so Jesus could get some water or if it meant she'd be right back, or because suddenly physical water wasn't the most important issue to her. Maybe the presence of this group of Jews frightened her, In any event, she was off, heading down the same dirt trail the disciples had just come up. John tells us what she declared when she came to the town.

I love the description of the woman's heart because notice that the first thing she does is tell others about the Lord—the very ones who had hurt her and talked about her. She went to the hateful people in the town to tell them God loves them. "Come with me," she said. "I've met Him. He's the Messiah. He laid out my whole life."

In reality, Jesus only had talked about her husbands. But that's not how she saw it.

"He knows me," she said. She went up the hill a child of Adam and came down a child of God.

With great love, she confessed, her life was changed, and in the Old Testament sense she was saved from her sin. She called Jesus "a Jew," "sir," and "a prophet." Then she went into town and said she had met "the Christ." She'd come a long way in twenty minutes, hadn't she? Touched by God, she began to share so much that the town came out to invite the Lord to stay the weekend so people really could understand who He was. Jews invited to stay in Samaria—who knew!

How thankful we are that the Lord loves us so much that He would go out of His way to come and find us where we live. If no one else cares about us, He does. If no one else comes to find us, He will. And if everyone else avoids us, goes around us, and is not a part of our lives, He loves us more than we could know. We are in many ways like this woman at the well, grinding away at life, hiding our hurts under a tough exterior, in fear living under isolation, sorrowful over our sin and often clinging to some religious hope in which we really have no confidence. But in the midst of her despair, Jesus sat at her well and showed her Himself. And as a result, she found life.

> In the meantime His disciples urged Him, saying, "Rabbi, eat." But He said to them, "I have food to eat of which you do not know." Therefore the disciples said to one another, "Has anyone brought Him anything to eat?" Jesus said to them, "My food is to do the will of Him who sent Me, and to finish His work."
> —John 4:31–34

If you've ever slaved over a hot stove to fix dinner for your family only to hear them say, "I'm not hungry," you know how the disciples must have felt. It was the middle of a hot day and they had gone into a Samaritan town to get Jesus some food—not a place they wanted to be. Have you ever wondered why they all went to get food? I think it was because they were either looking for or expecting trouble.

"What fills Me," Jesus said, "is doing the will of God." And as He had done with Nicodemus and the woman, He turns His conversation with the disciples to a spiritual plane and this time the illustration of food and eating and hunger is used to teach some hungry, thirsty guys.

Want to be revived? Start reaching out to others with the good news of who Jesus is. It's better than a vacation and more filling than a five-course meal. The disciples didn't see that, but they needed to learn that nothing will satisfy more.

When Paul in 2 Corinthians 5 spoke about the new birth experience, he said God has reconciled us to Himself and we are ambassadors for Christ. In other words, you get saved and then go tell others. That's the church's job. Nothing compares with doing the Father's will. It's supposed to be the hunger of our hearts and the satisfaction of our lives. Jesus had been physically hungry and tired—and yet when the door to share opened, it seemed He forgot all His temporal needs and began to share in the joy of meeting spiritual ones.

When the Devil told Jesus to turn stones into bread, Jesus said, "Man does not live by bread alone but by every word that goes forth from God's mouth." So too, He says here, "I'm most hungry to do My Father's will." That was what drove Him. That was what filled His heart. May it drive and fill ours as well.

God's will for us is certainly multi-faceted and spelled out for us in the Bible in several places, but here's one very clear direction we should embrace. God's will is that we share our faith and see to it that others hear about Him. And it is a work that truly satisfies. The disciples needed to learn that God was working and wanted to work through their lives to accomplish spiritual things. This discourse with the disciples paved the way for Jesus to set a principle of vision before them as they waited for the woman to return.

> "Do you not say, 'There are still four months and then comes the harvest'? Behold, I say to you, lift up your eyes and look at the fields, for they are already white for harvest! And he who reaps receives wages, and gathers fruit for eternal life, that both he who sows and he who reaps may rejoice together. For in this the saying is true: 'One sows and another reaps.' I sent you to reap that for which you have not labored; others have labored, and you have entered into their labors."
> —John 4:35–38

If you track months and times by the Jewish feast calendar, it would seem this might have been in April. The harvest came in September. If the fields had just been planted, the people would have been saying, "Four more months and we're going to the bank. We're going to cash in. We'll have enough money for the year." And although it is true physically that there is a gap of time between planting and reaping, Jesus said to the disciples that spiritually there was no need to wait four months because God is planting constantly.

If this was indeed April, the fields would have been barren and plowed under; the seed would have been in the ground, but nothing would have been showing above ground.

When Jesus said, "Look at the fields," the disciples would have said, "Yep, barren. Just like Samaria." But I think as Jesus said this, down the road, over the hill, and off in the distance came a woman with a town in tow because verse 39 tells us that many came out of the city to meet with Jesus, to invite Him to stay, and to ask more questions. Therefore, I think the Lord said, "Look up. Look over there. See those white robes coming over the hill? That's what I'm talking about. That's the fruit. We don't have to wait four months. There is work to be done right now."

Jesus wanted to give the disciples a very clear demonstration of a very important truth. That is, when it comes to evangelism, the fields are already white unto harvest. Yet we usually respond with several hundred reasons to do nothing about it.

"That person isn't ready."

"That guy's a real creep."

"That guy knows it all."

"That guy doesn't like me. I don't want to talk to him."

We don't think it will take just four months—we usually think it will take four years for someone to get saved.

We beg off with excuses because we don't have the spiritual vision Jesus had when He said, "Look around. The fields are white. There is work to be done today. There are needs to be met today. There are hearts to be reached today."

The "it will take years" mentality is an excuse we create to not do the work. It isn't something Jesus ever says. The disciples saw Samaritans. Jesus saw a field ready to be harvested. I think wherever God places us we usually conclude it is the most unlikely place for Him to move.

"My job? No one will get saved there. It's the most worldly place."

"My neighborhood? No one even comes out of the house."

"My school is so liberal."

"My family? They'll never listen to me."

We make excuses, telling ourselves that wherever God has placed us is the only place the fields aren't white.

Jesus said to work in the harvest, you've got to see one. Jesus always saw the harvest. Compare Him for a moment with His disciples. What a chasm of difference. When a woman washed Jesus' feet with her hair and tears, the Pharisees saw a woman with a bad reputation. Jesus saw an opportunity to minister. When the fathers brought their children to Jesus, the disciples saw an inconvenience. Jesus saw an opportunity to minister. From the blind beggars in Jericho, crying out for Jesus, to the demon-possessed man in Gadara screaming at the top of his lungs, Jesus saw fields white unto harvest.

How do you see the world? That's the issue.

What perspective do you have on evangelism? That's the question.

Do you start with the concept that the field is white, or do you assume no one is ready?

When Paul went to Corinth, he had a pretty rough go of it. In discussions with some men on Mars Hill, he tried quoting their poets and reasoning with them on a secular level. But nothing worked. Then, we read in Acts 18:9 that the Lord appeared to him at his lowest point and told him, "Don't be afraid. I'm with you. I have many people in this city to reach. You just keep talking."

Evangelism needs proper perspective. According to verses 36 to 38, we can't judge ripeness by appearance. We don't know if someone already has planted a seed or if someone else already has watered it. "You're going to be reaping where you haven't been planting," Jesus said to the disciples. "You're going to enter into someone else's labor."

Compared to the Old Testament prophets who gave their lives for the word of the Lord to be preached in Israel, the disciples were "Johnny-come-latelys"—yet it is both the reaper and the sower, the Lord said, who will rejoice together in that day.

The process is constant because you don't know in what state someone's heart is. Only God does. What is our job? We must have a spiritual perspective where we see the fields ready to harvest and be willing to go out and work rather than determine the place isn't ready.

The time to reap and the time to sow are now. Look up. Look around. Look who's coming down the road: some soon-to-be believers? Indeed! Putting things off has never been good in any kind of situation, but it's the worst when it comes to sharing your faith. The disciples wanted to wait. "Let's wait till we get to Galilee, where our people live. We speak their language. We like their food. We can stay at their houses. They love us."

But there's no gain in delaying sharing your faith.

> And many of the Samaritans of that city believed in Him because of the word of the woman who testified, "He told me all that I ever did." So when the Samaritans had come to Him, they urged Him to stay with them; and He stayed there two days. And many more believed because of His own word. Then they said to the woman, "Now we believe, not because of what you said, for we ourselves have heard Him and we know that this is indeed the Christ, the Savior of the world."
>
> —John 4:39–42

Rarely in the Bible do you find a wholesale coming to Jesus like this but I think it illustrates with an exclamation mark what Jesus had been teaching. The woman everyone hated—the one other women kept an eye on, the one who was a threat to their families—became the instrument through whom God spoke. Her testimony was only what she knew, yet many believed. Others were motivated to come and hear Jesus themselves. And when they heard Him speak, many more were saved.

We tell. God convinces. It was in the unlikely city of Samaria that Jesus was first called the Savior of the world. John was so taken by this that in 1 John 4, some 60 years later, he wrote, "We have seen and want to testify to you that the Father has sent His Son. He's the Savior of the world." John picked up that phrase in Samaria.

It's a wonderful lesson: we should look at the world not as a place of challenges and nuisance, irritants and bother, but as a place to minister. Who knows what seeds have been planted or what has received a good watering? There's reaping and sowing to do, followed by more reaping and sowing. You just gotta get out there and do it. God is ready to use you. But, like the disciples, we've got to get over what we see, because there's more to ministry than meets the eye.

God has much to be done. Whom will He use?

I hope it's you.

SECTION II

THE SECOND YEAR

Chapter 5

THE HEALING OF THE NOBLEMAN'S SON

John 4:43–54

After ministering to Nicodemus and the Samaritan woman, Jesus headed for Galilee, where He would begin His second year of ministry. From Matthew 4 and Mark 1 we know that following John the Baptist's arrest, Jesus went north with the express purpose of picking up where John had left off. Matthew writes, "From that time forth, Jesus went preaching, 'The Kingdom of heaven is at hand'" (Matt. 4:17). Mark 1:14–15 tells us that when John was put in prison, Jesus came to Galilee, preaching the kingdom of God. When John was arrested, Jesus purposely went to Herod Antipas' domain to stir things up, to be confrontational, and to demand that people listen. It was no longer a quiet ministry to individuals. Now it would become citywide and nationwide—which eventually would lead to the Cross and our redemption.

Josephus, the Jewish historian, wrote that at the time of Jesus, there were some 204 cities in Galilee with a population of over ten thousand people. It was a much more populated place than it is today. And as the Lord went north, the opposition continued to grow. The first event following His arrival in Galilee was ministry to a nobleman's son, yet another individual encounter with Jesus who comes for us personally. We read:

> Now after the two days He departed from there and went to Galilee. For Jesus Himself testified that a prophet has no honor in his own country. So when He came to Galilee, the Galileans received Him, having seen all the things He did in Jerusalem at the feast; for they also had gone to the feast.
> —John 4:43–45

The two days in verse 43 refer to the two days Jesus spent in Samaria at the Samaritans' request.

If you had been with Jesus that first year of relatively obscure ministry, you would have known it had been very fruitful. But the past couple of days had been awesome: you stop by, talk to a woman at a well, and pretty soon the whole town is begging you to stay. If there's ever a place of ministry you love, it's where people are open to hearing. Samaria was where the despised and rejected were, the ones who were persecuted. And they loved what they heard.

I always think the best job in the church is teaching new believers' classes because when people first get saved they love to learn. They're like vacuum cleaners. You say something and they write down every word. Samaria must have been like a new believers' class. But now Jesus and the disciples were off to Galilee, where it would be a much different story. In fact, Matthew reports that when Jesus showed up and began to speak, people began to ask one another, "Isn't this the carpenter, the son of Mary? Don't we know His brothers and sisters?" Soon they were despising Him for acting and talking like He was more than a child from a small town where everyone knew everyone.

Even as He left Samaria, Jesus knew what kind of homecoming He could expect. He knew what was waiting for Him. There would be rejection and opposition. Within only a week, people would be trying to kill Him. Kill Him! Imagine that!

You read these things and say to yourself, *Why go there at all? Why bother when people don't want to hear?*

The answer that Matthew gives us is that God has a heart for the lost. In chapter 4, he quotes from Isaiah 9 concerning Jesus' arrival in Galilee, saying the people sitting in darkness now saw a great light. There was an easier place to minister, to be sure. But there were people in Galilee whom God sought to reach and whom He loved, and the darkness had gripped their hearts and the Light was now coming to show them the way.

I think so often we determine God's will based on how easy things go. If it's blessed and easy, it must be God. If there are trials and difficulty, we can't be on the right track. But that's not true. Jesus went where the Father wanted Him to go—but to do so He left the place of blessing and receptivity to go to a place where, for the most part, many would refuse to believe in Him at all. Reaping had taken place in Samaria. Sowing would have to take place in Galilee.

> So Jesus came again to Cana of Galilee where He had made the water wine. And there was a certain nobleman whose son was sick at Capernaum.
>
> —John 4:46

The welcome Jesus initially received in Galilee had nothing to do with the message He preached—that people are sinners and they need forgiveness, and that the Messiah had come. Instead, the people were excited because of what they heard He had done in Jerusalem. Now that He was in town, they were sure they would catch one of His "performances."

Rather than being convicted by their sin, they were enamored with His reputation and work. There was no hunger for the Lord, no desire to follow Him, and no conviction of sin. There was just curiosity. They weren't looking to Jesus as the Savior of the world—they were looking at Him as a sideshow. If curiosity welcomed Him, soon unbelief would seek to silence Him.

But in the midst of this lukewarm reception came a man with a tremendous need. He was called a nobleman, but the Greek word *basilikos* means "a king's man." He was apparently a high-ranking officer in Herod's army, a Gentile who had traveled from his home in Capernaum some twenty-five miles away to come to Cana because he had heard Jesus was there.

We don't know how he got his information about Jesus. But we do know that even though all the people in Cana were excited about Jesus' arrival because of the miracles He had done, there was one man in town that day who was there because of the need he had. His young boy was on death's doorstep, gravely ill at home. It doesn't matter how wealthy, powerful, or tough you are. One day or another, you're going to have a need for the Lord in your life. On this particular day, this Roman soldier did.

> When he heard that Jesus had come out of Judea into Galilee, he went to Him and implored Him to come down and heal his son, for he was at the point of death. Then Jesus said to him, "Unless you people see signs and wonders, you will by no means believe." The nobleman said to Him, "Sir, come down before my child dies!"
>
> —John 4:47–49

Put yourself in this ruler's shoes. He had heard Jesus was in town. He had heard what Jesus could do. He had traveled all the way from his home to see if somehow he might persuade a man he didn't know to come with him miles out of His way.

What an agonizing five hours it must have been for this man. I'm sure he was going over and over in his mind, "If I find Him, this is what I'll say. This is the argument I'll make. This is the way I'll ask." He longed for, needed, and had to have an answer. This was as important to him as life itself. He simply had to persuade Jesus to come with him. And, like many who wait until tragedy strikes, he found himself having to find a God he didn't know and to consider seriously the claims of a God he hadn't considered.

But the Lord is all right with that. Better late than never—and He met him right where he was. Jesus' initial response to him might stop you in your tracks. Because it's written in plural, it means His words were not to the man only but to the crowd who, according to verse 45, was interested only in what it saw, not in who He was: "Unless you people see signs and wonders, you won't believe." Jesus' intent was that people would be attracted to Him who did the signs rather than His signs themselves.

Whenever you read the words *signs and wonders* in the Bible, they're always used to highlight aspects of Jesus' work. They were wonders in the sense that they were to draw attention to God's supernatural work. They were signs in the sense that they were to point to an individual: Jesus. What happens to many people, however, is they get caught up in the signs and wonders and not in the Lord. And that was certainly the problem for those in Galilee.

"Do a trick. Perform a miracle. Do something spectacular," they said to Him. They weren't there to *meet* Jesus. They were there to get something from Him that wouldn't speak to their hearts at all. So Jesus reprimanded them for being sign-seekers and not God-seekers—which must have broken His heart. Just up the road in Samaria, some fifty miles away, their was a town full of hungry-hearted people who believed in Jesus without so much as seeing a miracle. Now Jesus had come home here and the crowds were eager only to see a trick—except for that one man who needed much more!

The Lord uses signs and wonders to attract people to Him. But they are never the end. The end is knowing Him. If you stop at God's work and never come to know Him, you'll miss out on the life He came to bring. So Jesus didn't give the people what they hoped to see. He did, however, meet this man who, though weak in faith, was longing for help and had come looking for Jesus in the hopes of finding it.

> Jesus said to him, "Go your way; your son lives." So the man believed the word that Jesus spoke to him, and he went his way. And as he was now going down, his servants met him and told him, saying, "Your son lives!" Then he inquired of them the hour when he got better. And they said to him, "Yesterday at the seventh hour the fever left him." So the father knew that it was at the same hour in which Jesus said to him, "Your son lives." And he himself believed . . . .
> —John 4:50–53

Jesus' response moved the man to act in faith even though He said very few words to him. The man believed in the Person of Jesus and did as he was told. It was as if the Lord said to him, "You want Me to come to Capernaum? There's no hurry. I'm the Lord. Go your way, your son lives."

Pretend you are standing before Jesus with this man and notice his response. For him, believing was seeing. If Jesus hadn't been God, His words would have been cruel comfort. But if He was God, His words were all the man would need. To this man who had been running for five hours, out of breath, with a tear-stained face and anxious as could be, the Lord essentially said, "Relax. If you believe Me, you can go home in peace."

We know from what the servants said the next day that it was one o'clock in the afternoon when the man met with Jesus. Therefore, he could have said, "Thank you," ran right home, and been there in time for dinner. In fact, if there was ever a time to go crazy and buy a horse, that would have been a good time. Five hours away from the most important care of my life.

But Jesus said, "Slow down. Trust Me. He's fine." And the man did just that. He believed the word Jesus spoke to him and went his way, back to a normal pace of life. Whatever brought this nobleman to Jesus, hearing His words caused him to believe, and his act of faith changed his action of life. Why didn't he go home that evening? Because Jesus had said, "Go your way." And he believed Him. That's the kind of faith God wants to build—not the kind that would run home to see if He did it or not.

Want to live a stress-free life? Believe Jesus' word and go your way. That's where real life is found. If He said it, you can count on it. This nobleman found himself on the receiving end of God's goodness. While the town looked for miracles, he looked for God.

> . . . and his whole household. This again is the second sign Jesus did when He had come out of Judea into Galilee.
>
> —John 4:53–54

This man was now so convinced that his testimony and faith soon invaded his entire house. We see the same thing happening throughout Scripture. When the Philippian jailer believes, his family believes. When Crispus, the head of the synagogue, believes, his family believes. When Lydia believes, her family believes. In Psalm 103, David wrote that righteousness will carry down even to the children's children. It seems God likes to work that way.

In Matthew 8, there is another man who comes to Jesus. He's a Roman soldier. He has the same need as this man—one in his family was sick. He went to Jesus with his need and received from Him a healing touch. He also lived in Capernaum. But that's where the similarities end.

You might remember this story of the centurion with the servant who was sick. He'd been a great help to the Jews. He had even helped them build a synagogue in Capernaum, the ruins of which still stand on the shores of the Sea of Galilee to this day.

"Let Me come over and I'll heal him," Jesus said.

The nobleman said, "Lord, I know how authority works, and with that understanding, I know You don't need to come to my house. I know how far Your power extends. I know You're the Lord of all of these things. I know that if You just speak the word, my servant will be healed."

Jesus was amazed. "I have not found faith this great in all of Israel," He said. I wouldn't be surprised if this nobleman had told his story to that centurion. After all, they were both government officials.

"Go your way," Jesus said to the centurion. "Your faith has made him whole."

So here are two men—both Romans, both with tremendous need, both driven by love. Yet one came with very weak faith and Jesus had to convince him of whom He was: "You don't need Me to go there. I'm the Lord. I can speak from here, and twenty-five miles away your boy will sit up in bed and want Cheerios®." On the other end of the spectrum, the centurion came with such great faith that the Lord exclaimed He had not seen anything like it.

The nobleman is certainly the example of weak faith, the centurion of strong faith. Whom does God help? The awesome answer is both of them. So often, the Devil would like to convince you that if you had more faith, God could work in your life. That's a lie. God will work in your life through even the smallest faith in Him. Does He want to get you to a place where you don't run home? Yes. He wants to take you from John 4 to Matthew 8, from weak to strong. But He meets the needs of people wherever they are in that spectrum. All we need to do is believe Him.

Whether you're of weak faith or strong means little. Don't wait until you have more faith to seek Him. Just bring the faith you have and watch God work.

Chapter 6

JESUS GOES HOME

Luke 4:13–30
(Matthew 13:54–58; Mark 6:1–6)

So He came to Nazareth, where He had been brought up. And as His custom was, He went into the synagogue on the Sabbath day, and stood up to read. And He was handed the book of the prophet Isaiah.

—Luke 4:16–17

Jesus returned to His hometown. The people were thrilled He had come home. Nazareth was known as a backwoods kind of place. But the folks who had gone to the feast in Jerusalem and had seen His work were all talking about the hometown boy who had made good—phenomenally good! After all, He had opened the eyes of the blind.

I'm sure when He came into town there was a banner at the entrance that read "Welcome Home!" For a year, the news had filtered in about Him, and now He was here. But the welcome wouldn't last long because His message required believing in who He was and for these familiar folks, that was going to challenge them greatly.

Jesus' custom was to go to the synagogue. He placed great value on regularly going there to the place of worship, even though there were plenty of things in the synagogue that would have angered Him. The synagogues were outwardly religious but had very little love for God. In fact, it would be the leaders of these synagogues who would soon meet to try and figure out how to get rid of Jesus as He drew many to Himself.

I've heard people say, "I'm not going to church because it's just filled with hypocrites." And they're right! But praise the Lord for God's grace—or no one could come to church at all.

Paul wrote to the Hebrews in 10:25, "Don't forsake assembling together as is the manner of some." Although there will always be problems in churches, we need to be in fellowship. You'll never find things the way you wish they were. Jesus didn't—but He went anyway. It was His custom, His habit. It was vital to Him. What a great picture: God attending fellowship and worship.

I don't know if the synagogue in Nazareth usually was full, but I guarantee it was full this day because the hometown hero had come home and everyone wanted to see Him. "Wait till you see what He can do," they must have whispered expectantly.

In typical synagogue practice, there was a time of the reading from the Law, the prophets, and the books of wisdom from Job through Song of Solomon. These books were read

45

on a schedule. If you were asked to read in a synagogue, it usually would be because you attended and volunteered or it would be because you were a well-known visitor. Following the reading, there would be questions, comments, and interaction between the people and the one who had read. This day, Jesus was invited to read Isaiah 61, the scheduled passage. If you go to a synagogue today, you'll see Isaiah 61 is on the schedule four weeks before the Jewish New Year. Therefore, this would have been early September.

Jesus read a passage written by Isaiah in 683 B.C. about the purpose for His coming. He had come home to say, "Here's who I am and why I've come." It's a beautiful picture. It is also our message for the world: Here's why Jesus came; here's what He can do for you.

> And when He had opened the book, He found the place where it was written: "The Spirit of the Lord is upon Me, because He has anointed Me to preach the gospel to the poor; He has sent Me to heal the brokenhearted, to proclaim liberty to the captives and recovery of sight to the blind, to set at liberty those who are oppressed; to proclaim the acceptable year of the Lord."
> —Luke 4:17–20

The reader was allowed to choose which portion of the chapter to read. Jesus chose only a verse and a half, which would have taken about twelve seconds to read. He read verse 1 of Isaiah 61, half of verse 2, and then sat down. Why? Because He only read the part of the prophecy dealing with His first coming—the time of grace where God came to heal, deliver, and set free. In the middle of verse 2, the prophecy turns to the second coming of the Lord—when He will come to judge.

According to the words written here, we know Jesus read out of the Greek Old Testament, the Septuagint, a "modern" translation of the day.

Jesus, our example, said, "The Spirit of the Lord has come upon Me so I might preach good news to the poor and reach out to the lost." Certainly you and I are called and given the job of reaching out to every creature with the good news of Jesus, but we're not to even attempt it in our own strength. We're to do it in His. We need God's direction. We need God's empowering. We need God's boldness to rest upon us.

Jesus did preach the Gospel to the poor. This isn't a reference to the financial status of the hearer but to the spiritual condition of his heart. Jesus came to preach the Gospel to those who realize they spiritually have nothing to offer God (Matt. 5:3). "Blessed are the poor in spirit for theirs is the kingdom of heaven." To whom does Jesus come? To those who know they need Him. He would say to the religious folks later on, "I'm like a doctor but, because you don't believe you are sick, I can't help you" (see Matt. 9:12). Whom does the Lord save? Those who realize they don't have what it takes. That's us, right?

I remember reading that Lincoln said God must love common people because He sure made a lot of them. Later on, we'll read about the tax collectors and prostitutes gladly hearing Jesus while the rulers of the synagogue wanted nothing to do with Him.

When Mary was told she would bear the Messiah in Luke 1, she began to sing in spontaneous worship to the Lord. One of the lines in her song says, "He has filled the hungry with good things while leaving the rich empty" (Luke 1:53). That's what God came to do. Jesus came to feed those who realize they're poor in spirit.

When John the Baptist was arrested and had been in jail awhile, he sent one of his men to Jesus, figuring if Jesus was the Messiah and the program was to overthrow the Romans, he should be getting out of jail any day now, but it had not happened. In Luke 7, when this man came to Jesus, rather than answering his question directly, Jesus began to heal the sick, deliver those with evil spirits, and give sight to the blind.

Then He declared, "Go tell John the things you have been seeing and hearing—that the blind can see and the lame can walk, that the lepers are cleansed and the deaf can hear, that the dead are raised and the poor are hearing the Gospel." He knew John would recognize this prophecy of Isaiah 61 and the fulfillment of them in Jesus' work.

Jesus also came to heal the brokenhearted. If you've lived for a while, you've had your heart broken. It's hard to live in this world and not have that happen. There are winners and losers—but a whole lot more losers than winners in every field. Jesus came to heal, to put back together the aspirations that are lost when you discover what the world is all about.

"There's got to be more to life," you think. There is. And Jesus came to tell you what it is.

He also came to proclaim liberty to the captives. This is a phrase used often in Scripture, always to talk about being imprisoned in a spiritual sense. "I've come to set at liberty those who are bound by sin and can't escape," Jesus said. And Paul told the Corinthians that people are lost because the god of this world had blinded their eyes and held them captive.

"If the Son sets you free, you're free indeed," Jesus said in John 8:36. To the Galatians—a church that had been made free but was going back to its old ways—Paul wrote, "Stand in the liberty with which Christ has made you free. Don't go back to the entanglements and bondage you were once in."

I love the fact that, in Christ, you're free to do the right thing. People always ask what they have to give up to become a Christian. But it's not a matter of giving up the wrong things—it's a matter of having the ability to do the right thing, which you can't do if you're not saved.

Jesus came to set at liberty those who are oppressed. The word *oppressed* means "to be crushed." It's interesting to me that not only does Jesus save a life, but He restores it. In Joel 2, God said He would restore that which the canker worm had destroyed. God restores your sanity and purpose, joy and life. What an awesome message we've been given concerning what the Lord can do in the lives of those who look to Him. He ends by saying He came to proclaim the acceptable year of the Lord—and it's in the present tense. When is the acceptable year of the Lord? It's right now, while God still offers salvation by grace.

And He began to say to them, "Today this Scripture is fulfilled in your hearing."

—Luke 4:21

Or in other words: "This is Me. Isaiah wrote about Me. I have the ability to heal your broken heart and set you free from your sin, open your eyes that have been blinded by sin, and restore your life that has been destroyed in the process, to make you new. Today." Then He shut the book and sat down.

So all bore witness to Him, and marveled at the gracious words which proceeded out of His mouth. And they said, "Is this not Joseph's son?"

—Luke 4:22

That "all bore witness" means people saw and understood for themselves. It was personal. "I have come to heal the brokenhearted, to set at liberty the captives, to preach the Gospel to the poor." I am speaking to every one of you.

No hellfire and brimstone here. This was the Lord's announcement. It was meant to be great news for His hometown folks—and the Lord delivered it with great kindness. Yet as He spoke, in the hearts of the people there likely arose this problematic thought: *We know this kid. He's saying He's the Messiah? He made my dining room table.*

On the one hand, people were moved with great excitement that Jesus could indeed be the Messiah. But on the other hand, although His charm captivated them, their wonder clashed with His familiarity. They admired His words but they weren't affected by them. They admired His style, His attitude, and the way He presented Himself—but the things He said didn't affect their hearts.

Jesus said to these crowds at home, "I've come to preach the Gospel to the poor."

Yet no one in the synagogue said, "That's me."

"I've come to set at liberty those who are captive," He said.

Well, that isn't me, they all thought.

"I've come to proclaim liberty and heal broken hearts," He declared.

"But can You do one of those tricks You did in Jerusalem?" they said. "We want to see something cool."

Unfortunately, for the folks in Nazareth, their religion not only blinded them to the truth of the Gospel, it stirred them to anger.

The same is still true today. You can get away with sharing the Gospel with people as long as you stick to these things:

- God loves you.
- Jesus died and rose again.
- You can have life if you want it.

Where things usually go south is when you say, "By the way, you're the sinner for whom Jesus came. You need to personally apply this to yourself."

> He said to them, "You will surely say this proverb to Me, 'Physician, heal yourself! Whatever we have heard done in Capernaum, do also here in Your country.'" Then He said, "Assuredly, I say to you, no prophet is accepted in his own country.
>
> —Luke 4:23–24

It wasn't that the people in town that morning didn't have enough proof. They already had a year of testimony and witness. Instead, it was simply of choosing not to believe the evidence they had been given.

Jesus' works would have demanded consideration. But when you're religious, you stay put and just don't budge. So they began to murmur.

> "But I tell you truly, many widows were in Israel in the days of Elijah, when the heaven was shut up three years and six months, and there was a great famine throughout all the land; but to none of them was Elijah sent except to Zarephath, in the region of Sidon, to a woman who was a widow."
>
> —Luke 4:25–26

The people in Nazareth would have known this story from 1 Kings 17. During Elijah's ministry, a famine had caused thousands to die of starvation. God told Elijah to go to a Gentile city, where he would find a widow. When he found her he asked her:

"Do you have any food?"

"I have enough flour and oil to make one more meal for my son and me before we die," she replied.

Elijah, God's prophet, said, "Feed me first and you and your son will never have to worry again about having flour or oil. God will provide."

And this Gentile woman, without any Jewish history, background, or relationship with God, said to the prophet, "Fine. Take it."

She went home and made bread with her flour and oil and gave it to Elijah. And God responded by miraculously providing the flour and oil the woman needed each day, even as Elijah had prophesied.

What is Jesus' point to those sitting in the synagogue? This was a woman who had very little to go on, who had very little awareness of God, and who had only the reputation of a prophet who had spent very little time in her neighborhood—yet in her desperation she risked everything she had on God's promise. If she had had a couple of vats of oil and tins of flour in the house, she might have told Elijah to take a hike, knowing she could rely on her own reserves. But she was out of resources—and that's often the time when the good news of our Lord makes sense. She had no one to turn to, nothing to survive on. If this prophet could bring the blessing of God, then, in faith, she would do what he asked.

That she was a Gentile would have been offensive enough to the Jews. But that she was a woman made it even worse. Jesus didn't have to make the application. The people in Nazareth already knew it. If they wanted further proof of Jesus' claims to help the poor, blind, and embittered, all they had to do was trust Him. But that was the problem. In their eyes, they didn't need Him. They were good citizens of Nazareth. They went to synagogue every week. Therefore, to be unfavorably compared to a Gentile woman was an insult.

The comparison, however, was correct—for unlike the Gentile woman, they had so much evidence to go on but had brought such little response. Jesus gave them one other comparative to consider.

> "And many lepers were in Israel in the time of Elisha the prophet, and none of them was cleansed except Naaman the Syrian."
>
> —Luke 4:27

In 2 Kings 5, we're told of the Syrian army and how they had overthrown Israel. As a result, a Syrian general named Naaman had taken a Jewish girl into his house as a slave. Rather than being bitter however, she was sorry that her captor, the general, suffered from leprosy and suggested: "You ought to go to Israel. There's healing there."

Naaman in his desperation and having nothing to lose went and showed up at the palace of the king with money and gifts in hand. Finally summoned by Elijah to his home, the prophet directed him to go and dip seven times in the Jordan River and he'd be cleansed. Naaman, hearing this advice, was fit to be tied. "Who does he think I am, dipping in the Jordan?" he said. "We have cleaner rivers at home." He stormed off in anger and determined to leave this country immediately.

But one of his servants argued, "We've come this far. If he'd have asked you to do something difficult, you would have given everything. Give it a try."

So Naaman was persuaded. He gingerly went down into the Jordan and proceeded to dip seven times. As he arose out of the water the 7th time, he was absolutely healed. He rejoicing hurried back to the house of the prophet. "Now I know there is no God in the world except your God," he said to Elijah. He had so little to go on. But with his illness he went, and in going he found God's power and deliverance. Why? Because he had come to the end of himself. There was nothing he could do for his leprosy. He had to turn to God. And he did.

Both Naaman and the widow took steps of faith contrary to their own rationale. God honored their trust. Both had far less to go on than these Nazarenes who had heard about Jesus for the past year and had the scriptures given them by God which spoke of the coming Messiah. Both Naaman and the widow found it difficult to act in faith and yet both responded because they saw their needs as impossible to fix on their own. After all, some hope was better than no hope at all. God did not disappoint them; He won't disappoint you!

> So all those in the synagogue, when they heard these things, were filled with wrath, and rose up and thrust Him out of the city; and they led Him to the brow of the hill on which their city was built, that they might throw Him down over the cliff. Then passing through the midst of them, He went His way.
> —Luke 4:28–30

The citizens of Nazareth had heard enough. It was one thing to see a young boy from their neighborhood think He was God. It was another for Him to point His finger at them, tell them they were the problem, and compare them to Gentiles. That is why Jesus' sermon was followed not by a benediction or prayer, but by a riot as everyone in their collective religious wrath went after Him.

Up until this time, in everyone's mind Jesus had never done a thing wrong. He was the kid every parent wished his children were like. He was an honest, hard-working, dependable young man. But now, when He spoke about God's mercy and the need to repent, everyone began to turn. When He cut through the religious façade, all they could think about was killing Him.

They dragged Jesus out of town and to the high place of the city, intending to throw Him over a cliff. But if they wanted to see a miracle, He'd show them one: He'd disappear. Jesus will come back here at least once more. Matthew 13 and Mark 6 tell us of His return. But He will face the same difficulty of unbelief yet again. For now Jesus turned back to Capernaum—a town whose people believed and trusted in God—where most of the miracles recorded in the Gospels took place.

It is tragic when background, church tradition, and pride keep anyone from faith in Jesus, the only Way. Religion won't help. Jesus will. Traditions can't save. He can. The difficulty is, familiarity with the story can deaden you to the truth.

Don't miss out on the truth just because you're familiar with the story. Come to Jesus, for He alone can give you life!

Chapter 7

FOLLOW ME!

Mark 1:14–20
(Matthew 4:12–17; Luke 4:14–15)

Following John the Baptist's arrest, with great determination Jesus had come north. He passed through Samaria heading for Galilee to preach the message John had been preaching. If Jesus had predominantly ministered to individuals in His first year of public ministry, He would minister to the crowds and thousands of people in His second year. And as He did, the opposition would continue to grow more malicious and hateful. By the end of the second year, there would be meetings on a monthly and even weekly basis to see how He might be killed. The battle for men's souls raged on.

> Now after John was put in prison, Jesus came to Galilee, preaching the gospel of the kingdom of God, and saying, "The time is fulfilled, and the kingdom of God is at hand. Repent, and believe in the gospel."
>
> —Mark 1:14–15

Mark does not tell us here why John was arrested. He'll cover that in chapter 6. For now, he only mentions it to tell us what caused Jesus to come north. In chapter 4 of his gospel, Matthew quoted Isaiah 9 as the reason Jesus came. He says those who were sitting in darkness in Zebulun and Napthali had seen a great light. Those who were lost were now finding life. Jesus' arrival in the north was the fulfillment of that Isaiah 9 prophecy. Those who had sat in darkness were about to find a light even greater than John the Baptist.

The message Jesus came to bring is very clear and is written here in one verse. He came to declare that the time was at hand. There are several words for "time" in Greek. One of them is *chronos*, which means "clock." Another is *kairos*, which speaks of a time span or measure of time. It is in this time frame that salvation is available and this is the word Jesus uses here.

The response to this is the Greek word *metanoeo*, meaning "to turn around or to repent." *Metanoia* speaks of turning from the direction in which you have been heading to follow God's direction. The word *pisteuo*, or "believe," implies "placing all of your weight upon Him as your one hope."

That's the message Jesus came to preach. And in every city He visited, that was the Gospel He declared: "Good news, the kingdom of God is here. You've got a period of time now in which you can respond by repenting of your ways and believing in Me." That makes it very simple, doesn't it?

It's a great three-point outline to follow when you're sharing with your friends: The time is now. God is ready to rule. If He's going to rule in your life, you must turn and follow Jesus.

A lot of people conclude they are Christians because they go to church. We live, after all, in a Christian nation. At least it once was. But if you haven't repented and turned to Jesus with your sin, and believed in His sacrifice, you're not saved. Without Him there is no good news, but He brings good news to all who would hear His call. We are given here by Mark the calling of Jesus to the hearts of a few men he would use mightily.

> And as He walked by the Sea of Galilee, He saw Simon and Andrew his brother casting a net into the sea; for they were fishermen. Then Jesus said to them, "Follow Me, and I will make you become fishers of men." They immediately left their nets and followed Him. When they had gone a little father from there, He saw James the son of Zebedee, and John his brother, who also were in the boat mending their nets. And immediately He called them, and they left their father Zebedee in the boat with the hired servants, and went after Him.
> —Mark 1:16–20

If you're reading through this with an eye toward detail, you might think it strange and unusual for people to drop what they're doing without any kind of thought and simply follow Jesus. And you would be right—it rarely happened in the Scriptures. Most people have an understanding as to why they have decided to follow the Lord. No one follows Him blindly. He doesn't hypnotize or mesmerize. He calls us to make a decision about Him. These four men in our verses above had a year to think about who Jesus was, to watch Him, to question Him, and to understand the things He was teaching and mull over the things they had heard about Him. Yet they had been aware of Jesus for over a year by this time . . . a look back will show us how they got to this point of surrender.

Back in John 1:19–28, as Jesus began His public ministry, the apostle had covered a day in John the Baptist's life—when he had been confronted by the religious leaders in regard to who he was and had clearly told them, "I'm not the Messiah. I'm not Elijah the prophet. I'm just the voice of one sent out from the wilderness to tell people to prepare and make straight the ways of the Lord. I baptize with water, but there's another One coming and I'm not even fit to tie His shoelaces. He's going to baptize you with fire, with the Holy Spirit."

> The next day John saw Jesus coming toward him, and said, "Behold! The Lamb of God who takes away the sin of the world! This is He of whom I said, 'After me comes a Man who is preferred before me, for He was before me.'"
> —John 1:29–30

After saying to no one in particular, "I am the One sent to prepare and point out the way," John saw Jesus and said, "Behold, the Lamb of God who takes away the sin of the world." John didn't leave much doubt as to who Jesus was. He's the Lamb of God who came to die for our sins.

What a beautiful picture and type is this portrait of Jesus being the Lamb of God. Back in Genesis, Abraham took Isaac up to the mountain to be sacrificed according to God's Word. On the way up, Isaac said to his father, "I see the fire. I'm holding the wood. But where's the lamb?" He was looking for the lamb.

Here John the Baptist clearly declares, "Behold, the Lamb." And in the last book of our Bibles we find the church in heaven in Revelation 4, singing, "Worthy is the Lamb."

In Genesis 4, Abel brought a lamb to sacrifice for himself and God honored the sacrifice. In Exodus 12, we find a father sacrificing a lamb for his entire household at the Passover. By the time we come to the Gospels, we find our Heavenly Father sacrificing His Son, the Lamb of God, for the entire world.

John was older than Jesus, but in verses 15, 27, and 30, he says, "He's before me" because he wants us to understand that Jesus was no ordinary man. This was the Son of God, eternal in nature, in human flesh.

> Again, the next day, John stood with two of his disciples. And looking at Jesus as He walked, he said, "Behold the Lamb of God!" The two disciples heard him speak, and they followed Jesus. Then Jesus turned, and seeing them following, said to them, "What do you seek?" They said to Him, "Rabbi," (which is to say, when translated, Teacher), "where are You staying?" He said to them, "Come and see." They came and saw where He was staying, and remained with Him that day (now it was about the tenth hour).
>
> —John 1:35–39

John the Baptist was a true minister because he nudged people to Christ. At best, our calling is the same: get people to Jesus rather than seek to attract them to you or your personality or have them join your denomination or peer group. Bring them to Jesus. The most faithful servant is the one who helps people get to Jesus. John the Baptist did just that.

Who were these two disciples switching allegiances this day? Verse 40 tells us Andrew was one of them. No doubt the other one was John. John never mentions himself in his gospel account. He's been left very humble by the time he writes his account. From Luke, we also know Andrew and his brother, Simon, were business partners along with James, John, and their dad. This was one big company of fishermen.

John and Andrew went with Jesus and spent the evening with Him. By the time they awoke the following morning, both arose and headed out to tell someone else they believed they had found the Messiah.

> One of the two who heard John speak, and followed Him, was Andrew, Simon Peter's brother. He first found his own brother Simon, and said to him, "We have found the Messiah" (which is translated, the Christ). And he brought him to Jesus. Now when Jesus looked at him, He said, "You are Simon the son of Jonah. You shall be called Cephas" (which is translated, A Stone).
>
> —John 1:40–42

Andrew went to get his brother, Simon. John would get his brother, James. Whenever you see the word *Andrew* in Scripture, you always read "Simon Peter's brother" after it. To his credit, whenever you see Andrew in the Bible, he is always bringing people to Jesus. He might have been tempted not to share with Peter what he had discovered, because Peter always seemed to get the upper hand. But it's hard to keep Jesus to yourself. So he brought his brother, Simon. And as he did, Peter became the first person in the New Testament reached by a family member.

By observation, that is the single greatest way God works in reaching the lost: one by one by one. Those who have watched you and experienced what God has done in your life are the ones who most often will come. In this regard, Peter is the first convert. Later on, when there's no food, guess how the boy with the loaves and fish will get to Jesus? Andrew will bring him. Still later, when the Galileans want to meet with Jesus in Jerusalem, it will be Andrew who brings them as well. Make us more like Andrew, Lord!

When Jesus saw Simon, a very unstable, impetuous, emotionally driven man, He immediately changed his name as if to say, "You've wavered, but I'm going to make you solid." Cephas, or "stone," is Syrian for the Greek *Petros*.

> The following day Jesus wanted to go to Galilee, and He found Philip and said to him, "Follow Me." Now Philip was from Bethsaida, the city of Andrew and Peter. Philip found Nathanael and said to him, "We have found Him of whom Moses in the law, and also the prophets, wrote—Jesus of Nazareth, the son of Joseph."
>
> —John 1:43–45

In the days of Jesus, if you wanted to learn from a rabbi, you would ask if you could join his group and follow him. John the Baptist had his group. The Pharisees had their group. And Jesus went out to invite His group. You didn't have to ask Him. He'd ask you. Here quickly Jesus had six men following Him: two because John the Baptist had pointed them to Him, two who had reached their brothers, one because Jesus had invited Him with the words, "Come with us," and one brought by a friend. By the end of the first week of public ministry, Jesus has a crew of people who have begun to learn He is the Lord.

And what an interesting crew it was! There was Andrew, a very quiet and calculating kind of guy. There was Peter, hotheaded, impulsive, and outspoken, who would answer first and then wonder what the question was. There was Philip, who always seemed to look on the negative side of things. There was Nathanael, who the Bible indicates to teach was a brainy, bookworm kind of guy. And there were James and John, the sons of thunder, the rowdy guys.

We don't know how long these men traveled with Jesus or how often they spent days or weekends with Him. We do know they went back to work because, in the following year when Jesus comes to the Galilee after John's arrest (Mark 1:14–15) they're still running their fishing business. They knew of Jesus. They respected Him greatly. But they weren't with Him full time. They went with Him to the wedding feast in Cana. They were aware of the water being turned into wine, but they traveled away. For the next year, they seemed to find themselves again lost in their jobs and yet aware of Jesus.

When Jesus came north, He encountered Simon and Andrew, James and John, and gave them the invitation to follow Him. Immediately, all four of them did.

Think about this for a minute. Here were two sets of brothers along with a dad who had a very lucrative business that made a lot of money now being asked by the Lord to drop what they were doing and follow Him full time. We know they were successful because Peter was married and had a house in Capernaum, and John owned a home in Jerusalem and was able to take in Mary following Jesus' death. This departure to follow Jesus would have been like the entire upper level management in a business leaving at once. What happened to the business? I don't know. I do know what happened to the men: they were changed.

> So it was, as the multitude pressed about Him to hear the word of God, that He stood by the Lake of Gennesaret, and saw two boats standing by the lake; but the fishermen had gone from them and were washing their nets. Then He got into one of the boats, which was Simon's, and asked him to put out a little from the land. And He sat down and taught the multitudes from the boat.
>
> —Luke 5:1–3

What did Jesus teach? The message of Mark 1:15: "The kingdom of heaven is at hand. Repent. Believe. Good news." We don't know what the result was, but we do know there were so many people gathered on the shore listening that Jesus figured it was better to preach from a boat in the water than to try to stand on the shore.

> When He had stopped speaking, He said to Simon, "Launch out into the deep and let down your nets for a catch." But Simon answered and said to Him, "Master, we have toiled all night and caught nothing; nevertheless at Your word I will let down the net." And when they had done this, they caught a great number of fish, and their net was breaking. So they signaled to their partners in the other boat to come and help them. And they came and filled both the boats, so that they began to sink. When Simon Peter saw it, he fell down at Jesus' knees, saying, "Depart from me, for I am a sinful man, O Lord!" For he and all who were

with him were astonished at the catch of fish which they had taken; and so also were James and John, the sons of Zebedee, who were partners with Simon. And Jesus said to Simon, "Do not be afraid. From now on you will catch men." So when they had brought their boats to land, they forsook all and followed Him.

—Luke 5:4–11

After preaching from his boat, Jesus said to Peter, "Let's go fishing." The problem for Peter was that he had been fishing all night. As owner of the company, he knew all the fishing spots. He knew how the waters were and what types of bait to use. And one thing he knew for sure: you don't catch fish with nets during the day. At night, the fish come up. It's dark. They're not afraid. They eat off of the surface and you catch them with nets. But when the sun comes out, the fish go down into the darkness, and no net could reach three hundred to five hundred feet deep into the Sea of Galilee. It would be a worthless endeavor.

Yet Jesus said to Peter, "Let's go fishing." And over the last year, Peter had developed a great respect for Him.

"Lord, if it was anyone else, I'd tell them to go fly a kite. But it's You. All right. You want to go fishing? Andrew and I will take You out."

"Let's take some nets," Jesus said.

Peter, apparently, only took one. And as he let it down, it filled up so full that the boat began to list to one side. Peter, a very good fisherman, cried out for help. All night, he had caught nothing, but with Jesus it was a different story.

At this point, Peter realized Jesus wasn't only the speaker of Good News and the wise man who seemed to hold the religious at bay, but One who knew more about fish than even he did, One who controlled the whole situation. For the first time in Peter's life, what he knew about fishing caused him to surrender to the Lord now in his boat. He had known about Jesus for a year, but now he actually saw Him for who He was.

What was the first thing Peter saw when he saw Jesus? He saw himself as sinful. What was Jesus' message? Repent and believe. What was Peter thinking when Jesus was in his boat half an hour earlier preaching to the crowds? "Yeah, that's what He always preaches— the repent and believe thing. He's good at that. He's got that wired in."

But it never got to his heart until he saw the fish in the boat. The attitude with which he had set sail was wiped out by one incident as the Lord showed Himself to be wiser than Peter was at his wisest.

"Lord, depart from me. I'm sinful." It was Peter who spoke—but everyone there now felt the same way. Their lives were changed when they went from knowing about the Lord to actually *knowing* Him. When they got to shore, they left the best catch of the week, month, or maybe the whole year laying there for others to take. They forsook all, followed Him, and never went back—except for a moment when they returned to fishing after Jesus' death and He had to remind them again that they were supposed to be fishing for men.

A lot of people know the Lord in the sense that they know about Him. They listen to sermons, but nothing seems to penetrate. They can quote the right verses. They know the God of the baby in the manger and the resurrection at Easter. But He's not really their God.

Up to this point, Peter, James, John, and Andrew had been able to go on with their everyday lives and have Jesus simply be part of them. "Oh, we see Him now and then. Sometimes we have dinner with Him and hang out in the evenings. He's really cool." They had a good feeling about Him and they were quite comfortable with Him. But they weren't about to leave everything behind for Him. That required a revelation.

When they actually came to know the Lord, these four men left everything and followed Him with all they had. "I'm going to make you fishers of men," Jesus said. "Your job was once to catch fish, but your calling now is to catch the hearts of men." And over the next twenty-five years, these four guys would turn the world upside down for Jesus. Their lives would impact the planet from one end to the other as they preached the Gospel. When did it begin? When they finally surrendered all.

You might think you never can do any more than go to church. But there comes a time in your spiritual life when you come to meet the Lord who is revealing Himself to you in such a way that you're willing to give Him everything. And it is only then that God can begin to turn the world upside down with you. It isn't enough to have a passing acquaintance, head knowledge, general awareness, or respect for Him. The Lord wants us to have a love relationship with Him to the degree that we would forsake all else to follow Him.

Don't be satisfied just knowing about the Lord. Be sure that you're at a place where you would leave everything behind for Him. Know this, God wants to bring you closer.

Chapter 8

A Day in the Life of Jesus

Luke 4:31–44

Our text before us gives to us an unique picture of one day in Jesus' life—from morning through the afternoon into the late evening, and then before dawn again the following morning. Jesus' stamina for ministry and others knew no bounds.

> Then He went down to Capernaum, a city of Galilee, and was teaching them on the Sabbaths.
>
> —Luke 4:31

Although they were as unalike as two cities could be, Nazareth and Capernaum were very close geographically. In Capernaum, Jesus was believed on by many. As a result, He did many great works there. In Nazareth, His hometown, virtually no one believed in Him. The Lord goes where He's welcome. If He's desired, He's there. One of the last verses in our Bible tell us, "Whosoever will, let him come and drink freely of the water of life" (Rev. 22:17). If you want to, God wants to. If you need help, God has help. If you need life, God has life for you. Are you open to hear, receive, follow? If so, then He is more than ready to come and minister to you.

You will find this verified truth throughout Scripture. You can see it at work in the church. One arrives and listens to God's Word intently and with desire, and soon he is growing in faith and bearing fruit. Love, service, peace, and joy in the Lord become evident in His life. Yet right next to him sits a man who seems to be dying on the vine. Same service, same sermon, same pew—and yet such a different result. Maybe he's not yet so open to hearing what God has to say. Maybe he's not willing to obey the things the Lord wants him to do.

Maybe for him, it's routine, not love; religion, not relationship. The first man is a prime example of Jesus' invitation, "whosoever will." The other simply won't, has no desire to come to the Lord. God's Word promises to bring life, joy, peace, and rest—but it only can be accomplished in those who are hearers and then doers. Jesus went to Nazareth and they threw Him out of town. He went just up the road to Capernaum and they rolled out the red carpet. As a result, Capernaum became a place of great ministry. In fact, Jesus spent more time there than in any other city in Galilee and there are more recorded miracles from Him in Capernaum than all of the other cities combined.

Learn well the lesson that Jesus works where He's wanted. He would later tell the Pharisees, "I'm a doctor. If you're sick, I'm the answer. If you've got an illness, I'm the cure. But if you don't believe you are ill, I can't do you any good" (Luke 5:30–32).

Capernaum is located on the northwest shore of the Sea of Galilee. In Jesus' day, it was a thriving place. In fact, three of the major highways in the northern part of Israel passed through this city. The Lord made it His headquarters for the better part of two years. When Matthew writes in chapter 9 about Capernaum, he calls the city "His city." In Matthew 17, when Jesus has to pay taxes, He pays them in Capernaum. This is a place that was associated with Him. So when you read He went down to Capernaum, what a breath of fresh air it must have been for Him compared to Nazareth from which He had come. No wonder He went there every week and taught on the Sabbath.

The ruins of the synagogue in which Jesus preached are still standing today and are a part of our tour through the Holy Land. From Luke 7, we know a Roman centurion who had a good relationship with the Jews built it. That is why it's a synagogue with Jewish emblems and Roman architecture. This was the place Jairus will come to find Jesus later in Mark 5 to tell Him about his daughter who was dying and seek His help.

> And they were astonished at His teaching, for His word was with authority.
> —Luke 4:32

The word *authority* is the Greek word *exousia*, which means "right" or "privilege." When Jesus spoke, the crowd said, "Now here's a Man who seems to have a right to say these things. He has the ability to declare these things." They were convinced of Him by the assurance with which He spoke authority, because that's how He spoke. His heart was laid out before them.

The people were astonished because no one but Jesus had taught like this in the synagogues. What an awesome message! He spoke about heaven and hell as if He knew about them. He told how a broken heart could be fixed. He explained how sin could be dealt with and how fear could be resolved. And the people flocked to hear Him. According to Jesus, the scribes and Pharisees were only concerned with incidentals and externals of religion—yet He systematically took them to and through the Scriptures and taught them God's Word and His way of life.

Jesus had a great love for the people, and it showed. He was concerned for their welfare. He pointed them to the Father. The scribes and Pharisees were only interested in lording it over people. In Luke 20:46, Jesus said to the crowds, "Be careful of the scribes and Pharisees. All they want to do is walk around in long robes in the marketplace, receive greetings, the best seats in the synagogue, and the greatest places of honor at the feasts. Yet what they're really doing is preying on widows and making long prayers for a pretense." That's what the people were used to—and then Jesus came. No wonder they loved to listen to Him. He spoke with authority, and loved them enough to tell them the truth.

A couple of miles down the road from Capernaum, Jesus will later deliver what became known as His Sermon on the Mount and say at least six different times, "You have heard it said of old, but let Me tell you what that means . . . ." to differentiate the teachings of the religious and the Word of God. The scribes and Pharisees always quoted each other to establish their authority. Jesus simply spoke as God.

So touched were many by His message that, when the Pharisees eventually sent guards to arrest Him they returned empty-handed, declaring, "No man ever spoke like this Man" (John 7:46).

Every week, Jesus returned to speak—and every week, the people's hearts were moved. We are now taken by Luke to one particular Sabbath.

> Now in the synagogue there was a man who had a spirit of an unclean demon. And he cried out with a loud voice, saying, "Let us alone! What have we to do with You, Jesus of Nazareth? Did You come to destroy us? I know who You are—the Holy One of God!"
>
> —Luke 4:33–34

Imagine being at a church service when a demon-possessed man begins to screech out loud. That's worse than a cell phone going off! Yet true to form, wherever you find Jesus in the Gospels, you find the Devil following Him not far behind. I don't know if we see less of that today because we're too weak to get a response from hell, but we certainly see it in Jesus' ministry in the Gospels. Hell was upset because lives were being touched.

We're in warfare—of that I am sure. I'm also sure the Devil never misses a church service. If he doesn't come in, he'll wait outside the door to go home with you, because he doesn't like what God is doing in your life. Satan wants to destroy. Peter said that, like a roaring lion, he looks for those he can devour (1 Pet. 5:8).

Lions only roar when they're assured of victory, when they have their prey in their sights and cornered. Here, however, the Devil's cry was not one of victory but of fear: "Are You here to destroy us?" Every demon that meets Jesus in the Scriptures responds to Him with a mixture of fear and hatred as he begrudgingly confesses Jesus' lordship over him.

In Mark 5:6, we read that when the demon-possessed man saw Jesus coming, he ran to Him and worshipped Him. Most people believe the Devil is extremely powerful—but that is not the case when Jesus is around. The Devil is real powerful if it's just you and him. Then you lose. But you will be fine as long as you keep Jesus between you and the Devil!

> But Jesus rebuked him, saying, "Be quiet, and come out of him!" And when the demon had thrown him in their midst, it came out of him and did not hurt him.
>
> —Luke 4:35

I love the way Jesus confronted the situation: very calmly, very powerfully, and with tremendous love for the individual. The phrase "be quiet" or "hold your peace" can be translated from Greek as "be muzzled." Every time a demon cried out, Jesus silenced him.

"Come out of him," is only four words, but they were sufficient. After all, it wasn't an epic struggle. It was the Lord of creation and a created being—no contest. In defiance, the Devil threw the man down but didn't hurt him. He can terrorize us but he can't resist God's Word.

> Then they were all amazed and spoke among themselves, saying, "What a word this is! For with authority and power He commands the unclean spirits, and they come out." And the report about Him went out into every place in the surrounding region.
>
> —Luke 4:36–37

In verse 37, the word *report* means "echoes." The buzz began to echo throughout the country, and I suspect more and more people showed up at synagogue each week. What a work God was doing! And when God works, the world takes notice. Here in Capernaum, those seeking to be delivered, healed, and set free began to come to Him.

I think if the church is walking with Jesus, the city in which the church is planted ought to show the effects. In Capernaum, God was working. Lives were being changed. The demon-possessed were being delivered and echoes of it were resounding all around. That should be our testimony as well. We've got to be sure we're out there being a witness of God's work and that the echoes of His power are bouncing in every direction.

> Now He arose out of the synagogue and entered Simon's house. But Simon's wife's mother was sick with a high fever, and they made request of Him concerning her. So He stood over her and rebuked the fever, and it left her. And immediately she arose and served them.
>
> —Luke 4:38–39

Following the service in the synagogue, Jesus went to Simon Peter's house in Capernaum. Notice that Peter is married. In fact, 1 Corinthians 9:5 says he took his wife on many trips. Luke, being a doctor, is the only one who described Peter's mother-in-law's illness as a high fever. She might have had something like typhus. The disciples didn't demand that Jesus heal her or claim that He should. They simply asked Him. Just as we are instructed to pray for one another, they asked the Lord and left it with Him.

When the Lord rebuked the fever, not only was Peter's mother-in-law healed, but she was absolutely restored. The weakness of the fever left and she had enough energy to make grilled cheese sandwiches for everyone. When Jesus heals, He heals completely. I like the fact that Jesus was as ministry-minded at home as He had been in the synagogue.

> When the sun was setting, all those who had any that were sick with various diseases brought them to Him; and He laid His hands on every one of them and healed them. And demons also came out of many, crying out and saying, "You are the Christ, the Son of God!" And He, rebuking them, did not allow them to speak for they knew that He was the Christ.
>
> —Luke 4:40–41

After sunset on that Sabbath day, the travel restrictions of the Law were lifted. Because of the echoes throughout the community of what Jesus had done, many more people gathered, bringing the sick with them. The Lord had ministered in the morning, where a demon-possessed man had interrupted the service. He had healed Peter's mother-in-law in the afternoon. In the evening, the people lined up to be healed. And the Lord ministered to every need.

Luke writes that Jesus laid hands on every one of them singularly—that He took time with each individual. That's how God works. He's a Shepherd who loves His flock.

Notice also that God the Holy Spirit makes a clear distinction through Luke's writing here between the sick of verse 40 and the demon-possessed of verse 41. Many say today that all sickness is of the Devil. The fact is that all sickness is of the flesh. We're sick and we die because we've sinned. Sin has entered the world and death through it. Does the Devil use sickness? Yes. There are a couple of places in Scripture that this is mentioned—but predominately the issue is one of this sinful world.

We get sick because, as we get older, we wear out. Does God heal? Certainly. Does He tell us to pray for the sick? Definitely. But there are times when God has more important things to accomplish in our lives. To associate sin and sickness at every turn gives the Devil way too much credit I believe.

> Now when it was day, He departed and went into a deserted place. And the crowd sought Him and came to Him, and tried to keep Him from leaving them; but He said to them, "I must preach the kingdom of God to the other cities also, because for this purpose I have been sent." And He was preaching in the synagogues of Galilee.
>
> —Luke 4:42–44

Mark 1:35 adds, "Now in the morning, having risen a long while before daylight, He went out to a solitary place and there He prayed." As busy as He had been on the Sabbath, I think if Jesus wanted to sleep in, this might have been the morning. But He didn't. He got up well before dawn and hightailed it to pray. More work called for more prayer. More needs called for more prayer. Mark and Luke tell us that when the disciples found Jesus, they mentioned to Him that the crowd was calling for Him. But Jesus said He had to go to the next town so others could hear the Gospel and see God's work.

How many ministries do you know that would pull up stakes and move in the midst of great success? Jesus did. There were 204 cities in the Galilee region that needed to hear the Gospel. So from services in the morning to ministry at home in the afternoon to the long lines at night to prayer before sunrise—and then leaving to find more needs—Jesus' ministry life rolled on one day after the other.

I don't know how much time you spend with the Lord reading the Bible, seeking Him, or ministering to others, but I know that to the extent you're available, God will work through you. To the degree you believe in Him, you'll see His strength and power at work.

It's faith plus availability that God uses. If you follow Jesus and seek to obey His voice, you'll be busy. But as you seek first His kingdom and His righteousness, He promises everything else will be taken care of. If you put the effort into the things of God, He'll take care of the details of daily life.

Chapter 9

CLEANSING, HEALING, AND THE OPPOSITION

Luke 5:12–26
(Matthew 8:2–4; 9:2–8; Mark 1:40–45; 2:1–12)

In this second year of His ministry, Jesus' popularity grew daily—but so did the opposition. In the following stories from Luke that involve a leper, a paralyzed man with some friends who knew how to take off a roof, and some religious leaders who only knew how to criticize and find fault, God will teach us about faith and what kind of faith he honors. Let's begin here with the leper who came looking for Jesus' healing touch.

> And it happened when He was in a certain city, that behold, a man who was full of leprosy saw Jesus; and he fell on his face and implored Him, saying, "Lord, if You are willing, You can make me clean." Then He put out His hand and touched him, saying, "I am willing; be cleansed."
>
> —Luke 5:12–13

Leprosy is always a type of sin in the Bible and God uses it often to teach us much about sin's destructive ways and His ability to deliver us from it. Today, leprosy is known as Hansen's Disease. We can control leprosy with medicine, but in the days of the Lord, by the time people knew they had it, it was too late.

Sin is like that. It destroys you before you even realize you have it. And if you don't deal with it, it will wipe you out completely.

The leper here in Luke 8 saw Jesus and, having nothing to lose, ran right at Him, which for a leper was absolutely against the Law of the unclean separating themselves from others. "Cleanse me, Lord," he begged. "If You're willing, You can make me clean." With leprosy in the Bible, it's never healing that is addressed or required but rather cleansing. And that's what God does with our sin.

I appreciate this man's faith. We know the Lord did too. Usually when we get in very desperate places, to be able to say to the Lord, "Whatever You want is OK" is a hard statement to utter and mean. We typically have very specific instructions, don't we? "God, this is what I want You to do," we pray. "I don't want to take no for an answer. I'm afraid to trust You lest You do the wrong thing. Here's what I need . . . ."

How much has your faith grown when, like this leper, you say, "Lord, I'm in great need. If You want, if You're willing, then You can heal me. I know it's just a matter of Your will in my life." Notice in response that Jesus doesn't write this off as second-class faith. He honors it as genuine.

Over the last fifty years or so, there has been a faith movement in the church that has sought to redefine the kind of faith God honors. Part of this teaching says that if you don't have an adequate measure of faith you'll receive nothing from God but if you do, you can ask for whatever you want and get it. It's a good thing this poor leper hadn't heard that teaching, for he was willing to pray, "Lord, do whatever You want to do in my life. I trust You."

It is certainly no lack of faith to let God be God. You will find in the Bible folks who are not healed, though they have great faith. They die in faith. Others are raised up only to fall sick again. It's our hearts, the sin of our lives, and eternity that God wants to deal with as primary needs and they always overshadow temporal comforts and gains.

Mark writes in chapter 1 that the Lord was moved with compassion for this man. He just loved him. I like that, don't you? The Lord is moved by our needs. Luke tells us He touched him—which would have been against the Old Testament Law, except that when Jesus touched him, he immediately was made whole. I like that too. I think the Lord often wants to do so much more than that for which we're willing to trust Him. We're often unwilling to say, "Lord, do whatever You want to do." If we did, God could, and I suspect He would do so much more.

> Immediately the leprosy left him. And He charged him to tell no one.
> —Luke 5:13–14

After such a glorious and miraculous deliverance come these startling words from Jesus: "Don't tell anyone." Would you have been able to do that? If you hadn't been able to hug your children or wife in thirty years, you'd run home like crazy and tell everyone, wouldn't you? In many places throughout the Gospels, we find Jesus telling people not to tell anyone. Yet no one ever listened. If God's really done something in your life, you can't help yourself. You've got to tell someone, don't you?

Why did Jesus say this? I think because He sought to keep the crowds in check. His time wasn't up yet. He had to be able to move around and minister and this would keep the mob mentality at bay for a bit longer.

"Don't tell anyone," Jesus said, but the people couldn't help but tell. Today, He says, "Tell everyone," yet the church is so often silent. I wonder if it's because we're not all that thrilled over what God has done with us when we should, like the leper, realize God has saved us from a horrible eternity. If we were aware of His marvelous deliverance, how could we not shout it from the rooftops?

> "But go and show yourself to the priest, and make an offering for your cleansing, as a testimony to them, just as Moses commanded."
> —Luke 5:14

Jesus told him to go to the priest and offer the sacrifice required following the cleansing of leprosy instructions as specified in Leviticus 14. How often do you suppose they offered one of these sacrifices? It had been four hundred years since God had even sent a prophet into the country. No one was being healed of leprosy. And here comes this man to the temple asking to offer the offering of one cleansed of leprosy.

"Do you know anything about the leprosy offering?" the priests must have asked each other as they pushed the ladder to the bookcase to grab Volume 20 of the Law. No living priest had ever seen this. It was a section of the Law on which they wouldn't even have been tested in priest school.

If you look carefully, after this first leper was cleansed you will find more scribes, Pharisees, and priests gathering around Jesus. I think it was the talk of the temple: "We did the leprosy healing ceremony yesterday." "You did what?" "Yep, this man was sent in by Jesus to be checked and deemed clean!"

By the time we come to Acts 6:7, after the church had been born and things were moving forward, we read that the number of priests obedient to the faith were many. Here the seeds for their conversions were being planted. The Lord can do the impossible. He can change lives, even yours!

> However, the report went around concerning Him all the more; and great multitudes came together to hear, and to be healed by Him of their infirmities. So He Himself often withdrew into the wilderness and prayed.
> —Luke 5:15–16

Tell no one—but everyone knew! Notice that the busier Jesus got, the more He withdrew to pray. If you really want God to use your life big time, find time to pray and watch Him work. The worst thing you can do is become so busy in serving God that you forget where your strength lies. Jesus often withdrew to pray and so should we.

> Now it happened on a certain day, as He was teaching, that there were Pharisees and teachers of the law sitting by, who had come out of every town of Galilee, Judea, and Jerusalem. And the power of the Lord was present to heal them.
> —Luke 5:17

"Them" applies to the scribes and Pharisees. The fellow with leprosy knew he had a disease from which he couldn't deliver himself. He confessed. He came for help. If you're not saved and you're wondering if God wants to save you, He's willing. "Whosoever will" is a pretty big door. But if you're religious and refuse to take God's path through His Son, then you have no future and there is nothing God can do for you. Although His power is available, it will do you no good.

The Pharisees—or, literally, the "separatists"—were men who lived such outwardly religious lives that not only was everyone in awe of them, but no one could even hope to be like them. In the Sermon on the Mount, Jesus said to His disciples, "You better be holier than these guys if you expect to get to heaven on your own." He continued a bit later saying, "Outwardly, they look great. But inwardly, they're like sepulchers painted white, yet are full of rotten bones."

So here we see this picture of Jesus teaching the multitudes, while sitting on the outskirts of the crowds were religious folks who had great influence, but who bore a false message that deceived people and led them astray. Notice they don't sit with the crowd. They sit nearby. They want to hear what Jesus is saying to try and use it against Him—but they don't want to associate with the people pressing in at the doors and windows to hear Him speak. We're told in Mark 2 that this took place in Capernaum where Jesus spent a lot of time—maybe it occurred at Peter's house. We're also told that the crowd was so great that people were hanging out the doors and windows just to hear His voice.

> Then behold, men brought on a bed a man who was paralyzed, whom they sought to bring in and lay before Him. And when they could not find how they might bring him in, because of the crowd, they went up on the housetop and let him down with his bed through the tiling into the midst before Jesus.
>
> —Luke 5:18–19

I love this setting for our lesson. You have a huge crowd where no one can get in. You have the bad guys sitting out on the "fault-finding bench." And you have four men, according to Mark, who brought a paralyzed friend or family member that needed Jesus' healing touch. They however had come too late, it seemed. They thought the service started at ten, but it had begun at nine. And now they can't get in. Most folks would be upset and just leave, but if your need is great enough, you might instead reply, "Lord, it doesn't matter if I have to take off the roof to get to You, but get to You I must."

> When He saw their faith, He said to him, "Man, your sins are forgiven you." And the scribes and the Pharisees began to reason, saying, "Who is this who speaks blasphemies? Who can forgive sins but God alone?"
>
> —Luke 5:20–21

I imagine that as dirt fell through the roof and these sweaty faces peered over the edge, Jesus had a big smile on His face, delighted by their faith. When the centurion came on behalf of his servant, Jesus said He hadn't found that kind of faith anywhere. When a woman with an issue of blood snuck through the crowd to touch Jesus, He said, "Your faith made you whole." Of the ten lepers who were healed, Jesus said to the one who returned, "Your faith has made you whole."

God is looking for faith. The question is, how much faith is enough? And that's usually where people are in error. They tell you a certain level of faith is required. But is it? According to what we see in the Gospels, we don't need great faith—just a simple trust in Jesus.

So Jesus looked at this dangling man with great faith, loved what He saw, and dealt with this greatest need saying to him, "Your sins are forgiven." And I'm sure the guys on the roof hearing this were more than a little disappointed. They just wanted him to walk. But as we have mentioned, the Lord always goes after the important needs first.

Obviously this was a repentant man because Jesus doesn't arbitrarily forgive those who won't repent. But His words sparked an immediate response from those outside on "critic row." The Pharisees and scribes called what Jesus had done "blasphemy" and declared that only God can forgive sin—which is absolutely true. So what were they missing then?

> But when Jesus perceived their thoughts, He answered and said to them, "Why are you reasoning in your hearts? Which is easier, to say, 'Your sins are forgiven you,' or to say, 'Rise up and walk'? But that you may know that the Son of Man has power on earth to forgive sins,"—He said to the man who was paralyzed, "I say to you, arise, take up your bed, and go to your house." Immediately he rose up before them, took up what he had been lying on, and departed to his own house, glorifying God. And they were all amazed, and they glorified God and were filled with fear, saying, "We have seen strange things today!"
>
> —Luke 5:22–26

Notice Jesus answered their minds' objections, He knew their thoughts. I can imagine the crowd falling into a hush. Then He answered with an action. The crowd was amazed. The phrase "strange things" in the Greek translates as "paradox." In other words, the crowd couldn't make sense of it. Jesus looked like a man. But He was more. He was God. It stretched their understanding and moved their hearts.

According to Mark, the scribes and Pharisees responded a bit differently—they simply got up and left. They had the evidence. The Lord's power was there to heal them. They had the proof. But they didn't have the heart for Him.

What kind of faith brings God's forgiveness and mercy? The kind you find at the end of the ropes holding the bed of the paralyzed man. But notice that even though God's power is available, you can walk away. The crowds glorified the Lord. The healed man glorified God. The leper told everyone. But the scribes and Pharisees went back to the huddle and said, "How are we going to wipe out this man?" For now, they were silenced. But they wouldn't be silenced for long.

What kind of faith is God looking for from you? The kind that recognizes you have an internal illness called sin, and only He can forgive you. You can't work your way there. You can't make it better. You can't fix it. It's one of those paralyzing kinds of deals. You're stuck. You ask. He's willing. But if you don't step out toward Him, there's nothing He can do.

Tell others about Jesus. Who will listen? Many won't—but, oh, what joy for those who will. Someone shared Jesus with me and, I suspect, with you. Now, who will you be sharing with?

Chapter 10

A SICK TAX COLLECTOR

Mark 2:13–22
(Matthew 9:9–17; Luke 5:27–39)

As the second year of Jesus' ministry continued, the crowds and opposition both grew. A couple of events tied together by Matthew, Mark, and Luke highlight the difference between the Good News of the Gospel of Jesus Christ and the religious ways of man. What distinguishes salvation from religion? That was the confrontation Jesus faced. His call to a tax collector and acceptance of an invitation to dinner at his house paint the picture of the vast difference between a religious man and a saved one. Let's take a look.

> Then He went out again by the sea; and all the multitude came to Him, and He taught them. As He passed by, He saw Levi the son of Alphaeus sitting at the tax office. And He said to him, "Follow Me." So he arose and followed Him. Now it happened, as He was dining in Levi's house, that many tax collectors and sinners also sat together with Jesus and His disciples; for there were many, and they followed Him. And when the scribes and Pharisees saw Him eating with the tax collectors and sinners, they said to His disciples, "How is it that He eats and drinks with tax collectors and sinners?" When Jesus heard it, He said to them, "Those who are well have no need of a physician, but those who are sick. I did not come to call the righteous, but sinners, to repentance."
>
> —Mark 2:13–17

I don't think anyone likes taxes. We like the paved roads, the hospitals, and the police departments—but we like the IRS about as much as we like high blood pressure. Two thousand years ago, it wasn't any better. Historically, the Roman government determined how many people lived in any given area, as well as what kind of industry there was, and taxed accordingly. A poll tax was also collected, which began at age fourteen for boys and twelve for girls and lasted until the age of sixty-five. In addition, there were ground taxes: 10 percent of everything one had for grain; 20 percent for wine and oil. These were fixed amounts. Rome then sold the collection of these taxes to the highest bidder. The tax collectors, in turn, added additional taxes to those Rome established for their own personal income. For example, a person could be taxed for road use according to how many wheels were on his vehicle, for docking fees, and for sales.

It's not hard to understand why tax collectors were disliked. Not only did they work for Rome, the occupying power, but they often worked through extortion and were considered thugs and criminals. Everyone hated the tax collectors—or publicans, as they sometimes are called in Scripture—who got rich by leaning on others. In fact, there was no lower rung on the social ladder than that of the tax collector. Tax collectors were so despised by Jewish culture that they weren't allowed to testify in court or to go into the synagogue. This makes what Jesus did all the more remarkable because here, followed by throngs of people, He went out of His way to go to the tax office and say, "Hey, Matthew! Come join us!"

Jesus invited the one guy everyone loathed to follow Him. And the Bible says Matthew left it all behind. In fact, Luke uses an imperfect, active verb tense in Greek which means Matthew came, followed and never looked back.

Peter, James, and John had watched Jesus for a year. In the boat on the Sea of Galilee, they were convinced of who He was before they left their fish behind. We know their history, but not Matthew's. We know only that Matthew lived in Capernaum, where most of Jesus' miracles took place. So Matthew had a lot to see and think about, but we aren't told any of his background—only that when called, he followed.

I think I got saved more like Matthew than Peter. I don't remember thinking for years that I should get saved. I just remember going to my drug dealer friend's house. We were supposed to go out and buy some drugs, but he conveniently forgot to tell me he got saved the week before. So instead of buying drugs, I ended up at a Bible study at his house and got saved that night. Although Matthew had a powerful and wealthy life, evidently he knew there was no peace, no joy, and no satisfaction in it. So he was ready to take Jesus up on His offer. So was I.

From the standpoint of getting a crowd to follow you, Matthew would have been the wrong guy to pick. Everybody hated Matthew. The crowd would have thought, *If he's coming, I'm not.* I can see Peter saying, "That guy has hit me up for money I don't know how many times. I hate that guy. Pick anybody but that guy."

But Jesus chose Matthew anyway. Throughout the Gospels I so often see Jesus calling the person nobody wants—the outcast, the hurting, the hated, the frustrated, the criminal. Look at us. Nobody wanted us. But Jesus took us. That's good enough for me. And it was good enough for Matthew.

I'm always amazed at with whom the Lord associates. It's a trademark of His ministry. He went to Mary Magdalene the prostitute, Zacchaeus the tax collector, and the woman at the well. That's the difference between grace and works. Works define you as either a winner or loser in the eyes of the world. God sees you in His grace.

I remember learning in an art appreciation class about masters like Botticelli and Leonardo da Vinci. But there was also an artisan named Donatello, a sculptor in Italy. He ordered costly, massive marble pieces from Florence. When one particular piece arrived, there were so many cracks in it he felt it was beneath him to use it. So it sat in a warehouse for several years until a relatively new artist came by who asked for and was given this cracked piece which he took to his studio in downtown Florence, where he worked on it for two years. When he was finished, he invited the public to come see what he had made. This new artist turned out to be Michelangelo and his statue turned out to be David. I think it is an apt illustration of what God can do with us crack pots.

"Matthew?" He said. "I'll take him because I can make of him what no one else can." I love the way the Lord does that. Even if people despise and reject us, God has a plan for us. His love overwhelms my failures and sin.

I don't know what Peter and the other guys thought about it all, but here came a man whose life had been changed by his encounter with Jesus. And the first thing you see about Matthew is that he wanted to give Jesus a party in His honor so he invited all his other tax collector buddies to come over and hear about what he had found. Jesus was only too happy to go. He couldn't wait to minister. Yet outside sat the religious men—and in this we see the contrast between grace and religion.

"Oh, look who He's eating with now," the self-made religious men said. "How could this supposed man of God eat with this riffraff?" Ah, but that's exactly why He had come. Grace is available to everyone, but religion only to those who perform well. So outside sat the grumblers.

You might say to yourself, "I never would be like that." But I think we are. We decide to whom we can witness and to whom we won't. Who we think will hear us, who seems willing to listen, who we would rather not talk to at all. But Jesus came to bring life to all and any who turn to him. Just ask Matthew!

I remember reading that when England ran out of silver to make coins, Cromwell sent his men to find silver. The only silver they could find was in the statues of the saints in front of the churches. So Cromwell said, "Melt down the saints and put them back in circulation." I thought that was great. As saints, we've got to be out in the world reaching out to others because that's exactly what Jesus would do.

"The Son of Man has come to seek and to save those who are lost," Jesus said. Matthew knew he was lost. He knew he was a wicked, sinful, hard-hearted individual. And because he'd had enough of it, God could help. Until a person repents, there is no help to be had. The most difficult part of the Gospel for many to hear is not that Jesus is God but that they are sinners who need Him. Like religious people who depend upon their works for their stance before God and thus have great difficulty seeing a need for Jesus our Savior, so we, without confessing our sinfulness, will be left to ourselves without hope or help.

Matthew is the perfect example of how low God can reach. And how hopeful it should be for all of us that He can save us. I was thinking about my own salvation the other day as I was working on this passage. The first time I met Jesus, I wasn't standing proud—I was falling on my face. I wasn't rich—I was broke. I couldn't offer Him anything. But that's when the Lord called and received me to Himself. Look at Matthew. He's way out there, but he's aware of his need. And all it took was one word from the Master for him to leave it all behind.

> The disciples of John and of the Pharisees were fasting. Then they came and said to Him, "Why do the disciples of John and of the Pharisees fast, but Your disciples do not fast?" And Jesus said to them, "Can the friends of the bridegroom fast while the bridegroom is with them? As long as they have the bridegroom with them they cannot fast. But the days will come when the bridegroom will be taken away from them, and then they will fast in those days."
>
> —Mark 2:18–20

The second picture of performance versus grace is seen in the Pharisees' disciples, who went around practicing an outward religion in hopes that it would give them better standing with God. According to the Law, which was intended to drive people to the Lord, the Jews were to fast once a year on the Day of Atonement. But the Pharisees, who tried to make the Law a performance tool, said, "If once a year is good, twice a week is far better." So they taught everyone they should fast twice a week.

Of them, Jesus said in Matthew 6:17–18, "These guys are always running around with long faces like they're starving to death." They wore their religion on their sleeve. They were always showing off their religious ways to receive the honor of men.

"How come Your disciples are always laughing and happy and we're always sad?" they asked Jesus.

"Because I'm here," Jesus said. "They're like the best man or the maid of honor, or a bridal party at a wedding. I'm the bridegroom. They're happy I'm here." There will come a time when I am gone that they will fast and pray and seek Me. But for now I am with them and they rejoice to hear My voice.

There is a place for fasting, of drawing close to the Lord and denying the flesh, as seen in Isaiah 58. But it never is to be used as an exclamation point behind prayer, a notch in spiritual standing, or a way to manipulate God into giving us something we want. Fasting is not a work. It's a response. To the religious person, any kind of joy or carefree heart is a sure sign of sin. But not to Jesus. He had dinner with tax collectors, telling them how they could be saved. So Jesus turns to speak to these men about fasting and their religion, versus the grace of God in salvation freely given to us in Jesus Christ.

> "No one sews a piece of unshrunk cloth on an old garment; or else the new piece pulls away from the old, and the tear is made worse. And no one puts new wine into old wineskins; or else the new wine bursts the wineskins, the wine is spilled, and the wineskins are ruined. But new wine must be put into new wineskins."
>
> —Mark 2:21–22

Jesus gives here two illustrations for the same lesson. Everyone can relate to the first example. If you have a hole in an old pair of Levis and you put a new piece of denim over it, when you wash your jeans the new piece will shrink and your one-inch hole will be three inches large. It's just not a good practice. Neither is giving people the expectation that fasting as they had defined it, religiously working your way beyond the call of God towards Him, will bring life.

People in Jesus' day more easily understood the second example He used than we would. In that day, used wineskins even when empty would contain traces of yeast left over from the wine they once held. If you happened to pour a new batch of wine into one of these old wineskins, the new wine would react to the yeast in the skin and begin to emit gases. Pressure would build inside the skin, causing it eventually to burst.

"When it comes to the Gospel," Jesus said, "the only containers that will hold it are new wineskins—lives that have been changed." You cannot mix grace and works, for they are contrary and cannot be held in one heart together. It is either works or it is grace!

The scribes' and Pharisees' message was in error because they used the Law to construct a performance-based religion that says, "If I do this for God, I expect God to do this for me. And when I get to heaven, I expect a welcome because I've done pretty well." The problem with this is that there's no room for the Gospel because the Gospel says we're all sinners, incapable of doing good on our own, and the wages of sin is death.

One of the most difficult things in any church is for new wineskins to remain new. That is why you find that most revivals throughout history have taken place outside denominational settings. Denominations don't usually allow the flexibility necessary for God to work. In England, there are churches in downtown London that seat eight thousand people—and no one comes. There was a time three hundred years ago when they were filled to the rafters with worshippers. What happened? God was crowded out by tradition. The Word was set aside. Dependence on the Holy Spirit was gone. And all that was left were lots of empty seats.

There's a big difference between being religious and being saved. May we learn from Matthew the depth and length to which the Lord will go to take us in by His grace. And may we learn from the religious men sitting outside with complaints and arguments that until we become sick in our own eyes, the solution Jesus brings is of no value to us.

Chapter 11

JESUS AT BETHESDA

John 5:1–15

One of the characteristics of the Gospels is the substantial amount of time devoted to the on-going battle between religion and its adherents, and Jesus who came to call us to faith and a relationship with Him. You can't read three pages in any of the Gospels it seems without running headlong into another confrontation between those teaching that the way to heaven was based on good works and their accomplishments and Jesus sharing the message of the salvation He came to bring to man: His work vs. ours. We have a picture of that here and of how debilitating it can be to hold to your religion of performance when God has come to freely offer us His grace based on His work at Calvary.

> After this there was a feast of the Jews, and Jesus went up to Jerusalem. Now there is in Jerusalem by the Sheep Gate a pool, which is called in Hebrew, Bethesda, having five porches. In these lay a great multitude of sick people, blind, lame, paralyzed, waiting for the moving of the water. For an angel went down at a certain time into the pool and stirred up the water; then whoever stepped in first, after the stirring of the water, was made well of whatever disease he had. Now a certain man was there who had an infirmity thirty-eight years.
>
> —John 5:1–5

Although John writes that Jesus went up to Jerusalem, coming from Galilee, He would have been heading south. Yet nowhere in the Bible do you read of people going down to Jerusalem, because its glory sits high upon a mountain.

We're not told which feast this was. We do know from Leviticus 16 that there were three weeklong celebrations every year in Jerusalem that Jews were required to attend. They were designed to call and bring His people to worship God for His goodness, celebrate His provision, and remember His past work. In Leviticus, they were called the feasts of the Lord. Here they are called the feasts of the Jews. I think one of the reasons for this change in terms was due to the replacement of true worship by religion. People were still coming—sometimes in record numbers—but not with an open heart to serve God or honor Him. Many were now simply going through the motions and reducing the feasts to yet another way to work their way into God's favor.

Before the destruction of Jerusalem in 70 A.D., a wall surrounded the city. One of the gates in this wall was named the Sheep Gate, it being the place people came to purchase the sheep required for sacrifice. We're told in verse 2 that by the Sheep Gate was a pool with five porches, or porticos. For years, critics sought to disprove the Bible, saying they'd never been able to find the pools. In fact, if you read any Bible commentary written before 1880, it will make mention of the fact that no one had ever discovered these pools. In the 1800s, an excavation crew digging next to St. Anne's church found two pools—one fifty-five feet long, the other sixty-five feet long—with covered porticos running the entire lengths of the pools. There were five in all, just as John said.

We're told here in verse 3 that under these alcoves a great multitude of sick people lay—lame, paralyzed, blind. It was a place of tremendous suffering and sorrow, and located only a stone's throw from the Temple Mount. One could lie there and listen to the worship emanating from the temple and listen to the priests offer up prayers of confession of sin crying out for God's forgiveness. Up above in the temple, religion was in full force. But here, for these with the greatest need, there was none to help.

John records that this place had a folkloric reputation—and as the story went, the first person into the water after an angel "stirred" it would be healed. John doesn't endorse this superstition, and the Bible's teachings certainly would deny it. But John mentions it as the reason many people were gathered and lying there. We know that these springs were fed by the underground wells from Solomon's pool outside of town. Bubbling water, therefore, certainly would have been a very natural occurrence. But the picture John paints for us is that those who are hurting and in such distress with no hope will rely on nearly anything and look almost anywhere for help.

So you found here the blind, lame, and paralyzed, all waiting for God to move. But theirs was a false hope. Stirring waters don't heal—even if you have been so extremely ill for thirty-eight years. I would refer those who argue that as long as you're sincere, everything will be fine, to this man who had sincerely waited for nearly four decades to be healed and was waiting still. Only Jesus coming to Him delivered Him and it is ever so.

The number thirty-eight is interesting. In Deuteronomy 2, you find the nation of Israel being turned away from the Promised Land through unbelief. In verse 14 of that chapter, you read that for the next thirty-eight years they wandered in unbelief and died in the wilderness. It's the only other place in the Bible you see the number thirty-eight. It's a fascinating comparative, for thirty-eight years, this man had laid paralyzed, just as the people of Israel were paralyzed by their unbelief.

I don't know how long this man had been lying here in hopes of healing. He was, no doubt, the fixture at the pool. It is unlikely anyone had been there longer. He'd over time been abandoned and was now left clinging to a pathetic belief in agitated waters. The religious people were at the top of the hill going through the motions, the superstitious were at the bottom hoping in a myth. And neither could save lives temporarily or for eternity. Only our Jesus can do that!

When Jesus saw him lying there, and knew that he already had been in that condition a long time, He said to him, "Do you want to be made well?"

—John 5:6

I really love this picture. It's so typical of God's heart, isn't it? He goes to the place where people are in greatest need, finds the person who's hurting the most, and brings healing to those who have lived their lives with popular legends as their only hope, even though the legends have disappointed them for years.

Jesus knew the man's heart and the length of his suffering—a great reminder that the Lord always knows about you and your need. Salvation begins with God considering you—not with your considering Him. You're lost in sin. You're helplessly paralyzed. You're lying with people who can't deliver you. You've got a religion that won't satisfy you or touch your need. God takes note of you. It all starts with His understanding love.

Jesus went into the crowd—amongst the hopeless masses—and took the initiative as He always does, finding the one who needed Him most. Are we told of this man's repentance of his sin or his understanding of his need for God? No. But God knew where he was coming from. He always does. The woman at the well had a pretty tough exterior until the Lord was able to take down the fence. And there she was, all ready to be saved. Jesus knows you too. And He has life if you're willing. Maybe today you'll surrender!

Jesus' words to this man are very interesting because when He asks, "Do you want to be healed?" the question is literally, "Do you want to be made whole?" On the surface, the question would seem to have an embarrassingly obvious answer: "Yes! Maybe You can't see the impression I've made in the concrete from lying here so long. Of course I want to be made whole!" But that's not always the case. In fact, the Bible is full of stories—and so are our life experiences—of those who live with false hope in the face of deteriorating consequences of their lifestyles of sin and yet still don't care to change. They've fallen to the bottom of the barrel. But, when asked if they want a way out, they answer, "No, I'm all right. Just leave me alone."

"Do you want to be made alive apart from God that is the catalyst for bringing us to Him. Do you want to be made well? Do you want to be made whole? Do you want Me to change your life—not just make you better, but change your life?"

You would suspect that when you reach verse 7, that you would read the words, "I certainly do want to get well." Instead, what you read is a very typical answer of many people when confronted with change in their lives. They will explain to you why they haven't changed. "I'm so close to making changes," they'll say, "but there's my boss, my wife, the kids, my job, the weather. There's always something that interrupts me. But I'm so close to working this whole thing out."

You'd think that after thirty-eight years, you might get from this man, "Touch my life now Lord, immediately if not sooner." Instead, you read:

> The sick man answered Him, "Sir, I have no man to put me into the pool when the water is stirred up; but while I am coming, another steps down before me." Jesus said to him, "Rise, take up your bed and walk."
>
> —John 5:7–8

It is as if this man is about to say to Jesus, "Maybe You can hang around and help me into the water." This religious man's hopes had failed him. His answer declares, "I want help. But this is the only help I know."

It is at this point that Jesus says, "Let Me show you something else. . . ."

If Jesus waited for us fully to understand Him before touching our lives, no one would be saved. So He takes us from where we are. If you have hope and are looking up, He's ready to work. He'll bring this man here along, even though he doesn't have an awareness of anything but his helplessness. "I have a better idea than the mythical bubbling waters," Jesus said. "Why don't you just get up and walk?" And we don't hear this man arguing anymore.

> And immediately the man was made well, took up his bed, and walked.
>
> —John 5:9

John uses the Greek word, *peripateo*, meaning "to walk around or walk about." Jesus disappears into the crowd and this man takes off with his bed rejoicing! It is then we read of the ominous religious clouds quickly gathering.

> And that day was the Sabbath. The Jews therefore said to him who was cured, "It is the Sabbath; it is not lawful for you to carry your bed."
>
> —John 5:9–10

Can you imagine this man walking for the first time in thirty-eight years? Testing his legs, standing on his toes, big smile and tears of joy! To then hear someone shout at you, "Hey, it's the Sabbath, pal. What are you—crazy? You can't be carrying that bed."

This healed and joyful man unknowingly walked headlong into the indignant religious life of the city. If you look at the Ten Commandments and the explanations of the Sabbath throughout the Old Testament, the Sabbath amounted to a day of rest from labor so one might recognize that God is the One who provides everything, that life isn't dependent upon people but they are dependent upon God.

Once a person has faith in Christ, the Sabbath applies to his or her spiritual life as a Sabbath rest in the sense that we have ceased from our labors of trying to save ourselves and have come to rest in the finished work of our Lord Jesus Christ. But the religious leaders of Jesus' day were using reams of material written by generations past and still being written in that day of what constituted "work" on the Sabbath. Carrying one's bed certainly qualified. The problem, however, is that God never said that. But these men had made so many rules to cloud God's purposes that resting in God was no longer an option. There was simply too much work to be done memorizing man's rules!

They should have seen a man walking who had been lame for so many years as evidence that the Messiah was in town. After all, seven hundred years earlier, Isaiah had prophesied that when the Messiah came, the eyes of the blind would be opened, the ears of the deaf would be unstopped, and the lame would leap like deer.

But religion makes people blind both to their own need and to God's solution. Consequently, these thought it would be better that this man just rot in his sickness than walk around on the Sabbath.

> He answered them, "He who made me well said to me, 'Take up your bed and walk.'" Then they asked him, "Who is the Man who said to you, 'Take up your bed and walk.'" But the one who was healed did not know who it was, for Jesus had withdrawn, a multitude being in that place.
>
> —John 5:11–13

I love this man's answer because he doesn't respond to these religious men bound in their religious rules, "I think your biblical interpretation of the Sabbath is faulty." He doesn't argue with them or chastise them for their lack of sympathy. He simply says, "The Man who healed me told me to do it." That's the best argument there is.

When religious people want to know why you're like you are, just say, "Jesus told me to do it. He changed my life."

Jesus didn't tell this man to break the Sabbath. He did, however, ignore the man-made rules that accompanied it.

> Afterward Jesus found him in the temple, and said to him, "See, you have been made well. Sin no more, lest a worse thing come upon you."
>
> —John 5:14

If you hadn't walked for thirty-eight years, where would you go first? Home? To the track at the high school to see if you could really make those legs work? Or would you go to church? This man was very aware that God had touched his life. And he immediately headed to the place where he could worship Him. He made the right choice. He saw Jesus as the Lord and Jesus told him that more than healed, he had been made whole. Sin must now be resisted and refused and the Lord followed, His grace sufficient!

> The man departed and told the Jews that it was Jesus who had made him well.
>
> —John 5:15

I don't doubt that this man became Jesus' disciple. But first he went back to the religious leaders and told them it was Jesus who had healed him. What a blessed picture. In it, we see the folklore that couldn't help, the religious people who wouldn't help—and Jesus who alone can help to make man whole.

Chapter 12

JESUS SPEAKS TO HIS WOULD-BE ASSASSINS

John 5:16–47

We come to Jesus' longest discourse to date in the chronology of the Gospels, and it was delivered to people with money in their pockets and plans in their knapsacks on how to take Him out permanently. If you know people who think they can work their way to heaven, this is the passage you need to read to them, because in it Jesus tells us who He is, why He came, and how we can have life.

> For this reason the Jews persecuted Jesus, and sought to kill Him, because He had done these things on the Sabbath.
> —John 5:16

How hard do you have to be hit in the head before you think that somebody who got well after thirty-eight years of lying in bed was somehow offensive to God, or that you could just hear the Lord exclaim, "Oh, no! Now he's carrying his bed too"? Where does one go to get such a distorted concept of God, that He is nitpicky enough to want you better—but only on certain days of the week? Yet that is exactly what we read of the reaction of these religious folks to Jesus healing that man at the pools in our last chapter. Read John 5:15–16 together for context.

> But Jesus answered them, "My Father has been working until now, and I have been working." Therefore the Jews sought all the more to kill Him, because He not only broke the Sabbath, but also said that God was His Father, making Himself equal with God.
> —John 5:17–18

Jesus' answer to these men and their rules was, "My Father's still working, so if He's OK with it, I'm OK with it."

"Your Father? Wait a minute, who do you think you are, God?"

"Yes, I am."

And now they were going to kill Him for two good reasons—for working on the Sabbath and now, even worse, for making Himself equal with God.

When they tell you Jesus never claimed to be God, tell your Jehovah's Witness friends that He just did so right here.

I love Jesus' answers throughout the Gospels when confronted by the those bound in religion. Here they have rules about the Sabbath. But Jesus says, "God doesn't take the day off when it comes to ministry." Aren't you glad God isn't closed for the holidays? It's a good thing He's on duty twenty-four/seven because if He takes five seconds off, your breath which He holds in His hands will be available no more.

In Mark 2, we read that Jesus went on to tell these men that the Sabbath was made for man, not man for the Sabbath. In other words, the Sabbath wasn't intended as a vehicle we can use to score points with God, but was given to us as a blessing from God, for us to slow down, to stop and rest, and to consider Him and His total care and provision.

Hearing this made these angrier still. In fact, as you read through Scripture, from this point on you will repeatedly read of the cry of these religious leaders: kill Jesus. Jesus continued, "Let Me give you a little sermon before you try and kill Me again."

> Then Jesus answered and said to them, "Most assuredly, I say to you, the Son can do nothing of Himself, but what He sees the Father do; for whatever He does, the Son also does in like manner. For the Father loves the Son, and shows Him all things that He Himself does; and He will show Him greater works than these, that you may marvel. For as the Father raises the dead and gives life to them, even so the Son gives life to whom He will."
>
> —John 5:19–21

"Most assuredly" in Greek is where we get our word Amen, so be it and declares, "You can go bank on this." Imagine arguing with Jesus—God Himself—about where life comes from and telling Him the Sabbath rules had to be followed. Then imagine Jesus getting right in your face, saying, "Let Me tell you something. I'm not here on My own behalf. I've been sent by the Father. I don't do what I want; I do what He wants. The Father chose to heal this man on the Sabbath. Therefore, you're going to have to reckon with Him."

The Bible tells us that when Jesus came, although He was fully God, He emptied Himself of His dependence upon His divine attributes and was instead filled with the Holy Spirit. We're not God, but like Jesus can be filled with His Spirit. Jesus is our example and as such we are to walk as He walked: seeking the Father, doing His will, relying on the Holy Spirit to lead and empower us. One of the problems with sin is it makes us independent. It convinces us that we can handle things ourselves. Not Jesus. He was totally dependent on the Father. "The Father loves Me," He said. "He's not going to leave Me in the dark." And He won't do that to you, either.

"There will be greater works than seeing this man walking because the Father's will is that you marvel," Jesus continued.

Marvel is a great word. It means "to hold in admiration." God's work, healing, and miracles are to bring you to a place of admiring Him and saying, "You're the One I want to follow."

When I got saved, I said to my father, "Dad, I got saved. I'm going to heaven."

His answer was, "First you were into drugs, then you were into bikes, now you're into Jesus. What's going to be next?"

"Stick around," I said.

Fifteen years later, he said to me, "I want what you have." He had been able to see and watch the difference God's presence in my life had made. I'm a goof just like anyone else—but the Lord's light shines in my life and He is awesome.

"I'm going to do greater works than raising this man from his sick bed," Jesus declared. And sure enough, soon Jairus' daughter would be brought back from the dead by the work of Jesus. Later, the widow's son as well would be brought back to life. Even Lazarus would rise. The marveling had only begun.

In Deuteronomy 32:39, Moses said, "Before you go into the Promised Land, remember that there is only one God that can kill and make alive." When Jesus said, "I can give life," it's no wonder the religious leaders were angry. They were either going to have to submit themselves to Jesus as God or kill Him for lying. You can't be in the middle, can you? His claims too radical to ignore, their implications eternal.

> "For the Father judges no one, but has committed all judgment to the Son, that all should honor the Son just as they honor the Father. He who does not honor the Son does not honor the Father who sent Him. Most assuredly, I say to you, he who hears My word and believes in Him who sent Me has everlasting life, and shall not come into judgment, but has passed from death into life."
>
> —John 5:22–24

"The Father will not be the judge of man," Jesus said. "He's given that job to the Son and if you're going to honor the Father, you're going to have to honor the Son."

What were these religious folks doing in the temple? In reality they were trying to honor the Father, but were now seeking to kill His Son whom He had sent. You cannot have the Father if you ignore the Son, for it is He who sent Him for our salvation (Isa. 53:10).

Sometimes people ask us why we're always talking about Jesus. The answer is that He's right in the middle of God's plan—the Name above all names, the only name given whereby we can be saved, the Name to which every knee will bow.

> "Most assuredly, I say to you, the hour is coming, and now is, when the dead will hear the voice of the Son of God; and those who hear will live. For as the Father has life in Himself, so He has granted the Son to have life in Himself."
>
> —John 5:25–26

Jesus not only gives life but is its source. The religious man points to his performance and accomplishments. The believer points to Jesus, to life itself. The dead here are dead in sin, dead to spiritual things—all of us in other words.

"And has given Him authority to execute judgment also, because He is the Son of Man."

—John 5:27

"Son of Man" is a term often used in the New Testament as a title for Jesus. In the Old Testament this term is very unique to prophecy. So when Jesus said, "I'm the Son of Man," anyone who had read or had been taught the Old Testament would have been able to make the connection as to who Jesus was claiming to be.

"I know what you're going through," Jesus said. "As the Son of Man, I've faced sin and suffering and difficulty. And because I've been there, I can judge perfectly. If you want life, come to Me. I'll pave the way through the cross and My blood. If not, you're on your own—but you'll face judgment because I'm the solution God provided."

"Do not marvel at this; for the hour is coming in which all who are in the graves will hear His voice and come forth—those who have done good, to the resurrection of life, and those who have done evil, to the resurrection of condemnation. I can of Myself do nothing. As I hear, I judge; and My judgment is righteous, because I do not seek My own will but the will of the Father who sent Me."

—John 5:28–30

Death is not the end. Everybody's final destination depends on whether they have done good or evil—which is defined in God's Word as whether they have believed in Jesus as the Father's only provision for sin, or whether they thought they could take care of their sin on their own.

As this hostile crowd of murderers milled about, Jesus then spoke to them specifically about how they had plenty of evidence and reason to believe Him. They had chosen not to—they had made the call and they would live with the consequences.

"If I bear witness of Myself, My witness is not true. There is another who bears witness of Me, and I know that the witness which He witnesses of Me is true. You have sent to John, and he has borne witness to the truth. Yet I do not receive testimony from man, but I say these things that you may be saved. He was the burning and shining lamp, and you were willing for a time to rejoice in his light."

—John 5:31–35

When John the Baptist came on the scene, something happened that had never happened in Jewish culture. Jews came to be baptized. They agreed with God concerning their sinfulness and their need of a Savior. John was preparing the way. His strong preaching convinced many that needed help. Those who agreed were baptized by John, crying out for God's mercy.

When Jesus showed up and was baptized, when the Father confirmed who He was, John said to his disciples, "There He is—the Lamb of God who takes away the sin of the world. Follow Him." In saying this, Jesus reminded the crowd of John's testimony concerning Him. John's witness of Jesus had brought some to Him, but now the witness of His works should bring many more.

> "But I have a greater witness than John's; for the works which the Father has given Me to finish—the very works that I do—bear witness of Me, that the Father has sent Me."
>
> —John 5:36

Even greater than John's witness were the miracles, the signs, and the wonders in Jesus' life. How out of touch with reality would you have to be to doubt the word of One who opened the eyes of a blind man and made a paralyzed man walk? Yet the religious leaders rejected the evidence, a good indicator of how blinding and binding sin is. And if you reject the evidence that He is God, there's nowhere left for you to turn. You are now only able to weakly argue your religious rules, all the while ignoring the healed!

> "And the Father Himself, who sent Me, has testified of Me. You have neither heard His voice at any time, nor seen His form. But you do not have His word abiding in you, because whom He sent, Him you do not believe. You search the Scriptures, for in them, you think you have eternal life; and these are they which testify of Me. But you are not willing to come to Me that you may have life."
>
> —John 5:37–40

Jesus called on John the Baptist, His own works, and now the Words of the Father—Scripture itself—as witnesses of who He was. The religious folks had the Word, but the Word didn't have them. It didn't move them. As a result, although God stood before them in the Person of Jesus, they weren't able to recognize Him.

To these religious men fuming because a man was carrying his bed on the Sabbath, a man who had been paralyzed for thirty-eight years, Jesus said, "Search the Scriptures." It's a great word. It means "follow the track"—like a bloodhound on the scent. "Start studying because when you're all done following the track, you're going to end up right here with Me."

When the wise men came asking where the Messiah would be born, the scribes immediately knew chapter and verse. But they didn't go three miles to Bethlehem to see if it was true. Their heads were full, but their hearts were empty of love for God.

> "I do not receive honor from men. But I know you, that you do not have the love of God in you. I have come in My Father's name, and you do not receive Me; if another comes in his own name, him you will receive. How can you believe, who

receive honor from one another, and do not seek the honor that comes from the only God? Do not think that I shall accuse you to the Father; there is one who accuses you—Moses, in whom you trust. For if you believed Moses, you would believe Me; for he wrote about Me. But if you do not believe his writings, how will you believe My words?"

—John 5:41–47

"Religion is what people practice to honor themselves," Jesus said. He would later say to the religious leaders, "You love the best seats in the synagogue and being called rabbi in the marketplace. You love being honored, looked up to, and valued. But I'm not like that. I didn't come for the honor. I came to please My Father."

If you want to get right with God, that's what you'll do. You'll go to Jesus to please the Father. "When all is said and done," Jesus said, "I'm not going to accuse you of anything." The Bible will, though, because from Moses in the Pentateuch to John in Revelation, the declaration is that Jesus is both Savior and Lord. That's where the answer is. Search the Scriptures and you'll find Him, and without Him you will never find life.

Chapter 13

SABBATH DAY CONTROVERSIES

Luke 6:1–11
(Matthew 12:1–14; Mark 2:23–28; 3:1–6)

In this second year of Jesus' ministry, the crowds were gathering to Him in record numbers. In fact, we find people traveling some three hundred miles just to hear Him speak. The people loved what Jesus had to say. But as we have been studying, the religious folks did not. They often sought to ridicule Him publicly in an attempt to bring Him down a notch in the people's eyes. But His responses usually left them either ashamed angry, as He in great wisdom revealed both their wicked hearts and His great love.

The teaching of today's modern scribes and Pharisees is essentially the same: "God needs works to be satisfied. If you produce many, you can come to a place where God will welcome you into His kingdom." But the Bible teaches just the opposite—that man is sinful and cannot work his way to heaven or even draw near to God on his own.

We find this conflict constantly in Jesus' day as we do today. The issue of what we have done for God and is it enough, or do we need, as the Gospels teach us, the intercession of Jesus, His work for us to make us acceptable to Him? One area of tremendous conflict that highlighted this works vs. grace debate was the application of the Sabbath Law, which occurred weekly. In Luke 6, we come to two such Sabbath day controversies to learn God's heart to save us from our religious confidences:

> Now it happened on the second Sabbath after the first that He went through the grainfields. And His disciples plucked the heads of grain and ate them, rubbing them in their hands. And some of the Pharisees said to them, "Why are you doing what is not lawful to do on the Sabbath?"
>
> —Luke 6:1–2

The summarized commandment from the Old Testament regarding the Sabbath could simply be put, "Don't do any work on the Sabbath, keep it holy for the Lord." Yet the religious people had over the years taken on the task of defining "work" for us. Eventually they had thirty-nine major categories and thousands of sub-categories to define the work that could not be done. For example, if you had false teeth, you were not to put them in. That would be work. If you had a wooden leg, you were not to fasten it on. That would be work. The Law God had given so people could learn to know both Him and themselves had been replaced by man-made demands and an institution of works. Even today, there are many religious people who follow rules God did not write or authorize and, I think, quite frankly, hates because they all get in the way of the salvation He freely offers to men through faith alone.

For that reason, Jesus went out of His way to expose these false religious practices and hopes by ignoring them, breaking them. The religious leaders then inevitably came to Him and said, "Hey, what do you think you're doing?" He never broke or violated a single word of God's Law—He came to fulfill them completely. But He couldn't have cared less about the rules of man. He taught the religious leaders over and over again about the grace He was bringing for all men.

> But Jesus answering them said, "Have you not even read this, what David did when he was hungry, he and those who were with him: how he went into the house of God, took and ate the showbread, and also gave some to those with him, which is not lawful for any but the priests to eat?" And He said to them, "The Son of Man is also Lord of the Sabbath."
>
> —Luke 6:3–5

I love Jesus' answer to these religious guys: "Haven't you read the Bible?" I suspect they would have read it several times. But if you're only interested in making rules, you have very little need for the Word of God, and reading becomes selective to your own will and purpose . . . going to the Bible only to find support for what I believe!

The story to which Jesus alluded here is found in 1 Samuel. When God declared David would be king and King Saul got wind of it, he responded by trying to kill him. Feeling like he needed to get out of Dodge, David took a bunch of guys who had supported him and left town. But by the time they reached the tabernacle of the Lord, they were starving. So David said to the chief priest, "Give me the showbread." The showbread consisted of twelve loaves of bread that always sat in the Holy Place of the tabernacle before the Lord, representing these twelve tribes of God. The loaves were replaced each week and only the priests were allowed to eat of them, for they were holy or consecrated to the Lord. However, David and his men were hungry. So the Lord allowed them to eat the showbread. Why? Because the Law is designed for people's benefit—to convict them of sin and drive them to Jesus. Life takes precedence over Law. Need dominates decision. So their hunger was more important to God than the symbolism and lesson the 12 loaves held for the people.

"The bottom line is that what I'm doing is OK because I'm the Lord of the Sabbath," Jesus, in essence, said. And He put His finger on their problem when He said, "You don't even know your Bibles, and your decisions are not biblically based."

Luke then takes us forward to yet another Sabbath confrontation:

> Now it happened on another Sabbath, also, that He entered the synagogue and taught. And a man was there whose right hand was withered. So the scribes and

> Pharisees watched Him closely, whether he would heal on the Sabbath, that they
> might find an accusation against Him.
> —Luke 6:6–7

Jesus' enemies truly believed Jesus had both the capacity and the will to help anyone in need. That explains their constant watching of Jesus, looking for reasons to put Him to death. "Keep an eye on Him. If He heals on the Sabbath, this will be another nail in His coffin." They were convinced that if Jesus saw a need, He would help. And they were absolutely right. Revelation 2 says He walks through the church looking for needs. If you have one, God knows it and is more than willing to meet it. That's what He loves to do—even on the Sabbath, for the day of rest and acknowledgement of His Lordship is also to be a day of finding life and deliverance in Him and not ourselves . . . He not us: the very essence of the Sabbath lesson . . . resting from our own labors.

> But He knew their thoughts, and said to the man who had the withered hand,
> "Arise and stand here." And he arose and stood.
> —Luke 6:8

Just as Jesus had known the thoughts of the fence-sitters in Luke 5, He knew the thoughts of the scribes and Pharisees here in Luke 6. God always knows what's going on with us, even our thoughts and intents. He was not about to leave this needy man alone.

> Then Jesus said to them, "I will ask you one thing: Is it lawful on the Sabbath to
> do good or to do evil, to save life or to destroy?"
> —Luke 6:9

When Jesus said, "Hey, guys, before I do anything, I just want to ask if, according to your religious traditions, I can help this man," in response He received silence. Even these most opinionated, outspoken, loud-mouthed guys were tongue-tied. They chose to remain silent rather than have to defend their belief that God would let this man walk out the same way he walked in.

Mark 3:5 tells us Jesus looked at every one of them with anger and was grieved over the hardness of each one's heart. "How can you be like this? Look at this poor man who came to seek God—and your rules are going to send him away because your religion and tradition are more important than his welfare."

Mark 3:6 goes on to tell us that after Jesus healed this man's infirmity, the Pharisees went out and immediately consulted with the Herodians—the political leaders of Rome—concerning how they might work together to destroy Jesus. The Herodians were the occupiers, the Jews the occupied. They hated each other but would find unity only in their greater hatred of Jesus.

And when He had looked around at them all, He said to the man, "Stretch out your hand." And he did so, and his hand was restored as whole as the other. But they were filled with rage and discussed with one another what they might do to Jesus.

—Luke 6:10–11

Commanding a paralyzed man to shake hands was either the most cruel thing to do or the first step in God's work of healing. The man could have said, "Quit teasing me, I can't for my hand is withered." Instead, he simply sought to do what Jesus asked. And as he did, the Lord enabled him to do the impossible.

That's always the case. Sometimes we hear people say, "I don't know if I can quit smoking, or quit lying, or quit drinking, or quit cheating." Maybe they can't—but God can in you. In fact, whenever God asks you to do something, He'll enable you to do it. If you seek to obey, you stretch out your hand instead of arguing or making excuses.

Although we're not told of the reaction of the healed man (I can only imagine his joy), we are told of the religious leaders' reaction, for it is always the same. What happens to religious people when they hear the Gospel? They either get saved or they get mad. We do not read of anyone here proclaiming, "Wow! He just healed a withered hand. Who is this man? Leaves you blind and lost, doesn't it? It blinds your eyes and keeps you from the truth."

So instead of rejoicing with the paralyzed man, the religious leaders set up a Sabbath day meeting on how to murder Jesus. Apparently that didn't qualify as work.

Chapter 14

PRESSURE, PRAYER, AND PROVISION

Mark 3:7–19
(Matthew 10:1–4; 12:15–16; Luke 6:12–19)

As a growing number of people continued to come to Him, Jesus added to evangelism—telling the people how they could get to heaven, discipleship—training men who could carry His message forward. It is to that ministry of discipleship we look in this chapter as Jesus chooses the twelve apostles:

> But Jesus withdrew with His disciples to the sea. And a great multitude from Galilee followed Him, and from Judea and Jerusalem and Idumea and beyond the Jordan; and those from Tyre and Sideon, a great multitude, when they heard how many things He was doing, came to Him. So He told His disciples that a small boat should be kept ready for Him because of the multitude, lest they should crush Him. For He healed many, so that as many as had afflictions pressed about Him to touch Him. And the unclean spirits, whenever they saw Him, fell down before Him and cried out, saying, "You are the Son of God." But He sternly warned them that they should not make Him known.
>
> —Mark 3:7–12

After telling us two times in the first two verses that "a great multitude followed" Jesus, we are given an indication of just how far people were traveling to see Him. Idumea would have been 160 miles away. Tyre and Sidon were fifty miles up the coast. For literally hundreds of miles, the blind, lame, leprous, crippled, and demon-possessed did whatever it took to come to Jesus. I love the picture Mark paints in which simply hearing what the Lord was doing caused people to drop everything they had to find Him.

Jesus' primary reason for coming was to bring people to the place of repentance of their sin and to faith in Him as He would sacrifice His life for theirs. Unfortunately, as big as the crowds were, most folks were only there for temporary relief and not eternal life. They weren't there because Jesus was the Lord and they wanted to follow Him. They were there because He was real good at fixing your lame arm or feeding you breakfast when you hadn't had any. And as a result, most people left the same way they had come to Him, even from afar—spiritually dead.

Ministries today are often quick to point out how many people attend. But is largeness always an indicator of what God is doing—or is God's effective work far smaller than that?

A much smaller group in this huge crowd actually were there for all the right reasons. Yet I love the picture because Jesus was ministering to people who, for the most part, were taking advantage of His kindness and He continued to love them and be available to them. He wanted to give life. They just wanted to eat—and the moment He quit feeding them, they quit showing up. But in the midst of the crowds and in the midst of relentless religious opposition, Jesus chose some men upon whose shoulders He would lay the responsibility of the building of the church and carrying forth His message.

> And He went up on the mountain and called to Him those He Himself wanted. And they came to Him.
> —Mark 3:13

Luke writes of the same account that it came to pass in those days—the days of tremendous pressure—that He went up to the mountain to pray and continued all night in prayer. Jesus would only be on earth two more years, so He got away from the noise, went up into the mountains, and called these men to Him in the morning to give them great responsibility and privilege.

> Then He appointed twelve, that they might be with Him and that He might send them out to preach, and to have power to heal sicknesses and to cast out demons.
> —Mark 3:14–15

Out of thousands, Jesus appointed and trained twelve. They became the foundation of the church. Luke says they went from being disciples, or literally "learners," to apostles, or literally "ambassadors"—those sent to represent another.

The word *appointed* is a Greek word that means "to choose" or "to ordain." Notice that the apostles did not become apostles by a vote of the majority. There was no pulpit committee, no secret ballot, and no request for volunteers. God chose these men. And He chose you. If you think at times that you don't belong or fit in and wonder how God can use you, remember He picked you. Therefore, it's His problem how to use you. If you have no place here, He picked the wrong person—and He doesn't make mistakes.

Notice that these men's job was two-fold. They were to hang around Jesus, "be with Him" and then go out and minister with His power. What a great job description! Wherever the Lord went, they went. They learned by His example and were empowered by His presence.

So even as the crowds pressed in and the religious folks plotted, Jesus prepared the men He would use.

> Simon, to whom He gave the name Peter; James the son of Zebedee and John the brother of James, to whom He gave the name Boanerges, that is, "Sons of

Thunder"; Andrew, Philip, Bartholomew, Matthew, Thomas, James the son of Alphaeus, Thaddaeus, Simon the Canaanite; and Judas Iscariot, who also betrayed Him. And they went into a house.

—Mark 3:16–19

If I were picking a group of men to go out and reach the world, I would pick the famous people or celebrities of the day—the sports hero, maybe a finance guy to run the show, a lawyer for all the inevitable problems, and an advertising executive to draw the crowds. I wouldn't pick fishermen, traitors, and insurrectionists. This was a group of men that confirmed what Paul later wrote to the Corinthians, that God uses the foolish to confound the wise. Before you write yourself off as someone God cannot use, you're going to have to tear these verses out of your Bible, because He used these men.

When later Jesus began to speak in parables to illustrate spiritual truths, the very first words out of Peter's mouth in Matthew 15 were, "I don't get it. I don't understand it. I don't know what You're talking about."

And it was Philip who said to Jesus in John 14, "Show us the Father and we'll be happy. We just want to see God."

These guys didn't see things clearly. And if that weren't bad enough, they were also as proud as they could be. Even as late as the Last Supper, Luke tells us they jockeyed for positions of prominence in the kingdom. Four times in the Gospels, Jesus refers to His disciples as having "little faith." In fact, at the most difficult time of His life, Jesus asked His disciples to pray with Him for an hour. What did they do? Fell asleep.

Why would the Lord choose men like this? To assure people like us that we can be used as well! We aren't very qualified, very faithful, or very committed. We don't have much to offer that isn't covered by sin and self and a hundred other things. But if you give your life to the Lord, God can work. If we let God's Word and His Spirit fill our lives, we can be that which God wants us to be as part of His church. He chose us. He has His eye upon us. He knows who we are and has awesome plans for our life.

This list of disciples appears four times in the Bible: in Matthew 10, Mark 3, Luke 6, and Acts 1. In each of them, Peter is listed first and Judas last. There are always three groups of four and the first name in each group is always the same. Bartholomew is sometimes called Nathaniel; Judas, the brother of James is sometimes called Thaddeus; James, the son of Alphaeus, is sometimes called James the Less. The Lord joined together in these groups some very extreme personalities.

He put Peter, a guy who jumps first and wonders where the floor is later, with a guy like John who wouldn't move without thinking about whether or not it's going to work. He paired Nathaniel, who believed in Jesus the moment he heard about Him, with Thomas, the skeptic. He paired Matthew, the traitor who worked for the Roman government with Simon the zealot who belonged to the political group fighting the Romans. There must have been some pretty interesting discussions at night.

I don't think these men would have gotten along on any level except for their faith in Christ. Yet thirty years later, Paul wrote in Colossians 1 that the Gospel had gone throughout the entire world.

Misfits all—and yet in thirty years the whole world was reached by these men whose hearts God had touched. I hope the example here in Mark will convince you that you're "vessel material"—and if you allow God to fill you, He can use you mightily!

Chapter 15

POOR IN SPIRIT

Matthew 5:1–3
(Luke 6:20–26)

According to Mark 3 and Luke 6, after choosing His twelve disciples, Jesus went to the mountain, away from the multitudes, and taught His disciples what we know as the Sermon on the Mount. Luke tells us that when He was finished, He went down and stood on a level place with the crowd and gave them a shorter version of the same sermon.

The crowds were huge this second year of Jesus' ministry. The needs were everywhere. But the false teachers still taught salvation by works. They misinterpreted the Law and misused God's Word. It was a battle Jesus would fight continually, and I suspect it's still the biggest battle you will run into as a Christian sharing your faith. You will encounter religious people who somehow think they don't need God's help, that they can both live life and make it to heaven on their own.

In this context, Jesus sat down His disciples and gave them these three chapters of teaching—one of the longest sermons in the Bible—focusing first on salvation and then on the life of a believer, and He made one thing perfectly clear: religion cannot save you and you need His salvation if you ever hope to see or enter into His kingdom.

> And seeing the multitudes, He went up on a mountain, and when He was seated His disciples came to Him. Then He opened His mouth and taught them, saying . . . .
>
> —Matthew 5:1–2

If the multitudes were going to be reached, the disciples would have to be prepared. And the Lord's intention in giving them this sermon was to make sure they understood that salvation by grace is the only thing God will honor. This is not a sermon for unbelievers. It was delivered to the saints and was intended to make clear God's way of life. As you go through it, you will discover none of the attitudes and actions God requires of you is a natural tendency. In other words, left to themselves, this is not the way people would behave. Rather, these are God's works in the heart of the believer.

In the chapters that follow, you will hear God's word on how you should view yourself and handle your possessions, what a godly marriage should look like, the place of prayer and fasting, giving and forgiveness, and love and good works—and how they all fit together in God's plan. You will also read of the kingdom of heaven or the kingdom of God. One day when Jesus returns we'll see this kingdom over all the world. For now, we see it only in the lives of those who have submitted their lives to God as King.

> ". . . Blessed are the poor in spirit, for theirs is the kingdom of heaven."
> —Matthew 5:3

As Jesus sat down His newly-appointed disciples to tell them what real life is about, He began with the words, "Blessed are the poor." The Greek word for *blessing* is *makarios* and means "oh, how happy."

There are several words the Bible uses for "poor." One of them is a word that describes those who live from paycheck to paycheck—people who don't have a savings account or rainy-day fund. They just barely get by and are poor in the sense that they can't be very extravagant.

But then there is the word *ptochos*, which speaks of being so poor that you don't know where your next meal is coming from. This is the guy who wonders at lunch if there will be dinner and who doesn't have a friend to turn to or a phone call to make. There is no hope for him. He's on his knees, absolutely at the end of himself. This is the word Jesus used here.

How happy are people who realize they are without hope and totally destitute when it comes to their spiritual lives! Why? Because they will get the kingdom of heaven. They are the ones who are willing to hear the message and are ready to be saved. "Blessed are those who are in abject poverty when it comes to their spiritual hope," Jesus essentially said.

The problem with witnessing to people who are religious is that they are not abjectly poor spiritually in their understanding or outlook. They have all kinds of accomplishment going for them, they believe. Ask a religious person if he's going to heaven, and if he says yes, ask him why. What you will not hear is, "I'm poor." What you will hear is a list of personal achievements which are then often compared with individuals they have deemed far worse than themselves. Yet the Lord says we're blessed and filled with joy only when we come to a place of great poverty.

Poverty of spirit is a blessed place to be. But it is nothing that will come to you naturally. It is something only God can accomplish. It is a conscious awareness that you have nothing to offer God and it is the work of God's Spirit that shows you who you are.

In Luke 5, Peter, in the boat with Jesus, told Jesus he shouldn't be in His presence because of his sin. For three chapters, Isaiah prophesied woe to the people in the land before he said in chapter 6, "Woe is me. I'm a man of unclean lips." The centurion in Matthew 8 said he wasn't worthy that the Lord should come to his house.

Paul wrote in Philippians 3:4–8, "If anyone can brag, I've got even better credentials. But I counted all of those things but loss for the excellency of knowing Jesus Christ my Lord for whom I have suffered the loss of all things and count them but rubbish." If you look up the word *rubbish*, you'll find "cow patty." Dung! In other words, Paul said, "Everything I've accomplished means nothing compared to what God has made available to me."

It is only when people see God face to face that they see themselves empty. If I can come to that place in my life where I realize what I have to offer God is not sufficient, that I'm running on empty, then God says I can have the kingdom of heaven because then I'm in a perfect place to hear the Gospel. When Jesus said to the Pharisees, "I'm a Doctor but you're not sick so I can't help you," it wasn't that they weren't sick. It was that they didn't see themselves in need. If you're at the end of yourself, Jesus can begin to work. But if you're still coming to bargain with chips in hand to point out your good ways, there's nothing He can do.

In Isaiah 66:1–2, we read that when Isaiah stood before all of the people to tell them how big God is, the Lord said through him, "Everything you see, I have made. Everything around you exists because of Me. But this is what I will listen to and look for: one who is of a poor and contrite heart, one who trembles at My Word." In other words, He said, "I have made all of these things, but this is what I want, this is what My eye is looking for: not the constellation Orion, but a heart that trembles at My Word, that sees it is in absolute need of Me."

If that's you, you're blessed because wherever you find poverty of spirit, you find God bringing life. Are you poor in spirit? When you stand before God, do you come with a resume of your accomplishments to argue your case or do you come empty-handed? If you're empty, know that is something only God could accomplish in your heart. You'll never come up with that on your own because people's natural tendency is to stand on their own two feet.

If God can get hold of you and empty you, the blessings are just down the road, just around the corner. That's when the kingdom of heaven comes to you. That's when you are saved. You don't have what it takes—but He does. And that's a blessed place to be, for then Jesus will appeal to your empty hands and come to fill your heart to overflowing.

Chapter 16

MOURNING AND MEEKNESS

Matthew 5:4–5
(Luke 6:20–26)

I don't think we can understand the Beatitudes in isolation. They're all intertwined. In fact, even the order in which Jesus spoke them cannot be changed because it is the order they're given through which people find God's best for them and salvation in Jesus Christ.

> "Blessed are those who mourn, for they shall be comforted."
>
> —Matthew 5:4

If I'm poor in spirit, I realize I have nothing to offer God. And although He promises me His kingdom, I am still mournful over my condition. So contrary to the world that says the natural way for a blessed life is to forget your troubles, get happy, put on a happy face, take a pill, buy some shoes, or take a cruise, the blessed people in God's eyes are those who come to the end of themselves and are brokenhearted about the depth of wickedness and lack of goodness in their lives.

Not every type of mourning falls into this category. If your pride has been wounded, your stock has dropped, or the love of your life has broken your heart, that is not the mourning spoken of here. This mourning is a direct result of an awareness of sin. The Bible says the rich young ruler went away sad because he had great possessions. That's not the right kind of mourning. The right kind of mourning drives you *to* the Lord in your weakness, not away from Him.

Writing about his own experience with God, Paul said in Romans 7:18, "I know that in my flesh dwells no good thing. To will is present with me, but how to perform to do good, that I cannot find. And the things I want to do, I don't. The evil I wish to avoid, I find myself doing. Who will deliver me from this body of death?" Then he said, "I thank the Lord that, through Jesus Christ, I'm delivered. I'm free." Paul was a mournful man who recognized his own inability to do good. His grief over his sin turned him to Jesus and the cross.

One of the byproducts of mourning over our sinfulness and being comforted is that it turns you into an evangelist, because once you recognize how wicked you are and yet how readily God accepts you, you can't help telling others lost in sin about His love. After spending a year hiding his sin with Bathsheba, David was so sorry he said to the Lord, "Forgive me. My sin is ever before me. Restore unto me the joy of my salvation. Create in me a clean heart. Don't take Your Spirit away from me. I want to be changed so I can tell others about You." That's the kind of mourning that leads to comfort.

I'm glad the Lord didn't send the Holy Spirit to point out my sin, make me sad about it, and then just leave. He doesn't stop there. He turns me around and says, "Here's Jesus, the Lamb of God who takes away the sins of the world. You've failed, but He succeeded. He took your iniquity upon Himself and You're covered—so go tell this to someone else."

If you're poor in spirit and brokenhearted over your failures, that's a good place to be because it brings the comfort of our Savior to you. It also leads to meekness.

"Blessed are the meek, for they shall inherit the earth."

—Matthew 5:5

The Greek word for *meekness* is *praus* which can be defined as "strength under control." The word often was used in connection with taming a wild horse. If you try to ride a horse that's never been ridden, the chance of its letting you ride it is about zero. But if this horse allows you to sit on its back, although it has the capacity to absolutely destroy you, and if it submits to the reins and its strength is under your control, that is the definition of meek.

If you see yourself without an ability to please God and it breaks your heart, the natural consequence is you will submit yourself to Him. You will be in the place of meekness as you yield yourself to His will, direction, and authority.

Meekness is the byproduct of seeing my sinful life and mourning over it. If I do those two things, I only have one option left: I can't turn to myself. I can't turn to the world or anywhere else for help. I can only look up. And when God says He'll accept me, He'll help me, and He'll direct me, I inevitably say, "Then You can have my life. Without You, it was worthless. It wasn't going anywhere. So here, take it."

If I get through the first two of these Beatitudes, any stubbornness or cockiness, self-will or pride I may have had before I bowed before the Lord is obliterated. Although I have the capacity to rebel, I surrender because I know I don't have what it takes to live on my own. Meekness is not weakness. In fact, meekness is actually the place of greatest strength because it lets the God of the universe run the show.

Being meek isn't the same as being mild-tempered. Meekness is a work of the Holy Spirit that leaves a person surrendered to God and, in so doing, allows him or her to find God's will, while those who aren't surrendered are left to wander.

Psalm 25:9 says it is the humble God will guide in justice and the humble He will teach His way. In the first chapter of his epistle, verse 21, James wrote, "Lay all filthiness and wickedness aside and receive with meekness the implanted Word able to save your souls."

In David's dealings with Saul we see meekness. David could have killed Saul time and again. Instead, he said, "Lord, You handle it." That's meekness. Meekness will leave you much more patient and tolerant of the weaknesses of others because you're already hanging on to the Lord for your own failures.

If you see your condition and mourn over the consequence, and if you leave your rights and causes with God and live a life that is harnessed and under His control, trusting in His way, you'll be blessed. And there's even more blessing to come!

Chapter 17

HUNGERING, THIRSTING, AND MERCY

Matthew 5:6–7
(Luke 6:20–26)

"Blessed are those who hunger and thirst for righteousness, for they shall be filled."

—Matthew 5:6

After the first three Beatitudes—which are designed to empty us—we come to the fourth, which is given to fill us. In both the Old and New Testaments, the word *righteousness* means the same thing. It is that which God deems as right, that which pleases Him. The desire in the life of the believer filled with the Holy Spirit is to live in a way that pleases God.

Religious folks have all kinds of works with which they think God should be pleased, reasons God should consider Himself lucky to have them on His team. But not the believer. In the heart of the believer, the Holy Spirit produces a genuine desire to change. The truly saved person says, "I don't want to lie like I used to. I don't want to fly off the handle like I've always done. I don't want to be so caught up in the things of this world. I don't want to just go through the motions. I want a heart for God."

That is a blessed condition. And it is a condition found only in the life of someone who has been saved. People in the world desire to improve their lives only to the extent that it benefits them, not simply to please God. If it will do them good, they're all for it. But a heart that hungers and thirsts to please God is found only in the life of someone who has been saved.

Blessed are those who hunger and thirst for righteousness—who hunger to have their lives changed, to be filled. If I'm not poor in spirit, if I still think I can offer God something, if I'm not brokenhearted over the way I lived before I met the Lord, or if I think there are worse people than me in the world, there's probably very little hungering and thirsting in my life for God and His ways. It is to the extent that the first three Beatitudes apply to my spiritual life that I find myself empty and wanting to be filled.

Notice that the blessing is found in the very process of hungering and thirsting. We often get this backward because we easily mistake the end for the means.

"What is your goal in life?" I asked a man the other day.

"I just want to be happy," he said.

101

"How are you going to accomplish that?" I asked. "What is going to make you happy?"

He then proceeded to give me a whole list.

"What if that doesn't work?" I asked.

"I don't know," he said. "I just want to be joyful."

But there's no way to do that because joy and happiness are byproducts of something else. When you hunger and thirst to be right with God, you find there is great blessing in seeking Him—and as you do happiness follows as a byproduct. Desire to be pleasing in God's sight, seek Him and His ways and joy will overflow your heart.

Jesus applied the strongest Greek words there is, not the "I got home at five and dinner won't be on the table until five-thirty, so I'll probably starve to death" kind of hunger. It is rather the kind of hunger that says, "If I don't find something to eat today, I may not survive until tomorrow." It's scouring and scavenging and doing whatever you need in a desperate search for food to survive. Jesus said you will discover that kind of drive in your heart to do the things that please God, after you have been emptied of self and when you hunger so, you're a blessed person and nothing will be kept from you.

Maybe the best illustration I can come up with is that of the prodigal son. Jesus told the story of the boy who took his dad's inheritance and went to live in the world until his resources dried up. He tried to survive any way he could, finally taking a job feeding the swine, even looking longingly at the slop he was feeding them. It was in that condition he finally decided to go home. Hungering for his father's house he went humbly and discovered the love his father had for him. Soon he was blessed beyond belief!

How hungry are you to do what God says? The result of being poor in spirit, of a mourning heart and a meek life, is a hunger to be changed so acutely that nothing can deter you. To be hungry is to put yourself in the place where God can work.

In the last letter before his death, Paul told Timothy to flee youthful lusts and instead pursue righteousness, faith, love, and peace with those who call on the Lord out of a pure heart (2 Tim. 2:22). Flee, pursue, and look at the company you're in—those were Paul's three steps to hungering and thirsting.

If you want to be a football player, you work out, memorize the plays, learn to take a hit, and begin exercising with an eye toward the future. Likewise, if you want to know the Lord better, you will seek Him through his word, prayer, and faithful obedience. And like chocolate éclairs to a person trying to lose weight (I speak from personal experience), there are many things that can take away your spiritual appetite, things that of themselves are not problematic, but are hindrances to your hunger for God.

If you're hungering and thirsting after Him, you'll be committed to studying His Word because through it He'll tell you what He wants. If you're hungering and thirsting after God, you'll be praying because He has said he hears our prayers and wants us to come often. If you're hungering and thirsting after God, you'll be fellowshipping with other believers because you need their ministry and they need yours. Some people declare they don't have time to read their Bible, to pray or to go to church. Yet for everything else in their lives, their schedules seem to part like the Red Sea. If you're hungering and thirsting to be pleasing in God's sight, you will do and pursue everything you can to make that a reality because until that hunger is quenched, you're miserable.

"You will seek Me and find Me when you search for Me with all your heart," the Lord told His people through Jeremiah. But what we often find are people who want all of the benefits of knowing God for as little diligence as possible. "I want God to provide for me," they say. "I want peace. And I want perfect health. But I don't want to get up early and go to church. I don't want to read the Bible. And I don't want to go out and minister to anyone." They want the benefits—but they have no hunger. And because they have no hunger, they can't be filled.

Paul's advice to Timothy back in 2 Timothy 2 was to find some people hungry for the Lord and fellowship with them. How hungry are you? Paul was so hungry to know the Lord better that some thirty years after he was saved he said to the Philippians, "I'm not there yet, but I'm pressing on" (Phil. 3:12–14).

Blessed are those who hunger and thirst after righteousness, for they shall be filled. The word *filled* is the Greek word for glutted, fattened, and overflowing. It's the word that describes you twenty minutes after your Thanksgiving meal. If you want to walk with God and please Him, the more you desire Him, the more He will provide for you. There is never a lack to the hungry—only to the less-than-hungry. Which leads us to our next beatitude:

"Blessed are the merciful, for they shall obtain mercy."

—Matthew 5:7

The first four Beatitudes deal exclusively with our relationship with God—emptying ourselves to the point where He fills us with hunger to be more like Him. Beginning with mercy in verse 7 here however, the remainder of the Beatitudes deal with the effect our relationship with God has upon our relationships with others.

The word *merciful* in the Bible speaks of pity plus action, an understanding of the sordidness of a life and the ability to reach out to try to improve it. If the Lord fills us, as we've seen in the preceding four verses, we recognize that only the same work of God stands between those lost in sin and us.

If it weren't for the Lord, I'd be in the same boat as everyone else—no better, no smarter, no holier, and no more diligent. But I *am* saved, and that's all that makes me different. As a result, I empathize with those who aren't saved and who haven't been forgiven. I show them mercy. Grace in the Bible deals with sin as a whole. Mercy deals with the consequences of sin in its particulars. Grace gives me what I don't deserve: eternal life. Mercy keeps from me what I do deserve: judgment, hell, and separation from God.

Paul wrote in Ephesians 2:4, "God who is rich in mercy with the great love wherewith He has loved us, even while we were dead in our trespasses and sins has made us alive in Christ by His grace." God's mercy looked on you and your trespasses and, rather than giving you what you deserved, gave you what you did not. He didn't destroy you. He provided for you. He sent His Son.

In Psalm 103:8–10, the psalmist wrote that the Lord is merciful and gracious, that He hasn't dealt with us according to our sins or punished us according to our iniquities. That's a perfect definition of mercy and of grace plus action. It means that if I hear of someone who lied about me, rather than taking the world's approach and getting even with him, I can remember the mercy God shows me and say, "I used to lie a lot too. But God forgave me, so I'll just pray that the Lord changes his heart."

If you forgive men their trespasses, so will your heavenly Father forgive you," Jesus said. "But if you do not forgive them, neither will your heavenly Father forgive you" (Matt. 6:14–15).

"Wait a minute. If I don't forgive, I'm not going to be forgiven? That doesn't seem fair!" you might say.

Oh, really? You want everything from God but you don't want to pass anything along? That's not the way of the Lord. Mercy is a characteristic of the believer's life. Poverty of spirit produces mourning over sin, which produces a relinquishing of life, which results in a hunger and thirst for righteousness that we might be filled and begins to make me merciful even as we have received mercy.

Chapter 18

THE PURE, THE PEACEMAKER, AND THE PERSECUTED

Matthew 5:8–12
(Luke 6:20–26)

Continuing here with the beatitudes we have come to the final verses of them which continue to speak of how our relationship with God changes us. We have seen His work of making us merciful . . . we continue here in beginning in verse 8 with *purity*. That will be followed by becoming *peacemakers* and finally, if you're going to live for the Lord, *persecution* is bound to follow and how you respond reflects His presence in you.

> "Blessed are the pure in heart, for they shall see God."
>
> —Matthew 5:8

The minute we hear the word *pure*, we immediately think "sinless." But not only is that biblically incorrect, it's humanly impossible. As you go through the Bible, you see everyone falls short. Abraham hesitated in his faith. Noah got drunk one day. Moses disobeyed God about a rock. Job cursed the day he was born. David committed murder and adultery. Elijah fled from Jezebel. Peter denied Jesus. No one is pure in that sense. This word *pure,* however, literally means unadulterated, with unmixed motives, or sincere without pollutants.

The word *pure* speaks of single-minded commitment. God is looking to develop in your life a whole-hearted commitment to Him. In the parable of the sower, Jesus taught that God's Word falls on different types of hearts. Some of them are so hard, little gets in—and the Devil takes even that away before it has an effect. Others are like soil filled with rocks. They hear, but there's no real commitment, no real desire, no depth of soil. In others, the deceitfulness of riches and the cares of this world continue to choke out the Word much like thorns choke out a garden. For them, the Lord is only one of their many interests. But then there's the person with a pure heart who's ready to hear, willing to listen, and quick to respond. That's the heart in which God can produce fruit.

God made a great promise through Jeremiah's pen when He said in chapter 29, "You'll seek Me and find Me when you search for Me with all your heart." When your life is consumed with knowing God—not when God is a part of your life and you have a hundred other things to do, but when you surround your life with the things of God—you will be blessed. The Lord's promise here is though the divided heart will keep us hidden from God, a pure and single-minded heart will allow us to see much more of Him.

Moses wanted to see God so much that he asked the Lord to let him do so. "In your body, with your ever-present sin, if you look at Me, you'll explode," the Lord answered. "But I'll put My hand over your eyes and go by quickly. Then I'll pull My hand away, and you can see where I've been" (Exod. 33:18–23). But even seeing only the "after-burners" of where God had been, put humble Moses on his face.

God's promise here is that we will see Him clearly in our daily life. We of course won't see Him literally face to face until the day we're in heaven, but we can see His presence with us and His working in us, even through the trials we face. It is such a comfort to see God's hand at work in our lives, but it is hidden until our lives are in His hand, until our hearts are pure, unadulterated, and single-minded. If you want to see God in your life clearly, you have to devote yourself to Him completely.

From getting saved, to mercy to meekness, to hunger, to purity of heart in our lives—the Lord now brings us to the work of the church in the world.

> "Blessed are the peacemakers, for they shall be called sons of God."
> —Matthew 5:9

An outgrowth of our salvation should first and foremost be peace. That is, the consequence of our being saved is that you greatly begin to desire to see others saved as well. You become a peacemaker. You take God's Word to the world. It is an action that the Bible says assures you that you are a child of God.

When Paul wrote in Ephesians 6:15 about the battle believers fight with the Devil, he said, "Make sure your feet are shod with the preparation of the Gospel of peace." In other words, wherever your feet take you as a Christian, make sure you bring along the good news, the Gospel message that can bring peace to the hearts and souls of men.

Do you want to be assured that you are a child of God? One aspect is to see how often you share your faith, because the natural consequence of your salvation is that God's love for the lost now fills your heart. Blessed is the man who is out there sharing his faith. Blessed is the woman who takes it upon herself to speak up. They are the children of God.

"You're blessed if you're out there being a peacemaker because that's what the children of God do," Jesus said to His disciples. How horrible it would be if you knew the way out of trouble but didn't tell someone he or she was headed for disaster.

Yet as we go forth bearing this precious Gospel to a lost world, we will, like our Lord, encounter much resistance and even persecution. Jesus addresses that here.

> "Blessed are those who are persecuted for righteousness' sake, for theirs is the kingdom of heaven. Blessed are you when they revile and persecute you, and say all kinds of evil against you falsely for My sake. Rejoice and be exceedingly glad, for great is your reward in heaven, for so they persecuted the prophets who were before you."
> —Matthew 5:10–12

The final Beatitude is the direct result of those that preceded it. The cost of being a witness, of living your life for Jesus in the world, is that it will cause trouble. One of the reasons the Lord set His apostles aside and spoke to them here on the mountain is that they had already faced—and would continue to face with increasing hatred—persecution for their faith and hope.

The word *persecute* in Greek is an interesting one. It means "to chase after with evil intentions." You're blessed when people pursue you with only wickedness in mind. That makes sense only to the extent that you're living for Christ. If you don't live for Jesus, you can fit right in. But try living for Jesus in the world and it's hard to fit in. It is the difference between night and day, darkness and light, the work of God's Spirit and the Devil himself.

So to His apostles who were just about to begin following Him full-time, Jesus said, "Blessed are you when you are persecuted for righteousness' sake. You should be extremely happy. You should greatly rejoice." And the promise given here at the end of the Beatitudes is the same given at the beginning: the kingdom of heaven. It's come full circle.

The suffering we are to endure is the suffering that comes from lining ourselves up with Jesus. Before He was arrested, Jesus said to His disciples in John 15:18–20, "I want you to know that if the world hates you, it's because it hates Me. And the only reason it hates you is because you're hanging around with Me." The persecution that is blessed is the one that comes to you solely through your association with Jesus.

Unfortunately, we can also face persecution because we're self-righteous, obnoxious, arrogant, loud, demanding, and foolish rather than loving, godly, and kind. Yet that will bring no blessing, for it is not attached to my walk with Jesus and sharing His love.

If you go through the Bible, beginning with Cain and Abel, you'll find believers in every generation suffering at the hands of unbelievers. Yet persecution did not deter them and should not deter you. It should bless you. It should tell you very clearly that God is at work and He's using your life. You have entered into Jesus' labors.

Are you being persecuted for your faith? If you're walking with God, you ought to be. The guy at work who brings doughnuts and wishes everyone a nice day makes the people around him feel they could do that too if they wanted to. But when you come along and say, "I'm not really very nice but the Lord has changed my life and He could change yours too," suddenly your life convicts them because you're not taking credit for it yourself. When you say, "I'm a sinner saved by grace," people don't know what to do with you except hate you, because you didn't change yourself. Your pointing to Jesus puts them in the position of being a sinner too.

For more than 120 years Noah built an ark, and we read in Hebrews 11 that as he did that, he warned the world of things not seen as yet. He lived a godly life but people turned away. I'm sure the tour buses came by and pointed to silly Noah. "Yeah, he's been at it for eight years now. He's just a lunatic with a big old boat two hundred miles from water."

Blessed are you when you're persecuted for righteousness' sake. Rejoice and be exceedingly glad. Why? For two reasons: First, you're in good company. The prophets were persecuted too. And, secondly, there's a glorious reward waiting for you. One day in heaven, you're going to rejoice at having been faithful to the Lord.

The Beatitudes are designed to take you from getting saved to living for the Lord—not by your works but by faith in Him.

Chapter 19

THE CHURCH IN THE WORLD

Matthew 5:13–16
(Mark 9:50; Luke 14:34–35)

The focus of the Sermon on the Mount was very clear. It was designed to delineate the difference between grace and works, between the Law that couldn't make a person righteous and the Gospel that could. Having finished with the Beatitudes, the Lord continues to address the church, the body of saints, and the believers in Him in the verses that follow. What is the church to be like in the world? On the heels of sharing our faith, and finding persecution as we studied last time, come these words of Jesus to the saints about their influence in the world.

We get great insight into God's heart by looking at these verses. Jesus gives us two very specific illustrations of what we should be accomplishing and how we should be affecting the world. Both of His illustrations are unique to the culture of His day; both of them speak about influence.

As a Christian, your life either will influence others to get closer to God and be more desirous of the things of God, or by your influence you're going to push away those who potentially would believe in Him. When Paul wrote the last of his two letters to the Corinthians, he said, "We are to God the fragrance of Christ among those who are being saved and among those who are perishing. To the saved, we are the fragrance of life. To the perishing, we're the fragrance of death. But either way, rather than peddling the Word of God, we are sincerely speaking in the sight of God in Christ" (2 Cor. 2:15–17). That's the calling of the church. And, as the Lord looks at us as part of His body, this is what He hopes to see: a people so filled with Him, they become His vessels through whom He can reach the world.

Peter said it this way in 1 Peter 2:9: "We are a chosen generation and a royal priesthood, a holy nation, a special people that we might proclaim the praises of Him who has brought us out of darkness into His marvelous light." Ultimately, we gather as the church to worship, but the work we do is outside the walls and it is to those places God would send us. Jesus continued with His disciples by saying,

> "You are the salt of the earth, but if the salt loses its flavor, how shall it be seasoned? It is then good for nothing but to be thrown out and trampled underfoot by men."
>
> —Matthew 5:13

What a glorious picture. The Lord is so good at using things we can see and understand to explain spiritual truths often hidden from our eyes! Salt is vital to our lives. I always think of it as being God's antiseptic for everything that's rotting. You find it everywhere—from the soil, to rocks, to our blood. Even our drinking water is purified by it. If you don't have enough salt, your life won't be long on this earth. And in Jesus' day, it was one of the most vital commodities known. In fact, the disciples' mindsets would have been very much different than ours because, to them, salt preserved their very food.

In a culture that relied heavily on raising and slaughtering one's own cattle, salt was absolutely essential because it provided the only preservative for all the meat one wasn't able to eat immediately. Even in the first century, the practice of cutting meat into strips and soaking it in a salt solution so the salt would retard the bacteria growth caused meat to be able to last for days rather than for a few hours. The Romans often paid their soldiers in salt rather than gold. That's where the phrase, "He's not worth his weight in salt" came from. In fact, the root word in Greek for *salary* is *salt,* for salt was of such tremendous value.

Today with our refrigerators and freezers, with markets and expiration dates, we don't think about salt very much. Now it only comes up if the food is bland or the doctor tells us to lower our salt intake. Potatoes without salt? I'm thinking if the doctor ever tells me that, I'm going to pray the Lord takes me home right away!

We now put so many preservatives in our food that it has a shelf life longer than us. Yet in the days of Jesus, salt was the single most important thing you could have when it came to food preservation. So when Jesus said to the disciples sitting at His feet, "You are the salt of the earth," they immediately would have thought of that salt as a preservative. Even the salt they used on the meat couldn't stop the rotting, but it could slow it down.

One thing God's word teaches us about the world is that it is getting worse, not better. Part of the church today teaches "kingdom theology," which basically says we're here to make things better and prepare the earth for the Lord—and when everything's ready, He'll come. But that is an unbiblical view. When the Lord gave the vision to Nebuchadnezzar in Daniel 2 about all of the kingdoms that would follow his, an increasingly inferior metal represented each successive empire. In fact, clear back in Genesis, God said one of the reasons He would destroy the earth was because the imagination of people's hearts continually was evil. Yet while the world rots around us morally, ethically, and spiritually, the church is placed in its midst as salt—as a preservative. God's Word in your life and the Spirit upon and within your life cause the rotting of sin to slow down in the world around you—you come into the room and they don't tell the dirty joke because you're there. You live in the culture and God brings blessing because you are present. You share your faith and others come to Jesus.

When Paul wrote the last of his two letters to the Thessalonians about how one day the antichrist will come, he said in 6:7 that the Holy Spirit's restraining work in the church is what keeps lawlessness from having its way entirely in the world. In other words, we're the vessels God uses so the world can hear about Christ. Our lives and our influence, are salt in the world. As we pray, make friends, get involved, and reach out, wickedness is slowed. What kind of preserving influence are you having as a Christian in your world? Are you the one who slows down the wickedness of sin—or are you part of it? God wants to salt the world through us, His church.

Secondly, salt provides flavor and produces thirst. As you go out into the world and live for Jesus, people see that you're happy, at ease, upbeat, and hopeful—and they become thirsty for what you have. In 2 Kings 2:19–21, when the people said Jericho was a beautiful place, Elisha said it wouldn't be for long because the water had gone bad. "Bring me a new bowl and put salt in it," he said. Then he poured the salt into the headwaters and said, "The Lord has healed the water." And Scripture records that the water was healed according to the word Elisha spoke.

Likewise, if the Lord has changed your life, you make life taste good. Will there be battles? Sure. Opposition? You bet. Difficulty? Guaranteed. But salt is only good if it's poured out. It doesn't have any influence in the shaker. That's why Jesus wants to pour you out into the world.

Thirdly, salt heals. At the Dead Sea, the saltiest place on the planet, there's a sign that tells you if you have any cuts, you should be ready for pain. Salt stings, but it makes you better. It hurts, and then it heals. That's what our witness does in the lives of others. The healing of repentance follows the sting of conviction. "Let your speech be with grace, seasoned with salt," Paul said to the Colossians (Col. 4:6). Our speech should have an impact. It should preserve and flavor, make thirsty and heal the lives of others.

"If the salt loses its flavor, what good is it?" Jesus asked. If you and I as believers live in the world in such a way that people rotting in sin around us aren't attracted to the Lord in our lives, if they're not hungry for what we've been given and don't want what we have, if no one asks to get saved or even seems to notice that we are, we have a problem. When Jesus moves in, people notice. Lives change. Jesus continues,

> "You are the light of the world. A city that is set on a hill cannot be hidden. Nor do they light a lamp and put it under a basket, but on a lampstand, and it gives light to all who are in the house. Let your light so shine before men, that they may see your good works and glorify your Father in heaven."
> —Matthew 5:14–16

The second example Jesus gave, much like the first, still focuses on influence. If you're in Israel at night on the Sea of Galilee and get turned around, you can simply look for the largest cluster of lights on the side of the mountain some eight hundred feet above the lake: the city of Tiberius—and even from twelve miles out, you'll immediately have your bearings seeing their lights. You can't miss Tiberius. It's a city of lights on a hill. Being in the north in Galilee, Jesus could have been referring to Tiberius. I don't know, but His point is very simple: lights on a hill are clearly seen.

Some people want to be light without being salt. That's a problem because what you do will speak so loudly that no one will be able to hear what you say. That is why salt comes first, then light. A little light at the end of a dark tunnel is all you need to get down the road. Even as the world gets darker, we shine all the more brightly.

According to the Bible, people without the Lord live in darkness. When you come around filled with the Spirit and living a life that's been changed by the Lord, there will be conflict because now you're in the light. Jesus told Nicodemus, "Men love darkness rather than light." Therefore, many people won't want any part of the Gospel message you bring. The Gospel is good news, but only if you've first heard the bad news. You might be able to go out to the street and convince some guy strung out on heroin that his life ought to change without even talking about sin. But it's hard to tell the company vice president making a million dollars a year with his three-car garage, three talented kids, and beautiful wife that he needs Jesus.

The purpose of light is to expose and then to provide direction. This means that as Christians we have to live our Christian lives on our sleeves. If you're a believer who's never told anyone you're saved, it's like putting a light in a closet and shutting the door. It doesn't help anyone.

Am I making it easier for people to find the Lord, or am I hiding the fact that I know the way? As light, we're supposed to be drawing people to Jesus as they see us and find the way. As salt we slow the rotting of sin, produce thirst in those who see us, and bring healing to lives destroyed by sin. Use us, Lord, to honor You!

Chapter 20

THE CHRISTIAN AND THE LAW

Matthew 5:17–20

The intention of the Sermon on the Mount was to define how to get to heaven—to differentiate man's plan vs. God's plan, man's way vs. God's ways, religion vs. relationship, works vs. grace. It is the crux, the center of everything we learn as Christians. Therefore, what began as a battle between Jesus and the religious leaders of His day became the Lord's training ground for His saints on how to go out and share their faith. The plan of God for His Law was to make sure everyone was convinced not only that they were lost, but that they could be found in the grace of Jesus Christ.

> "Do not think that I came to destroy the Law or the Prophets. I did not come to destroy but to fulfill. For assuredly, I say to you, till heaven and earth pass away, one jot or one tittle will by no means pass from the law till all is fulfilled. Whoever therefore breaks one of the least of these commandments, and teaches men so, shall be called least in the kingdom of heaven; but whoever does and teaches them, he shall be called great in the kingdom of heaven."
> —Matthew 5:17–19

In the Old Testament, the Law is divided into 3 categories: the ceremonial law, the judicial law, and the moral law. The ceremonial law was given to Israel by God as a way to deal with their sin. How does an unholy people meet with a holy God? Through the sacrificial system outlined in the ceremonial law. The people would come to the Lord, sacrifice in hand, realizing that they were on holy ground and that without the shed blood, they wouldn't be able to come at all, to stand before Him. The ceremonial laws governed the worship, sacrifice, and attendance at the sanctuary. And in so doing, they painted a picture of what Jesus would come to do.

The author of the letter to the Hebrews said if the blood of bulls and goats could remove sin, the people could have done it once and for all. But since it couldn't, every day of every week the priests continued to slaughter the animals the people brought in their stead. In Jesus, however, God once and for all provided a sacrifice as the Lamb of God laid down His life. The sacrifices in Jerusalem stopped with its overthrow in 70 A.D., and have not begun again since. They are indeed no longer necessary because Jesus the Messiah has come—not to destroy the Law but to fulfill it in our behalf.

The judicial law governed the civic, social, and interpersonal relationships of the nation—how people were to deal with each other and how they were to relate to the heathen nations around them. The judicial law dealt with everything from paying for the damage caused by a runaway ox to the death penalty. It outlined the righteous way to live, the way a nation ought to operate. The principles encased in the judicial law are those of love and mercy, accountability, integrity, and honesty.

Everywhere, however, where God speaks about the effect of the Law, the reference is to the moral law of God. This moral law doesn't change. It's still applicable to all men and is designed to convince men of their sin. Paul said he had done fine with the law until he got to the part that said, "Thou shalt not covet." Coveting says, "I want what you have." It's not a behavior; it's an attitude. And, at that point, Paul realized his need for a Savior. Whatever righteousness he found in performing the Law as he understood it, the simple word about coveting reduced him to a sinner who needed a Savior.

The difference between a religious person and a Christian is that the religious person will seek to keep the Law in his own strength and then offer his best efforts to God as evidence of his good intentions. "Look at all I've tried to do, at all I've tried to accomplish," he would declare.

That was as true in Jesus' day as it is today. Ask your family and friends if they're going to heaven, and they'll say yes on the basis of what they've done or on what they intend to do. Jesus, however, says, "Look at the moral law. See yourself absolutely destitute and realize you're poor in spirit. Only then can you find life."

Once Jesus saves us, changes our hearts, and gives us His Spirit, then we can obey the moral law—not through our own abilities, but through the work of God in our lives. The unbeliever can count to 10 when he's angry—but God will see the steam. In the life of the believer, on the other hand, God removes the anger altogether and replaces it with forgiveness, love, and mercy founded on His goodness and based on the understanding of how much God has forgiven us.

Many of the Jews returned from the Babylonian captivity unable to speak Hebrew. Consequently, they needed someone to tell them what the Word of God said. These teachers took it upon themselves to go one step further than teaching what the Word of God said, they began to interpreting what it meant as far as they were concerned. As a result, they held many generations hostage as they misinterpreted the Scriptures and the gap between God's Word taught in context and their interpretation grew with every succeeding generation.

The scribes and Pharisees, for example, had misled the people by redefining the Law as nothing more than a tool to make themselves presentable to God. And when it came to the commandments they couldn't keep, they simply rewrote them in a way that they could keep, without concern for God's intent and purpose in sending His Word. So we read Jesus here saying,

"For I say to you, that unless your righteousness exceeds the righteousness of the scribes and Pharisees, you will by no means enter the kingdom of heaven."
—Matthew 5:20

I don't know how the disciples were doing up to this point, but when Jesus said, "You've got to do much better than these guys who are known for being the most spiritual guys around, if you ever ever expect to get to heaven," I'm sure some of them fell over onto the ground. Surely, there was no one in the culture who appeared as holy as the scribes and Pharisees. In fact, the very word *Pharisee* means "distinct or separate."

For years, the Pharisees walked amongst the people as the separate ones and had absolute influence in the culture for setting the standard of outward holiness. People looked to them for spiritual guidance, for understanding of the language, for the teachings of God. The Pharisees looked the part, dressed the part, acted the part, seemed the part. The problem for them was that God looked past their robes and cloaks, past their long faces on fasting days, past their righteous faces on prayer days and right at their hearts to see what they were really like. The Pharisees plotted to kill Jesus because religion will never make room for faith, and Jesus was a threat to their chosen way of life.

As you go through the Gospels, you become quickly aware of how the Pharisees loved attention, how they were self-serving, how they preyed on widows, how they liked the chief seats. Yet Jesus will say to them, "You are like white-washed sepulchers. You look good on the outside, but if we dig, there's a dead man inside" (Matt. 23:27). So they plotted to kill Him because religion won't make room for faith.

In Luke 16, Jesus will say to those gathered against Him, "The things you highly value are an abomination in God's sight. You justify yourself before men, but God knows your heart." And that's the argument that the Sermon on the Mount makes. Religion breaks God's Law. Relationship with Him fulfills it for He accomplished perfectly the righteous demands of God that the Law sets forth.

In Matthew 2, when the wise men from the east showed up, they came to Herod and said, "We've been following the star of the Messiah. Where is He supposed to be born?" Herod, not knowing, looked over his shoulder at the scribes who worked for him and said, "We got a Bible question here. Where's the Messiah supposed to be born?" The scribes didn't say, "We'll have an answer by morning." No, they immediately said, "Micah 5:2 says He'll be born in Bethlehem."

That was all the magi needed to hear. They ran out of the house with great joy, headed for Bethlehem, 3 miles up the road. The scribes, on the other hand, went back to their coffee break. They had a head full of knowledge that never got to their heart, and so even hearing of the star, and the possibility He had been born, meant nothing to them. No wonder Jesus saves His most scathing words for the scribes and Pharisees, angry at these men who hold others in bondage by their religion, prohibiting them from finding life.

David's last words to his son, Solomon were, "Know the God of your fathers and serve Him with a loyal heart and willing mind for the Lord knows your heart and understands the intent of your thoughts. Seek Him with everything you have and you'll find Him. Refuse to do that and He'll forsake you forever." He didn't say to Solomon, "Here are some good works you can do. Here are some brownie points you can earn. Here are some ways you can get God on your side." He said, "Make sure your heart is right with God because that's where God looks."

Through Jeremiah, the Lord said to the people, "I am the Lord who searches the heart and tests the mind." God's judgment against man's sin will be based on man's heart. Outward appearance means nothing to God. He sees man from the inside out. The law might be kept outwardly, but by a sinful heart it fails within. We need a Savior, and Jesus has come to save us.

Chapter 21

ILLUSTRATION 1:
MURDER BEGINS IN THE HEART

Matthew 5:21–26
(Luke 12:57–59)

How does man get to heaven? That was the battleground. The scribes and Pharisees—the religious folks of that day—insisted that their performance was their ticket. They not only used the Law as a gauge to measure their own righteous behavior, but also taught it to others in such a way that it could actually be kept and that one day they could stand before God on the grounds of their accomplishments. Jesus, however, came to say that, because man is inherently evil, sinful, and fallen, whatever good works he might do certainly cannot erase or deliver from the sin in his life. And, as the battle between Jesus and the religious folks raged over relationship with God by faith versus man's performance-oriented work, the Law came into question constantly.

What is the Law all about? From God's standpoint, it is to convict man of sin. From the religious man's standpoint, it is a barometer of religious performance. Jesus gave the Sermon on the Mount with one intention: to convince His disciples, and later the multitude, that man needs a Savior, that grace keeps a life, and that mercy rather than works opens the gates of heaven.

We love performance. We love to brag about what we've done. The scribes and Pharisees were the epitome of this. So is religion. But Jesus came, saying, "The rules were not meant to make you righteous. They were meant to convince you that you're sinful and need help." God wants to bring you to a place where your relationship with Him is based on faith, where your hope for the future is based not on your works but on His. To that end we read,

> "You have heard that it was said to those of old, 'You shall not murder, and whoever murders will be in danger of the judgment.'"
>
> —Matthew 5:21

"You have heard it said . . . but I say . . ." Jesus will follow this same formula in each of the following 5 examples to differentiate between what the scribes and Pharisees taught and the actual purpose of God with regard to the Law. Both in Exodus and Deuteronomy, where the 10 Commandments are laid out by the Lord, the 6th commandment is "Thou shalt not murder." Old Testament Law made it clear that the life of the one who took a life would itself be taken. So far, so good. The rub will come in the next few verses when Jesus says that, in teaching this 6ᵗʰ commandment, the scribes and Pharisees limited it only to behavior . . . outward behavior and did not apply it at all to what motivated murder in the heart, hatred, jealousy, self etc . . .

> "But I say to you that whoever is angry with his brother without a cause shall be in danger of the judgment. And whoever says to his brother 'Raca!' shall be in danger of the council. But whoever says, 'You fool!' shall be in danger of hell fire."
>
> —Matthew 5:22

In comparing His teaching to that of these religious men, Jesus said that not only is murder sin—but so is everything that leads up to it and will go on to outline the kinds of attitudes that not only lead to murder but that, in God's eyes, reveal the true nature of our heart. Anger is not the way God works. When you get saved, He gives you a new heart. He doesn't tell you to count to 10. He tells you to turn the other cheek.

In verse 22, Jesus refers to anger without a cause. A lot of people say they have a good reason to be angry, yet wherever you find righteous anger in the Bible, it always has the glory of God as its focus—never self, never personal. If you are angry that God's ways are being trampled underfoot, wonderful. But the minute your anger becomes one of protection of self and selfish interests, it's no longer righteous. You're to be dead to yourself and not require payment. It is the Lord's responsibility to balance the books, not yours.

"The wrath of man cannot accomplish the righteousness of God," James will write in the first chapter of his epistle. Anger is not the way God works. Yet as the Holy Spirit moves in, we are changed and enabled to keep the Law—not by our own resources, but by His strength. I'm able to love those who hate me. Why? Because God loves me and has shown such mercy to me, I am only asked to show to others what God has shown to me and by the work of His Spirit, I'm able to do what I could never have done alone.

The word *raca* is an Aramaic word that can best be translated "brainless idiot." It was a derisive epithet of the day provoked by an action. The person who used it was in danger not of judgment or of hell but of the council. In other words, even the religious Sanhedrin would agree that it was the wrong way to respond. Even wicked people agree you can't call people names every time something goes wrong. In this we see that not only actions but exclamations of disgust are forbidden. Interestingly, whenever the Lord gives us a list of sin in the Bible, murder is often listed right after evil speaking because it's from the heart that evil thoughts and murder proceed. In Romans 1, Paul writes that the heart is filled with envy, murder, and strife. The teaching of religious folks when it came to the 6ᵗʰ commandment was concerned only with overt behavior and outward action, yet Jesus says it is the anger of the heart that curses a man for offending him in some manner . . . today maybe someone cuts you off in traffic.

Jesus' second example took it a step further when He talked about calling someone a fool. It is a Greek word that says that, after an assessment over time, you've come to the conclusion that someone is completely worthless. Unlike the word *raca*, the word "fool" springs not from an immediate reaction based on emotional response but rather from a determined conclusion that a person is not worth having around.

So whether it's a spontaneous eruption or a settled determination, whether it's being upset for a moment or viewing someone over a period of time and concluding he's not salvageable, the hatred in man's heart is irrefutable proof of his sinfulness, his violation of the law and his need for a Savior.

> "Therefore, if you bring your gift to the altar and there remember that your brother has something against you, leave your gift there before the altar and go your way. First be reconciled to your brother, and then come and offer your gift."
>
> —Matthew 5:23, 24

In the Old Testament, fellowship with God was based on sacrifice. Praise, prayer, and worship all required sacrifice. The scribes and Pharisees brought offerings day and night, but in the Lord's eyes, it was all worthless because their hearts were wrong. In Luke 18, it will be a Pharisee who prays, "God, I thank You that I'm not like that guy over there. I'm holier than he is. I do glorious things." Jesus said whether you bring offering, prayer or worship, if you remember that someone has a problem with you, seek to restore fellowship with him before continuing in your sacrifice because God is more interested in the heart than the sacrifice of a man with a hard heart of hate and sin.

Isaiah was sent to a religious nation who had lost its relationship with God. In Isaiah 1:11, the Lord said, "To what purpose are all these sacrifices to Me? I've had enough of this." For the lost, the Law is intended to drive them to Christ that He might save them. For the saved, however, it's intended to draw them to Christ that He might change them. The religious man will always hate, but the man who is truly saved will seek to restore and walk in God's love, putting on this new man.

> "Agree with your adversary quickly, while you are on the way with him, lest your adversary deliver you to the judge, the judge hand you over to the officer, and you be thrown into prison. Assuredly, I say to you, you will by no means get out of there till you have paid the last penny."
>
> —Matthew 5:25, 26

In Jesus' day, it was the plaintiff's responsibility to physically bring the defendant to court. So, the idea here is, if you let a problem go without resolution, you may find yourself in court at the mercy of a judge who may throw you in a place where you have to pay the price for your bitterness. How much better to fix it before you get to that point. Seek peace and do it quickly so you might find yourself in a place where God can bless.

Chapter 22

ILLUSTRATION 2: ADULTERY

Matthew 5:27–30

The second example of how the scribes and Pharisees had rewritten the Law to accommodate their works concerned the issue of adultery:

> "You have heard that it was said to those of old, 'You shall not commit adultery.' But I say to you that whoever looks at a woman to lust for her has already committed adultery with her in his heart."
>
> —Matthew 5:27–28

There are very few things in our American culture that are as obvious as the liberal views people have taken with regard to sexual activity. When I was a kid, adultery was something only whispered about. It was that shameful uncle no one mentioned. But today it has become part of the fabric of our society. It is the subject of most humor, a way of life that seems to convey freedom. Yet, conveniently, no one seems willing to discuss the sorrow and suffering it brings to lives, family and children alike.

Jesus said we can know we are sinners because we look with lust at a woman, even before the act of adultery as we know it has taken place. The religious person might say, "We're clear if we don't act on our lust"—but Jesus said otherwise. Anyone who has ever been involved in an adulterous relationship will agree that it was sinful thoughts that eventually led to sinful behavior and lust that led to action—and that the fruit of that lust it is never pleasant for long.

The word *look* here is the word for "imagination" or "the mind's eye." The word for *lust* speaks of "the desire for that which is forbidden." In other words, the Lord says if you begin to imagine, entertain, and examine those things God has forbidden, it is sin whether or not the action is carried out. This ought to leave all of us deciding quickly that we need some help. We can't do this on our own, and we need a Savior.

When the Lord asked Adam why he was hiding, Adam said, "Well, Lord, the woman You gave me brought of the tree and I ate it."

When Moses left Aaron in charge for six weeks, the people complained that they needed to worship a god. So Aaron made them a calf. When Moses came back and asked what was going on, Aaron said, "The people were scared. They wanted a god. I took the gold they gave me, threw it in the fire, and *poof!* out came a calf. It wasn't me. It was a miracle." Yeah, right.

There's always an excuse for sin, isn't there? But sin doesn't come from someone else. It comes from the corruption of our own hearts. In chapter 1:14–15 of his epistle, James put it in order, saying, "Each one of us is tempted when we are drawn away by our own desires and we are enticed. When that desire conceives, it brings forth sin. And if that sin fully grows, it will bring forth death."

The first step is desire. Where does sin start? In wanting that which God forbids. Then deception follows. The phrase "drawn away" is from the Greek for "setting a trap." The word *entice* means to "set the hook." In other words, there is a drawing away through the promise of things to come and the bait oftentimes is that we'll have a better life, that we'll have things the way we want them. After all, we've got to take care of ourselves, don't we?

Desire takes the bait and disobedience follows—either through action or imagination. Sin is born and if you pursue it long enough and are drawn to it often enough, it will bring death—to your marriage, your family, and your relationship with God.

Sometimes Christians ask, "How close can I get to sin and still not sin? Where's the line?"

My answer is, "Get as far away from the line as you can because the Devil seeks to bring you down, and the further removed from his domain, the better."

But what is bad about lust is also good in the sense that if I am convicted of my sin, I am driven to go to the Lord for help, and God does something wonderful: He gives me a heart that can overcome lust. And with my abiding in Him and relying on His strength to work in me, I can find deliverance from a heart of sin. That battle is what Jesus addresses next.

> "If your right eye causes you to sin, pluck it out and cast it from you; for it is more profitable for you that one of your members perish, than for your whole body to be cast into hell. And if your right hand causes you to sin, cut it off and cast it from you; for it is more profitable for you that one of your members perish, than for your whole body to be cast into hell."
>
> —Matthew 5:29–30

If what Jesus said in verse 28 upset His disciples, what He said in verse 29 would have done them in. "What in the world is He talking about?" they must have wondered.

Was Jesus offering a physical solution to a spiritual problem? No. If your right eye goes, you'll still have a left eye; if your right hand goes, you'll still have a left one. If you're going to start cutting, you'll be cutting for a long time because sin runs very deep. It would be nice if a surgery existed that would remove sin altogether. But in this flesh, we'll always be fighting sin.

So what was Jesus saying? He wasn't talking about self-mutilation but about self-evaluation. He was talking about what the eye looks at, what the hand touches, and where the feet lead. He was telling us to do whatever it takes to keep from stumbling in these areas because we're responsible for what we look at, what we handle, and where our feet take us. If any of these things lead you away from God, they are signposts on the road to hell. Get off that road.

Taking half-measures in dealing with temptation is not very productive. If you're going to walk with the Lord, you'll have to make victory over your flesh your greatest goal. As a Christian with a new heart, you can win the battle. Jesus said it might take extreme measures to extract yourself from places of stumbling. However, He also said it's worth doing because the gain will be eternal.

Chapter 23

ILLUSTRATION 3: DIVORCE

Matthew 5:31–32
(Matthew 19:9; Mark 10:11–12; Luke 16:18)

Jesus placed the illustration of marriage and divorce between the illustrations of adultery and taking of oaths. The formula He followed for the first two He follows again: "They say . . . but I say . . . ."

> "Furthermore it has been said, 'Whoever divorces his wife, let him give her a certificate of divorce.' But I say to you that whoever divorces his wife for any reason except sexual immorality causes her to commit adultery; and whoever marries a woman who is divorced commits adultery."
>
> —Matthew 5:31–32

According to the scribes and Pharisees, the most important issue in divorce procedures was paperwork. They came to this conclusion based on four verses in Deuteronomy 24 where God gave a Law to Moses to protect women from indiscriminate divorce. In Matthew 19, the Pharisees themselves raised the issue of divorce in an attempt to trap Jesus, when they asked Him if it is lawful for a man to put away his wife for *any reason*. Posed before a large crowd, it was a well-calculated question, because divorce was as volatile an issue as it is today. There were those who maintained that to leave a marital relationship for any reason was sin. The other extreme position held that God's desire for people to be happy justified any reason for divorce.

I love how Jesus answered this powder keg of a question for it is impossible to corner our Lord—try to put the Lord in a corner and pretty soon, you're the one there. "Have you not read, that which made them at the beginning made them male and female?" He asked. "For this cause shall a man leave father and mother, and shall cleave to his wife: and they shall be one flesh. Therefore, what God has joined together, let not man separate."

Jesus responded to their loaded question by taking them beyond the culture, beyond the argument of the day, beyond even Deuteronomy 24 and back to the beginning. "Hey, religious guys, don't you read your Bible?" He asked. "You should know what God's heart is about marriage and the fact that when Adam and Eve were created, He did not create any spares." One man. One woman. One flesh. Had they broken up, divorced, given up, or quit, we wouldn't be here. The human race would have ended. But they were brought together as one in the marriage God ordained. More than a sexual union, marriage is a covenant God honors.

"Why, then, did Moses command that a certificate of divorce be given?" the Pharisees asked.

"It was because of the hardness of your hearts that Moses permitted divorce," Jesus answered. "But from the beginning it was not so." In other words, divorce is not God's will but in Deuteronomy 24 was a concession to protect the abuse women were suffering at the hands of their husbands.

In every culture, including that of God's people, there was an ease by which the husband, the patriarch, could move a woman out of his house because women had virtually no rights. The problem for the woman was the culture didn't allow her to live alone. Not allowed to work, she had very little recourse other than to quickly marry someone else. Therefore, the Law provided women protection from being treated like a yo-yo at the whim of a husband who, after impulsively kicking her out, just as impulsively would demand she come back.

The Pharisees had made divorce merely a paperwork issue. Jesus said, "It's not a matter of writing. It's a matter of the heart."

The crowd realized that Jesus' definition of Deuteronomy 24 was very strict. According to Matthew 5 and 19, Jesus said that because sexual immorality brings death to the marriage bond, it is the only reason God allows divorce.

I'm sure divorce isn't the unpardonable sin. Divorce and adultery are both forgivable. But whenever you willingly sin and hope to clean it up later, I think you and God will have to discuss how that works out for you. I think it's very dangerous to be flippant with grace.

One thing that both God and men love is mercy. God loves giving it. We love getting it. Through the life of Hosea, a prophet God called to marry a prostitute, God illustrated His love for us despite unfaithfulness in our lives. God doesn't throw us out. He remains faithful. But without repentance, there can be no restoration. Therefore, if the Devil gets you to fall into sexual sin, turn and repent. God will restore. The Devil will lose. And you'll win.

Chapter 24

Illustration 4 and 5:
Oaths and Retaliation

Matthew 5:33–42

"Again you have heard that it was said to those of old, 'You shall not swear falsely, but shall perform your oaths to the Lord.' But I say to you, do not swear at all: neither by heaven, for it is God's throne; nor by the earth, for it is His footstool; nor by Jerusalem, for it is the city of the great King. Nor shall you swear by your head, because you cannot make one hair white or black. But let your 'Yes' be 'Yes,' and your 'No,' 'No.' For whatever is more than these is from the evil one."

—Matthew 5:33–37

As in the preceding three illustrations, Jesus repeated the teaching of the scribes and Pharisees and then contrasted it with His own. The words *swear* and *oath* in verse 33 were interchangeable Greek words and literally spoke of a promise made. In the Law, the third commandment read "You shall not take the name of the Lord in vain." We tend to think this means we shouldn't curse. But the word *vain* speaks of making a promise that isn't kept.

When Moses sat down the tribal leaders in Numbers 30:2 he said, "This is what the Lord has commanded: If a man makes a vow to the Lord or swears an oath to bind himself to some agreement, he should not break his word but should do everything he says." Several years later, in Deuteronomy 23:21 he said to them, "When you make a vow to the Lord, do not delay to pay it for the Lord will require it of you and it would be sin for you not to complete it."

The purpose of the third commandment is to convince us that we can't keep our word. We can swear any kind of oath we want, but the weakness of our flesh never allows us to be truthful and honest. What the scribes and Pharisees had done was make it so you could swear and not have it be binding, depending on what you swore. For the Pharisees, if divorce was a matter of paperwork, oaths were a matter of semantics. You could not swear to God but you could swear on your mother's grave. You could not involve God's name in what you swore, but anything else was fair—like crossing your fingers. They provided ways whereby people not only could skirt conviction by their dishonesty but actually work the system so they could lie without appearing to lie.

When my kids were little, they wouldn't tell the truth, but they wouldn't necessarily lie either. "Well, you didn't ask us that," they'd say. "You didn't mention the matches and fire." That's what the Pharisees were teaching. And rather than feeling guilty and turning to a Savior for help, they were trying very hard to manipulate the system in such a way that they could lie in their sin and yet still be fine in the Lord's eyes. They eventually wrote chapters of opinion as to what you could swear by and what you couldn't.

Jesus said, "You've heard this teaching of theirs, but I say don't swear at all. Your yes and your no should suffice as evidence of a heart that's been changed."

The problem with oath taking is people swear to the Lord out of desperation. "Lord, if You'll just do this one thing for me, I will _____." But the minute the crisis passes and the difficulty subsides, we immediately forget. That's using God's name in vain and Jesus says very clearly that it is better not to make a promise than to make one you don't keep.

In 5:12 of his epistle, James said, "Above all, brethren, don't swear. Don't swear by heaven or earth or any other oath. Just let your yes be yes and your no be no, lest you find yourself falling into judgment."

If you're in a position where you often have to take oaths for people to believe you, it is evidence that you are not very honest. "No, I swear to God this time . . . ." What about the last time?

There are times in the Bible and in society where oath taking is both necessary and required. If you testify in court, you are required to take an oath that includes severe consequences if you lie. When you get married, you take an oath. Oath-taking is such a serious thing that when the Lord wanted to convince us of His promises, we read in Hebrews 6 that He Himself took an oath so we would believe His Word to us.

Be known as one who keeps your word, because in Christ you can be honest and trustworthy. The breaking of an oath and the twisting of intents and words are characteristics of sinful hearts where wicked people try to cover up their wicked ways. Jesus put the emphasis on the wicked heart rather than on the spoken word.

> "You have heard that it was said, 'An eye for an eye and a tooth for a tooth.' But I tell you not to resist an evil person."
> —Matthew 5:38–39

The fifth example of the misuse of the Law by the scribes and Pharisees concerns retaliation. The quote in verse 38 is found in three different places in the Old Testament. It is first found in Exodus 24, in the Lord's instructions to the judges of the day concerning how to deal with criminals and offenses. In Deuteronomy 19, it appears again as a deterrent to further crime. Finally, in Leviticus 24 the Lord said the punishment should fit the crime. In other words, it's an eye for an eye—not two legs for an eye. It's not oppressive. It's not lenient. It's appropriate.

ILLUSTRATION 4 AND 5: OATHS AND RETALIATION

The Pharisees, however, interpreted incorrectly this Law to teach that people had an obligation to get even. The problem is, God never meant the idea of an eye for an eye to apply to an individual. It was only given for the corporate structure of a society—the courts, legislators, and leaders. God intended it to restrict crime in a society, to make the punishment fit the crime, and to be applied so society as a whole could be safe from criminals and offenses.

The Pharisees, however, loved to apply this Law personally. Who wouldn't? Retaliation and revenge seem to be the natural way of people driven by sin. You don't have to teach your kids to get even. They'll seek that all on their own:

"Why did you hit him?"

"Because he hit me."

How do you handle a violation of your rights? The natural person without God is quick to get even. But the Lord taught that it would be better if you died to yourself.

What is the appropriate response to personal injury or personal suffering? The state has an obligation to protect you with an eye for an eye, a tooth for a tooth. Romans 13:1–4 tells us, "Let every soul be subject to the governing authority because there is no authority except it be given from God. And God appoints those who exist. They are there to give direction. You don't need to be afraid of them if you do good." God's purpose is to protect. But in your personal life, you have another choice to make. In fact, in Luke 9:23, Jesus said, "If any man come after Me, let him deny himself, take up his cross, and follow Me."

The Pharisees' teaching made room for hate in the heart. Jesus, on the other hand, said, "But I say to you . . ." and then gave four examples in four verses of the differences in personal response between those who have been touched by God and those who haven't when it came to loss, personal rights and self-interest.

"But whoever slaps you on your right cheek, turn the other to him also."
—Matthew 5:39

Stay in context or you'll go astray. This is certainly no mandate from Jesus never to resist evil. In fact, if someone breaks into my house and threatens my family, I'll minister to them with all I can to help them see their idea was a bad one. But when it comes to personal suffering, what can you do? This isn't something you can ask someone else to do. This is what God asks you to do. Can you take abuse or evil without looking to get even, but rather simply turn away? You can if you're saved. You can't if you're not. And because the Pharisees made room to get even, they weren't convicted of their sinful selfishness at all, for they had taught these things by removing the Law and its conviction

When Alexander the coppersmith hounded Paul in Ephesus, Paul said to Timothy, "Alexander has done me much harm. May the Lord repay him for his works" (2 Tim. 4:14).

Paul could have gone to court and tried to fight back with a lawsuit. But when it came to personal attack, he said instead, "God, You handle it. You deal with this man. You give him what is required."

When Peter wrote about Jesus' suffering, he said (1 Pet. 2:23), "When the Lord was offended, when He was reviled, He didn't revile again. He didn't commit any sin. No deceit was in His mouth. He didn't threaten when He suffered. He just committed Himself to the One who judges righteously."

That's quite a different approach, isn't it?

This isn't talking about societal response or even a response when it comes to the protection of others. It's talking about self-protection. If you are offended, can you turn the other cheek—or will you follow the worldly way of retaliation and defend yourself at all costs?

Die to self. Let God handle the situation. He can judge while you show mercy. He can repay while you forgive. The Lord will set the books straight. There's a government for the sake of the nation and for the sake of the nation the government has to be just. But for the sake of the lost, the church has to be merciful. That's the distinction Jesus makes. So the religious rewrite the rule so they might keep it outwardly, but the Law was given to show us we cannot keep it inwardly, for we are sinners. Yet in Christ we can overcome the flesh and obey, even in these areas where we without Him would fall each time. Next,

> "If anyone wants to sue you and take away your tunic, let him have your cloak also."
> —Matthew 5:40

This is an interesting example because, according to the Law in Exodus 22, if someone sued you or you owed something, you could be required to give up your shirt. But no one could keep your coat overnight because you wouldn't be able to get warm. Here, however, the Lord says, "If they want your shirt, give them your coat as well."

"Wait a minute," you protest. "That's more than they deserve. I know my rights."

So does the Lord. If the insistence is on getting everything that's coming to you and never giving an inch, that's not the heart of God. That's the way of the world and I suspect for you, when it comes to your standing before God, you really don't want everything that is coming to you.

Stay in context. If someone is suing you for doing well, get a good lawyer. Fight for that which is right. But never be driven by selfish ambition or gain because the Lord can provide far more than you can ever get for yourself. The question is, would you rather win your case or win the lost?

> "And whoever compels you to go one mile, go with him two."
> —Matthew 5:41

As an occupying power, the Romans had absolute rights over your existence and one of the ways they applied their dominance was a law that stated they could make a Jew carry their packs, swords, or armor for one mile. In fact, this was the law used to compel Simon of Cyrene to carry Jesus' cross. It was the law. He had no choice.

ILLUSTRATION 4 AND 5: OATHS AND RETALIATION

Can you imagine the long faces and grim looks as people waited to get to the end of the mile? But Jesus said, "If they make you go one, tell them you'll go two." Do more than is required. Why? Because your heart's been changed. There's no selfishness left. The Lord is now in charge. That's the issue. That's always the issue.

So what do we do? We do extra. You've probably known people at work who reason very clearly that they're not paid enough to do more than the bare minimum. But we ought to be the best employees and those most interested in serving, not getting. That, however, can only be reflected in the heart of someone who's been truly saved!

> "Give to him who asks you, and from him who wants to borrow from you do not turn away."
>
> —Matthew 5:42

Finally, staying in context, the issue here is how to handle personal possessions when it comes to giving or lending to others. Again, this is an attitude of one who only looks out for himself versus that of a vessel God can use, an individual who is either self-absorbed or willing to help others, saved or lost.

John said, "If we have the world's goods and see our brother in need and shut our hearts from him, how is God's love dwelling in us?" (1 John 3:17). It's a matter of the intent of the heart in a life that is changed vs. the heart of a legalist who knows nothing but the rules.

The Law is the way the world works. But Jesus gave and set the example of God's work in a heart that removes self from the equation.

Chapter 25

ILLUSTRATION 6:
LOVE YOUR ENEMIES

Matthew 5:43–48
(Luke 6:27–36)

The religious leaders of Jesus' day took God's Law, which was designed to make men see themselves as sinful before God and turn and cry out for His help, and twisted and corrupted it in such a way that it became an instrument to prove they were worthy of heaven solely by their works. So Jesus began to teach the people the difference between what the religious folks taught and what God's Word intended. He gave them six examples from the Law itself that were designed to convince people of their sin and how the religious leaders had misinterpreted the heart of God by rewriting the Law so it could be kept on the exterior and not applying it all to the heart.

By the time you come to Matthew 6–7, this truth is applied to religious activities—prayer, giving, and fasting—and to the state of the heart in that process. But before that, here in chapter five, we come to the final example that is intended to convince the apostles—and us—that we need a Savior if we're ever going to live the way God intends.

> "You have heard that it was said, 'You shall love your neighbor and hate your enemy.' But I say to you, love your enemies, bless those who curse you, do good to those who hate you, and pray for those who spitefully use you and persecute you, that you may be sons of your Father in heaven; for He makes His sun rise on the evil and on the good, and sends rain on the just and on the unjust."
> —Matthew 5:43–45

In each example, Jesus first quoted the position of the religious teachers of the day and then corrected them, saying to His disciples, "Here's what God intended and also what only He can accomplish in your heart."

"You've heard it said that you should love your neighbor and hate your enemy." Nowhere in the Bible will you find that verse. You will, however, find, "You shall love your neighbor as yourself" in a number of places. But everywhere you find "Love your neighbor," you will read the words *as yourself*.

I don't know if anyone could love himself as much as the scribes and Pharisees loved themselves. Maybe that's why they left that part out altogether. As for the second portion, "You shall hate your enemies," you'll never find that anywhere except in the misguided, fabricated, misdrawn conclusions of the religious person who wants to make a performance out of his religion.

In Jesus' day, the religious leaders had defined a neighbor as a close friend or family member—but always a Jew and, more specifically, someone of the same tribe. Yet if you go through the Old Testament to discover God's heart in the Law, you'll find He often spoke of blessing the stranger. In Leviticus 19, Moses said, "If a stranger comes to dwell among you, don't mistreat him. You used to be strangers in Egypt. You know what that was like. Love him as yourself." God's heart for the people was that they might receive and entertain those outside, but who, by definition of the religious folks, would never have been received.

Who would think hating one's enemies would be a Bible verse? Only the person who uses logic rather than spiritual insight. The word *hate* is used in Scripture, but not as a personal hatred but rather a hatred for people's rebellion against God. In Psalm 139:22–23, David said, "Lord, I hate them who hate You. I hate them with a perfect hatred and count them as my enemies." That's not a personal hatred. It's a hatred for the sinfulness and wickedness that reproaches God.

"Love your enemies." If Jesus had said, "Tolerate your enemies," that would have been all right. "Don't kill your enemies" would have been acceptable. But He said, "Love your enemies." And He didn't use a word that meant to put up with them. He used the word *agape*, the selfless giving love that acts solely for another's benefit. Agape is the love God showed us when He died for our sins. Agape is the love God places in the hearts of those in whom He has taken up residence. It's not affection. It's not a natural tendency. It's not a feeling. It's an action where you place others before and above yourself in the hope that they gain something even if you gain nothing.

Religious people make up rules so they can satisfy their wicked hearts. Love your neighbor. Hate your enemy. That just makes sense. But God asks us to love our enemies with the love He shows us. As you begin to measure your life against Jesus' commands, you fall miserably short—and that's the point. The Law is designed to dress you down—not dress you up—to bring you to the end of yourself so God might help you stand.

I think if we were sitting at Jesus' feet we might be overcome at this point with wanting to stand up and say, "Wait a minute. This is ridiculous." Verse 44 is both impractical and impossible unless God changes my heart. I automatically dislike people who treat me poorly, don't you? We automatically dislike people who curse us, use us, and lie about us. We do not, by natural consequence, love them, because the natural man doesn't know anything about that.

Jeremiah wrote in 13:23 that if an Ethiopian could change the color of his skin or a leopard could change its spots, then people might be able to do good, those accustomed to doing evil (sinners). In Romans 8, Paul said the carnal mind is God's enemy and is not subject to the Law of God. But if we turn to the Lord in faith, God promises to give us a new nature. He'll do the impossible. He'll change our spots.

Rather than twisting the Law to make it work in our own ability, God changes us from the inside so we can be, as Paul said to the Corinthians, new men and women, renewed in knowledge according to the image of the One who created us.

We can have God's heart and love. Things can change. The proof of this new birth is found in the doing of the impossible: in dying to self and loving our enemies. It is against my nature to love my enemies, but it is according to my new nature to do so even as God has loved me. Jesus will say that love is the single greatest evidence that we're His disciples. Why? Because it's so unique, so different, and so unlike the world.

It's the love you find in Abraham for Lot—to whom he offered the first choice of land. It's the love Joseph showed for his brothers who sold him into slavery. It's the love of King David who, seeing Saul sleeping in the cave, let him walk rather than cut off his head. It's the love you find in Stephen's heart before that final rock hits him in the head, when he cries, "Lord, don't lay this sin to their charge." Is it easy? No. Is it possible? Only if you're saved.

If you love like this, you'll be a child that resembles your Father. God wants an identifiable likeness in love between you and Him. If you're saved and walking with our Lord, you'll be able to treat others as He does. He sends His blessing upon those who curse Him. He sends heat, warmth, and life-giving sunshine even upon those who despise Him. He waits for them to come around and gives them plenty of opportunities to repent.

If you do the same, there is proof of sonship. Judgment will come from the Lord eventually. But that's not your job. Yours is to bless those who hate you and let God work out the rest.

> "For if you love those who love you, what reward have you? Do not even the tax collectors do the same? And if you greet your brethren only, what do you do more than others? Do not even the tax collectors do so?"
>
> —Matthew 5:46–47

I don't suspect there could have been a worse group of people than tax collectors that Jesus could have used as an example. The tax collectors were Jews who went to work for the Romans to collect taxes from their fellow Jews. And if that weren't bad enough, they increased the taxes they collected in order to earn their own income. They worked for the enemy and gouged their own people. They were the lowest of the low. No one liked these guys—but if you limit your love to friends or family, you're no better than the worst in society.

> "Therefore you shall be perfect, just as your Father in heaven is perfect."
>
> —Matthew 5:48

If you can be perfect, you don't need to be saved. But if this convicts you, you have no other choice than to come to Jesus and ask Him to save you from yourself and your sin. Paul was saved for thirty years when he wrote to the Philippians in chapter three, "I haven't got there yet. I'm not perfect, but I'm pressing forward for the goal and the high calling of Christ."

Fortunately, God sent His Son to pay for our failures. Jesus used the issue of loving our enemies as the final example to convince us that we need Him desperately, for the Law demands a life we cannot give. But in Him we can find a life that obeys it.

Chapter 26

HOW AND WHY I DO WHAT I DO

Matthew 6:1–4

In Matthew 6, the subject of Jesus' teaching remains the same: the difference between religion and relationship, works and grace when it come to our salvation and how those positions affect how I look at my walk with God. But the focus here narrows to why we do what we do and with what kind of heart we do it. Jesus said religious men are very interested in practicing their religion outwardly to be seen by others, to be acclaimed as religious, and to be honored for their devotion. He said the entire scope of their religious habit and pursuit has an ulterior motive, whereas a believer in Christ has only one interest: God's glory. And as such, his or her religious practices are pursued in a completely different way and with an entirely different heart.

In the process of His teaching however, Jesus will tell us that the danger we face as believers is to nonchalantly begin to practice our faith in such a way that we no longer do so to honor Him, but merely out of habit. The Lord clearly differentiated between the two, but clearly warns us because the enemy is very sneaky. If he can't get through the front door, he'll try to enter through the back door of your life. If he can't get you to stop worshipping altogether, maybe he can have you coming to worship in a way that puts your interests before God's. In every instance however, it is relationship that alone brings life and value to any religious exercise or practice. The heart condition determines the acceptability of everything else.

> "Take heed that you do not do your charitable deeds before men, to be seen by them. Otherwise you have no reward from your Father in heaven."
> —Matthew 6:1

As this comparison unfolds in the first four verses, Jesus begins by asking, "Why are you doing what you're doing?" It is certainly true that every religion in the world has various outward practices that constitute their own approach to God. Muslims teach in the Koran that prayer, self-denial, and devotion to God in the outward sense constitute true religion. Buddhists have their prayer wheel; Catholics their rosary. But Jesus took His disciples aside and, speaking with great authority as their Lord, told them any other motivation for seeking Him except for love and obedience for His honor is not only something that will fail to reach God but will, in actuality, offend and dishonor Him.

In chapter five, Jesus said to the disciples, "Let your light so shine before men that, when they see your good works, they might glorify your Father." In other words, there's a way to do things correctly, where the Lord receives honor and the result of your spiritual life brings God glory. He says the same thing here, but now in the context of the daily approaches people take toward God. There is certainly a way to practice faith that draws attention to oneself. Not every good deed is done in secret. For the unsaved man, his entire life is lived looking for the world's applause rather than God's rewards because he has no relationship with Him and is still dominated by his flesh, by self. Sitting on the throne. His religion is self-sufficient, self-absorbing, and self-generated.

When you hear someone pray, "Father, this morning at three A.M. when I was up early before dawn seeking You," you don't hear "seeking You." You hear "up at three A.M." The issue is whether we are seeking God's glory or our own. The nature of the old man is that he loves to be thought of as spiritual. The true believer, however, is only interested in what God thinks. People look at outward behavior and may or may not be able to tell whether you're interested in applause or not. But God knows.

Even as Christians there is a way to do the right thing in the wrong way. So Jesus says right here in the beginning, "Take heed"—which is a very solemn, serious, somber warning. In other words, "Be on guard against, and watch out for an attitude where you begin to do spiritual things in a carnal or fleshly manner for fleshly rewards."

In Luke 18:9–14, Jesus gave an example of a Pharisee who showed up at the temple to pray. The Pharisee's prayer was telltale of the condition of his heart. He prayed, "Lord, I thank You that I'm not like that guy over there. I thank You that I fast twice a week and that I give tithes of all I possess." But Scripture concludes "he prayed with himself" (Luke 18:11). Across the way stood a tax collector so ashamed of his sin and aware of his failure that he was unable to bring himself to even look up, lest God would strike him dead. "God be merciful to me a sinner," he prayed. And Jesus called him just.

> "Therefore, when you do a charitable deed, do not sound a trumpet before you as the hypocrites do in the synagogues and in the streets, that they may have glory from men. Assuredly, I say to you, they have their reward."
> —Matthew 6:2

In the Greek theater of Jesus' day, actors wore masks to convey their emotions. These actors were called *hupokrites:* actors with masks that had an emotion upon them: happy, sad, devious . . . It is where we get our English word hypocrite from, for the actor was simply playing a part. Here Jesus borrowed that term to speak of the person who gives in such a way that everyone notices. This person doesn't care about God or the things of God. He or she is interested only in the applause of others even as the person hides behind the mask of devotion to God. The scribes and Pharisees may have posed as devout worshippers, concerned with the needs of the poor and the glory of God. But deep within,

135

they were indulgent, fleshly folks who longed for the recognition and applause of others. I think Judas was the ultimate hypocrite. After all, he was a man who could fit in so well among the disciples for three and a half years that no one suspected he was a thief and would betray their Lord. Even at the Last Supper when Jesus said, "One of you is going to betray Me," no one said, "I bet it's Judas." Instead, each wondered if it was he.

This religiosity that hides wickedness is no new kind of hypocrisy. It has been with us from the fall of man. Abel had a true heart for God that followed by faith. Cain, on the other hand, just went through the motions and when he was called on it, he became angry, eventually killing his brother in hopes of lightening the conviction, That too failed.

Jesus used the example of giving because within the society, giving had become a big deal. In His day, thirteen brass treasure chests, trumpet-like in appearance with the wide end at the base and the narrow end pointing upward, stood in the treasury of the temple. These chests had slits in them wherein people would deposit their offerings. The wealthy would bring bags of shekels carried by slaves and a trumpet would sound in the street to announce their arrival. And you can imagine the noise created as they poured their bags of money into the slots of these brass chests.

Mark 12 and Luke 21 tell us that one day, Jesus sat down in the treasury to watch the people give. In the midst of the parade came a widow with two mites—the smallest denomination possible. And without fanfare or a trumpet sound, these two mites fell into the bucket. But it was this woman to whom Jesus directed the attention of His disciples. "These men have given of their excess," He said. "But she has given of her very sustenance. Therefore, she has given more than them all." And in that temple treasury, Jesus differentiated between what was given and how it had been brought to Him.

Not only what we give but *how* we give is of utmost importance to the Lord. Some come with great fanfare as if to say, "Look at me and look what I've done." Yet this woman gave quietly. She only had two mites. She could have kept one for food. But her faith in the Lord and her love for Him caused her to give everything. No one took notice—except God. The others had their reward. She would be getting hers down the road.

Are we careful that when we seek to do things that draw us nearer to God we do them in a way that brings the Lord honor and hides our actions from others—or do we blow the trumpet? You can blow the trumpet in a hundred different ways. You can sing a bit louder than everyone else. You can give so your name is on TV. You can raise your hands in worship, all the while thinking of the Grand Slam at Denny's. You can give so that your name is inscribed in the walk of faith, engraved on a pew, or chiseled on a plaque. But those who are enticed to give that way will one day find the Lord unhappy with their gift because He's interested in our honoring Him rather than in our honoring each other.

> "But when you do a charitable deed, do not let your left hand know what your right hand is doing, that your charitable deed may be in secret; and your Father who sees in secret will Himself reward you openly."
>
> —Matthew 6:3–4

So often we subtly congratulate ourselves for our faithfulness. "When I was praying at four this morning, the Lord told me . . . ." or "Brother, we went out to witness and there weren't many of us, but I was there. In fact, I was there early." We should hide from ourselves anything of which we might be proud because even our own service to God can cause us to stumble. We don't want to be the Pharisee who looks across the room and says, "I rarely sin like that guy over there. At least I'm more faithful than He is. I attended. I came. I sacrificed." It is impossible for your left hand not to know what your right hand is doing. But don't break your arm patting yourself on the back either. Give simply. Do it to please the Lord—then forget what you've done.

If someone can keep a record of your good behavior and godly service, there's no need for the Lord to do so. He keeps the books, doesn't He? And one day in heaven, there will be rewards that will be brought forth for behavior. Our works will be placed in the fire to find out what sort they are. The wood, hay, and stubble will go up in smoke—but the gold, silver, and precious stones will bring a full reward.

What is God looking for from you as His people? He looks for service that isn't broadcast. The reward for this will be far greater than anything we might have been fishing for otherwise. The open reward of God for a life of service in secret is exactly what you want, and He desires as well, for then He is honored and you will used by Him.

Chapter 27

LESSONS ON PRAYER

Matthew 6:5–15
(Luke 11:2–4)

As Jesus distinguished between the religious practices of religious men and the faithful practices of believing saints, He spoke of our motives for behavior and God's acceptance of one and not the other. The first example He used dealt with giving, while the last one will deal with fasting. In the middle He gives us this example of prayer.

I am convinced most Christians don't know how to pray very well. They want to pray. They know they should pray. Most, when they have to pray, do. But hopefulness in prayer, or the feeling that they have accomplished something when they pray, escapes many of us. I think if you look at Jesus' teaching to His disciples, you can't help but learn that prayer is an awesome gift from God—one you can look forward to, be involved with, and use constantly to draw near to God and bring Him your life.

> "And when you pray, you shall not be like the hypocrites. For they love to pray standing in the synagogues and on the corners of the streets, that they may be seen by men. Assuredly, I say to you, they have their reward."
>
> —Matthew 6:5

A religious person's prayers tell us one can actually pray or worship outwardly and do very well, while inwardly what he or she really wants is the honor of others, the praise of many, and the recognition of his or her peers. God has very little to do with this kind of prayer because from His perspective, prayer without a relationship with Him is nothing more than a charade and a fleshly vying for attention and accolades.

Jesus said the prayers of religious men fall short in two basic categories. First, their motivation for prayer is wrong. They don't come to seek the Lord. They don't come to look to God. They don't come to honor Him. They simply come so others can see and hear them. Secondly, as we will see in verse 7, their doctrinal understanding of prayer is wrong. They think long, repetitious prayers give them a better chance of God hearing them. The motivation for a religious man's prayers is usually self-honor and recognition. The doctrine for religious prayers is the more, the merrier, and the better chance they have of being heard in heaven. But Jesus taught the saints just the opposite.

To the Jew, prayer had always held an extremely important place in their history. The Shema—Deuteronomy 6's declaration that God is one God—was prayed every morning

138

and every night at nine. The Shemmonith—the eighteen prayers that took about thirty minutes to recite—were prayed daily at nine in the morning, noon, and three in the afternoon. These prayers were designed to remind men of the goodness and love of the God they served. But these prayers for many degenerated into simply an exercise of words religious people rattled off while their minds were actually in Fiji. During the appointed times of prayer, the scribes and Pharisees would be sure they found themselves in public places so as they stopped to pray, everyone would take note. Their prayers were for public consumption—Jesus called this hypocrisy.

When Peter and John came to the temple in the book of Acts, they came at the hour of prayer. And while the hypocrisy continued inside, a man who had been sitting at the gate outside was healed. Amongst a people flaunting their spirituality, the Lord was still working through those honest men like Peter who looked to the Lord for help.

Religious men will pretend to be interested in prayer, when in reality their prayer lives exist only to be seen, heard, or admired by others. If you don't know the Lord, this makes sense because without knowing Him, prayer holds no other value than to impress others of our spiritual status. But so sin's subtlety and wickedness is seen in this area of mixing prayer which, by definition, is a confession of dependence on God, with pride, which is the defiant declaration of confidence in myself.

How different public prayer might be if people only spoke to God and weren't concerned about what others listening thought. God isn't moved or honored by men's applause anyway. That's why Jesus said, "Don't pray like the hypocrites."

> "But you, when you pray, go into your room, and when you have shut your door, pray to your Father who is in the secret place; and your Father who sees in secret will reward you openly."
>
> —Matthew 6:6

The type of prayer God desires from us is one that focuses attention solely upon Him. But be careful that you don't read into this that all public prayer is wrong. That's not what this verse teaches at all. Jesus prayed in public a lot, surrounded both by believers and unbelievers. Paul did the same thing in many different places. The idea here is that prayer, however and wherever it is engaged, should be for the purpose of coming to the Lord and seeing Him rather impressing others. Prayer has God as its focus, but religious men can't focus on God because they don't know Him. So their focus is on others and on their own "much" praying, as Jesus now addresses.

> "And when you pray, do not use vain repetitions as the heathen do. For they think that they will be heard for their many words. Therefore do not be like them. For your Father knows the things you have need of before you ask Him."
>
> —Matthew 6:7–8

In addition to their wrong motivation, the second problem with a religious man's prayers is wrong doctrine. Because they have no biblical view for their prayers, they conclude that, like everything else in their life, things work best when invested with sweat equity. For them, if five prayers are good, a hundred must be better. Until you know God, that's all you know. The problem is, the Lord calls those prayers vain—empty, worthless, and without value.

The truth is, God isn't moved by any perspiration on our part. There is no "marathon of prayer" reward. There is no prayer repetition that will impress God. In fact, when Solomon wrote Ecclesiastes, he said in chapter five that we should never be rash with our mouths and that our words before God should be few. Our dialogue with Almighty God ought to be very reverent. How much better for us to ask ourselves, "What in the world am I doing here?" rather than engage in an ongoing chatter mistakenly called prayer in hopes of impressing the Lord or wearing Him down.

This doesn't, however, mean you shouldn't repeat a prayer. The Bible is filled with repeated prayers. Facing separation from His Father, Jesus spent three hours praying, "Take this cup away from Me. Nevertheless, not My will but Thine be done."

In 1 Corinthians 12, Paul prayed at length three different times about his thorn in the flesh. The author of Psalm 119 prayed, "Lord, teach me Your statues" no fewer than seven times. It was the cry of his heart; a desire that wouldn't go away. But you can't badger God into answering. You can't talk God into something. You don't need to explain to Him how important a situation is. You don't need to impress Him with the volume of your speaking. God wants fellowship, not empty exercises.

In 1 Kings 18, we read that in the worship of Baal, people made the same request over and over. Because they had no relationship with God, they were left only with prayers they were taught or exclamations they had learned. When Paul upset the Ephesians in the book of Acts, the whole city gathered together with one voice and cried out, "Great is Diana of the Ephesians" for two hours, because that's all they knew.

Even as believers, sometimes we think we have to inform or direct God on how to come to our aid. While it is true that God wants us to bring everything to Him, it is for our benefit that we are invited to come in prayer, not His. Although we're to cast our cares on Him, prayer is not a place to convince God of our needs. It's a place to come to rely on Him to meet them. How important is prayer? It's the place where your relationship with God is most developed because it's where faith becomes real.

When Paul was knocked to the ground and taken blind into Damascus in Acts 9:10–11, the Lord said to a man named Ananias, "I want you to go down to the street called Straight and inquire at the house of Judas for a man named Saul of Tarsus because, behold, he's praying." Now according to his Jewish faith, Paul was a man who had been praying for years. As the self-described "Hebrew of Hebrews and Pharisee of Pharisees," he would have been more diligent to meet at the nine, noon, three, and evening prayers than anyone else. But for the first time in his life, now converted, he was crying out for God from his heart and the Lord said, "Check this out: he's praying." This kind of prayer got through to God. This kind of prayer was acceptable to the Lord. This was real praying—and God made note of it.

According to Luke, Jesus gave this outline that begins here in Matthew 6:9 after His disciples had watched Him pray. In Luke's account, this outline was given between Jesus' teachings on the value of sitting at His feet and that of asking, seeking, and knocking. The disciples had watched Jesus pray both late into the night and oftentimes before dawn. In Luke 9:18 we read, "As He was praying alone and His disciples were with Him . . . ." In other words, they were with Him physically but not where He was spiritually, and they wanted to be, wanted what He had when it came to fellowship with His Father in prayer.

They said, "Lord, John taught his disciples to pray. Why don't You teach us to pray? We'd like to learn to do what we see in Your life." In answer to their request, we are given this model, which is commonly called "the Lord's Prayer." But it's not. Jesus wouldn't have prayed, "And forgive us our debts," because He had no sin. The Lord's prayer is actually in John 19. This one is really the disciples' prayer, because the Lord gave it to them in answer to their request to be taught to pray.

If you asked Jesus to teach you to pray, I'm sure you wouldn't be surprised if He gave you a thousand-page book on prayer. Yet He gave the disciples neither a thousand pages nor even a thousand paragraphs. He gave them sixty-four words. And in them we find everything we need to know concerning the scope of, approach to, and content of prayer. You can make a quick outline of this prayer by noting there are three petitions for God's glory followed by three petitions for our own need, followed by one statement of faith that God can handle it. It's a wonderful outline to follow.

> "In this manner, therefore, pray: Our Father in heaven, hallowed be Your name."
> —Matthew 6:9

Notice where prayer begins: with a realization that we have a relationship with God. Why do unbelievers' prayers not please God? Because although they're directed toward Him, they're uttered by people who don't know Him. One of the benefits of being saved is I can pray. If I've given my life to Jesus, I have access into the Father's presence. The curtain is torn, the door is open, and I can talk with God because Jesus has paved the way, removing my sin with His blood. This is a tremendous benefit we have as Christians. But note that before I lay out my concerns or run down my list of requests, I am, according to Jesus' outline, to stop and consider to whom I'm speaking and how I got there.

Praying in his eighties at a time he really needed to hear from God regarding the future, Daniel spent thirteen verses in chapter three of his letter praising the Lord for all He is. It's not until verse 17 that he says, "Oh, yeah, here's why I've come today." He began his prayer by reminding himself to whom he was speaking.

In the Old Testament there are only seven references to God being our Father. In the New Testament, there are seventy. "Our Father" is an intimate and welcoming term, but it would cost Jesus His life for us to be able to use it. The familiarity with God as our Father is balanced by the fact that He is our Father in heaven, that He is our Lord.

For five chapters, Isaiah said, "Woe is this. Woe is that. Woe is you." Then, in chapter 6, he met the Lord and his message changed to "Woe is me."

In chapter 40, Job said to the Lord, "I know I'm vile. I don't know how to answer You, but I think I'll put my hand over my mouth." He slowed down when he realized in whose presence he stood.

In this outline of prayer, Jesus said, "First come recognizing to whom you belong and how you got there."

If you can grasp the meaning of "Father in heaven," it will be the greatest stride you ever make toward maturity in prayer because knowing you're talking to a God who loves you, cares for you, and knows all about you will give you great hope, great encouragement, and great confidence, before you ever ask for anything at all.

Secondly, Jesus said you should be interested in "hallowed be Your name." The word *hallow* means to honor, glorify, and set aside as distinct. The purpose of everything that follows in my prayer should be to honor and glorify God. When Jesus faced the greatest crisis of His life, we read in John 12:27 that as He talked to His disciples on the way to the cross He said, "It is for this hour I have come. Therefore, Father, glorify Thyself." In the worst of times, Jesus' prayer was that His Father be glorified.

Ultimately my prayer life must focus on the fact that I need to glorify God's name. In the Bible, the name referred not so much to a title but rather as a description of character. God used plenty of names in Scripture to reveal Himself, but the one He used most often consists of four Hebrew consonants: YHWH, the tetragramaton. No one knows how to pronounce it because there are no vowels. But it is Jehovah, Yahweh, or some form of that and means "the One who becomes" or "the One who is."

To Abraham, who was to offer his son, Isaac, on Mount Moriah, God revealed Himself as Jehovah-Jireh, "the God who provides." When Moses and the people were to battle a much stronger army, God revealed Himself as Jehovah-Nissi, "the Lord your banner." To Gideon, terrified to go into battle, the Lord said, "I am Jehovah-Shalom," or "the Lord your peace." To Jeremiah, overwhelmed by the people's sins, the Lord revealed Himself as Jehovah Tsidkenu, "the Lord our righteousness."

When I pray, I should be so interested in honoring the Lord that however God chooses to answer or respond to my prayer is secondary to what I really want, which is that my Lord be honored. If that means not getting my way, great. If that means changing my ideas, fine. All I should want is for the Lord's name to be glorified.

"Your kingdom come, Your will be done on earth as it is in heaven."
—Matthew 6:10

In the big picture, the phrase "Your kingdom come" speaks of the Lord's future rule over the earth. On a practical level, it means I should pray with the understanding that this life isn't all there is. When Isaiah wrote about the Child that would be born, the Son that would be given, he said the government would rest upon His shoulders and there would be no end of an increase of His government. The Lord is coming back to establish His kingdom—and when He does, things will get better. This means I can't be so shortsighted in prayer that everything revolves around what happens next Tuesday at eight. As I pray, I've got to realize that because my Father in heaven has a kingdom He's going to establish, there is a future to anticipate, and His plans work towards that time.

In a more personal sense, God's kingdom is already here. In Luke 17:21, Jesus said, "The kingdom of God is within you." I look forward to the day the Lord will come to rule and reign on this planet. But in many ways, He is already on the throne, for He rules in our lives. He's the head of the church. He rules in our hearts. And the extent to which I understand this is the extent to which I'll pray, "Lord, may Your kingdom come in my life. May Your will be done in my life."

God never told us to pray that our will would be done in heaven, yet I think that's how most of us pray. "Here I am, Lord," we say. "I've got a lot of ideas. I hope You can run with a few of them for me." We tell God what we want, what He should do, and how He should do it. Then we wait. And if He gives us what we want, we say, "Amen! Praise the Lord! Isn't God good?" But if He comes up with anything else, it's, "Oh, I'm having a bad week. God's not listening to me."

As a Christian, prayer is a place for me to seek heaven on earth, not the other way around. But I have found that the more precious something is to us, the less likely we are willing to let God be the Lord over it. For example, if someone I hardly know is sick, I pray, "Lord, if You want to heal him, great. But if You want to, take him home to be with You, You know best." But if it's my kid who's sick, I pray, "Lord, heal him. Now!"

Yet Jesus in His prayer outline says to me, "Ask that the Lord's will be accomplished, that His will be done."

Before I get to the place of asking God for what I want, I have to come to the place where I can say, "God, I want what You want. I've been born again. You've brought me out of the darkness and into the light. You're my Lord. Have it Your way"—regardless of what He chooses. And lest you think that is always easy, think of how Jesus struggled hour after hour in Gethsemane.

It isn't easy to let God be God, to be afraid of what He might choose to do, and to surrender to Him. But if you're going to pray, "Your kingdom come," you're really praying, "My kingdom go." That's not an easy, once-and-for-all process. But it's a daily practice that will bring great fruit.

In verse 11, we come to three petitions for ourselves. Verses 11 and 12, and the first part of 13, cover the present, past, and future in our lives with regard to prayer. But notice it is worship, submission, and giving thanks to the Lord that bring us to the place where we can now bring our concerns before Him.

In Acts 4, the early church leaders are beaten by the government and sent home with a warning not to preach anymore. Scripture records that they went to the church, gathered everyone together, and for five or six verses prayed about this very present danger. I love their prayer because it begins with, "You're almighty God. You knew this was going to happen. You saw this from day one. You understand all we're going through. Lord, we want strength to stay the course." They followed the outline from Matthew 6. They acknowledged who God is, sought His will, and then let Him know their needs and concerns.

In each of the following three requests, almost all of the verbs are present active imperative—which means we are to pray now, pray later, and keep praying. Some Christians pray for daily needs weekly. God, however, wants a daily relationship.

> "Give us this day our daily bread."
>
> —Matthew 6:11

Although God knows what we need before we ask, it is to our benefit to develop a dependence upon Him that is very real to us, because we are by nature very independent, aren't we? And spiritually, independence is sin when it comes to a relationship with God. God calls me to pray daily, because I need to learn that He is involved in every part of my life. And if I will learn to do this, by the time I get to verse 25, where the Lord starts talking about worrying, I won't need to worry because I meet with God every day about my life.

When we go to Israel, we check in with the troops in whatever area we're in just to say, "Here are our plans for today. What do you think?" They look at their intelligence reports and usually say, "It's a good day. Have a great time." But if they said, "Maybe you could go somewhere else today and go there tomorrow," we'd be foolish to do otherwise. The same is true with the Lord. We've got to check in every day, because we want to go to the right places. We want to do the right thing.

If your refrigerator is full and you have enough money in the bank to pay your bills for the next couple of months, you might think you don't have any needs and, therefore, have no need of prayer. What needs do you have? How about breathing? According to Daniel 5:23, the Lord holds your breath in His hand. If He nods off for a moment, you'll be nodding off for a long time! I need the Lord to direct me on the right path and to protect me from the things I'm facing. He wants to be part of my life, and that's a good thing because I desperately need Him in my life.

How does God usually meet our needs? How does He provide our daily bread? Most often by giving us a job. I talked to a fellow whose business was having a difficult time. As we talked, he began to realize he wasn't running it to honor the Lord. Yet he wanted God to bless it. As I reminded him, when we seek the Lord for our daily needs, it shines a light on our own lives so we can see if we are doing things right in God's eyes. We have to do our part. "Give us this day our daily bread" puts me in the position of asking, "Am I doing the things I'm supposed to do to allow God to bless my life?"

"Give us this day our daily bread." The manna the children of Israel were given as they journeyed through the wilderness had an expiration date: midnight. The same is still true. Daily needs must be prayed for daily.

> "And forgive us our debts, as we forgive our debtors."
>
> —Matthew 6:12

The prayer for daily bread is a prayer for the present. Praying for forgiveness is a prayer for the past. "Forgive me my debts, or sins." What sins? The sins I committed since the last time I prayed. This is a necessity I think few Christians practice. We ask the Lord to save us. We get saved. We say, "All my sins are forgiven!" And then we go on with life and never once say, "Lord, I'm not doing the right thing here." Yet throughout the Bible, God teaches us that sin can interrupt fellowship with Him.

As his child, my father loved me no matter what—but there were times I was in my room and he wasn't speaking to me because I'd totally disobeyed him without concern for his will. It's the same with the Lord. I'm saved, but sin interrupts fellowship. I've got to walk in the light. I've got to be washed in the blood. I've got to stay in contact—every day.

At the Last Supper (John 13) when Jesus began washing feet, Peter said, "You're the Lord. I'll wash Your feet."

"If I can't wash your feet, you don't belong to Me," Jesus answered.

Then Peter had a change of heart. He wanted a bath. But Jesus said, "You're already cleansed, washed, and saved. But you've got to have your feet washed, because every day you walk through dirt."

That's us. We live in the world. We fall short. We need to maintain a relationship with God and we do that by confessing our failures so we can continue to be dependent on His grace. But here, as well as throughout Scripture, the Lord directly attached forgiveness and mercy to our willingness to extend them to others.

God is so concerned that you don't get a hard heart that He wants you to consider your own sin every day as you pray. That's why Paul told the Colossians that they should bear with one another and forgive one another. And if anyone had a complaint, as Christ forgave that person he or she was to do the same. He told the Ephesians in chapter four to let all bitterness, malice, clamor, and evil speaking be put away from them. Instead, they were to be kindhearted, forgiving one another as Christ had forgiven them.

Why? Because that's God's nature and heart for His people.

Do you consistently consider your own sin and your unwillingness to forgive others? That's how God would have you pray. You can't claim mercy for yourself and then withhold it from others.

In Matthew 18:21–22, Peter thought he had it all figured out. "Lord," he said, "I think I should forgive someone seven times"—which was six times more than anyone else was willing to do.

But Jesus said, "Peter, it should be seventy times seven." Then He told the story of a guy who had a twenty-million-dollar debt he couldn't pay. Rather than throwing him into a labor camp, however, his lender forgave his debt completely. As you can imagine, the guy went whistling out the door—until he caught up with a guy who owed him twenty bucks.

"Where's my twenty bucks?" he asked.

"I don't have it right now," came the reply.

"Fine. I'll call the police and you'll be in labor camp by morning."

When the lender of the twenty million heard about this, he called in the debtor and said, "I shouldn't have forgiven you. You're a rat." And he forced him to work off his debt.

This is only a nice story—until you get to Matthew 18:35 where you read, "So shall My heavenly Father do to you if, from your heart, you do not forgive your brother his trespasses." No wonder Jesus told us to confront this daily.

> "And do not lead us into temptation, but deliver us from the evil one."
>
> —Matthew 6:13

In this petition for our future, the words *lead* and *deliver* are present-tense verbs. As such, this also is to become a daily petition: "Wherever I go today, Lord, I don't want to fall into the trap of the evil one."

Trials, or temptations, are very interesting in the Bible. James studied them carefully and concluded that we should be grateful when we fall into different kinds of trials, because the testing of our faith produces patience, and if patience has its perfect work, we won't lack a thing.

God tries our faith so He can prove to us how genuine it is, so we might become strong. Nothing gets strong without resistance. It is resistance that produces strength. Therefore, if there is no resistance to faith in your life, you won't be very strong. The minute something goes wrong, you'll fall apart because you won't be used to clutching to the Lord. God allows trials in our lives with the intention of strengthening us and providing us a measure whereby we can begin to see that He's been at work in us.

The Devil, however, has other plans for our difficulties. He wants those same trials to trip us up and take us away from faith. Consequently, the best prayer for the future—whether that future is ten minutes away or next week—is, "Lord, keep me away from the evil one. I don't ever want to fall into the trap where the things that are meant for my good turn out to be used by the enemy for my destruction."

I love this prayer because no matter what comes our way, we can look to the Lord and say, "I know You meant this for good. What do You want me to learn through it?"

"For Yours is the kingdom and the power and the glory forever. Amen."

—Matthew 6:13

Jesus' outline for prayer ends with our saying, "When all is said and done, Lord, it's Your kingdom. It's Your power. It's Your glory. I just want to be part of it."

It's a beautiful prayer, a perfect way to pray. But I believe its greatest value is not in the words prayed as a prayer but rather the outline it gives us for how we should pray, even as the disciples had asked of Jesus.

"For if you forgive men their trespasses, your heavenly Father will also forgive you. But if you do not forgive men their trespasses, neither will your Father forgive your trespasses."

—Matthew 6:14–15

The prayer for forgiveness is the only portion of the prayer on which Jesus elaborated. Here, after the "amen" is said, He returned to verse 12 as if to underscore its importance. Every day when we pray, isn't it interesting that we are to think about our own sin and unwillingness to forgive others? If that has to come up every day, I'm assuming it's because we have a very difficult time forgiving. We're much better at asking for forgiveness than giving it, aren't we? Yet His words here demand we respond seriously and soberly for His grace and forgiveness we all need desperately.

Chapter 28

Fasting: Food for Thought

Matthew 6:16–18

"Moreover, when you fast, do not be like the hypocrites, with a sad counte-nance. For they disfigure their faces that they may appear to men to be fasting. Assuredly, I say to you, they have their reward. But you, when you fast, anoint your head and wash your face, so that you do not appear to men to be fasting, but to your Father who is in the secret place; and your Father who sees in secret will reward you openly."

—Matthew 6:16–18

In His third comparison between the religious man and the believer, Jesus turned to the practice of fasting. According to the Law, fasting was required only once a year on the Day of Atonement when the entire nation gathered to acknowledge their dependence upon God's mercy and grace for the forgiveness of their sins. By Jesus' day, however, the Jews had increased the requirement to fasting on Monday and Thursday of every week. And as with the bringing of offerings and the offerings of prayer that we have already discussed, the religious person would approach fasting with the same spirit of being sure others knew of his sacrifice. That's why Jesus said, "If you're fasting, wash up. Smile. Don't let on that you're seeking the Lord in secret."

Notice that Jesus didn't say it was wrong to fast. He said it was wrong to fast simply to be seen.

I think the very words *when you fast* suggest that the Lord expects us at some time to fast. Following are four reasons for fasting drawn from biblical examples.

There is no ordinary occasion in the Bible for fasting. You never find someone saying on a Tuesday, "This looks like a good day to fast. I've got to get groceries tomorrow anyway." In the Bible, fasting is always attached to extraordinary circumstances. Whether it is in conjunction with a grave situation, tremendous distress, or deep humility accompanied by tears, fasting is the voluntary action of a believer who has turned to God in faith.

When the people in Zechariah's day finally got the message that they needed to turn to the Lord, in Zechariah 8:19, the Lord said to the people through the prophet, "I want you to set aside the fast you have proclaimed in the fourth, fifth, seventh, and tenth month." The people had repented. There was no need at this point for fasting. There was only need for great rejoicing. So the Lord said, "Put those self-imposed fasts aside."

148

In Matthew 9:14–15, John's disciples didn't understand the behavior of Jesus' disciples. "John taught us to fast," they said. "And we see the Pharisees fasting. How come Your boys don't fast?"

"Can the friends of the bridegroom mourn as long as the bridegroom is with them?" Jesus answered. "But the days are coming when the bridegroom will be taken away from them, and then they will fast."

It does appear that the Lord would have us to be people who approach Him with fasting from time to time as He leads. By definition, a fast can either be absolute—where you don't eat or drink anything—or it can be the giving up of certain foods. In chapter ten, Daniel gave up only dessert. That wouldn't be a bad idea even for non-spiritual purposes! The length of time for fasting also changes. In the Bible we see one-day, three-day, and three-week fasts. Moses did a forty-day and even an eighty-day fast without any food or water. I suggest God lead you before trying that!

The first reason to fast and the one found most often in Scripture accompanies repentance. When you were in school with a big test coming up, if your mom offered you breakfast you might have said, "I can't eat. I have that big test." Your stomach was churning. You lost your appetite. I think in much the same way godly repentance robs us even of our desire to eat. Being right with the Lord becomes all that matters and we find ourselves setting aside daily food for the sake of our real appetite: to make our lives right with God.

When the Lord sent the prophet Joel to those who were living in great defiance, he counseled them in Joel 1 to return to Him with all of their heart with fasting, weeping, and mourning. Fasting is the heart's intention acted out in life. Joel called the people to a true repentance that would be accompanied by fasting. He said in the same chapter, "You should rend your heart and not your garment. It's no good to wear sackcloth, throw dust on your head, tear your clothes, and outwardly look like you're sorry if you're not." This wasn't supposed to be some religious posturing but the effect of the people's true sorrow over the fact that they had failed to follow their God.

In 1 Samuel 7, Samuel said, "If you'll return to the Lord with all of your heart and get rid of your false gods, God will answer your prayer." The people heeded his counsel and gathered together and fasted that day, saying, "We've sinned against God." The association is hard to separate. Repentance and fasting often are found in the same place.

It was Nehemiah in chapter 9 who gathered the people together, read to them from the Bible that they hadn't heard for years, and focused their eyes again upon the Lord. And we read that the people fasted and confessed their own sins and those of their fathers. Even in Leviticus 23, in the description of the Day of Atonement, God said it was a day to make atonement through confession and sacrifice.

When God knocked Saul, who was such a terror to the early church, on his backside outside Damascus and left him physically blind, he fasted for three days and three nights. After his whole life had become unraveled in a matter of moments, and realizing his path was absolutely wrong, Paul knew food was the least important thing to him at that point.

Understanding that everything he had done had been in error, he repented and sought God. God, in turn, sent help because Paul's hunger for the Lord was evidenced in part by his lack of hunger for his daily bread.

When Jeremiah sent Baruch to read God's Law to the people, Jeremiah 36 records that as the people heard the Word, they proclaimed a fast. The Word got in. Hearts were broken. And the people turned back to God.

When Jonah was sent to the Ninevites, the people listened to his message, and from the king down everyone believed God. He proclaimed a fast so widespread that they wouldn't even let their animals eat. The people cried to God in fear, desperation and hope and, much to Jonah's chagrin, God heard their prayers and relented from His anger.

The second reason to fast as seen in Scripture is often associated with times of great distress—even when sin or rebellion is not the cause. When the Jews heard of Haman's plan to destroy them because Mordecai had failed to bow down and worship him, they called a fast. The nation was at risk. It was a time like never before. And in their distress, God responded.

In 2 Chronicles 20, as Jehoshaphat faced a million-man army, he called the people together to seek the Lord. They proclaimed a fast and the Lord gave them great victory.

Before Ezra was allowed to take a contingent of people from Babylon to Jerusalem in order to rebuild and repopulate the city, he had been bragging to the king about how great his God was. So when the king gave him gold and building materials, Ezra was reticent to ask for government protection as they made their way across seven hundred miles of desert. Instead, he gathered the people and proclaimed a fast so that his witness wouldn't be compromised. As a result, God's hand was with them for good and they arrived safely, with gold and materials intact.

Third, you will find fasting in the Bible as an expression of grief. When Moses, Saul, Jonathan, and Solomon died, Scripture records that there was great weeping accompanied by fasting. Hearing from someone who had come back from Jerusalem about how the city was laid waste and the name of the Lord was disgraced, Nehemiah was so grief-stricken that he fasted and prayed. As Nehemiah sought the Lord, God began to open doors for him to be part of the solution.

Finally, fasting is seen in connection with intercession. In Psalm 35, David wrote that when his enemies were sick, he humbled himself with fasting.

When Moses came down from Mt. Sinai and found the people worshipping a golden calf, he threw down the tablets the Lord had given him, dealt with the people, and then went up to get a second edition of the Law. That meant forty more days of no eating or drinking. When he described it later in Deuteronomy 9, he said he was afraid of the anger of the Lord on behalf of the people.

When the seventy years of captivity were almost over, we read in Daniel 9 that it was with prayer and fasting that Daniel sought the Lord on behalf of the people.

I don't know how much love you have to have for someone else to quit eating. Aside from breathing, it's the thing we like most. But these four reasons ought to motivate us to pray and ask the Lord how we might incorporate this practice into our lives.

In Isaiah 58, we have the definitive chapter in the Bible on fasting. It gives us both sides of the story: the religious aspect versus the preferred aspect of truly seeking God. Through Isaiah, the Lord said to the people, "You pretend to seek Me and My ways. You're going through all the religious activity, but your prayers aren't heard on high because there's no corresponding lifestyle. I'm not fooled, nor am I impressed." Then Isaiah goes on to describe the type of fast that pleases the Lord:

> Is not this the fast that I have chosen: To loose the bonds of wickedness, to undo the heavy burdens, to let the oppressed go free, and that you break every yoke? Is it not to share your bread with the hungry, and that you bring to your house the poor who are cast out; when you see the naked, that you cover him, and not hide yourself from your own flesh? Then your light shall break forth like the morning, your healing shall spring forth speedily, and your righteousness shall go before you; the glory of the Lord shall be your rear guard. Then you shall call, and the Lord will answer; you shall cry, and He will say, "Here I am."
> —Isaiah 58:6–9

What good reasons to fast! What a mighty promise of God!

Should we fast? I think the Bible indicates that Jesus expects us to. How long should we fast? When should we fast? How often should we fast? I think those are determined solely by God's work in your heart. But the motive has to fall in line with what God establishes in His Word: repentance, great distress, grief, or intercession. If any of those are part of your life, Isaiah 58 becomes a wonderful place of promise because it seems to me there is great power to be found in extreme circumstances by devoting time to the Lord in prayer and fasting.

I hope God will show you when and where. I know there's a lot to be gained by seeking Him.

Chapter 29

YOUR TREASURE AND YOUR MASTER

Matthew 6:19–24

Beginning here in verse 19, the topic of Jesus' teaching changes from private devotion to public life as He gives His disciples some examples of how their relationship with Him should affect the way they were living.

A relationship with Jesus ought to be seen. It ought to be measurable. It ought to change lives. It's kind of like Numbers and Deuteronomy. Numbers is the Law. Deuteronomy is the life. We're to live out what we know.

A life lived with God is more than just spiritual devotion. It's a daily practice. When they are in trouble, religious men have a religion that fails them. They may pray, but they don't know to whom. Neither do they know if there will be an answer. They may look up, but all they see are clouds, because they don't have God's promises. So at some point along the way, they are failed by their religion. But those who know the Lord have peace, because they have God's promises and hang on to God's power and find God's peace and presence when they are most needful of Him.

> "Do not lay up for yourselves treasures on earth, where moth and rust destroy and where thieves break in and steal; but lay up for yourselves treasures in heaven, where neither moth nor rust destroys and where thieves do not break in and steal. For where your treasure is, there your heart will be also."
> —Matthew 6:19–21

These verses seem to me to be revolutionary for believers. Therefore, I'm not surprised they always are met with great resistance. We don't like them because they are a challenge to our western way of life. According to the Scriptures, neither earthly riches nor the lack of them has anything to do with being wealthy from God's perspective. The only treasure that will last is the treasure that awaits you in heaven, not the one you gather together here on the earth.

The word *treasure* is one of those all-inclusive terms defined by its context. Here it speaks of that which is valuable to you. The way this verse is written in Greek, it is not a suggestion or a recommendation that we store up treasure in heaven—it's a command. Jesus didn't say, "This would be a good idea." He said, "Do this."

To "lay up" could be translated "to store, horde, gather, stockpile, or accumulate." As believers, we're not to make this our goal upon the earth. Instead, we're to store, horde, and accumulate treasures in heaven where they are safe. Notice that the Lord gave a couple of reasons for this. The stuff we store on earth is subject to erosion, rotting, and thievery. It just doesn't last. Nothing you have or can see lasts—not even yourself. Everything is rotting away. Whether through biological function or natural disaster, it one day will be gone. Whether illness steals it, the economy robs you, or some guy breaks in and takes it from you, it's leaving. So the Lord's counsel gives us some absolute wisdom: don't horde treasure on earth.

Yet you can take those very things and store them in heaven where they are not only kept for you, but are protected from the debilitating effects of life on earth. In 1 Peter 1 we read that our inheritance is incorruptible and undefiled.

Certainly God is not prohibiting you from doing well in business and being wise with your finances. In fact, the Bible is filled with injunctions to be responsible, to lay up for a rainy day. When Solomon wrote Proverbs 6, he said, "Look at how industrious ants are. They work all summer to get ready for the winter. Be like the ant. Plan ahead. Be wise in what you do."

In Romans 12:11, Paul said, "You shouldn't be slothful in your business. You should work hard." He told the Corinthians to "lay up for your children rather than having them lay up for you" (2 Cor. 12:14) and to his disciple Timothy he wrote, "If you don't provide for your own family, you're worse than an unbeliever" (1 Tim. 5:8).

Laying up treasure in heaven is not a matter of being irresponsible, lazy, or undependable on earth. It is, rather, a question of where your values lie because, according to verse 21, whatever storage unit you choose has great consequence. If it's the one on the earth, that's where your heart will end up. But if your treasure is in heaven, your heart will be there and you will have true riches.

So little did Esau value his spiritual birthright as firstborn that he sold it for a bowl of stew. Centuries later, the Gadarenes valued Jesus' work among them with such little regard that they asked Him to leave when He upset their illegal pig-raising business in Matthew 8. Like Esau and the Gadarenes, if the ultimate purpose and goal of your life and the driving concern and preoccupation of your thoughts are with temporary, worldly treasures, know that you are absolutely out of God's will, because it is His desire that you value Him who can give you eternal life.

Although we try in vain to prove otherwise, the Bible teaches that our heart is singular in its ability to focus and it only can be completely occupied with one thing at a time. We think we can play both sides of the fence—that we can fill our lives with a lot of things and keep them in balance.

But Jesus said otherwise. Here He said, "You can either store up treasures on earth or you can store them in heaven, but you can't do both because you can only serve one thing at a time. And if you choose the former, remember that the moth eats it, the rust destroys it, and thieves will steal it. Everything on earth has an expiration date—including you."

We tend to admire people who are good shoppers. We read *Consumer Reports* because we don't want a washer that's going to break down in eleven years. We want one that will last the full nineteen. We applaud the guy who buys the car with the best gas mileage and the smallest need for repair at the lowest price—yet Jesus says what we value will affect not the next nineteen years but our eternal destiny. When it comes to the spiritual side of our lives, we have difficulty translating eternity into daily behavior. It's not a matter of what you have or don't have. It's a matter of who has you. Where's your heart? Where's your treasure? Who's your Master?

I think one of the strongest proofs of how blinding sin can be is the difficulty Christians have with putting this truth into action. We nod in agreement and then we act like the world. Yet to invest in the world is foolish. We're supposed to be much wiser. We're supposed to store our treasure in heaven.

That your heart follows your treasure is a very appropriate message for our culture because statistics show that, materialistically, you and I have more available to us than any generation that has ever lived. Shopping malls were unheard of fifty years ago. Today, if you go to the Midwest to a town of two thousand people, there will be three of them. They're everywhere. We love them. They open early on Thanksgiving so we can shop for Christmas. Shopping has become the national pastime.

"What are you doing?" we ask.

"We're going to the mall," we answer.

"What are you buying?"

"Oh, we're just going to look around."

"What are you looking for?"

"We're going to wander around to see if something exists that we don't know about so we can buy it."

According to the U.S. Bureau of Economic Analysis, in 1958 Americans spent 7.5 percent of their income on non-necessary items. Today, that figure has risen to 30 percent. In the last thirty-five years, we have gone from spending forty-two billion dollars a year to three-quarters of a trillion dollars just to entertain ourselves. Even actuary figures reveal that money is destructive rather than helpful for most. As wages increase, so do the numbers on suicide, divorce, and infidelity. Money can take a toll. Materialism grips the heart of our nation and is Jesus' warning to the saints to live differently.

Paul hit the nail on the head when he wrote to Timothy that those who desire to be rich fall into the snare of foolish and hurtful lusts that drown people in destruction and perdition (1 Tim. 6:9). The love of money is the root of all evil, he went on to say. Obsession with money is the motivation behind the drug dealer, the thief, and the white-collar criminal. It drives this country. It drives the world. But it shouldn't drive you because the ultimate price of loving temporal things is destruction.

And maybe the saddest part of the equation is that many Christians live pretty much like the world does and then say, "God has blessed me" without ever realizing that somewhere along the way they set their hearts on their material blessings rather than on Jesus. In Luke 12:15, Jesus said life doesn't consist of the abundance of things we possess. There is no culture that needs to hear this more than ours.

Want to know if you're investing in heavenly things or earthly things? Let me suggest you look at your checkbook and see where you spend your money. How much money do you spend every year to get the Word of God out to someone through missionaries, church, a Bible for your friend at work, or Gospel tracts for your back pocket? According to Isaiah 55, the Word doesn't return empty. Therefore, supporting any aspect of getting God's Word to people is guaranteed to reap huge dividends.

Before I became a pastor, my father and I invested together in the stock market and in apartment buildings. He developed in me the habit of getting up every morning and, even before I got dressed, seeing how the stocks were doing. But as a twenty-two-year-old, it drove me crazy because my heart would rise and fall with the stock market, the mortgage rate, and the occupancy level. And while some mornings I said, "Oh, it's going to be a good day," there were just as many when I said, "Oh, no. I might as well just go back to bed." Where your treasure is, there your heart will be also. If you're occupied with the things of God, pleasing Him will be the determining factor of any given day.

How can you invest in heaven? You can begin by taking a proper view of this life. Hebrews 11 tells us we're like pilgrims walking through the world. We're looking for a city made without hands whose Maker is God. We're just passing through. We're holding on to things lightly rather than tightly because this is not our home. Who would spend a million dollars fixing up a house he's only renting? You have to have the proper view of life not to get caught up in all of this.

Second, you have to stay in fellowship with God. In Luke 10, Martha was so busy in the kitchen that she was distracted with serving. Mary, on the other hand, was just spending time with Jesus. When Martha asked Jesus to tell Mary to help her, Jesus said, "Martha, just one thing is necessary and Mary has chosen it" (Luke 10:41–42). The right view of life and true fellowship with God will make you a good steward of the blessings He gives you.

> "The lamp of the body is the eye. If therefore your eye is good, your whole body will be full of light. But if your eye is bad, your whole body will be full of darkness. If therefore the light that is in you is darkness, how great is that darkness!"
> —Matthew 6:22–23

The topic hasn't changed because verse 24 is still part of the same discussion concerning material versus heavenly treasure. If your eye is on the things of God, focused on God's will and on eternity, you will be single-minded and full of light. You won't get caught up in the culture in which you live or the values of that culture. "Thy Word is a lamp unto my feet and a light to my path," the psalmist wrote (Ps. 119:105).

On the other hand, if you're driven by materialism and earthly treasure, darkness will rule your outlook. As such, you'll be vulnerable to making the wrong choices in numerous areas because you'll have faulty vision, blurred perspective, and a divided heart. In Proverbs 28:22, we read that a man with an evil eye will seek hastily after riches, not remembering the poverty that awaits him. He doesn't have a long-term view. He can't see past the nose on his face.

> "No one can serve two masters; for either he will hate the one and love the other, or else he will be loyal to the one and despise the other. You cannot serve God and mammon."
>
> —Matthew 6:24

Mammon is literally the god of wealth. This verse hits the nail on the head for us because most of us think we can have it both ways, that we can take advantage of both the present and then the eternal world. Jesus, however, says we cannot. We either worship God or riches. We're either heavenly-minded or earthly-minded. We either serve God or mammon. Look at the comparison:

- One master demands a walk by faith, the other by sight.
- One demands you humble yourself, the other that you fill yourself with pride.
- One tells you to set your affection on things above; the other says, "Look to the earth."
- One wants you to look at unseen things by faith; the other hands you a catalog of the world's goods.
- One wants you worried about nothing; the other wants you worried about everything.
- One wants you to be content with what you have; the other wants you to thirst again and again and again.
- One will leave you ready to give your life for others, the other to hang on selfishly only for yourself.
- One wants you to look to the Creator; the other tells you simply to enjoy the creation.

Where your treasure is, there's your heart. Where's your treasure? Who's your master? If God is your Master, then money is your servant. But if money is your master, you're in big trouble, for he and all things of this world are extremely ruthless taskmasters.

Chapter 30

WHY I DON'T HAVE TO WORRY

Matthew 6:25–34
(Luke 12:22–31)

Here in our next study, Matthew 6:25–34, the topic from our last chapter continues unchanged, but the focus of the illustration is different, so we might clearly see these truths. In these ten verses, Jesus focuses on the essentials of life—eating, drinking, and clothing—the things we can't do without—rather than focusing upon the luxuries. You can sum up these ten verses in four words found early in verse 25: *Therefore do not worry*. We find them repeated in verses 31, and 34. I think because we are so slow to learn, the Lord often repeats Himself for our benefit—especially in the area of worry.

What we're going to learn first is that it's unfaithful to worry, because we have a Master in heaven who can do anything. Secondly, it's unnecessary to worry, because we have a heavenly Father who loves us and will care for us. Thirdly, it's unreasonable to worry, because worry cannot accomplish a single thing. And, finally, it's unwise to worry because we have a good future ahead of us, and we can rest in God's care.

> "Therefore I say to you, do not worry about your life, what you will eat or what you will drink; nor about your body, what you will put on. Is not life more than food and the body more than clothing?"
>
> —Matthew 6:25

The word rendered *life* (psuche) is often translated *soul* and represents everything you are physically, emotionally, and spiritually. In other words, if God is your Master, there is no need to worry in any area or for any reason. Worry is the sin of distrust in God and, as such, becomes perhaps the greatest sin in the life of the saint. The word *worry* comes from an old German word that means "to choke yourself." What a great picture. Jesus' word to the believer is that he is to live far differently than those who simply have a religious persuasion but do not know God. Religious men will find comfort in their religion as long as things go well. But when they are without hope, there's no place for them to turn. Believers, on the other hand, have great hope and never need to worry.

Worry is produced when I don't have what I think I need, what I think I should have, or what I wish I could have. In other words, worry is the result of a lack of contentment. In Philippians 4, Paul, thirty years a Christian, said, "I've learned in whatever state I am to be content. If that means being abased, fine. If that means abounding, that's fine too. In everything and all things I've learned how to be full and to be hungry, to abound and to suffer need" (Phil. 4:11–13). Paul learned to be content. Worry overtakes us oftentimes simply because we're not willing to learn to be content. We wish things were different. We don't like the way God is running the show.

In 1 Timothy 6:7–8, Paul essentially said, "We brought nothing into the world and surely we'll bring nothing out of it. Let us, therefore, be content with food and clothing while we are here." But, oh, how often that becomes our greatest difficulty. The earth is the Lord's and the fullness thereof, Paul declared in 1 Corinthians 10:26. Yet even though we serve a God who loves us and promises to meet our every need, we seem to find ways and reasons to worry endlessly.

Rarely do you find people in western culture who have nowhere to live, nothing to wear, and nothing to eat, although unfortunately it is becoming increasingly more common. Yet the majority of today's population doesn't exist in that condition. In Jesus' day, however, many did. There really was no middle class. You were either very poor or very wealthy. The majority of people spent much of their time simply existing—finding grass to graze their animals, slaughtering a lamb to cook for stew, curing meat to be able to eat another day, or finding a water source. An inordinate amount of time was spent just staying alive. Unlike those in Jesus' day, we in America don't worry about this because we have more than we need. Our refrigerators are full. We have enough clothes to last a hundred years if we don't outgrow them. So we don't find ourselves imprisoned by daily necessities.

But the lesson doesn't change. Listen closely to Jesus' words. He was saying to His disciples, "Don't worry about your daily necessities. There are more important things in life than that." This, of course, would have startled them. After all, what's more important than eating, sleeping, and clothing?

In Psalm 127:2, the psalmist declares, "It is vain for you to rise up early and go to bed late just to eat the bread of your sorrowful labors because the Lord gives His beloved sleep." I love this picture because the world is constantly struggling to get what it thinks it needs. But you and I can have a life that is restful, carefree, and dependent upon God.

"Don't worry about your life," Jesus told His disciples. Then He gave them some reasons why.

> "Look at the birds of the air, for they neither sow nor reap nor gather into barns;
> yet your heavenly Father feeds them. Are you not of more value than they?"
> —Matthew 6:26

Maybe even as Jesus spoke these words, a flock of birds flew overhead. "Look at the birds," He could have said to His disciples. Birds have no intricate plan for wealth. They don't have a garage or a storage shed. They don't have an IRA or a retirement account. They don't even have a doggy bag for the food they don't eat. They pretty much have to eat, move on, and hope they can find their next meal. Yet you'll never see a bird with gray hair. God cares for them.

"Look at the birds," Jesus said. "Your heavenly Father takes care of every one of them and you're a whole lot more important than they are because they weren't made after His image. They're not destined for eternity. You are. They don't have a heavenly Father. You do."

> "Which of you by worrying can add one cubit to his stature?"
> —Matthew 6:27

The word *stature* refers not to height but to life expectancy. If you can add a day to your life, we all should start worrying. But you and I know that far from adding to your life, worry only robs you of life. I read somewhere that Charles Mayo, founder of the Mayo Clinic, was driven by the desire to provide good medical attention for people so they'd stop worrying about their health. "I've never seen anyone die of hard work," he said. "But I've seen millions die of worry."

If you faithfully walk with God and seek to do well, you'll live out His full plan for you. But you won't live a minute past that because there is a pre-determined expiration date on your life. You might be forty or 140—but one day you're coming off the shelf. Your worrying and fretting will not prolong that date by a moment.

> "So why do you worry about clothing? Consider the lilies of the field, how they grow: they neither toil, nor spin; and yet I say to you that even Solomon in all his glory was not arrayed like one of these. Now if God so clothes the grass of the field, which today is, and tomorrow is thrown into the oven, will He not much more clothe you, O you of little faith?"
> —Matthew 6:28–30

The word *consider* is a great Greek word that means "to study carefully." Perhaps it was as He pointed to the beautiful wildflowers that covered the Israeli hillside that Jesus said, "How do these grow? Do they worry? No, they just hang around."

When we go to Israel in the springtime, everything is beautiful with the flowers on the hillsides in bloom. But the guides say, "Be glad you're here now because eight weeks from now it'll look like the Sahara." In the days of Jesus, landowners would use the dried flowers as fuel for their ovens. So Jesus' point is, if they're just going to end up burning anyway, why would God spend so much time making flowers look good? That's just the way He is. Therefore, if He cares for the lilies of the field like that, if He provides for things that have no longevity, will He not much more clothe those who have an eternal future?

Jesus called His worried followers "you of little faith." Four times you'll find this description in Scripture and all four are directly applied to those fretting over the necessities of life, as if God either doesn't know or doesn't care about them.

If you picked up your kids from Sunday school and said to them, "We're going out to lunch," and they fell to the ground, saying, "Oh, Daddy, please help me to believe you. Are you really going to feed me?" anyone in earshot probably would question the care you give your children. You'd feel very embarrassed. Likewise, worry is not a trivial sin to God because it says, "I don't believe You. I don't trust You. I don't think You're telling me the truth." God's ultimate plan for you is that you would rest in the contentment of His provision without worry or fear. The world will have all kinds of anxieties because they do not know God. But as believers, we can rest from worry.

> "Therefore do not worry, ..."
>
> —Matthew 6:31

It is impossible to rewrite that so it doesn't mean "Don't worry."

> ". . . Saying, 'What shall we eat?' or 'What shall we drink?' or 'What shall we wear?' For after all these things the Gentiles seek. For your heavenly Father knows that you need all these things. But seek first the kingdom of God and His righteousness, and all these things shall be added to you."
>
> —Matthew 6:31–33

In a spiritual context, the term *Gentiles* refers to unbelievers. In other words, Jesus was saying, "Don't be like the lost who have to relentlessly pursue the daily necessities of life." Those who have no hope in God can only hope in what they see. But as believers, we have something far better. We have a heavenly Father who knows our needs.

God makes a deal with you. He says, "You just seek Me first and I'll make sure that your food, clothes, drink, lodging, and all of your temporal needs are taken care of." What a great promise! So often we find that people have very little time to seek the Lord because they're so busy with the necessities of life. You can work a hundred hours a week and kill yourself to pay your bills and buy more stuff—or you can seek the Lord and let Him provide that which He will. Jesus doesn't tell us to be slothful and lazy. He does, however, say that worry is a driving force that is to characterize only the lost.

Verse 33 simplifies your life, doesn't it? There's just one needful thing, one *first* thing to do. There can't be ten things that are first. There's only one: to seek the kingdom. In Psalm 34, David wrote that the young lions lack and suffer hunger. Now if lions are old, maybe they're no longer able to hunt. But young lions have ambition and power and strength. Therefore, if there's anything that shouldn't starve, it should be them. But the Lord says even they have hunger. On the other hand, the psalmist adds to this that those who seek the Lord shall not lack any good thing. This means that although the king of the jungle will have bad days, the one who seeks the Lord need not.

"Therefore do not worry about tomorrow, for tomorrow will worry about its own things. Sufficient for the day is its own trouble."

—Matthew 6:34

To say that tomorrow will worry about itself is not fatalistic. It is simply the truth, because God has only promised to give us strength for today. We have enough to do with letting God have today. We don't need to borrow from next week.

Deuteronomy 33:25 says, "As your days, so shall your strength be." God doesn't give you grace for a week from Friday. He gives you grace for today. So why worry? We have a Master who loves us and a Father who knows us, and we can have faith because He's promised that we have a future waiting for us. Therefore, worry is unwise, unnecessary, unreasonable, and unfaithful. You don't need to do it. Will you worry? Sure but hopefully less so as we rest in Him. If you'll keep these things in mind, you'll head farther down the road to the peace God wants you to have in His care.

Chapter 31

JESUS ON JUDGING

Matthew 7:1–12
(Luke 6:37–42)

As we come to the concluding chapter of the Sermon on the Mount, we see Jesus continuing to point out the difference between the man who is saved having come to the end of himself and the man who's still trying to work his way to heaven, even if it means changing the rules in the process. In Matthew 6, the Lord looked at the behavior of the believer versus the behavior of the unbeliever and said when the unbeliever performs his religious duties, he does so to be praised by others. He doesn't know God, so he needs to find satisfaction elsewhere. He gives, serves, fasts and prays, always with the thought of how others view him and what kind of impression he is making upon them. The believer simply loves the Lord and wants to serve Him. Therefore, he doesn't need anyone else's credit or applause.

Here in Matthew 7, Jesus addresses two issues as He continues setting the religious man beside the saved man. The first topic is, as a believer, how do I make determinations concerning people around me? And secondly, how do I do so in light of the fact that I'm supposed to be bringing the Gospel to the world? The Gospel tells us people are sinful, that they are on their way to hell and that they are not going to make it to heaven without God's help. Those are pretty harsh messages. How do I present them as a sheep among wolves?

The first twelve verses of Matthew 7 answer those questions. They're all about judgment, and prayer for wisdom as we judge.

"Judge not, that you be not judged."

—Matthew 7:1

What does Jesus mean by "judge not"? The phrase itself means to discern, choose, select, or determine. Depending on the context in which it is used, there are shades to the meaning. There are certainly plenty of places in the Scriptures where God emphatically tells us to judge or make judgments. In fact, in verse 6 Jesus said to these same men, "Don't cast what is holy before the dogs." That requires a judgment, doesn't it? And in verse 15, He said to beware of false prophets who come in sheep's clothing and that we'll know them by their fruits. That requires judgment, doesn't it? So when you read "judge not," you want to be sure you understand what Jesus meant in the context of all He had been teaching.

In Matthew 18:15–20, in speaking about church discipline and inter-personal relationships, Jesus said, "If you find a brother in sin, you should go to him yourself in private and minister to him. Maybe he'll listen to you and you can bring him back. But if you've gone several times and he won't listen, take a few men who can help encourage him. If that doesn't work, you may have to bring him before the church. And if he won't listen to the church, he should be put out of the church." All of those steps require judgments to be made. So that's not the kind of judgment the Lord forbids here in Matthew 7.

John wrote in his second epistle that if someone said Jesus wasn't God no one should receive him or bless him, because whoever did would share in his evil deeds. That requires a judgment to be made.

Paul told the Galatians that even if an angel came preaching another gospel, they were not to listen. He wrote to the Romans that they were to take note of those who caused division in the Body of Christ. He wrote to the Corinthians that they were to stay away from the immoral person, the adulterer, the covetous person, and the drunkard in their midst who called themselves brethren.

With so many examples of the Lord calling us to make good decisions as Christians who want to follow Him, how can we then apply His words here? Well, a quick overview of His Word to us will help us get it right.

For one thing, God never allows us to judge to condemnation. That is, we're not to decide what the ultimate result of a person's life is going to be or where he or she is going to spend eternity. We can warn them, but only God can judge their hearts. But we are called to judge and identify others for the purpose of restoration. That is, after careful self-examination we're to humbly help others who are caught in the snares of sin.

The judgment God does not allow you and me happens when we take on the kinds of things the scribes and Pharisees took upon themselves—where, in a matter of moments, we determine the eternal destiny of an individual simply by observation and often by wicked prejudice. You have probably met people who have an opinion about everyone and everything. All you have to do is ask, and they'll be happy to give it to you—sometimes they'll do so even without your asking! Too often we draw conclusions or make determinations based only upon appearance. We judge people on the basis of financial status or family history, on personal conviction or political persuasion.

Oftentimes, we judge when we don't have all of the facts. We even have a name for this: jumping to conclusions. In both Genesis 11 and 18, we see God bringing great judgment upon the earth. One is at the Tower of Babel; the other is at Sodom and Gomorrah. In both cases, however, before He judged, He said, "I'm going to come down and see if all I'm hearing about this place is right." It's interesting to me that the Lord said, "I'm going to check it out." He already knew. After all, He's God. But He gives us an example. He checked the facts.

Jesus began this issue by telling the disciples not to judge lest they be judged. But the application of not judging is restricted to those things only God knows. For example, I can say to you, "Without Jesus, you're not going to make it to heaven" because the Bible says that's the Gospel I'm supposed to declare. However, I can't determine that you're not really saved, that you had a wrong motive for doing something, or that your heart is divided at any given moment. We tend to want to do that. We tend to read into things. But that's off limits. That's God's place. He alone knows the thoughts and intents of the heart. He alone knows why we do what we do. He alone knows where we're headed.

Eventually, as believers, we'll come to the place of the bema seat that the Bible describes in 1 Corinthians 3, where our works will be tried by fire to see what sort they are. Whatever we did with the right heart or attitude, and whatever we did for God's glory rather than our own, will make it through the fire. And for those we will be rewarded. But I'm sure a lot of us are going to show up at the reward ceremony with baskets only to walk away with handfuls. "Go ahead, Lord, fill it up," we'll say, empty basket in hand. But when we look inside we'll realize we could have carried our rewards in our pockets.

The unbeliever will stand before the Lord, who will open the book of works and no one therein will have done enough to be received into glory. Because his name is not found in the book of life, he'll find judgment. So for both the believer and the unbeliever, there's a final judgment coming. Yet until then, I cannot nor am I allowed by God to seek to determine a person's motives, the purpose of his heart, or his devotion or lack thereof, because those are things only God can know.

> "For with what judgment you judge, you will be judged; and with the measure you use, it will be measured back to you."
>
> —Matthew 7:2

I don't like this verse because it says that the attitude with which I judge is the attitude God will use in dealing with me. One of the problems of our flesh is that it will have us believing we are far superior to others most of the time. We love it when people fail, because then we can feel better about ourselves. But one day we'll stand before God and we won't be able to say to Him, "I didn't really know what I was doing," because He'll say, "You sure acted like you did. You determined this guy's motive was wrong, that guy's attitude wasn't right, and the other guy was going to hell in a hand basket. You decided all of this. You told everybody. Now I'm going to deal with you as if you knew all the things you said you knew."

Judgment is like a boomerang. You throw it out and it comes right back at you. Haman built gallows from which to hang Mordecai because Mordecai wouldn't bow down to him. But by the end of the story there in Esther, it was Haman hanging from his own gallows. To judge for condemnation is dangerous for the person you're judging because now he or she has to suffer your bias. But it's far worse for you because, in so doing, you'll be tightening the noose around your own neck.

"And why do you look at the speck in your brother's eye, but do not consider the plank in your own eye? Or how can you say to your brother, 'Let me remove the speck from your eye' and look, a plank is in your own eye? Hypocrite! First remove the plank from your own eye, and then you will see clearly to remove the speck from your brother's eye."

—Matthew 7:3–5

Not only do we have a poor view of others, but we have a poor view of ourselves, though for ourselves we make many concessions and come with great patience. This explains why the sins in my life look a lot better than the same sins in your life. If I hit my thumb with a hammer and lose my temper, I have good cause. But if you lose your temper, you're just not in control of yourself. I look at the same sin differently because the two-by-four in my eye distorts my vision. Whether you have a splinter or a log in your eye, neither one is good for your eye. But the analogy is very clear. I can't help you get the splinter out of your eye until I get the two-by-four out of my own.

When David had hidden his sin with Bathsheba over a year, Nathan, the prophet, was sent by the Lord to him. In fear the king would not hear, Nathan devised a story. "David," he said, "I need your advice on something. There's a rich guy down the road with flocks of sheep and herds of cattle. But when some of his friends dropped by for dinner, rather than killing one of his many sheep he went next door, stole his poor neighbor's one and only pet lamb, and fed it to his guests. What do you think I should do?"

"That guy's gotta die!" David bellowed.

"That guy's you," Nathan said. "You took Uriah's wife."

And David was broken.

That's always the way it is. Self-righteousness is blind. So when it comes to judgment, you must first give extremely serious thought to your own sin and shortcomings, struggles and difficulties before you venture out on some mercy mission of aid to others. James wrote in 1:23 that if you're just a hearer of the Word and not a doer, you're like a guy who looks in the mirror, sees all the problems, and then goes his way, refusing to comb his hair, brush his teeth, or wash his face.

Years ago, we put a tape packet together on the topic of self-deception, taken from the book of James. It's the worst seller of any series we've ever made. In fact, I think the only ones we've sold are to people who buy them for their friends! But this should make sense because none of us thinks we're in need of help. The fact, however, is that until we see our own sin, confess our own weakness, and look to God to straighten out our own lives, we'll be in very poor position to help others.

In Psalm 51:10–13, David said, "Lord, I need You to create in me a new, clean heart and to give me a right spirit. Don't take away Your Holy Spirit. Restore the joy of my salvation and uphold me with Your Spirit. Then I can teach transgressors Your ways and sinners can be converted." When could David speak to other sinners about God? When his own life was right with God in repentance, resting in His grace—not until then.

"Do not give what is holy to the dogs; nor cast your pearls before swine, lest they trample them under their feet, and turn and tear you in pieces."

—Matthew 7:6

In the context of the scribes and Pharisees who had been hounding His footsteps and those of His disciples, Jesus was especially relevant when He said to His disciples, "You can't condemn. But you don't have to be naïve, either."

In Jesus' day, dogs weren't pets. They were wild and dirty and sometimes dangerous and should be avoided. As for swine, they were unclean animals Jews absolutely stayed away from. In the context of these last twenty verses of the chapter, which speak of sharing our faith, Jesus said, "There can come a time when as you're giving the Word out you realize the response is continuously disingenuous and disrespectful. At that point, you have to make a judgment and decide whether or not the people with whom you're sharing are in a place where you should continue to reach out to them." As He sent His disciples out, more than once Jesus said, "If they won't hear you, move to the next town." There is a time to speak and a time to share. There is also a time to wipe the dust from your feet and move on.

"Ask, and it will be given to you; seek, and you will find; knock, and it will be opened to you. For everyone who asks receives, and he who seeks finds, and to him who knocks it will be opened. Or what man is there among you who, if his son asks for bread, will give him a stone? Or if he asks for a fish, will he give him a serpent? If you then, being evil, know how to give good gifts to your children, how much more will your Father who is in heaven give good things to those who ask Him! Therefore, whatever you want men to do to you, do also to them, for this is the Law and the Prophets."

—Matthew 7:7–12

Connected to the topic of judgment is the topic of prayerful fellowship with God to ask, seek, and knock to determine what you should do and how you should go about it.

In the end, regardless of how we are treated, we are to love others not to the degree that they love us, but to the degree we would like to be loved by them and, as we learn here in the Gospels, as Jesus has loved us. Only the Lord's people can have this, where they set aside condemnation and, instead, seek after restoration and bringing folks to Christ.

The world doesn't need to see Christians judging everything. They need to see Christians loving Jesus because He's the only source of love and the only One who gives life.

Chapter 32

How Do I Get
to Heaven from Here?

Matthew 7:13–14
(Luke 13:24)

We have come to the final point Jesus made in this sermon He gave to the apostles He had chosen in the second year of His public ministry. From chapter 5 on, whether the subject was praying, giving, fasting, storing up treasures on earth rather than in heaven, passing judgment on everyone but yourself, or worrying about daily cares, Jesus set the concerns of the religious person on one side and those of the believer on the other. And He addressed the men sitting before Him as those who would believe and trust in Him.

By the time you arrive here at the end of these three chapters, Jesus will ask, "What path will you choose? What gate will you go through? Which road will you follow? Will it be the easy one—where you do your best and run with the crowd—or will you walk with Jesus as the only way of life?" It's a fitting end because the argument has been made, the lessons taught and now only your decision awaits with eternity hanging in the balances.

We make lots of decisions each day. Most of them are fairly trivial and inconsequential, but when it comes to believing in God and how we follow Him, we've got to be sure we have that right. You can pick the wrong major in college and change it again the next semester. You can pick the wrong friends and move on. But if you make a mistake concerning whom you're going to believe and why, there is an eternal consequence. So after three chapters of instruction, Jesus tied it all together and said, "Come and follow Me." Yet in keeping with God's sovereign will, He always has allowed people to make their own decisions. That's God's heart: here's life; come, follow Me; now it's your call.

In Moses' final instructions to the people before Joshua took them into the Promised Land, he said in Deuteronomy 30:19, "I call heaven and earth as a witness against you this day. I've set before you life and death, blessing and cursing. Choose life so that you and your descendants may live."

After entering the Promised Land, Joshua again asked the people to make a choice. Would they serve the gods of the Canaanites and Egyptians—or would they turn to the One who had brought them out of Egypt? Like Moses, Joshua called the people to make a choice based on evidence.

On Mt. Carmel, it was Elijah who, in the confrontation with the prophets of Baal, said to the people, "How long are you going to falter between two opinions? If Baal is god, follow him. But if Jehovah is God, you must follow Him."

In this passage, Jesus spoke about a simple choice. It's clearly laid out. It isn't confusing. There isn't any small print. It's between the many false ways to God and the one true way Jesus offered. You can't come to God any way you want. You can only come the way He prescribes. The choice is either God's way or man's way.

There have always been only two systems of religion. There has been the predominant one where you write your own rules, follow your own ways, and figure God will accept whatever it is you're putting out there. Then there's the other, smaller group that realizes they can't do anything for God but hang on to what He has done for them. There are only two camps—the religion of faith or the religion of works; the religion of heart and sincerity, or the religion of hypocritical practice. And there is a very stark contrast between the two.

That is why, in the verses that follow, we see two ways, two gates, two destinations, two kinds of trees, two kinds of people, two kinds of builders, two kinds of foundations, and two kinds of houses. In every illustration, there are always only two: man's way or God's. And in all of the preaching and presentation of the Gospel, the Bible always demands a choice between those two.

> "Enter by the narrow gate; for wide is the gate and broad is the way that leads to destruction, and there are many who go in by it. Because narrow is the gate and difficult is the way which leads to life, and there are few who find it."
>
> —Matthew 7:13–14

The word *enter* in verse 13 is in the aorist imperative tense in Greek and, therefore, speaks of a specific action and definite behavior. In other words, there's a point in time when a choice is made. Notice that the command is not to study the gate but to enter it. There are certainly lots of people who greatly admire Jesus but never receive Him as their Lord. They don't enter in. They watch, analyze, talk about, think through—but they never say, "Lord, I believe in You. Save me."

Jesus' command is that, of the two gates, we are to pick the narrow one. Every person enters into one gate or the other. Jesus' plea to us is, "Come through this way. Take the right gate—God's gate. It's the only one that leads to life." Jesus said He is the way, the truth, and the life. That's the narrow gate. The world has a hundred ways to go—all works-based. That's the broad road. But the narrow road we preach is Jesus. Whenever we go out and teach, witness, or share, we proclaim that the only way you ever reach heaven is through Jesus Christ.

It's a narrow message, isn't it? But it's not narrow because we're exclusive or narrow-minded, although we are accused of that. It's narrow because God said it's the only way to go. "I alone am the door," Jesus declared. "If you try getting in any other way, you're a thief, a liar, and a robber."

The Gospel's message is narrow because Jesus made it that way. It's a small passage. It allows for only one way: faith in Him, rather than works and faith in them.

Paul said there is only one God and one Mediator between God and man: the man Christ Jesus. The gate is narrow and, as such, doesn't give you many options. Not only that, but you must come through the gate by yourself. Only one person at a time passes through. And as passing though a turnstile, you can't bring a lot of baggage with you. You can't bring self-will, and you've got to leave your self-confidence behind. You've got to leave your works in the back room and come with nothing but faith in Jesus in hand.

When questioned by the rich young ruler who wanted eternal life, Jesus got to the heart of the matter when He said, "Empty your pockets and squeeze through the narrow gate." But the gate was evidently too narrow for him. Salvation is always the exchange of all that we have for all that He has. That's the issue Jesus wanted to address with His disciples. The narrow gate requires repentance and faith, not works. The wide gate, on the other hand, represents all of the various means people have decided will lead to God. To enter the wide gate they can come in together—you can bring your friends and you can bring your baggage and your varied accomplishments. And through it, most people apparently pass, everyone agreeing this certainly is the right way. Yet salvation isn't accomplished by public opinion. A vote or a group movement doesn't save you. Coming to Jesus by faith saves us personally.

There are not only two gates, but these gates lead to two ways: one that is broad and the other that is difficult. There are few on the hard and the narrow and many on the wide and broad. Every city seems to have a Broadway avenue or road. So does every life. The politically correct thing these days is to embrace the broad way: Does it feel good for you? Does it seem right to you? Then it must be OK. The broad way is all-inclusive. Many beliefs are embraced and all are welcome. There are lots of traveling companions, but where does this way really lead?

Both roads in fact lead to eternity. Both promise there will be good at the end—but only one in reality has a reward and a welcome. Hell is at the end of one; heaven at the end of the other. Ask people about heaven and how they're going to get there, and you will find that everyone has an idea which often has nothing to do with Jesus the narrow gate. "I've been good," they'll say. "My family has always been church people. I come from the south. I'm an American. There are lots of reasons I'm going to heaven."

The broad way is very indulgent, very permissive, and very self-oriented. There are few rules and even fewer requirements. All you need is religion—and it doesn't really matter which one you have, as long as you're sincere about it.

On the broad way, sin is OK, truth is moderated by circumstance, and God's Word is set aside. It's praised but not studied, admired but not followed. The broad way is the path of least resistance. It doesn't require commitment or sacrifice. It's all downhill from here. The traveler on the broad way says, "I'll live like I want, show up with great need, and God will be good to me."

The narrow way, on the other hand, Jesus described as difficult. It's a hard path because it demands that you deny yourself. It demands that you take up the cross. No one will be found in heaven who stumbled in by accident. You won't hear anyone say, "I was trying to go left, but there was a door on the right so I entered in, and here I am!" It doesn't work that way. It's a difficult path that requires hunting and searching, dedication, commitment, and desire.

In Luke 13 when someone asked Jesus if there are only a few being saved, He said, "Strive to enter in to the narrow gate for many will seek to enter but won't be able" (Luke 13:24). The word *strive* comes from the word for "agonize." Most folks, when they get saved, come forward or pray with someone because they've come to the end of themselves, and see they lack goodness, and Jesus is the Way. Whether it's a conscious or unconscious war within, someone who truly comes to know the Lord comes after a long struggle with life and purpose, meaning and peace, searching for truth.

In Acts 14:22, Paul said it is through much tribulation that we enter into the kingdom of God. It's not so easy to live for Jesus. Try it in your college class or work environment. God's way of salvation is remarkably simple, but it's not easy. We pay nothing for our salvation, yet coming to Jesus costs everything. He pays the price but wants our whole life. It's really not a fair exchange—He's getting ripped off as far as I can tell! But I'm not arguing. To say yes to Jesus means to say no to the world. To follow Him may mean persecution, ridicule, or some measure of tribulation in this life. It's a difficult path once you make a commitment to Christ. Jesus said, "In the world you'll have tribulation. They'll hate you because they hated Me." He warned us ahead of time. But He also said, "Come follow Me. I'll give you life."

Every religion except Christianity follows the same spiritual way that leads to the same spiritual end because they're all based on "I can do it myself." Christians are the only people who say, "I didn't do it. I couldn't do it. I haven't been able to do it. This is what God did for me." There are two gates, two roads, and two destinations. The broad way narrows into a horrible pit, while the narrow way opens up to a broad glorious eternity.

Finally, we read of two groups. The Lord distinguished them by the words *many* and *few*. Going through these two gates, traveling down these two roads, and ending up at two destinations are two groups of people. The broad road has the most travelers—the majority and the "in" crowd. The minority are those who trust in and believe in Jesus Christ as Lord and rest in His accomplished work. At the end, many will claim to have been followers of Jesus but will be shocked to find that they will not be allowed to go in. There will be surprises on the day people stand before God because their religions—the ones so many embraced—will fail them. Jesus said many will say to Him, "Lord, haven't we prophesied in Your name, cast out demons in Your name, and done many wonders in Your name?" If they are even half true, those are some ambitious accomplishments! But Jesus said He'll say to them, "I never knew you. Depart from Me. I don't know who you are." Yikes!

Jesus will welcome the other group, passing one by one through the narrow gate and finding only sparse support along the way. Jesus called them His little flock. But notice that the believers are not few in number simply because the gate is too narrow or the road is too small to accommodate them all. The Bible teaches that God wants every person to be saved. Heaven is big enough. God wants everyone to be there. It's just that very few people by comparison respond to His invitation. To His disciples, Jesus said, "Take the tough road, the smaller route, the narrow path. Follow the difficult way. Come and have life with Me."

Speaking for the Lord, Isaiah invited the people to come to the narrow gate. "Seek the Lord while He may be found," he said in chapter 55:6–7. "Call upon Him while He is near. Let the unrighteous man forsake his ways and his thoughts. Let him return to the Lord, for He'll have mercy upon him. Let him return to our God for He'll abundantly pardon." I love the scripture in Hosea 11 where the Lord, in having to deal with a wayward people, said, "How can I give you up, Ephraim, or hand you over, Israel? My heart churns within Me, and My sympathy for you is stirred."

So to these twelve men sitting at His feet, Jesus said, "Pick the right gate. If it's the broad way, that's the wrong choice." There's only one way to heaven and it comes through Jesus. At the end, you can't blame your neighbors, your friends, your parents, your wife, or kids. It's your choice. Jesus' call is to make the right one.

Chapter 33

BEWARE OF FALSE PROPHETS

Matthew 7:15–20
(Luke 6:43–45)

As Jesus sat down with His disciples and gave them this first sermon, He talked about the difference between God's way of life and ours, God's way of salvation and everything else, and faith in Him versus self-accomplishment. If Jesus isn't the hope and if the Law is being misused, if works are the trust or if people begin to pretend to believe when they don't, there's a great danger looming ahead and it is eternal in nature. So Jesus warned them and directed them to be watchful and careful because even the right road is lined with danger and difficulty. One great challenge is the enemy and his hordes of false teachers and prophets drawing men away from God and His wonderful Word.

> "Beware of false prophets, who come to you in sheep's clothing, but inwardly they are ravenous wolves."
>
> —Matthew 7:15

False prophets are nothing new. Wherever God works, the Devil is sure to follow. In Genesis you find God creating Adam and Eve in the garden and giving them everything. But because people need to choose to walk with God, they were to signal their choice to obey Him by not eating from the Tree of the Knowledge of Good and Evil. Seizing this opportunity to deceive, the Devil said to Eve, "God's not very good to you, is He? He doesn't want you to be as smart as He is." The challenge to God and His Word and His love is first seen here.

Before he handed off the people to Joshua, who would take them into the Promised Land, Moses said, "When you get there, if a prophet comes to you and says, 'Come and let us go follow these other gods,' don't follow him even if he performs signs or wonders. God is testing you to see if you'll love Him with all your heart and follow His ways alone." The warning was that the determining factor shouldn't be the reality of the power or miracle, but whether what was taught and spoken lined up with the Word of God.

God spoke to Isaiah in chapter 30:10 and said, "This people is a rebellious people. They say to the seer 'Don't see' and to the prophet, 'Don't prophesy. Tell us smooth things, ones we like to hear.'" The heart was hardened to hear the truth.

In his second epistle, John said, "There are a lot of deceivers going out in the world who say Jesus isn't coming in the flesh. But they are of the spirit of antichrist" (2 John 7). In

Romans 16:17, Paul said, "Be careful of those who cause divisions and teach doctrines contrary to what you've learned." To Timothy, he wrote that the Spirit expressly said in the latter days that people would depart from the faith and instead give heed to doctrines of demons. In Acts 20:29, he said, "I know that after I depart, savage wolves will come in among you to destroy the flock."

There's a large market in the world today for the false prophet and his message. As in the days of Isaiah, many only want to hear what will make them feel better, not what will heal them for good. They want pleasant words. They want doctrines that don't require any change on their part. They want to hear what's nice rather than what God says is good for them. The narrow road is fraught with danger from these men.

In the Old Testament, two things always distinguished a true prophet of God: first, he had a divine commission and, second, he had a divine message. And even when the prophet was weak or faltering, the Lord's Word was always accomplished. The false prophet, on the other hand, merely claimed to be sent from the Lord—and therein lies the danger. In Jeremiah 5:31, the Lord said to His people, "The prophets are prophesying falsely. They're speaking from their own hearts, not from Mine. Yet no one turns away from their wickedness."

Here we're told that under the guise of a shepherd, the false prophets try to sneak in among the sheep of God to slaughter them. And before you think this is overstatement, think back thirty years to Jim Jones and Guyana. His ability to talk a thousand people into killing themselves, and then convincing them it was God's will, ought to tell you there is a real battle for people's hearts and there is real wickedness behind the false teacher.

The scribes and Pharisees were classic examples of false prophets. Rather than bringing people closer to Jesus and presenting the Word of God to them, they sought to lead them astray. "You are a bunch of hypocrites," Jesus said to them in Matthew 23. "You will travel over land and sea to make one proselyte, and when you convert him, you make him twice the son of hell that you are."

Here Jesus ends this last portion of the Sermon on the Mount by declaring, "Beware of anyone hawking another way, pointing to another path, or trying to drive you down any other highway than the narrow road." The word *beware* is an interesting word because it doesn't just mean "take notice." It means "be on guard; put up a fence because there's something harmful nearby." False prophets are more than wrong. They're dangerous to your spiritual well being. That is why it is foolish to spend much time listening to, reading about, or immersing yourself in false prophets' doctrines. They are ravenous wolves.

In Israel, wolves were the sheep's most common enemy. They always followed the flock, waiting for one to be tired or a little out of step. Like ravenous wolves, false prophets pounce on easy prey. *Ravenous* is a word that, if used concerning an individual, speaks of an extortioner or swindler. If it is used concerning an animal, it speaks of a complete lack of mercy. In other words, the false prophets not only will destroy you like a wolf, but will seek to make merchandise of you for their own gain. They're not looking to serve the

Lord—only themselves—while always on the prowl for new victims. To accomplish this, they come in sheep's clothing as your friend or helper. And if your defenses are down, you will easily be led astray. The dogs and swine of verse 6 are easy to recognize, but these folks in sheep's clothing certainly are not.

The Old Testament prophets often wore very coarse, rough clothing. They did this because they wanted to separate themselves from the luxury of regular life as well as to define their message as rubbing our flesh the wrong way, an irritation. It was an outward display of an inward reality. Even John the Baptist wore camel's hair clothing. It wasn't comfortable but it was part of his message. Shepherds, on the other hand, wore woolen clothing, made from the wool of their flocks. As such, their clothes were the fruit of their ministry. In light of this, notice that the false teacher doesn't impersonate a sheep. He impersonates a shepherd. He pretends to be concerned about others, but is only out to feed himself. No wonder Paul wrote to the Corinthians that false apostles are deceitful workers and can even transform themselves into angels of light.

It's the deceptive appearance that often trips us up. False prophets can appear pleasant and positive, encouraging and welcoming. They speak like Christians. They know their Bibles and use them well. They are often most identifiable by what they do not say. Most false prophets take very few positions on anything of note because to do so is to diminish their audience, their potential crowd—and that they can't afford. So their message is to attract the masses and it can change to make sure that is what it does. Beware of them. Be careful. Be on guard.

> "You will know them by their fruits. Do men gather grapes from thornbushes or figs from thistles? Even so, every good tree bears good fruit, but a bad tree bears bad fruit. A good tree cannot bear bad fruit, nor can a bad tree bear good fruit. Every tree that does not bear good fruit is cut down and thrown into the fire. Therefore by their fruits you will know them."
>
> —Matthew 7:16–20

In this business of the extremely deceptive and dangerous wolf in sheep's clothing, Jesus said, "Let Me give you a method by which you can get beyond the dignified appearance." Notice that in both verses 16 and 20, we're told we'll know them by their fruits because people's nature and character eventually comes out. But fruit takes time to grow. If you hear someone for the first time and don't know what to think, just wait. You'll find out. You don't have to make up your mind immediately. Just be careful.

Paul said the Bereans were nobler than the Thessalonian believers, for not only did they readily receive the Word, they then searched the Scriptures to see if what was taught was so. They were on guard. They were diligent. They didn't buy it just because the guy on TV with a fancy suit said so. A prophet over time will show either that he is a man of God or that he's not. And because fruit takes time to grow, discernment might take some time as well before the heart's true condition becomes evident. The Lord says very clearly that good trees can't bear bad fruit. Does that mean that, as believers, we won't sin? Of course not. Do we fall short? Absolutely. Stumble? Yep. But the preponderance of our live will make the heart visible: if it is of God or not?

As you go through you Bible, you will see at least three areas of fruit inspection that make the truth known. The first one is character—the inward motive, the standard, and the conviction by which someone lives his life. The scribes and Pharisees told the people they were God's servants even as they plotted to kill Jesus. They wouldn't go into Pilate's judgment hall because they didn't want to defile themselves in a Gentile place. But they had no difficulty sending Jesus there. They were phonies and it showed. The fruit of their life was evident and continued over time.

In the long run, the false prophet's actions will always betray him. That is why there is something to be said about longevity of ministry. If you belong to Jesus and follow His Word, your life will bring forth the fruit of the Spirit and it will show in a hundred different ways. If, however, you don't belong to Him, your life will eventually show that as well.

False prophets can hide behind their biblical hocus-pocus for a while. But they can't hide forever. In 2 Peter 2, Peter wrote an entire chapter on false prophets, describing them as being wells without water, as clouds with only a promise of rain, and as dogs that return to their own vomit. In other words, after his prophecies and promises come up empty, the false prophet will eventually return to his nature of self-service.

In addition to character, a prophet is known by his creed. False prophets do not have a strong or clear theology based on the Scriptures, because they want to be all-inclusive so they can fish from the biggest pond. In Jeremiah 6, the Lord said false teachers prophesied peace when there was no peace. Paul said to Timothy that the time is coming when people won't endure sound doctrine but will raise up teachers who will tell them what they want to hear: that everyone goes to heaven, that all someone can do is his or her best, and that if there's anything wrong in someone's life it was his or her parent's fault. People love to hear those kinds of messages, but the problem is, they don't help anyone get to heaven because the road there is a narrow one and His name is Jesus. False prophets attract those who want illusions rather than the truth, encouragement without correction, and cheap grace rather than a contrite heart. Beware of false prophets. Their messages are filled with gaps—the greatest one being how to get to heaven.

You'll know them by their character, their creed, and, finally, by the crowd that follows them. False prophets attract people who are like themselves—superficial, self-centered, and unscriptural in their orientation. In 2 Peter 2, Peter wrote that many will follow their destructive ways and, because of them, their own converts will blaspheme the truth in the world. You can tell a lot about someone by the folks who follow him or her.

There are two gates, two roads, and two types of teachers. Make sure you're listening to the right one.

Chapter 34

SAYING, HEARING, AND DOING

Matthew 7:21–29
(Luke 6:46–49)

After three chapters of differentiation between faith and works, between God's grace and people's efforts, between the broad way and the narrow road, Jesus concludes this first sermon with two illustrations that both say, "You want to be sure of the road you're on because eternity is a long time." Jesus turns from the subject of unsound teachers to that of unsound hearers because not only can false prophets deceive us, we can deceive ourselves. It is human nature to look at ourselves with a bias, so in the following two examples, Jesus lays out the difference between someone who truly knows Him and someone who merely agrees with Him but doesn't follow Him.

Jesus' closing words to these men He had chosen call them to reject the religious way of life and, instead, to be of those who walk with God in faith in His work. I think the bane of Christianity always is those who say they're saved but live otherwise, those who are in church but have no relationship with the Lord. Jesus told a parable in Matthew 25 about ten virgins waiting for the Lord to return. He called five of them foolish because, when He returned, they had no oil in their lamps. Oh, they had lamps. They were pretty sure they were ready. But they weren't. The five that were ready went in. The five that weren't were left out.

What would cause people to be so deceived that they actually think one day they're going to end up in heaven when, in reality, they're not? Is it just a poor understanding of what Jesus said that gets people thinking everything's fine—or is it an unwillingness to be honest with themselves? Those who go through life oblivious to their sin will, at the end of their lives, appear before the Lord, saying, "I'm here! Open the door," only to hear Him say, "I don't think you're on the list."

When Paul wrote to the Corinthians, he said, "Examine yourselves to see if you're in the faith. Be sure." Likewise, Jesus ended this portion of His sermon by illustrating clearly what Paul would later write to the Corinthians "Be sure of where you stand" (2 Cor. 13:5).

In even the weakest of saints there is a desire to be more like Jesus, a hatred of the sin in their own lives, and a desire for God's Spirit to work in and through them. On the other hand, you will not find this in even the strongest religious man. No matter what people claim, there must be a corresponding lifestyle for that claim to be genuine.

The most frustrating thing to me as a pastor is watching people come to the Lord when they need something only to walk away when they get it. "Give me a husband." "Pay my bills." "Heal my sickness." "Thank You, Lord. I gotta go."

The Lord is looking for something more than that. He's looking for a relationship with you because the narrow road that leads to life consists of fellowship with Him through His Son. There is no substitute.

These words with which Jesus ended His sermon are very scary to me because they speak of self-delusion—what I think of myself, versus what God thinks of me. And His point is very clear: You can confess verbally you're a believer; you can mentally agree that the Bible is right—but if your life isn't being changed, and obedience from your heart isn't brought forth, there is no assurance that you know the Lord.

> "Not everyone who says to Me, 'Lord, Lord,' shall enter the kingdom of heaven, but he who does the will of My Father in heaven. Many will say to Me in that day, 'Lord, Lord, have we not prophesied in Your name, cast out demons in Your name, and done many wonders in Your name?' And then I will declare to them, 'I never knew you; depart from Me, you who practice lawlessness!'"
>
> —Matthew 7:21–23

In Jesus' day, the word *Lord* was a title of honor not necessarily having to do with devotion. It was like "Sir" or "Mr." When the word is repeated, however, it becomes a title of devotion. "Didn't we do glorious things in Your name?" people will ask. These people will think everything is fine until the day of judgment when they discover that the Lord they've been calling "Lord" isn't answering the door.

When Jesus went down to the crowds in Luke 6 and gave this same message, He said in verse 46, "Why do you say, 'Lord, Lord' to me and do not the things I say?" I think these are very sobering words because the folks to whom Jesus is referring devoted themselves to doing these things—but not in a way that honored Him or came from faith. They had the right words in their mouth, but there was still sin dominating their heart, as evidenced by the word *lawlessness*, which is a description of someone who is not saved and who has no law, no rule, no boundaries, and no one to obey.

A profession of faith and a practice of lawlessness are not compatible. If you go to the beach all week, people won't have to ask where you were when you go back to work the following Monday. Your suntan will tell them all they need to know. Likewise, if you get saved, it shows. It shows in obedience. Slowly, methodically, your life will change. If I know God loves me and I am saved, my life will head in His direction and my lawless nature will slowly but surely fade away.

How did these people do these great works of God if they didn't know Him? In Acts 8, Simon the sorcerer captivated the city with his good works, yet he didn't know the Lord. In Acts 18, the sons of Sceva made their living casting out Devils, yet they didn't know

Him either. How can people do these things? God spoke through an unsaved Balaam and a reprobate King Saul. He even spoke through a donkey—but that doesn't mean Balaam, Saul, or the donkey knew Him. Ultimately, these people in Matthew got exactly what they wanted. They didn't want to know the Lord. Therefore, they wouldn't have to spend eternity with Him.

> "Therefore whoever hears these sayings of Mine, and does them, I will liken him to a wise man who built his house on the rock: and the rain descended, the floods came, and the winds blew and beat on that house; and it did not fall, for it was founded on the rock. But everyone who hears these sayings of Mine, and does not do them, will be like a foolish man who built his house on the sand: and the rain descended, the floods came, and the winds blew and beat on that house, and it fell. And great was its fall." And so it was, when Jesus had ended these sayings, that the people were astonished at His teaching, for He taught them as one having authority, and not as the scribes.
>
> —Matthew 7:24–29

The doing of God's Word brings life to the house, while the not doing of it leaves the house subject to ruin. Notice the two builders. Both are "churchgoers." Both sat in the pew and took notes. Both lived their lives in ways they were convinced were right. Their pursuits and expenditures, their words and deeds, all became building blocks for their lives. And, for a while, both houses seemed to stand.

No one purposely builds on sand. Everyone wants a secure foundation for the greatest investment of his or her life. But when the storm arose, the house built on sand fell. For all appearances, it looked like the house next door that was built on the rock. But the storm proved it wasn't. The foolish builder, although mentally agreeing with God's Word, didn't allow it to change the choices he made and the priorities he set. The foolish builder today has also heard the Word. He knows the Christmas story. He knows who Moses is. He gets a pretty good score on the "Bible category" on *Jeopardy*—but his life doesn't change. He doesn't know a Scripture verse from a phone number. He doesn't have the Word in his heart. And because it doesn't matter to him, it doesn't affect the way he lives. Yet he is convinced he's fine, and God is pleased, simply because he goes to church.

The fellow who builds his house on the rock is the one who acts on the Scriptures. His life is lived in obedience. The verse that talks about the Word of God being a light to our path is only helpful if you go to the light. What's the last thing you prayed about changing in your life because you read it in the Bible and you know that's what God wants? What priorities are different in your life from those of the unsaved person with whom you work? What changes are in the works right now? What is God doing with you now because of your relationship to Him?

The one who hears the Word and does it can build confidently on bedrock. Bedrock is wonderful to build on because it doesn't shift. Sand, on the other hand, keeps moving—and there's no shortage of sand being sold by oceanfront real estate agents and false prophets. The Rock is Jesus, and whether we build on rock or sand is determined solely by our reaction to His Word. We either obey it or we don't. The mark of any true saint is that he longs to hear what God has to say and then he greatly desires to do it.

James said the one who hears God's Word and doesn't obey it is like a guy who looks in the mirror but doesn't do anything about what he sees. That's why he said, "Be a doer of the Word and not a hearer only."

At ninety years of age, John wrote in his first epistle, "By this we know that we know Him: if we keep His commandments" (1 John 2:3).

If you really want to be sure you're saved, do what God says. People who obey God from a true heart do so not because someone else is pressuring them to do so. They obey Him because He is at work in their lives. It's the evidence of salvation. In fact, John went on to say, "If I don't keep His commandments, then to say I know Him makes me a liar." It's black or white. It's one or the other.

Are you saved, or are you fooling yourself by living in sin and disregarding God's Word? If you're the latter, your house may indeed feel fine for a while. But eventually trouble will come. That's why, in the last letter before he was killed, Peter told us to be diligent and to make our calling and election sure.

Are you saved? That's the question. You don't want to play church, because not only will your house fall, but the fall will be eternal.

Chapter 35

WHO'S THE BOSS?

Luke 7:1–10
(Matthew 8:5–13)

Following Jesus' three-chapter sermon on the difference between the religious man and the man of faith, we come to the account that Matthew and Luke give about His arrival in Capernaum.

> Now when He concluded all His sayings in the hearing of the people, He entered Capernaum. And a certain centurion's servant who was dear to him, was sick and ready to die.
>
> —Luke 7:1–2

Capernaum was Jesus' headquarters in Galilee. In fact, more recorded miracles took place in this one city than anywhere else in the Gospels. In Jesus' day, Capernaum was a fairly large city with a population of roughly twenty-five thousand people—among them this centurion. Centurions were Roman soldiers in command of a hundred men whose job it was to ensure Roman rule was applied throughout the empire.

Wherever you turn in Scripture, you always will find centurions presented in a positive light. In Matthew 27:54, when Jesus died on the cross, it was a centurion who said, "Truly, this was the Son of God." Following Jesus' resurrection, a centurion named Cornelius was the first Gentile to hear the Gospel. And it was a centurion named Julius who let Paul, a prisoner, visit his friends and family and be refreshed by the church. Wherever you turn, it seems centurions always had a favorable relationship with God. And the one in the passage before us is no exception.

> So when he heard about Jesus, he sent elders of the Jews to Him, pleading with Him to come and heal his servant. And when they came to Jesus, they begged Him earnestly, saying that the one for whom He should do this was deserving, "for he loves our nation, and has built us a synagogue."
>
> —Luke 7:3–5

This was a remarkable man, to be sure. He was, after all, working for the occupiers, the Roman government. He had to enforce Roman law in a Jewish state, and yet he had befriended the Jews in such a way that when his servant's life was in jeopardy, the Jewish elders themselves were willing to go to Jesus—not exactly their favorite man—on his behalf. The Jewish elders were at odds with this would-be Savior, this so-called prophet. Many even had joined in seeking how they could kill Him. They didn't like Him. He was emptying their synagogues. People were listening to Him instead of them. Yet for this centurion's sake, they swallowed their pride, set aside their prejudice, and came to Jesus.

We are given three testimonies of this centurion in these ten verses. The first is from his friends, the Jewish elders, in verse 4. They told Jesus the centurion was deserving because he loved their nation and had even built them a place of worship. Their opinion was far different from his own, but I think both their opinion and presentation accurately reflected the heart of most religious people who perceive of their relationship with God as being a give and take proposition and that, at some point, He owes them. This barter system of religion is a common view in people's hearts that, unfortunately, can even creep into the life of the saints.

Jesus had just finished saying, "If you'll build your house on the rock, your house will stand." Yet immediately, here comes the religious thinking heaven can be had for a price. Whether it was praying, giving, or serving—it was all offered to God as a reason for Him to act on their behalf. But all of that is misguided because a true relationship with God is not like earning American Express travel points. In Philippians 3:4–6, Paul essentially said, "If you think you have something to offer God, I have more. I was circumcised on the eighth day, of the stock of Israel, of the tribe of Benjamin, a Pharisee; I was blameless." Paul had a whole list of stuff he thought he could offer God that would benefit Him. But then he said that when he met Jesus, he counted it all but dung. At that point, he declared, "I want to be found in Him not having my own righteousness which comes through the Law, but the righteousness that comes from God by faith" (Phil. 3:9).

The elders here, however, weren't at that place. They related to the Lord solely on the basis of merit, performance, and goodness. Most men still do. They sit on the throne of their accomplishments, waiting for God to respond and reward. But do we really want what we deserve? No! The wages of sin is death! We want what we don't deserve. We want life!

> Then Jesus went with them. And when He was already not far from the house, the centurion sent friends to Him, saying to Him, "Lord, do not trouble Yourself, for I am not worthy that You should enter under my roof. Therefore I did not even think myself worthy to come to You. But say the word, and my servant will be healed."
>
> —Luke 7:6–7

I love Jesus' response to the elders' plea. Although He wasn't going to come out of an obligation or to pay off a credit debt, His love for any crying out for Him will find His willing response. As He drew closer to the centurion's house, the centurion sent his friends to give Jesus the second opinion about the centurion we find in the story: his own. "Lord, don't trouble Yourself. I'm not worthy," the centurion said through his friends. The words *not worthy* in verse 7 are the exact opposite of the word *deserving* in verse 4. "I'm not deserving," the centurion said. "In fact, I didn't even feel I was deserving enough to come to You personally or to speak to You about this directly." He wanted Jesus' help because verse 3 tells us it was he who went to the elders to see if somehow they could persuade this Jewish healer to come to his house for his servant's sake. But in the process, as the elders went out to do his bidding, this man realized he was in no position to be asking for anything.

It's an interesting picture because the centurion didn't look to his accomplishments for his hopes of getting Jesus to help. He saw things more clearly. The elders had nothing but good to say about him. His own opinion, however, was far more precise. Put yourself in this centurion's shoes. He was facing some very desperate times with a servant he cared about so deeply that, in verse 7, Luke didn't use the word for *servant*; he used the word for *son*.

His humility and awareness of who he was before God however put the centurion in a position where he didn't feel worthy. "I need Your help," he said to Jesus, "but I don't deserve it. I want Your help. I must have Your help—but I can't earn it." Then he explained his outlook, which thrilled Jesus' heart:

> For I also am a man placed under authority, having soldiers under me. And I say to one, "Go," and he goes; and to another, "Come," and he comes; and to my servant, "Do this," and he does it.
>
> —Luke 7:8

The centurion's explanation was really a further definition of his faith. As a man in a place of power and leadership, he had been stationed in this city by Caesar himself to enforce the authority of Rome over a captive people. He was a man who had to report to headquarters. He had to give an account for his behavior. He had to apply the law he had been sent to uphold. In that position, however, he also had been given authority—to command his soldiers and command their service.

The Bible teaches us that a person will never rule well unless he first has been ruled. I think that becomes very obvious observing human nature. You can't rule well unless God rules your heart—and the centurion understood this. If one has no sense of being ruled or having someone to answer to, men in power can soon become tyrants.

"Submit yourself to your husband as unto the Lord," Paul wrote to the wives in Ephesus. But he goes on to say that the head of every man is Christ. How can a man be a good husband? By being ruled by Christ. In other words, he's going to have to be under authority to be in authority. The fellow who's not under authority, yet still wants power to throw his weight around, will make a horrible husband and a miserable home. But once your life is in Christ's hands, you can rule well with great care as the Lord would.

Implied, of course, in the centurion's statement is the fact that he saw Jesus as Lord over the illness, over His creation, and over this terrible suffering. And he recognized that all of the world must obey Him. It's quite a statement of faith. Rather than come on the basis of his own accomplishments, he recognized Jesus as God and said to Him, "Just say the word. You're in authority over these things. It's up to You." And it was this confident faith and denial of self that must have caused Jesus to smile. After all of the opposition and rebellion and all of the conflict, unbelief, and difficulty He'd had with entire groups of religious folks, here was a Roman centurion who had it absolutely right.

> When Jesus heard these things, He marveled at him, and turned around and said to the crowd that followed Him, "I say to you, I have not found such great faith, not even in Israel!" And those who were sent, returning to the house, found the servant well who had been sick.
>
> —Luke 7:9–10

The third opinion we find about this centurion is the one opinion that really matters: God's. We see Jesus marveling only twice in the New Testament—here and in Mark 6 when the people of His hometown wouldn't believe in Him. In Mark 6, He couldn't believe that they wouldn't believe. Here He marvels at the great faith of this Roman centurion who saw Him as the One in authority to whom he could turn and find hope without a list of reasons why he deserved the help. What a breath of fresh air his confession was!

"I haven't found this great faith even in Israel," Jesus said. Israel had thousands of years of biblical history and relationship with God. It was a culture, nation, and people that had, from their very inception, believed in only one God. They should have known better. This Roman, on the other hand, came from a culture that worshipped everything that moved. There was a god for everything—and yet he saw only one true God. He saw Jesus. He was well ahead of the curve, wasn't he? And it's exactly this kind of faith you and I need to have to please God because, according to Hebrews, he that comes to God must believe that He is and that He is a rewarder of those who diligently seek Him.

In Matthew 28:18, as He was about to ascend into heaven, Jesus said to His disciples that "All power has been given to Me in heaven and earth." Jesus has all authority—and we are saved when we place our lives in His capable hands. That's when life really begins. That's when God's blessing comes. And that's when I begin to learn that, although I can't earn this, I can receive life from Him.

In 2 Chronicles 14:11, as King Asa faced a million-man Ethiopian army, he prayed, "Lord, it's nothing for You to help whether by many or by few. So help us, Lord. Don't let man prevail against You." Asa had it right. Numbers matter little when the battle is the Lord's.

I don't know what it is that keeps us from learning it is nothing for God to move. It just requires our trust. If I have a headache, I'll ask the Lord to heal me. But if I have cancer,

I think of it as an entirely different matter—as if God is saying, "Boy, that's a hard one. I don't know if I can do anything about that." If I need ten bucks, I say, "The Lord will provide!" But if I need a hundred, I say, "Oh, no. I'm in big trouble." Yet for the centurion, God's authority set him free in faith. His servant was dying. It was out of his hands. But it wasn't out of God's hands. And that's how he approached Jesus: "It is nothing for You, Lord. I recognize Your authority." God is thrilled when you, like the centurion, arrive in that place of faith and understanding.

Gideon had thirty-two thousand men to fight against the Midianites. But the Lord said, "That's too many. If anyone is afraid, tell him to go home." Twenty-two thousand said, "Thanks!" and left.

But the ten thousand that remained were still too many for the Lord. "Get them to drink out of the river and see how they drink," He said. "Those who put their faces in the water, set to one side. Those who drink with their hands so they can keep their eyes on the horizon, put in another group."

God told Gideon to send home the 9,700 who put their faces in the water. Gideon was left with only three hundred so he would know the victory was the Lord's.

For God, there is no degree of difficulty. He is the Lord. He is the authority. And if God can free you from a restrictive heart of fear that wonders what next and draw you to Himself, then you can say with the centurion, "Just say the word, Lord. It's up to You. I can rely and rest totally in what You would do."

The Lord is worthy. He is capable. Mountains will move at His Word. Seas will roll back at His direction. The big question you've got to answer is, how do you know Him?

Chapter 36

THE WIDOW OF NAIN
MEETS THE LORD

Luke 7:11–17

We come now in our chronology to the story that took place the day after the centurion's servant was healed. This time Jesus would work without invitation. No one would ask Him for His help. But we are given one of those beautiful portraits of our Lord, framed in seven verses—God's love and His concern for us.

> Now it happened, the day after, that He went into a city called Nain; and many
> of His disciples went with Him, and a large crowd.
>
> —Luke 7:11

The word *nain* means "beauty." The town of Nain was located about fifteen miles from Capernaum along the Sea of Galilee. The crowds were huge now as Jesus' ministry and words brought people from everywhere to be with Him.

> And when He came near the gate of the city, behold, a dead man was being
> carried out, the only son of his mother; and she was a widow. And a large crowd
> from the city was with her.
>
> —Luke 7:12

As they arrive at the gate of this walled city, two crowds will collide—the one with Jesus and the one with a woman going out to bury her only son. Luke used a word we often find used in the New Testament and always with the same implication. The word *behold* demands we "pay particular attention" because this is a very unique situation. No doubt this colliding of the crowds was something God had orchestrated and intended. Had Jesus come either a few minutes earlier or later, He would have missed them entirely. But He came right at that time because He had something He wanted to accomplish.

I love the Bible's teaching about God's timing—yet there are times I hate it in my own life. I know everything God does is perfect, that He never misses a beat, but I so want to hold up my watch and say, "Lord, look what time it is," because He seems to move so slowly. I read in the Bible about God answering even as people prayed. Yet very rarely do I experience that. Yet to learn that God's timing is perfect, even for you, is to make great strides in spiritual maturity.

185

I think about Abraham being called to offer his only son on Mount Moriah. It was a three-day journey of carrying wood and answering questions from Isaac concerning the offering. It isn't, however, until the climax of his obedience to God in Genesis 22:10 with Abraham's outstretched hand holding the knife to slay his son that the Lord cries out, "Wait a minute, Abraham. I know now that you love Me, that you wouldn't keep your only son from Me." Talk about last minute reprieves . . . Abraham then lifted up his eyes and there, behind him in the thicket, was a ram caught by the horns. The Lord would provide a sacrifice for him, later in Jesus for all of us, but the timing for Abraham! Whew!

A couple of chapters later, Eleazar, Abraham's servant, was sent by Abraham back to his original home, out of the Promised Land, to find a bride for his son Isaac. He was not to look anywhere but among God's people—but how would he know which woman to choose?

As he arrived into town he came first to a place where women gathered with water pots at a well, and there he prayed, "Lord, You've got to show me which one. There are a lot of them!" We read in Genesis 24 that as he finished praying, there came Rebekah. And God answered his prayer in such a way that Eleazar didn't doubt she was the one. But it happened in the nick of time—at exactly the right time!

When Ruth came home with Naomi, impoverished and in need of work, Naomi said to her, "Go ask the master of the field if you can follow the reapers and pick up what's left." And we read in Ruth 2 that as Ruth went out to do this, it "just so happened" that she came to the field of Boaz—the man who eventually would be her husband, and the one who would appear in David's lineage, in the ancestral line to Jesus.

Often as God works, only the believer can appreciate and recognize His guiding hand and perfect timing. Everyone else just sees life going by. Yet the believer can say, "Look what God did!" It seems to me that the early church was very aware of God's timing. Paul was arrested in Jerusalem for preaching on the steps of the Antonio Fortress, and the crowd wanted him killed. The Romans decided to transfer him to Caesarea, on the coast, where they could keep him until they tried him. Hearing of their plan, forty religiously zealous men made an oath to go on a hunger strike until they had laid an ambush and killed Paul along the way. We read in Acts 23 that Paul's sister's son overheard these forty men making this plot and alerted Paul. What is the likelihood of a kid hanging around a bunch of plotting murderers? Not very high—unless it's part of God's plan.

It is so important to learn that our lives aren't just luck or happenstance in God's hands. God orchestrates. He plans. He looks ahead. Therefore, if we're smart, we'll keep our eyes open to see what He might be doing and learn to rest in His perfect ways!

When we first purchased our church facility, it was completely overgrown and had an archaic pump system that didn't work very well. Whenever it rained, we had to be there all night to help pump out water from the property as it crawled towards the buildings. The thing was built in 1610 or something, so our first job was to get this pump repaired. After a couple guys looked at it, the cheapest price we could get to fix it was twelve thousand dollars. But we hardly had twelve dollars! We were just glad to be in the building, even if we had to turn off the lights between services to keep the costs down. So that Sunday morning I came into church and told everyone, "We gotta pray. This pump thing is ridiculous."

Following the service, a guy came up and said, "I work on that kind of pump. Could I take a look at it?"

"Sure!" I said. "How long have you been in the church?"

"Well, I'm just visiting," he said. He went down, looked at it, came back Monday and said, "It'll be forty-five dollars."

The day we expanded our services, we needed to open eight more classrooms for the kids. That week, we had eight applications for teachers.

It's fun to watch God work. But you'd miss it if you weren't paying attention. People come to church and say, "Your message spoke exactly to me." Yeah, isn't that lucky? To the world, that's the way it looks. But to the eyes of the believer, we know what God is doing. He has perfect plans and perfect timing. We read in Proverbs that people's hearts can plan their ways, but the Lord will direct their steps; that into the lap the lot is cast, but the decision is the Lord's; and that there are many plans in people's hearts, but it is the Lord's counsel that stands.

In Acts 4, as the disciples went out and begin to minister, the Holy Spirit was poured out and people were saved by the thousands. After the disciples were arrested, threatened, and beaten, they prayed, "Lord, we know that both Jews and Gentiles are gathered against You to do whatever Your hand and purpose have determined beforehand." In other words, "Yes, there's opposition, but God, we know You're in charge. We know You're in control."

Paul told the Romans (v. 8:28), that all things work together for good to those who love God and are the called according to His purpose. In Ephesians 2:10, Paul said we are His workmanship, created in Christ Jesus to do good works which He has created beforehand that we should walk in them. So as we come in our text to these words *It happened* and *behold* we should pay close attention as these two groups come together, reminded that God's in charge and things don't just happen. Sometimes we lose sight of this because we're so busy bemoaning what He's doing or complaining about our lot. But we're the poorer for it because God wants us faithful, not foolish; thankful, not complaining.

There could be nothing more different than these two crowds. The folks with Jesus were boisterous and excited. They had seen Him heal the eyes of the blind. They had watched Him minister to the sick and cast out the Devil from the lives of the possessed. He had fed them all when they were hungry.

"Let's hang around with Jesus. He's awesome. I can't wait to see what He's going to do next!" they must have said. They talked loudly with excitement of their experiences one to another.

And then we see this somber crowd coming out of the city, carrying an open casket of an only son. The crowd was supportive, but what could they really say to bring comfort to a mother who was already a widow, making at least her second trip to the graveyard?

Her husband had been lost, and now her only son. I've always thought this would be a great painting—the two crowds at the city gate and the difference in their expressions as Almighty God faced the wages of sin.

> When the Lord saw her, He had compassion on her and said to her, "Do not weep."
>
> —Luke 7:13

This is the first time Luke uses the word *kurios*, or *Lord*, to refer to Jesus. As the centurion already had learned and as the widow was soon to learn, Jesus is indeed Lord over all. In this huge throng of people, He turned to the one who was hurting the most and, noticing her, moved with great compassion for her.

I love this picture of Jesus' concern. I talk to people so often who wonder if God really cares. Their lives are very difficult, their situations only get worse, and they've been praying, yet God doesn't seem to answer. Look what Jesus did at this city gate.

Hebrews 4:15 tells us we don't have a high priest who cannot be touched with the feeling of our infirmities. Rather, He was tried in every way we are, yet without sin. God cares. I love Isaiah 63:9, which says that in all of our affliction, He was afflicted. God suffers with you. In His love and pity, He redeems us, bears us, and carries us.

Don't ever come to the wrong conclusion that because you have yet to see God work, He doesn't care. He cares very much. As a Father pities His children, so the Lord pities those who fear Him. It is a matter of timing, His perfect timing, wait upon Him!

I also love the fact that the Lord's eye was drawn to this woman whose heart had been broken. I don't know about you, but most of the time suffering isolates people. If you lose someone you love, no matter the comfort offered by others, you really feel alone. Suffering removes everything else. And yet the Lord's there. He understood what this woman was going through. It was her suffering that moved His heart. I think it's important we learn that Jesus pays attention when no one else does, and He knows what's going on when no one else can.

Later on, when Paul writes to the Philippians about church life, he says to the saints, "Don't just look out for your own needs. Look out for the needs of others." That's a God-quality because that's what the Lord does. It is often because we lose sight of the compassion of God's heart that we become depressed when things are difficult.

As He looked at this woman who was in such pain, Jesus said something to her that, in light of her circumstances, sounded almost cruel. He said, "Don't cry."

Excuse me? Don't cry? she must have thought. *If I can't cry now, when should I? I don't know what else I have left in life. I can't think of a better time to cry.*

Don't cry? It's an unreasonable suggestion—especially when in first century culture, wailing was customary. And the louder one's cry, the deeper the concern.

Don't cry? It makes no sense. It doesn't compute. It's an unreasonable suggestion—unless it's the Lord who issues it.

As you read through your Bible, you'll find a lot of things the Lord said that run counter to common sense. For example, we are told to rejoice in trials. I hate trials. When they're gone, then I'll rejoice. But that's not what the Lord said. He said to rejoice in them. He also said to be anxious (worry) for nothing. Yeah, right. Or, love your enemies? I identify my enemies by the fact that I hate them. If I started loving my enemies, I'd lose track of them!

Why should I stop worrying and complaining, hating, and weeping? Because the Lord said so. He knows our hearts, needs, and the ways of life.

> Then He came and touched the open coffin, and those who carried him stood still. And He said, "Young man, I say to you, arise."
>
> —Luke 7:14

Jesus stopped the procession by grabbing the casket, which was set on planks and raised overhead, as the boy was being carried to the grave. According to Numbers 19, touching this dead boy's casket would have made Jesus unclean. If the boy arose however, no harm, no foul. But otherwise, Jesus would have had to offer sacrifice before He would have been unable to worship in the temple.

Notice that no one had asked Jesus for any help. If you read Luke alone, you will find that up to this time, everyone who had been healed by the Lord had asked for help: the woman with the hemorrhage, the fellow with the leprosy, the paralytic, and the servant to the centurion. There was always, "Lord, help us." But not here. This man was dead. And the attitude you find around all of these funerals is that it's too late now. Is it?

Jesus stopped the procession. And though He was not asked to help, with love as His motivation and as God come in the flesh, He said to the woman, "Don't weep" and to the young man, "Get up." He talked to this dead guy as if he was still alive.

Why? Because he was. The Bible teaches that we are spirits but we are placed in bodies. Our bodies are only our houses. When you die, the house dies. But your spirit goes to stand before the Lord. If you died without Jesus, you will then die again a second time, as you are sent to eternal judgment in hell. If you died believing and holding to Jesus, saved by Him, your dying really will not be death but just a change of address. You will continue to live, but now in God's presence with joy forevermore.

> So he who was dead sat up and began to speak. And He presented him to his mother.
>
> —Luke 7:15

The entire procession must have stopped just to revive all of the people who fainted. The point is, Jesus, the Lord has the ability to command dead people's spirits to sit up and talk and to return to their bodies. And Jesus, seeing the result of sin, presented Himself as the One in whom we can find victory over death. He brings life. One word from Him and the dead rise.

We do not find a long incantation where Jesus said, "All right, let Me work up some power. This is going to be a tough one." No, it's simply, "Arise. Let's go." And people responded.

> Then fear came upon all, and they glorified God, saying, "A great prophet has risen up among us"; and, "God has visited His people."
>
> —Luke 7:16

How did the people's reverential fear manifest itself? They began to glorify God by recognizing Jesus. They called Him a great prophet. It had been four hundred years and nearly ten generations—twice as long as America has been a nation—since Israel had had a prophet. Then John the Baptist was sent. And now Jesus was there. When Zechariah prophesied at the birth of his son, John the Baptist, he said, "Blessed is the Lord God of Israel who has visited and redeemed His people." The Word had become flesh. Jesus had come. He had visited His people.

> And this report about Him went throughout all Judea and all the surrounding region.
>
> —Luke 7:17

Judea was eighty miles south, but good news travels fast. The best the world can offer is a good funeral. But Jesus offers eternal hope. Through all of our hurt, He brings us to a place where we can meet His grace.

To us He would say, "Don't cry; trust Me. Don't worry; look to Me. Don't fear; rest in Me." Is it an unreasonable request? Only if He's not God. But if He is, it would be unreasonable to do anything else.

Chapter 37

Doubt and the Believer

Luke 7:18–23
(Matthew 11:2–19)

In Luke 7:17 we read the news that Jesus' ministry had traveled eighty miles south to Judea. But Matthew wrote that John the Baptist, imprisoned 150 miles away at Makarios by the Dead Sea, heard reports of what Jesus had been doing as well. John had been imprisoned six months earlier because he had spoken out against Herod's adulterous relationship with his brother Philip's wife. Hearing reports about Jesus, John sent two of his disciples to ask Him if He was truly the Messiah. Jesus entertained John's doubts with real grace and answered them with great hope.

I hope if you struggle with doubts you'll realize that God is very interested in answering them. God doesn't mind your doubts and questions. What He minds is unbelief and disobedience. That's the line you don't want to cross.

> Then the disciples of John reported to him concerning all these things. And John, calling two of his disciples to him, sent them to Jesus saying, "Are You the Coming One, or do we look for another?" When the men had come to Him, they said, "John the Baptist has sent us to You, saying, 'Are You the Coming One, or do we look for another?'"
>
> —Luke 7:18–19

The reports John was hearing about what Jesus was doing didn't line up with what he was looking for, because his understanding—like that of most people in the first century—was that when the Messiah came He would be a political deliverer. He would boot the Romans out and restore rule to the Jews, they thought. So it created some doubt for John when after he had been sitting in jail for six months Jesus still hadn't come to bail him out, nor had the political machinery been moving in any positive direction.

When God seems inactive, we tend to doubt. When God doesn't come through on our timetable, we wonder where in the world He is. *Maybe I've got it all wrong*, we think. *After all, I've been praying. I've been waiting. I've been asking. I've been reading. I've been doing a lot of stuff. And as far as I can tell, God hasn't been doing a thing.*

Scripture makes a very clear distinction between honest doubt and stubborn unbelief. The first God meets with everything He has; the other, He chastises and deals with as sin.

191

When Abram was brought out of the land of the Chaldeans and into the Promised Land, God told him amazing things: a great nation would come of him, the land would be given to his seed, and the Messiah would be born from his lineage. In Genesis 15:8, he asked the Lord for proof. And, as we read the chapter, we see the Lord immediately encouraged the little blossoming hope and faith Abram had. Years later, however, still childless, he thought he had run out of waiting time. So rather than believing God, he had a child on his own: Ishmael. That wasn't honest doubt. That was deliberate disobedience. And God chastised him for it.

When the Lord called Gideon to lead the nation in war, he was doubtful. So he said, "Lord, if I lay out this fleece and in the morning it's wet even though the ground is dry, that would be a good sign that I was indeed called to be the leader." And the Lord graciously did what Gideon asked. He met his doubts and fear with encouragement. But then Gideon wondered if the wet fleece and dry ground were just an accident. So he asked the Lord to make the fleece dry and the ground wet—and the Lord did that too. This wasn't unbelief. This was honest doubt. And God was perfectly fine with helping Gideon along the way. So the Lord told him to sneak down to his enemy's camp and listen to what they were talking about. When Gideon did, what did he hear? He heard one soldier tell another that he was sure the sword of the Lord (and the sword of Gideon!) would kill them all. As a result, Gideon's heart was encouraged. The Lord led Gideon through all of his doubt with as much support as he needed, because He saw in him a genuine willingness to want to learn God's ways rather than a hard heart that didn't want to obey.

After Lazarus died, Martha said to Jesus, "Lord, If You only had been here, my brother wouldn't have died."

"Martha," Jesus answered, "I am the resurrection and the life. If you die while believing in Me, you'll live. And if you live believing in Me, you'll never die. Do you believe that, Martha?"

"Yes, I believe," she said. "You're the Messiah. You're the Savior."

Then Jesus said, "Come with Me and I'll show you My glory." They then went to the graveyard where Jesus ordered the stone in front of Lazarus' tomb rolled away.

"Lord, that's a bad idea," Martha protested. "He's got to be stinking by now."

But Jesus said, "Martha, I told you that if you believe Me, you'll get to see who I am."

No rebuke, only encouragement for Martha wanted so much to believe. She just had lots to learn about God.

I think sometimes the faith teachings that have traveled around the country for the last few decades have destroyed our concept of God's opinion about our trust. Some television preachers loudly declare, "If you have enough faith . . . ." But I don't have that much faith. Whatever amount they want, I don't have it. The Lord, on the other hand, comes along and talks about my faith like this: "If you just have faith the size of a grain of mustard, you can say to the mountain, 'Get in the ocean,' and it will go."

I think the Lord's concept of faith is very different from ours. If you ask someone how much he or she believes you and the person pinches his or her fingers together and says, "About that much," that wouldn't be good. Yet that's all the faith the Lord requires from us.

Thomas didn't show up the night of the resurrection evening dinner because he was still so distraught over Jesus' death. The next day, the disciples said, "You should have been here. Jesus is alive! He showed up!"

"That might be," Thomas said. "But unless I see the prints of the nails in His hands and stick my hand in the wound in His side, I'll never believe."

Was this honest doubt? Yes. Thomas had followed Jesus for years. For him, the cup was always half empty at best—but he had the right heart. So the next Sunday, when Jesus came to dinner again, Thomas was there. Thomas needed some help—God helps those who have honest doubt.

In Acts 12, the church in Jerusalem met together to pray after Peter was arrested. James already had been killed and Peter was slated to be next. So the church held an all-night prayer meeting. Some time during the night, the Lord sent an angel to get Peter out of jail. Knowing they were praying, upon his release Peter went right to where the church was meeting and knocked on the door. The girl who answered was so excited to see him that she left him standing outside while she told everyone he was at the door.

"It can't be Peter," the church said. "He's in jail."

"But it is Peter," she insisted.

"It's probably his spirit," the believers said. "He's probably dead."

The question is, how much faith would these saints exercise if they couldn't even believe it when their prayers were answered? Yet God certainly honored their prayers because, although their faith might have been weak, it was real.

God blesses those with honest struggles to grow because He wants us to know Him. The whole process of question and answer establishes our trust in God, gives us an answer for the hope that lies within us, and pushes us to find out what's true and what's not.

John had prophesied of Jesus, "He's coming with a winnowing fan in His hand. He's going to cleanse the floor, gather the grain, and burn the chaff with unquenchable fire" (Luke 3:17). But when he was told that "all" Jesus had been doing was eating with sinners, healing the servant of a Gentile, and raising a single boy from his casket, he thought Jesus might not have been who he thought He was. But who else could possibly have done those things, John?

Most doubt is the result of a misconception of who God is. That was certainly John's problem. Like most first-century believers, he thought that when the Messiah came, He only was coming once and was going to take over. You will find that idea in the mindset of everyone who followed Him. That is why the disciples fought with each other to see who would be the greatest in the kingdom and who would get to sit in a position of authority with Him when He began to rule. Although He said it a hundred times, they never heard Him say, "I'm going to die and rise." It went in one ear and out the other because it didn't match the conception they had of the Messiah.

"He was wounded for our transgression," Isaiah had written of the Messiah in chapter 53:5. But all they could see was what he had written in chapter 9—how the government would be upon His shoulder and of His kingdom there would be no end.

There would be a first coming and a second coming—but they saw only one.

Psalm 22 talks in very specific terms about the crucifixion, which wouldn't be employed as a method of capital punishment until a thousand years later. But no one applied this to the Messiah either. Instead, they said it was an allegorical description of suffering and they turned to Zechariah 14, where they read He would fight against the nations and rule the world. That was the Messiah for whom they were looking and that was John's mindset as well.

Why do we have doubts? Sometimes it's because, like John, we operate under a misconception of what God should do and should be like. One solution to doubt is to go back to the Scriptures and find out what God really says. Find out God's heart and plans. Let the Bible be the light for your path.

John could have just quit, but he wouldn't quit so easily. He would go ask:

> When the men had come to Him, they said, "John the Baptist has sent us to You, saying, 'Are You the Coming One, or do we look for another?'" And that very hour He cured many of infirmities, afflictions, and evil spirits; and to many blind He gave sight. Jesus answered and said to them, "Go and tell John the things you have seen and heard: that the blind see, the lame walk, the lepers are cleansed, the deaf hear, the dead are raised, the poor have the gospel preached to them."
>
> —Luke 7:20–22

Rather than saying to the two young men sent from John, "I'm the Messiah. Tell that quitter to hang in there," Jesus met honest doubt with great hope. "Tell John what you've seen and heard," He said, adding that the lepers were cleansed and the dead raised back to life—two things only God could do.

We find in the Bible that God often places great emphasis on His work to support His Word. In John 5, Jesus said, "I have an even greater witness than John: the works My Father has given Me to do and to finish testify of who I am." He said the same thing in John 14: "If you don't want to believe My Word, look at My works because they will convince you of who I am."

It's one thing to say to the dead, "Get up out of the grave." It's quite another to see that happen.

Instead of answering John's disciples' question, Jesus revealed Himself more fully to them. I often have found in Scripture that the answer to honest doubt and questions is a greater revelation from God to us about Himself. In this way, we are forced through our doubts to grow up in our faith.

In 2 Corinthians 12:9–10, when Paul received a thorn in his flesh because of all that had been revealed to him, he said he prayed again and again for the Lord to get rid of it. God, however, didn't do that. Instead, He said to Paul, "My grace is sufficient for you and My strength will be made perfect in Your weakness."

"I get it," Paul said. "From now on, whenever I'm weak, I'm going to rejoice because I know that when I'm weak, He's strong." The answer didn't change, but Paul did.

When Asaph wrote Psalm 73, he began by saying, "I know God is good, but I've been having trouble with what's going on around me. The rich are getting richer. They never have a sick day in their life. They curse everyone around them and shake their fist at God. Yet they seem to have a great life. I don't get it." But then he said, "I almost slipped in my stand with God until I went into the sanctuary and considered their end." Asaph's honest doubt and tremendous difficulty brought him to a greater awareness of who God is. And that's usually the case.

The solution for most doubt is that we get more information. We study a bit harder, we pray a little longer, and we search the Scriptures a little deeper—only to discover that God is not at all like we thought. The misconceptions are corrected. Not only are we better off for it, but we have an answer for people as to why we hope as we do. Doubt is all part of growing up. You can't get around it.

After Job had struggled with the reason God allowed suffering in his life, God finally revealed Himself to Job. Then Job said, "I've heard about You with the hearing of my ear, but now I see You with my eye." Job's struggles became his answers.

> "And blessed is he who is not offended because of Me."
>
> —Luke 7:23

"Tell John he's blessed if he's not offended because of Me," Jesus said. The word translated *offended* is *skandalon*. It means to "to cause to stumble." John's idea and expectations didn't fit Jesus' ministry. But Jesus said, "Don't let this trip you up, John. Look to Me."

Doubts are usually borne out of misconceptions God corrects through His Word. The result of doubts is usually that we're hungrier to find answers in the Lord. But ultimately we have to take the stand of just trusting God, don't we? I know all I know—but there are some things I just don't know. We read in Deuteronomy 29:29 that the things revealed belong to us, but the hidden things belong to God. Therefore, I must not stumble over the things He doesn't reveal.

You can come to know God's heart, but He's not liable to explain to you what He's doing. There's a great verse in Job 33 that says God is greater than man. Therefore, who do we think we are to contend with Him? He will not give an answer for all of His actions.

As parents, our kids continually ask us, "Why?"

And we always answer, "Because."

"Because why?" they push.

"Because I said so," we answer.

But wouldn't it be great if they said, "I don't understand this, but Dad, you're the smartest guy I know, so I'm going with you"? We'll never hear that—but that's what we hope to hear. So does the Lord.

At some point, after my misconceptions are corrected and all of my hunger to know has driven me to find better answers and a better understanding of God, I'm left to simply trust Him and hand over my doubt to Him. In Psalm 18:30, David said, "As for God, His way is perfect; the word of the Lord is proven." Honest doubt is certainly something God can use. It will correct any misconceptions you have about God because it will drive you to seek Him in His Word. God never turns away from those who seek to know Him. Honest doubters eventually end up with a clearer revelation of who God is, an assurance of His ways, and a stronger faith on which to stand.

John didn't get out of jail. In fact, he was beheaded. But he died in faith. And he saw God's goodness. One day in glory we will meet John and rejoice with Him before the Lord.

Chapter 38

JESUS SPEAKS OF THE FAITHFUL AND THE NOT SO FAITHFUL

Luke 7:24–35
(Matthew 11:2–19)

After John's disciples left to tell him what Jesus had told them, Jesus turned to the huge crowd filled with both believers and doubters to give testimony to John's faithfulness and to give them yet another opportunity to believe.

> When the messengers of John had departed, He began to speak to the multi-tudes concerning John: "What did you go out into the wilderness to see? A reed shaken by the wind? But what did you go out to see? A man clothed in soft garments? Indeed those who are gorgeously appareled and live in luxury are in kings' courts. But what did you go out to see? A prophet? Yes, I say to you, and more than a prophet."
>
> —Luke 7:24–26

Jesus defended John in very glowing terms. Was John a vacillating kind of guy? Was he like one of the reeds by the river that leans whatever direction the wind blows? No. John had been solid as an oak. Here was a man who had preached one message faithfully for a year. Everyone who came—rich, poor, powerful, weak—heard the same message. John was not wishy-washy at all. Nor had he lived a life of ease and comfort to try and benefit from his ministry. He was a tough, rugged individual who hadn't minced words or played favorites. Thousands had listened to the message he preached and had gone to the Jordan River near Jericho to be baptized, agreeing they were sinners in need of a Savior. Jesus let the crowd know in very clear terms that the message John had preached was a message on which they could rely.

I would think that had John the Baptist been able to hear what Jesus said after his disciples left, he would have been greatly encouraged. The enemy often badgers us when we have had momentary doubts or fears. The crowd might have said, "Oh, he's got cold feet, does he?" But not Jesus. Jesus said John was a prophet and more. I love the fact that even when other people think we've failed, God knows the truth about us.

> "This is he of whom it is written: Behold, I send My messenger before Your face, who will prepare Your way before You. For I say to you, among those born of women there is not a greater prophet than John the Baptist."
>
> —Luke 7:27–28

John would have liked to have heard this part too. "He's the greatest prophet that's ever been born," Jesus said. Now if I told you to write down the greatest prophet of all time, I'm sure you wouldn't pick John the Baptist. You might pick Moses. Moses was the lawgiver. He got to see God. His face even glowed. Or maybe you'd choose Elijah. He performed more miracles in the name of the Lord than any other Old Testament prophet. He saw the future. He even got raptured—Old Testament style. Maybe you'd pick Daniel. Daniel had such vision that he was able to declare the very day Jesus would come riding into Jerusalem to present Himself as the Messiah. He had such great insight that, without Daniel, we never could begin to understand the book of Revelation. I'd even pick Isaiah over John, Jeremiah over John, or Ezekiel over John.

But there are a couple of things mentioned here that tell us from where John's greatness came. The first was his message, the second his proximity to Jesus.

John the Baptist was the last of the old-time prophets. Luke 16:16 says the Law and the prophets were until John, and since then the kingdom of heaven. So John was the last guy in a long line of men who came to proclaim the acceptable year of the Lord. And John stood as the door between the old and the new. After John, following Jesus' death and resurrection, the church was born. But up until then, the prophets foretold of His coming—and John was the last of them, for Jesus was now in their midst.

Not only that but John's message was different from the other prophets because they only could say, "One day the Lord is coming," while he could say, "He's right here." He could point Him out. He was that close. He was there to usher in the coming of the Messiah. "Behold the Lamb of God who takes away the sins of the world," John said. "I must decrease. He must increase. Follow Him." John saw firsthand the end of his prophesies standing before him. Therefore, the position he had and the message he was given made him the greatest of all prophets because he got to point out and see with his own eyes the One whom he had been sent to declare as His forerunner.

I like verse 27, where Jesus says of John, "He's the fulfillment of Scripture." And then He quotes from Malachi 3:1. Not many folks have their birth and subsequent ministry spelled out in the Bible before they're born. Wouldn't you love to open the Bible and see a verse with your name in it and what you are supposed to do? John had biblical precedent; he was called to this unique ministry and position and he knew it.

When Jesus spoke to the people about John in Matthew 11, He said, "If you're willing to receive this, this is Elijah to come." Yet in John 1, when the religious leaders asked him if he was Elijah, John said he wasn't, that he was simply a voice in the wilderness calling to make straight the path of the Lord.

So what did Jesus mean? Here again you see the importance of an understanding of the difference between Jesus' first and second coming. From Malachi 4:5 we know Elijah will be one of the two witnesses that comes before Jesus returns. John the Baptist preceded Jesus in His first coming; Elijah will precede His second coming. The Lord blended these two teachings together so the people might understand that John was not Elijah, but he was like him in regard to the Spirit that was upon him, the power God gave his life, and the message He was given to preach.

> "But he who is least in the kingdom of God is greater than he."
>
> —Luke 7:28

The Lord had allowed John a place of honor as a point man of great privilege. He preached one message: "Come and be saved. Come and repent of your sins. The Messiah is coming. Prepare your heart." But all of that took place prior to Jesus' death and resurrection, which means the Holy Spirit was not yet given. John had the Holy Spirit upon him. We, however, have the Holy Spirit within us. Therefore, from the Lord's perspective, as glorious as John's place was, we have an even better place because we have a relationship with God where the Holy Spirit dwells in us. More blessed than being an eyewitness and more blessed than being a direct fulfillment of prophecy is the fact that we have Jesus living in us by faith. So in the kingdom of God the least has the greater privilege, the greater position, and the greater message.

> And when all the people heard Him, even the tax collectors justified God, having been baptized with the baptism of John. But the Pharisees and lawyers rejected the will of God for themselves, not having been baptized by him.
>
> —Luke 7:29–30

Hearing Jesus' testimony thrilled many of the people's hearts. They had agreed with John that they were sinful and needed help and that the Messiah was soon to come. But there was also the religious group who refused to admit they were sinners, refused to admit they needed forgiveness, refused the message of John, and so refused Jesus—the One for whom John had come to pave the way. And these in the crowd had missed God's outstretched arm of grace because they were lost in their self-righteous religious ways.

Verse 30 says they rejected God's will for themselves. What was God's will for them? That they confess their sin and turn to Jesus by faith. What is God's will for us? The same thing. They weren't only rejecting John the Baptist's counsel. They were rejecting God's will for themselves. Likewise, for you to refuse Jesus is to reject God's will for you.

During my thirty years of pastoring I have had occasion to speak in places where as a pastor I was not well received. It used to bother me but it doesn't anymore, because I realize at some point it's God's Word they don't like and it is not personal. It's not my word they're rejecting but His. It is my standing with Him and His Word that brings.

> And the Lord said, "To what then shall I liken the men of this generation, and what are they like? They are like children sitting in the marketplace and calling

to one another, saying: 'We played the flute for you, and you did not dance. We mourned to you, and you did not weep.' For John the Baptist came neither eating bread nor drinking wine, and you say, 'He has a demon.' The Son of Man has come eating and drinking, and you say, 'Look, a glutton and a winebibber, a friend of tax collectors and sinners!' But wisdom is justified by all her children."

—Luke 7:31–35

To speak to the heart of the scribes' and Pharisees' rejection both of John's message and His own, Jesus used the illustration of kids playing in the street. A lot of times, kids won't play unless it's their idea and they can have their way. It is like the old phrase "it's my ball, so we play my game." In Jesus' illustration, the kids said, "We pretended we were at a wedding but you wouldn't dance. So since you didn't like the happy stuff, we pretended we were at a funeral. But you didn't like that either."

Applying the analogy, John *was* more like a funeral. He was a somber man with a sobering message. He lived in the desert. He ate wild locusts. He spoke often of sin and repentance and didn't cut corners. One had to travel some thirty miles into the desert just to find him. And the religious declared of him, "This guy's possessed of the Devil."

Then the Son of Man came and Jesus by His illustration said He was just the opposite. He came to people's houses for dinner. He came to weddings. He talked to tax collectors. Prostitutes asked Him for forgiveness. He laughed. He was available. Yet the religious said of Him, "He's a glutton and a drunk. He's too accessible to sinners."

Jesus rarely spoke of what His critics said about Him. But these accusations were apparently so well known that He used them as a teaching tool to say, "Look how unreasonable these people's attitudes are who will not hear the truth, no matter how it is presented." Whether the message came from a serious prophet like John or a more accessible Savior, Jesus, the religious community rejected it.

Jesus ended by saying children of wisdom would see the truth in both and rejoice all together. But children of folly are set in their ways and no amount of bridging the gap will work, because their hearts are hard and their minds made up.

If men reject the message of the Gospel, don't blame the messenger. There is nothing the messenger can do or say that will open the heart. People in Jesus' day had it both ways—and the hard hearts of some rejected them both.

The issue is usually not so much one of presentation but rather of the message itself. When Paul was in jail writing to the Philippians, he said in chapter 1, "I've been noticing that there are some folks preaching Christ out of envy and strife; others seem to have a good will. Some preach Christ out of selfish ambition; others preach Him out of love. I really don't care what their motive is as long as Christ is being preached." In other words, it doesn't matter what drives the message. It is the preaching of the Word that brings life.

Wisdom is known of her children. There is a difference between childlikeness and child-ishness. Jesus recommended the first but not the second. There was wisdom to be found in listening to John the Baptist's call to self-evaluation and confession of sin. There was wisdom to be found in Jesus' message of grace and mercy. But the scribes and Pharisees wanted neither. Since they didn't see themselves as sick, they didn't need a doctor. They were wise in their own eyes.

Isaiah said God's Word never returns to Him void. So share it freely. There will be those who think they don't need to hear it—but there also will be many who are wise and child-like enough to realize they do. Bless your Word, Lord, as we share it with others!

Chapter 39

JESUS LOVES SINNERS

Luke 7:36–50

I n Matthew 11, we come to a discussion Jesus had with the crowd just before He went
to the Pharisee's house for dinner. I'm sure it is the message He gave and the prayer
that followed that prompted the woman we'll meet later in our study in Luke 7. Here is
the Matthew passage and its context:

> Then he began to rebuke the cities in which most of His mighty works had
> been done, because they did not repent: "Woe to you, Chorazin! Woe to you,
> Bethsaida! For if the mighty works which were done in you had been done in
> Tyre and Sidon, they would have repented long ago in sackcloth and ashes. But
> I say to you, it will be more tolerable for Tyre and Sidon in the day of judgment
> than for you. And you, Capernaum, who are exalted to heaven, will be brought
> down to Hades, for if the mighty works which were done in you had been done
> in Sodom, it would have remained until this day. But I say to you that it shall be
> more tolerable for the land of Sodom in the day of judgment than for you."
>
> —Matthew 11:20–24

In the group following Jesus were many simply looking for reasons to find fault and
reject Him, or worse. He had just said the religious leaders were like kids playing in the
street who were never satisfied. Here He spoke of cities like Capernaum and others who
had seen His power and glory clearly demonstrated. "You had so much light," He said.
"If the city of Sodom had had that much light, it never would have fallen to judgment.
Therefore, one day you're going to receive greater judgment because you have been given
greater light."

> At that time, Jesus answered and said, "I thank You, Father, Lord of heaven and
> earth, that You have hidden these things from the wise and prudent and have
> revealed them to babes. Even so, Father, for so it seemed good in Your sight.
> All things have been delivered to Me by My Father, and no one knows the Son
> except the Father. Nor does anyone know the Father except the Son, and the one
> to whom the Son wills to reveal Him. Come to Me, all you who labor and are
> heavy laden, and I will give you rest. Take My yoke upon you and learn from Me,

for I am gentle and lowly in heart, and you will find rest for your souls. For My yoke is easy and My burden is light."

—Matthew 11:25–30

The chronology now shifts to Luke 7, where we see a woman coming to Jesus. I don't doubt it was this prayer of Jesus recorded by Matthew that convinced her He would welcome even a sinner like her, if she was to humbly come to Him with her sordid life. Let's turn to Luke 7:

Then one of the Pharisees asked Him to eat with him. And He went to the Pharisee's house, and sat down to eat.

—Luke 7:36

Out of the crowd listening to Jesus came a Pharisee who invited Him to dinner. We gather, even from this terse one-verse statement, that this was no friendly invitation. By the time the story is finished, we'll know for sure that this was not an invitation offered by a man looking for answers and thinking he had found them in Jesus. Rather, it was an invitation offered by a man who wanted to embarrass Jesus in front of his friends. This was a setup. Jesus knew it but graciously went anyway.

In the culture of the day, when you arrived at someone's house, your host would always do three things for you: kiss you on both cheeks in greeting, wash the dirt from your dusty sandaled feet in welcome, and place a drop of fragrant oil upon your head to cover the sweat odor and make you a sweet-smelling fragrance in their home. Jesus received none of these common courtesies because this was a dinner designed to embarrass Him and paint Him as the fool, and set Him up. Yet He graciously stayed.

And behold, a woman in the city who was a sinner, when she knew that Jesus sat at the table in the Pharisee's house, brought an alabaster flask of fragrant oil, and stood at His feet behind Him weeping; and she began to wash His feet with her tears, and wiped them with the hair of her head; and she kissed His feet and anointed them with the fragrant oil. Now when the Pharisee who had invited Him saw this, he spoke to himself, saying, "This man, if He were a prophet, would know who and what manner of woman this is who is touching Him, for she is a sinner."

—Luke 7:37–39

This woman of the streets, a prostitute everyone knew, came to Jesus in the house of the Pharisee while He sat at dinner, and she was weeping. What was she doing in the Pharisee's house? Verse 37 says when she knew Jesus was there, she came. I suspect from Matthew's account that she might have been the one in the crowd who might have been the one most delighted when Jesus said, "If you're heavy laden, I can give you rest."

"That's what I need," she thought to herself as she heard Him speak. "I'm so tired of the way I'm living. I've made wrong choices. I don't want to live like this anymore." I think right then and there she came to a saving faith in Jesus.

However, when the crowds dispersed, Jesus was gone. "Where did He go?" she must have asked.

"To Simon's house for dinner," someone replied.

She was ready in heart now to go to Him. But that would require some real effort because she knew the Pharisees would hold up a woman like her in scorn. Still, she came looking for Jesus. Why risk the rejection and ridicule? Because her hurt was greater than her worry, and her love for Him greater than her fear of them.

If you love the Lord more than you fear people, you'll have a great life because you'll be able to discover what God wants to do. I've had people call the church office and say, "I was in church Sunday and I meant to get saved, but I didn't want my friends to think I'm weird, so can you pray with me on the phone now?" But isn't having your friends think you're weird better than God having to judge you in your sin? This woman came to a point in her life where all she wanted was what Jesus had to offer, even though it meant she would have to walk into a religious home where she would most likely be judged. I love this picture, for even as Jesus paid the price to be there, she was willing to pay the price to come to Him.

We're told that when she arrived, she stood behind Jesus at His feet because that's the way the guests would have reclined around the dinner table. Overcome by her sin, Jesus' promise, and the judgment of the religious men in the room, the woman couldn't stop crying. And as her tears fell on Jesus' dirty feet, she realized He had been ignored. So she took down her hair—a taboo in the culture—and began to wash His feet as a servant would. This was worship from a heart that finally had found rest in Him. By the time she was finished, His feet were the cleanest and He smelled the best of anyone in the room because He didn't get just a drop of fragrant oil—He got an entire bottle. All of the common courtesies Simon had failed to extend to Jesus, this woman, driven by love, gave Him.

Around the table Simon and his buddies sat, watching. And at least in Simon's mind, this was enough to confirm what he had suspected all along: that Jesus was a phony. *This is not the Messiah*, he thought. *If He were, He certainly wouldn't let such a wicked woman get so close to Him.* And smugly, untouched by the woman's demonstration of devotion and repentance, Simon sat in judgment of Jesus.

And Jesus answered . . . .

—Luke 7:40

The only question to which you can tie this is Simon's thoughts in verse 39. In other words, Jesus knew Simon's heart as well as the heart of the woman sitting at His feet, and He now responds verbally and loudly for all to hear, to Simon's inner thoughts.

. . . and said to him, "Simon, I have something to say to you." So he said, "Teacher, say it."

—Luke 7:40

I suspect it was a rather sarcastic Simon who said, "Go ahead. Say whatever it is You have to say. I've seen through You, phony."

> "There was a certain creditor who had two debtors. One owed five hundred denarii, and the other fifty. And when they had nothing with which to repay, he freely forgave them both. Tell Me, therefore, which of them will love him more?" Simon answered and said, "I suppose the one whom he forgave more." And He said to him, "You have rightly judged."
>
> —Luke 7:41–43

The story Jesus told was of two men in debts that neither of them could repay. This is by illustration one of the clearest presentations of the Gospel, for many people think they only owe fifty denarii and so that is something they can handle eventually. That was Simon's problem. If he was a "fifty denarii" sinner, the woman was certainly of the "five hundred denarii" type. But Jesus' point is, "They're both unable to pay." The issue for Simon was that he didn't see himself very deeply in debt. But the wages of any sin is death—regardless of whether that sin is small or great. People make broad distinctions when it comes to external sins. We allow for some and disallow others. Jesus' question when it came to the absolution of debt was, "who's happier, the one forgiven little or the one forgiven much?" The Pharisee answered correctly and indeed anyone who realizes his great sin and finds great mercy in God will love God all the more. And it was that realization that had driven this woman in tears into a Pharisee's house, and to her knees washing Jesus' feet.

It is, by the way, much harder to reach "fifty denarii" sinners with the Gospel of Jesus Christ because they think they're fine. They don't think they owe that much. It's when you find out you are a "five hundred denarii" sinner that you really begin to worship. I hope that's you. I hope you know God has washed your slate clean and you owe Him everything, for only then you can come to church with joy, worship with honesty, and study the Word with hunger. But until you get to that place, there is very little that will drive you other than perhaps a sense of obligation.

"Who will love more?" Jesus asked Simon. And the tepid "I suppose" in Simon's answer was proof of his lack of care or willingness to listen to Jesus at all.

> Then He turned to the woman and said to Simon, "Do you see this woman?"
>
> —Luke 7:44

As He turned to the woman, Jesus continued to talk to Simon. I love the question because Simon thought he knew all about her. He saw a repulsive, sinful woman he thought he should despise because he knew what she did for a living. But Simon only saw the woman's past. He didn't see her conversion. He couldn't tell what was in her heart. And not only was he wrong about the woman, but he was wrong about Jesus as well. He had mistaken Jesus' accessibility, love, patience, and tolerance for a lack of personal holiness and discernment. Simon also was wrong about himself because he didn't see himself as a debtor to God for sin he couldn't repay. He didn't see himself in need of a Savior in the least. Simon sure was wrong about a lot of things.

> "I entered your house; you gave Me no water for My feet, but she has washed My feet with her tears and wiped them with the hair of her head. You gave Me no kiss, but this woman has not ceased to kiss My feet since the time I came in. You did not anoint My head with oil, but this woman has anointed My feet with fragrant oil. Therefore I say to you, her sins, which are many, are forgiven, for she loved much. But to whom little is forgiven, the same loves little."
> —Luke 7:44–47

What a powerful insight. This is the application of the parable of man's sinfulness as Simon sat in judgment of every heart except his own. Why did this woman love Jesus so much? Because not only did she realize her sins were many, she realized God could forgive them. If you don't see your need for God's forgiveness, you're going to have very little love. But because this woman realized how far down she had fallen and how far God had brought her, she loved Jesus deeply, while Simon only could sit on the sidelines and scoff.

That's the trouble with Simons. They don't see themselves but they think they see everyone else perfectly—and it's always in a bad light. I love the idea that forgiven sins cause great love. The folks most on fire for the Lord, most willing to tell someone else about Him, most willing to risk being rejected or ashamed, and most willing to look like fools are those who see most clearly what Jesus has done for them. You don't have to tell them to go to church, read their Bible, or pray. They do all of those things because they have great love for the One who has received them, forgiven them and loves them so.

John wrote that we love Him because He first loved us. In 1 John 4:11 it says if He loved us like this, so then we should love one another. The intolerant person is usually the one who is unaware that God has washed clean his or her own slate. But once you know that, you're very tolerant with people who struggle and fail because you know personally that the Lord can and will forgive. In fact, the love you show for others in their weakness tells you a great deal about the forgiveness you have received.

> Then He said to her, "Your sins are forgiven." And those who sat at the table with Him began to say to themselves, "Who is this who even forgives sins?" Then He said to the woman, "Your faith has saved you. Go in peace."
> —Luke 7:48–50

"Your sins are forgiven. Your faith has saved you. Go in peace," Jesus said to the woman. She was accepted in God's love by faith in Him. And while the whole table formed opinions in their minds about her, Jesus assured her that she was fine.

Did Jesus tell the woman that her works had saved her? No, that was Simon's department. Was it her love that saved her? No, that was simply a response to what God had done. It was her trust and faith in what she had heard outside that saved her. She had been heavy laden with sin. She had come to Jesus. And she found rest.

Whether you are a big sinner or a little sinner in the world's eyes, you are simply a sinner in God's eyes. But Jesus can make you clean. Simon left this dinner still deciding he could do it alone. But the woman went on to real life.

Chapter 40

THE UNPARDONABLE SIN

Mark 3:20–35
(Matthew 12:31–32; Luke 11:14–21)

I n Mark 3, we find Jesus returning to Peter's house in Capernaum. From Matthew's account, it would appear that this is only the beginning of what would turn out to be a very long day.

> Then the multitude came together again, so that they could not so much as eat bread. But when His own people heard about this, they went out to lay hold of Him, for they said, "He is out of His mind."
>
> —Mark 3:20–21

The words *came together* are in the present tense indicative, which in Greek means there was no let-up. The crowds just kept coming so that Jesus and His disciples didn't even have time to eat. The word *again* suggests this wasn't an isolated event. It seemed to happen quite a bit. And news of this reached Jesus' family. The word used here by Mark translated "lay hold of Him" means "to arrest." In other words, His family wanted to forcibly take Jesus home. No doubt they loved Him. But they thought He was suffering delusions and so before He hurt anyone else or Himself, they wanted to help Him. They were sure it would be for His own good. After all, He'd been running into the religious leaders and causing a lot of trouble. There had even been talk about having Him killed.

As you go through the Gospels, you conclude Jesus' family didn't believe in Him until after the resurrection. Jesus spent His three-and-a-half-years in ministry with a family who were not yet convinced. They were kind to Him. They loved Him. But they were mistaken about who He was.

In *The Quest for the Historical Jesus*, Albert Schweitzer mistakenly concluded after reading the Gospels that it was Messianic delusions that crushed Jesus. The same charge was leveled against His followers. When Paul stood before Festus and began to share Jesus with him, Festus proclaimed, "Paul, you are beside yourself. Your large amount of learning has made you mad"—in other words, "You've lost your mind." People said the same thing about Luther, Spurgeon, and Wesley. And if we open our mouths much for Jesus, they're probably going to say that about us.

Jesus' family's view was that He had lost His mind. The crowd's view was that they needed Him day and night. And there was a third group—the scribes and Pharisees—who said He was possessed by the Devil:

And the scribes who came down from Jerusalem said, "He has Beelzebub," and, "By the ruler of the demons He casts out demons."

—Mark 3:22

Matthew tells us a man who was blind and mute was brought to Jesus. When Jesus healed him, the multitude said He must be the Son of God. But the Pharisees said, "No, this man is possessed by Beelzebub." Beelzebub either means "lord of the flies" or "the lord of the house." In either case, the title was ascribed to an idol that was supposedly the ruler of the demonic world. The word for *said* is in the imperfect tense, which means they said it again and again. So every time the crowds brought up a healing or another of Jesus' works, the scribes and Pharisees dismissed it as being of the Devil.

So He called them to Himself and said to them in parables: "How can Satan cast out Satan? If a kingdom is divided against itself, that kingdom cannot stand. And if a house is divided against itself, that house cannot stand. And if Satan has risen up against himself, and is divided, he cannot stand, but has an end. No one can enter a strong man's house and plunder his goods, unless he first binds the strong man. And then he will plunder his house."

—Mark 3:23–27

Matthew tells us in chapter 12:25 that Jesus knew the thoughts of the men who were attributing His power to the Devil. Summoning them, He gave them a parable. The word *parable* is derived from two Greek words that mean "to throw alongside." Parables set physical illustrations alongside spiritual truths. Jesus used parables to explain but also to hide truth, because He didn't want people who didn't believe to be even more responsible for what they had heard. Yet at the same time, He wanted those who loved Him to be abundantly clear about what He was saying. So to answer the Pharisees' thoughts as well as to instruct the crowds, Jesus said, "How can Satan cast out Satan and expect to take over?" Jesus used the word *Satan* rather than Beelzebub because He knew the Devil stands behind every idol.

"Satan can't be fighting against himself and expect to have much of a kingdom left," Jesus said. He applied the same logic to a nation at war with itself or a family divided against itself. And then He gave them a parable that required them to look at the only other conclusion to which they could come about Him—not that He was driven by Beelzebub but that He was God Himself.

"No one can enter into a strong man's house and rob him unless he first is able to bind the strong man," Jesus said.

Who's the strong man? Satan.

What is the house? The kingdom of Satan set up in men's hearts.

So you have the Devil, the world that he rules, and this man that has been bound. John later wrote that the Son of God was made known that He might destroy the works of the

Devil. We are saved because God has broken the bondage the Devil was able to lay upon us through our sin. We didn't free ourselves. God freed us. We can't battle the Devil and win. But God can. And the very fact that Satan was being defeated ought to have told the religious community that Jesus was the stronger of the two.

Jesus' logic left the Pharisees speechless. In fact, Matthew intimated that they went away shaking their heads. Before they left, however, Jesus gave them a heavy warning, one that was very important for them to hear:

> "Assuredly, I say to you, all sins will be forgiven the sons of men, and whatever blasphemies they may utter; but he who blasphemes against the Holy Spirit never has forgiveness, but is subject to eternal condemnation"—because they said, "He has an unclean spirit."
>
> —Mark 3:28–30

Jesus wanted to be sure the men who accused Him of being in a league with the Devil understood that there would be grave consequences for maintaining their position. And the lesson is for us as well. For whenever there was an extremely important consequential statement, Jesus used the word *assuredly*. After getting their attention, Jesus gave them (and us) what has commonly been called the doctrine of the unpardonable sin, a sin that cannot be forgiven.

This doctrine has often been misapplied in history and misunderstood in the church. Therefore, I believe it's important we understand it because we not only find it here in Mark 3 but also in Matthew 12 and Luke 12. Jesus brought it to bear on those who were rejecting Him and accusing Him of being in league with the Devil, a sin that He declared would leave man without hope.

What is the sin that's unpardonable? The Bible is filled from cover to cover with sins that are not unpardonable. David was a liar, adulterer, and murderer. Yet when his sin with Bathsheba was discovered, Nathan the prophet said he wouldn't die. Jesus forgave the woman who washed His feet with her tears even though she had committed many sins. The prodigal son who ran off to live in sin was received back home and restored. Peter denied the Lord with swearing and cursing on three separate occasions—yet he was forgiven. Paul spent many years killing Christians and locking up their families. Yet when he repented, he was forgiven. Even on the cross as Jesus was crucified, referring to those who drove spikes through His hands and feet and spat in His face, He said, "Father forgive them." They hadn't committed the unpardonable sin either, although how much more horrible could it have gotten?

What then is the unpardonable sin? In verse 28, Jesus identified it as blasphemy of the Holy Spirit. The work of the Holy Spirit in the world is to bring people to Jesus (John 16:8–11). Now if the Lord sends the Holy Spirit to tell you God loves you, Jesus died for you, and you must believe in Him but you repeatedly reject His voice, there's no hope for you because you've turned away from the one door that leads to life.

It's the Holy Spirit whose work it is to turn you to Christ. If you blaspheme Him, and constantly put off His Word, His plea, and neglect what He says to you, you end up in a place where there's no return. You can't go to Jesus because you've written Him off. What do you have left then? A hundred other solutions—none of which will bring life. All sin is forgivable except the continual rejection of the message of the Holy Spirit who calls you to turn to Jesus as your Lord and Savior.

This sin, however, takes time. To exasperate God's grace takes a lot of time. Notice that even the wicked scribes and Pharisees who were, on occasion, planning to kill Jesus hadn't arrived at that place yet. "If you continue on this road, if you continue in this manner, if you stay this course . . ." Jesus warned them.

God sent Moses to Pharaoh with one miraculous proof after another that he was God's messenger. For a while, Pharaoh's little magicians were able to duplicate the miracles, but eventually they couldn't mimic what God had done. When the Lord called Pharaoh to turn, to believe, to let go, and to respond, Pharaoh wouldn't. By the time we get to Exodus 10:27, it was a matter not only of unwillingness but inability. Because Pharaoh *would* not respond, he ultimately *could* not respond. He had put himself in a position where there was no longer any way out. He crossed the line. He dove headfirst into hell.

Where is that line? I don't know. I do know it's way out there, because God is so willing to give life. But Genesis 6:3 tells us that God not always will strive with man. So if you continue to resist Him, you eventually will find yourself at some point in your life dead to the things of God.

I've had believers tell me they think they've blasphemed the Holy Spirit. But if they're saved, that's impossible because their very belief in Jesus proves otherwise. That they worry about it at all is proof as well, because the description of someone who has crossed the line is that he or she is no longer sensitive to the work of God's Spirit.

C.S. Lewis, in his book *The Case for Christianity*, wrote that due to Jesus' claims, one has to conclude He was either a lunatic, a demonically driven liar, or that He is, in fact, the Lord.

And that's exactly what was happening in Peter's house. We see Jesus' family thinking He was a lunatic. We see the religious people saying He was in league with the Devil. But we see Jesus declaring, "I'm the Son of Man. I'm the Lord."

> Then His brothers and His mother came, and standing outside they sent to Him, calling Him. And a multitude was sitting around Him; and they said to Him, "Look, Your mother and Your brothers are outside seeking You." But He answered them, saying, "Who is My mother, or My brothers?" And He looked around in a circle at those who sat about Him, and said, "Here are My mother and My brothers! For whoever does the will of God is My brother and My sister and My mother."
>
> —Mark 3:31–35

When Jesus' family arrived in Capernaum from twenty-five miles away in Nazareth, the crowd was so large they couldn't get inside to see Him so they passed a message in to tell Him they were outside. But I'm sure no one in the chain that passed the message to Jesus expected Him to respond the way He did when He looked around at the faces of the believers sitting by Him and gestured to His disciples with His hand, saying, "Here's My family." It was a startling statement, not only because in every culture family is important, but because in Hebrew culture, family reigned supreme.

"The world was made by Him but the world didn't know Him," John wrote. "He came to His own and His own didn't receive Him. But to as many as received Him, to them He gave the right to become the children of God, even to those who believed in His name who were born not of blood nor of the will of man or of the will of the flesh but of the will of God." That is why Jesus said, "This is My family. Believers belong to Me."

And so before the crowd, Jesus corrected the scribes, the Pharisees, and the opinion of His own family. He set aside the charges of being a liar and a lunatic, and instead declared by word and action that He is the Lord.

Chapter 41

HOW DO YOU HEAR?

Luke 8:1–15
(Matthew 13:1–23; Mark 4:1–20)

As we continue on this very busy day of the Lord, Luke gives to us here a general statement about Jesus' Galilean ministry.

> Now it came to pass, afterward, that He went through every city and village, preaching and bringing the glad tidings of the kingdom of God. And the twelve were with Him, and certain women who had been healed of evil spirits and infirmities—Mary called Magdalene, out of whom had come seven demons, and Joanna, the wife of Chuza, Herod's steward, and Susanna, and many others who provided for Him from their substance.
>
> —Luke 8:1–3

I find it very interesting that as Jesus went from city to city bringing good news, the company of those who took care of Him grew. Not only the apostles, but several women mentioned by name, were driven to serve Him because of the work God had done in their lives.

Mary from Magdala, which is just a couple of miles north of Tiberius and south of Capernaum, was one of four Marys we see in the Bible. She is the epitome of the truth that if God has forgiven you much, you love much. This Mary was at the cross and the tomb, and was the first to see the resurrected Lord and to tell the disciples He had risen.

Joanna was a woman we also find at the tomb Easter Sunday with a group of women coming to finish the burial job. We know that her husband was an accountant for Herod.

And though we know nothing of Susanna except her name, the Lord certainly knows much. In addition to Mary, Joanna, and Susanna, there were many others.

These unnamed lovers of Christ took care of His food and lodging, mended His clothes, and helped in any way they could. Did Jesus really need their help? Does He need ours? No. We need His help. This group met the Lord's needs because He already had met theirs. They supported His work with their hands because of the work He had done in their hearts. The One who would feed five thousand from five loaves of bread and two dried fish obviously didn't need anyone to provide for Him, but He loves to work that way, doesn't He? As the Lord ministers to you and you begin to give to God's work, do it out of love because you want to, not because you think He needs you.

And when a great multitude had gathered, and they had come to Him from every city, He spoke by a parable: "A sower went out to sow his seed. And as he sowed, some fell by the wayside; and it was trampled down, and the birds of the air devoured it. Some fell on rock; and as soon as it sprang up, it withered away because it lacked moisture. And some fell among thorns, and the thorns sprang up with it and choked it. But others fell on good ground, sprang up, and yielded a crop a hundredfold." When He had said these things, He cried, "He who has ears to hear, let him hear!" Then His disciples asked Him, saying, "What does this parable mean?" And He said, "To you it has been given to know the mysteries of the kingdom of God, but to the rest it is given in parables, that seeing they may not see, and hearing they may not understand."

—Luke 8:4–10

As the crowds grew, among them were still these religious men who were out to discredit Jesus. After reasoning with them and then warning them about the road they were on, Jesus began to tell stories, or parables to them. By definition, a parable is a story of a physical nature that is placed beside a spiritual truth. And by making the comparison between the two, spiritual truths can be understood.

For the disciples, these became great times of learning. For anyone not interested in what Jesus had to say, however, the intent of the parables was two-fold. First, they hopefully created curiosity to know what God had to say. But secondly, they hid the truth from those who were unwilling to hear it so that they would not be responsible for it.

In four verses, we have the parable of the sower. According to Mark's account, when the disciples said, "Lord, we don't know what You're talking about," He said, "If you don't get this parable, you won't get any of the others." In other words, this is the one you want to understand so you can take what you know and apply it to the rest. In Bible school, this would be known as "expositional constancy." It means that the definition Jesus gave to the symbolic use of things in one parable is to be applied consistently to each.

Here in verses 11 through 15, Jesus gives the explanation—the standard by which you can study all the other parables as He uses this one as the constant.

"Now the parable is this: The seed is the word of God."

—Luke 8:11

Go back to verses 5 through 8 and every time you see the word *seed*, read it as "God's Word." A sower goes forth to sow God's Word. Sometimes God's Word falls by the wayside. Sometimes God's Word falls among the thorns. Sometimes God's Word falls on rocky ground. This means that as we share the Word with the lost, we actually are sowing seeds in their hearts. We don't know what kinds of hearts they have, but we do know what seed we're sowing.

I think if we truly believed the seed is the Word, we would stick with Scripture rather than relying on some clever argument or our ability to argue persuasively in our sharing. In Jesus' parable, the sower didn't go out to sow his own opinion. He went out to sow God's Word. It's not your argument that has power. It's God's Word that has power.

The writer to the Hebrews will say in chapter 4 that God's Word is sharper than any two-edged sword. It alone can get right to the heart of any matter.

> "Those by the wayside are the ones who hear; then the Devil comes and takes away the word out of their hearts, lest they should believe and be saved."
>
> —Luke 8:12

The first heart is characterized by a path through a field that, because it had been trodden down and often stepped on, it was as hard as it could be. Consequently, the birds of the air, which Jesus identified as the Devil, were able to take away whatever people had heard because the seed was unable to penetrate the hard grounds of their hearts. They make it through the church service, but their response at best is so short-lived that it is not long before the influence of what they hear is removed from their life altogether.

> "But the ones on the rock are those who, when they hear, receive the word with joy; and these have no root, who believe for a while and in time of temptation fall away."
>
> —Luke 8:13

The second type of soil is a thin layer on top of rocks. Because 90 percent of the country of Israel is on limestone, there are places with as little as three inches of soil before that bedrock is encountered. Consequently, without much soil to retain water, growth in that soil becomes extremely difficult. So the Lord used this very clear picture to say there were some folks in the crowd who, although they heard the Word, had no depth, no ability to put down roots or get nutrients from it. They received the Word with joy. There was an emotional response—but no substance to keep them going.

Emotional responses bring great release and make people feel close to God—but that's not repentance. Repentance isn't a feeling. It's a choice. Both in the Bible and in history, we see that surface conversions are always found on the fringe of true spiritual revival. There will be folks whose lives are truly changed and then there will be a lot of fringe-dwellers who, like the crowds in Jesus' day, will leave when the temptations come and the difficulties begin. Someone hears a message and he's in tears. Next week, he's back with a Bible big enough to choke a mule. He has eleven bumper stickers on his car. He shows up two hours early for every service. He stays three hours late. He can't get enough of it. And then, a month later, we never see him again. He's up. He's down. And then he's gone.

Emotions are fine if they're rooted in knowledge. But they can be dangerous if they hide non-existent faith. God will carry you around for a while, but then He sets you down and says, "Now walk by faith." You can't sustain faith on emotion—which is why I think a lot of people run from church to church, looking for their next "high." Eventually the feelings fail, the newness wears off, and the temptation arises to pick up and start all over again somewhere else with something else. The truth, however, is that, according to Philippians 1:6 if God began a work in you, He'll complete it.

> "Now the ones that fell among thorns are those who, when they have heard, go out and are choked with cares, riches, and pleasures of life, and bring no fruit to maturity."
>
> —Luke 8:14

These hearts last a little longer than the first two groups. They stick around for a while, but their commitment is being constantly compromised by competing interests. Jesus' description of this in a physical sense is like trying to plant in a field in which there's a lot of thorns, a lot of weeds, and a lot of things to choke out the seed's fruitfulness. There are folks who hear God's Word, but their entanglements in the world are their spiritual undoing. The crops compete for space.

Jesus identified three specific thorns that are able to make the Word of no effect: the cares of this life, the deceitfulness of riches, and pleasure. The word *care* is from the general Greek word for "worry" and speaks of daily worries about the necessities of life. There are some who never can grow in God's Word because they are constantly preoccupied with the day-to-day cares of the world. Jesus said to His disciples, "Don't take any anxious thought for tomorrow." Yet for these, when God wanted to do a work through them, always had a reason why they didn't have the time.

If it isn't daily necessities that crowd out the Word, it's the pursuit and deceitfulness of riches. We see plenty of examples of this. There's the rich young ruler, the rich fool, the rich man, and Lazarus. And each of those rich men were on the wrong side of God's best. They showed great devotion to business, but it was at the expense of their eternal state.

And finally, if it isn't worry or work, it's leisure or pleasure that crowds out the Word. We are a pleasure-driven society to be sure. Solomon had enough money to buy everything he wanted, yet he wrote in Ecclesiastes 2:1 "I said to my heart, go find joy where you can find it. Enjoy pleasure to the full. I did—and I'm empty."

"I can't go to church," we say. "I have to go to dinner with my friends. I have to be home watching the playoffs. I'm too busy entertaining myself." Unlike pleasure, growth takes time. There's no immediate payoff. You have to wait around awhile for the fruit to come forth.

I find this parable tremendously enlightening because it tells me there are hard-hearted, shallow-hearted, and emotional responders—that there are hearts that have so many things going on that they can't respond to the truth of the Gospel or the things of God.

"But the ones that fell on the good ground are those who, having heard the word with a noble and good heart, keep it and bear fruit with patience."

—Luke 8:15

Fortunately there are also willing hearts. The word *noble* means "pure." The word *good* "agreeable, open trustworthy." This is a heart that is soft, a heart that has depth and a willingness to learn and sees itself in need of God's help. The deceitfulness of riches isn't deceiving this heart. And while pleasure may be a part of its life, it's not life itself. This heart bears much fruit. But it takes a while.

What a great lesson. I think as we go out to share, we should understand that there won't always be people who say, "All right! I want to be saved!" In fact, according to this parable, three out of four times no one gets saved. But the one who does brings forth abundant fruit. People in ministry sometimes have a tendency to overrate their success. Yet it seems to me that the numbers don't necessarily mean you're bearing much fruit because even though Jesus had a huge crowd, He realized they weren't all in.

The fact that a lot of people turn away, however, is no reason to stop sowing because that's what we've been called to do. Look at the four soils: a hard heart who can't wait to get out of church, wishing he'd never come; an emotional hearer who even now sits with goose bumps but has no heart for God; a divided heart who finds that Jesus and the things of God are but a small part of a big life; and a whole-hearted believer, the only one in all of the examples who is saved and the only one who brings forth good fruit.

Solomon wrote in Ecclesiastes 11, "In the morning, sow your seed and in the evening don't withhold your hand. Who knows what will prosper—if it's this or if it's that or if both will be good alike." That's what we must do. We must faithfully sow the Word—and see what happens.

Chapter 42

HE SPOKE TO THEM IN PARABLES

Matthew 13:10–17, 24–52

In Matthew 13, we find six parables Jesus gave crowds that numbered in the thousands on this long day that had begun with the healing of a blind and mute man back in (Mark 3:20–35).

> And the disciples came and said to Him, "Why do You speak to them in parables?" He answered and said to them, "Because it has been given to you to know the mysteries of the kingdom of heaven, but to them it has not been given. For whoever has, to him more will be given, and he will have abundance; but whoever does not have, even what he has will be taken away from him. Therefore I speak to them in parables, because seeing they do not see, and hearing they do not hear, nor do they understand. And in them the prophecy of Isaiah is fulfilled, which says, 'Hearing you will hear and shall not understand. And seeing you will see and not perceive; for the hearts of this people have grown dull, their ears are hard of hearing, and their eyes they have closed, lest they should see with their eyes and hear with their ears, lest they should understand with their hearts and turn, so that I should heal them.' But blessed are your eyes for they see and your ears for they hear; for assuredly, I say to you that many prophets and righteous men desired to see what you see, and did not see it, and to hear what you hear, and did not hear it."
>
> —Matthew 13:10–17

As Jesus changed His method of communication with the crowd to that of speaking in parables, the disciples wondered why. As seen here, the answer is basically two-fold. First, those in the crowd who didn't want to hear from the Lord didn't need to be responsible for even more truth that they would simply refuse with hard hearts. Therefore, in His mercy, because they didn't respond to the light they had been given, Jesus hid the truth from them with these parables. God is very merciful. If you're not going to live, believe, and walk with what you have, there is no sense piling up punishments for later, because to whom much is given, much is required.

On the other hand, for the believers, the parables were illustrations that made the truth easier to understand and remember. In Matthew 21:33–46, Jesus told a parable of wicked vineyard keepers and Matthew recorded that the scribes understood it to be about them. So in addition to hiding truth from those who would not believe and sharing truth with those who would, sometimes Jesus used parables to speak to resistant hearts. When Jesus' words and works don't arouse our interest, maybe the stories will. So great is His love for us that God doesn't turn away from us very easily, leaving no stone unturned in reaching out to us.

The statement being made in the following parables is this: the kingdom of heaven is far smaller than the perceived church. Remember that Jesus was speaking to huge crowds and not everyone in those crowds loved or wanted Him. There were sign-seekers, accusers, and even some plotting His death. Others came just for the free food. The same is true today. The church looks large. But in reality, the believers in the church are much smaller in number. Just being in the crowd doesn't mean you are saved! We jump ahead of the parable of the sower which we saw last time to this second parable:

> Another parable He put forth to them, saying, "The kingdom of heaven is like a man who sowed good seed in his field; but while men slept, his enemy came and sowed tares among the wheat and went his way. But the grain had sprouted and produced a crop, then the tares also appeared. So the servants of the owner came and said to him, 'Sir, did you not sow good seed in your field? How then does it have tares?' He said to them, 'An enemy has done this.' The servants said to him, 'Do you want us then to go and gather them up?' But He said, 'No, lest while you gather up the tares you also uproot the wheat with them. Let both grow together until the harvest, and at the time of harvest I will say to the reapers, "First gather together the tares and bind them in bundles to burn them, but gather the wheat into my barn."'"
>
> —Matthew 13:24–30

Jesus gave the explanation of this parable six verses later, after having shared two more short parables (Matt. 13:31–35): the parable of the mustard seed, and the leaven, each supporting the lesson of this parable of the tares sown amongst the wheat here before us and ones to which we will return in just a few moments.

> Then Jesus sent the multitude away and went into the house. And His disciples came to Him, saying, "Explain to us the parable of the tares of the field." He answered and said to them, "He who sows the good seed is the Son of Man. The field is the world, the good seeds are the sons of the kingdom, but the tares are the sons of the wicked one. The enemy who sowed them is the Devil, the harvest is the end of the age, and the reapers are the angels. Therefore as the tares are gathered and burned in the fire, so it will be at the end of this age. The Son of Man will send out His angels, and they will gather out of His kingdom all things that offend, and those who practice lawlessness, and will cast them into the

furnace of fire. There will be wailing and gnashing of teeth. Then the righteous will shine forth as the sun in the kingdom of their Father. He who has ears to hear, let him hear!"

—Matthew 13:36–43

This second parable says the Lord has a field—the world—and He is sowing good seed. And yet as the seed is being sown, the enemy comes at night to sow tares among the wheat. In Jesus' explanation, we are told the enemy is the Devil and the tares are unbelievers who infiltrate the field, God's work. When the servants began to see the cream-colored buds appear, they knew there would be wheat. But dark-colored buds indicated tares. As the fruit became evident, the workers asked the owner of the field if they should pull up the tares. But the owner said, "If you start trying to separate the crop now, you'll pull up the good seed as well and all will be lost."

Sometimes that's what we try to do in churches, isn't it? We try to determine who's who. But we really can't do that. Our job is just to sow good seed and let the Lord separate the tares. Billy Graham used to say that only a relatively small percent of the hundreds of thousands that came forward in his crusades actually stayed with the Lord. If you looked at the altar call, however, you'd say, "We're gaining ground!" But the Lord's viewpoint is that among the wheat are sure to be tares.

This parable lays out for us the fact that although God is willing to let the field grow, eventually the tares will be judged and the righteous will be able to enter the kingdom. Those who only profess to be Christians make the kingdom look larger than it really is, but separation is God's work in God's time.

While the parable of the sower spoke of quality of the individual heart, here Jesus referred to quantity, illustrated by a field of wheat infiltrated by the Devil and looking far more prosperous and full than it really was when it came to fruit, wheat! Pew sitting, Bible toting, and a sticker on the car won't help. We've got to have a relationship with God—and God knows who belongs to Him. What Jesus said to His disciples was, "Look around. See how big the crowd is? That's what the kingdom of heaven is like: big crowd, but a smaller harvest of wheat." Jesus had huge crowds, but knew every heart.

To reinforce this, He told another parable:

Another parable He put forth to them, saying, "The kingdom of heaven is like a mustard seed, which a man took and sowed in his field; which indeed is the least of all the seeds; but when it is grown it is greater than the herbs and becomes a tree, so that the birds of the air come and nest in its branches."

—Matthew 13:31–32

Although a mustard seed can produce a plant, it never grows to be a tree. Like the field of wheat, the picture here is of something that looks bigger than it actually is. And like the tares, the birds of the air nest in it. From the first parable that sets the standard for interpretation, we know the birds represent evil and the evil one.

Again, saying you're a Christian doesn't make you one. And because of the claims of many, like the crowd following Jesus, the perceived kingdom of God is very large. But the true kingdom is obviously much smaller.

In Jesus' letters to the churches in Revelation 2–3, you'll find this same warning. Those who are hanging on to Christ by faith, those who are walking with Him in obedience, are the ones assured of a future with Him. But Jesus said there will be a lot of folks who will say, "Didn't we cast out Devils in Your name and do great works?" only to hear Him say, "Depart from Me. I never knew you." They took comfort in showing up on Sundays, but had no relationship with God.

> Another parable He spoke to them: "The kingdom of heaven is like leaven which a woman took and hid in three measures of meal till it was all leavened."
> —Matthew 13:33

If the parable of the mustard plant spoke of outward size and expansion, the parable of the leaven speaks of inward development and false doctrine. Throughout the Bible, with only one exception, leaven is always representative of sin. The chemical process of yeast is that it works through fermentation, or rotting. That makes it a pretty good picture of sin because sin gets in and begins to rot, but we don't even notice it until we've swollen from its effects.

During Passover, the Jews had to get rid of every trace of leaven in their homes before celebrating the deliverance of the Lord. Only in the Pentecost offerings was yeast allowed, because it spoke of abundance.

In Matthew 16:6,11–12, Jesus said false teachers brought leaven into the lives of those who heard them. They had a religious covering for the leaven (sin) of their lives. It had infected them and was through them infecting others. Jesus warned the people to beware of their leaven. Through this parable of the leaven, He said, "Part of the reason for the swelling of the church is that it allows sinful teachings." One of the methods Satan uses to lead people astray is to work within the church and begin to tolerate sin, teach doctrines not of God, set the Word aside and so "welcome all comers" with no call to repentance whatsoever. As a result the church looks full, but is this the true church of Jesus Christ?

When Paul wrote his second letter to the Corinthians, in chapter 11 he said, "I worry about the fact that someone actually might come and preach to you another Jesus that we haven't been preaching or that they might offer to you a different spirit which you haven't received." Most cult leaders grew up in fundamentalist churches. They usually came from truth and a background of being taught the Word of God. Yet they drift so far that they become leaven the enemy uses. It is only when the Lord returns that His kingdom of hearts that are truly submitted to Him will be seen.

All these things Jesus spoke to the multitude in parables; and without a parable He did not speak to them, that it might be fulfilled which was spoken by the prophet, saying: "I will open My mouth in parables; I will utter things kept secret from the foundation of the world."

—Matthew 13:34–35

According to verse 36, the parables, which begin here in verse 44, were given to the disciples apart from the crowds. God was sharing His view of the crowds with those men that would be overseers in the years to come. Yet though the crowds were deceptively large because many in it were not with Jesus, does not mean He didn't love each one and come to bring them eternal life. It is His value of the soul of man that Jesus sets before us in the following parables.

"Again, the kingdom of heaven is like treasure hidden in a field, which a man found and hid; and for the joy over it he goes and sells all that he has and buys that field."

—Matthew 13:44

To the disciples, Jesus said, "I give My life for the world, the field. Why? To get the treasure." The teaching to the disciples is that all who believe in Him are the treasure. The good news for every saint is that even if he or she had been the only treasure in the entire field, Jesus would have come. No one can ever say God saves only a few. He doesn't. He'll save anyone who comes. He gave His life for the entire world, yet those who believe Him out of the world is a small percentage and they are indeed His treasure.

"Again, the kingdom of heaven is like a merchant seeking beautiful pearls, who, when he had found one pearl of great price, went and sold all that he had and bought it."

—Matthew 13:45–46

There are many pearls from which to choose but this master, this Savior, knows the value of the real pearl: the church, the believers, and the saints. And it is for them He gives all that He has. He is under no misconception about who truly loves Him and who is just along for the ride.

"Again, the kingdom of heaven is like a dragnet that was cast into the sea and gathered some of every kind, which when it was full, they drew to shore; and they sat down and gathered the good into vessels, but threw the bad away. So it will be at the end of the age. The angels will come forth, separate the wicked from among the just, and cast them into the furnace of fire. There will be wailing and gnashing of teeth."

—Matthew 13:47–50

As many of the apostles were fishermen, the illustration of the dragnet would certainly have been an appropriate one for them. A dragnet is a net that is thrown into the water. After it is pulled around the lake, it is brought up with fish inside—along with some rocks and weeds. Jesus said that's like the kingdom of heaven. We go into the world and throw out nets. We preach the Gospel. We sow the seed. We don't know what kind of soil it falls into or what is in our nets—but we keep sowing and we keep pulling our nets around. It's not our job to quit trying; it's our job to quit separating. God can do that. I'll just stick with the Gospel because that's the bait.

The Lord gave these parables to His disciples against a backdrop of several thousand people clamoring for His attention because He saw the success of His work very differently than they did. And the same is true today. You are either in the church only in the sense that you are in the physical building, or you belong to the church as the bride of Christ. You are either in Christ or you are not. There is no third category. There is an "in" and an "out." There is an "of" and a "not of." You want to be sure you're right with God because ultimately when you go to the Lord you won't take the crowd with you and try to argue as a group. There are no class action suits with God. You don't file on behalf of many. You go alone. And your life is hung in the balance.

God would have us see that the true church is smaller than the claimed church. Yet for those who love and believe Him, Jesus' willful and glad sacrifice saved us. Now our job is to pull the net around. His job is to figure out what we caught.

Chapter 43

A LATE-NIGHT BOAT RIDE

Mark 4:35–41
(Matthew 8:23–27; Luke 8:22–25)

The day had begun in Capernaum at Peter's house, where Jesus ministered to a man who was possessed by the Devil and left blind and mute. With everyone watching, Jesus made the man whole. Pressed for an explanation, the religious leaders said the only way Jesus could have pulled this off was to have been in league with the Devil. Jesus was both very merciful and very angry with them. He warned them that to stay on that route was to cut themselves off from ever finding life. He then began to speak to them about the kingdom through a series of parables.

Before Jesus comes to the end of this day, we see Him getting away from the crowds to go across the Sea of Galilee to Gadera. From all that the Gospels tell us, it would appear that the only reason Jesus did this was to minister to one man, because the minute He did, He came right back to where He had started. Jesus goes a long way out of His way to reach those who are hungry to know Him—even on a very long day like this one we have been following in the Gospel accounts.

> On the same day, when evening had come, He said to them, "Let us cross over to the other side." Now when they had left the multitude, they took Him along in the boat as He was. And other little boats were also with Him. And a great windstorm arose, and the waves beat into the boat, so that it was already filling. But He was in the stern, asleep on a pillow.
>
> —Mark 4:35–38

I like the fact that the disciples took Jesus "as He was." I think He had to have been tired! In His humanity, He certainly gave His all every day. With the crowds pushing and shoving and the spiritual warfare He had to face, He had to have been just worn out. As tired as He was, His last words to His disciples were, "Let's just go over to the other side."

So the disciples hoisted the sail and set off with a little flotilla of admirers tagging along. Jesus went to the stern, grabbed a boat cushion, lay on a very hard seat, and soon was fast asleep. From where He was to where He was going was roughly seven miles, a trip that could take several hours. But what a great picture. Here's our Lord sound asleep. He knew what was waiting for Him on the other side: a very violent, dangerous man who would come running right at Him the minute He got off the boat. For now He would get some rest. The old adage of the serviceman, sleep while you can!

Notice from verse 35 that Jesus had definite plans. He said to His disciples, "Let us go over to the other side." He didn't say, "Let us go under," although a few minutes later, I'm sure, the disciples thought He had! I like the fact that as I get into the boat of life in my walk with God on any given day, I don't know what lies ahead—but my Lord does. And as long as He's in the boat with me, I'm fine. That's not always an easy lesson to learn. We like it when there's smooth sailing. Then we say the Lord's with us. It's when it's really rough that we wonder where He is or what He meant, or is He wrong or did He lose control . . . I assure you He has not and so does our text before us.

Even with all of the lessons the disciples had learned that long day, there was one left to be added: when God is with you, don't get too upset about the storm. Here without warning, a huge storm arose on the Sea. Matthew, in describing the storm, used the word for "earthquake." The Sea of Galilee began to pitch and roll so violently that even these seasoned fishermen thought they were in desperate straits.

The Sea of Galilee is almost seven hundred feet below sea level, surrounded not only by hills but mountains. The Golan Heights, for example, rises several thousand feet. Between the Sea of Galilee and the Mediterranean is a thirty-mile ravine that acts like a wind tunnel. Twenty miles to the north of the Sea of Galilee is Mount Hermon, which is 9,200 feet high and very cold. So as the cold air off Mount Hermon runs underneath the heat of the desert, the pressure builds through the ravine, creating the likelihood of very bad weather. In fact, in ten minutes, the Sea of Galilee can go from being a placid lake to being an ocean with ten to fifteen-foot waves. These storms weren't unknown, yet when you read that a bunch of fishermen were beginning to panic, you should know this was quite a storm. When men who earn their living on the Sea of Galilee think they're going to die, that's a problem. These seasoned veterans were entertaining thoughts that this could be the end—and through it all, Jesus was sound asleep. That which terrified and terrorized the disciples didn't bother Jesus at all. He was, after all, going over to the other side.

That's the way life is. The stuff that bugs you doesn't bug God. He doesn't sweat, start to wring His hands, or hope you make it through the next episode. He knows everything that's coming. The trials of life that come raging in like waves, causing us to feel like our boats are sinking, don't upset Him at all. In fact, He oftentimes steers us right into them because He has lessons for us to learn in them. There's no way we'll learn to trust God unless we have to. We're not going to do it on our own or willingly. We'll only do it as we're pushed into it. That's where the disciples were. And what was worse to them was that Jesus seemed totally oblivious to their concern. They were panicking and He was out like a light. They were praying for help. He didn't seem to answer.

The interesting thing to me is that here were twelve men the Lord was training and teaching to take over when He would be gone, who were in this mess simply because they were obedient. Jonah ended up in a storm because he was disobedient. But these guys were right where they were because the Lord said, "Let's go over to the other side." And they set sail to do just that. They did what God said to do. But in so doing they came face to face with this monstrous storm.

Sometimes Christians think that if they're walking with the Lord, things will be easy. Wrong! Things will be fine, but they won't necessarily be easy. I remember somewhere in *The Chronicles of Narnia* one fellow asking Aslan the lion, "Is it safe?"

"Who said anything about safe?" the lion answered.

Just because you're walking with the Lord doesn't mean there won't be any storms. It just means that when the storm is over, you'll still be afloat and while it rages, God has good purpose and will see you though for His glory.

Here these men were in a position where their expertise at handling storms in a boat was overwhelmed by the intensity of the storm itself. And that's usually when we start praying—when our expertise runs out. As the sails tattered and the guys bailing water were losing ground, they finally went to Jesus for help. Yet notice in despair they still believed Jesus would be their help. He might for now have been their last rather than first resort, but they do now turn to Him, though with but miniscule faith and much chagrin.

> And they awoke Him and said to Him, "Teacher, do You not care that we are perishing?" Then He arose and rebuked the wind, and said to the sea, "Peace, be still!" And the wind ceased and there was a great calm.
>
> —Mark 4:38–39

Why didn't the disciples wake Jesus earlier? I suspect it was for the same reason we don't pray right away. We're very self-confident. But that's something we have to lose if we're going to do well with the Lord. We've got to lose the "I can trust in me" mentality and instead learn to trust in Him. But that's not easy because the flesh loves self-confidence. So the disciples waited until they really didn't know where else to turn. Maybe they used the excuse that Jesus was tired and they didn't want to bother Him. But "I don't want to bother the Lord" seems like a pretty weak excuse to me because the Bible is full of Him saying, "Bother Me."

Luke 8:24 recorded that they said, "Master, we're perishing." Mark 4:38 added, "Don't You care?" That's the wrong conclusion, isn't it? They felt that Jesus' sleeping meant He didn't care, which is, by the way, what you usually hear from people when God doesn't answer their prayers fast enough.

When the people of Israel complained that God didn't care, He sent Isaiah to say to them, "Zion is saying, 'The Lord has forsaken me. The Lord has forgotten me.' But can a nursing mother forget her child? Even if she could, I never could forget you. In fact, I've engraved you on the palms of My hands and you are before Me continually" (Isa. 49:14–16). To the argument that God would write them off, He said, "I've written you on

My hand. To the argument that says, 'You don't care about me anymore,' He says, 'Even human nature and all of its attachments will fail before I will fail you.'"

I like the fact that what the storm couldn't do—wake Jesus—was accomplished with just one word from one of His own. This reminds me of a recent situation at home when our five grandchildren, including a new baby, were visiting. These kids together can certainly make some noise! Throw in the dog and turn on the TV and it's really loud! But their mother was tuned in to her baby crying.

"Hear the baby?" she asked.

"No! I can't even hear myself think!" I answered.

Just like a mom and her child, all the noise in the world won't keep God from hearing you.

"Why isn't God doing something?" That's a familiar complaint. But I suggest we be careful not to make the same mistake and accuse God of sleeping while we're suffering because that is never the case. He's on board in our situations. Just because He hasn't acted doesn't mean He won't—and just because He's been silent in a situation doesn't mean He doesn't have time to calm the storm.

The guys came with accusations in their mouths and Jesus woke up. He spoke to the wind and the waves, and the storm stopped. The sea became glass. The Greek phrase for "Be still" is "Put a muzzle on it. Knock it off." Immediately, things were painfully quiet. I love the picture. Here was Jesus, quiet as can be, talking to twelve guys dripping wet and out of breath. They needed to learn that unexpected storms were not out of God's hand, and just because He didn't do something right away didn't mean He wasn't in charge.

> But He said to them, "Why are you so fearful? How is it that you have no faith?"
> And they feared exceedingly, and said to one another, "Who can this be, that even the wind and the sea obey Him!"
> —Mark 4:40–41

The account of this story in Matthew 8 says that before He spoke to the waves, Jesus said to the men, "Why are you afraid and have such little faith?" I'm glad I wasn't part of that group—they always were getting in trouble! It's not surprising that their fear of the storm immediately turned to fear of the Lord because the minute God works, the outlook absolutely changes. It's no longer us but Him who is in focus.

I find that seems to be the case so often. When our faith fails us, we can say and do the dumbest things. It's not that we don't love the Lord, but anything we might have learned we lay aside for the sake of freaking out. Then when God calms the storm, we want to say, "I knew He was going to do that." But the Lord says, "No you didn't." And then we're embarrassed, wondering why we panicked in the first place.

You can't sink if the Lord is on board. The answer for fear is to rest in His presence even in the storm. That's a lesson we have to learn.

"Take heed how you hear," Jesus said in Luke 8. What value or weight do you give that which you're hearing? If the Lord is the Lord and His Word is life, then how you hear His Word will be far different from how you hear the word of your professor, the newscaster, or the latest author because they don't carry the same weight or value or authority as the Lord's Word.

Maybe you're in a storm right now. You've been bailing water; you're close to panic, and, if the truth were known, you're pretty mad at God for sleeping through the whole thing. You can't wake Him up no matter how hard you scream. But one word from Him will turn your fear into worship. The good thing is, you can hear that word even before your situation gets better. Even as the wind might howl, if you listen, you'll hear Him say, "I will never leave you nor forsake you. I'll give you peace that passes understanding. You'll be more than a conqueror through Me."

Listen carefully because how you hear is as important as what you hear.

Chapter 44

MAN OF THE TOMBS

Luke 8:26–39
(Matthew 8:28–34; Mark 5:1–20)

In the story before us, we come to the end of the very long day that began when, after healing a man that was born deaf and blind, Jesus was accused of being in league with the Devil. This particular account can be found in all of the synoptic Gospels—Matthew, Mark, and Luke—and is one that gives us great insight into the Devil's character and his will to seek our destruction. Let's join the man of the tombs!

> Then they sailed to the country of the Gadarenes, which is opposite Galilee. And when He stepped out on the land, there met Him a certain man from the city who had demons for a long time. And he wore no clothes, nor did he live in a house but in the tombs.
>
> —Luke 8:26–27

It is about a seven-mile trip across the Sea of Galilee from Capernaum to the town of Gadara, which used to be called Gergesa. Because the tribe of Gad had settled there, it was known as the Gadarene area. It was the first of ten cities called the Decapolis that moved inland from the Mediterranean and were basically Gentile towns, this one having a Jewish enclave. But it is also an interesting place on the Sea of Galilee because it is the only site where there are cliffs above the lake. Everywhere else along the Sea of Galilee, the land is only gently sloped. But not here. The cliffs are high enough where a fall from them would be fatal.

The man who met Jesus, possessed by many Devils, causes me to wonder if the storm at sea hadn't been demonically driven, because the only reason that Jesus crossed the sea was evidently to heal him. This man came running to meet Jesus the moment His foot touched the shore. And we are told that he had had demons in his life for a long time.

For "unclean spirits," Mark used a Greek word that means "that which perverts or destroys." Here is a man whose life was being destroyed by the Devil—emotionally, physically, and spiritually. This should not be surprising because whenever the occult rises in a culture, so does mental illness, drug use, pornography, and suicide. The Devil certainly looks to destroy. It's what he desires and what he knows.

If you take the three gospel accounts together, we see quite a bit about this poor man. Although he used to have a home and family, he now was living in isolation in a graveyard consisting of caves in the side of a hill. He was an extremely violent man. Passersby ran when they saw him because he had a tendency to hurt, chase, or threaten people. He had tremendous power that could tear the shackles and chains meant to restrain him.

Luke tells us that once in a while, the Devil himself would drive him into the wilderness where he would wander about aimlessly. Mark tells us he would gash himself with stones. Out of control, out of his senses, self-destructive, scarred for life—what a picture of what the enemy of our souls would do to us if given half a chance!

The Bible teaches us that the primary work of the enemy is that of deception and subtlety. When Paul wrote about the Devil in 2 Corinthians 11:13–14, he said Satan likes to transform himself into an angel of light. Most of the Devil's work in society today tends to be misdirection—offering people another Gospel, another Jesus, another way of life. But in the cases of demon possession seen in the Gospels and in the book of Revelation, when the Devil is allowed to fully take over, we are given the clearest picture of his intent, of what he would like to accomplish if allowed. It is one of harassment and harm, destruction and opposition, isolation, unending misery and death.

When Paul wrote to the Ephesians in chapter 6:11–18, he said of our battle with the Devil that we should be wise and strong in the Lord and in the power of His might, and that we should put on the whole armor of God so we can stand against his wiles. He said the Devil comes against us in forms of principalities and powers, in rulers of darkness, and in spiritual hosts of wickedness—different rankings of demonic forces that have as their common goal the destruction of man and God's work in the church. The good news, however, is once you're saved, the enemy can no longer seek to dwell in you for you have become a vessel filled with the Holy Spirit.

"Greater is He that is in you than he that is in the world," John declared (1 John 4:4). At the church, we sometimes get calls from believers who think they're possessed by the Devil. But that's impossible. God doesn't rent out rooms. He takes the whole building. When He moves in, the Devil has to move out. You can be harassed. You can be oppressed. The Devil can try to do a great many things, but what he can't do is take over a life that's been given to the Lord.

If you want to know how you're supposed to approach anything that has to do with the Devil, the Bible gives us three Rs: recognize, resist, and then rejoice in the victory God provides. We're told to stay away from anything that relates to the occult, spiritism, or an ungodly lifestyle. In cultures where there is a tremendous hunger and willingness to practice voodoo magic, it seems the Lord at times allows men to experience what they are seeking . . . No one, however, would want what this man had.

> When he saw Jesus, he cried out, fell down before Him, and with a loud voice said, "What have I to do with You, Jesus, Son of the Most High God? I beg You,

> do not torment me!" For He had commanded the unclean spirit to come out of the man. For it had often seized him, and he was kept under guard, bound with chains and shackles; and he broke the bonds and was driven by the demons into the wilderness.
>
> —Luke 8:28–29

When Jesus said in John 10:10 that the thief comes only to kill, steal, and destroy, He wasn't kidding. The Devil has only that as his agenda. Even as temptation may on the surface look promising—in the long run it will wipe us out.

Notice that when Jesus showed up, the Devil needed to retreat. Jesus had only to put one foot on the land and this man fell down in worship. I love this picture because it dramatically shows the Devil is no match for Jesus.

Notice also that the demons in this man immediately recognized our Lord, calling Him the Son of the Most High God. In fact, in nearly every case in the Bible where Jesus has a conversation with someone who is demon-possessed, the demons always acknowledge who He is. They recognize His authority and beg for mercy. James 2:19 tells us that the Devil believes God and trembles. Yet it's not enough for us just to believe Jesus is God intellectually. We must submit to Him willingly. And that's where the Devil went the other way.

"Have mercy upon us," the demons cry. Isn't that an interesting request, considering what they had done to this man for so many years—ruining his life and his family and stealing his sanity and dignity? Now they want mercy?

Matthew 8:29 added that the demons also said to Jesus, "Don't torment us before our time," which tells us the enemy knows his time is short. He knows what's coming and he knows what is awaiting him. He knows his days are numbered. The trouble he's making is done with a cognizance that this is not going to go on forever.

> Jesus asked him, saying, "What is your name?" And he said, "Legion," because many demons had entered him. And they begged Him that He would not command them to go out into the abyss.
>
> —Luke 8:30–31

A Roman legion consisted of six thousand men. That doesn't mean there were six thousand demons in this man's life. Satan is a liar, after all. But it does appear there were quite a few—enough to drive two thousand pigs off a cliff. Mark tells us there was an innumerable amount of demons. One alone would have been bad enough—imagine this!

In addition to begging not to be tormented before their time, the demons added that they didn't want to be sent to the abyss. The Greek word for this is *abusso* and is a reference to the bottomless pit wherein demons are kept until they are judged and cast into the lake of fire.

We get a few looks at this place in the book of Revelation. It is from there that thousands of locust and scorpion-like demons will be released to torment those on the earth for five months. We are also told that Satan will be bound for a thousand years in the *abusso* during the time Jesus reigns on the earth.

I am thrilled with this picture of Jesus' authority. We never can beat the enemy on our own because he's a lot stronger and smarter than we are. But once the Lord steps into the equation, there is never a protracted battle. In fact, even the battle of Armageddon is over in a couple of words. It didn't take weeks or months for this man to be released. All it took was one word from Jesus: "Go."

> Now a herd of many swine were feeding there on the mountain. So they begged Him that He would permit them to enter them. And He permitted them. Then the demons went out of the man and entered the swine, and the herd ran violently down the steep place into the lake and drowned.
>
> —Luke 8:32–33

Mark tells us this herd numbered two thousand, which represented a huge business enterprise. The value of them must have been astronomical in that day. It would appear this was a Jewish community apparently raising for profit animals that were unclean and forbidden by Jewish law in Deuteronomy 14. So in the process of delivering this one man, Jesus also pretty much put an end to an illegal cottage industry there.

> When those who fed them saw what had happened, they fled and told it in the city and in the country. Then they went out to see what had happened, and came to Jesus, and found the man from whom the demons had departed, sitting at the feet of Jesus, clothed and in his right mind. And they were afraid. They also who had seen it told them by what means he who had been demon-possessed was healed.
>
> —Luke 8:34–36

I can understand the reaction of the herd keepers. No one would believe them if they said the pigs under their care became simultaneously demon-possessed and ran off a cliff. So to absolve themselves of the responsibility, they quickly got to the herd's owners and kept around the eyewitnesses for firsthand testimony. On arrival, the owners not only didn't find their herd, but saw this man whom they had known to be violent and out of his mind sitting at Jesus' feet, clothed and in his right mind, his dignity restored. It left many in fear—who is this Man? In fact we read this amazing response from the townspeople:

> Then the whole multitude of the surrounding region of the Gadarenes asked Him to depart from them, for they were seized with great fear. And He got into the boat and returned.
>
> —Luke 8:37

Now don't you think that if you found a violently insane man you'd had to deal with for years completely delivered, you might want to say, "Lord, could You hang around for a while? My daughter hasn't been feeling well and maybe I could talk to You about how my life has been going." You'd think this miracle would have stirred up some manner of hunger within the people. After all, when Jesus had ministered to the woman at the well in Samaria, we read in John 4 that when she went into town to tell everyone what had happened they came out to see Him and said, "Could You stay with us?" Not this town. They said, "You've got to leave." And instead of fearing the Lord in the sense of wanting to believe and follow Him, they wanted to get rid of Him because His power and authority were a tremendous threat to their way of life.

"You've ruined our business," they said. "You are apparently a bigger God than the one that used to dwell in this guy and we really don't want You messing around with our lives." Their fear was in their loss rather than in their sin. They weren't ready to change or repent, because they placed less value on deliverance than they did on their financial hopes.

I think the last sentence in verse 37 might be one of the saddest in the entire Bible. If you don't want Jesus in your life, He'll leave. He goes back down to the boat. He didn't argue with the people nor did He break down the door. He knocked, but they refused to open. To those who are hungry, He can help. But to those who don't want Him, He'll just go on to the next town.

> Now the man from whom the demons had departed begged Him that he might be with Him. But Jesus sent him away, saying, "Return to your own house, and tell what great things God has done for you." And he went his way and proclaimed throughout the whole city what great things Jesus had done for him.
>
> —Luke 8:38–39

This is the only man in the entire Gospel record whose request to follow Jesus was denied. Why was he not allowed to go with Jesus? Because Jesus wanted him to remain in this town that had rejected Him as a witness of what He had done and of what He had wanted to do for them. Throughout the Bible this is the way we find God working most often in the area of evangelism. He changes a life and then He leaves the person in his old environment to be a light.

I have found that when most Christians first get saved they want the Lord to come back immediately. "Lord, I'm saved," they pray. "Let's get outta here. Let's wrap this up. We don't want to be here five more minutes."

But the Lord usually says, "No, you go back home and be a light. You're not the person you used to be—under the influence of the enemy, in torment and struggle, in darkness, and in bondage. You're free. Go back and tell them what I've done for you."

I think every time this guy walked to the store in this Gadarene town, people said, "There's the guy who used to be possessed by the Devil. But Jesus delivered him." If you asked, he'd tell you. And one day in heaven, I suspect we'll see him sitting with a group of saints from his area—the fruit of his ministry.

Maybe you think you can't be a witness because you don't know what to say. But you don't need to be a Bible scholar to bear witness of Jesus. Just go and tell people the great things God has done for you—how He's changed your life. This guy didn't know much more than, "I was possessed and then the Lord came. But with one word—'Go'—to the demons inside me, Jesus delivered me. And with another word—'Stay'—here I am."

Mark adds in chapter 5 that this man didn't stop with his own town but began to work his way through the Decapolis region, which is interesting because only one of the Decapolis cities is on the western side of the Jordan. The other nine were on the eastern side, which meant they were entirely Gentile cities. This man then might very possibly have been the first missionary to the Gentiles the Lord sent!

I know most Christians would rather just get on the boat and leave the area—escape the rat race. I think for some of us our greatest desire for the Lord to come back is not necessarily so we'll be with Him but so we'll be out of here. This guy wanted to be with the Lord, but the Lord said, "Stick around. I've got work for you to do here. I need a light in a dark place." That's really where God sends us. The only criterion is that you experience God's work in such a way that you have a story to tell. The change in this man's life was dramatic. So was the change in ours. We were dead; now we're alive. We were lost; now we're found. We were living for ourselves; now we live for Him.

Will everyone listen? No. But there will be enough who will that our lives will have great value to God's plans. Like this man of the tombs, our testimonies can reach a country. All we need to know is what God has done for us and what He promises to do for others. Then we need to shout it from the hilltops!

Chapter 45

THE DESPERATE FIND JESUS

Luke 8:40–56
(Matthew 9:18–26; Mark 5:21–43)

After healing the man from Gadera, Jesus returned to Capernaum, where there were two people who desperately needed Him to work in their lives. We read:

> So it was, when Jesus returned, that the multitude welcomed Him, for they were all waiting for Him.
>
> —Luke 8:40

What a contrast to verse 37 where the multitude had said, "Get out of here." Here we see an open-hearted group of folks gathered to meet Him, waiting for Him!

Years ago, when we went to Holland to help establish an outreach fellowship, the people were so closed to the Gospel that they actually lit on fire the tracts we handed them—right in front of us. We had been there for three days ministering when the police called one night, saying, "We found three tracts on the beach. They're yours. Come and get them or you'll go to jail." But when we went to the Philippines and began to simply share the Gospel, many hearts turned to Jesus and were saved. We have experienced great open-mindedness in some parts of the world and yet hard hearts elsewhere.

On one side of the lake, no one wanted Jesus to stay. On the other side, they couldn't wait for Him to return.

> And behold, there came a man named Jairus, and he was a ruler of the synagogue. And he fell down at Jesus' feet and begged Him to come to his house, for he had an only daughter about twelve years of age, and she was dying. But as He went, the multitudes thronged Him.
>
> —Luke 8:41–42

In this group of people waiting for Jesus to return was one of the synagogue rulers. In Luke 7:1–2, a group of men from the synagogue had come to Jesus asking for His help in healing a centurion's servant. It very well could be that Jairus had been a part of this group. We don't know Jairus' position concerning Jesus. We do know that he lived in the town that saw more miracles than anywhere else. I am sure that if Jairus believed in Jesus, he did so quietly because the cost was so great. And if he didn't, he was at least aware of all that had been going on.

Back in Luke 4:33–37, there had been the demon-possessed man who had walked right into the service and whom the Lord healed in front of everyone. No doubt Jairus would have been there. There had been a demon-possessed man left blind and mute delivered as well just up the street from the synagogue in Peter's house that the whole town knew about. Luke wrote that in addition to those men, Jesus healed many others. But it is difficult to determine where Jairus' heart was in regard to the Lord—until now that is. On this day we find him waiting for Jesus' boat with tremendous anxiety because his daughter was dying. Regardless of what he might have thought about Jesus up to this point, from this point forward his only hope is in Him.

It does seem that extreme circumstances quickly weed out of your life the things that are relatively unimportant. Everybody else might be talking about the high price of gasoline, but when your daughter is dying you don't care about the price of gas, how busy the freeway is, or the guy next door who can't seem to turn down his stereo. Suddenly you cut to the chase and the things of value are recognized, while everything else is put on the back burner. Here was a religious leader who now swallowed his pride even though he had great status in town, and who turned his back on all of the social pressure that might have otherwise caused him to reject Jesus or at least keep his distance from Him. He said goodbye to the religious establishment, because after this day, he no longer would have a job in the synagogue. He had taken a stand with Jesus and, before a huge crowd, fell on his face, begging Him for help. With panic in his voice and tears in his eyes, he laid everything aside that everyone else might have counted valuable to seek to redeem the one thing that mattered to him the most.

Jairus had left the house that morning going to look for Jesus. "Where is He?" he must have asked the first person he could find.

"He's gone," came the answer.

"Where did He go?" Jairus pressed.

"I don't know. But we think that's His boat coming over there."

"Stand back," Jairus might have said. "I need to talk to Him first."

Of the many hundreds there, it was Jairus who seemed to be agonizing the most. He would have been given priority as the ruler of the synagogue. People would have backed away. He would have been allowed access. So here he was, with his robes of authority and his religious persona, in the dust of the road, crying out to the Lord.

Mark 5 tells us, and Matthew 9 fills in the blanks, that when Jesus landed, Jairus said to him, "My daughter is at the point of death. Could You come and lay Your hand upon her that she might be healed?" In response, Jesus turned and went with him. But then Mark records the same thing that is recorded here: that as He turned to go, the crowd pressed in around Him.

Suddenly Jairus was being suffocated and there was no time to waste. His daughter was dying. But crowds don't move very quickly and a crowd this large may not move at all. Everything seemed to have come to a standstill.

236

God paints for us this very desperate picture. In the midst of it all stood Jairus so beside himself, Jesus so willing to help, and the crowds so demanding, and they all became a backdrop for what happened next. With no time to lose and every moment a seeming eternity, Jesus now stops dead in His tracks. Certainly Jairus must have thought he hadn't made it clear to the Lord just how seriously ill his daughter was. Let's go Jesus, no time to waste! What in the world is going on here?

> Now a woman, having a flow of blood for twelve years, who had spent all her livelihood on physicians and could not be healed by any, came from behind and touched the border of His garment. And immediately her flow of blood stopped.
>
> —Luke 8:43–44

In addition to Jairus, there was another desperate person in the crowd: a woman who had been hemorrhaging for twelve years. It was chronic and persistent, severe and debilitating. And because the Law said blood was unclean, her illness ostracized her as well. No hugging her children or her family, no going to synagogue, and no hanging out with everyone for dinner. She was on her own and by herself. If that wasn't bad enough, the cultural bias of the day attributed this type of illness to an immoral lifestyle. So not only had this woman put up with this illness for twelve years, she'd also had to endure all of the allegations, accusations, and crowd whispers as well.

Doctor Luke tells us she had spent everything she had on doctors. Mark adds that she had suffered many things at the hands of these physicians. It would seem she went to doctors with cash in hand, looking for hope, and was given all kinds of promises of what they could do if only she'd pay first. And now she found herself twelve years later out of money and literally out of hope.

Like Jairus, she too had run out of options. Unlike him, however, she wasn't ready to fall down in front of Jesus before the crowd and ask for help. She was just as desperate, but she was convinced that if she could but touch the hem of His garment, all would be well. So she put her plan into motion. She pushed through the crowd, broke the ceremonial law, and grabbed one of the tassels that hung from Jesus' robe.

In Numbers 15:37–41, God told His people through Moses that they were to put blue tassels on the hem of their clothes so that every time they looked at them they'd be reminded of heaven. Everyone wore them, and Jesus was no exception.

For the word *touch*, Luke used the word *haptomai*, which means "to cling or hold on to." After the woman accomplished her mission, she turned to leave because she didn't want to be seen. By being in the crowd at all she had broken the ceremonial law—and right in front of Jairus, ruler of the synagogue, no less. Yet as she touched the edge of Jesus' garment, we read that her flow of blood stopped. Mark wrote that she felt she was healed. She knew without a doubt God had just touched her life and healed her!

> And Jesus said, "Who touched Me?" When all denied it, Peter and those with him said, "Master, the multitudes throng and press You and You say, 'Who touched Me?'"
>
> —Luke 8:45

"Who touched Me?" Jesus asked. His disciples must have thought He certainly was kidding.

It could have been him or him or her or them, they must have thought. *All of them, probably.*

They couldn't distinguish between the pressing of the crowd and the touch of faith. But God can. God is very aware when faith is activated—when we look to Him with all we have, as weak as we might be. Jesus knew His power had gone forth to meet a need in faith, and He wasn't going to let the woman get away without speaking to her.

> But Jesus said, "Somebody touched Me, for I perceived power going out from Me." Now when the woman saw that she was not hidden, she came trembling; and falling down before Him, she declared to Him in the presence of all the people the reason she had touched Him and how she was healed immediately.
>
> —Luke 8:46–47

I don't know if the woman looked back and Jesus was looking right at her or if the crowd parted and she was the only one standing there. I am positive she just wanted to get away. *"Keep moving. Keep moving. Don't look back,"* she must have said to herself. But Jesus persisted.

So she came trembling and fell down before Him in the spot Jairus had been only a moment earlier. It was hard for her to do this in the crowd. Women weren't to speak publicly in that culture. Besides, she had one of those "questionable" illnesses. She had snuck in among the crowd and, in so doing, had defiled many.

Then there was Jairus, who if looks could kill was saying, "I wish you were dead. You're holding us up. My daughter needs help."

No one seemed to be happy she was there. No doubt she really was going to get it now! But her desperation had brought her and Jesus would welcome her.

Jesus stopped this woman. She was caught. But the only reason He called her out is that He didn't want private disciples. The same is still true. The opinions of others shouldn't matter to us. We should be interested in only one opinion: God's.

> And He said to her, "Daughter, be of good cheer; your faith has made you well. Go in peace."
>
> —Luke 8:48

What more loving response could she have heard? Her hand may have touched Jesus' robe, but it was her heart that touched Him. He saw her faith, her persistence, and her desire. Her faith was far from perfect. She took what she needed and left. But Jesus will meet us right where we are and this was enough for Him when it came to this suffering woman. "It's your faith, not My tassel that has made you whole," He said.

> While He was still speaking, someone came from the ruler of the synagogue's house, saying to him, "Your daughter is dead. Do not trouble the Teacher." But when Jesus heard it, He answered him, saying, "Do not be afraid; only believe, and she will be made well."
>
> —Luke 8:49–50

As He stood speaking with the woman, the most horrible news arrived from Jairus' home. His daughter had died and it was too late! Jesus quickly turned to speak words of encouragement to Jairus. The verb tense literally reads, "Don't be afraid. Keep trusting Me." This would imply that when Jairus had come, he was trusting the Lord in the way God intended. But with this latest report, his faith would have all but disappeared. Whenever you find great faith on display in the Bible, it is always opposed by only one thing: fear. There is fear that we don't believe that God can do what we're asking, fear that we're wrong in even asking, fear that we've got it all backward, and fear that maybe it's too late. No doubt that is why Jesus' first words to Jairus were, "Don't be afraid." Jesus with that continued to head towards Jairus' home.

> When He came into the house, He permitted no one to go in except Peter, James, and John, and the father and the mother of the girl. Now all wept and mourned for her, but He said, "Do not weep, she is not dead, but sleeping." And they ridiculed Him, knowing that she was dead. But He put them all outside, took her by the hand and called, saying, "Little girl, arise."
>
> —Luke 8:51–54

He arrived at the house to find that the professional mourners already had set up shop. In that culture, weepers were hired when there was a death in the family because the louder the weeping, the greater the love. When Jesus got there, He told the weepers they could go home. "She's not dead," He said. "She's just sleeping."

The mourners began to laugh. "Hey, You're talking to professionals here," they said. "We don't even go on the clock until the person is really dead—and we've already been wailing for quite some time."

But Jesus kicked them out and brought in His inner circle along with Mom and Dad to wake up the sleeping little girl.

Jesus uses the term *sleeping* of saints when they die to explain that they're not dead but at rest in Him. He only used the word *sleeping* of unbelievers when He talked about their spiritual condition. Mark tells us in 5:41 that Jesus grabbed the girl by the hand and said, "Talitha cumi." Literally translated, "Little lamb, arise." I wouldn't be surprised if this was the same endearing term Mom and Dad had used to wake up their little girl every morning.

> Then her spirit returned, and she arose immediately. And He commanded that
> she be given something to eat.
>
> —Luke 8:55

People sometimes ask for the biblical definition of physical death. Here it is: when your spirit leaves your body, you're physically dead. You can keep the body breathing and the heart beating, but the test of brain activity is a pretty good one because it is our souls that think and choose and process information. When the Lord takes the spirit, the flesh just becomes an old place to dwell. Here in this little girl's body, now dead because her spirit had departed, it is the Lord Himself who demanded that the spirit return. And when the spirit moved back into the body, the body immediately was able to act again. She sat up immediately.

"Give her something to eat," Jesus said.

"That's kind of trivial," you might say. No, it's not. The body requires food to function. She probably hadn't eaten for quite some time. She could have used some food! There would be no miracle necessary when simply eating would suffice. What balance between the miraculous and the mundane.

> And her parents were astonished, but He charged them to tell no one what had
> happened.
>
> —Luke 8:56

The crowds had been huge and growing yet Jesus had many more months of ministry ahead. The crowds were filled with religious folks and the sign-seekers, many there for all the wrong reasons. So during this period, Jesus often told people not to say anything regarding His work in them and for them so more folks would not be attracted to Him simply due to a miracle. But as you might suspect, these parents didn't listen to that part at all. How could they have really? Matthew 9:26 says the report of this went everywhere. They just couldn't hide what God had done.

Like Jairus, we can have the wrong religion and feel very comfortable—until it can't meet the issues of life and death. Or like the woman, we can allow social stigma to keep us from coming to Jesus—until we have spent all we have to no avail.

Hopefully, there comes a point in our lives where the desperation in our hearts outweighs our reasons for not coming to the Lord. And in our desperation, we will find Him. But why wait until we're desperate? Here two desperate lives collided on a lakeside, both looking to Jesus, both tugging on Him for time, both stretched to the limit—and both made whole. Won't you come to Him today?

Chapter 46

ANOTHER OPPORTUNITY LOST

Mark 6:1–6
(Matthew 13:54–58; Luke 4:16–24)

The following story in the chronology reflects on two lessons: First, God doesn't give up on us so easily. Second, it's very dangerous to become so familiar with Him that we begin to settle in and find ourselves losing out on what He has available for us.

On the one hand, the Lord is very willing to keep coming to us. But on the other, once we know Him we have to be willing to keep coming to Him.

Here in Mark 6, Jesus went back to where He had grown up. All three of the synoptic Gospels record that whenever the Lord met with those from Nazareth, He always had a difficult time—and the event before us would prove to be no exception.

> Then He went out from there and came to His own country, and His disciples followed Him. And when the Sabbath had come, He began to teach in the synagogue. And many hearing Him were astonished, saying, "Where did this Man get these things? And what wisdom is this which is given to Him, that such mighty works are performed by His hands!"
>
> —Mark 6:1–2

After healing Jairus' daughter, Jesus left Capernaum and traveled twenty-five miles to His hometown of Nazareth. This time He arrived not as the "hometown boy made good," but as a rabbi with a group of students in tow.

From the way these verses are written, it appears He did very little street ministry in town that week. Maybe this time He was quietly gathering people so He might once again offer them life in this place where, on His previous visit, the townspeople had tried to throw Him off a cliff. This is a good lesson for us on not giving up so easily when people refuse to hear, because Jesus went back even to the places where people were trying to string Him up. God is patient and merciful and so should we His people be.

On the Sabbath He was able to speak to the entire city. And the initial reaction was, in many ways, like it had been the first time. The people were amazed and astonished basically at two things: His wisdom and His power. He was different from the scribes and Pharisees. He was able to do what no one else had done. He had no formal education. He hadn't gone to the best schools in Jerusalem. He didn't have a diploma from the rabbinical college. Yet His insights and interpretation of the Scriptures and the ideas He expounded stopped people in their tracks. He was wiser than the rest. He spoke exactly to people's needs.

And if that wasn't enough, stories about Him were everywhere. Someone would say to someone else, "Did you hear what took place in Capernaum last week? Apparently some little kid died and His parents called Jesus—and the kid sat up and started talking!" Everyone was aware that He had done some amazing things.

Yet the townsfolk's astonishment was tempered by a familiarity with Him that bred contempt. Therefore, rather than saying, "Maybe He's God," they began to say, "We know Him. He can't be God."

> "Is this not the carpenter, the Son of Mary, and brother of James, Joses, Judas, and Simon? And are not His sisters here with us?" So they were offended at Him.
>
> —Mark 6:3

Our biblical accounts seems to indicate that Joseph died when Jesus was a young man. If this is true, as the oldest son Jesus would have been obligated to go to work to provide for His family. He would have become the village handyman. He could have built the cabinets in your kitchen! Knowing Him like this for years, the townspeople were now "offended" at Him. The Greek word for *offended* is *skandalon*. It means "to trip over." The people couldn't reconcile the wisdom they were hearing with the fact that it was coming from someone they had watched grow up.

When it comes to human relationships, the saying that familiarity breeds contempt is absolutely correct because we're all sinners. In other words, the closer you get to an individual you respect or admire, the less you like him because the more you see his flaws. That's inevitable. But that isn't true with Jesus because He doesn't have a single flaw. Therefore, to know Him is to love Him all the more. He has no sin to uncover, no failure to excuse. The townspeople were offended—but they should have been convicted.

> But Jesus said to them, "A prophet is not without honor except in his own country, among his own relatives, and in his own house."
>
> —Mark 6:4

Jesus quoted a very well known proverb. Usually the greater distance from home you are, the greater honor you're given. I think part of the reason I had such a hard time witnessing to my parents was that they were the ones who changed my diaper and told me two plus two was not eleven. What could I possibly know that they didn't?

What is the danger of familiarity? For us as Christians, the greatest danger is becoming complacent and dull in our spiritual lives because we've become comfortable with the way we practice our faith. The joy with which we once approached the Lord gets lost in the familiarity with the habit. And although there is motion, the emotion of it falls by the wayside because we forget the privilege we have of talking with God, coming to worship, and knowing our sins are forgiven. Because we are no longer awed by His love, spiritual disciplines become a chore. We become comfortable with our habits instead of hungry for the Lord—and our spiritual lives suffer as a result.

> Now He could do no mighty work there, except that He laid His hands on a few sick people and healed them. And He marveled because of their unbelief. Then He went about the villages in a circuit, teaching.
>
> —Mark 6:5–6

Jesus marveled at the people's unbelief. What in your life causes God to marvel? I have known folks who have seen God's power and have had answers to prayer and yet still seem to have a very nominal relationship with God. I don't understand that. I don't understand why you ever would have to ask a Christian if he was going to church. I would think going to church would be a given. Are you reading your Bible? Given. Are you praying? Given. What in the world is wrong when you have to tell the saints of God to do these things?

Notice in verse 5 that the people's unbelief hindered the work Jesus wanted to accomplish. Don't get this wrong. God could work if He wanted to because, being omnipotent, He is governed only by His own will.

If God had willed to work, He could have. It isn't that He couldn't have worked—it's that He wouldn't have worked because the atmosphere in which He works is that of faith. To perform a miracle in the absence of hearts trusting Him would only have hardened the people's hearts all the more. Yet Jesus responds even to the smallest amount of faith.

Years ago, we were in Hungary teaching in a Bible school for a week. On the way home through Budapest, the church's pastor was away with his wife on their anniversary so he asked me to teach Sunday morning. Pastors, like others who speak publicly, rely on their emotions, facial expressions, and energy to communicate, but the minute one has to speak through an interpreter, all those things become useless. As I taught I also discovered that my three words in English my require 10 in Hungarian. So the flow, the mannerisms, the cultural examples all fell by the wayside and I was left with, in reality all I needed, the pure Word of God.

"Be sure to give an altar call at the end of the service," the pastor had said.

When I got to the altar call, I was sure nothing would happen. But I dutifully said, "If you want to give your life to Jesus, you can come forward right now"—and a dozen people immediately rose and came to the front. I learned yet again how powerful is God's Word.

The next week, I gave the same message to a church in Chicago. I was at my charming best. I used illustrations all of the Chicagoans would understand. I worked in White Sox jokes and Cubby fan jokes. I talked to them about their mayor. I had it all covered. But as far as I could tell, there was absolutely no response. Yet again I was reminded that God's work has nothing to do with me and everything to do with His Word and faith in Him.

Jesus marveled at the unbelief of the people of Nazareth, because He gave them God's Word yet they didn't hear it. He wanted to do so much more. He came to bring life. But a few sick folks were all that were willing to believe.

Familiarity certainly can keep you from the joy of knowing the Lord. And a lack of faith will hinder all that God wants to do. God looks for faith, so we need to keep our relationship with Him alive and well. If we can stay close to the Lord and not let the practice of our faith become familiar, God can do great things. If that's hindered, it's not Him who's hindering it. It's us because God is more than willing. In fact, as He did in Nazareth, He'll come back again and again looking to do His work.

Chapter 47

Learning to Serve By His Power

Mark 6:7–13
(Matthew 10:1–42; Luke 9:1–6)

As we come to Mark 6:7, Jesus is about to take His disciples from sitting and learning to going and doing. In the first year of His ministry, He was in Jerusalem, where the crowds were small. After John the Baptist's arrest, however, He took up the torch and came into the Galilee area. The crowds grew immensely—as did the opposition. Here in Mark 6, we are coming to the end of His one-and-a half-year ministry in Galilee. His last year would be spent heading south into Jerusalem and the surrounding areas. Now, with His last year upon Him, Jesus would take His disciples to the next step.

Up to this time, they had been able to sit around and say, "Boy, that was cool. Did you see that?" But now they were going to have to get up and, relying on His power, act on His Word. It's one thing to come to church and learn, but if that's all you're doing, not only are you not finding God's best for your life, but you'll never get beyond getting fat in the Lord. Ministry doesn't end with you. It ends with your going out and allowing God to use you.

In Luke 10, a little bit down the road, Jesus sends out seventy of His disciples two by two as well. But this time He sent only the twelve. They went out and preached that the kingdom of heaven was at hand. They called people to repent and turn in faith to Jesus, the Messiah. In the process, God empowered them to minister to the sick and to see people freed from demon possession.

In verses 7 through 13, we see the disciples' marching orders. Only the last two verses give us the result of it all. And for the most part, in all of the Gospel accounts the marching orders were what God put His greatest focus upon. He focused less on the result of their ministry and more on their willingness to do what He asked of them.

If you read this account in Matthew, you find that directly following His appearance in Nazareth, Jesus began heading through the cities and villages in Galilee and teaching in the synagogues, and that He was moved with compassion because the multitudes were like sheep that had no shepherd. So the disciples' ministry originated in the heart of God. He saw people as lost and wanted to send His own to them with good news of salvation and hope.

That hasn't changed. That's still the heart of God for lost man and still the call from God for each of us.

> And He called the twelve to Himself, and began to send them out two by two, and gave them power over unclean spirits.
>
> —Mark 6:7

I don't know about you, but I think if I had been one of those twelve guys, I might very well have balked at this. They had been to Nazareth twice. The first time, the townspeople had all but killed Jesus. The next time, they all but chased Him out of town by their unbelief and rejection of Him.

"I'm going to have you do what I do," Jesus told the twelve.

I'm sure I would have said, "Why? You're doing it just fine. I don't want to have to face that kind of stuff!"

Yet notice that the Lord equipped and empowered them. He gave them power, the Greek word here is *exousia*, meaning a privilege of power and authority based on relationship. These twelve very ordinary guys in training with Jesus are now given the privilege of serving God by His power upon their lives.

Whenever I read about this commissioning, I long for the outpouring of the Holy Spirit upon us so we too might go out in His strength to meet needs. It would be very wrong for us to excuse ourselves from serving Him just because we feel we can't. "I don't know what to do. I don't know what to say. I don't think I'm very prepared" translates only to "I'm unwilling to go."

Yet it is the Holy Spirit's work not only to save us but to prepare us to serve God that sets Christianity apart from every other religion. For example, Buddhists can tell you the problem with the world is its materialistic outlook. Yet Buddha has no power to deliver you from it. He can point out the problem; he just can't fix it. In all of the human religions, the incredibly frustrating thing is there is always a problem but never a solution. Not one that works where the power brought to bear is beyond yourself.

When Jeremiah wrote in chapter 13:23 about people trying to do good when they basically are wicked, he said, "If the Ethiopian could change his color or the leopard could change his spots, maybe you who are accustomed to doing evil could do good." In other words, if people could change their very nature, they'd have a chance. But religion can't change our nature. Only the Holy Spirit can. He can put a new heart within us. He can empower us to live for God. But we can't.

"Without Me, you can do nothing," Jesus said.

"Through Christ, I can do all things," Paul proclaimed.

In going out, the disciples experienced both sides of that truth. Jesus gave them power and privilege to deal with the Devil and disease, to preach the kingdom, and to call men to repentance. He gave them might and He gave them right.

Notice the disciples were sent out two by two. More than anything else, this would provide encouragement for them. When John the Baptist sent out His disciples, He sent them out two by two as well. When Jesus later sent out the seventy, it was two by two again. I think that's a great way to learn. We need encouragement as we step out to serve, and joining others in that task makes it easier for us all.

As Jesus sent out these twelve, He gave them a very specific task. In fact, Matthew added that Jesus said, "Don't go to any of the Samaritan cities. Just go to the lost sheep of the house of Israel and preach to them that the Messiah is here." Later on in Matthew, when Jesus sent out the disciples, He would say, "Go into all the world." But not now. For now, it was a very specific work in a very specific field.

The same can be true for you. You may not be called to reach the world, but how about your own town. If not that, try your street. Get a vision for what God's plans are and then get to work in His power. I love watching people being stretched when the Lord puts them in places where they aren't necessarily comfortable. It's a blessing because I have to do that too. Ministry can be improved on and the only way you can do that is to try and fall down and try again.

Jesus sent the disciples out for a while. He followed up behind them and bailed them out when needed. Then He listened to what they learned and taught them more only to send them out again.

> He commanded them to take nothing for the journey except a staff—no bag, no bread, no copper in their money belts—but to wear sandals, and not to put on two tunics.
>
> —Mark 6:8–9

On this first journey, the disciples were reduced to the clothes on their back because they needed to learn that God would provide all of their needs, and this minimum provision would provide maximum opportunity to trust Him. They wouldn't have to beg. They had might. They had right. And they had the promise that where God guides, He provides. The same is still true today. The place we see God work in the greatest sense is when we have nothing with which to help Him.

When our church first began many years ago, we had four or five couples in a home study and we decided to rent some space in a school gymnasium. But if there was ever a place where you could find nothing going right, that was it. It was always dirty. And, invariably, baseball practice took place in the field behind us during our services. We'd close the windows to keep out the noise—but it was 100 degrees inside and no air conditioning. So we opened up the doors and windows and tried to talk over the noise of baseball games and cheering parents. We only had metal chairs and most of them didn't sit straight. We had two classrooms to use for the nursery and Sunday school, but if the schoolteacher forgot to leave her key, we were out of luck. We had only a sandwich board for a sign. How could this possibly work, I thought to myself more than once. Yet within a year, we had five hundred people in attendance each week. I remember sharing with the elders that when you have nothing to use or depend on, then God can work—and work He did, and has continued to do.

Our present sanctuary originally seated only eighty people. In order to remodel, we had to move out and tear it down. We set up a large tent in the yard. Again, I complained to no one in particular.

"Nobody's going to want to sit in a tent," I whined.

It was hot. The lighting was bad. The noise was endless. It was a seven-month building project and it couldn't have been more miserable, and yet we've never grown as much as we did during those seven months. When you are reduced to trusting God, He is able to do some great things. It is only when we have other options that we can hinder His work in us.

We stress capacity and ability. Jesus stressed His power on His disciples' lives.

> And He said to them, "In whatever place you enter a house, stay there till you depart from that place. And whoever will not receive you nor hear you, when you depart from there, shake off the dust under your feet as a testimony against them. Assuredly, I say to you, it will be more tolerable for Sodom and Gomorrah in the day of judgment than for that city!"
>
> —Mark 6:10–11

Jesus sent out His disciples with these parting words: "Stay where you're welcome and leave when you're not." Shaking the dust off one's feet is a symbolic act that says, "I'll just leave that here and go somewhere else." Paul modeled this exactly in Acts 13:14–51. When the people in Antioch didn't want to hear him, he headed to Iconium.

> So they went out and preached that people should repent. And they cast out many demons, and anointed with oil many who were sick, and healed them.
>
> —Mark 6:12–13

"Change your mind about Jesus," the disciples preached. "I know you think He's a troublemaker, but He's not. He's the Savior. And change your mind about yourselves. You think you're good, but you're not. You need a Savior." And as they preached, God's power fell.

Notice this order because it never changes in the Bible. The miraculous work of the Holy Spirit is always in support of the preaching of the Word. It is never a means in and of itself to attract people. If you really want to see God's power in your life, share His Word. That's where His power is found. He will honor it even above His name!

Chapter 48

DEATH OF A CONSCIENCE

Mark 6:14–29
(Matthew 14:1–14; Luke 9:7–9)

We are coming closer to the final year of Jesus' public ministry, as Jesus will soon head south to Jerusalem and the cross. In Mark 6:30, He gathers His disciples together and asks them what they learned while they were on their missionary trip. Then He teaches them again the things He wanted them to learn. But before that, Mark insets this report of how Herod was affected by what he had heard about Jesus. A year and a half earlier, Herod had ordered John the Baptist's execution. But now, hearing what Jesus had been doing, his conscience was stirred yet again. And through this, we are given a fairly complete picture of how God works with people's consciences.

The conscience can be a very good thing if we pay attention to it. God, by His Holy Spirit, certainly uses it to bring conviction. But if we turn it off and constantly turn away, we may find ourselves, like Herod, with no place to turn, because God only waits for so long.

Not only was John the Baptist's birth miraculous, but early on he understood God's plan for his life was to be the herald of the Messiah to come. He moved to the desert, wore the camels' hair robes of the prophets, and ate grasshoppers and wild honey. And as he began to preach, God began to work and people began to come by the thousands to admit they were sinners.

To the soldiers who asked what they could do to get right with God, John said, "You guys should quit intimidating and falsely accusing people. And you should be content with your wages" (Luke 3:14). When the scribes, Pharisees, and Sadducees came to see him in the wilderness, he said of them, "Here comes the brood of vipers. Who has warned all of you to escape the judgment that's to come?" (Luke 3:7). He was a no-nonsense kind of guy, so it's small wonder that when Herod developed an illicit relationship with his brother's wife John told him, "God won't put up with this." As you might suspect, his message was not well received by those in power.

Herod Antipas was one of the sons of Herod the Great, who had died. Herodias was the daughter of Antipas' half-brother, Aristobulus. When she married another of Herod's half-brothers, Philip, she became both niece and sister-in-law to Herod. He talked her into leaving her husband for him, and they moved back to the Galilee area where he was assigned the job of overseeing the regions of Galilee and Perea.

Now King Herod heard of Him, for His name had become well known. And he said, "John the Baptist is risen from the dead, and therefore these powers are at work in him." Others said, "It is Elijah." And others said, "It is the Prophet, or like one of the prophets." But when Herod heard, he said, "This is John, whom I beheaded; he has been raised from the dead!"

—Mark 6:14–16

With the disciples out in pairs, there were six cities at any given time in the Galilee area that had someone preaching. So it is not surprising that word of Jesus' miracles and messages reached the ears of those in the palace.

It seemed everyone had an opinion about Jesus. Some thought He was Elijah—the prophet the Scriptures said would come. Others thought he was the prophet Moses talked about when he promised the Lord would send a prophet like him who would lead the people into life.

Whatever else He was to the people, Jesus was the first prophet they'd seen in four hundred years. And whatever else they thought about Him, Herod had only one thing in mind: a guilty conscience wrapped in superstition that convinced him the man he'd killed a year and a half earlier had come back to haunt him. Others had different opinions, but Herod would not be swayed by any of them.

"I've killed him—and this is my punishment," Herod emphatically declared. And in so doing, he sounded a lot like Shakespeare's Lady Macbeth as she washed her hands, crying in vain for the bloodspots to go away.

When confronted with our sinfulness, we really have only two options: We can repent and say, "God, You're right. I'm wrong. I shouldn't have done it this way. Forgive me and help me serve You." Or we can seek somehow to justify or hide what we've done so we can put our conscience to rest. Most folks choose the latter. But conscience is a gift that every person receives. People know right from wrong innately. So although we can hide or ignore our sin for a while, it eventually emerges from the deep recesses where we have tried in vain to bury it.

David spent a year trying to hide the fact that he had killed Uriah, Bathsheba's husband. For a year, he was sick, out of the public eye, and unable to make speeches or reign effectively. Yet he remained unwilling to repent. He wrote in Psalm 32:3–4, "When I kept silent, my bones grew old. My vitality turned into the drought of summer. I groaned day and night. I never had a day's rest." That's what conscience does and that's so often how God reaches us. By the time Nathan the prophet confronted David, David's conscience had brought him to the point where he was more than ready to throw himself on God's mercy. In Psalm 51:3,12, he said, "Lord, I acknowledge my sin to You. Against You only have I sinned. Now restore to me the joy of thy salvation."

The conscious awareness of sin is certainly a gift from God, because it is almost always through the conscience that He works to drive us back to Him. People can pressure you or try to correct you but only God truly can convict a heart.

A year and a half had passed since John had been killed and Herod's conscience had been working overtime. Now, with Jesus doing all of these glorious things and with the disciples preaching simultaneously in multiple cities, it flared up again and all he could think about was his sin. Did he turn to the Lord? No. The pricks of his conscience were so bad that he decided instead that his only choice was to kill Jesus like he had killed John, in order to silence the voices he heard in his head.

We're told in Luke 13:31–32 that on that very day, some of the Pharisees had come to Jesus, saying, "You should get out of town because Herod is trying to kill You."

Jesus' response was, "You go tell that fox"—and He used the female term, *vixen*, perhaps in reference to Herod's wife, who ran the show—"I'm going to deliver people from demons and I'm going to heal the sick today. On the third day, I'll be perfected." In other words, "On the third day, I'll be resurrected—but I'm going to work until then."

An aroused conscience is only good if it draws you to the Lord in repentance, seeking mercy. If our conscience dies, so do we.

In the fourth chapter of his first letter to Timothy, in verses 1–3, Paul said that in the last days there will be those who depart from the faith. They will follow seducing spirits and doctrines of demons; they'll speak lies in hypocrisy and their consciences will be seared as with a hot iron. In other words, there comes a time in people's lives when a conscious conviction from God is no longer effective as sin renders it insensate, unable to respond. At that point, sin can be pursued without feeling any remorse. They can do the wrong thing and not be sorry. They can continue on in wickedness without being bothered by it. Like a hand burned in the fire that has been scarred and lost its feeling, so a seared conscience can no longer warn of the path of destruction we have chosen.

We certainly see this in our culture today where more and more sin is tolerated with less and less guilt. We become dead to the very conscience that should bring us back to God.

> For Herod himself had sent and laid hold of John, and bound him in prison for
> the sake of Herodias, his brother Philip's wife, for he had married her. Because
> John had said to Herod, "It is not lawful for you to have your brother's wife."
> —Mark 6:17–18

A year and a half earlier, when John declared Herod's marriage to Herodias sinful, Herodias was furious. She leaned on her husband to arrest John, who was thrown into the dungeon of a palace. The paranoid Herod had built it surrounded by 240-foot-high walls on a bluff above the Dead Sea. Being thrown into that place would be like being thrown into a hole in Death Valley—hot, miserable, and dry. No wonder John had sent messengers to Jesus asking in so many words why He hadn't come to rescue him.

> Therefore Herodias held it against him and wanted to kill him, but she could
> not; for Herod feared John, knowing that he was a just and holy man, and he

protected him. And when he heard him, he did many things, and heard him gladly.

—Mark 6:19–20

God's Word, delivered by John, had two completely different effects on Herodias and Herod. In Herodias, it produced an innate hatred that wouldn't go away. In fact, the imperfect tense in verse 19 tells us she didn't just hate John that day—she hated him every day. She was not going to let this go until he was dead.

Contrast that with Herod's reaction. This very innocuous ruler, whose wife seemed to have his number, now drew a line in the sand and said, "I'm not moving on this point. I don't care if you want him dead. I like him. In fact, I fear him. And the words he speaks touch my heart. I know he is a just man." The word *just* means "without fault." Herod's conscience was being stirred. As a result, he defied his wife—something he didn't do very often—and preserved John's life. For eighteen months, Herod watched over John and often went to see him.

What a picture of a man to whom God has begun to speak! After all, it isn't often we see a king go to someone in prison chains and say, "Got a minute? There are some things I've got to work out. Could you help me?" Not only did Herod go often, but when he heard John, we read that "he did many things." He actually began to respond to the things he heard. Yet, his actions didn't result in repentance and as a result, eventually, the opportunity and work of his conscience began to fade.

Generations earlier, another king, King Saul, was not aware when the Holy Spirit was taken from his life. Likewise, Samson got up one day to fight the Philistines only to find he had lost God's power, and he was not aware God had departed from him. Herod spent eighteen months hearing John gladly and doing a number of things. But he failed to do the one thing required of him—surrender to Jesus as Lord. So we read:

> Then an opportune day came when Herod on his birthday gave a feast for his nobles, the high officers, and the chief men of Galilee. And when Herodias' daughter herself came in and danced, and pleased Herod and those who sat with him, the king said to the girl, "Ask me whatever you want, and I will give it to you." He also swore to her, "Whatever you ask me, I will give you, up to half my kingdom." So she went out and said to her mother, "What shall I ask?" And she said, "The head of John the Baptist!" Immediately she came in with haste to the king and asked, saying, "I want you to give me at once the head of John the Baptist on a platter."
>
> —Mark 6:21–25

This passage shows what happened when Herod listened but didn't act, and meanwhile Herodias had continued to plot. The day of Herod's birthday was her open door. Like most Roman parties, this one was attended by men only. In verse 21, we see a list of the men who came—political leaders, military men, and the social registry of the chief people in the area. They were all there, the "A list." Most of these parties went on for days and got louder and drunker as they went. I don't suspect this one was any different.

Into this mess, as part of her plan to kill John, Herodias, a very wicked woman, was willing to send her own daughter to dance a dance that usually a prostitute danced. All of the men, drunk with wine, leering and cheering, were greatly pleased. So Herod said to the girl with the bravado before his supposed friends and admirers "What do you want from me? I'll give you whatever I have up to half my kingdom"—which is kind of an interesting promise since he had no kingdom at all but only a job he was assigned. In Esther 5:3,6, the king said the same thing to Esther, so maybe it was simply a colloquial expression.

Having been put up to this by her mother, and not knowing how to respond, she turned and asked her mom. Imagine a mother saying to her daughter, "Tell him you want the head of a prisoner." The daughter, however, didn't seem to be bothered by this. In fact, she added the words "at once" and "on a platter." Like mother, like daughter.

> And the king was exceedingly sorry; yet, because of the oaths and because of those who sat with him, he did not want to refuse her. Immediately the king sent an executioner and commanded his head to be brought. And he went and beheaded him in prison, brought his head on a platter, and gave it to the girl; and the girl gave it to her mother. When his disciples heard of it, they came and took away his corpse and laid it in a tomb.
>
> —Mark 6:26–29

Herod was greatly distressed. In fact, the word for "exceedingly sorry" used here is found in only one other place in the entire Bible: the Garden of Gethsemane, where Jesus said to His disciples, "I am sorrowful unto death. Pray with Me. Watch with Me."

Here was a man whose conscience had been moved for so many months and yet, at this moment, as much as he had been blessed, he knew he'd been duped. In front of all of his buddies, he was in a horrible dilemma that produced great distress. He knew the right thing to do. But he had made a brash promise, shot off His mouth, and, more concerned about what his drunken buddies thought of him than anything else, he immediately ordered John's execution.

How often do we find people in church with aroused consciences as God begins to work His work of drawing men in their sin to find forgiveness at the Cross. Their consciences are awake and God's Word is getting through. They're not saved yet—but they're thinking about it. But at the point of decision, rather than turning to God they worry about what others might think if they do. *What will my wife say? Or my business partner?* And they run for the hills to escape their conscience and the Spirit's conviction.

John the Baptist was a very simple, faithful, courageous, righteous man ministering to a very flamboyant, foul man who had no spine. John lost his head but kept his life. Herod just lost everything. That was a year and a half earlier. Now we read that when Herod saw Jesus and the disciples, all he could think about was the day he killed John the Baptist. "I know John has come back from the dead," he said. "Those are the kinds of words he spoke. That is the kind of power he had." But would Herod repent? No.

The last time we see Herod in the Bible is in Luke 23. Pilate sent Jesus to Herod during His trial. And Luke records that when Herod saw Jesus, he was thrilled because he had heard many things about Him and hoped to see Him do a miracle. His conscience no longer was awake, and he had no fear of seeing a ghost. All Herod could say was, "I'd like to see a trick."

As Herod began to question Jesus, Jesus didn't respond. So Herod's soldiers put a robe on Him and mocked Him. Without an active conscience, Herod could mistreat an innocent Man for play. Eventually he sent Jesus back to Pilate, with the words, "I find no fault in Him. Do what you want. I don't care." Maybe the most telltale sign of his dead conscience was that Jesus had nothing to say to him at all. It was too late for Herod!

You have to go a long way before the Lord stops talking to you. But Herod is proof that you can get there if you work hard enough at it. With his conscience dead and God no longer speaking to him, Herod went on to infamy and a horrible death instead of a life that could have been.

The progression of a conscience's death is a sobering picture. Don't let it happen to you.

Chapter 49

I'm Your Sufficiency

Mark 6:30–44
(Matthew 14:13–21; Luke 9:10–17; John 6:5–13)

Earlier, in Mark 6, Jesus had sent out His disciples, filled with His strength and anointed by His power, to go before Him to the Galilee cities to minister to the people. It was a road trip that enabled them to begin to see how their lives would be after His death and resurrection. Here in verse 30, we see them returning from this "field trip." After de-briefing them, Jesus immediately put them in another situation designed to reinforce what they had learned, that their own strength was insufficient and they would have to depend upon Him. I don't know what it is about us Christians that, like the disciples, we learn to depend on God one time, only to forget the next. So Jesus teaches them here again with this miracle recorded in all four of the Gospels.

> Then the apostles gathered to Jesus and told Him all things, both what they had done and what they had taught. And He said to them, "Come aside by yourselves to a deserted place and rest a while." For there were many coming and going, and they did not even have time to eat. So they departed to a deserted place in the boat by themselves.
>
> —Mark 6:30–32

We have no idea how long the disciples were out or any details as to their discussion with Jesus upon their return. In Luke 10, when the seventy went out two by two, there is an account of what Jesus wanted them to learn. But we don't have that here. All we hear is Jesus saying to them, "Why don't we get away for a little while?"

It interests me that the disciples had worked to a point where they were just worn out. I find that often Christians today try to do as little as possible, which is such a different picture than what we see here. These guys were tirelessly giving it their all to the point where Jesus said, "You need a break." So He got them in a boat and they set sail from Capernaum, headed to the Bethsaida area four miles across the lake—a region known today as the lower Golan Heights, still a fairly desolate place.

> But the multitudes saw them departing, and many knew Him and ran there on foot from all the cities. They arrived before them and came together to Him. And Jesus, when He came out, saw a great multitude and was moved with

compassion for them, because they were like sheep not having a shepherd. So He began to teach them many things. When the day was now far spent, His disciples came to Him and said, "This is a deserted place, and already the hour is late. Send them away, that they may go into the surrounding country and villages and buy themselves bread; for they have nothing to eat."

—Mark 6:33–36

This is an interesting picture of the crowd's hunger. For Jesus and the disciples, it was a four-mile boat ride. But for the crowds, it was an eight-mile trip by land. Yet so eager were they to be with Jesus that they were able to beat Him there. And by the time the disciples were docking the boat, there were probably ten thousand people waiting for Him. The disciples may have been frustrated by the crowds, but they were not a bother to our Lord. They were needy and He wanted to be their Shepherd. He wanted to love and care for them. The apostles, having just returned from their first missions excursion, may have learned many things—but they hadn't yet learned this heart of love God has for man. The Holy Spirit would eventually bring that love to dwell in their hearts after they were born-again.

Jesus knew many in the crowds were not there seeking forgiveness of their sin, but only a handout or to see an awesome display of His power. In fact, in John 6:27, in the sermon Jesus gave this big crowd the following day, He said, "You guys are really putting a lot of effort into following Me, but not because you've seen the signs and figured out who I am, but rather because I give you food. You shouldn't work so hard for the food that perishes, but rather for that food that leads to eternal life which I can give you." Yet even though He knew the crowd was gathered primarily for selfish reasons, Jesus still wanted to spend His day ministering to them because He had compassion for them.

The Greek word for *compassion* speaks of a feeling in the gut. It's an emotional word rather than simply a commitment word. It isn't only that Jesus loved them. That's a choice. It's that He felt compassion for them. The poor, the weak, the needy, the sick, the lost—Jesus felt for them in the pit of His stomach. They were, after all, sheep in need of a Shepherd.

Sometimes it's not a big compliment to be called a sheep. Sheep are, after all, some of the dumbest animals in the world. If you walk a bunch of them in one direction and turn the corner where they don't see you, they'll stop. Even though they can hear you, if they don't see you, they'll lie down and die. If they don't have any food on this side of the street and there are acres of food on that side of the street, they'll never go there on their own. They are absolutely dependent animals. So are we in our needs for Him.

Jesus here immediately set about caring for the sheep by teaching them, telling them, I'm sure, about salvation and life. Luke adds in chapter 9 that He healed as many as needed healing. And for the apostles, the training continued. But now they would have to serve the people at a time when it was a great imposition to them, tired and just back and needing some rest. We truly have the heart of our Lord when we are willing to serve when it's inconvenient, because convenient service is worth very little to the Lord. If I come only when I feel like it, if I stick around only when I've got nothing else to do, or if I give only when I have extra, the love that motivated me is not a love for God but a love for me. It is a willingness to serve others when we could be serving ourselves that displays His love.

So the disciples watched Jesus minister to the people with great joy while they steamed at how they were losing precious personal time. Finally, late in the afternoon, the disciples said to Him, "We're in a place that has no food. Let's get rid of these folks."

We know from John it was Passover time, April or May. If it got dark at five-thirty, maybe it was three or four o'clock at this point. I'm sure the disciples felt very good about their suggestion to send the people home. That always seemed to be their solution. Later when a Canaanite woman came with her demon-possessed daughter, the disciples said to Jesus, "Could You just send her away? She's bothering us." And when the parents brought their children for Jesus to bless, the disciples told them to get lost. So it's no wonder that here the disciples' counsel to Jesus regarding the people was to simply, "Send them away."

> But He answered and said to them, "You give them something to eat." And they said to Him, "Shall we go and buy two hundred denarii worth of bread and give them something to eat?"
>
> —Mark 6:37

Instead Jesus said to them: "Give them something to eat." John tells us Jesus asked this of them to test them. He already knew what He would do, but it was a challenge for the disciples to practice what they had been learning. This is the only place in the entire Gospel record where Jesus asked for advice. It's not because He was lost—but because the apostles needed to grow and learn, on-the-job so to speak.

We should learn from this that when God puts us in a place where our faith is tried or where our knowledge of God is put to the test, it is never for His benefit but always for ours. He's not saying to us, "Hang in there. I'll come up with something." He knows what He's going to do. All He's waiting for is us to learn to trust Him.

Jesus could have called for a "manna drop." But He wanted His disciples to learn to accomplish His will in His strength. And if we're going to grow in our relationship with Him, we have to learn to be dependent on Him more, not less. The apostles had been with Jesus almost two and a half years by now. They had seen it all. But none of them said, "Lord, we don't know where to get enough food to feed the people—but You do. Lord, we don't have what it takes to meet their needs—but You do."

We know from John 6:5 that Philip got the question first. Why Philip? For one thing, he had grown up in this area. Therefore, it might have been that Jesus said, "Hey, Philip, you're from around here. Where do we get food so these people can eat?"

Note Jesus asked Philip, "Where?" But Philip answered with "How much?"

We read in verse 37 that it would have taken two hundred denarii worth of bread to give everyone something to eat. A denarius was roughly a day's wage. So Philip likely voiced the disciples' combined wisdom and said to Jesus, "We think that nine months' worth of income could barely feed everyone even a little piece of bread." What he should have said was, "Lord, it is beyond me." But he stops at the obvious conclusion. He doesn't say, "Lord, this is impossible for us but not for You" because the "brain trust" did what most brain trusts do: they relied on themselves.

Unfortunately, we as His people can do the same thing. We begin in faith but quickly fall back to resort to our works. We need constant reminders to trust in the Lord and not ourselves. We read about the children of Israel coming out of Egypt experiencing the same problem. If there was anyone who could have written a book on how big God is, based on what they had seen and learned, they could have. As He brought them out of Egypt, God miraculously parted the Red Sea, and yet the very next day, they thought they were going to die. We do the same thing. When we are hit with financial pressure, marital disagreement, parenting difficulty, or job insecurity, what do we do? Like Philip, we begin to compute and strain and see the whole thing as a math equation that's impossible to solve. We never get to the Lord being our help.

Instead of running to Jesus and saying, "You can do this," Philip did some mental arithmetic and showed his ignorance. He factored in the size of the crowd and the price of bread—everything but the fact that the Lord was standing right in front of Him. It's an amazing picture of how soon we can forget, and Philip just back from his first ministry tour seeing the power of God at work.

In the Bible, the number two hundred is most often used in the context of the insufficiency of people's ability—unable to accomplish God's purposes. We see it with Achan in Joshua 7, Absalom in 2 Samuel 14, the apostate Micah in Judges 17, and the world's armies in Revelation 9. The number two hundred always seems attached to those trying to do things without God. The same is certainly true for two hundred denarii here.

Yet Philip's conclusion is revealing, for it speaks to our hearts. We declare we trust God for eternity, but panic worrying about next month's rent. We trust Him with forever, but not with tomorrow. I think we're better off having faith than a calculator, because faith sometimes overwhelms the figures. And all of the human resources we can muster will soon fail if we fail to factor Jesus into the figures. Let's continue reading:

> But He said to them, "How many loaves do you have? Go and see." And when they found out they said, "Five, and two fish."
>
> —Mark 6:38

Again, we know from the other Gospels that Andrew was the fellow who first came to Jesus and said, "I found a kid with some lunch." Apparently the boy didn't tell Andrew how much he had. So Jesus sent Andrew back to find out how much the young man had. Andrew is an interesting guy in the Bible for whenever we see him, he's always bringing someone to Jesus. He had a very persuasive personality and a gift from God. I think any man who can talk someone out of his lunch in an area where there is nothing to eat and it's getting late is pretty persuasive indeed!

The boy had five loaves made of barley grain—the least desirable little pita breads the poor ate—along with two smoked sardines. Andrew, like Philip, hit the wall of unbelief and said, "But what are these among so many?" Andrew's arithmetic went a little bit differently than Philip's. Philip was overwhelmed by the great demand; Andrew stumbled at the small supply. Like Philip, Andrew left the Lord completely out of his figuring as well.

I love the picture of these two apostles looking over Niagara Falls and being worried about where they would get a drink. But lest you are too hard on them, we should consider our own responses. God has made such great promises and has accomplished so much in our lives—yet we sometimes still forget to take into account the Jesus factor.

I like the little boy because it seems to me he was the only one who did what he should have done: give up what he had, as little as it was, and put it in Jesus' hands. I bet when he went home later with fifty lunches and a great story, God used his testimony.

But notice that the insufficient from the hands of the insignificant becomes both sufficient and significant the moment it passes through Jesus' hands. What Philip didn't count on, and what Andrew couldn't see, was that no matter how little we have, if Jesus touches it, it's enough. God used a little boy with a big sling to rid Israel of a monster. A little slave girl in a foreign country helped deliver a powerful leader from his leprosy. A virgin girl from a poor village brought forth the Messiah. Once God touches us, look out!

Ten thousand people and twelve worried apostles added up to an impossible task as they wore out their fingers on their calculators. But throw in one boy willing to give Jesus his lunch, and the stage is set for God to work.

> Then He commanded them to make them all sit down in groups on the green grass. So they sat down in ranks, in hundreds and in fifties. And when He had taken the five loaves and the two fish, He looked up to heaven, blessed and broke the loaves, and gave them to His disciples to set before them; and the two fish He divided among them all. So they all ate and were filled. And they took up twelve baskets full of fragments and of the fish.
>
> —Mark 6:39–43

I love the picture of the apostles as Jesus now puts them to work to facilitate His miracle. As servants they headed back and forth from Jesus to the ten thousand people now sitting in groups of fifties and hundreds that needed to be fed. Can't you just hear the people yelling, "Hey, Philip! More bread over here!"? Yet this miracle was all but hidden from the crowd. It had been accomplished without fanfare. There were no flying angels. There was no shaking earth. It was really for the benefit of the apostles Jesus was training so they might learn for the second time who their source was to be.

Every time the bucket was empty, the disciples had to run up the hill and get more from Jesus. Filled, they'd run down the hill and were emptied again. Yet they always ended up back with Jesus. Likewise, if we run to Him with what we have, He uses us to meet the needs of others far beyond ourselves. But we have to keep returning to Him.

As a result, the people not only ate, but they were filled. The Greek word *chortazo* means they were stuffed. From John 6 we realize many of these people were there just because of the free meals. Therefore, we presume these were eating like crazy and kept the disciples running back and forth for quite some time.

It's just like the Lord to supply our needs and still have plenty left over. In verse 43, we have this wonderful picture of the twelve apostles with twelve baskets of leftovers. Twelve baskets meant every apostle had a personal lesson from Jesus in his hand. "Hey, Philip, what was that number again? Hey, Andrew, what is it that we had?" I can just see Jesus laughing. One didn't think the boy's food was enough. The other didn't think he had enough money in the treasury to feed everyone. Yet they each ended up with their own basket full of leftovers. Our God is an awesome God!

> Now those who had eaten the loaves were about five thousand men.
> —Mark 6:44

Matthew 14:21 added "beside the women and children." Many more thus than 5000. We need to learn that God has resources far beyond our capacity. The Lord didn't say to Philip, "Where are we going to get food?" because He needed help, but because Philip needed to learn that the help was standing right in front of him. He didn't say to Andrew, "How many loaves and fish do we have?" in hopes that He'd have enough to feed everyone, but so Andrew might see that what little he had would be sufficient if God was in it.

Don't ever excuse yourself by thinking you have too little. Just give what you have. The Lord never asks for more than that, He just asks for you and your trust.

Years later, Paul wrote to the Corinthians, "We have this treasure in earthen vessels so that the obvious work of God in our lives might be for His glory and not our own." God loves to put us in that kind of spot. Did the disciples learn their lesson? The storm that followed would answer that question.

How long does it take to learn the lesson that we need to give what we have to the Lord and trust Him? Apparently a long time. How important is it? It's the only miracle in every one of the Gospels. It was hearing this story for the first time that I gave my life to Jesus—so I'll never forget it. Now if I could just remember the lesson each day!

Chapter 50

STORM SENSE

Mark 6:45–56
(Matthew 14:22–36; John 6:15–21)

Jesus had just fed thousands. And with twelve baskets of leftovers in their hands, the disciples had learned that God could do much with very little. We pick up the story here in Mark 6:45.

> Immediately He made His disciples get into the boat and go before Him to the other side, to Bethsaida, while He sent the multitude away. And when He had sent them away, He departed to the mountain to pray.
>
> —Mark 6:45–46

If you were only reading Mark's gospel, you might wonder why Jesus would chase off His disciples so quickly or why He wouldn't sit down with them and talk about what they had just learned. But John 6:14–15 fills in the details. After seeing Jesus feed thousands, some in the crowd concluded He was the prophet Moses had promised. In Deuteronomy 18:15,18, Moses had prophesied, "The Lord your God will raise up for you a prophet like me from your midst. Him you shall hear." For centuries, the Jews believed that when the Messiah came, He would be a man like Moses. But that wasn't to be the case. Jesus would be like Moses in the sense of being a deliverer and bringing people out of bondage to sin. Yet He was God come in flesh while everyone looked for a man. Yet because Moses had brought manna in the wilderness to feed a hungry nation, and Jesus had brought bread and fish in the desert to feed a hungry crowd, they thought He surely must be the one, and decided then and there to make Him king.

John said Jesus perceived what their plans were and He immediately moved His disciples out of the way. What the coup-planning men failed to realize was that Jesus the Prophet and Jesus the King first came to be Jesus the Lamb, who would take away the sins of the world. He had come to die. He hadn't come to rule the earth—not yet. First things first. If there was going to be a crown, it would be a crown of thorns. If there was to be a kingdom, it would not be of this world. What they wanted was external and temporary. What He came to bring was internal and eternal.

Very few in the crowd saw Jesus as the Savior come for sinners. The connection between Him and the crowd was missing in most hearts. Most of the folks were not at all aware of their needs. If they had been, they would have been begging for mercy—as you and I did when we got saved. For now, they were just plotting to make Him king for their own purposes, none of them spiritual in nature.

There is no shortage of people who will follow Jesus as long as they can control the action. They don't mind Jesus being God and Jesus being King as long as He does what they want. When they pray, expect answers immediately if not sooner. But the minute the Lord does something other than what they want from Him or imagined He would do, they quit following.

Knowing how hard it is to stop a crowd from doing what it wants, Jesus sought to shield His disciples from the will of the world. They had a lot to learn. Following this crowd's will only would have taken them one giant step backward. I suspect the disciples sensed what was going on and didn't want to leave. But Jesus sent them to a place that would have been seven miles away on the other side of the lake. Meanwhile, five thousand men somehow were dissuaded from making Him king. He was able to go up to the area of what is known today as the Golan Heights, where He had a view of the entire Sea of Galilee below. And there He began to pray. No doubt He prayed for the disciples and for the zealous, misled crowd; He prayed for the lost that they would see Him for who He was; and He prayed for the final year of public ministry, which was just around the corner, with Calvary waiting at the end.

> Now when evening came, the boat was in the middle of the sea; and He was alone on the land. Then He saw them straining at rowing, for the wind was against them. Now about the fourth watch of the night He came to them, walking on the sea, and would have passed them by.
>
> —Mark 6:47–48

The Sea of Galilee is seven hundred feet below sea level. It's an interesting location as it is surrounded by mountains on every side except the west. The west side has a big valley that runs seven hundred feet up to the Mediterranean Sea, creating a giant wind tunnel. As the disciples rowed, the wind became a real problem. They encountered this wind even though they were rowing in the very direction Jesus had told them to go. In other words, this storm came upon them even as they were being obedient to the Lord.

This being Passover time, April or May, there would have been a full moon. So as Jesus prayed on the mountain, He no doubt had a very clear view of His disciples. He watched them struggle against the wind, but it wasn't until the fourth watch—between three and six A.M.—that He came for them. If they had left at six that evening, they would have been on the water for nine hours. And if that wasn't bad enough, John added that they had rowed only three or four miles. After eight or nine hours of rowing, they had made it only halfway across.

Halfway to anything is horrible, isn't it? Being halfway finished with painting your house is the worst because you still have an equal amount of work to do. Being halfway done with the dishes is no good either. Can you imagine twelve guys in a rowboat for nine hours realizing that they only had gone halfway? The storm was terrible and they were straining. The word *straining* speaks of physical distress. Everything hurt and they were beat!

This wasn't a storm that scared them like the last one. This was more the storm that broke them. Here they were, trying to do what Jesus said. To their credit, they didn't turn around. They were going to obey one way or the other, even though turning around would have gotten them back to shore very quickly. They didn't quit. They were going to stay the course. They sought to do what Jesus had told them to do but had already forgotten the lesson from shore: when asked to do what you cannot, look for the Lord to do it!

It was impossible for them to heal the sick, to cast out the Devil, or to feed the five thousand on their own. It was now becoming impossible to row across the lake. At what point should these apostles in training have simply started praying for help? Jesus was praying for them, watching them, concerned for them—but apparently, from all we read, they were doing none of the same. They were determined to do what God wanted. But they were not willing to do it by looking to Him for help. They were physically committed, giving it their all, but spiritually still weak and out of touch.

Some people use the fact that we need God's help to excuse themselves from doing their best. "I can't really do anything," they say, "because I'm really nothing anyway." That is like saying, "I'm not even going to try." You've got to do your best—but never apart from the relationship you have with God.

The entire time they were rowing, on the floor of the boat sat twelve baskets of leftovers, which should have been a tangible reminder that the last time this happened, Jesus came through.

This time before He came to the rescue, however, He left them out there for quite some time. "Doesn't God care?" we cry. "Doesn't God know? Doesn't He understand?" In the entire Bible you never will find God placing His people under duress without a great purpose in doing so. God doesn't waste suffering. If there is suffering to be had, there's glory to be gained. These men could have been rescued at midnight or at three A.M. But maybe at that point they still had some energy left. Maybe they wouldn't have been at the end of themselves. Jesus pretty much let them row themselves out.

God doesn't do anything but so in the end, we know Him better and have more confidence in His love—but that isn't always so clearly seen while we're in the storm.

What did this storm do? It kept the disciples from the worldly approach to Jesus the multitude employed. But what it had not yet accomplished was convince them to look to Him for help. I suspect if there are no storms in your life, you don't pray much. You probably skip more church services too. There is no way that your spiritual life blossoms if life is a breeze. Your spiritual life blossoms when God leans on you, when you pray out of necessity, and when you seek God out of pressure. At those times you want the Lord's help because things are not as they should be. At those times you learn that in order to serve God, you require His strength. All of those things work for your good.

Storms wear out the flesh and drive us to the Lord. But in the midst, when things are dark, we are tempted to ask, "Where is God?" And I'm sure these rowers had wondered the same thing a time or two throughout the night.

In all of his distress, Job in chapter 30:20–26 said to the Lord, "I cry out to You and You don't answer me. I stand up and You don't regard me. I look for good, and evil comes to me. I wait for light, and darkness falls." But in Psalm 112:4, the Lord said to the people, "To the upright, light will arise in darkness with grace and compassion." Job's conclusion was wrong because he wanted God to come at midnight, when the Lord had planned for his good to wait to work until three A.M.

It takes time to learn to trust God, especially when circumstances are dark and we seem to be getting very little help or making much progress, though we're right where God put us. "Why is this happening?" we might ask. Because there is no shortcut to learning to trust God would be my reply. There's no easy way to grow up. We have a name for physical pain as kids grow: growing pains. "I once grew four inches in a year and everything hurt." Growing four inches spiritually in a year will have everything hurting too—but with great purpose.

Why doesn't the Lord deliver us at once? Because the God who is in charge of everything can afford to wait until we run out of options. He doesn't say, "I've got to be done by Tuesday or the clouds will roll in and I'll be out of power." No, He can wait as long as it takes for you to run out of energy and look to Him.

When Paul wrote his second of two letters to the Corinthians, he said in chapter 1:8, "I don't want you to be ignorant about the trouble we ran into while we were in Asia, how we were burdened beyond measure and despairing even of life. We had a sentence of death in ourselves so that we might learn not to trust in ourselves but in God who raises the dead." At least in his struggles, Paul was able to put two and two together and say, "I know God is allowing this so I'll learn to depend on Him all the more."

The disciples were in the process of learning this firsthand, and so Jesus watched them struggle. They must have been at the end of their ropes when, sometime after three in the morning, He walked on the water towards them and would have passed them by. Due to the Greek construction of the verse, we don't know whether this means Jesus would have passed by without saying a word had they not responded, or that His intention was to get out in front of them so they could see Him better. I do know the lesson Jesus taught them is that when He gets on board, things are fine.

> And when they saw Him walking on the sea, they supposed it was a ghost, and they cried out; for they all saw Him and were troubled.
>
> —Mark 6:49

Phantasma is the Greek word for ghost, or phantom. These tough fishermen began to scream. When they last had come face to face with the fact that their sufficiency was insufficient, Jesus had told them He could do it. Twenty-four hours later, they still hadn't figured that out. They had not been praying. They were not crying out to the Lord. They were suffering needlessly because they were unwilling to seek God to help them do what He had asked them to—get across to the other side.

Isaiah 30:18 gloriously declares, "He will be exalted and He will have mercy and the Lord will wait to be gracious. Blessed are those who wait on Him." God waits for us to wait on Him so He can bless us. The disciples weren't waiting on the Lord. They still were busting themselves up, trying to do what God wanted.

> But immediately he talked with them and said to them, "Be of good cheer! It is I; do not be afraid."
>
> —Mark 6:50

I love the picture! Everyone was panicked. But not Jesus. They were terrified. He was happy. "Come on, boys," He said. "It'll be all right. It's just Me."

Matthew tells us in chapter 14:28–29 that Peter then said, "Lord, since it's You, command me to come and walk on the water toward You." I don't know how close to the boat Jesus was, but we know He was far enough away earlier for the disciples to think He was a ghost.

"Come," Jesus said. And Peter did.

We're great at Peter-bashing, but Peter's the only guy besides Jesus in all of history who has walked on water. Stepping out of the boat and into the wind and waves, Peter began to walk toward Jesus, eyes on Him. Yet when he looked away and saw the waves and the unlikely place he found himself, he began to sink and immediately cried, "Lord save me!" Jesus quickly picked him up and put him back in the boat.

Peter got his eyes off the Lord and unto the surrounding circumstances. His motive must have been right, for the Lord invited him to come. But then he got out there and the whole thing changed. It seems like he might have been the summary of the lesson itself because that's exactly what the disciples were doing. They were trying to do the right thing. But they didn't have their eyes on the Lord.

Mark didn't cover this part of the story, as he got his account from Peter, and I suspect Peter conveniently left this part out.

> Then He went up into the boat to them, and the wind ceased. And they were greatly amazed in themselves beyond measure, and marveled. For they had not understood about the loaves, because their heart was hardened.
>
> —Mark 6:51–52

To their credit, John says when Jesus got into the boat, the disciples were glad to see Him. It wasn't that they didn't love Him. They had just failed to look to Him when impossibility set in. Does that ring a bell with you?

Matthew recorded that as Jesus got in the boat, they began to say, "Truly, You are the Son of God." The minute Jesus got on board, the wind stopped, the waves stopped, the disciples worshipped, and they were able to get to the other side without further incident. I think it was a good lesson for these boys that even if they were seeking to obey God's will, it was much easier sailing with their eyes on Him than trying to row on their own.

> When they had crossed over, they came to the land of Gennesaret and anchored there. And when they came out of the boat, immediately the people recognized Him, ran through that whole surrounding region, and began to carry about on beds those who were sick to wherever they heard He was. Wherever He entered, into villages, cities, or the country, they laid the sick in the marketplaces, and begged Him that they might just touch the hem of His garment. And as many as touched Him were made well.
>
> —Mark 6:53–56

John tells us it was the next day that Jesus gathered the big crowd that kept running around the lake to speak to them about what they should be chasing after, rather than trying to make Him king.

I think this story in Mark should convince you that if there's a trial in your life, it's for a good purpose. In the process, the Lord never loses sight of what we're going through. He waits that He might bless us once we wait on Him. He is not oblivious to our suffering. He's not out of touch. His timing is perfect. But I think sometimes in the midst of the storm what we can best do is to stop rowing and start listening for His voice.

Commit your ways to the Lord, Psalm 37:5 says. Trust in Him and He'll bring it to pass. The hard thing is to learn the lesson and remember it. I know you have it now. I hope you'll have it tomorrow at three in the morning.

Chapter 51

JESUS: THE BREAD OF LIFE

John 6:22–71
(Matthew 8:19–22; 10:36; 16:13–20;
Mark 8:27–30; Luke 9:18–21)

We come now to a discourse that was interrupted several times by an increasingly hostile crowd whom Jesus tolerated so they might hear and know who He was. The conversation began on the seashore outside the town of Capernaum.

> On the following day when the people who were standing on the other side of the sea saw that there was no other boat there except that one which His disciples had entered, and that Jesus had not entered the boat with His disciples, but His disciples had gone away alone—however, other boats came from Tiberias, near the place where they ate bread after the Lord had given thanks—when the people therefore saw that Jesus was not there, nor His disciples, they also got into boats and came to Capernaum, seeking Jesus.
>
> —John 6:22–24

The crowd that had wanted to make Jesus king had traversed around the lake or sailed across to seek for Jesus. No one knew where He had gone, but they knew He hadn't gone on the boat. They concluded He must have gone back to Capernaum because that's where He spent most of His time. And whatever it took, they were going to take that seven-and-a-half-mile boat ride to the other side.

What a picture as thousands clamor to be near Jesus, and only a few with spiritual hunger for Him. Most still driven by free meals, and not His message of forgiveness of sin and the offer of eternal life. There was not yet for these any desire for a changed heart. No one was hungry to be righteous. They were only hungry for breakfast!

I think sometimes people go to church just to see what God might do for them. They aren't there to repent, to turn away from their sin, to line up with His will, or to go His way. They have needs and if He could fill them, oh, that would be wonderful. So up until the time He comes through, they're in church. But the minute He does not, they're off to something or someone else.

> And when they found Him on the other side of the sea, they said to Him, "Rabbi, when did You come here?" Jesus answered them and said, "Most assuredly, I say

to you, you seek Me, not because you saw the signs, but because you ate of the loaves and were filled."

—John 6:25–26

When the crowd found Jesus, they asked Him how He had gotten there. But Jesus didn't answer the question. Instead, He turned it around and said, "Why are you here? Why did you expend such effort to get to where I am?" Their eyes were looking for Jesus, but their hearts were looking for gain. And Jesus put His finger directly on the problem. "You're interested in Me not for who I am or for why I have come, but only for your own gain."

All of Jesus' miracles and signs had adequately proved who He was. It's one thing to say, "I'm God." It's another thing to prove it. And the crowd, if they had been with Jesus for any length of time at all, certainly had seen that. No one before had opened the eyes of the blind. No one before had instantaneously healed leprosy. No one had fed ten thousand with a single lunch. The miracles attracted the people for their gain—but they did not attract them to the Miracle Worker Himself. Jesus said, "You have proof, but you're not responding to it."

The same is still true. How often do you find spiritual truths about Jesus set aside for the sake of something else far short of that? We celebrate Easter every year, a worldwide celebration of Jesus' resurrection from the dead. But if He really walked out of the grave, shouldn't the whole world worship Him?

One thing for sure—verse 26 tells us that God knows the reason we're seeking Him. I don't know why people come to church. But God does. He knows what we're looking for and what is driving us. This crowd, for the most part, was focused on the material. Their concern was for the physical, and their zeal was for the carnal. They would do whatever it took to get the handout, to receive the food, and to be taken care of. They would run around the lake and pay for a boat ride if necessary to get to Jesus before it was time to eat again. I don't want to miss out!

> "Do not labor for the food which perishes, but for the food which endures to everlasting life, which the Son of Man will give you, because God the Father has set His seal on Him."
>
> —John 6:27

Jesus said to this crowd, "Quit working so hard." What were they doing? Running around the lake, sailing over in a panic, pushing and shoving, asking Him how He got there. "Relax," He said. "You should show the same kind of resolve, hunger, and drive that you have shown for food in seeking the things of God." It is amazing how much effort we are willing to expend pursuing temporal gain. It usually consumes much of our life. The things we work hard to buy are perishable. They come with an expiration date.

When I do weddings, I'm always jealous of how good we can look when we are young. It seems that only lasts a few years, however, before you begin to look like the rest of us for

268

the next 60 years. If I had known then what I know now, I'd have taken a lot more pictures early on and then broken the camera at thirty. I was a good-looking guy! You wouldn't know that to see me now—but that's just the way life goes. Everything is perishable. And yet we are consumed with and overwhelmed by the gain of things that don't last. We are constantly aware of higher mortgages, increased credit card balances, and an endless list of things that have to be replaced. Yet when it comes to our spiritual lives, it is extremely difficult to convince people to spend more than an hour a week in church, in prayer, in the Word, in ministry outreach . . .

It can get so bad that by the time we are done pursuing the temporal, we have very little energy left for anything else. So Jesus spoke to their effort for temporal gain, "Do not labor like this to fill your stomach with food that perishes, because God has provided food that will last forever." *Perishes* is a present-tense verb that means all that is temporal is even now rotting away and wearing out. These guys had eaten the night before, but it was morning or later, and they were hungry again. And at lunchtime, they'd be hungry yet again. It's interesting that most of the things we buy or try to possess satisfy us only for a little while. You just have to look in a mirror to know that things aren't getting better!

"Don't spend your time on non-essentials," Jesus said. "Rather put that kind of effort into securing what you desperately need. Reorder your priorities. Only I can give you life. I'm the One the Father has sealed. I'm the only One on whom rests His stamp of approval."

> Then they said to Him, "What shall we do, that we may work the works of God?"
> —John 6:28

This is always like people. "You think we're ungrateful?" the crowd asked. "Just tell us what to do and we'll do it." When confronted with anything having to do with God and salvation, most people operate on a barter system. They say to God, "I'll show up at church and You'll answer my prayers. I'll throw a couple of bucks in the offering plate and You'll pay for the boat." They think salvation is based on a merit system. They never see grace. Grace has a way of escaping us, because one of the Gospel's biggest offenses is that it removes people from the equation, while sin wants to make us the center of attention.

In Acts 2, when Peter spoke about Jesus and death in his sermon on the Day of Pentecost, the people cried out, "What shall we do?"

The Philippian jailer who, thinking his charges had escaped, was terrified for his life and said to Paul, "What can I do to be saved?"

Even the prodigal son came home with suggestions on how he could work off his debt.

"What shall we do to do the works of God?" the crowd asked. Religion always has an answer to verse 28. Islam will tell you to follow the five pillars of faith. The Buddhist will give you eight steps to Nirvana. The Hindu will hand his mantras to you as a way you can do what needs to be done. And the religious person will cite the Ten Commandments—even though God gave them to convince us we can't keep them. But Jesus has an entirely different suggestion for you:

> Jesus answered and said to them, "This is the work of God, that you believe in Him whom He sent."
>
> —John 6:29

In verse 28, the crowd used the word *works*. Jesus answered with the singular word *work*. We all have to do just one thing. That kind of limits our playing field, doesn't it? That puts us all in one category. We all have to do just one thing: believe In Jesus. It's the word for *faith* throughout the New Testament and it always means the same thing: to put all your eggs in one basket or to hang the entire weight of your body on one support. To the Philippian jailer, Paul said, "Believe on the Lord Jesus Christ—and you will be saved."

To the crowds gathered at Pentecost, Peter said, "Men and brethren, you need to repent of your sin and go and be baptized in the name of the Lord Jesus—and you'll receive the Holy Spirit."

The prodigal son never did have to work as a slave. The father's ring and robe were given in grace to this one who now knew he didn't deserve it.

John 6:29 is one of the verses we should know well when we go out to share with others, because people invariably want to know what they have to do to earn their salvation.

> Therefore they said to Him, "What sign will You perform then, that we may see it and believe You? What work will You do? Our fathers ate the manna in the desert; as it is written, 'He gave them bread from heaven to eat.'"
>
> —John 6:30–31

Hearing that the only thing they had to do was believe in Jesus, the crowd asked Him what He would do to prove He was right—as if He hadn't done enough already. They had seen so much, yet notice miracles don't produce faith. They can only support faith. According to the Bible, it is hearing God's Word that produces faith. But in their anger and self-defense, the people went back to their Old Testament history and argued that bread from heaven was nothing new to them, that for forty years God had fed their fathers manna in the wilderness. That's true. Psalm 78:24 says, "He rained down manna on them to eat." But in the verses preceding that, we read "the Lord was furious so a fire was kindled against Jacob and anger also came up against Israel, because they did not believe in God and did not trust in His salvation."

Who was given food from heaven? Rebellious, disobedient, hard-hearted folks who could have been in the land enjoying God's blessing, but whose lack of faith had kept them out.

"What sign are You going to do to prove You're any different from anyone else? We've always gotten food from God," the crowd arrogantly said.

If I were Jesus, I'd have left by now. Fortunately I am not, and fortunately for me, His grace and mercy are everlasting.

> Then Jesus said to them, "Most assuredly, I say to you, Moses did not give you the bread from heaven, but My Father gives you the true bread from heaven. For the bread of God is He who comes down from heaven and gives life to the world."
>
> —John 6:32–33

As Jesus' love is so longsuffering, rather than leave the crowd, He corrected them, by saying, "It wasn't Moses who gave you manna. He was the instrument but My Father was the source. Likewise, He is the source of bread for you—and I am the bread."

> Then they said to Him, "Lord, give us this bread always."
>
> —John 6:34

Like the illustration of living water given to the woman at the well, the spiritual truth of Jesus' illustration about bread sailed right over the heads in the crowd.

> And Jesus said to them, "I am the bread of life. He who comes to Me shall never hunger, and he who believes in Me shall never thirst."
>
> —John 6:35

This is the first of seven "I AM" statements John recorded. "Who shall I say sent me?" Moses asked the Lord.

"Tell them I AM." In Hebrew, it's *Yahweh* or *Jehovah* and means "the Becoming One." It is that name that is placed before other attributes of God throughout the Old Testament. Jehovah-Shalom means "God has become my peace." Jehovah-Tsidkenu means "God has become my righteousness."

"I AM the bread of life," Jesus declared. "Believe in Me. Come to Me. I alone can satisfy the hunger of your soul."

> "But I said to you that you have seen Me and yet do not believe."
>
> —John 6:36

"You've seen Me and yet you refuse to believe in Me," Jesus said. And unless they believed in Him, their situation was hopeless because there was nowhere else for them to turn. They had the proof, the evidence, and had seen all they needed to determine He was Lord. It was now a matter of the heart and the will.

"All that the Father gives Me will come to Me, and the one who comes to Me I will by no means cast out. For I have come down from heaven, not to do My own will, but the will of Him who sent Me. This is the will of the Father who sent me, that of all He has given Me I should lose nothing, but should raise it up at the last day. And this is the will of Him who sent Me, that everyone who sees the Son and believes in Him may have everlasting life; and I will raise him up at the last day."

—John 6:37–40

Jesus made two points here. The first one is that God's plans aren't going to be frustrated. He's going to accomplish His will—and His will is for men to be saved. The invitation has been issued. The door is open. You can come if you want. Just examine the evidence. Second, if you do come, you can be assured God will raise you on the last day. I love the order in verse 40: Look to Jesus, believe in Him, find life, and have a future.

Jesus said to a very hungry crowd looking to Him to feed them, "Here's the kind of hunger God wants you to have and it is the hunger I've come to feed."

The Jews then complained about Him, because He said, "I am the bread which came down from heaven." And they said, "Is not this Jesus, the son of Joseph, whose father and mother we know? How is it then that He says, 'I have come down from heaven'?"

—John 6:41–42

When you see the term *the Jews*—especially in the book of John—it is not a reference to the nation, the people, or the worshippers as a whole. It is always a reference to the leadership bound by their religious ways. It was the scribes and Pharisees who were there to infiltrate the crowd, to make people disinterested, to deflect the undeniable work of God, to keep people from following Jesus—and eventually to have Him killed.

As Jesus taught, these men began to complain. "What are we listening to this guy for?" they said. "He didn't come from heaven. He came from Galilee—and Galilee is hardly heaven! Don't listen to Him. Listen to us."

Jesus therefore answered and said to them, "Do not murmur among yourselves. No one can come to Me unless the Father who sent Me draws him and I will raise him up at the last day. It is written in the prophets, 'And they shall all be taught by God.' Therefore everyone who has heard and learned from the Father comes to Me. Not that anyone has seen the Father, except He who is from God; He has seen the Father."

—John 6:43–46

Rather than defend Himself on a personal level, Jesus said, "If you're going to hear Me, it will be because the Father in heaven is doing a work in your life. You'll listen and believe Me only when My Father begins to reveal the truth to you." In other words, it isn't an intellectual process by which people are saved. It isn't an intellectual practice through which people come to know the Lord. If people are going to get saved, it will have to be by spiritual revelation because salvation always begins with God.

In Romans 3:11, Paul said there is no one who seeks after God. That means if God had left us to ourselves, we never would have been saved. If God doesn't come knocking on our door, we remain in darkness, we stay lost, and we're doomed to hopelessness. But when the Lord in His love comes knocking, we're given the opportunity to respond.

In verses 39 and 40, Jesus had said, "This is the will of the Father. Those He gives Me will come and anyone who comes will get in." Here in verse 43, we see the other side of that equation: God calls; people respond. God offers; people receive. God loves; people believe. None of us got saved by accident. None of us stumbled in by chance. So you can be sure that if you're saved, it's because God came looking for you. You weren't capable, because of sin, to find Him on your own.

> "Most assuredly, I say to you, he who believes in Me has everlasting life. I am the bread of life."
>
> —John 6:47–48

Most assuredly is from a Greek word that means, "You can count on this." Jesus relied on His work, the Spirit's work, and God's Word to bring people around. It's a good thing to know when we go out and share with folks that the pressure isn't on us. We're the messengers, not the Savior. We're the deliverers of good news, not the converter of the heart. If the pressure was on us, we'd quit for sure. But I'll be happy to tell anyone what God can do if man will simply turn to Him by faith.

> "Your fathers ate manna in the wilderness, and are dead. This is the bread which comes down from heaven, that one may eat of it and not die. I am the living bread which comes down from heaven. If anyone eats of this bread, he will live forever; and the bread that I shall give is My flesh, which I shall give for the life of the world."
>
> —John 6:49–51

Manna is what the crowd claimed their fathers had received from God. Jesus said, "Although manna brought temporary relief, I'm here to bring eternal life. I'll break My body for you. It will be life for the world, for everyone, for anyone."

It's interesting what people think they need. At two years of age, my grandchildren are absolutely sure of what they need. As a kid, I knew what I needed too. And for my parents to convince me of what I really needed was almost impossible. "You need a good night's sleep," they'd say. Wrong. "You need to eat your Brussels sprouts." Really wrong! "You need to sit up straight." Nope.

"You need Me for life," Jesus said. And they responded, "No, what we need is health and wealth, an easy life and green lights, a raise and a promotion, less work and more money. I need a lot of things but none of them have to do with You."

Americans eat because it's time. Most people in the world eat because they're hungry. Hunger drives them to eat. And Jesus used that analogy for these folks who had run all night to perhaps get a meal.

> The Jews therefore quarreled among themselves, saying, "How can this Man give us His flesh to eat?" Then Jesus said to them, "Most assuredly, I say to you, unless you eat the flesh of the Son of Man and drink His blood, you have no life in you. Whoever eats My flesh and drinks My blood has eternal life, and I will raise him up at the last day. For My flesh is food indeed, and My blood is drink indeed. He who eats My flesh and drinks My blood abides in Me, and I in him. As the living Father sent Me, and I live because of the Father, so he who feeds on Me will live because of Me. This is the bread which came down from heaven—not as your fathers ate the manna, and are dead. He who eats this bread will live forever." These things He said in the synagogue as He taught in Capernaum.
>
> —John 6:52–59

Rather than backing off the analogy, Jesus just pressed it harder. His body and blood are where we find life. The shedding of His blood and the sacrifice of His body must be appropriated for our spiritual life, just as food is for our physical life. Without His sacrifice, we don't have life. But if we eat or partake of Him, we have eternal life.

It's a clear illustration. Man fell into sin by eating forbidden fruit. We are brought to life by eating of the Son of Man, by depending totally on Him. Although most of us are extremely busy, we usually find time to eat. We'll skip prayer, Bible study, and church—but somehow we always have time to "grab a quick bite." Why are we so weak? Maybe it's because we're not so hungry to have fellowship with God.

In verse 53, the words *you eat* are in the aorist tense. That means it's a one-time action with consequences that last down the road. In verse 54, the word *whoever eats* is in the perfect tense, which speaks of ongoing eating to find ongoing sustenance. So here the tenses of the verbs indicate that we give our lives to Jesus once, and then we come back to Him for daily nourishment. It is that faith, that relationship, and that trust that bring real life to us in our daily partaking in fellowship of our Savior and Lord.

Eating is analogous to intimacy, to abiding, and to faith. But you have to hunger. In the Ethiopian famine a few years ago, three-ton hippos traveled sixteen hundred miles to find food. Why then is it we can't drag our two hundred pounds two miles to church if it looks like rain? Are you hungry for the Lord? Jesus said to these folks for the third time, as He compared manna to His broken body that only the latter was eternal.

> Therefore many of His disciples, when they heard this, said, "This is a hard saying, who can understand it?" When Jesus knew in Himself that His disciples complained about this, He said to them, "Does this offend you? What then if you should see the Son of Man ascend where He was before?"
>
> —John 6:60–62

After talking about His broken body and shed blood, Jesus talked about His resurrection and ascension.

> "It is the Spirit who gives life; the flesh profits nothing. The words that I speak to you are spirit, and they are life. But there are some of you who do not believe." For Jesus knew from the beginning who they were who did not believe, and who would betray Him. And He said, "Therefore I have said to you that no one can come to Me unless it has been granted to him by My Father." From that time many of His disciples went back and walked with Him no more.
>
> —John 6:63–66

After being presented with the Gospel, some people say, "That's hard to understand." It isn't hard to understand. It's the easiest thing possible: Believe in Jesus. It's not a hard saying. It's a hard heart that's the problem.

Jesus was not going to let these people off so easily. "Don't try and make this a physical issue," He said. These are spiritual words for spiritual realities. "You're only going to believe when My Father works in you." I like the fact that Jesus didn't stop to explain Himself. He just gave them the truth. But for the sixth time during the course of this one conversation, Jesus said to the scribes and Pharisees, "Believe in Me." And, for the sixth time, they chose not to.

It interests me that as these people began to leave, Jesus didn't run after them, saying, "Maybe I used the wrong analogy. Let Me give you something else to think about." There's no striving, no persuading, and no trying to talk someone into life. Instead, He said, "If My Father is speaking to you, you'll hear. If you hear, you'll come. And if you come, you'll be received."

> Then Jesus said to the twelve, "Do you also want to go away?" But Simon Peter answered Him, "Lord, to whom shall we go? You have the words of eternal life. Also we have come to believe and know that You are the Christ, the Son of the living God." Jesus answered them, "Did I not choose you, the twelve, and one of you is a Devil?" He spoke of Judas Iscariot, the son of Simon, for it was he who would betray Him, being one of the twelve.
>
> —John 6:67–71

"Want to go back to your former ways?" Jesus asked His disciples.

"Where else can we go?" Peter answered. "We have come to believe and we know that You are the Christ, the Son of the living God."

The disciples were in the dark about a lot of things. But they were right about Jesus. And if you're right about Jesus, everything else will clear up. If you're wrong about Him, nothing will.

There were two groups: one that stayed with Jesus and one that walked away. We certainly want to know which group we're in and how hungry we are for life.

Chapter 52

Truly Clean!

Mark 7:1–23
(Matthew 15:1–20)

The ongoing confrontations between Jesus and the religious leaders of His day point out the difference between what man decides the way to God should be, versus God's declared way as found in faith in His Son. This particular confrontation before us took place after the discussion with the crowds in John 6.

> Then the Pharisees and some of the scribes came together to Him, having come from Jerusalem. Now when they saw some of His disciples eat bread with defiled, that is, with unwashed hands, they found fault.
>
> —Mark 7:1–2

The religious leaders had made an eighty-plus-mile trip from Jerusalem because Jesus had become a real problem for them. Thousands, if not tens of thousands, of folks were following Him—not all for the right reasons, but all caught up with and talking about who He was and why He had come. The religious machinery in Jerusalem saw Him as a tremendous threat to their power, influence, and income. That is why several times in the Gospels we see these spiritual leaders coming from Jerusalem, sent by the Sanhedrin, the governing body, with one intention: to discredit Jesus in the people's eyes.

It is this group that showed up here again from Jerusalem to find fault. These theological "hit men" had politeness in their voices, but their position was one of superiority. They gravely looked down on the disciples who had the audacity to break their hand-washing law. Because Mark wrote primarily to Gentile believers, he explained this Jewish practice:

> For the Pharisees and all the Jews do not eat unless they wash their hands in a special way, holding the tradition of the elders. When they come from the marketplace, they do not eat unless they wash. And there are many other things which they have received and hold, like the washing of cups, pitchers, copper vessels, and couches.
>
> —Mark 7:3–4

A compilation of the Jewish oral law, known as the Mishnah, was written down between the years 70 and 200 A.D. It was a huge book containing instruction on every type of religious practice. The rabbis had divided the Torah, the Law, into 613 specific decrees from God. Prohibitions made up 365 of the decrees, and another 248 were positive declarations. But when they wrote the oral law, they took each of the 613 commandments and expanded them to thousands. As a result, anything having to do with God's love or people's sin was buried under a mountain of man-made laws God never intended.

For example, you couldn't look in a mirror on the Sabbath because if you saw a gray hair you might be tempted to pull it out and that would be work. You couldn't wear false teeth on the Sabbath because if they fell out you'd have to pick them up and that would be lifting a burden. You could spit on the ground but not on the dirt because that would be irrigating the soil.

But the longest section in the entire book is the section dedicated to cleanness and uncleanness. It required 186 pages to tell us how to be clean. Yet these 186 pages grew out of less than twenty verses in the Old Testament. Some of them had to do with the preparation Aaron and his sons were to make before they offered sacrifice as priests. Some had to do with the cleansing that exposure to the blood of the sacrifices would require. But by the time the oral law kicked in, it was assumed that everyone had to clean everything in a certain way if they were going to be pleasing in God's eyes. The Mishnah contained thirty-five pages for ceremonial pot-washing alone. Can you imagine these religious men teaching that God's great concern was how clean the pots and pans were?

Jesus was infuriated with these teachings that hid the grace and mercy of God under the labors of man. It was inevitable He would clash with the religion of the scribes and Pharisees sooner or later. Here He would use their complaint to teach that what matters to God is a pure heart—something we can never accomplish on our own. God has to do that in our lives and no amount of outward or external scrubbing will do (Jer. 2:22).

> Then the Pharisees asked Him, "Why do Your disciples not walk according to the tradition of the elders, but eat bread with unwashed hands?" He answered and said to them, "Well did Isaiah prophesy of you hypocrites, as it is written: 'This people honors Me with their lips, but their heart is far from Me. And in vain they worship Me, teaching as doctrines the commandments of men.'"
>
> —Mark 7:5–7

I imagine that this confrontation between Jesus and the very scary-looking officials with their fine robes and distasteful looks certainly backed up the crowd a bit because most were wary of these men.

"Uh-oh. Jesus is in trouble now," they must have whispered. "They are from Jerusalem. Step back. Pretend you don't even see what's going on."

The question the Pharisees asked wasn't one of faith but of ritual. "How come Your boys aren't following the rules?" they asked.

"First of all," Jesus answered, "you have a heartless religion. Second, you are absolutely wrong when you interpret the Law to make these kinds of rules, because washing your hands can't possibly cleanse the wickedness in your hearts."

Then He quoted a seven-hundred-year-old prophecy out of Isaiah 29 that said that when worship is made with the mouth only, detached from the heart, it is vain. "Vain" meaning empty or worthless.

"You're pretending to be spiritual but you're not," Jesus said. "You're pretending to be holy but you're not. You're pretending to love God but you don't. You're hypocrites."

Calling these robed men hypocrites must have scared everyone within earshot. They were, after all, the most powerful group in the nation.

In Genesis 4:3–7, when God said to Cain and Abel, "Here's how you're to worship and here's how you're to come," both Cain and Abel showed up—but only Abel listened to God and did as God asked. Cain just brought an offering he thought God should be happy with.

To Abel, God said, "This is good."

To Cain, He said, "This is not acceptable."

Cain got angry. *I came all this way and brought all this stuff and You don't accept it?* he must have thought. *Who do You think You are?*

"Who do you think *you* are?" God would have answered. "If you do it right, you'll be accepted."

Cain had gone through the motions and yet had done what he wanted. He had provided a religious way to God—but we can't come to God any way we please. Only God can prescribe the way to come. And never did He prescribe this ongoing scrubbing and washing.

> "For laying aside the commandments of God, you hold the tradition of men—the washing of the pitchers and cups, and many other such things you do." He said to them, "All too well, you reject the commandment of God, that you may keep your tradition."
>
> —Mark 7:8–9

"Not only is your own worship empty, but you're responsible for teaching others this futile way," Jesus said. I can just see the religious leaders' blood begin to boil. Then He gave them an example:

> "For Moses said, 'Honor your father and mother'; and, 'He who curses father or mother, let him be put to death.' But you say, 'If a man says to his father or mother, "Whatever profit you might have received from me is Corban"'—'(that is, a gift to God), then you no longer let him do anything for his father or his mother, making the word of God of no effect through your tradition which you have handed down. And many such things you do."
>
> —Mark 7:10–13

The Old Testament Law clearly taught that they were to honor their parents. To "honor" meant to respect and obey, to provide for and care for. So as parents grew older and had needs, their grown children were to help meet them. The Pharisees, however, taught that whatever was "Corban" or, literally, "dedicated to the Lord," was to be used at the owner's discretion as to how he felt the Lord's leading. In this way, money, goods, or property could be off limits even to one's elderly parents. Jesus said, "You've handed down this tradition simply as a way to skirt the Law. There's no desire to know God. There is no coming to the Lord for wisdom or to the Bible for direction. There is only a manipulation of the things of God to serve yourselves."

It's interesting to me that religious people often are religiously zealous about religious practices—but there's no conviction of sin, no desire to be saved, no need for a Savior. Everything is performance-driven, which is true of most religions and is certainly true of these scribes and Pharisees that had come to challenge Jesus. Yet Jesus made His closing arguments by drawing the crowd in even closer.

> When He had called all the multitude to Himself, He said to them, "Hear Me, everyone, and understand. There is nothing that enters a man from outside which can defile him, but the things which come out of him, those are the things that defile a man. If anyone has ears to hear, let him hear!"
>
> —Mark 7:14–16

Here is the basic truth of God: Spiritual defilement doesn't come from outside our lives. It arises from within. Sin comes from the heart, not the diet. So the next time someone tells you Jesus was a vegetarian, tell them it doesn't matter what He ate. Nor does it matter what we eat. It's the heart God is interested in. Externals have no impact. Jeremiah said the heart is so desperately wicked that people have trouble even knowing their own hearts. Solomon wrote in Ecclesiastes that the hearts of the sons of men are filled with evil and there is madness in their hearts all the days of their lives.

As a Christian, you read this and say, "Of course." But to a crowd that had been led by religious influence all of their lives, this was a huge challenge to the status quo. "You mean we don't have to wash like that? You mean God doesn't require 186 pages of cleanliness? What does He want?"

A clean heart.

By the time you come to Acts 10:14, where the Lord tells Peter to eat of those animals in his dream that were unclean by law, Peter still will say, "I'm not eating anything unclean!" It took Peter awhile to fully be free in God's grace, because he'd been indoctrinated so long by a religion that blinded the eyes and bound the heart only to itself.

> When He had entered a house away from the crowd, His disciples asked Him concerning the parable.
>
> —Mark 7:17

Between verses 16 and 17 here in Mark, Matthew 15 fills in a couple of verses for us that tell us that when they got into a house away from the crowd, the disciples asked Jesus what He had meant about defilement versus what it means to be truly clean.

> So He said to them, "Are you thus without understanding also? Do you not perceive that whatever enters a man from outside cannot defile him because it does not enter his heart but his stomach, and is eliminated, thus purifying all foods?" And He said, "What comes out of a man, that defiles a man. For from within, out of the heart of men, proceed evil thoughts, adulteries, fornications, murders, thefts, covetousness, wickedness, deceit, lewdness, an evil eye, blasphemy, pride, foolishness. All these evil things come from within and defile a man."
>
> —Mark 7:18–23

To Jesus, the legalism, tradition, and hypocrisy of the religious attacks against Him were from people who were caught up in the externals of life, blinded to the truth of God that said, "It's your heart that's in trouble."

It is still the message of the Gospel today. The real issue is the heart's sinfulness, a sinfulness that is measurable and quantitative. To prove this, Jesus gave us a list of thirteen categories of sin. The first seven are plural and speak about behavior. The last six are singular and speak about attitude because sin isn't just behavior—it's attitude as well. It's a pretty complete picture. Many of these terms are listed in this same order in several places in the Bible where God talks about people's nature apart from salvation.

Evil thoughts refers to corrupt thinking. *Adulteries* is the word for unfaithfulness in marriage. *Fornications* is a more general word for any sexual sin. *Murders* speaks of both hate and bitterness. *Covetousness* is interesting because in the Bible it refers not only to an insatiable desire for more for oneself, but also the desire that others would have less. *Blasphemy* means to speak evil or to slander. *Pride* is self-exaltation. Jesus ended with the word *foolishness*, which speaks of thoughtlessness with regard to spiritual issues.

If you are committed to the idea that people are basically good, you shouldn't read the Bible because it will change your mind. The Bible says people are basically evil, that sin has destroyed them, and that they have no hope or future apart from God. Isaiah 64:6 says even our righteousness—the very best we can do—is no better than filthy rags. "There is none righteous, not one. There is none that seeks after God. We've all sinned and fallen short of His glory," Paul wrote in Romans 3:23.

When John the Baptist came on the scene in Matthew 3:10, he said, "When the Lord comes, He'll lay His ax to the root of the tree." In other words, "He'll get to the root of the problem." And the root of the problem is this: It isn't a better religion people need—it's a changed life. It's not a different set of rules that's required—it's a new heart. You can wash all day long and still be filthy. You can show up every Sunday for church, sit in the right spot, and say the right things and still never be saved. You have to have a relationship with God—and it all begins with faith in Jesus. Satan's plan is to use religion to blind us to our real need. Therefore, we've got to be aware whenever religion begins to replace God's Word and when lip service begins to be enough. We need a new heart, a new birth, a new beginning. The good news is that Ezekiel prophesied in chapter 36 that Jesus would come for that very reason. Have you been born-again?

Chapter 53

JESUS AND TWO GENTILES

Mark 7:24–37
(Matthew 15:21–31)

After sparring with the scribes and Pharisees, Jesus went northwest to a predominantly Gentile area known as the Decapolis—a place where these religious men from Jerusalem would not follow Him.

> From there He arose and went to the region of Tyre and Sidon. And He entered a house and wanted no one to know it, but He could not be hidden. For a woman whose young daughter had an unclean spirit heard about Him, and she came and fell at His feet. The woman was a Greek, a Syro-Phoenician by birth, and she kept asking Him to cast the demon out of her daughter.
> —Mark 7:24–26

In Lebanon today, there is still a Tyre and Sidon and, as in the days of Jesus, it is still a very Gentile area—a place then where hundreds of gods were worshipped. The disciples, no doubt, were concerned as to why they were there. But Jesus had gone there to rest. However, when He got there, it became just like everywhere else He went—a place filled with needs that touched the heart of our God!

In Mark 3 we read that there already were a lot of folks from Galilee who were traveling across the border to hear Jesus. In fact, Luke tells us that following the Sermon on the Mount Jesus gave to His disciples, He came down to speak to a larger crowd among whom were many from Tyre and Sidon. And although they hadn't been given specific promises because they were not part of the chosen people, they went home with reports of the wondrous, miracle-working teacher they had encountered. So when Jesus came into the area, He again encountered crowds hungry to see Him.

Mark here draws our attention to one particular woman who lived in an area the Syrians controlled. Having grown up in a Greek culture, she spoke a language that certainly would have been foreign to this group. Matthew added in chapter 15:22 that she was a Canaanite, a descendant of people who had been slated for God's judgment in the Old Testament days because of their great sin. From a condemned group, she came to a Gentile town to see a Jewish man surrounded by Jewish disciples who didn't have much time for her at all, as evidenced by the fact that the preferred first-century Jewish epithet for Gentiles was "dogs"—not pet dogs, but scavengers. In fact, some rabbis taught that God created Gentiles only as fuel for hell.

Religious intolerance isn't new. And yet God's heart is always the same: He comes for all of His creation, for everyone needs Him. Why did God choose the Jews? He said it wasn't because they were smarter, better looking, more faithful, or more godly than everyone else, but simply so that through them the world would know who the Messiah was.

To that nation He gave promises, prophets, signs, and wonders so no one would miss His arrival. Unfortunately, the people chosen to deliver the message became proud and exclusive, thinking they alone were in and everyone else was out. But that wasn't the Lord's intention. He always had the world on His heart.

The disciples were going to have to learn that—beginning here on the road with Jesus as He focused on this one woman who came to Him and fell on her face, asking for help with her demon-possessed daughter. She interrupted. She was persistent. She was loud. She wasn't taking no for an answer. Nothing could deter her or keep her away. She was there because her need was too great and her options limited to the One who had delivered others.

Matthew 15:22 records that as she fell at Jesus' feet, she said, "Have mercy upon me, O Lord, Son of David." This Gentile woman—who knew a different god for every day of the week—used a Jewish title for the Messiah and said, "I am looking for mercy from You, the promised One." As far as we know, she had never seen Him, never spent time with Him, never watched Him work, or never listened to one of His sermons. Yet her words were as near the truth as any had spoken.

We read in Matthew 15:23 that Jesus answered her "not a word." Even as she continued to cry, there was no response from our Lord. He seemed to be completely indifferent to her plight. The next thing Matthew records is the disciples saying, "Lord, could You please get rid of her? She's bothering us."

I always think that if people could just meet Jesus, they'd get saved. The problem is they meet us first. Like the disciples, we're often not His best representatives.

The disciples were at their usual best but Jesus seemed so different from before. Why? Didn't He care about her pain? Of course, He did—as we'll see in a minute. But His silence drew out a couple of things, the first of which was her faith. Second, the disciples needed to learn they weren't the only choice, the only nation, or the only ones. Jesus had come to reach the world.

I think the fact that this woman persisted in faith even though she ran into some difficulty should tell everyone that it isn't lineage, nationality, or skin color that gives someone an advantage with Jesus. It's faith. She cried out and kept on because her need was greater than any obstacle. Matthew tells us Jesus finally said to her, "I am here only for the lost sheep of Israel." In other words, "First things first. I've come for the Jews."

She then fell on her face and worshipped Him, saying, "Help me, Lord. (The word she used for *Lord* means 'boss' or 'the one in charge.') I don't care who's first or second. My daughter needs Your help. Please don't turn me away. Please don't put me off. If You are the Lord, You can help." In her persistence, her belief in Jesus became evident.

> But Jesus said to her, "Let the children be filled first; for it is not good to take the children's bread and throw it to the little dogs."
>
> —Mark 7:27

The "children" were the house of Israel. "Bread" was the Gospel and the declaration of who Jesus was. For "dogs" Jesus didn't use the word for scavenger, which was the usual word used to refer to a Gentile. He used the word for puppy. As opposed to the religious leaders' hatefulness, Jesus welcomed her to Himself, saying, "God has a plan for the Jews—but His heart is for the world." After all, although no one wants a wild dog in his house, everyone likes puppies.

Speaking to the Jews in Rome in Acts 28:28, Paul said, "I want you to know that salvation of God has been sent to the Gentiles." God's plan was for the church to be born. Therefore, this Gentile woman begging for help would fit right in.

> And she answered and said to Him, "Yes, Lord, yet even the little dogs under the table eat from the children's crumbs."
>
> —Mark 7:28

If you ever wanted to find a humble heart coming to the Lord, this is certainly one. Recognizing the place of Israel, this Gentile woman came to Jesus solely on the basis of mercy. She didn't demand attention because she thought she deserved it. She was happy with crumbs. And it is to that humble response that Matthew records Jesus saying, "O, woman, great is your faith. Let it be done to you according to your desire."

> Then He said to her, "For this saying go your way; the demon has gone out of your daughter." And when she had come to her house, she found the demon gone out, and her daughter lying on the bed.
>
> —Mark 7:29–30

God loves persistence in faith because true faith is persistent. Jesus told the story of a woman who presented her case in court to a judge who cared neither what God nor man thought. But because she kept coming back, he helped the woman only to get her out of his hair. Jesus set this judge in opposition to Himself and said, "If you can get wicked people to do the right thing just by nagging them, how much more can you move the hand of a God who wants to help by simply coming in persistent prayer?"

True faith is both persistent and passionate. Yet it is always based on grace rather than works. I like the fact that this woman knew nothing in her could convince Jesus to help. But due to her willingness to sit at the chosen family's feet and catch the crumbs falling off the plates, Jesus said, "What great faith." She was one of the first Gentiles in the Gospels to enter the kingdom.

The disciples were amazed when Jesus sat and spoke to a woman at a well in Samaria. This was an even more remote area than Samaria, without even a synagogue in sight. Yet faith knows no boundaries, and faith is what Jesus honors, no matter where He finds it.

> Again, departing from the region of Tyre and Sidon, He came through the midst of the region of Decapolis to the Sea of Galilee. Then they brought to Him one who was deaf and had an impediment in his speech, and they begged Him to put His hand on him. And He took him aside from the multitude, and put His fingers in his ears, and He spat and touched his tongue.
>
> —Mark 7:31–33

If you walk from the Tyre area on the northern side of the Sea of Galilee toward the east, you will find remnants of the ten Gentile cities known as the Decapolis. They shared the same currency, ruler, and trade agreements. They also formed the dividing line between the Gentiles to the north and the Jews to the south.

Here, among a mixture of Jews and Gentiles, Jesus again made Himself known. Seven hundred years earlier, Isaiah had written in chapter 35:5 that when the Messiah came He would open the eyes of the blind and the ears of the deaf. Therefore, to the Jews, Jesus should have been the proof of the Scriptures. To the Gentiles, He was the assurance God was very interested in them.

Although we know nothing more about this deaf man who was brought to Jesus than the fact that he had lost his ability to speak plainly—which might suggest he'd gone deaf rather than he had been born deaf—we do know Jesus was able to heal him. This being in the vicinity of Gadera, it could be that it was the witness of the once-demon-possessed man living in the Gadera tombs that was the catalyst to stir these townspeople to bring this deaf man to Jesus.

The scant information we are given in the account directly preceding this one as to how the demon-possessed girl was delivered is contrasted with the abundance of information we are given here. After removing the man from the crowd, Jesus stuck His fingers in the man's ears, spat, touched his tongue, looked up to heaven, sighed, and spoke. That seems like an awful lot to go through, doesn't it? Does the Lord need to stick His fingers in your ears and spit before you get well? Of course not. But all of these actions must have spoken very loudly to this man who could only see and not hear. Jesus never followed a pattern for healing, I think so we wouldn't attempt to recreate His actions, but rather simply seek the Healer, not His various methods.

> Then, looking up to heaven, . . .
>
> —Mark 7:34

Jesus took this man of great need away from everyone else and looked up. We must do that as well. Looking up and seeing our Father and relying on Him will prepare us for any ministry He has planned for us.

> . . . He sighed, . . .
>
> —Mark 7:34

Sighing is an emotional response that carries with it an involuntary physical response. Your chest rises and falls; your face takes on a different expression. Even though he was not able to hear Jesus sigh, this man was able to see in Jesus' sigh His concern for him.

I think as we go out to minister to others, we must be moved by the suffering they face and weep with those who weep. In chapter 9, Jeremiah, known as the weeping prophet, said, "Lord, I wish my head was filled with water so that my eyes could cry day and night for my people." I don't think the Lord means for us to get through this life with dry eyes. What breaks your heart? What moves you to sigh? That's probably where you'll find your ministry. It was the way Nehemiah discovered his (reads Nehemiah 1).

> . . . and said to him, "Ephphatha," that is, "Be opened."
>
> —Mark 7:34

Then finally, Jesus spoke, for it is always His Word that brings life.

> Immediately his ears were opened, and the impediment of his tongue was loosed, and he spoke plainly. Then He commanded them that they should tell no one; but the more He commanded them, the more widely they proclaimed it.
>
> —Mark 7:35–36

Tell no one? We have read that before haven't we? And as before that simply didn't work. It never does. If God has touched you, even if He says, "Don't say a word," you can't help but share it. I am moved by the fact that these whom God ministered to, when told to keep quiet, could not, but were compelled to tell all of His glory. Today we are sent to tell all of His glory and we rather see many who simply choose to keep quiet. God help us.

> And they were astonished beyond measure, saying, "He has done all things well. He makes both the deaf to hear and the mute to speak."
>
> —Mark 7:37

How would God have you reach the world? If you have eyes that look up in prayer, a heart of compassion, hands that reach out, and a willingness to declare His Word, He could use you to turn your world upside down. Use us, Lord, in every place you put us!

Chapter 54

NURTURING SPIRITUAL UNDERSTANDING

Mark 8:1–26
(Matthew 15:32–39; 16:1–12)

We now come to a series of lessons where the Lord will tell us that although He is very patient with nurturing our spiritual understanding, at some point, we must respond with what we have learned, make progress, show growth and practice living out what we have received from our Lord.

> In those days, the multitude being very great and having nothing to eat, Jesus called His disciples to Him and said to them, "I have compassion on the multitudes, because they have now continued with Me three days and have nothing to eat. And if I send them away hungry to their own houses, they will faint on the way; for some of them have come from afar." Then His disciples answered Him, "How can one satisfy these people with bread here in the wilderness?" He asked them, "How many loaves do you have?" And they said, "Seven." So He commanded the multitude to sit down on the ground. And He took the seven loaves and gave thanks, broke them and gave them to His disciples to set before them, and they set them before the multitude. They also had a few small fish; and having blessed them, He said to set them also before them. So they ate and were filled, and they took up seven large baskets of leftover fragments. Now those who had eaten were about four thousand. And He sent them away, immediately got into the boat with His disciples, and came to the region of Dalmanutha.
>
> —Mark 8:1–10

Back in Mark 6, Jesus had fed five thousand men plus woman and children north of the Sea of Galilee in what today is called the Golan Heights area. Here we see an almost identical miracle. In fact, many Bible commentators say they are one and the same. But the texts themselves would say otherwise. Look at these comparisons:

There were five thousand men in Mark 6.
Here there are four thousand.

In Mark 6, the people had been with Jesus for only one day.
Here they had been with Him for three.

In Mark 6, the people sat on the grass in the springtime.
Here they sit on the dirt.

In Mark 6, there was one prayer offered for both bread and fish.
Here there is a separate prayer for each.

In Mark 6, the crowd was mostly Jewish.
Here they are mostly Gentile.

In Mark 6, there were five loaves and two fish.
Here there are seven loaves and a few fish.

In Mark 6, there were twelve small baskets of leftovers
Here there are seven large hampers of leftovers.

If that isn't enough to convince you, Jesus will say in verses 19 and 20 that they were two separate occasions,

So twice in a matter of weeks, Jesus multiplied bread to feed hungry people. And through repetition, the disciples were to learn to trust Him. Here in Mark 8, with no food for a hungry crowd, they should by now have been able to say to Jesus, "Maybe we can find a little food. We know You can multiply it even as You did before." But instead, they balked again at the same obstacles that had stopped them previously. We are slow to learn, aren't we?

Three days into the wilderness, this miracle took place in much the same way as it had before: through Jesus' hands, the meager became more than enough for all. Every hungry mouth and heart was filled. By the time the disciples left the area, they had witnessed two overwhelming miracles that involved multiplied thousands of people. But they too were slow to learn from them. Help us God!

I remember the first day I touched a hot stove because it's the only time I did it purposefully. That day there was an immediate, permanent lesson for me. Unfortunately, we don't seem to learn permanent spiritual lessons as quickly. So we are destined to have to learn them over and over again.

> Then the Pharisees came out and began to dispute with Him, seeking from Him
> a sign from heaven, testing Him.
>
> —Mark 8:11

We are told in Matthew 16:1 that along with the Pharisees came the Sadducees. If you ever had wanted to get together two people who disagreed on nearly everything, it would have been a Pharisee and a Sadducee. The Pharisees were the religious men. They had hundreds of rules to follow and were big on outward tradition. Although they rejected God's Word, they looked for heaven. The Sadducees, on the other hand, had no desire for or belief in an afterlife. To them, this was it. This was all there was. They were the humanists, the rationalists, and the liberals of their day who lived for power and wealth.

As different as these two groups were, they were united in their hatred of Jesus because He posed a threat to both of their ways of life. So they approached Jesus and began to argue with Him, demanding proof that He was whom He claimed to be. After all He had already done, you conclude they were not interested in the truth. They had plenty of information—but they lacked the heart for God to respond to it. So to discredit Him in front of His followers, they chided Jesus, saying His works weren't proof enough.

> But He sighed deeply in His spirit, and said, "Why does this generation seek a sign? Assuredly, I say to you, no sign shall be given to this generation."
>
> —Mark 8:12

The word for *sighed* we have seen before and is an interesting Greek word, which literally speaks of the outward manifestation of a broken heart. Matthew 16:2–3 records that as Jesus asked, "Why is this generation always seeking a sign?" that He added, "When it's evening, you will say, 'It's going to be fair weather because the sky is red.' And yet in the morning, you say, 'Now it's going to be foul weather because the sky is red.' You hypocrites. You know how to read the sky but you can't discern the signs of the times. No sign shall be given this generation except the sign of the prophet Jonah. As he was three days and three nights in the heart of the earth, so shall the Son of Man be."

The Pharisees should have known better. They had the Scriptures. They could have searched through it and seen the promises of the Messiah and where He came from and what He would do, etc. They could have received Him by faith in what had been spoken of Him. But they didn't. Five times in the Gospels—in Matthew 12, Mark 8, Luke 11, John 2, and John 6—every time they asked Jesus for a sign, He gave them this one sign because signs wouldn't convince them. Miracles don't save—faith saves. Even the miracle of Lazarus being raised from the dead wasn't enough to persuade the chief priests. Rather than turn to Jesus, John tells us in chapter 11 they tried to kill Lazarus.

> And He left them, and getting into the boat again, departed to the other side.
>
> —Mark 8:13

After telling the Pharisees and Sadducees that no sign would be given to them except for the sign of Jonah—which spoke of His resurrection—Jesus departed. I can think of nothing more tragic than to have the Lord depart from a life. But he who ignores the obvious and refuses what he has been given can end up with nothing at all.

> Now the disciples had forgotten to take bread, and they did not have more than
> one loaf with them in the boat. Then He charged them, saying, "Take heed,
> beware of the leaven of the Pharisees and the leaven of Herod." And they reasoned
> among themselves, saying, "It is because we have no bread."
>
> —Mark 8:14–16

I don't know if the rapid departure took the disciples by surprise so they didn't have time
to shop. I also don't know what had happened to the seven large hampers of leftovers. But
whatever the reason, the disciples only had one loaf of bread—hardly enough for thirteen
hungry men. When Jesus began to speak to them about the wickedness of the men He
had just left behind, they mistakenly assumed He was chiding them for forgetting to bring
lunch.

Throughout Scripture, leaven—or yeast—is always emblematic of sin. So Jesus' warning
was of the sinful influences and practices of legalist and humanist doctrines embodied by
the Scribes and Pharisees. But the disciples misapplied Jesus' warning because, like us, they
failed to apply what they had just learned. Twice they had seen Jesus feed thousands. They
had even been the waiters. Yet here they were worried about food for thirteen, and Jesus
could certainly not have been lamenting the fact they forgot to get bread for them all.

If we add Matthew's account to this passage, Jesus asked these men ten rapid-fire questions—all of them designed to remind them of what they already should have learned:

> But Jesus, being aware of it, said to them, "Why do you reason because you have
> no bread? Do you not yet perceive nor understand? Is your heart still hardened?
> Having eyes, do you not see? And having ears, do you not hear? And do you
> not remember? When I broke the five loaves for the five thousand, how many
> baskets full of fragments did you take up?" "Twelve." "Also, when I broke the
> seven for the four thousand, how many large baskets full of fragments did you
> take up?" And they said, "Seven." So He said to them, "How is it you do not
> understand?"
>
> —Mark 8:17–21

Aside from the sleeping apostles in Gethsemane, and Peter arguing with Jesus about the
cross at Caesarea Philippi, we do not find elsewhere Jesus being as stern with His disciples
as He is here. Jesus is extremely tolerant and patient. After all, we're still here, aren't we?
But after two and a half years of observing Him firsthand, the disciples needed a wake-up
call. The word *perceive* means to give something concerted thought. To *understand* means
to put the facts together. "Are your hearts so thick-skinned and calloused?" Jesus asked.
"Why are you discussing bread? Can't you think anything through?"

The disciples were not hard-hearted due to lack of love for Jesus. They had left home,
family, and income, and risked life and limb, to follow Him. Lack of love wasn't the issue.

Lack of listening was. They weren't paying much attention. Their repeated exposure to His ways and His Word were without reflection or application—and it left them dull.

What have you permanently learned this year that has affected your life so you'll never be the same? When Joshua led the people into the Promised Land, he had to take all two million or more of them across the Jordan River at flood season. To do this, the Lord miraculously rolled the river upstream some thirty miles. As they crossed, Joshua sent the priests back into the riverbed to gather twelve large stones and bring them to the shore. He piled these stones of remembrance one on top of the other and called the spot Gilgal, or literally, "The Lord will roll away our reproach." Over the next several years as Joshua became the leader of the campaign to overthrow Canaan, he would return to this same spot time and again to remind himself that God can do the impossible. I think we all need a Gilgal—minds and hearts filled with lessons from the past that will help us do better in the future as we remember His glorious work in our behalf.

> Then He came to Bethsaida; and they brought a blind man to Him, and begged Him to touch him. So He took the blind man by the hand and led him out of the town. And when He had spit on his eyes and put His hands on him, He asked him if he saw anything. And he looked up and said, "I see men like trees, walking." Then He put His hands on his eyes again and made him look up. And he was restored and saw everyone clearly. Then He sent him away to his house, saying, "Neither go into the town, nor tell anyone in the town."
>
> —Mark 8:22–26

The healing of the blind man here in chapter 8 is very similar to the healing of the deaf man in chapter 7. I love the way the Lord took this man along—because more important than sight to a blind man is faith in God. So a healing in steps, not because our Lord was weak or low on power, but because God encourages our faith each step of the way. How good our God to help us grow. Just ask Gideon (Judges 6–7) who weak in faith was, however, willing in heart, and God sent many encouragements to him so he might go forth in His name to do great things in faith!

Afterwards, why did Jesus say, "Don't go into town"? Because, according to Matthew, the Lord had given up on Bethsaida. If the works that had been done there had been done in Tyre and Sidon, they'd have repented long ago, Jesus said. So to this blind man He said, "Go home. Don't go back into town. Nobody's listening."

At your home, office, or neighborhood, however, there's still time.

Chapter 55

WHO DO YOU SAY THAT I AM?

Luke 9:18–26
(Matthew 16:13–27; Mark 8:27–38)

Nearing the end now of two and a half years of public ministry spent primarily in the area of Galilee, Jesus dramatically changed both His message and behavior toward His disciples as He began to head south toward Jerusalem. Up until this point, the crux of His message had centered on who He was. At this point, however, it changes to why He had come. As the ministry in Galilee drew to a close, Jesus would, for the first time, tell His disciples He had come to die. The final approaching year loomed large, and His disciples still had much to learn.

> And it happened, as He was alone praying, that His disciples joined Him, and He asked them, saying, "Who do the crowds say that I am?" So they answered and said, "John the Baptist, but some say Elijah; and others say that one of the old prophets has risen again."
>
> —Luke 9:18–19

We know from both Matthew 16:13–20 and Mark 8:27–30 that this conversation between Jesus and His disciples took place about as far north in Israel as one could go at the time—a place called Caesarea Philippi. Half of the water in the Jordan River comes through the headwaters at Caesarea Philippi, making for a very lush and beautiful setting.

When Jesus asked His disciples who people said He was, I think they must have only told Him the best of what they had heard because there were plenty of people who wanted Him dead, plenty who thought He had lost His mind, and plenty who didn't think much about Him at all. "They think maybe you're John the Baptist come back from the dead. Or maybe Elijah, or one of the other prophets of old who has resurrected," they said. Whatever the crowds thought, the possibility that He was a prophet risen from the dead suggested they thought Jesus was, at the very least, supernatural. Even though, being Jewish, they had thousands of years of prophesies, signposts, and promises; even though they had a timeline to follow; and even though they had seen Jesus' works, His identity as the Messiah stilled seemed to escape them.

There were a couple of reasons for this. First, their hope and expectation of the Messiah was very unlike God's plan. Beginning years earlier, the teaching had always been that when the Messiah came, He would be a political ruler who would set the Jews free and make Israel the center of world power once again. So people looking for the Messiah were looking for a political figure who could dominate crowds and had a political agenda. And Jesus just didn't fit that bill. He came quietly. He ministered to individuals and was available to them personally. He didn't show any interest in politics or power. In fact, He talked about the heart and sin, about blindness and the Devil, about heaven and hell. There was no effort to get votes. There was no campaign trail. So the people missed Him.

Second, when someone comes to know God personally, it is because God takes the first step. The Bible says it is only by divine revelation that we come to recognize Jesus as God. There is always a balance between God revealing Himself and our response to His revelation. But it is always in that order. God has to reveal Himself first. Sin will keep you from ever discovering God. Only God can save you from the blindness and darkness of sin—and the good news is He wants to do just that. So He speaks to your heart by sending the Holy Spirit.

One thing is obvious from the disciples' report of what the crowds thought: you cannot find Jesus by public opinion. Even today, everyone has an opinion about Jesus and they're not afraid to tell you what it is. But you can't follow the crowd. There are millions of people who embrace Islam, for example. Islam teaches that Jesus is probably the greatest of the prophets. That's what the crowd in Jesus' day thought, too. But that's not enough to save you.

Men like Thomas Aquinas and C.S. Lewis did a good job of taking what Jesus said and saying to the people, "You can't write off Jesus as a good prophet because the claims He made are too absurd. He can't simply be a good guy if He's saying He's God. He can't simply be a good man if He's saying He's the only way to heaven. He can't simply be a prophet from God if He's emphatically declaring, 'Without Me, you end up in hell.' His statements are way too radical and make Him either a liar, a lunatic—or else He must be the Lord."

If Jesus is crazy, we should all run away as far from Him as possible. If He's lying, we should all wake up and come back to reality. But if He's the Lord, we should all bow down and surrender our lives for His great love and sacrifice.

> He said to them, "But who do you say that I am?" Peter answered and said, "The Christ of God."
>
> —Luke 9:20

Matthew 16:16 records Peter's answer as, "You're the Christ, the Son of the living God." Both Matthew and Luke 16:20 use the word *Christ*, the Greek word for the Hebrew *Messiah*. In other words, "You're the Messiah, the One we are looking for, the Anointed One." Peter spoke what everyone else in the group was thinking.

"We believe You're the Messiah," Peter answered. Did the disciples understand fully what this meant? Absolutely not. They too still looked for a political ruler, still fought about who was going to be in His cabinet, and still anticipated with great hope the overthrow of the Roman oppression. They didn't understand the "Savior" part of Jesus' coming. But they were on the right track. They were listening to the Scriptures. God was speaking to their hearts. And they were on the way.

Matthew records that when Peter said, "You're the Messiah," Jesus said, "You didn't come up with that on your own. That's information you can't discover apart from God leading you to those things." I've always taken great comfort in this as a pastor because there can be a lot of pressure to wonder if I made the Gospel clear enough, to wonder if I could have studied more or used a better illustration. But knowing it is only Jesus who truly can draw people to Himself takes the pressure off me. So I can study and pray and do my best, but must never forget that unless God by His Word and Spirit reaches the heart, I am unable to accomplish a thing.

Peter received spiritual revelation but the interesting thing to me is he didn't know he had been given it. People often think that when God speaks there are a lot of things that need to happen. The sun has to set. The room has to get dark. The hair on the back of their neck has to stand up. They have to get a cold chill. And then an echo chamber has to be turned on. But it doesn't work that way. Peter had been watching and praying, learning and listening—and through these natural paths, God had been speaking. Slowly but surely, the light was being turned on and he was able to see Jesus was the Messiah.

The disciples had a lot left to learn—but they were moving forward. The next year would be revolutionary for them as they would discover that Jesus wasn't going to stay and rule now, but that He had come to die as the Lamb of God for the sins of the world, and by His death would provide an open door for all men to be saved. One day He'd return to do all that they were hoping for—but not yet.

Matthew 16:18 tells us that, in response to Peter's declaration, Jesus said, "You are Peter. On this rock, I will build My church and the gates of hell will not prevail against it." The Catholic Church in which I was raised has taught this to mean that Jesus here made Peter the head of the church. The Scriptures themselves, as well as the context of the verse, don't lend themselves to that interpretation, however. Either Jesus is saying, "You are Peter, the pope, the ruler, the smartest guy in the group because you spoke up first," or He is saying, "You are Peter and it is upon the rock of your testimony of who I am that the church will be built." Interestingly, the original word for *Peter* is *Petros*, meaning "pebble" or "a little stone."

When Peter himself years later wrote about the church, he said, "The church is gathered like a bunch of living stones that make a building. But the foundation, or cornerstone, is Jesus" (1 Pet. 2:4–6).

When Jesus said here, "Upon this rock I will build My church," He didn't use the word *petros*. He used *petra*, or "boulder." In other words, He said, "Peter, you're one of the pebbles in the work, one of the living stones in the building, but I am going to build My church upon your testimony that I am the Promised One, the Savior, the Messiah. And when that takes place, the gates of hell won't be able to prevent its growth."

Matthew 16:19 records that Jesus went on to say, "I will give you the keys of the kingdom so that whatever you bind on earth will be bound in heaven and whatever you loose upon the earth will be loosed in heaven." Again, the Catholic Church has taught that this gives priests the right to forgive sins. The problem with that position is we find this authority delegated to the disciples in more than one place. As Peter and the disciples were sent forth, Jesus gave them the responsibility to tell others who He was. The responses of those who heard the message determined whether they could be forgiven or remain in their sin.

The words *binding* and *loosing* are rabbinical terms that mean to cut off and set free. As followers of Jesus, we have the ability to say to people, "I know how you can go to heaven. I know how your sins can be forgiven. The Bible says if you go to Jesus, your sins will be cleansed. On the other hand, if you don't go to Him, you'll be stuck with your own sin."

Only God can forgive sin. But we are the vessels through which He declares to the world the way to be forgiven. The church is commissioned to tell all men that only God can forgive their sins through Jesus Christ who died for each of them.

> And He strictly warned and commanded them to tell this to no one.
> —Luke 9:21

Why did Jesus want His disciples to keep silent? I suggest it was because the understanding that the Messiah first had to be a Savior before He could be a ruler, that He first had to die before He could reign, was foreign to them and they needed to understand it better than they did. They weren't ready yet, but after the resurrection, beginning on Pentecost, they would be sent out with others to preach that exact truth, which would by then have gripped their hearts. For now Jesus' time had not yet come and neither had theirs. Then came this bombshell:

> Saying, "The Son of Man must suffer many things, and be rejected by the elders
> and chief priests and scribes, and be killed, and be raised the third day."
> —Luke 9:22

"Son of Man" is the title Jesus used to refer to Himself because it speaks of His humanity. "I'm going to suffer and be killed by the religious leaders, but three days later, I'll rise," He said. This statement must have hit His disciples like a ton of bricks. Virtually every time He spoke to them of His death He also declared He would rise again on the third day. Yet not once do we ever read of any of the disciples responding to words of His resurrection. Apparently, they heard "die" and stopped listening.

In Matthew's account, this was so upsetting to Peter that he said, "You can't die. We won't allow that."

"Get behind Me, Satan," Jesus answered.

Why would He say that to the same guy who only moments earlier had declared He was the Messiah? Because in saying He couldn't die, Peter was voicing his own plans rather than God's. Before we get saved, He has to bring us around to His way of thinking, because our way of thinking is that we can work our way to heaven. Our way of thinking is that Jesus is a nice prophet that we talk about once in a while, but hardly depend upon for our future and life. We have to be brought to understand that without His death, we will never have life. Peter was voicing the world's idea of salvation and Satan's greatest lie: you can do it yourself.

> Then He said to them all, "If anyone desires to come after Me, let him deny himself, and take up his cross daily, and follow Me. For whoever desires to save his life will lose it, but whoever loses his life for My sake will save it. For what profit is it to a man if he gains the whole world, and is himself destroyed or lost? For whoever is ashamed of Me and My words, of him the Son of Man will be ashamed when He comes in His own glory, and in His Father's, and of the holy angels."
>
> —Luke 9:23–26

Jesus addressed the conflict between His purpose for coming and the reason His disciples thought He had come. That's the crux of discipleship. We only do well with the Lord to the extent that we follow His ways. The world has an idea of how things should be—most people will even try to correct how God has been doing things. But if I truly want Jesus to be the Lord, I have to submit to Him as such. That means I start to take orders rather than give them. I surrender, seek to know His will, and ask for help to be obedient to Him each step of the way.

A life of faith in Jesus means I follow Him. I do what He says. And when I don't agree, He's still right. I may not get it—and a lot of times I don't—but my only option is to leave it with Him.

To the disciples sitting at that beautiful place in Caesarea Philippi, Jesus said, "I'm going to die."

"Die? You can't die," they insisted.

"If you want to follow Me, you are going to have to deny yourself," Jesus answered. "If you don't agree with this, you'd better get off the boat now, because this is where we're headed. This is the way of God. You take up your cross daily."

Things had been relatively smooth up to this point. Jesus and the boys had lots of friends and supporters. But it was going to get a lot harder for the disciples in the months to follow. As Jesus headed for Jerusalem, there were going to be many threats, violence, and even death. This was going to be a costly trip for everyone, especially our Savior.

What brought Jesus to the cross? The fact that He claimed to be God. When the crowd picked up stones to throw at Him, Jesus said, "Which of the good works am I getting stoned for?"

"We're not stoning You for good works," the crowd answered. "We're stoning You because You claim to be God."

It was Jesus' identification as God that brought the cross. For us, the cross appears anytime we identify with Jesus in a world that wants very little to do with Him. I've heard people take the concept of bearing the cross out of context. "He's my cross to bear," a dad will say of his rebellious teenage son. Wrong. He's your son. The cross is only the result of your identification with Jesus to the world. When we suffer shame for standing with the Lord or bearing His name in our business, ethics, or behavior, that is picking up our Cross. Standing with Jesus is what is clearly taught here.

A lot of evangelicals today see Christianity as a way to benefit or enhance their own lives. Jesus, however, said following Him isn't a matter of enhancing our lives but of losing them.

What is the highest ambition you have in life? In priority, at the top of your list, what do you want more than anything else? "If you're ashamed of Me, I'll be ashamed of you," Jesus said. Later in Luke 12:8, He said, "If you confess Me before men, I'll confess you before My Father. If not, I won't."

If Jesus is a fraud, why follow Him? If He's only a good guy, He is one among many. He has to be more than that. He has to be the Savior, Lord, Messiah, and the Promised One in order for you to leave behind everything to follow Him. But only as you do will you find real life. For the disciples, the upcoming year would be life changing and would require life surrender. All but Judas would pass the test. I suspect the Lord is preparing you today as well for what lies ahead. To be ready however, we must die to ourselves, pick up our cross and follow Him daily.

Chapter 56

THE TRANSFIGURATION

Luke 9:27–36
(Matthew 17:1–8; Mark 9:2–8)

E ight days after Peter's declaration at Caesarea Philippi, we come to an event that was previously unique to the Old Testament: an appearance of the shekinah glory, or the presence of the glory of God in a visible form.

> "But I tell you truly, there are some standing here who shall not taste death till they see the kingdom of God." Now it came to pass, about eight days after these sayings, that He took Peter, John, and James and went up on the mountain to pray. As He prayed, the appearance of His face was altered, and His robe became white and glistening. And behold, two men talked with Him, who were Moses and Elijah, who appeared in glory and spoke of His decease which He was about to accomplish at Jerusalem.
>
> —Luke 9:27–31

I think one of the things I learn about our Lord as I read through the Bible is that He has always desired to be with us intimately in fellowship. For example, after choosing Israel to be the people through whom He would work, God brought them out of Egypt. As they journeyed, they were able to see a visible representation of Him in the cloud that led them through the wilderness. For the next forty years, if the cloud moved, they moved. If it stayed put, so did they. In this way, they began to experience how God would protect and be with them. Even at the crossing of the Red Sea, it was the cloud that had stood between them and the approaching Egyptians.

One of the most intimate encounters a person ever has had with the Lord was when Moses was called to Mt. Sinai to receive the Law. As the people watched, he disappeared into the cloud that covered the mountain. For nearly six weeks he was with the Lord before coming back with the tablets. As he returned from Mt. Sinai with his face aglow, the people could see he had been with God. We read in Exodus 33:8–10 that as the cloud stood at the tabernacle door when Moses and God spoke, the people marveled in the doorways of their tents. They fell on their knees in worship, because this was God meeting with people.

"Lord, I'd really like to see You better," Moses said.

"If you see Me, because you're sinful, you'll die," God answered. "But I'll put you in a crack of the rock and I'll put My hand over your face. Then I'll come by and as soon as I'm gone, I'll pull My hand away and you'll be able to see where I've been." As God did what He said, Moses was blown away by God's "after-burners" (Exod. 18:20–23).

In the books of Exodus and Leviticus, Moses was given intricate details of a tabernacle the people were to build, where God would meet with them. When it was finished and the dedication took place, the cloud of God's presence so filled the tabernacle that even Moses wasn't able to enter (Exod. 40:34–35).

In the centuries that followed, including the many years in the wilderness, this meeting tabernacle was carefully disassembled and reassembled as the people moved so it could go with them. Years later, having conquered the world by God's grace, David was frustrated that the Lord's presence was relegated to what was by then a well-worn tent. Although he wanted to build God a permanent structure, the Lord wanted his son to build it instead. So David gathered the funds and materials instead. When Solomon came to the throne he was able to finish the job in seven and a half years.

On the day of the dedication, fire came down from heaven, consuming the offering. It was God's glory filling the temple and signaling to the people that God was in their midst. As recorded in 1 Kings 8:27–40, Solomon stood outside and prayed, "Lord, I know You don't live here. The heaven of heavens can't contain You. Everything we see You've made, but we know this is a place of meeting. When we pray toward this house, hear from heaven. Heal Your people. Deliver them from their enemies."

For a time, the people came and met with God through the blood of the sacrifices that were shed. Unfortunately, however, after awhile the temple lost its significance in the people's minds. As the Queen of Sheba came, Solomon was proud to show her the glorious temple he had built. But after seeing it, she blessed him rather than the Lord.

Over the next couple of hundred years, the temple became a place where people ignored, rather than sought God. It degenerated into a religious prop and lacked any true benefit as the place they could come to have a relationship with God. By the time we get to the book of the prophet Ezekiel, approximately four hundred years had passed and the temple had become a place the elders used to carry out their debauchery.

In Ezekiel chapters 8, 9, and 10, we witness the slow and painful departure of God's glory. From the holy of holies out to the holy place, out the tent gate to the place of offering outside, out the entrance of the entire compound, and finally up to the Mount of Olives, the Lord looked back over a place He so wanted to be with His people. And for the next many hundreds of years, although there was a temple in Jerusalem, God's presence had vacated it. No prophet was heard. No prophet would come. Four hundred years of silence from heaven followed.

The New Testament opens with the exciting news that God wanted to show people His glory again. It was the shepherds in the field on that glorious night who saw the angel of the Lord appear, announcing the Savior had been born in Bethlehem. John 1:14 wrote that the Word became flesh and dwelt among them and they beheld the glory of the only begotten of the Father, full of grace and truth. The shekinah glory of God had been brought to earth in the Person of Jesus. For thirty years He lived in obscurity before stepping into the public eye, where God's glory was revealed again. He was the Lord over nature as He calmed the storms, the Lord over the Devil as the demons were cast out, the Lord over life as He healed the sick and raised the dead, and the Lord over His creation as He fed the multitude.

But He was also the Messiah who had come to die to save us. And this the disciples needed to understand. So eight days after Peter's great confession, Jesus took three of His disciples up a mountain. Tradition in Israel says the Transfiguration actually took place on Mount Tabor. The problem is, Mount Tabor is not a mountain. It's just a hill. Matthew said in chapter 9:2 that Jesus went onto a high mountain. I think Mount Tabor has been identified as this place simply to accommodate tour busses since it is only forty-five minutes from Jerusalem. But Caesarea Philippi, where Jesus and His disciples had been seven days earlier, is at the base of Mount Hermon, the largest mountain in Israel. It's not nearly as easy to get to by bus.

I truly believe it was Mount Hermon Jesus and His disciples climbed that day. And as the tired disciples slept, Jesus prayed. As He did, we read in verse 29 that His face was altered. Mark uses the word *transfigured*. The Greek word is the word for *metamorphosis* and means "to change appearance from within." Like Superman revealing the "S" on his chest, Jesus pulled away the flesh for a moment and said, "I'm God Almighty. I'm the One who has come for you. I'm the One of whom you have testified." And God's glory was revealed to these disciples.

In verse 30, we see Moses and Elijah appearing with Jesus for a Bible conference. Both men had been on Mount Sinai—Moses several times to meet with God and receive the Law; Elijah on Mount Horeb, another name for Sinai, following his showdown with the priests of Baal in 1 Kings 19:8. Both men had seen God's glory in spectacular ways. Both had famous departures—Moses buried on Mount Nebo by God and Elijah riding off in a chariot of fire. Moses was the lawgiver. Elijah was one of the greatest miracle-working prophets who ever lived.

But standing between Moses and Elijah, between the Law and the prophets, was Jesus—the fulfillment of both. And they were talking about His decease or, literally, His "exodus" that would take place in Jerusalem just a year from then. The focus of their discussion was that the Lord, in all His glory, had come to save and to die, and would rise again. The Greek tense for the word *spoke* in verse 31 suggests this was quite an extended conversation. And the disciples slept nearly all the way through it.

> But Peter and those with him were heavy with sleep; and when they were fully awake, they saw His glory and the two men who stood with Him. Then it

> happened, as they were parting from Him, that Peter said to Jesus, "Master, it is
> good for us to be here; and let us make three tabernacles: one for You, one for
> Moses, and one for Elijah"—not knowing what he said.
>
> —Luke 9:32–33

Imagine waking up to the sight of Jesus shining and glorified, talking to Moses and Elijah. I don't know how long the disciples sat and watched, but when it looked as though the meeting was coming to an end, Peter spoke up. Mark wrote in 9:6 that because Peter didn't know what to say and was extremely afraid, he blurted something out. "Good thing we're here, Lord," he said. "Let's build churches. Let's put up tents."

> While He was saying this, a cloud came and overshadowed them; and they were
> fearful as they entered the cloud. And a voice came out of the cloud, saying,
> "This is My beloved Son. Hear Him!"
>
> —Luke 9:34–35

Jesus didn't answer Peter, but as he was speaking, the Father rolled in on a cloud, overshadowing the mountain. Matthew wrote in chapter 17 that when this happened, the disciples hit the deck and began to worship.

The cloud that passed by Moses in the cleft, that occupied the tent of meeting, that filled the temple on dedication day, and that slowly moved away from the place of worship was none other than the Son of God who had now come to give people light. Jesus revealed His true self, as His flesh was laid aside so the disciples might know that the fulfillment of all that the Law and prophets had foretold was He who had come to give His life not many days from now.

> When the voice had ceased, Jesus was found alone. But they kept quiet, and told
> no one in those days any of the things they had seen.
>
> —Luke 9:36

"Listen to Him," the Father commanded. And, as if for emphasis, when the cloud disappeared, so had Elijah and Moses. The shekinah had departed—yet Jesus still stood before them. And now they knew Him better.

Although I'm sure he didn't put this together that day, years later when the Lord directed Peter to write two letters to the scattered saints running for their lives from persecution, he said, "We haven't been following some cunningly devised fables. We were eyewitnesses of His majesty." Peter may not have gotten it at the time, but he did later.

The Feast of Tabernacles was one of three yearly gatherings in Jerusalem everyone was required to attend. At the end of this feast, a huge candelabra was mounted to the side of the temple that represented the pillar of fire, God's shekinah glory, that had led the people through the wilderness. Seven or eight months after His transfiguration, Jesus attended the

Feast of Tabernacles and, on the morning after the last day, stood before the smoldering candelabra and declared, "I am the Light of the world. If you follow Me, you won't walk in darkness, but you'll have the light of life." There couldn't have been a more emphatic way to say, "I am the glory of God. I am the One you can follow. Turn to Me. I'll give you life."

God doesn't forsake His people. He's available. If you want to know Him, look to Jesus. If you want life, follow Him. Did the disciples understand? They didn't then, but they did eventually. At that point, all they could do was hide what they had seen in their hearts and spend the next year listening as they put those things together. But we have it, don't we? We can walk in the light. We can follow Jesus. He's God's glory come to man. He's all we need. Stay close to the Light. Follow Him.

Chapter 57

TRUE GREATNESS

Luke 9:37–50
(Matthew 17:14–23, 18:1–6; Mark 9:14–40)

As the time drew closer for Jesus to turn south and head directly for Jerusalem and the cross, He continued to prepare His disciples to be those through whom He would do His work in years to come. God wants the world to see Him and He chooses to use us. As I look around, I wonder how in the world that's going to work—yet God prepares us just as He prepared the disciples. I am glad the success depends upon Him and not us!

> Now it happened on the next day, when they had come down from the mountain, that a great multitude met Him. Suddenly a man from the multitude cried out, saying, "Teacher, I implore You, look on my son, for he is my only child. And behold, a spirit seizes him, and he suddenly cries out; it convulses him so that he foams at the mouth, and it departs from him with great difficulty, bruising him. So I implored Your disciples to cast it out, but they could not."
>
> —Luke 9:37–40

Mark 9:9–13 tells us that as they were coming down from the Mount of Transfiguration, Jesus said to Peter, James, and John, "I don't want you to tell anyone the things you've seen until the Son of Man is raised from the dead."

After asking each other what He was talking about, the disciples said to Jesus, "The scribes say Elijah has to come first."

"Elijah will come first," Jesus answered. "But it is written concerning the Son of Man that He'll suffer many things and be treated with contempt."

Again Jesus touched on the issue of death, which would become very much clearer in the next thirteen months before the cross.

The disciples came down the mountain not yet understanding what Jesus was speaking about, but filed away the information in their hearts for later. At the bottom of the mountain, trouble waited. In fact, Mark writes that when Jesus returned to the disciples, there was a great multitude gathered around them with the scribes disputing with them. Peter, James, and John had just seen the most glorious vision—and yet as they came off the mountain, all they heard was yelling and confrontation.

Mountaintop experiences are great. I love listening to people who come back from retreats or short-term mission trips where the focus of their lives the past few days or weeks had intensely been the things of God. But there's nothing magical about those times. It's just that without television, phones, or a garage to tinker in, more time is spent seeking the Lord. The more He has of our attention, the greater His work in us.

Yet because we're to be lights in a dark place, God has placed us in the daily grind of the world. And the three disciples who had seen firsthand God's shekinah glory on the mountain were jolted back to the demands of daily life the moment they heard the din of the crowd. It interests me that the Devil waits, it seems, at the bottom of every mountain-top experience. Many times I've had great joy in teaching the Bible and seeing people get saved, only to get ripped off before I arrived home because I got behind someone going eight miles an hour on the road.

It only had been a month or two earlier that the disciples had come back from their first field trip, having been sent out two by two with instructions to go through the Decapolis cities to preach the Gospel, heal the sick, and cast out demons. Truly they had experienced God's power in their lives. Yet now, just a few months later, facing what had to have been a very similar situation, nothing seemed to work for them. No power, no authority—just embarrassment as the religious folks used the disciples' inability to heal the boy as an argument that Jesus was a fraud not worth following.

The Gospels paint a very dark picture of this young man's suffering. His father said the demons left him with great difficulty, or "with less frequency," as the original would translate. It seems the episodes were only getting longer and more difficult. Later after the disciples left this place, they sat in a house and asked Jesus why they were unable to cast out the evil spirit. According to Mark, Jesus said, "This kind can only come forth by prayer and fasting." Unfortunately, I think a lot of Bible commentators have misinterpreted this to say there is a specific procedure for exorcisms the disciples hadn't followed. But this premise is based on a false assumption that because God and the Devil are equals, it is hard for God to get the upper hand. The fact is that God and the Devil are anything but equals. God is almighty, while the Devil is a created and now fallen angel. At best, he does what he's told. So I don't think the issue Jesus addressed with His disciples was their failure to follow the proper exorcism format.

Instead, I believe the Lord was saying to these disciples, "If you're going to have power with God, you're going to have to have fellowship with Him." Prayer and fasting represent two aspects of a Christian's life that push him toward the Lord and the things of God. The disciples had been given power. But if they were to continue to have that power, they had to remain in intimate contact with God, not simply presume that because they were apostles when the need arose they could act with His power.

When they returned from their missionary trip, they seemed to have come back full of themselves in many ways, arguing about greatness and who would be in charge of what. They were supposed to be learning, however, that God only can use those who look to Him. Apparently, the disciples this day were still preoccupied with themselves and not so occupied with the Lord. But they learned. We have to learn, as well. You can't build your house in the storm. You'd better be in fellowship with God before the rain comes.

By the time the events in the book of Acts take place, the disciples had realized where their devotion needed to be and, as a result, we can see God's power resting mightily on their lives to bring His touch to hurting lives.

> Then Jesus answered and said, "O faithless and perverse generation, how long shall I be with you and bear with you? Bring your son here."
>
> —Luke 9:41

Jesus quoted from Deuteronomy 32:5, where Moses warned the people about a lack of faith that would grab hold of them in years to come. Jesus applied this warning to the religious folks, the crowd, the complainers, and maybe even the disciples, asking, "How long shall I put up with you?"

I understand that. I wonder how long He'll put up with me too! I'm so thankful He does and that His mercies are new every morning. If not for God's mercy He would have thrown up His hands long ago and just given up, wouldn't He? But He is patient!

> And as he was still coming, the demon threw him down, and convulsed him. Then Jesus rebuked the unclean spirit, healed the child, and gave him back to his father. And they were all amazed at the majesty of God.
>
> —Luke 9:42

"The majesty of God" is the same phrase Peter used later to describe the Transfiguration. In other words, as Jesus healed the demon-possessed boy, the glory that Peter, James, and John had seen on the mountain, the crowd saw in Jesus' work and power. I love the picture because I can see the scribes and Pharisees walking away, muttering, "Curses! Foiled again."

The world is supposed to see Jesus in us. "Let your light so shine," He said, "that men might see your good works and glorify your Father in heaven." To the Philippians, Paul wrote, "You should be a blameless and harmless nation, children of God without fault in the midst of a perverse generation among whom you shine like lights in the world" (Phil. 2:15).

We often can experience our God work mightily on the mountaintop—but it's when we come down to where the people live, where the Devil works, and where deliverance is necessary that God can do His best work through our lives if stay in fellowship with Him.

> He said to His disciples, "Let these words sink down into your ears, for the Son of Man is about to be betrayed into the hands of men." But they did not understand this saying, and it was hidden from them so that they did not perceive it; and they were afraid to ask Him about this saying.
>
> —Luke 9:43–45

The crowds were cheering. The response was favorable. The argument was stopped. The religious people were quieted. But this wasn't the way it would remain. In fact, from this point on, every time the crowds cheered, Jesus was quick to say to His disciples, "Don't be fooled by the response. I'm about to be betrayed and killed. Soon enough, the crowds will be calling for My death."

This didn't register with the disciples. Why? I suggest it was due to their presupposition that the Lord was coming to rule. Therefore, anything else just wasn't heard but tuned out.

To the honest questioners in the Bible, God always had an answer. Whether to Nicodemus or the woman at the well, honest, serious questions were answered with honest, serious answers. The disciples didn't get it yet, but were sincere in their confusion and the Lord responded in patience and love. But the Lord took them through this time and whittled away at their preconceived ideas so they could come to know Him as He is.

> Then a dispute arose among them as to which of them would be greatest. And Jesus, perceiving the thought of their heart, took a little child and set him by Him, and said to them, "Whoever receives this little child in My name receives Me and whoever receives Me receives Him who sent Me. For he who is least among you all will be great."
>
> —Luke 9:46–48

We are told in the other Gospels that on the road as they walked, the disciples argued about who among them was the greatest. When Jesus asked them what they were talking about, they said it was nothing. After failing at healing the demon-possessed boy and being cornered by the religious folks, the disciples' arguing about being great is surprising. But I suspect Peter might have said to the other disciples, "So you couldn't help that boy, huh? We leave you behind for one day and look what you got yourselves into."

"Well, a lot of good you were doing up on that mountain," the other disciples might have countered.

"Oh, we had stuff going on," Peter would have answered, "but we're not allowed to talk about it. Who's the greatest? At this point, it must be me and James and John."

Knowing what was in their hearts, Jesus sat a young child down in their midst as an illustration for His disciples.

"Want to be great?" He said. "Receive the lowly, the helpless, the insignificant, the ones who are of no apparent benefit to you. The greatest in the kingdom are those who serve the weak and dependent, the ones without status, the ones who are helpless."

> Now John answered and said, "Master, we saw someone casting out demons in Your name, and we forbade him because he does not follow with us." But Jesus said to him, "Do not forbid him for he who is not against us is on our side."
>
> —Luke 9:49–50

Look at the disciples for a minute. First they loved themselves so much that they weren't depending on the Lord and ended up powerless. Then they loved their own concept of Jesus' work so much that when He said He was going to die, they said, "No way." Then they didn't love each other enough to keep from arguing about who was the greatest. And if all that wasn't bad enough, they were critical of someone else's ministry, which at that moment was going far better than theirs was.

Jesus said, "Let God use them. You're not the only show in town."

God will use those who depend on Him and will bless those who are in fellowship with Him regardless of their denominational label.

In the book of Numbers, Moses had been complaining to the Lord that the work was too big for him and he couldn't keep up with it. The Lord said, "Bring seventy of the men who have proven themselves before the congregation and I'll take some of the Spirit I've put on you and put it on them. Then they can help you." In the morning, of the seventy who had been chosen, sixty-eight showed up while two stayed in their tents. But when the Spirit of God fell, all seventy began to prophesy.

Joshua, Moses' helper, said, "Tell those two who didn't come out to be quiet. Who do they think they are? They didn't follow the rules."

But Moses said, "Joshua, are you upset for my sake? I wish every man had the Spirit of God upon him."

When Paul heard about people mocking his preaching, he said to the Philippians 1:15–18, "I hear people are preaching Christ. Some are preaching in pretense, some in truth. But I'm just glad the Word is going out. God will work out the details. His Word brings life."

Better that we are wise and rejoice, as long as Jesus is being exalted and people are following Him. As long as the Word is paramount, we're all right. Sing the way you want. Stand on your head if you like. Wear whatever works for you. Use whatever style you want. The methods change with the culture. But the message never does. Neither does God's power or His Word by which men hear the good news of our Savior Jesus.

Chapter 58

THE STAGE IS SET

Matthew 18:1–14
(Mark 9:33–50; Luke 9:46–50; 15:3–7)

We have come to the end of Jesus' first two and a half years. As you might be able to surmise, much of the Gospel records are devoted to His final year as He turned south from Galilee and toward Jerusalem and the cross. Jesus focused on why He had come and what He planned to do as He prepared His disciples for what they didn't expect—His death on the cross.

Matthew 18 follows the Mount of Transfiguration story and comes before Luke 9:51, where we're told Jesus steadfastly set His face toward Jerusalem. The chapter before us developed out of the arguing among the disciples as to who would be the greatest. It's a stern chapter in many ways, but at the same time it shows us God's heart for the church and how we are to relate to one another. It is kingdom living in a most practical sense.

> At that time the disciples came to Jesus, saying, "Who then is the greatest in the kingdom of heaven?" Then Jesus called a little child to Him, set him in the midst of them and said, "Assuredly, I say to you, unless you are converted and you become as little children, you will by no means enter the kingdom of heaven. Therefore, whoever humbles himself as this little child is the greatest in the kingdom of heaven.
>
> —Matthew 18:1–4

Mark 9:33 tells us in his connecting verses that it was on the road to Capernaum from the foot of the Mount of Transfiguration that Jesus asked His disciples, "Why are you arguing among yourselves?" Mark 9:34 records they didn't say anything. Yet when they got to the house in Capernaum and sat, it was then that they asked Jesus, "Who is the greatest in the kingdom?"

For illustration purposes, Jesus took a little child and said, "Here you go: the greatest." A little kid? No, the spirit of a little child—the trust, the confidence, the humility, the dependence. The one who has faith and dependence upon God rather than confidence in himself is the greatest. Faith brings greatness.

> "Whoever receives one little child like this in My name receives Me."
>
> —Matthew 18:5

Jesus said, "I stand with My own. If you bless them, you bless Me. If you love them, you love Me." The disciples were all trying to be better than each other. Jesus, on the other hand, identified with others. And it's this identification that sets the tone for the entire chapter.

> "Whoever causes one of these little ones who believe in Me to sin, it would be better for him if a millstone were hung around his neck, and he were drowned in the depth of the sea."
>
> —Matthew 18:6

The Greek word for *stumble* as we have spoken about before is *skandalon*, a word that means to trip or cause someone to veer off course. Here Jesus was saying, "If You're the cause of God's children getting off track, to doubt Him, to question Him, to forsake Him—it would be better if you jumped into the water with cement 'floaties.'" Wow!

Jesus said, "You guys are arguing about great? Here's great: faith in Me, identification with Me, and blessing others through Me. Don't be a cause of sin or you'll walk the plank."

> "Woe to the world because of offenses! For offenses must come, but woe to that man by whom the offense comes!"
>
> —Matthew 18:7

There isn't a single place in the Bible that I am aware of where God uses the word "Woe" and then something good follows! Here Jesus said, "Woe to anyone who causes His children to struggle." We can expect this of the world, because it is run by the Devil and its appeal is to the flesh. But there is woe for the believer who causes this to happen.

> "If your hand or foot causes you to sin, cut it off and cast it from you. It is better for you to enter into life lame or maimed, rather than having two hands or two feet, to be cast into the everlasting fire. And if your eye causes you to sin, pluck it out and cast it from you. It is better for you to enter into life with one eye, rather than having two eyes, to be cast into hell fire."
>
> —Matthew 18:8–9

Here Jesus said something that is exaggerated, offensive, and startling—yet at the same time it makes us see how seriously He takes the sin of causing others to stumble. Obviously these verses are not to be taken literally because, for example, if you cut off one hand, you still would have the other. That isn't the issue. The issue is the length to which you should go to be sure you are not causing others to veer off course in their walk with the Lord. For example, you may feel at great liberty to have a drink at dinner. Yet the problem enters when the person next to you does not have that liberty because he had a drinking problem for thirty years before he met Jesus. Though the analogy is not designed to be literally followed, it is very clear that self-denial for the sake of God's children is so important to Him that it would be better for you to go into eternity without all you felt you should have had in this life, rather than risk causing others to stumble in your pursuit of your liberty in Christ.

I have to believe that Jesus' words made a tremendous impact on these twelve guys sitting there looking at Him, all red-faced from their arguing an hour before.

> "Take heed that you do not despise one of these little ones, for I say to you that in heaven, their angels always see the face of My Father who is in heaven."
> —Matthew 18:10

The word *despise* in Greek is *kataphroneo*. *Phroneo* is the word for *brain*. *Kata* is the word for *next to*. Therefore, the word literally means "to think less of than you should or to despise." Angels watch out for God's children—and they tattle. So take heed. Pay special attention. Don't mess with God's kids, for to do so has you messing with Him.

> "For the Son of Man has come to save that which was lost. What do you think? If a man has a hundred sheep, and one of them goes astray, does he not leave the ninety-nine and go to the mountains to seek the one that is straying? And if he should find it, assuredly, I say to you, he rejoices more over that sheep than over the ninety-nine that did not go astray. Even so it is not the will of your Father who is in heaven that one of these little ones should perish."
> —Matthew 18:11–14

A shepherd doesn't want to lose a single sheep. In this example, one sheep would be 1 percent of the value of his flock. Likewise, when a believer goes astray, the Father pursues him with a shepherd's diligence. He looks for him with unconditional love and rejoices with emotional love.

So rather than finding fault with someone who doesn't measure up, seek to restore him. It doesn't mean you approve of sin. It means you're willing to go with forgiveness and bring back any who have gone astray so God's grace might make new!

Chapter 59

CHURCH DISCIPLINE

Matthew 18:15–22

After establishing the truths that causing God's children to stumble is a bad idea and that the heart of the Father is to restore those who are straying, Jesus went on to give us the most definitive verses in the Bible on church discipline and church relationships.

At its best, the church is a place where believers come to grow and stay strong. And if the Lord has His way, we would walk each day together down this narrow road that leads to life. Church life is not about who can be smarter, wiser, or better than the next. It's about grabbing each other and holding on to each other so no one is left behind.

> "Moreover, if your brother sins against you, go and tell him his fault between you and him alone. If he hears you, you have gained your brother."
>
> —Matthew 18:15

The Greek word for *trespass* is the word for "missing the mark." Therefore, the sin referred to here isn't just about someone who hurts people's feelings or rubs them the wrong way. It's a sin that is constant and committed without repentance, one that is missing the mark God has set in His Word for us. And if God makes us aware of this type of sin in someone's life in the body, He wants to use us as His vessel to confront, to go after the sheep that has strayed, and to seek to restore them with Jesus' heart of love.

There are people in every church who think their ministry is to tell everyone else what they're doing wrong. That's not what is described here. It's not a ministry of rebuke God is interested in but rather a way to keep His children from stumbling. The words *against you* do not suggest against us personally but literally among us, toward us, or in our sight. If we become aware of sinful practices in the lives of the saints, we're to have the heart of God and be the vessel He can use to address it.

His first direction to those who are aware of ongoing sin, is to go talk directly to the one who is off course and missing the mark. And because God has put us in the position of knowing about it, once we confront and restore that person, our relationship with them will be strengthened. We will have won a brother or sister back to the Lord. God will have used us to bring one of His sheep back into the Lord's light once again. When Paul wrote to the Galatians, he said, "If a man is overtaken in a trespass, those of you who are spiritual should seek to restore him in a spirit of gentleness."

James wrote the same thing, saying, "If one wanders from the truth and you're the one that brings him back, you'll cover a multitude of sin." There is benefit to being involved in a church. People think sometimes they can get by without it. I don't think you can—not very well. God didn't give us a body for nothing. But correction is to be done with a spirit of humility, love, and restoration.

If we see someone fall into sin, we're to go and talk with them. The word translated *go* is in the present imperative tense in Greek. That means we're to go now, go again tomorrow, and follow it up on the third day. Don't just go once. Make repeated efforts to try and bring this brother or sister around. The word *tell* is in the aorist imperative tense in Greek, which means to say it straight, no beating around the bush.

Some people are good at Bible-thumping. Other people just want to love us without saying anything. But if we see someone about to fall off a cliff, love would dictate us to warn him, wouldn't it? So Paul wrote to the Ephesians that we should speak the truth to one another in love. We need both. We need truth and love. That means we are to talk to the lost sheep consistently and repeatedly to try to restore them to the flock. This requires involvement and taking a stand.

A lot of people don't like this. They will beg off from this responsibility. They'll say, "How can I address someone else's sin when I'm a mess myself?" But I'm pretty sure we're all in church because we know we're in need of His rescue! It's a matter of helping each other to move forward in the things of the Lord. If you're walking with Him, God wants to use you to help others to do the same. Of course, Jesus said we're not to help someone get a speck out of his eye if we have a two-by-four in our own. But once we have dealt with our own sin, we can see clearly to help someone else. We're to go on God's behalf to beckon these saints to return to their Lord. We're to get involved, risk criticism, and risk losing a friend for the sake of gaining a brother or sister.

The term "gained a brother" is a Greek term for accumulating wealth. In other words, we'll have valuable treasure if we involve ourselves in restoration. That's the biblical work of the body—not to overlook sin but to actively seek to help people live holy lives. How awesome it would be if the church would seek to minister to itself. It's the heart of the Father. It's what God wants.

> "But if he will not hear, take with you one or two more, that by the mouth of two or three witnesses every work may be established."
>
> —Matthew 18:16

If you've become involved in restoration only to be shunned, refused, and maligned, what do you do next? Step 2 is to turn up the love and turn up the accountability. Go again and again—same verb—but this time take a few godly folks with you to confirm and establish the position taken. Here Jesus quoted from the Old Testament Law, Deuteronomy 19:15, about witnesses establishing truth.

I would suggest you don't take your best friends because that would look like a gang confrontation. The Lord wants the erring brother or sister properly represented. He wants to repeat the efforts, keep it small, and do it with dignity and love—but have some greater accountability. And the hope is that with a couple more people involved who will stand on the Word of God and His ways, the problem can be resolved.

> "And if he refuses to hear them, tell it to the church. But if he refuses even to hear the church, let him be to you like a heathen and a tax collector."
> —Matthew 18:17

If after repeated efforts to seek to restore someone living in sin nothing has been accomplished, eventually we need to involve the church leadership. So if you think the church is a safe harbor to live in sin, think again.

This is the hardest step and it presumes that lots of work has been done beforehand. At this point, the erring brother or sister is asked to leave the church. And although this last step is very dramatic, it is a decision the person who continues to live in sin makes for themselves. These are the clear steps for our ministry to one another. When we get to verse 17 here, the issue of the Lord's heart is still one of restoration. Even this isn't the end of the line.

In over 23 years as senior pastor, we've asked only three people to leave our fellowship. One man had decided to move in with a woman from the church, although both were married. People had talked to them, but to no avail. So they told the leadership.

"What are you doing?" I asked the man.

"You can't tell me how to live," he said.

"You're right," I said. "But I can tell you that you're not welcome here."

He's still gone. But the other two folks have come back, repentant.

When Paul wrote his first letter to the Corinthians, he said in chapter 5:1–5, "I've heard that you're allowing someone living in sexual immorality to fellowship with you. Rather than mourning, you guys are proud of your tolerance. I'm not there in the body but I'm with you in spirit and my judgment is that this guy should be put out of the church."

But by the time Paul wrote his second epistle to the Corinthians 2:6–11, the man who had fallen into sin had repented, broken off the relationship, and asked for forgiveness. So when Paul wrote the second letter, he said the punishment the church had inflicted was sufficient and they were now to forgive him, comfort him and receive him back into fellowship.

What happens when someone who knows the Lord is asked to leave a fellowship due to ongoing sin in their lives? The Lord would want them to see as their back into the world, which is where they have been living anyway, and say, "This stinks. Nobody loves me here. Nobody supports me here. I have no hope here, no promise here. I'm going back to church. But to go back there, I know I've got to walk with God." So even the taste of the world and deliverance to the Devil's kingdom will drive us back to repentance.

The Lord's purpose in all of this is to say, "Rather than worrying about if you're great, one of your greatest responsibilities in the church is to see that you all make it together." We're to pick up the stragglers and help the weak. We're to stand with the ones who are having difficulty and cover the sins of those who are struggling because they ought to be encouraged.

God loves restoration. Does it work? Of course. A healthy body ministering to itself by following Jesus' words will help even the weak to be strong.

> "Assuredly, I say to you, whatever you bind on earth will be bound in heaven, and whatever you loose on earth will be loosed in heaven."
> —Matthew 18:18

Jesus promises to support and stand by the difficult decisions we sometimes need to make regarding those who call themselves saints but are living very sinful lives. By the time you get to the point of telling the person they are not welcome to fellowship with you any longer, you can't help but wonder if you're doing the right thing.

Three times—in verses 18, 19, and 20—Jesus' answer is, "I'm giving you the authority to represent Me in this manner and I will stand with you in heaven concerning whatever is decided upon the earth."

The words *loosed* and *bound* are found in several different places in the Bible. In both Luke 24 and John 20, we find two accounts of the evening of the resurrection. As 120 believers hid out in fear, Jesus popped into their midst, breathed on them, and said, "Receive the Holy Spirit. If you forgive the sins of many, they're forgiven. If you retain them, they're retained." In so doing, He gave to the church—to the 120—the authority to declare to the world how sins can be forgiven.

Today as a Christian, we have every right to say, "Want to know how to get to heaven? I can tell you how. This is the only key, the only door, the only way . . . ."

If someone says, "I don't believe that. I think that if I do this, that, and the other, I'll get to heaven," we can say with absolute authority that no amount of works will get them there.

John used the words *retain and remit*. When we remit a bill, we pay it. Jesus remits—pays the price—for the sin of anyone who asks Him for forgiveness. To "retain" means "to hold on." Therefore, if we say to someone, "Because you don't have Jesus in your heart, you're still in your sin," even if he argues that he goes to church every week, we have the authority to declare that his sins are still retained.

I think it's a comfort to know from Jesus' own lips that if the body is pursuing holiness, we'll make it. After being a Christian for thirty years, Paul wrote to the Philippians in chapter 3, "I haven't got there yet—but I'm pressing on." So it will take awhile. We won't get completely holy until the day we stop breathing—but we've got to keep trying to head in that direction.

"Again I say to you that if two of you agree on earth concerning anything that they ask, it will be done for them by My Father in heaven."

—Matthew 18:19

This is such an important issue that Jesus said, "If you're having doubt, be assured that if two of you agree on earth concerning anything, it will be done by the Father in heaven." The word for *agree* in Greek is *sumphoneo*, from which we get our word *symphony*. No one is singing his or her own tune. It's a symphony where everyone plays the same notes.

In the Old Testament, the responsibility of judging wasn't handed over to individuals but to the government. Individuals tend to operate on the basis of vengeance. But the government was to operate on the basis of protection. We see the same thing in the New Testament. Romans 13:1–5 says God established governments so society would be protected from evildoers. And the same is true in the church. When the church collectively agrees that sin can't go on, when it is led by prayer, much consultation, and love, God honors the steps taken. He longs to restore—but when push comes to shove, He is willing to stand with the church in order to protect His people.

"For wherever two or three are gathered together in My name, I am there in the midst of them."

—Matthew 18:20

I have heard people use this verse to say, "If there's just two or three of us, God will hear our prayer." But that's out of context. This is in the context of church discipline. God hears us even if we're praying by ourselves. So I don't think this verse is properly applied to prayer meetings. It is, however, an assurance that this difficult decision is the one God would have us make if it goes this far, and that He will bless those who stand upon it.

Then Peter came to Him and said, "Lord, how often shall my brother sin against me, and I forgive him? Up to seven times?" Jesus said to him, "I do not say to you, up to seven times, but up to seventy times seven."

—Matthew 18:21–22

I don't doubt that Peter was the loudest in the "Who's the greatest?" argument. So maybe he was trying to make up for that when he asked Jesus, "How do I determine repentance? How much do I have to tolerate? How often do I have to forgive?" According to the Jewish Law of the first century, people were required to forgive three times. So Peter bumped up that number 133% and came to seven. I'm sure he expected Jesus to congratulate him for his insight and to tell him he was definitely on his way to being the greatest. Instead, Jesus said something that stopped Peter in his tracks and that followed the teaching of what Jesus had just said and set the stage for the parable to follow.

One of the interesting things about forgiveness from God's point of view is that He never asks of us any more than He's given us. In other words, you never will be asked to forgive someone for more than God has forgiven you. No matter who offends you, what bothers you, or who hurts your feelings, you have a lot less to write off than the Lord does with you. With forgiveness from God comes His demand to now forgive others.

Paul wrote in Ephesians 4:32 that we should be kindhearted and tenderhearted, forgiving one another just as God in Christ forgave us. In Colossians 3:13, he said, "If you have a complaint against anyone, for Christ's sake, forgive them even as God has forgiven you." Aren't you glad God doesn't count when it comes to your sins? Would you be here if seven was the magic number?

With all of the wisdom God gave him, Solomon wrote in Proverbs 19:11 that man's glory is to overlook a transgression. In other words, the ability to forgive is the glory of God at work in our lives.

"Father, forgive them," Jesus said from the cross. "Father, don't lay this sin to their charge." Stephen echoed, even as the rocks stained with his own blood piled up around him.

That's exactly what God asks of us His people. Yes, we need holiness. But we need mercy as well. Therefore, every step of discipline has to be taken in light of support and restoration. That's God's desire. He doesn't want us to lose anyone along the way.

I think Peter's question was an honest one. What's the limit of forgiveness? After David's sin with Bathsheba, he wrote in Psalm 51:4, "Lord, against You and You only have I sinned and done this great evil." It all began with sin against God. Then it was reflected in the way he treated Uriah. Sin is always first against God, and because He is willing to forgive, we're obligated to do the same. We rely on God, and God, relies on us to pass forgiveness to each other.

Why does the Devil attack the church so frequently? Because the fellowship of the saints is the place of greatest strength for the church.

Chapter 60

THE PARABLE OF
THE UNFORGIVING SERVANT

Matthew 18:23–35

In the last portion of this chapter that deals with the way the church is to interact, Jesus gives to us a parable about forgiveness. It is so convicting maybe we should just go through it as quickly as possible. Just kidding, let's take a look.

> "Therefore the kingdom of heaven is like a certain king who wanted to settle accounts with his servants. And when he had begun to settle accounts, one was brought to him who owed him ten thousand talents."
>
> —Matthew 18:23–24

The phrase, "the kingdom of heaven," is most often used to speak of God's rule in men's hearts. To illustrate this, Jesus gave a picture of a king who had set a time to take account of his servants and their debt.

In the Old Testament, when men were made slaves for whatever reason, Jewish Law required that they could only be kept so for a limited time before they were to be set free. If, however, their master treated them well, they could request to become a permanent slave—a slave by choice. In the New Testament, a slave by choice was called a *doulos*. Interestingly, *doulos* is the word God uses most often to speak of you and me—those who have, by choice, come to Jesus as their Lord. It's also the word used for the servant here in the parable.

At the king's direction, this man who was in huge debt, some ten thousand talents is brought before him. Ten thousand is the largest number in the language. So when Paul wrote, "You have not many fathers but you have ten thousand instructors," or when John went to heaven and saw ten thousand times ten thousand worshipping, it's a number that's as big as it can be. To add emphasis, Jesus put an "s" on the end. He made it plural. To translate "ten thousands talents," the word *zillions* will do. This man was standing before God with an incalculable debt and without a plan on how to pay it back, the debt of course representing people's sin before God.

As this fellow was called before the Lord, he was reminded first and foremost of his inability to settle his own account. On the day of reckoning, he was in trouble.

"But as he was not able to pay, his master commanded that he be sold, with his wife and children and all that he had, and that payment be made."

—Matthew 18:25

There's nothing wicked about this. It was first-century justice, comparable to bankruptcy or foreclosure in our day. A man could spend his entire life working of this debt as a slave. This debt, however, was so large that this man never would have been able to do it. The consequence of his debt, of his sin, was that he had lost everything.

"The servant therefore fell down before him, saying, 'Master, have patience with me, and I will pay you all.'"

—Matthew 18:26

Facing the imminent loss of everything he counted valuable, the man didn't ask for justice. Nor did he deny his debt. He simply asked for more time. "I know what I've done. I know what I owe. If you could just give me some more time, I'll pay everything," he said.

His is a response seen throughout the Bible from people who become aware of their sin:

"What must I do to be saved?" the Philippian jailer asked.

"What do I have to do to have it all?" the rich young ruler wondered.

Maybe you did the same thing. When you realized you were in trouble with God, maybe you began to make Him promises. That's the natural way of people. When sin convicts us, we immediately want to make it better. We don't comprehend the impossibility of paying off our debt, because we do not yet see that the wages of sin is nothing short of death.

This man pleaded for more time. Reason would tell us that will make no significant difference while emotion says it has to. But I have found that when people start wanting to make God promises because they realize their sinfulness, they're pretty close to being saved. They're right about themselves—just in error of how to make it work out. They still see themselves, rather than the Lord, as the solution.

The fortunate thing in the whole picture is that this king is a good king, a loving king, a "for you" not an "against you"—a king who came to save, not to destroy.

"Then the master of that servant was moved with compassion, released him, and forgave him the debt."

—Matthew 18:27

When God's love meets the inescapable judgment of sin and produces a new life, it's an awesome picture, isn't it? More time is not what he needed; forgiveness of his debt alone would deliver him. This guy went in with his head on a platter and walked out with his head held high. He went in crushed under the weight of his sin and walked out free. He was released and forgiven solely on the basis of the king's love.

People come in sometimes for counseling and say, "I don't think God can forgive me." But the Bible says absolutely the opposite. God is able to forgive. God is willing to forgive. God loves to forgive.

The servant said, "Give me more time and I can make it right."

The Lord says, "Let Me make it right for you right now."

Forgiveness always begins with a willingness on our part to admit we're sinful. And because this man realized his position, he met with God's mercy and found God's grace.

> "But that servant went out and found one of his fellow servants who owed him a hundred denarii; and he laid hands on him and took him by the throat, saying, 'Pay me what you owe!' So his fellow servant fell down at his feet and begged him, saying, 'Have patience with me, and I will pay you all.' And he would not, but went and threw him into prison till he should pay the debt."
>
> —Matthew 18:28–30

This man, however, has yet to come to the understanding that his forgiveness by the Lord now obligated him to show like mercy to others for far less transgressions. I read it and say he must have had rocks for brains, because he walked out of the "You're forgiven" meeting, saying, "All right, who owes me stuff?" It was the antithesis of what he had just received. We shake our heads when we read this—and I think the Lord shakes His head when we do the same thing! He went after someone who was a fellow servant—a bond slave, someone, like him, who also needed grace and who also had to look to the cross.

Depending on the rate of exchange, a hundred denarii may have been twenty bucks. In fact, it's such a small amount that this guy easily could have worked it off. Instead, the servant laid hands on him and demanded immediate payment. The words of the fellow servant in verse 29 are the same words uttered by the forgiven man three verses earlier, and therefore should have been a reminder to him of where he himself had once been.

The lesson is obvious. Whatever debt you ever will be required to forgive someone else will pale in comparison to the debt God has forgiven you. And the restoration God is seeking among fellow servants is one that is based on all He has given us. It really should be a no-brainer, shouldn't it? Unfortunately, it isn't—as evidenced by our tendency to want grace for ourselves but judgment for others.

The man gave his fellow servant no mercy. He gave him justice. It was legal. It just wasn't God-like. God expects more from us.

> "So when his fellow servants saw what had been done, they were very grieved, and came and told their master all that had been done. Then his master, after he had called him, said to him, 'You wicked servant! I forgave all that debt

because you begged me. Should you not also have had compassion on your fellow servant, just as I had pity on you?'"

—Matthew 18:31–33

Before we wonder why the servant was unable to show his fellow servant the same love and grace he had received, we would do well to listen to our own voices, for example saying, "I love You, Lord." Followed by, "Hey! Get out of my parking spot, pal. Please bless my finances and my family, Lord." Followed by, "Hey you. Get out of my way. Your blinker wasn't on!" It doesn't make sense. Why do we think forgiveness stops with us?

"And his master was angry, and delivered him to the torturers until he should pay all that was due to him."

—Matthew 18:34

The price for unforgiveness is torment. The Bible teaches that unforgiving hearts end up wicked, angry, and bitter. You always can identify unforgiving people. They're the most unhappy people in the room. They never can rejoice in the joy of their salvation because they have too many lists to keep, too many people to point fingers at, and too many hurts to remember.

"So My heavenly Father also will do to you if each of you, from his heart, does not forgive his brother his trespasses."

—Matthew 18:35

Unforgiveness isn't an issue of losing your salvation. It's an issue of losing your peace and the fellowship it brings.

"How many times must I forgive?" Peter got his answer in this parable.

On the day you stand before the Lord, you're not going to care about justice. You're just going to hope that everything the Bible says about mercy is true. That's what the rest of us are counting on from you as well. That's what God requires of His people. That is true greatness, for in forgiveness we are most like our God.

SECTION III

THE FINAL YEAR
OF MINISTRY

Chapter 61

HEADING FOR THE CROSS

Luke 9:51–62
(Matthew 8:19–22)

W e come now to the final year of Jesus' three-and-a-half-year public ministry, as He turns from Galilee in the North towards Jerusalem and His appointment with the cross. At this point, a lot of things change—among them His determination, the conflict, and the training of the disciples. In their gospels, Luke and John devoted more time to this final twelve months than to the other two and a half years combined. Our first verse sets the tone.

> Now it came to pass, when the time had come for Him to be received up, that He steadfastly set His face to go to Jerusalem.
> —Luke 9:51

Notice the specific language. The time had come for what? For Jesus to ascend. The time was coming when He would go back to the Father. But between here and there lay a year of conflict, training, and betrayal. Jesus' eye was on the end. His eye was on the reward and the prize of faithfulness: the church would be born. Lives would be changed. But don't think for a minute that this turning to Jerusalem was easy for Him. As a man, this was as horrifying as it could be.

He steadfastly set His face. In other words, He determined with great resolve that this is where He would go. Writing about the coming Messiah seven hundred years earlier, Isaiah wrote in 50:5–7, "The Lord God has opened my ears. I was not rebellious. I didn't turn away. I gave My back to those who struck Me and My cheeks to those who plucked out My beard. I didn't hide My face from the shame and the spitting, for the Lord God will help me. I won't be disgraced. I have set My face like a flint so I wouldn't be ashamed." In order to accomplish our salvation, Jesus struggled in the flesh through all of these things He would face. But the greatest pain would be His separation from the Father. He'll mention the physical pain very little. He'll mention separation from the Father a lot.

When Mark recorded this same turning in chapter 10:32, he said that as they were on the road heading for Jerusalem, Jesus went before them and the disciples were amazed and afraid. The style had changed. The step had changed. The look had changed. The urgency had changed. So Jesus pulled them aside and began to tell them what was waiting for them at the end of the road they were on.

Later when the disciples tried to argue with Him that they could pay the price for sitting next to Him in government, Jesus said, "I have a baptism to be baptized with but how distressed I am until all of this is accomplished." The word *distressed* means to be discouraged or to be under great pressure. Jesus knew what was waiting—and everyone recognized it. There was a steely determination with purpose and understanding that followed His every step. But never conclude this was easy for Him—it was not!

> And sent some messengers before His face. And as they went, they entered a village of the Samaritans, to prepare for Him. But they did not receive Him, because His face was set for the journey to Jerusalem.
> —Luke 9:52–53

As some of the disciples were sent ahead of the group to make lodging arrangements in a Samaritan town, they found themselves walking a path they usually avoided. The conflict between the Jews and Samaritans had grown so strong over the years that if a Jew was traveling from the north to the south, he would first head east, cross the Jordan River, and come down on the eastern side of the Jordan, known at the time as the area of Perea, before coming back into Jericho and over to Jerusalem.

The animosity between the Jews and the Samaritans went all the way back to 722 B.C. During that time, Israel was a divided nation—the northern kingdom of Israel and the southern kingdom of Judah. Due to idolatry and unfaithfulness, in 722 B.C. God sent the Assyrians to take the Jews in the north into captivity. The Assyrian practice was not to kill people but to transplant them. So they moved the Jews into Gentile lands where they didn't know the culture, couldn't speak the language, and didn't particularly like the food. Then they took Gentiles from other defeated places and moved them into Samaria—today known as the West Bank.

Therefore, aside from a few Jews left behind—the poor and infirm—Samaria was basically filled with transplanted, defeated Gentiles. We read in 2 Kings 17 that these Gentiles asked the Jews left behind who their God was and what they needed to do to make Him happy. The problem for the Jews was they didn't know the answer because they had lived their entire lives worshipping false gods. But they shared the little they remembered. This was incorporated into the Gentile religious practices, and eventually the Samaritan way of life was born.

When the Babylonians began to overthrow the kingdom of Judah in its first of 3 major invasions beginning 116 years later, the Jews were taken to Babylon for seventy years. When they were allowed to return in 536 B.C. under Ezra and others, the Samaritans offered to participate to rebuild the temple. But according to Ezra 4, they were rejected as half-breeds and their services rebuffed. As a result, whatever rift had begun already was then set in stone. The Samaritans set about writing their own Bible. They rewrote the Pentateuch. They built a new place on Mount Gerazim to worship. They set up their own feast days. And they became the hated foes of the Jews to the south.

One of the Samaritan tactics with the Jews was to offer lodging to anyone leaving Jerusalem. But to those headed for Jerusalem, the motels mysteriously would all be full. This is what the disciples ran into here.

> And when His disciples James and John saw this, they said, "Lord, do You want us to command fire to come down from heaven and consume them, just as Elijah did?"
>
> —Luke 9:54

No doubt there was a reason James and John were called the "Sons of Thunder." I suspect before they came to know the Lord they liked to fight and had a reputation for doing so. Not much talk, just action. So now, "in the name of the Lord," they wondered if they could use God's power to get even. There, is of course, much violence in the name of the Lord amongst those who do not know Him. Doing the wrong things for the wrong reasons these religious peoples will declare, "there's a biblical reason for this," but it is devoid of true biblical mandate. Our anger and His power is not a mix God can use.

Here both James and John weren't completely out of touch with God's Word. There is the story in 2 Kings 1 about Elijah facing Ahaziah's messengers who were sent to arrest him. "Lord, they're bothering me," Elijah said. And the Lord consumed all fifty who had come. When Ahaziah sent a second group, they met the same fate. So James and John's request for fire from heaven was not without precedent.

But I am sure James and John hated the Samaritans as much as the Samaritans hated them. I suspect everyone is prejudiced to some extent, although most will deny it. But one of the things God certainly sets about to do once we are saved is deliver us from the prejudices of our heart and fill us with His love. So Jesus responds:

> But He turned and rebuked them, and said, "You do not know what manner of spirit you are of. For the Son of Man did not come to destroy men's lives but to save them." And they went to another village.
>
> —Luke 9:55–56

James 1:20 tells us that says the wrath of man will not accomplish God's righteousness. It literally means that if we're angry and about to do something for the Lord in our anger, we can be assured we are in the wrong place, for that is not the way God operates. The fruit of the Spirit is longsuffering and meekness, gentleness and goodness. If we're going to follow the Lord, we had better learn to show mercy when we suffer reproach, instead of always reaching for lightning bolts.

Jesus said to Nicodemus in John 3:17 that the Son of Man came not to condemn the world but that the world through Him might be saved. To a larger group in John 12:47 He said, "If you listen to Me and hear My words and you don't believe Me, I won't judge you, because I didn't come to the world to judge the world. I came to save it. But the Word will judge you." In other words, the believer's reputation must be one of mercy. Judgment can come from a hundred different sources, but mercy must come from the body of Christ who represent God.

In Acts 8, when the Gospel reaches this area known as Samaria, the apostles in Jerusalem hear about the revival. Guess whom they send to check it out? You are right! Peter and John. These men who wanted to call fire down upon its people are now sent by God to preach Jesus and life to them. The one who wanted to destroy the town now had to lay his hands on the sick and pray for them. There is no room in the church for preachers who preach hell and hope you go there. To seek and to save those who are lost should be our heart, and we should be willing to suffer much for the sake of the Gospel.

> Now it happened as they journeyed on the road that someone said to Him, "Lord, I will follow You wherever You go." And Jesus said to him, "Foxes have holes and birds of the air have nests, but the Son of Man has nowhere to lay His head."
>
> —Luke 9:57–58

As they walked, Matthew 8:18–22 tells us it was a scribe, a student of the Law, who came to Jesus with a mouthful of commitment. "Wherever You go, I'm going," he said. Jesus' response to him was that he didn't understand how much that would entail. In other words, this wasn't the best time to sign up.

Lest you take the next verse on a purely literal level, Jesus had plenty of places to stay. He stayed at Peter's house in Capernaum for up to two years. In the Bethany area around Jerusalem, He spent so much time at the home of Mary, Martha, and Lazarus that when Lazarus became sick, they assumed He would come right away. The issue was not physical habitation. It was a call for those who would follow Him to count the cost. Few hearts were open for His presence. Today it is still a minority who have been saved by faith in Him, born-again with the Holy Spirit dwelling within them. Additionally, He was speaking of this not being His home, and then not being ours as we follow Him.

"If you're going to follow Me in this world, you're not going to be very comfortable here," Jesus said. "You're not going to be at home. There's no place here to truly rest." If you're going to follow the Lord, your eyes are going to have to be higher than the horizon. They'd better be looking up, because if you're going to live as a Christian in this world, there will be a lot of dissonance between you and the world—a lot of discomfort and a lot of unease.

No one who commits to following Jesus is going to have it easy. If we're going to walk with the Lord we're going to know the discomfort of difficult people, of giving until it hurts with nothing in return, and of denying ourselves so someone else can hear the Gospel. We're going to feel out of step with modern culture and like an outsider looking in. There's no way to speak up for Jesus in a world that wants nothing to do with Him, without being aware of the discomfort and separation.

> Then He said to another, "Follow Me." But he said, "Lord, let me first go and bury my father." Jesus said to him, "Let the dead bury their own dead, but you go and preach the kingdom of God."
>
> —Luke 9:59–60

The second example of three would-be followers was of someone Jesus invited to follow Him. We are told in Matthew 8:21 that this man was a disciple, someone who had been in the crowd for a while. This time, however, Jesus wanted to elicit from him a commitment of involvement. His response to Jesus' invitation was to say that his father had died. I don't think that's literally the case because Jesus' words, if he was truly dead, would have been very insensitive and contrary to everything we know of God's heart regarding family. I think it was a matter of, "I have responsibilities at home. My father's still around—but one day, when he's dead and gone, I'll be available."

To those who are constantly involved with the physical things of a life that ends in death and have little or no involvement with the things of God that end in eternal life, Jesus said, "There is an urgent need for us to go from receiving to doing, giving out."

There seems to be no shortage of excuses for not becoming involved in serving our Lord. "When my house is paid off . . . When my kids finish school . . . When the job demands ease up . . . When I'm a bit older and have more time . . . I'll serve God," people say. The problem, however, is that we never will have more time than we do right now, and we only have today to count on anyway! There will always be something that will demand our attention. If we're going to serve the Lord, it will be because there's urgency in our hearts over the calling of God which looms large before us in comparison to this life, which will soon be past.

If counting the cost deterred the gentleman in Jesus' first example, the second put off his calling by finding other pressing matters in his life. He didn't deny Jesus or His call. He just didn't want to do it right then. "Spiritually dead people can be involved with spiritually dead things," Jesus said. "But those who are alive spiritually need to pursue spiritual life."

I think there is a tremendous need for the church to follow the Lord with a dedicated and hungry heart. Jesus said the fields were already white unto harvest. We need not wait for them to ripen. Often Western Christians tend to be very casual about their faith. I remember being in the Philippines when Marcos was being overthrown and there was much unrest, but the church there was on fire for the Lord. Jesus was their hope, their life. If they were to survive another year, He would have to be the One to intervene.

For us, all too often Jesus is a sidelight, filling the gaps in our lives. But there's a whole world around us dying in sin. The church has been given open doors and the truth to preach. Other things easily can deter us, but Jesus' warning is that we should act while He calls and the fire is hot! Time is short, and no excuse will lengthen it.

Put this calling next to the calling of Matthew, who was at his tax collection job and very successful at that. When Jesus said, "Follow Me," Matthew said, "I'm in" (Matt. 9:9). And he left it all behind. Or go to Peter, James, and John who, on the day of a catch of fish so large it took all of them and all of their strength to land the net on shore, they too left it all behind when Jesus said, "Follow Me. I'll make you fishers of men." There was no "Give us sixty days to broker the fish and sell the equipment." They just walked away. They left the physical for the spiritual, the temporal for the eternal.

If you're going to be on the road with Jesus, not only will you have to live a life that's filled with mercy for the lost, but you're going to have to live with urgency because tomorrow is no guarantee for anyone. The very thought you can put something off until then is a presumptive act on your part. After today, eternity waits! Finally:

> And another also said, "Lord, I will follow You, but let me first go and bid them farewell who are at my house." But Jesus said to him, "No one, having put his hand to the plow, and looking back, is fit for the kingdom of God."
> —Luke 9:61–62

The third man, like the first, came to offer his service. But like the second man, he had some other things to do first. They seem to be simple requests—yet they again strike a death blow to the service God is seeking from His own.

If we're going to follow Jesus it must to be our first and primary concern, because looking back will not move us forward. Our relationship to the Lord must precede everything else. If our businesses or our hobbies are first, we cannot be available for Him.

Jesus must be first. And if He is, everything else will take care of itself. But if He's not, we've got more problems ahead than we realize. The issue of going back to say goodbye to his family was not the issue at which Jesus was pointing. It was the promise of following with the excuse of not following yet.

The excuse used in our text: "Let me first . . ." is often the greatest difficulty we find in following the Lord. The author of the letter to the Hebrews 11:39 talked about the believers who died in faith not having received the promises. But seeing them far off, they embraced them, he said, and confessed they were strangers and pilgrims in the earth. They sought a homeland and if they had in mind the homeland from which they had come, they would have occasion to return. But they declared they wanted a heavenly country, so God is not ashamed to be called their God and has prepared for them a place. In other words, whatever I used to have, I don't need anymore. I now must find what God has for me.

What do we need to travel on the road with Jesus in this life? Tender mercy and a steadfast commitment willing to accept hardships. We need to have a sense of urgency and a single eye where no sacrifice for His kingdom is too great. After all, He went down this road for us first.

Three examples—two volunteers and one who was invited. You'll find yourself in one of them. When all is said and done, you want to be the one who sets your face like Jesus to follow Him no matter what. There is work to do, the fields are white, and God longs to pour Himself into your life, and then out of your life for His glory. Are you available?

Chapter 62

JESUS VISITS JERUSALEM

John 7:1–31

J esus' final year is not linear in the sense that it took Him a year to travel the seventy-five or eighty miles to Jerusalem from the Galilee region. But we find Him more and more often in the south, in Judea, and in Jerusalem in particular, spending a great deal more time with the disciples talking about death, the cross, and the resurrection—and spending many hours facing off with the religious leaders who controlled Jerusalem.

Back in John 5, when Jesus was in Jerusalem previously, He had gone to the pool of Bethsaida on the Sabbath to minister to a man who had been laying there for most, if not all, of his adult life. When Jesus healed him and told him to take up his bed and walk, the Pharisees decided then and there that because He had told this man to carry his bed on the Sabbath, that Jesus was a lawbreaker, not the Messiah, and worthy of death. In this part of the country, the cost for the disciples to follow Jesus into Jerusalem was about to go way up.

> After these things Jesus walked in Galilee; for He did not want to walk in Judea, because the Jews sought to kill Him.
>
> —John 7:1

If you go to Israel today, you will find that Galilee is still a much more relaxed place than Jerusalem. Not only is the population smaller, but the strict interpretation of the Law is not so prevalent. So although He was headed for Jerusalem, it wasn't yet fully time for Jesus to be arrested and killed. Therefore, He didn't look for direct confrontation but exercised caution. I find that a good lesson because sometimes, under the guise of faith, we will attempt to do some dumb things. Go where the Lord leads you, but no further, and then rest in Him.

> Now the Jew's Feast of Tabernacles was at hand. His brothers therefore said to Him, "Depart from here and go into Judea, that Your disciples also may see the works that You are doing. For no one does anything in secret while he himself seeks to be known openly. If You do these things, show Yourself to the world." For even His brothers did not believe in Him.
>
> —John 7:2–5

The Feast of Tabernacles, celebrated in September or October, lasted eight days and was designed for the nation as a whole to commemorate God's provision during the forty years they were in the wilderness. Each family would build a booth or temporary tent-like structure in which they would stay, signifying how the Lord had provided shelter for them in the wilderness. Like a spiritual camp, it was a family affair that brought millions of people to the capital.

Back in Galilee, Jesus' brothers thought the Feast of Tabernacles would be a great place for Him to make Himself known. So they said to Him, "If You want a following like we think You do, You'll never get it up here in the backwoods of Galilee. You've got to go where the people are. In fact, there's a built-in opportunity coming. The Feast of Tabernacles would be an awesome place to show who You are. Why don't You go up and make Yourself known? It's where the action is." Yet in verse 5, we see the motivation for their suggestion was actually a taunt, because they didn't believe in Him.

I find it amazing they could live with Jesus for thirty years and somehow not have an inkling of who He was, who he might be. He never lied. He never lost His temper. He didn't join others in wrong activities. He could be trusted in His business. He was a loving son to His mother. He was a hard worker. He did everything right.

If you're trying to witness to your family and are frustrated that they're not paying attention, look at Jesus' experience. His family tells you that spiritual truth is only spiritually revealed. So don't give up in your witnessing. Keep praying, because it may take awhile. Fortunately, about a year later, in Acts 1:13–14, Jesus' family is among the 120 gathered believers in Jesus gathered in the Upper Room, waiting for the promised outpouring of the Holy Spirit. It just took the resurrection to convince them. It usually does—because to serve a God that is dead is a worthless practice.

> Then Jesus said to them, "My time has not yet come, but your time is always ready. The world cannot hate you, but it hates Me because I testify of it that its works are evil. You go up to this feast. I am not yet going up to this feast, for My time has not yet fully come." When He had said these things to them, He remained in Galilee.
>
> —John 7:6–9

Jesus' answer to His brothers was one of timing. Their suggestion was based on their own ideas being not yet submitted to God. They were on their way to a religious festival without really knowing the God of the festival. Jesus was different. His life was in the Father's hands. He was led by the Spirit. He followed God's timetable. His brothers were part of the world's system so they fit right in, but not Jesus. His life and words caused difficulty even with religious men, because He talked about sin and responsibility. His way of life brought conviction.

We're to be in the world but not of it. We're to be the salt of the earth and bring the Word of God to bear and to testify of who Jesus is. Christians shouldn't be comfortable in the world. For them, being with the church ought to be a much more comfortable place. There's no way to be acceptable to a world that hates God if you're walking with Him. It doesn't mean you have to be obnoxious or foolish—but your very commitment to the Lord will bring some opposition.

> But when His brothers had gone up, then He also went up to the feast, not openly, but as it were in secret. Then the Jews sought Him at the feast, and said, "Where is He?" And there was much complaining among the people concerning Him. Some said, "He is good"; others said, "No, on the contrary, He deceives the people." However, no one spoke openly of Him for fear of the Jews.
> —John 7:10–13

As the blind in unbelief headed out, Jesus followed behind, but not to be exposed. By law, He had to go. That was His religious responsibility. It would have been sin to avoid going, but He didn't have to go with trumpets blaring. He went "undercover" to avoid the big conflict at that point, instead of in the manner His brothers had suggested.

After seeing the family's attitude toward Jesus, we also see the attitude of those in the crowd concerning His identity—from good man to liar and perhaps everything in between. But regardless of their position, no one was willing to take much of a stand because of the tremendous fear they had of the religious leadership.

> Now about the middle of the feast Jesus went up into the temple and taught. And the Jews marveled, saying, "How does this Man know letters, having never studied?"
> —John 7:14–15

As Jesus exposed His position in the middle of the Feast, the people gathered in Jerusalem couldn't believe what they were hearing from what they assumed was an uneducated man. He wore a homespun robe and spoke with a distinctly Galilean accent. He hadn't graduated from any of the many yeshivas in town that would have given Him a diploma that validated His teaching. Yet as He sat down to speak, no one could fathom what they heard. They marveled!

When Peter and John are arrested and brought before the Sanhedrin for healing a lame man, we read in Acts 4:13 that although the Sanhedrin assumed they were uneducated and untrained, they also realized they had been with Jesus. Paul was the best in his class and the Lord mightily used his wisdom and education. But don't think for a minute that if you don't have a good education God can't use you, because Peter, John, and the others are examples of people who were empowered without having taken much part in the educational process.

Jesus answered them and said, "My doctrine is not Mine, but His who sent Me. If anyone wills to do His will, he shall know concerning the doctrine, whether it is from God or *whether* I speak on My own *authority*. He who speaks from himself seeks his own glory, but He who seeks the glory of the One who sent Him is true, and no unrighteousness is in Him.

—John 7:16–18

"How am I so smart?" Jesus replied to their fascination. "I've been hanging around My Father, listening to what He says. I'm just quoting Him." Jesus had been raised with the Scripture from His youth. As seen in the Sermon on the Mount, He was aware of the common misinterpretations of the Law. He rightly divided the word of truth. He shared the full counsel of God's Word—yet none of this came from His formal education. It came from fellowship with His Father.

In Galatians 1:12, Paul said, "When I came to preach to you, I didn't come with wisdom according to men. The Gospel I taught you came from revelation through Christ." God honors His Word. That's always the case. Some of God's greatest tools through the ages have been those without much of a formal education because the fundamental condition for spiritual growth is simply a genuine desire to act on God's Word once we are saved and He fills us with the Holy Spirit.

Of the other teachers, Jesus said, "If someone is making it up as he goes, he wants glory for himself. But if the source of his information is the Lord, then it's God's glory he's after and he'll be right. There won't be any unrighteousness driving him." Religious speakers who seek their own glory come with their own message—but those who seek the Lord bring His message to bear.

"Did not Moses give you the law, yet none of you keeps the law? Why do you seek to kill Me?" The people answered and said, "You have a demon. Who is seeking to kill You?"

—John 7:19–20

These religious leaders standing in the crowd thought they had been very secretive about their plans to have Jesus killed, and yet Jesus knew exactly what was going on all along. Not only that, in verse 25, the people said to each other, "Isn't this the man they're trying to kill?" It seems their plan was common knowledge. Yet when confronted, they denied it, again accusing Jesus of being possessed by the Devil.

Jesus answered and said to them, "I did one work, and you all marvel. Moses therefore gave you circumcision (not that it is from Moses, but from the fathers), and you circumcise a man on the Sabbath. If a man receives circumcision on the Sabbath, so that the law of Moses should not be broken, are you angry with Me

335

because I made a man completely well on the Sabbath? Do not judge according to appearance, but judge with righteous judgment."

—John 7:21–24

Jesus said, "You will circumcise a child on the eighth day even if it falls on the Sabbath. So how much more appropriate is it for Me to heal a man paralyzed for thirty-eight years on the Sabbath? Isn't that what God would want?" It's an interesting picture, because religion and its rules are always devoid of compassion.

Now some of them from Jerusalem said, "Is this not He whom they seek to kill? But look! He speaks boldly, and they say nothing to Him. Do the rulers know indeed that this is truly the Christ?"

—John 7:25–26

We are shown the hearts of everyone from the family to the leaders, from the general folks to the locals. But notice that everyone needs God's grace to see the Lord. "Isn't this the one the religious leaders have been talking about killing?" the people asked. "Maybe they've decided He really is the Messiah because He's sure getting away with it." But throughout the Gospels we read that the only hesitation these religious leaders showed in grabbing Jesus immediately was worry over the people's reaction.

"However, we know where this Man is from; but when the Christ comes, no one knows where He is from." Then Jesus cried out, as He taught in the temple, saying, "You both know Me, and you know where I am from; and I have not come of Myself, but He who sent Me is true, whom you do not know. But I know Him, for I am from Him, and He sent Me."

—John 7:27–29

"You might know physical things but you don't have spiritual insight. You think you know about Bethlehem and Nazareth but you don't really know where I've come from," Jesus said.

Therefore they sought to take Him; but no one laid a hand on Him, because His hour had not yet come. And many of the people believed in Him, and said, "When the Christ comes, will He do more signs than these which this Man has done?"

—John 7:30–31

As time went on, more people believed in Him as they saw His power displayed. The religious leaders grew increasingly hostile; soon violence would be their only option.

Chapter 63

WHO IS HE?

John 7:32–8:1

In John 10:11, the Jews had asked concerning Jesus, "Where is He?" But in the text before us, Jesus will answer the question, "Who is He?"

> The Pharisees heard the crowd murmuring these things concerning Him, and the Pharisees and the chief priests sent officers to take Him.
>
> —John 7:32

After failing to apprehend Jesus themselves, the religious leaders gave orders to the temple police to bring Him in. Notice that the Pharisees and the chief priests were in this together. That's important because most of the chief priests during Jesus' days were Sadducees. Sadducees didn't believe in life after death. On the other hand, the Pharisees believed in life after death and judgment for sin. Though the Sadducees and Pharisees were diametrically opposed in outlook, they both were interested in keeping their power, authority, income, and status. So they aligned themselves together against Jesus.

> Then Jesus said to them, "I shall be with you a little while longer, and then I go to Him who sent Me. You will seek Me and not find Me, and where I am you cannot come." Then the Jews said among themselves, "Where does He intend to go that we shall not find Him? Does He intend to go to the Dispersion among the Greeks and teach the Greeks? What is this thing that He said, 'You will seek Me and not find Me, and where I am you cannot come'?"
>
> —John 7:33–36

We don't know how long the temple guards listened to Jesus, but we are told in verse 45 that Jesus' words so moved their hearts that they didn't arrest Him. As they stood and listened, Jesus told the crowd He would be with them for only a little while longer before He would be leaving, that He would be going back to the One who had sent Him, and that when He left, they would try to find Him but they wouldn't be able.

The result of unbelief is that heaven's doors are locked. There's only one way in, one hope, one life, and one direction we can take. Jesus declared, "I am the Way and I'm only here for a little while. You're going to have to make your decision about who I am in the time you're given."

337

Following His resurrection, Jesus appeared to a number of groups and individuals. But every one of them was a believer. According to the Bible, He never once appeared to the religious unbelievers who had plotted His death. So today you can share the Gospel with others, but if they refuse and turn away from Jesus and His offer of life, each refusal hardens the heart a bit, dims the light, and over time can extinguish it all together.

As the Lord spoke through him, Solomon wrote in Proverbs 1:24–28, "Because I have called you and you have refused Me, because I have stretched out My hand and no one has regarded, because I have had My counsel disdained, I'm going to laugh at your calamity and mock when your terror comes like a storm and a whirlwind. Then you'll call but I won't answer. You'll look for Me diligently but won't find Me." Those aren't words from a hateful God who can't wait to get even. They are instead a warning from a loving God who won't wait forever.

You're given a life. You've got to make the best of it. You've got to make your choices now. Jesus, I'm sure with great sadness, said to the crowds at the temple, "You've only got now."

As the religious crowd plotted to rid themselves of Jesus, there was coming a day when they would wish they had been with Him rather than against Him. It's a tragic truth, but it's fair. God invites each of us to come to Jesus to be saved. He's knocking. But at some point the knocking ceases. If nothing else, the day you die, the opportunity is gone.

At least for the moment, devoid of hunger for spiritual understanding and with great confidence in their own power, some in religious power began to wonder aloud where Jesus was going to hide from their control. "Maybe He'll go to the Decapolis cities, the northern cities above the Sea of Galilee," they scoffed. "Maybe He'll try and teach the heathen because we religious folks certainly aren't buying any of this. What does He think? He can't run from us!"

Prophetically, Scriptures tell us that once He was refused by His own nation, Jesus would turn to a nation that would bring forth fruit and would believe in Him. So the national opportunity for Israel would pass until after the Rapture. But the individual opportunity is still here for everyone. "Seek the Lord while He may be found," Isaiah wrote in chapter 55:6. "Call upon Him while He is near"—which would imply that there's going to be a time when that's not the case. But for now, you can come to Him!

> On the last day, that great day of the feast, Jesus stood and cried out, saying, "If anyone thirsts, let Him come to Me and drink."
>
> —John 7:37

According to Alfred Edersheim, author of several historical books on the life and times of Jesus, during the Feast of Tabernacles the priests would walk around the temple with pitchers in hand to the pool of Siloam, or literally the pool of "He who has been sent," where they would fill their pitchers They would then pour out the water on the temple steps, signifying that God had given His people water out of the rock. They did this every day for seven days. The eighth day, the last day of the Feast, commemorated the nation's arrival in the Promised Land, where they were given wells they hadn't dug, houses they hadn't built, and vineyards they hadn't planted. Therefore, on the eighth day the priests marched around the temple seven times but poured out no water, because in the Promised Land they found in God's goodness all they would ever need.

It was on this last day of the Feast that everyone, ready to return home, crowded around the temple for the final time. It was then that Jesus cried out, "If you're thirsty, you can come to Me and drink. He who believes in Me, out of His heart will flow rivers of living water," as He invited the people to celebrate God's deliverance not to a physical land, not to a Promised Land, but to a promised life.

I've got to believe that in that religious crowd there were a lot of people who were very thirsty for the things of God. But the system didn't minister very well to their thirst. There were plenty of rules and regulations—but not much love. There was no shortage of demands—but not much grace. "If you're thirsty, come to Me," Jesus said, putting Himself right at the center of the equation. To this group remembering the water from the rock that had been given to their forefathers, Jesus identified Himself as the Rock, the One who gives life, the only One who, in this wilderness called life, satisfies thirst.

> "He who believes in Me, as the Scripture has said, out of his heart will flow rivers of living water." But this He spoke concerning the Spirit, whom those believing in Him would receive; for the Holy Spirit was not yet given, because Jesus was not yet glorified.
>
> —John 7:38–39

In hindsight, John understood it was God's intention to send the Holy Spirit to indwell those who believed in Him and then flow through them to a world that was lost.

> Therefore many from the crowd, then they heard this saying, said, "Truly this is the Prophet." Others said, "This is the Christ." But some said, "Will the Christ come out of Galilee? Has not the Scripture said that the Christ comes from the seed of David and from the town of Bethlehem where David was?" So there was a division among the people because of Him.
>
> —John 7:40–43

Some heard Jesus' words and believed. Others, however, had a problem. Prejudiced against the north, they saw Galilee as Hicksville. Besides, Scripture said the Messiah would come from Bethlehem. But what they hadn't bothered to do was find out that Jesus had been born there. Had they done so, the very Scripture that turned them away would have brought them closer. But they weren't interested enough. Hindered by unbelief, hindered because they weren't thirsty enough to check out the facts, and unwilling to listen, they turned off the message.

Now some of them wanted to take Him, but no one laid hands on Him.

—John 7:44

If the first group heard the message and the second group was hindered by it, the third group just hated Jesus and wanted to silence Him. But they wouldn't get rid of Him that easily, for He loved them too much to leave. Throughout his gospel—in 5:18, 7:1, and 10:39—John points out the futility of people's efforts to get rid of Jesus.

"You're not going to speak to me? Don't you know I have the power to crucify You?" Pilate later asked Jesus.

"You don't have any power over Me at all unless you are given it from My Father in heaven," Jesus answered. He wouldn't be taken. He's always in charge. When He would go to the cross, it was because He chose to go. It was time!

> Then the officers came to the chief priests and Pharisees, who said to them, "Why have you not brought Him?" The officers answered, "No man ever spoke like this Man!"
>
> —John 7:45–46

When the temple police returned empty-handed, the religious leaders were beside themselves. "You're armed," they said. "This is your turf. You have great authority. What's the problem?" The problem was that although they had gone to silence Jesus, He had silenced them. His gracious words and powerful manner had stopped them in their tracks and they were taken in.

Jesus didn't talk like the religious leaders who simply quoted each other's books. He spoke as if He had written the whole thing, as if He knew all about it. If they were anything like the police in our day, these temple guards might have been very cynical because of their constant exposure to liars, cheaters, and crooks. But they said of Jesus, "He's for real! He's awesome!"

> Then the Pharisees answered them, "Are you also deceived? Have any of the rulers or the Pharisees believed in Him? But this crowd that does not know the law is accursed."
>
> —John 7:47–49

Look at the Pharisees' reaction to some honest policemen who were touched by Jesus. "So you're as dumb as the rest? You don't see any of us smart guys buying into His little game, do you? Look, if Jesus was the Messiah, we'd tell you. But He's not. As for the crowd, they're just a bunch of cursed people who don't know anything about what the Law says." The wise, learned, well-educated men turned on everyone but themselves.

> Nicodemus (he who came to Jesus by night, being one of them) said to them, "Does our law judge a man before it hears him and knows what he is doing?" They answered and said to him, "Are you also from Galilee? Search and look, for no prophet has arisen out of Galilee."
>
> —John 7:50, 51

"Do you see a single man among us who believes in Jesus?" the Pharisees had asked. But no sooner had these words left their uneducated mouths than Nicodemus spoke up. One of them, a member of the Sanhedrin, a man with great pull and seniority, after secretly meeting with Jesus two years earlier had become convinced that Jesus was the One for whom they were waiting. He wasn't ready to speak publicly yet at this point—there was still a lot at stake. But after the cross, he was one of the first ones to declare his faith.

I'm sure it cost Nicodemus something to make even this moderate defense of Jesus. He branded himself at this point as a sympathizer of Jesus among a group of hateful men who constantly were having meetings to see how they could kill Him.

Every time John mentioned Nicodemus, he added the words "at night." But soon it was Nicodemus in the twilight and then Nicodemus in the daylight. Grace takes time. He might not have been making progress as quickly as we would hope, but he was making progress nonetheless. He challenged his own party, saying, "We're biased. We're not playing fair here. We're breaking the law ourselves by judging Him before we hear Him. That's not the way the Law works." Rather than listening to reason, however, these were in no mood for a lecture. Their position was tenuous at best and Jesus was shaking the foundations. So, threatened with reason, they reacted with hatred.

"You're uneducated too," they said—even though he was one of their leaders. "You better study the Bible. No prophet has ever come from Galilee." That's wrong. Elijah and Jonah, to name two, had come from Galilee. But hatred and unbelief lack respect, honesty, openness, and a willingness to learn. It blinds every heart.

> And everyone went to his own house. But Jesus went to the Mount of Olives.
>
> —John 7:53, 8:1

This is an interesting comparison because with the Feast over and with the tents being taken down and families on their way en masse to go home, most of the folks had missed a great opportunity to be right with God. Many had listened—but many had not.

The officers went to their houses. The Sanhedrin, Nicodemus, and the people of Jerusalem went home. The lights went on. Dinners were started. Beds were made. But Jesus had no place to lay His head. He had come to serve, not to be served. So the very next thing we read in John 8:2 is that early the next morning, Jesus was back again, continuing to press home the point—He had come to bring life to anyone who would hear!

Chapter 64

JESUS' MINISTRY AT THE TEMPLE

John 8:1–59

In chapters 7, 8, 9, and the first part of chapter 10 of John, we are given a record of approximately eight days in the life of Jesus' ministry. During the Feast of Tabernacles and in the days following, we see ongoing conversations between Jesus and the religious leaders, messages to the gathered crowds, and a constant invitation to come to Him because He was their only hope.

At the end of the Feast of Tabernacles, everyone from out of town had gone home. Jesus, however, had gone up to the Mount of Olives.

> Now early in the morning He came again into the temple, and all the people came to Him; and He sat down and taught them.
>
> —John 8:2

If the authorities thought they could scare off Jesus, they were dead wrong. Twice in one day they unsuccessfully had tried to trap Him. But Jesus was not finished yet—so the very next morning, bright and early, He was back in the temple. And the people who were there early to seek the Lord found themselves sitting at His feet.

It must have been great to come to the temple after years of nothing but rules to find a smile on this rabbi's face and a word of hope in His mouth. He was ministering to the people in the same place that, eighteen years earlier, He had said to Mary and Joseph, "I must be about My Father's business."

> Then the scribes and Pharisees brought to Him a woman caught in adultery. And when they had set her in the midst, they said to Him, "Teacher, this woman was caught in adultery, in the very act. Now Moses, in the law, commanded us that such should be stoned. But what do You say?" This they said, testing Him, that they might have something of which to accuse Him.
>
> —John 8:3–6

Into this beautiful picture of ministry at the temple came religious leaders with just one thing on their minds: destroy Jesus one way or the other. This time they came bringing with them a woman who, I'm sure, was fearful and in tears. Setting her in front of Jesus and in view of the large crowd, they said she had been caught in the very act of adultery. John makes it clear immediately that they were interested neither in holiness or the woman. They simply had come to trap Jesus, exploiting her for their own purposes.

From a biblical standpoint (Lev. 20:10), adultery in the Old Testament was a breach of the Law that, provided there was eyewitness testimony, was punishable by death. In this case, the charge was grossly unfair because if the woman had been caught in the act, the man should have been there as well. But he was nowhere to be found.

"The Bible says we should put her to death," the religious leaders announced.

Yet in Jesus' time, the occupying Roman forces did not allow the Jews to carry out capital punishment. Although they took it upon themselves occasionally, they had no legal right to do so. This was nothing more than grandstanding in front of a big crowd for the sake of discrediting Jesus. At stake was this woman's life or, at the very least, her reputation—along with Jesus' credibility and everything He taught about the Law and mercy.

It is a good lesson to us, for when we share the Gospel with people, they sometimes have difficulty bringing justice and mercy together. How can God forgive an unrighteous person? Seems impossible to us and it us, but not to Him. He sent His Son. He paid the price. Jesus is the answer to that otherwise impossible dilemma. If these men thought they could ensnare Him they were mistaken, because even early in the morning Jesus is pretty good at answering questions.

> But Jesus stooped down and wrote on the ground with His finger, as though He did not hear. So when they continued asking Him, He raised Himself up . . . .
> —John 8:6–7

"Aha! Now we've got Him. Let's yell a little louder," the religious leaders said. They obviously didn't know that this One writing on the ground was the One who had written the Law with His own finger on tablets of stone.

I love the picture. Look at the players. There is the Savior who came to seek and save all of us lost in sin. There is a guilty sinner, the poor woman who neither could defend herself nor clear her name. There is the Law that demands death for sin. And there's the enemy, delighting in accusation.

The enemy mistook Jesus' silence for weakness. That is a bad decision. When Solomon wrote Ecclesiastes, he said because God's sentence is not speedily exercised against an evil work, a person's heart will be fully in them to do evil. In other words, God is very patient—by the time our lives are over, we won't be able to say, "I didn't have a chance to change." God gives us enough rope to hang ourselves and enough invitations to be made free in Him. He invites us to come—then waits to see what our choice will be.

> . . . and said to them, "He who is without sin among you, let him throw a stone at her first." And again He stooped down and wrote on the ground.
> —John 8:7–8

Finally, Jesus stopped writing and stood up. "All right. Let's kill her," He said. "That's what the Law demands. The guy without sin can start." According to the Law, the eyewitness to a capital offense had to throw the first stone in order to verify he was telling the truth. "Let's get eyewitnesses up here first," Jesus said.

> Then those who heard it, being convicted by their conscience, went out one by one, beginning with the oldest even to the last. And Jesus was left alone, and the woman standing in the midst.
>
> —John 8:9

The Bible talks a little about God's finger. It says God wrote the Ten Commandments with His finger. It also says that on Belshazzar's last night as king of Babylon, it was God's finger that wrote, "You've been weighed in the balance and your kingdom is found wanting" on the palace wall.

I don't doubt that as Jesus seemingly was ignoring the scribes and Pharisees' accusations, there upon the ground God's finger was writing out the secret sins of those who had brought the woman to Him. As a result, one by one, these men suddenly remembered they had to be somewhere else, they were late for work, or they hadn't had breakfast.

The Bible says conscience is God's gift to us and that it operates in everyone's life—believer and unbeliever alike. Your conscience doesn't leave you alone. It shines the light on your sin and only begins to lose power if you constantly turn it off. Paul told Timothy (1 Tim. 4:2) that we can come to a place where our consciences are unresponsive, like something burned with a hot iron. If we can sin without being convicted, that's a danger sign. The conscience is a great gift by which the Lord calls us to Himself.

> When Jesus had raised Himself up and saw no one but the woman, He said to her, "Woman, where are those accusers of yours? Has no one condemned you?" She said, "No one, Lord." And Jesus said to her, "Neither do I condemn you; go and sin no more." Then Jesus spoke to them again, saying, "I am the light of the world. He who follows Me shall not walk in darkness, but have the light of life."
>
> —John 8:10–12

How much clearer could this picture have been for these crowds? The only One who could throw stones didn't. The only One qualified to bring death offered life instead. And far from condemning her for her sin, Jesus said, "Don't sin anymore. Here's how: Follow Me and you won't have to live in darkness. The light will be on. The way will be clear. I can be your life."

Jesus used this confrontation as a lesson to the crowd gathered around Him: "You're never going to find life following religious men in the darkness. You have to believe in Me."

Verse 20 tells us this confrontation took place in the treasury area of the temple. In the first century, during the Feast of Tabernacles, priests hung huge candelabras on the Court of the Treasury's walls and burned them every night, signifying the pillar of fire. Jesus made His declaration the day after this feast was over. The candles were out—the wall still blackened from the flames—and the smell of smoke still in the air. Standing in front of this wall, Jesus said, "I am the light of the world"—and I don't doubt the people made the connection between Him and the light that had led their forefathers through the wilderness.

> The Pharisees therefore said to Him, "You bear witness of Yourself. Your witness is not true." Jesus answered and said to them, "Even if I bear witness of Myself, My witness is true, for I know where I came from and where I am going; but you do not know where I come from and where I am going. You judge according to the flesh; I judge no one. And yet if I do judge, My judgment is true; for I am not alone, but I am with the Father who sent Me. It is also written in your law that the testimony of two men is true. I am One who bears witness of Myself, and the Father who sent Me bears witness of Me."
>
> —John 8:13–18

When the arrest hadn't worked, when the trap hadn't worked, and when they had nothing left to argue, the Pharisees were reduced to foolish bickering. "You can't say who You are. Others must testify," they said to Jesus. Yet if we go back and look at all that had taken place here, we see He had revealed the hearts and sins of a whole bunch of religious accusers. He had healed and delivered and made new a broken woman. They had all they needed to go on. But when we don't want to hear the truth, we'll always find a reason not to believe. We'll bicker. We'll argue. But Jesus' bottom line is always the same: "If you want life, follow Me. You won't walk in darkness. I can provide forgiveness."

The problem with the Pharisees, Jesus said, was they had no spiritual insight. It was true the Scriptures said every word was to be established in at least two witnesses' mouths. But the Pharisees failed to take into account the Father's witness, as heard from heaven at Jesus' baptism and seen in His works. And yet with infinite patience and great love, Jesus just kept ministering to them. He does the same with you. If you're not a Christian and you're still breathing, God is patient, isn't He? What are you waiting for?

So He told these who opposed Him over and over again that His judgment was not clouded or tainted by self as theirs was, that He was God in the flesh, and that He had the testimony of His Father.

> Then they said to Him, "Where is Your Father?"
>
> —John 8:19

As we read the rest of the chapter we will clearly see their implication. In verse 41, they will say, "At least we weren't born out of wedlock." For now Jesus tolerates their wickedness in His love for them.

Jesus answered, "You know neither Me nor My Father. If you had known Me, you would have known My Father also."

—John 8:19

Jesus' answer was that those who know God would know better than to ask that kind of question. They would know Him if they knew the Father. They did not!

> These words Jesus spoke in the treasury, as He taught in the temple; and no one laid hands on Him, for His hour had not yet come. Then Jesus said to them again, "I am going away, and you will seek Me, and will die in your sin. Where I go you cannot come." So the Jews said, "Will He kill Himself, because He says, 'Where I go you cannot come?'" And He said to them, "You are from beneath; I am from above. You are of this world; I am not of this world. Therefore I said to you that you will die in your sins; for if you do not believe that I am He, you will die in your sins."

—John 8:20–24

In John 7:33–36, Jesus very sorrowfully said to this same group, "You're going to look for Me later and wish you could find Me, but it will be too late." Here He said the same thing: "Your problem is that you're all about this life and nothing more. You have no ear for eternal things. And if that continues, you'll die in this world because that's where you live. But if you believe that I am, you can escape it."

Jesus reduced salvation to one issue, and He used the title God most often used for Himself: I AM.

"Who shall I say sent me?" Moses had asked.

"Tell them it was I AM," God had answered.

Jesus used the name for God to refer to Himself—and His audience understood exactly what He meant. In fact, by the end of the chapter, they pick up stones to stone Him because of this claim.

The singular issue for heaven is a belief that Jesus is God, who has come to save you from your sin. And that places all of the cults in the same basket, because they don't. They have a hundred other explanations for Jesus, but that He is God is the one that makes all of the difference. It's a non-negotiable point. Here in the temple, Jesus said very clearly, "I am God and if you believe in Me, you'll have life. If you don't, you'll die in your sins." That's hard to misread.

> Then they said to Him, "Who are You?"

—John 8:25

In other words, "Who do You think You are?"

346

And Jesus said to them, "Just what I have been saying to you from the beginning."

—John 8:25

Every word, miracle, healing, deliverance, and sermon validated who Jesus was. The problem was not a lack of information. The problem was not a lack of proof. The problem was a lack of belief.

"I have many things to say and to judge concerning you, but He who sent Me is true; and I speak to the world those things which I heard from Him." They did not understand that He spoke to them of the Father. Then Jesus said to them, "When you lift up the Son of Man, then you will know that I am He, and that I do nothing of Myself, but as My Father taught Me, I speak these things."

—John 8:26–28

"You're going to know eventually," Jesus said. From the cross and the resurrection forward, the greatest argument for Christianity is the empty tomb. That's the ultimate proof. You don't need anything else. He was dead. Now He's alive. So I'll follow Him until I find something better.

Jesus overcame death even as He said He would. The graves were opened. The dead were seen in the city. The temple veil was torn. The rocks cracked. The sky darkened. The earth moved. He was the One. The Pharisees weren't yet connecting Jesus with the Father. But the resurrection would be the final proof.

"And He who sent Me is with Me. The Father has not left Me alone, for I always do those things that please Him."

—John 8:29

"I always do those things that please the Father," Jesus said. What pleased the Father? Offering forgiveness to the woman thrown in front of the crowds pleased Him. Jesus had helped this woman out of the temple with dignity and joy, forgiveness and mercy, because it pleased the Father to save her. And it pleased the Father to save us. Angels rejoice when people get saved. All of heaven enjoys that more than anything else.

As He spoke these words, many believed in Him. Then Jesus said to those Jews who believed Him, "If you abide in My word, you are My disciples indeed."

—John 8:30–31

There is a kind of believing that doesn't save. Mental agreement or general awareness is not the kind of belief God is looking for in your life. He wants belief that grabs His Word and follows it wholeheartedly, belief that is convinced of who He is, and belief that will give one's life for His sake.

There are a lot of examples of folks in the Bible who "believed." Maybe Judas is the best one. He hung around the disciples for three and a half years and not one of them suspected he was a bad guy. In Acts 8, Simon the sorcerer believed and was baptized. But a couple of weeks later, when Peter and John came from Jerusalem to pray for people to be filled with the Spirit, Simon's true heart was revealed when he offered to buy the Holy Spirit's power to manipulate the people.

"If you abide in My Word, you are My disciples indeed," Jesus said. The original word for *indeed* is the word for *genuinely* or *sincerely*. In other words, following God's Word is a definitive mark of a true disciple. True believers honor God's Word, hide it in their hearts, and make it a part of their lives.

In the 1800s, a man from France named Blonden stretched a 1,200-foot metal cable 200 feet in the air over Niagara Falls. Every day, he, his wife, and their children would walk across the cable as crowds gathered and paid to watch them defy death.

"Do you think I can walk across and back?" Blonden would ask them.

"Yes!" the crowd would roar.

"Do you really believe that?" he'd ask.

"Yes!" the reply would thunder back.

"Then who will be the first to get on my back?"

Silence.

If we really believe in Jesus, we should be able to "get on His back." We should walk with Him—because that's the only kind of faith that saves. In verse 3, it said these believed. But by the time we come to verse 59, they are trying to kill Jesus.

In the parable of the sower (Matt. 13:18–23), some of the seed of God's Word fell on stony ground. And because shallow earth tends to be warmer and more conducive to growth, it immediately sprang up—only to wither and die under the eventual heat of the sun. There are a lot of people who when they initially hear about God or the things of God say, "That's what I want." But because there is no heart attachment, no moving of faith, and no dependence on God, they don't make it very long. The true believer is going to follow God and hang on to Him for dear life.

> "And you shall know the truth and the truth shall make you free."
>
> —John 8:32

If you believe in Christ, then you receive His Word. You know the truth, you follow it, and it sets you free—from your sin, the world, and temptation. You become an overcomer.

> They answered Him, "We are Abraham's descendants, and have never been in bondage to anyone. How can you say, 'You will be made free'?"
>
> —John 8:33

Politically, this was a senseless boast because the nation itself had been in bondage in Egypt for 430 years. During the time of the judges, they were under someone else's control more often than on their own. After Saul, David, and Solomon, the Assyrians came, followed by the Babylonians, Medes and Persians, and Greeks and then the Romans. Even as the Pharisees spoke, they were under Roman control. They should have said, "We've never been free for long"—because they spent more years under someone else's rule than they did under their own.

I suspect the Pharisees were speaking religiously rather than politically. "What do we need to be freed from?" they said.

From a spiritual standpoint, that's still often the universal argument that is made: "The Lord needs to save others, but I'm OK. I know there are some folks who need His help. I'm just not one of them."

> Jesus answered them, "Most assuredly, I say to you, whoever commits sin is a slave of sin. And a slave does not abide in the house forever, but a son abides forever. Therefore if the Son makes you free, you shall be free indeed."
> —John 8:34–36

The same Gospel that tells us we can be free in Christ also tells us we're bound to sin. Jesus used the word *enslaved*. Most folks don't see themselves that way. Even if they admit to sin, they'll say, "But I can take care of it if I want."

Sin has a way of convincing us we can stop anytime we want even as it further destroys us each day. Jesus said to these very self-secure, proud, and religious folks, "If you're sinning, you're a slave. You're not free. You are bound by that sin that works in you. The lust of your flesh, the Devil's influence, and the drive of a wicked mind, they all control you." Yet it's hard to convince the religious in the temple that they're dead in their sins.

These men were as wrong about their personal lives as they were about their national history. They weren't free. They were bound. And I think most folks, if you could spend five minutes with them, would have to agree that they are as well. If people could make a promise to do better and turn over a new leaf and it would work, we could have a problem sharing the gospel of Jesus. But instead people make fresh New Year's resolutions every year because they didn't keep those from the previous year.

If the bondage of sin were not a reality, you could make one choice to straighten out and be done with it. But it doesn't work that way, because sin is more powerful than we are and only Jesus genuinely can make us free.

Sometimes in sharing with people we hear, "Well, if I get saved and give my life to Jesus, what will I have to give up?" The answer is, "Bondage." Get saved and for the first time you'll be able to do something you've never been able to do before: obey God.

You can't be a slave to sin and live in His house because slaves aren't part of the family. But the Son will make you part of the family. He'll break the power of sin.

> "I know that you are Abraham's descendants, but you seek to kill Me, because
> My word has no place to you. I speak what I have seen with My Father, and you
> do what you have seen with your father."
>
> —John 8:37–38

Jesus acknowledged the Pharisees were physical descendants of Abraham, but that made their rejection of Him all the worse. They should have known better. They had the Scriptures, God's promises.

There are many today who consider themselves Christians simply because their parents went to church and they have grown up in religious households. But if there is an inconsistency between your religious claim and your actual behavior, Jesus said the reason is God is not your Father and His Word finds no place in your heart. You have a different father you're following—and he's misleading you.

> They answered and said to Him, "Abraham is our father." Jesus said to them, "If
> you were Abraham's children, you would do the works of Abraham. But now
> you seek to kill Me, a Man who has told you the truth which I heard from God.
> Abraham did not do this. You do the deeds of your father."
>
> —John 8:39–41

Approximately 25 percent of the book of Genesis tells the story of Abraham. Growing up in an idolatrous home, he responded to God's calling to separate himself. Then, following the Lord by faith to a land where he had never been, he spent the rest of his life in Canaan, supported by God's promises that one day succeeding generations would inherit it. Near the end of his life, he even was willing to put his son on the sacrificial altar because he believed God would raise the dead if necessary to fulfill His Word that through Him his descendants would come innumerably.

Abraham was God's friend, James 2:23 said. These were not. Even though they had four thousand years of Old Testament history to identify Him, they did not accept what Jesus had to say about who He was. The time, place, and why He had come were all laid out in Scripture. But they simply chose not open to it.

> Then they said to Him, "We were not born of fornication; we have one Father—
> God." Jesus said to them, "If God were your Father, you would love Me, for I
> proceeded forth and came from God; nor have I come of Myself, but He sent
> Me."
>
> —John 8:41–42

Jesus swept aside all of their wicked insinuation by saying, "If you truly were Abraham's children, you would believe in Me." Peter said the same thing in Acts 3:22 when he reminded us Moses said a prophet would follow one day who would be like Moses. But if the people wouldn't hear the Prophet that was to come, Moses said, they would be utterly destroyed from among the people. He warned them about hearing, about paying attention, and about listening to what God has to say.

> "Why do you not understand My speech? Because you are not able to listen to My word. You are of your father the Devil, and the desires of your father you want to do. He was a murderer from the beginning, and does not stand in the truth, because there is no truth in him. When he speaks a lie, he speaks from his own resources, for he is a liar and the father of it. But because I tell you the truth you do not believe Me."
>
> —John 8:43–45

The issue in rejecting God's Word, which Jesus was sharing, was that they still were being driven by the wrong spirit: the Devil. It's not a truth the world particularly wants to embrace, but God only sees the world in two camps: those who belong to Him and those who do not. There is a place of death and a place of life. There's not a third place. Either the Lord is your God and you've come to Him, or you're still under the auspices and influence of the Devil who runs this world. You can go to the beginning of the Bible and see him at work in the garden. You can go to the end and see him seeking to destroy everyone who believes in God, and God Himself, if that were possible.

We need a new Father. We need to get into a new family. This guy's not taking care of us. He stands in opposition to God. And Jesus tells them very plainly that they had a way out but chose not to follow it.

> "Which of you convicts Me of sin? And if I tell the truth, why do you not believe Me? He who is of God hears God's words; therefore you do not hear, because you are not of God." Then the Jews answered and said to Him, "Do we not say rightly that You are a Samaritan and have a demon?"
>
> —John 8:46–48

This is both a racial and spiritual slur because the Jews believed the Samaritans were defiled and would never get into heaven. If that weren't enough, the religious leaders also accused Jesus again of being possessed by the Devil.

> Jesus answered, "I do not have a demon; but I honor My Father, and you dishonor Me. And I do not seek My own glory; there is One who seeks and judges. Most assuredly, I say to you, if anyone keeps My word, he shall never see death."
>
> —John 8:49–51

The original term for *most assuredly* is the word for *amen*. It means this is a settled, unshakable fact. Isaiah uses the word *amen* in chapter 22 to speak about a peg placed in a wall at **a secure place** that can hold weight. That is why saving faith is often defined as that trust on which you hang your entire weight.

I'm amazed at the graciousness Jesus extends to these mean-spirited men.

> Then the Jews said to Him, "Now we know that You have a demon! Abraham is dead, and the prophets; and You say, 'If anyone keeps My word he shall never see death.' Are you greater than our father Abraham, who is dead? And the prophets are dead. Who do You make Yourself out to be?" Jesus answered, "If I honor Myself, My honor is nothing. It is My Father who honors Me, of whom you say that He is your God. Yet you have not known Him, but I know Him. And if I say, 'I do not know Him,' I shall be a liar like you; but I do know Him and keep His word. Your father Abraham rejoiced to see My day, and he saw it and was glad."
>
> —John 8:52–56

"Abraham's dead. The prophets are dead. You really think You're going to give us life? It hasn't worked so far," the religious leaders said.

And yet Jesus answered them still. "Abraham rejoiced to see My day," He said.

When did Abraham see Jesus? Some suggest this is a reference to Melchizedek found in Genesis 14:18–20. Others say it refers to the meeting with the three angels at his tent before they went to destroy Sodom and Gomorrah (Gen. 18). Jesus meant what He said in any event, that Abraham saw Jesus' day and rejoiced.

> Then the Jews said to Him, "You are not yet fifty years old, and have You seen Abraham?" Jesus said to them, "Most assuredly, I say to you, before Abraham was, I AM." Then they took up stones to throw at Him; but Jesus hid Himself and went out of the temple, going through the midst of them, and so passed by.
>
> —John 8:57–59

In answer to their question as to how He, a young man, could have seen Abraham, Jesus said, "Before Abraham was, I AM." They understood this was God's name—a name so holy the scribes wouldn't write it without changing pens and taking a shower between each letter. For Jesus to use this name was, to them, blasphemy. After all, Leviticus 24:16 says he who made himself out to be God was to be killed. But it's only blasphemy if it's untrue. So Jesus left and chapter 9 tells us it was as He passed by that He came across a man born blind.

Chapter 65

WHO IS REALLY BLIND?

John 9:1–41

The ninth chapter of John is all one story, a wonderful story told in great detail. It is one of the seven miracles around which John chose to build the Gospel as he later wrote (John 20:31), "so you might believe in the Lord Jesus Christ and, believing, you might find life through His name." It is the only miracle mentioned in the Bible where someone born blind was given sight, making it not only a miracle of restoration but of creation as well.

This is such a great lesson because the recipient is a spiritual picture of all of us. We are born blind to God because of sin. Romans 3:11 says there is none who seek after God. That is why there's no way out unless God looks for us. When I first got saved, I thought the Lord was lucky to have me. Now I know I'm just lucky to have Him.

> Now as Jesus passed by, He saw a man who was blind from birth. And His disciples asked Him, saying, "Rabbi, who sinned, this man or his parents, that he was born blind?" Jesus answered, "Neither this man nor his parents sinned, but that the works of God should be revealed in him."
>
> —John 9:1–3

I've always liked Jesus' toughness. The last verse of John 8 says the Jewish leaders took up stones to throw at Him but He passed by them. I think if someone were trying to kill me, I might go home for the night. But not Jesus. As He passed by, there was another need. So He stopped, because that's what He does. The gates of hell will not prevail against the church He plants, and no one will frustrate His purposes. When we're serving the Lord it might be rough along the way—but there's victory waiting because God's work will continue, no matter the resistance or opposition.

So here as Jesus and His disciples passed by, they came to a man who was blind from birth. The disciples' question about him presupposes that all such disability is the direct result of a specific sin. Their assumption might have been based on Exodus 20:5, where we read that parents' sins often were visited on the third and fourth generations. Even today we hear this same assumption from those who say, "I drink because my dad always drank," or, "Depression runs in our family. That's why I'm always depressed." Though we can learn and inherit much from our parents and homes, sin is a personal issue for which each of us must answer.

We love placing blame—yet when the Lord sent Ezekiel to Israel at a time they weren't doing very well, He said, "Why do I keep hearing the old proverb that the children's teeth are on edge because the fathers ate sour grapes? I don't want to hear that saying anymore." We die for our own sin. We answer to God for our own lives. In Exodus 20:6, immediately after God had declared that the sins of the parents are visited on following generations, God said He gives mercy to thousands. So there's always a way to break the cycle for anyone who turns to the Lord and finds His mercy.

Sin certainly brought into the world everything that is wrong with it. From Genesis 3 forward, we find every sorrow, difficulty, and hardship known to mankind. And it's all the result of sin. But Jesus in His answer to His disciples question sweeps aside the idea that there is always a direct link between specific suffering and specific sin. The only purpose for this young man to be born blind was for God to glorify Himself through it.

On the surface, this might seem grossly unfair. We look at someone like this man born blind and wonder how fair that really is. From Jesus' perspective, however, the things we go through in this short life are always used to bring us to Himself, to salvation and eternal life. In other words, if you held a hundred years in one hand and eternity in the other, you would thank the Lord that He deals with us in the years of our flesh for the purpose of eternity. God desired to bring this blind man to Himself. That's worth it, isn't it? The blind man couldn't see it yet, and we might not agree, but by the time the whole story is told, it will be clearly seen as worth every difficult hour he had suffered.

The book of Job is a long debate between a group of men who believed there is always cause and effect, and Job, whose tremendous calamity in his life included a disease that couldn't be healed, the loss of ten children in a day, and a wife about ready to give up on him and his God.

"What did you do wrong?" his friends asked. "It must be something horrible."

"I don't know of anything horrible," Job said.

"Well, God would never allow this to happen to anyone who hadn't done something horrible."

But that wasn't the case. Job's friends would learn that there are times God allows suffering for an eternal purpose of which men may or may not be aware. God always prioritizes the spiritual over the physical, the permanent over the temporary. As a result, by the time we're done with John 9, there will be one more saint walking with the Lord and telling the rest of the world who Jesus is!

> "I must work the works of Him who sent Me while it is day; the night is coming when no one can work. As long as I am in the world, I am the light of the world."
>
> —John 9:4–5

The disciples wanted to talk philosophy. Jesus wanted to go to work. There was an urgency about Jesus' ministry, a desire to help and serve. I'm amazed how often Christians will sit around and talk Christian theory while doing nothing. They'll quote Bible verses to each other while the world walks by. It's imperative to learn—equally so that having learned we go out and do!

> When He had said these things, He spat on the ground and made clay with the saliva; and He anointed the eyes of the blind man with the clay. And He said to him, "Go, wash in the pool of Siloam" (which is translated, Sent). So he went and washed, and came back, seeing.
>
> —John 9:6–7

I suspect Jesus' methods of healing varied with specific purposes because we're method people and He doesn't want us copying methods. He wants us following Him. So one time He made clay and the person was healed. The next time He spoke or laid His hand on someone to heal him. If we were to develop churches based on Jesus' methods, we'd have towns of partially right churches. There would be the "Spit and Be Healed Fellowship" or the "Speak and Be Healed Congregation." But that's not the issue. The issue always is the Healer, Jesus.

I love the way the Lord works because the method doesn't matter. What matters is that He is honored, He is exalted. Whether we are healed as someone lays hands on us and prays for us, or the doctor gives us the right medicine, praise the Lord. Either way, it's His doing.

Put yourself in this man's shoes. He hears Jesus. He's told to do what seems to be nonsense. And he obeys. It is a strange method, isn't it, to stick dirt in the eyes of a man who can't see?

Why did Jesus choose this method this time? Maybe it was so that by the time the blind man returned from washing the dirt from his eyes, Jesus would have time to go and the rest of the story could take place as it did.

> Therefore the neighbors and those who previously had seen that he was blind said, "Is not this he who sat and begged?" Some said, "This is he." Others said, "He is like him." He said, "I am he." Therefore they said to him, "How were your eyes opened?" He answered and said, "A Man called Jesus made clay and anointed my eyes and said to me, 'Go to the pool of Siloam and wash.' So I went and washed, and I received sight." Then they said to him, "Where is He?" He said, "I do not know."
>
> —John 9:8–12

Such a miracle was unheard of. It left the neighbors talking among themselves and doubting their own eyes to the point that the blind man had to confirm he was who they thought he was. "You're not the same guy," the neighbors said. "How is it that you can see?" The neighbors asked "How?" but the once-blind man wanted to talk about Who.

Not quite knowing what to do with him, the neighbors took him to the temple to meet and seek answers from the religious rulers. They'll know, won't they?

> They brought him who formerly was blind to the Pharisees. Now it was a Sabbath when Jesus made the clay and opened his eyes. Then the Pharisees also asked him again how he had received his sight. He said to them, "He put clay on my eyes, and I washed, and I see." Therefore some of the Pharisees said, "This Man is not from God, because He does not keep the Sabbath." Others said, "How can a man who is a sinner do such signs?" And there was a division among them. They said to the blind man again, "What do you say about Him because He opened your eyes?" He said, "He is a prophet."
>
> —John 9:13–17

Like the neighbors, the Pharisees asked how the blind man could see and concluded that whoever had healed him could not be of God because, according to Section 126.815 of the code, there could be no healing of eyes on the Sabbath. Some of the more sane and rational there, however, said, "Wait a minute. He can see. Nobody could do this but God. It doesn't sound like the work of an evil man." And in their collective wisdom—or lack thereof—a fight broke out. Meanwhile, this poor man who had just received his sight probably looked like a person watching a tennis match, turning his head back and forth between the arguing factions. If this is what seeing is all about . . .

Finally, they asked him what he thought and he said, "I think He's a prophet."

Under pressure of these bullying hardliners, he showed the character of one God had truly touched. He'd been healed for an hour, but he was growing by the minute. And all the while, I'm sure he was listening for the voice that had healed him.

> But the Jews did not believe concerning him, that he had been blind and received his sight, until they called the parents of him who had received his sight. And they asked them, saying, "Is this your son, who you say was born blind? How then does he now see?" His parents answered them and said, "We know that this is our sin, and that he was born blind; but by what means he now sees we do not know, or who opened his eyes we do not know. He is of age; ask him. He will speak for himself." His parents said these things because they feared the Jews, for the Jews had agreed already that if anyone confessed that He was Christ he would be put out of the synagogue. Therefore his parents said, "He is of age; ask him."
>
> —John 9:18–23

After arguing among themselves, the religious leaders decided to ask the man's parents if he was, in fact, previously blind. "This is our son," the parents said, "and he was born blind. But how he is able to see now, we don't know. Ask him, he is old enough to speak for himself."

What a sad picture. Here are parents who, according to John's insight for us, were so terrified of the religious machinery that they were unwilling to rejoice with their own son who could now see. John tells us the reason is that anyone who stood with Jesus in any of His claims was to be put out of the synagogue. This was a severe consequence. It was being totally ostracized. For anyone standing with Jesus, there would be no job, no doctor, no support, no children coming over to play, no one coming over for dinner, and no greeting on the streets.

You would think the parents would have said, "I don't care about your rules. Look at our son! He can see!" But the fear and frowns of the religious establishment caused them to shrink away. The religious folks had made up their minds. The parents were now terrified. How difficult the fear of man can make our decision to follow Jesus.

> So they again called the man who was blind, and said to him, "Give God the glory! We know that this Man is a sinner." He answered and said, "Whether He is a sinner or not I do not know. One thing I know; that though I was blind, now I see."
>
> —John 9:24–25

"Whatever conclusion you smart guys come up with, go ahead. I just know I can see." This was the only answer the once-blind man could give. I'm sure the men in the robes asking the questions could have out-quoted the Bible for him, out-argued him, out-muscled him, and out-politicized him—but they couldn't refute his answer.

> Then they said to him, again, "What did He do to you? How did He open your eyes?" He answered them, "I told you already, and you did not listen. Why do you want to hear it again? Do you also want to become His disciples?"
>
> —John 9:26–27

Great answer, true logic. He was learning fast. He was taking a stand. And his use of the word *also* indicates he already had decided that once he found the Man who healed him, he was going to become His disciple.

> Then they reviled him and said, "You are His disciple, but we are Moses' disciples. We know that God spoke to Moses; as for this fellow, we do not know where He is from."
>
> —John 9:28–29

357

Two chapters earlier, when Jesus told this same crowd He was the Son of God, they said, "We know You can't be the Son of God. We know where You're from." Here, however, they said, "We don't know where He came from." They at least should have stuck to their argument! So the young man who had never been able to see now saw more clearly than everyone else.

> The man answered and said to them, "Why, this is a marvelous thing, that you do not know where He is from; yet He has opened my eyes! Now we know that God does not hear sinners; but if anyone is a worshiper of God and does His will, He hears him. Since the world began it has been unheard of that anyone opened the eyes of one who was born blind. If this Man were not from God, He could do nothing."
>
> —John 9:30–33

I love his testimony. He said, "This is marvelous to me. You are supposed to be in tune with God and what He's doing, but somehow this Man slipped by you and got to me. And now I can see, and you have no clue who He is?"

Then he began quoting the Bible to the Bible guys. "We know God doesn't listen to sinners (Ps. 66:18) yet we know His ears are opened to the righteous (Ps. 34:17). Since the world began, this has never happened." This guy was obviously a man who, although he was blind, had been seeking God—which is always a prerequisite for seeing Him!

Although there are countless miracles throughout the Old Testament, there is no record of a blind man's eyes being opened. The healing of blind eyes is unique to the New Testament. It is unique because it is a miracle associated exclusively with the promised Messiah.

"It is the Lord who opens the eyes of the blind," the psalmist declared in Psalm 146:8. If there was anyone who should have known Jesus was the Messiah, it ought to have been the people reading the Old Testament. They ought to have been the ones keeping an eye out for the One who healed the eyes of the blind.

I love this ex-blind guy. He was preaching. He was teaching. Ninety minutes in, and he was growing like a weed!

> They answered and said to him, "You were completely born in sins, and are you teaching us?" And they cast him out.
>
> —John 9:34

Without an argument, all the religious leaders were left with was anger and insult and pride. Yet when religious people throw you out, go to Jesus, for He will receive you.

> Jesus heard that they had cast him out; and when He had found him, He said to him, "Do you believe in the Son of God?" He answered and said, "Who is He,

Lord, that I may believe in Him?" And Jesus said to him, "You have both seen Him and it is He who is talking with you." Then he said, "Lord, I believe!" And he worshipped him.

—John 9:35–38

What a picture. At last, the One whose voice the man recognized showed up. "I'm the Son of God," Jesus said. "You've heard Me already. You see Me now." And as a result, having gone from testifier to preacher, this man turns to worship Him—it had been an awesome few hours in his day . . . coming to Jesus will do the same for you!

And Jesus said, "For judgment I have come into this world, that those who do not see may see, and that those who see may be made blind." Then some of the Pharisees who were with Him, heard these words, and said to Him, "Are we blind also?" Jesus said to them, "If you were blind, you would have no sin; but now you say, 'We see.' Therefore your sin remains."

—John 9:39–41

Ultimately, the Lord can only be the light of the world to those who admit they're in darkness. Although He comes to find us, our response is required. And the response is very simple: We don't have what it takes. We can't do it on our own. We need Jesus.

"I'm a doctor," Jesus said in Mark 2:17, "If you're well, I can't do anything for you." If you think you're all right and have life all figured out, the Lord can do very little for you. Although He's able to open your eyes and give you life, He won't because you're still thinking you can do that for yourself. But when you run out of options and ideas and realize you're not as clear-sighted as you thought you were, then He can do great things as He did for this blind man who got thrown out of the religious system—and tossed right into heaven.

Chapter 66

JESUS, OUR GOOD SHEPHERD

John 10:1–21

There are many analogies found in the Scriptures and that is especially true of the Gospels. If you ever conclude God doesn't want you to know Him, just read the Gospels and you'll see instead that He uses every possible angle to make Himself known—likening Himself to light, to water, to bread, to being the door . . . He wants you to know Him, and thus the endless pictures for us to learn to know Him by.

One of the most often used analogies is that of a shepherd. We find it in almost every book of the Bible. It is an understandable analogy because there has never been a shortage of shepherds. In fact, in the Israel of Jesus' day, shepherds made up 80 percent of the work force. When we read in Mark 12:37 that the people heard Him gladly, it's an indication that they clearly understood what He was saying and could relate to what He was communicating.

Abel was a shepherd. Moses was a shepherd for a time. So was David. And today, whether you're in the Galilee, the Golan Heights, or the Sinai, you see Bedouins everywhere, grazing their flocks. The landscape in that regard looks extremely similar.

The shepherds of Jesus' day looked very distinct. Wearing one-piece tunics with ropes around their waist, they were dressed simply for the job at hand. Over their shoulder was a bag in which they carried dried fruit to coax the little lambs to follow. Also in this bag were rocks in case a coyote got too close. Shepherds carried a rod and a staff—used both to protect the obedient sheep and to correct those that strayed. But sheep are as dumb as doorknobs, which is why I'm always amused that the Lord calls us His sheep, though I am not surprised, considering how slow I am to learn.

If a lamb wandered off repeatedly, the practice of the shepherd was to break one of its legs and then carry it on his shoulders for the five or six weeks its leg took to heal. When the lamb was finally able to walk on its own, it never again would leave the shepherd's side. The Lord does that with us. He'll slow us down sometimes only to get us to stay close to Him, so we quit running off away from Him on our own.

In first century practice, there were basically two types of sheepfolds—one for the city and one for the countryside. The sheepfold in the city was a permanent, fenced enclosure with a guard on duty and a gate that could be locked. In verses 1 through 5 of John 10, it is this type of sheepfold to which Jesus referred. In verses 7 through 14, however, He refers to the second kind of sheepfold—the one shepherds would build when they were in the middle of nowhere and wanted to bed down for the night. This type of enclosure was made simply of rocks and brush. It was temporary and provided only a basic protection and fence for his flocks. The shepherd himself would lie across the doorway.

> "Most assuredly, I say to you, he who does not enter the sheepfold by the door, but climbs up some other way, the same is a thief and a robber. But he who enters by the door is the shepherd of the sheep. To him the doorkeeper opens, and the sheep hear his voice; and he calls his own sheep by name and leads them out. And when he brings out his own sheep, he goes before them; and the sheep follow him, for they know his voice. Yet they will by no means follow a stranger, but will flee from him, for they do not know the voice of strangers."
> —John 10:1–5

If you didn't use the door to get into the sheepfold in the city, it was a pretty good bet you were a crook. In the first century, sheep stealers would go to city pens, jump over the wall and slit the throats of three or four of the lambs, throwing the bodies over the fence to their accomplices, and quickly running off. It was relatively easy, and there was meat to eat for months.

Through this analogy, the people understood Jesus' implication that the scribes and Pharisees were false shepherds who had no regard for the sheep—as seen with the blind man they most recently had been cast out from the synagogue. To them, Jesus said in Matthew 23, "You will not only refuse to enter the kingdom of heaven, but will try to keep everyone else out as well."

"Say to the shepherds, 'Woe to you, shepherds. You're supposed to feed the flock, not yourselves. And yet you have scattered them. I'm going to visit you for the evil of your doing,'" the Lord told Jeremiah in chapter 23:2.

In Ezekiel 34:1–15, He said the same thing when He said, "Woe to you who are supposed to feed My flock."

Jesus used the picture of the sheepfold in the city, saying, "Robbers and thieves come in through other ways. But to the good shepherd, the honest shepherd, and the real shepherd, the door would be opened. The guard would recognize him as would his sheep. His voice would draw them out."

Jesus had come through the right channels. He had all the Messianic credentials. He'd been born of a virgin in Bethlehem of the seed of Abraham, of the tribe of Judah. He had revealed His power. He had opened the eyes of the blind. One plus one should have equaled two for these Pharisees. But they refused both the declaration and the demonstration of God's truth, power and love.

Jesus said He knows His sheep by name personally and, knowing Him, they follow Him willingly. Jesus is the shepherd who goes before us. Hebrews 4:15 tells us He's been tempted in every way we have, yet without sin. He knows the way and He's coming again to get us.

Jesus used this illustration, but they did not understand the things which He spoke to them. Then Jesus said to them again.

—John 10:6–7

I like the fact that Jesus didn't say, "You bunch of dumb sheep." Instead, He patiently gave them another illustration, that of the sheepfold in the country:

"Most assuredly, I say to you, I am the door of the sheep. All who ever came before Me are thieves and robbers, but the sheep did not hear them. I am the door. If anyone enters by Me, he will be saved, and will go in and out and find pasture."

—John 10:7–9

The word *door* in verses 7 and 9 is singular. In other words, Jesus said, "I am the only door you can walk through to get in because there isn't any other way to enter." One church. One Savior. One Lord. One flock. Those who offer other ways are thieves and robbers. In verse 8, Jesus wasn't talking about David, Moses, or the prophets, because they all pointed to Him. But those who point to anyone other than Jesus are wolves in sheep's clothing, thieves, and robbers.

The ark Noah built had only one door. When he entered the ark with his family, it was the Lord who shut the door. The tabernacle, the place of God's presence in the Old Testament, had only one entrance—it led by the altar of sacrifice. It was also the only access available.

It would have been foolish to leave six openings in an enclosure meant to hold sheep for the night in the middle of nowhere. Likewise, Jesus provides one Door—Himself—so He can watch over and protect His sheep.

The invitation to enter in is as broad as the way is narrow. Anyone can come, but everyone must come through the same door.

"The thief does not come except to steal, and to kill, and to destroy."

—John 10:10

The purpose of the thief, of the Devil himself, is to destroy God's work, to offer alternatives to faith, and to keep people away from Jesus. Speaking through the prophet Zechariah 11:16, the Lord spoke of a shepherd who does not care for the land and seeks to cut off the people in it. He doesn't seek for the young. He doesn't heal that which is broken. He doesn't feed that which stands still. He just eats the flesh of their fat and tears their hooves asunder. It's a description of the antichrist to come.

The Devil comes to rip us off. The religious person falsely offers and entertains himself alternatives to Jesus. But Jesus is the only door.

"I have come that they may have life, and that they may have it more abundantly. I am the good shepherd. The good shepherd gives His life for the sheep."

—John 10:10–11

How do I know Jesus is the door? How do I know Jesus—not Buddha, Mohammed, or Joseph Smith—is the good Shepherd? Jesus' answer to "What makes You so special?" is "I'm going to die and rise again. I'm giving My life for you and then offering you life in Me. Top that."

"But a hireling, he who is not the shepherd, one who does not own the sheep, sees the wolf coming and leaves the sheep and flees; and the wolf catches the sheep and scatters them. The hireling flees because he is a hireling and does not care about the sheep. I am the good shepherd; and I know My sheep, and am known by My own. As the Father knows Me, even so I know the Father; and I lay down My life for the sheep."

—John 10:12–15

In Israel even today, shepherding businesses are family-owned and operated. Jesus used this as a distinction between a true shepherd and a hired hand whose motivation for caring for the sheep was monetary gain rather than love. As opposed to a true shepherd, the hireling did his job around his coffee breaks and vacation schedule. And if there was a wolf he had to fight on behalf of the flock, he most likely said, "I don't get paid nearly enough to risk my neck for these dumb sheep. Good luck with that wolf, guys. I gotta go."

"And other sheep I have which are not of this fold; them also I must bring, and they will hear My voice; and there will be one flock and one shepherd."

—John 10:16

This speaks of the church—Jews and Gentiles alike, but all with the common denominator of Jesus as their Lord.

"Therefore My Father loves Me, because I lay down My life that I may take it again. No one takes it from Me, but I lay it down of Myself. I have power to lay it down, and I have power to take it again. This command I have received from My Father."

—John 10:17–18

Here is God's heart: He not only needs to give His life, but He is willing to give it on your behalf. All of the Gospels testify to Jesus' voluntary death. When Peter cut off the servant Malchus' ear, Jesus said, "I have angels I can call. I have reserves. But I'm not calling them because I've come for this purpose" (Matt. 26:52–54).

When the soldiers came to arrest Him, He said, "Who are you looking for?"

"Jesus," they said.

When He answered, "I AM," they all fell over backwards. He knocked them down so He could tell them when they got up that He would go willingly. Just because they came with a lot of back-up didn't mean they'd get Him. They got Him because He wanted to be "got" (John 18:1–8).

> Therefore there was a division again among the Jews because of these sayings. And many of them said, "He has a demon and is mad. Why do you listen to Him?" Others said, "These are not the words of one who has a demon. Can a demon open the eyes of the blind?"
>
> —John 10:19–21

As always, the Gospel leaves people in two camps: the believers and those who refuse to believe even the obvious evidence. Jesus came on the scene as a Lamb going to the slaughter for the sheep. We, the sheep, have a Shepherd who was first a Lamb that was slain so we could realize God's love is for real and His Word is trustworthy. He declared, "I alone am the door into the sheepfold." Only a ridiculous claim if He hadn't died and risen again. The minute He came from the grave, all of His wild claims became perfectly reasonable, didn't they? And any other voice that would point to any other way but Him was seen for the lie it held out in protest.

David wrote, "The Lord is my shepherd, I shall not want" (Ps. 23:1). "I won't lack anything. I don't need anything else. He's all I need." In Old Testament days, if you wanted to have fellowship with God, you had to bring a lamb to be slain. It had to be a perfect lamb with no defects. As you came to worship, the priest would put the lamb on the table and carefully examine the offering. He wouldn't examine the worshiper. He'd examine the lamb.

Today, if you want to stand before God, you would rather He check out the sacrifice than you because Jesus is perfect. God looks at Jesus—and we get in. God checks Him out—and we get in. I fully expect to be welcomed into heaven with open arms because the Sacrifice offered on my behalf is perfect.

As a sheep, whom you choose to follow is up to you. But I would listen for Jesus' voice. It's the only one worth following, the only One who can lead you to eternal life.

Chapter 67

Sent Out as His Ambassadors

Luke 10:1–16

From Luke 10 through Luke 18 we come a period in Jesus' ministry covered almost exclusively by Luke alone. It is called the Perean ministry, referring to the territory on the eastern side of the Jordan River in which much of it took place. Located today in and around Amman, Jordan, it was on the main trade route from the north to the south and was comprised of primarily Gentile towns.

> After these things the Lord appointed seventy others also, and sent them two by two before His face into every city and place where He Himself was about to go.
>
> —Luke 10:1

"After these things" puts this verse just after Jesus had met three different individuals on the road who had varying degrees of commitment to Him. Some of them He invited to follow. Others came and offered themselves. All of them did so with a half-hearted diligence and lots of excuses in the mix.

God's way of reaching the lost world is to use the church, His people. You might think that's a bad idea—especially if you look around the church! You might think sending angels would be a much better alternative. At least they'd get the message right and they'd be at it night and day since they don't have to sleep. But that wasn't God's choice. He chose you and me.

As Jesus was ready to go through the Perean towns, He chose seventy others to go before Him, to be the advance team, and to begin ministering before He arrived. They were sent out—in contrast to those who were hindered by their excuses in Luke 9:57–62. A year and a half earlier, Jesus had sent the twelve out, also two by two. We know all the names of the twelve but not one of these seventy. In fact, we don't know anything else about them other than they were willing to be used.

That ought to encourage every one of us. Even if no one knows who you are, God can use your life richly because His Spirit is still being poured out. And it is still His method of reaching the lost.

In Greek, the word *sent* is the root word of *apostle*. The basic meaning of *apostle* is "one who has been sent out on a commission or as an ambassador." Of the twelve, Jesus referred to them as disciples up to the point He sent them out in Matthew 10:1. After that, He referred to them as His apostles. In Greek, *disciple* is a word for *student*. That's how God works. He has you sit and learn, but not as an end in itself—only as part of the process. The end is that you go out and do. It isn't enough for you to go to church every week to be able to quote verses so you can correct people when they're wrong. If you're not doing what you learn, then you've short-circuited God's plans to disciple you and send you out as an ambassador. God's investment in the people He saves is that through them the world can hear about His Son. So we sit and *learn*—then go and do.

I suspect it was with great joy that Jesus sent out these thirty-five pairs because He looked forward to a year down the road, after His death and resurrection, when the church would be born and the believers, in the power of the Holy Spirit, would fan out in every direction doing just this work. Within thirty years, Paul would write in Colossians 1:6, "The Gospel has come to you as it has come to every corner of the globe."

For now, however, it was still the time of preparation. As Jesus sent out these seventy, He gave them, in many ways, the same directions He had given to the twelve: "Go two by two. Tell people the kingdom of heaven is at hand. Find out how open or interested in the Gospel they are. If there's a willingness to hear, stay. If there isn't, keep moving, because it's time to get the word out."

I note the fact that He sent them out two by two. In fact, with very few exceptions in the Bible, you will find successful ministry carried out by teams of people. Solomon, who didn't always walk in the wisdom God gave him, wrote in Ecclesiastes 4:9 that two are better than one because if one falls there is another to pick him up—but woe to the one who is alone when he falls. Moses went with Aaron, Joshua with Caleb, Peter with John, Paul with Barnabas, and these seventy in pairs—appointed by Jesus to go before Him into the cities to which He eventually would come. In this, they were much like the church as we go out into the world to say, "The Lord is coming. Here's how you can be ready."

> Then He said to them, "The harvest truly is great, but the laborers are few; therefore pray the Lord of the harvest to send out laborers into His harvest."
> —Luke 10:2

Jesus desired that as they went they would be led by this vision of the work that lay ahead. He said, "I want you to see the world as a ripe field ready to pick fruit." And whether it's the white of a cotton field, or oranges falling off the tree in a citrus orchard, from God's point of view the world is a very fruitful place for ministry. It isn't as gloomy, dismal, or barren as we might suspect by looking around. From God's vantage, the problem is not the harvest—it's a shortage of laborers.

In three different places Jesus used relatively the same language. Early in His ministry He sat in Samaria with a woman at a well and ministered to her while the disciples went into town to get food (John 4). Upon their return, they were surprised to find Jesus talking to a woman—and a Samaritan at that. When she went running for town, they said, "Hey, Lord, You want something to eat? We got fries."

"I'm not hungry," Jesus said.

"Who brought You food?" the disciples asked.

As He pointed to the woman heading for town with the good news about who He was, Jesus answered, "My meat is to do the will of Him that sent Me. You have a saying that there are four months until harvest. But look. The field is white already."

What seemed like the most difficult place in the disciples' eyes for ministry, amongst the Samaritans, was the most successful in God's. Maybe you see your job, home, family, friends, or neighbors as unreachable. But the Lord says you should see it as white unto harvest. I think we need to change our attitude. And I think the reason we haven't explains why the laborers are few.

I was saved in 1973 at the tail end of the hippie movement. No one was ministering to us at all. People had pretty much written off my generation as foolish and foolhardy. Yet when the Gospel began to be preached, not a few came to Jesus, but tens of thousands who are still doing well today. From the outside we looked unsalvageable. From God's perspective, however, He couldn't wait to get in there because the fruit was ripe. I think if you see your world as a white field as opposed to a field that needs four months of work, you'll see fruit everywhere just waiting to be harvested.

When Jesus came into town directly before He sent out the twelve, Matthew said in chapter 9:36–38 that He was moved with compassion for the people because they looked like sheep without a shepherd—scattered and weary. "The harvest is plentiful," He said to the disciples. "There's plenty of work to do. It's the laborers we can't find."

I find so often that when we are confronted with our responsibility as His people to share the Gospel, that excuses come readily. But that's not new.

When the Lord told Moses he was to lead the people out of Egypt, Moses said, "That's a really bad idea, Lord. Since I've known You, I've never spoken publicly. I'm bad at speaking. I've got a slow tongue.

"Moses, who made your mouth?" the Lord asked. "I'll be with your mouth. I'll tell you what to say" (Exod. 4:10–12).

The Lord called Jeremiah at eighteen years of age to speak to the nation on His behalf. "I'm just a young man that no one will respect or hear," Jeremiah protested.

"Before you were formed in the womb, I knew you," the Lord answered. "And before I set you apart, I already had ordained you to be a prophet. So don't say you can't speak and don't tell Me you're too young, because where I send you, you shall go, and what I command you, you shall speak" (Jer. 1:4–10).

"Go your way; behold, I send you out as lambs among wolves."

—Luke 10:3

To the seventy Jesus said, "Just because there are few to help doesn't mean you shouldn't go. Pray for more laborers, but for now, you go. And as you go, realize you'll be in a very difficult place. Lambs against wolves isn't a fair fight. In fact, if you're a betting person, bet on the wolves—that is unless the Lord's on the side of the lambs."

"Carry neither money bag, knapsack, nor sandals; and greet no one along the road."

—Luke 10:4

Unless it's the Lord who's telling you this and what follows, it's not very good advice for most trips. It was limited in this case to Jesus' desire to teach anyone who would serve Him that it would be Him doing the work and providing the means. Later on in Luke 22:35–36, He said, "You who are going out should buy some shoes and take some cash. If you don't have a sword, you should think about buying one for protection." For now, however, the lesson was to be that of faith in His provision and urgency for the task at hand.

When Elisha heard that the son of a woman to whom he had ministered had died, he said to his servant, "Here's my staff. Run and put it on his forehead. And if anyone wants to talk to you, you don't have time" (2 Kings 4:17–30). In other words, "Don't be interrupted or turned away from the work that is set before you. Don't let the day to day salutations slow you down from the important work at hand."

I think Christians today sometimes are not driven by this same sense of urgency because we don't look at the world from God's point of view. We just figure we'll do it tomorrow. We aren't stirred by the fact that sitting next to us in the restaurant are people who may be headed for hell. These seventy were to look to Jesus to sustain them and to be driven by the urgency of the work before them, the souls of men hanging in the balances.

"But whatever house you enter, first say, 'Peace to this house.' And if a son of peace is there, your peace will rest on it; if not, it will return to you. And remain in the same house, eating and drinking such things as they give, for the laborer is worthy of his wages. Do not go from house to house. Whatever city you enter, and they receive you, eat such things as are set before you. And heal the sick there, and say to them, 'The kingdom of God has come near to you.'"

—Luke 10:5–9

The marching orders had to do both with the message and their behavior. The message was very simple: "The kingdom of God is near. In fact, He's coming right behind us. He'll be here on Thursday." As for their behavior, they were to minister to the people in God's name and rely upon His power to work. They were not to go from house to house in an effort to "upgrade" their accommodations. They were to eat whatever was put before them, which would have been no small issue considering these Jewish men were going into very Gentile towns.

> "But whatever city you enter, and they do not receive you, go out into its streets and say, 'The very dust of your city which clings to us we wipe off against you. Nevertheless know this, that the kingdom of God has come near you.'"
>
> —Luke 10:10–11

If a city did not welcome them, they were to move along to the next town. If the Lord opened the doors, great. If not, they were to leave the same message behind.

> "But I say to you that it will be more tolerable in that Day for Sodom than for that city. Woe to you, Chorazin! Woe to you, Bethsaida! For if the mighty works which were done in you had been done in Tyre and Sidon, they would have repented long ago, sitting in sackcloth and ashes. But it will be more tolerable for Tyre and Sidon at the judgment than for you. And you, Capernaum, who are exalted to heaven, will be brought down to Hades."
>
> —Luke 10:12–15

Jesus said any town that refused them would bear culpability before God some day. If seventy people filled with the Spirit and God's power came into town tomorrow healing the sick, praying for the possessed, and proclaiming the Gospel, it would seem odd if someone said, "You must all leave immediately. You're causing way too much trouble." But that's what happened in some of the cities to which they came. And if their anointing and power were refused, we shouldn't be surprised if some today won't listen to the message we bring.

Jesus said to them that had Sodom, Tyre, and Sidon seen the power of God the way Chorazin, Bethsaida, and Capernaum had, they would have repented. First Corinthians 3 teaches that there are degrees of reward in heaven. According to Luke 12, there are also degrees of punishment in hell as well. Tyre and Sidon historically were known for selling Jews into slavery. Capernaum, the site of Jesus' headquarters for two and a half years, witnessed more miracles than any city. But no amount of information can make up for an absence of faith in the hearts of people who refuse to believe.

> "He who hears you hears Me, he who rejects you rejects Me, and he who rejects Me rejects Him who sent Me."
>
> —Luke 10:16

Ultimately, the difficulty you and I have to face as Christians sharing the Gospel is that the message isn't ours. It's God's. And God's message is not always so easily received. If Jesus is rejected, you're rejected for bringing the message.

The fields are white for harvest but the laborers are few. We're like lambs in the midst of wolves. So we're going to have to go prayerfully and dependent on the Lord to open the door. We're going to have to share the Gospel and minister in the Lord's name, all the while realizing the judgment is God's and the refusal is spiritual, not personal. But if they hear us, they'll hear Him.

From what Jesus said, some will hear us and we'll find open doors. Many will not, and they'll find judgment with God based on the opportunity they've squandered. That's out of our hands. But our obligation to represent the Lord is something we can't refuse.

The fields are white. Are the laborers ready?

Chapter 68

REAL JOY!

Luke 10:17–24

Jesus had sent seventy apostles into the Perean area on the eastern side of the Jordan. We don't know how long they were gone, but in the passage before us, we see the debriefing Jesus had with them upon their return. He lets them share and then shares with them the main lesson He wanted them to learn, one we need to learn as well.

> Then the seventy returned with joy, saying, "Lord, even the demons are subject to us in Your name."
>
> —Luke 10:17

I love the picture of these seventy men coming back with great joy because it rings true with me that, as a Christian, my greatest joy has always been when God uses my life. That's as good as it gets. To even think that God would even want to involve us in His work is a remarkable thought. We will never discover while sitting in church how God can empower our witness, for that we are going to have to speak up. If you've ever begun to share and felt God's power as the words came at the right time to the right person, you know it's no wonder these seventy came back with grins and excitement, knowing the Lord had miraculously used their lives. And I don't doubt that when Jesus said, "So, how did it go?" every one of them wanted to talk first.

Most of the testimonies, it seemed, focused on the power of God at work to heal and deliver. We love power almost more than anything else. We love telling the stories of God's actions and the strength He demonstrates. Therefore, it's not surprising that when the seventy had to boil it down, the one thing that stood out in their minds was that Jesus' name had driven the Devil out! In response you might think Jesus would have said, "That's great!" But that's not what He said:

> And He said to them, "I saw Satan fall like lightning from heaven. Behold, I give you the authority to trample on serpents and scorpions, and over all the power of the enemy, and nothing shall by any means hurt you. Nevertheless do not rejoice in this, that the spirits are subject to you, but rather rejoice because your names are written in heaven."
>
> —Luke 10:18–20

I find this to be a very interesting response. The seventy came back with testimonies of experience, but Jesus wanted them to find joy in the permanence of the work He would do for them. "Satan is a fallen angel," He said. "I was there when he fell." He used a term that describes the way lightning lights up the sky before it completely fades away. Satan was a brilliant star at one time, created by God to serve Him. But he fell and is no more in that place of honor.

"How are you fallen from the heavens, O Lucifer," Isaiah 14:12 had written seven hundred years earlier. Ezekiel wrote in chapter 28:11–19 about a chief cherub, an angel, who led the worship in heaven with great authority and power. But when he wanted to take God's place, he was thrown out of heaven along with a third of the angels who sided with him. Today, according to the Bible, Satan still has access to God's throne. In Revelation 9, we're told his greatest joy is to point out your faults to God. Indeed, you and I are in spiritual warfare with the Devil. But the outcome is never in doubt. He's a defeated enemy.

The seventy wanted to talk about their experience with power—and, indeed, it must have been thrilling to witness. But Jesus wanted them to know that His authority over Satan was a given. One day Satan will be put out of heaven completely. In Revelation 9, the door is finally shut—and then it's just a matter of time before he's put away for good. The Devil's future is pretty grim. He's on borrowed time. But one day, he'll be gone and you'll be free. So as much as you should rejoice in the victory God brings, it's misplaced in the sense that those victories are but temporary ones. There is a more permanent victory for you.

With the word *nevertheless* Jesus, rather than raining on the disciples' joy, simply sought to direct their hearts to something far more glorious and permanent that God had done for them: their names were written in heaven! Despite all the power we receive from the Lord, our greatest joy ought not to be the experiences we have because of Him, but rather our relationship to Him. Almost every joyful experience we have is temporary. "I prayed and I got a new job!" we say. But that's temporary. The job's going away and so are we, eventually.

Every experience of God's work is wonderful—but it's all temporary. We really only have one permanent joy: that we're going to heaven. In fact, you could end every sentence you ever speak with, "But I'm going to heaven." It would change your life. When people ask how you're doing, you could say, "I got a flat tire—but I'm going to heaven!" Heaven is permanent. It's dependable. And it's freely given to those who believe in Jesus Christ. It's to be our source of great joy.

Unfortunately, when we look for joy in other things—experiences, deliverance, power—we can be disappointed because God doesn't always come through immediately. There are times we're just told to wait, and times we don't understand what God is doing at all. But we can know this: we're going to heaven. It's not that we're disconnected from real life. It's that overshadowing it all is the fact that we're leaving. It's kind of like the week before a vacation. When work piles up around you, you don't care—you're going on vacation.

Jesus said we shouldn't find great joy in power but in our destination. The disciples were new to all of this. They were caught up in the experiences. I remember as a young Christian I talked less about knowing Jesus than about what I was doing, because I knew Him. But now I know that even if God doesn't move today, and even if He doesn't answer today, my eternity is still secure.

In Matthew 7, Jesus said some will one day show up at heaven's gate, declaring, "Have we not cast out demons in Your name?" I suspect every day they went home feeling pretty good about themselves—until they showed up and Jesus said, "I don't know you."

"But we had power," they probably protested.

"Yes," He answered, "but you didn't have Me."

Of the wise men following the star to look for the newborn King, I remember someone commenting that what drove them was the thought that, "To see His star was good, but to see His face was better." That's why they never stopped moving. They couldn't wait to see Him. So we follow and serve and minister by His strength, but our joy is to be with Him one day in glory. Our names are written in heaven.

So Jesus redirected the joy of these seventy. And as He watched their smiling faces, He began to pray:

> In that hour Jesus rejoiced in the Spirit and said, "I thank You, Father, Lord of heaven and earth, that You have hidden these things from the wise and prudent and revealed them to babes. Even so, Father, for it seemed good in Your sight."
> —Luke 10:21

The word *rejoiced* is very interesting because in verse 16–20 it spoke of the character, attitude, or permanence for it. Yet the word for *rejoice* here in verse 21 is a different word that speaks of an emotional response. I suspect Jesus looked at these seventy grinning faces and said, "Father, this is awesome. What a great idea to put Your Spirit in the lives of these men." Even though they didn't have it all quite figured out, seeing them gave Him great joy.

And with this joy, Jesus began to pray, "Father, it's such a good thing that the little believers, the babies, would be filled with the Spirit and see these great things while the wise of the world—the guys who think they know better, the self-righteous, the religious—have no understanding at all." Here standing before Him were tax collectors, fishermen, unlearned folks, and ones without society's status. But what they had in common was a faith in Jesus and the humility to go out and do what He had said. Even if they understood little else, they were the foolish of the world who would confound the wise. So Jesus rejoiced over these seventy who had come back. I see Him chuckling to Himself, "All right! This is great! Look, Father, what You're doing!"

"All things have been delivered to Me by My Father, and no one knows who the Son is except the Father, and who the Father is except the Son, and the one to whom the Son wills to reveal Him."

—Luke 10:22

"Father, thank You for revealing to these the truths of Your Spirit and of Your power—and for using Me as the source of revelation," Jesus prayed. You can't come to God and know Him without Jesus. You can't come to know Jesus without His revealing Himself to you. And here, sitting before Him, were unlearned, no-name, inconsequential people in the world's eyes but who were of great value to God. And though they were still learning, they were already the joy of Jesus' heart—as are you. And their joy was that He had written their names in heaven.

Then He turned to His disciples and said privately, "Blessed are the eyes which see the things you see; for I tell you that many prophets and kings have desired to see what you see, and have not seen it, and to hear what you hear, and have not heard it."

—Luke 10:23–24

For centuries there had always been the promise of the coming Messiah. Now He was here—and these had great privilege because they could listen and watch. So can we. The Devil has to submit in Jesus' name—his fate sealed. You're just beginning. For the Devil, the worst lies ahead. For you, this is as bad as things get. The Devil knows this and therefore will do everything he can to thwart what God is doing in your life. But when it's all said and done, you can still loudly say, "Yeah, but I'm going to heaven!"

Chapter 69

BUT A SAMARITAN . . .

Luke 10:25–37
(Matthew 22:34–40; Mark 12:28–34)

Jesus thanked the Father for choosing to show His truths to those who were simply faithful instead of those the world esteemed wise and learned. Here in our text, one who would be considered wise in the world's eyes came to Jesus—not to learn from Him but to make himself look good. Yet like everyone else in this final year of Jesus' ministry discovered, if you came to Jesus, regardless of your agenda, He would seek to steer the conversation to how you could get to heaven.

> And behold, a certain lawyer stood up and tested Him, saying, "Teacher, what shall I do to inherit eternal life?"
>
> —Luke 10:25

In the Bible, almost all lawyers were scribes. Experts in the Law of Moses, scribes devoted themselves to applying God's Word, specifically the Law, to the people's lives. Unfortunately, because God's Law is impossible to keep, they rewrote it in such a way that, if they worked hard enough, it actually could be kept by those who devoted their lives to following it.

The problem was not that the Law needed adjusting. According to Psalm 19:7, it's perfect. The problem is, we're not. So, faced with God's righteous demands, we have to throw up our hands and say, "We can't do this." Then we go to Jesus. He saves us and gives us His Holy Spirit—who enables us to do the very things the Law requires. The Law never was intended as a way to make us holy. It was intended for us to see our unholiness and turn to faith in Christ.

This lawyer, or scribe, had studied God's Law and had joined with other scribes and Pharisees who over the years had sought to reinterpret what God demanded, thus removing the need for a Savior. Both in the Old and New Testaments, those who talk about the Law usually refer to the Shema—the declaration in Deuteronomy 6:4–5 that we should love the Lord with all our heart, soul, mind, and strength—as well as the declaration in Leviticus 19:18 that we should love our neighbors as ourselves. Of the Ten Commandments, the first four deal with man's vertical relationship to God. The last six deal with our horizontal relationship to our neighbor. In other words, the essence of the Law is love for God that produces love for others.

The lawyer's background was the Law. Testing Jesus was his purpose. Luke used an interesting word for *test*. It's only used a couple times in the Bible—always in a negative sense and always with the intention of disproving or discrediting. When Satan tempted Jesus to worship him in the wilderness in Luke 4:12, Jesus said, "You shall not tempt the Lord your God" and He used this word for *test*. When Paul wrote to the Corinthians, he said, "We should have faith in God and not be like those in the wilderness who tested God." Again, he used this word *test* as a word of unbelief, rejection, and refusal. And that's the way this lawyer came. That's what drove his heart. He wanted to make a name for himself publicly so he asked Jesus a good question with a bad motive: "What shall I do to inherit eternal life?"

It's a great question—one to which I hope you have the answer. There are a lot of things we can be wrong about—like whether or not our favorite team is going to win the championship. We can be wrong about that without much consequence. But if we're wrong about how we get to heaven, the consequences are eternal.

So in this final year of ministry, we often find Jesus engaging individuals by asking in many ways the same question of them, "Where are you going and how are you going to get there?"

I think it's a great question to ask when we're out witnessing to people—to say to them, "How are you going to get to heaven?"

Those who think they'll make it there usually will explain that it is because they're better than other people. "I don't drink as much as my neighbor," they'll say. "I don't cheat or steal like a lot of people I know." In other words, "I've pretty much earned it. I deserve it. God owes it to me."

In the world's eyes, entrance to heaven is based on a point system. That is why almost every religion is performance-driven—not God's performance, but our own.

"What must I accomplish in order to have eternal life?" the lawyer asked. The term *eternal life* is used in the Bible in two ways that are practically interchangeable. One deals with length, duration, or quantity of time. But just as often God used the term to talk about quality rather than quantity, about a life characterized by peace, joy, and love. When the rich young ruler came to Jesus, he asked, "How can I have what You have?" When Nicodemus came, he asked the same thing. They used the term *eternal life* in terms of quality of life—the kind of life produced in someone who knows God. They saw it in Jesus.

When the lawyer asked how he could have eternal life, I don't doubt he was asking about both quality and duration. But he really wasn't interested in an answer to either. He was interested in discrediting Jesus and hoping to have a debate with Him about what Jesus taught versus what the lawyer thought he knew. Jesus' answer however, turned the tables back to the lawyer and his supposed field of expertise:

> He said to him, "What is written in the law? What is your reading of it?"
> —Luke 10:26

"What do you think the Bible says?" It's a great response, isn't it? If we're out witnessing to people, we should ask them what God says about heaven and how they can get there: on what authority do you form your beliefs? In almost every situation where Jesus met people who were hungry to know the truth, He told them point blank. But those who came challenging Him with some hidden agendas, He sought to bring to the place where they either admitted they already knew what God wanted or admitted they didn't, in which case He shared the truth with them. Jesus asked what the lawyer thought and how he saw it so He might then minister to him.

The shift from works to grace requires confrontation with God's demands and our inability to meet them. These two things cannot be set aside. The lawyer wanted to argue from performance. Jesus said, "What do you see in the Bible? You're an expert of the Law. That's your job. You spend your life making these kinds of decisions. How do you understand or make application of these things?" The Lord was drawing out this man to admit he fell short. Admitting poverty of spirit is needed if we are to come to Jesus.

> So he answered and said, "'You shall love the Lord your God with all your heart, with all your soul, with all your strength, and with all your mind,' and 'your neighbor as yourself.'"
>
> —Luke 10:27

The lawyer answered the question perfectly. You love God with everything you have and, as a result, you love others. If your relationship with God is right, everything around you eventually will be right, as well. But if you forsake your relationship with Him, nothing else will matter. Unfortunately, what so often happens is when people want to change their lives, they only try to change the horizontal aspect. "I'd be happy if I could get a new wife, a new job, a new car, or a new house," they tell themselves. "Then I'd be able to love other people." But until we get saved and the Holy Spirit moves in, the problem is not a wife, job, car, or house. The problem is us. That is why we have to love God with all we have before we can love our neighbor.

> And He answered him, "You have answered rightly; do this and you will live."
>
> —Luke 10:28

"You're exactly right," Jesus said to the lawyer. "Now just do that." But isn't that the issue? The lawyer couldn't! Most people will agree that God's demands are right. But when you ask them if they live up to them, the best they can say is they try. It is the admission of failure to meet God's righteous demands that brings salvation. Blessed are the poor in spirit. They're the ones who see God because they're the ones who recognize they don't have what it takes. They're the ones who come to Him for salvation.

If the lawyer had said to Jesus at this point, "You know what? I can't do that. I know what the Law says. God knows I've tried to keep it. But I can't," I think Jesus would have said to him, "Come to Me if you're heavy laden and I'll give you rest. Take My yoke upon you. It's easy. My burden is light." And He would have given him life. But unwilling to admit failure, the lawyer's only other option was to change the subject:

> But he, wanting to justify himself, said to Jesus, "And who is my neighbor?"
> —Luke 10:29

In verse 25, the lawyer wanted to test Jesus. Here he wants to justify Himself. You've heard people do this before. You share with them and they say things like, "Well, if God is so good, there can't be a hell." That's a reasonable answer—if you don't want to repent. "No one knows for sure," they'll say—and that gets them off the hook because, after all, they don't have to do anything if "no one knows for sure."

If you've ever taken a class in debate, you know if you're losing your best bet is to change the course of the debate, change topics, change tactics, or change focus. And that's exactly what the lawyer did. He didn't want answers. He just wanted to cover himself because he realized he was on the spot. The rich young ruler had asked, "Which laws?" This lawyer asked, "Which neighbor?" Neither one of them said, "I need help."

What follows in the next seven verses is Jesus' parable of the Good Samaritan. Unfortunately, most of the time it is taken out of context and taught as an illustration of the importance of good works. As evidenced by a lawyer who wouldn't repent and two religious men in the parable who did the wrong thing, however, it teaches that a person's heart only can be changed by faith in God. The most despised person in the culture—the Samaritan—was able to please God. Why? So people like the lawyer might understand that religion won't help but a relationship with God will. It is faith, not religion, His work, not ours that can determine our love for others . . .

Jesus already had brought the lawyer to the brink of saying, "I need help." The lawyer, however, sought to change the subject and Jesus followed along with Him, still driving home the same point, now in the form of this parable: Now He puts the lesson in a story:

> Then Jesus answered and said, "A certain man went down from Jerusalem to Jericho, and fell among thieves, who stripped him of his clothing, wounded him, and departed, leaving him half dead. Now by chance a certain priest came down that road. And when he saw him, he passed by on the other side."
> —Luke 10:30–31

Jerusalem is three thousand feet above sea level. Jericho is twelve hundred feet below sea level. The road from Jerusalem to Jericho was a very dangerous road through wilderness areas frequented by thieves and robbers. This priest would have been leaving Jerusalem after serving the Lord. The Law demanded that we have mercy, even upon a stranger. The priest might have been one of the lawyer's friends. They would have written the law together. But religion did this priest very little good as far as love was concerned.

> "Likewise a Levite, when he arrived at the place, came and looked and passed by on the other side."
>
> —Luke 10:32

The Levites responsibilities were to arrange the other parts of the temple services. In the parable, unlike the priest, the Levite actually went over and looked at the man in his suffering before deciding he didn't want any part of the problem. He handled religious services and followed its rules and order, but love escaped him as well.

> "But a certain Samaritan, as he journeyed, came where he was. And when he saw him, he had compassion."
>
> —Luke 10:33

To the Jewish mind, the Samaritans were among the most hated people on the face of the planet. We have covered them at length in other chapters but here Jesus takes a Samaritan and makes him the hero of his story, for it sets great contrast between religion of performance and faith in action with His love.

> "So he went to him and bandaged his wounds, pouring on oil and wine; and he set him on his own animal, brought him to an inn, and took care of him. On the next day, when he departed, he took out two denarii, gave them to the innkeeper, and said to him, 'Take care of him; and whatever more you spend, when I come again, I will repay you.' So which of these three do you think was neighbor to him who fell among the thieves?"
>
> —Luke 10:34–36

Because the definition of *neighbor* was only a deflection of the original discussion, Jesus' point was not for the lawyer to identify his neighbor. The point was for him to see it was a matter of the heart, that religion couldn't make him a neighbor, but God could. Jesus made it so obvious that I don't think anyone could have missed the right answer.

> And he said, "He who showed mercy on him." Then Jesus said to him, "Go and do likewise."
>
> —Luke 10:37

It's either the law or it's mercy. It's either rules and performance or the gift and grace of God. We have no idea what happened to this man. We know the rich young ruler went away sad. We know this lawyer just went away. But the conflict isn't confined to these ten or twelve verses. It is found in this last year of Jesus' ministry nearly every time He stopped to talk to an individual. No matter what direction they came from, the conversation centered on works vs. grace, the law vs. mercy.

It's mercy or it's law. It's grace or it's works. We have to choose. Jesus brought this lawyer as far as he would go. He'll bring us as far as we will follow.

Chapter 70

WHO'S IN THE KITCHEN WITH MARTHA?

Luke 10:38–42

The lives of these two sisters who, along with their brother, came to know and dearly love Jesus teach us that if it comes to fellowship vs. service, God would have us set aside all the doing for Him in order to simply sit and spend time with Him. He longs for our fellowship long before our service.

> Now it happened as they went that He entered a certain village: and a certain woman named Martha welcomed Him into her house. And she had a sister called Mary, who also sat at Jesus' feet and heard His word.
> —Luke 10:38–39

Mary and Martha were sisters who lived in a house with their brother, Lazarus, in Bethany, just over the hill from the top of the Mount of Olives. Because they lived so close to Jerusalem, in this final year of His ministry Jesus stayed with this family quite often. They were sure He was not just a good man or prophet. They were absolutely convinced He was the Messiah. When Lazarus became sick a little while later, Mary and Martha sent a servant to find Him with only a few words: "The one You love is sick." They had come to believe in Jesus—and that grew as the days continued.

From everything we can gather from Scripture, Martha was a woman who not only kept an immaculate house but could make tamales like nobody's business. Hers was the house you'd like to visit because that was where you would get treated like a king. And motivated even further by her love for Jesus, she was extremely busy every time she knew He was headed in their direction. There were sheets to change, food to prepare and, like everyone with a servant's heart, she wouldn't have rested until everything was just so.

James wrote that if we're only a hearer of the Word and not a doer, we are deceived about our walk with God. I think James could have made Martha the poster child for his book for she was certainly a busy, serving, loving individual. Yet the danger for all of us who love Jesus is that over time we can slowly begin to substitute our service for fellowship with him. The Lord would rather spend time with us than see us running around like a chicken with its head cut off, wearing ourselves out for Him.

In the letter to the Ephesian church found in Revelation 2:1–7, Jesus said, "I know your works, labor, and patience. I know you can't bear those who are doing evil. You labor hard for My name's sake and you never become weary." This sounds just like Martha, doesn't it?

Sixty years after the church at Ephesus was established, they were still as busy and engaged as a church should be. Yet in His love for His people, Jesus then said, "But I have a problem with what you're doing. You have left your first love"—or literally, "You're not doing it for the same reason you used to."

The Ephesians had replaced fellowship with busyness and service. And all of their works, labor, patience, discernment, perseverance, diligence, the hating of sin, the suffering for His name, and the "no quit" in them was not good enough for the Lord. He wanted fellowship, not service, because service from a heart out of fellowship meant nothing to Him. I am sure that, unbeknownst to her, Martha had fallen into that trap, and so can we. When we come to Jesus and are saved, we always begin with fellowship. But all too often we remove ourselves from that and begin to "do" for God rather than "be" with Him as our primary concern. And He would rather just the opposite.

The great love that drove you to Jesus, that caused you to walk down the aisle, raise your hand, or go into a prayer room and surrender your life to Him; the responses to God's love for you; the "I just want to be with the Lord" love—can be subtly but surely replaced by serving without love and turning from grace to works again. I have found that sometimes folks in the church who have been serving for a long time can fall into that trap not because they don't love the Lord, but because they do. But when the love that caused them to sign up to do whatever it is they're doing in service for Him becomes a "have to" rather than a "get to," it uncovers the problem that must be addressed. So here we read of Martha:

> But Martha was distracted with much serving, and she approached Him and said, "Lord, do You not care that my sister has left me to serve alone? Therefore tell her to help me." And Jesus answered and said to her, "Martha, Martha, you are worried and troubled about many things. But one thing is needed, and Mary has chosen that good part, which will not be taken away from her."
>
> —Luke 10:40–42

Martha was overly preoccupied with all she had to do. "Martha, Martha," Jesus said. Most of the time when Jesus repeated things it was to men because I think we men are slow to listen. But this time it was Martha, a woman, who wasn't paying attention. "Why are you so upset?" He asked. "Why are you troubled about so many things?"

Martha was serving Jesus, the One she loved. But what she failed to realize was Jesus was longing for something else. And it wasn't that every knickknack be in the right place. It wasn't that the vegetable platter had the radishes cut into flower patterns. The salad didn't have to be a work of art. He had come to visit Martha. He had come to spend time with her. And that's what He wants from us as well. He would rather spend time with us than see us out of fellowship and serving Him. For Martha, serving had taken a place of greater value than simply loving Jesus. What used to be a joy was causing her turmoil. It had become a demand that left her angry and frustrated that she was unappreciated. It produced bitterness, strife, faultfinding, and a martyr complex.

I can see her bursting through the kitchen door, sweating, apron on, exasperated, flour sticking to her face, and feeling fully justified about what she was about to say. Initially, she wasn't going to say anything. But this had gone too far. It had been nearly an hour that Mary had been sitting at Jesus' feet as if nothing needed to be done.

"Lord, don't You care?" Martha cried. "She's left me to serve alone. Tell her to help me! There's iced tea to be made, rolls to brown, a table to set. Dinner doesn't make itself!"

When fellowship with God is replaced by service, we can quickly become judgmental of others' less than diligent behavior. I've seen people quit serving in ministry because they thought no one was helping them. But in reality, if they were doing it for the Lord, why would that cause them to stop? The Lord certainly hadn't abandoned them. If fellowship with God drives us, everything's fine. But if service replaces fellowship, we get Martha.

Not only did Martha get angry with her sister for not helping, but she accused Jesus of not caring about her. If that was the point to which her service had driven her, she should have stopped doing everything and gone back to where she started—just loving Jesus.

Martha had forgotten her first priority—and because she had, it was the work for the Lord she became most interested in and everyone was to blame, even Jesus. Mary, on the other hand, took full advantage of Jesus' presence. She had spent some time helping prepare, but once He knocked on the door, that was it for her. She was going to sit at His feet, intently listen to every word, give Him her full attention, just enjoy Him.

Jesus said Mary made the right choice. To the Ephesian church, Jesus gave three words: *remember, repent,* and *return.* They were to remember how it used to be when they simply longed for fellowship with Him. They were to repent and change direction. And they were to return to their first love.

Often when I've asked people over the years if they're new at church, they'll say yes and tell me where they're from. When I ask if they're involved in serving anywhere they sometimes say, "Oh, no! In our last church, we did everything. We're not doing anything anymore. We're burned out."

All right, Martha, I think to myself. *Relax!* How can we get burned out loving God? It seems to me that He burned out loving us—yet He's still available. The only way we can get burned out loving God is if we put service before fellowship.

"One thing is needed," Jesus said to Martha. We think there are a hundred things to be done on any given day. There aren't. There's only one.

To the rich young ruler, Jesus said, "You're only missing what you're looking for by one thing: Come and follow Me."

When questioned about Jesus' healing on the Sabbath, the blind man said, "I know this one thing: I can see."

Paul said to the Philippians in 3:12–14, "I haven't arrived yet, but I do this one thing. I press on."

David wrote in Psalm 27:4, "One thing have I asked of the Lord. I want to sit in His presence."

If we have that one thing in order, everything that follows is fine. But if we have that out of order, we find ourselves not only occupied with worry, but angry with everyone around us—and eventually we even could turn on God as well. It's not that serving the Lord is wrong, but substituting serving and busyness for fellowship is more than wrong and will only bring bitter disappointment.

All of us lean toward being Martha because we're work-oriented. To be Mary takes faith. But the way of abundant life begins with a devotion to the Lord. Then the service that comes from that relationship will be sweet and powerful. But until then, you'll feel like Martha. Work on fellowship with God—and all the other stuff will follow.

Chapter 71

LORD, TEACH US TO PRAY

Luke 11:1–4
(Matthew 6:9–15)

On the heels of Jesus' word to Martha about the importance of fellowship comes a lesson on prayer, a place we are called to have that intimate fellowship with God each day. Sometimes this is known as the Lord's Prayer. But it would better be entitled the Disciples' Prayer for it provided them an outline for prayer that could revolutionize the way we pray as well.

> Now it came to pass, as He was praying in a certain place, when He ceased, that one of His disciples said to Him, "Lord, teach us to pray, as John also taught his disciples."
>
> —Luke 11:1

Certainly the greatest teaching tool Jesus used was Himself. His disciples learned much just by being "with" Him. And as they spent time with Him day after day, one thing they noticed about Him was His prayer habits. If we go through the Gospels and take note of all of the times we see Jesus praying, we find Him praying often and under all kinds of circumstances. Before He chose the twelve disciples, He spent the night in prayer. After being thrown out of the Capernaum temple, when the disciples woke up before dawn the next morning, Jesus already had left to pray. Before the Transfiguration, He prayed. Before He headed to Jerusalem, He prayed. In the Garden of Gethsemane on the night of His betrayal, He prayed.

Praying with Jesus late at night, the disciples nodded off, but He didn't. They were hungry to have what He had. "Lord, teach us to pray," they said.

If I had been a disciple, I'm not sure I would have said that. I mean, Jesus had fed thousands with just a few loaves of bread. He had opened the eyes of the blind. He had cured leprosy and cast out demons. Even some who had died were raised. Therefore, I think I might have said, "Teach me about that leprosy thing. That looks cool" or "I'd like to raise a few guys out of the graveyard." I'm afraid I'd have wanted something more spectacular. Not the disciples. Prayer was what impressed them the most. It was so much a part of Jesus' life and had such an influence on His ministry that they were able to connect the two in their observations of Him.

The disciples had heard from John the Baptist's disciples that he had taught them to pray. I find this to be interesting, because our thoughts or impressions of John the Baptist might have been his lifestyle or bold message along Jordan. Yet of the many things his disciples remembered about him, it was his teaching on prayer they valued most.

If Jesus prayed so much that the disciples noticed, and if His forerunner was also one found constantly in prayer, then I think the church ought to take note. How much do we really pray? I don't know how your prayer life is—if it's good or poor, constant and rich, rare and sporadic, an "emergencies only" situation, or something you do on a regular basis. I don't know if I were to ask your children how much you pray what they would say from your example.

I do know the disciples wanted to learn to pray more, to pray better, and to pray like Jesus. So in response to their request, He gave them the outline that follows. The fact that He taught it in the Sermon on the Mount and that there are at least portions of it mentioned in other places as well suggest to me that it wasn't such an easy lesson to learn. It needed to be repeated to them—just as it does to us.

> So He said to them, "When you pray, say: Our Father in heaven . . . ."
> —Luke 11:2

The order is important. It's given the same way every place you find it. This outline for prayer begins with relationship. *Father* is a relationship word. According to the Bible, the only prayer God hears from the lost is the prayer to be found, forgiven, and saved. So first things first. Paul wrote to the Ephesians in chapter 2 that through Jesus we have access by the Spirit to the Father. The letter to the Hebrews tells us we have a high priest touched with the feelings of our infirmities, tempted in every way we are, yet without sin. And by Him, by Jesus, we can come boldly before God's throne to find His mercy and grace in time of need.

Jesus is the door into glory. If we try to pray apart from Him, no matter what may come our way, we have no access for we have not come through the Door. Yet once we are saved, we become children of God. Kids always have access to their parents. God's never too busy for us either. We'll never hear Him say, "What are you doing here?"

So prayer always comes from, and because of, our relationship with God through His Son, Jesus. Paul wrote to the Romans that God doesn't given us the spirit of bondage to fear, but the spirit of adoption whereby we can cry, "Abba, Father" or literally, "Daddy." My confidence in my earthly father knew no bounds. He could do anything in my eyes. Today, it is my Father in heaven that I know to be able to do all things. He is Almighty and my Father. Awesome! So Jesus says that as a believer in Him I must begin praying by realizing to whom I am coming. Before we start rattling off our lists of things we think we must have, we should stop to consider to whom we're speaking for it will change the way we pray. *Our Father in heaven*: oh, this is going to be good!

> ". . . hallowed be Your name."
>
> —Luke 11:2

After remembering to whom we're speaking, we should make sure we understand why we've come. The word *hallowed* means "to make holy" or "to be honored." Jesus tells us that we want to be sure our desire in prayer is that God's honor is our concern. We should want Him to look good in all of this; we should want His will to be accomplished. Therefore, if we're asking for something that will not work out for His glory, no matter how much we ask He will say no, and we should say amen. Think of it this way: Just because your kids ask nicely if they can play on the freeway, your answer always will be no. The same is true of God. He must be glorified in us!

In John 12:28, Jesus cried out, "Father, glorify Yourself." When we are all done here, we want to leave behind a trail of God being glorified. At the point when we're more interested in God's glory than our lists of demands, our prayer lives change, because what we want is what He wants. What an outline Jesus gave them—and we've just begun!

> "Your kingdom come. Your will be done on earth as it is in heaven."
>
> —Luke 11:2

In heaven, there are no detractors. The Lord runs the show. Here on earth, however, not everything is yet under His feet, although He can come and take it whenever He wants. "Father, have Your will here like it is in heaven." What a great prayer! In the strictest sense, prayer is never designed by God to bring our will to pass, but to bring His will to pass in us and then through us.

We usually approach prayer thinking somehow that if we can learn the right prayer method, we will have success in our request. But one of the greatest flaws to me in the "name it and claim it" and "health and wealth" doctrines that have run across the country for the last twenty-five years is that they see God as a vending machine and us as the supplier of the quarters who can pull the arm and get what we want by praying in a certain manner. But that's not the prayer of the Bible. Prayer is all about us discovering what God's will is and going His way.

That doesn't mean we can't bring our needs to God. The Bible clearly says we are to do this. Yet they come later in the outline, after: "Your kingdom come, Your will be done!" God is not a genie in a magic lamp. He doesn't follow our instructions. We're to follow His. And prayer is all about discovering what He wants. Prayer is not about our telling God what to do. Nor is it about our informing God what's going on. Did you know He knows what we're going to say before we even show up? We'll never hear Him say, "What? You're kidding! I didn't know that!" God already knows what we need.

Why, then, do we have to keep asking? The simplest answer is because He said to. "Pray without ceasing," Paul told the Thessalonians. The longer answer is that, in so doing, we build a daily relationship with God where the events of our lives are attached and brought to Him in prayer, so he might be honored and His will accomplished.

"This is the confidence we have in God, that if we ask anything according to His will, He hears us. And if He hears us, we know we have the petitions we desire of Him," John wrote in his first epistle. God knows our desires and needs—yet prayer will conform us to His will, so He might then move mightily in our lives.

"Lord, not my will but Yours be done." That is the greatest step of faith we can take. If you have ever lost sight of your young child for but a moment at the store or the beach, you know your heart rate can go from normal to three thousand in two seconds. And then when you find them, what is the first thing you say? "If you do that again, so help me . . .!" You were terrified! But who suffered more when that child was in "disappearance mode"—you or them? They didn't even realize they were lost, but you were dying. It's the same with God. If we don't discover His will and instead are lost, His heart breaks. He knows what our needs are. So be sure you know whom you're speaking to and why you've come, and be sure your greatest desire is that His will be done in your life. Now we turn to our needs:

"Give us day by day our daily bread."

—Luke 11:3

The word *give* here is in the present active imperative voice—which means it's an action that constantly is being repeated. A daily part of our prayer lives ought to be a continual looking to the Lord for *daily* needs—not only food, but whatever we need to be sustained each day. I love the simplicity of it. God wants to be involved day to day with my every need and I need to give Him my day so I can watch Him provide constantly.

Someone told me once he didn't like to bother God with little things. There are two problems with that. First, God said He wants us to ask Him to meet our every need. Second, with God everything is a little thing. There are no big things for Him. Daily prayer for daily needs will eliminate the day's anxieties. Let Him be actively involved with your life daily, and in so doing your fellowship with Him is strengthened and maintained. From daily bread to daily forgiveness:

"And forgive us our sins, for we also forgive everyone who is indebted to us."

—Luke 11:4

The Bible teaches that the moment we're saved, our sins—past, present, and future—are forgiven. When we came to the Lord, He didn't just look back at our sin, He looked ahead to our future failures and yet took us anyway. The Lord promises that what He starts He's going to finish and that one day He'll present us faultless before His throne. So once we turn to Christ, our salvation is never in jeopardy. Our fellowship with God, however, depends on confession of sin, because sin gets in the way of a believer's relationship with the Father.

If your kids are always acting up, you may have a hard time wanting to bless them. Instead, you might have to take away their allowance, phone, or TV. I remember getting everything taken away as a kid. It seemed like I was always losing privileges to my stuff! It wasn't that my parents wanted to take things from me. They just wanted me to straighten up and fly right. It's the same with the Lord. If we walk by faith, seek Him, and turn from sin, we'll have fellowship with Him and experience His grace, joy, and peace. But let sin enter the picture and all that will be broken. Whatever He wants to do He can't because we've stepped out of fellowship with Him.

Because we're in a place where we're depending on God to forgive us each day to keep our fellowship with Him unhindered, so He wants us to apply that to our relationships with others each day in prayer as well: forgive, restore, grace and mercy.

I think the fact that we are told to do this every day suggests we have a great need for this in our daily practice. Forgiveness is not a natural part of our lives. Yet every time I say, "Lord, forgive me," I have to stop and think if I have something I haven't forgiven. So serious is this that Jesus said in the Sermon on the Mount, "If you don't forgive men their trespasses, the Father won't forgive you" (Matt. 6:14–15). Again, this is not about our salvation being lost. It's about our fellowship with God being broken.

"Bear with one another," Paul told the Colossians in 3:13, "If you have a complaint against anyone, because Christ forgave you, you forgive them." It will keep us strong and close to the Lord. It is in the daily outline of prayer Jesus gives to his own.

"And do not lead us into temptation, but deliver us from the evil one."
—Luke 11:4

James 1:13 tells us the Lord never tempts us with evil. But in my daily prayer and seeking to have Him direct my life, I have to ask that God overrule my choices if I'm going in the wrong direction. I can pray—and then walk out of God's presence and do whatever I want all day long. Or I can seek the Lord to be sure that if there's a place of weakness that would cause me to stumble, He will overrule me and take me somewhere else.

The Devil loves to lay traps. He looks for our weaknesses. He tests us to find out where we might fall. And he's always waiting. Therefore, we shouldn't run off on our own. God never will give us what we can't handle—but that's provided we're walking with Him. If you're on your own, you'll come across all kinds of stuff you can't handle. But if you walk with the Lord, He promises to keep you in the place you need to be.

It was a pretty short outline Jesus gave His disciples when they asked Him to teach them to pray—only a few words long. But if you'll use it, your prayer life will be solid. You will become a prayer warrior as you discover God's will for your life each day. You don't want to just give God your list—you want to give Him your life.

Chapter 72

ATTITUDE IN PRAYER
Luke 11:5–13

After giving His disciples an outline for prayer, Jesus used a couple of stories to teach them about what attitude and understanding they should bring to prayer each day. In them, He addressed a couple of really important questions: "Why do we have to persist in prayer?" and "Why doesn't God always answer right away?" My experience is that God rarely answers right away. In fact, I'd like to buy Him a watch for Christmas. "Come on, Lord," I say. "It's late. What are You doing?" All kidding aside though, both persistence in prayer and God's delays are good and necessary as we learn here.

> And He said to them, "Which of you shall have a friend, and go to him at midnight and say to him, 'Friend, lend me three loaves; for a friend of mine has come to me on his journey, and I have nothing to set before him'; and he will answer from within and say, 'Do not trouble me; the door is now shut, and my children are with me in bed; I cannot rise and give to you'? I say to you, though he will not rise and give to him because he is his friend, yet because of his persistence he will rise and give him as many as he needs."
>
> —Luke 11:5–8

In the desert culture of Jesus' day, many people built homes relatively close to one another and, due to the heat of the day which was oppressive, would often travel at night. This practice, however, sometimes conflicted with the obligation people felt to feed and house anyone who came to their home. So the picture for the disciples was clear: You have someone drop in late at night because he has been traveling. He gets to your house and you have an obligation not only to take him in but to feed him. The problem is, you have no food. Whatever they had was eaten by the family before they went to bed—and the cupboards were bare.

Within the culture, in daylight hours everyone's doors were open—like when Abraham saw the three visitors approach as he sat in the door of his tent (Gen. 18). But when the door was shut, to knock meant it was an emergency. Most of the houses—especially those of the poorer people—had two floors. The animals slept on the bottom floor and the people slept upstairs on one mat. So to get up and answer the door would have required more than just waking up one person. Every person and animal would stir. To this fellow with the visitor, his lack of bread was an emergency. His neighbor, however, didn't see it as pressing, so in a kind way he basically tells him to, "Get lost."

After painting the picture, Jesus put it in perspective in verse 8 when He said that although the friend would not rise because of relationship, he would rise because of persistence. The Greek word for *persistence* means "shameless"—to have no guilt and in this case, no guilt about pushing until you get what you want. "I've had enough of your pounding on the door. You're waking up the whole neighborhood!" the neighbor eventually said. And the man in need got his three loaves—although the rate of speed at which they were be delivered to him flying out the door is anybody's guess!

I often have heard this story taught as a lesson that if we will just keep knocking and be persistent in our prayer, we'll get what we need. The problem with that teaching, however, is that it doesn't picture the God of the Bible. If this were an issue of comparison rather than contrast, God would be the man lying in bed. When we came with our needs to Him, there would be a pretty good chance we could be bothering Him. He could be busy. He could have had a long day. He could be upset we didn't come earlier. If that weren't enough, He might not even see our needs the same way we do. So our friendship with God at that point would have no value. We'd only be able to get something from Him if we made pests of ourselves—and what we got would be given begrudgingly, if at all.

Does that sound like God? We know God better than that. Psalm 34:15 says His ears are open to the righteous and their cry. Jeremiah tells us the righteous cry and the Lord answers and shows them great and mighty things they knew nothing about. Paul said in Philippians that if we let God know our needs with thanksgiving, His peace will fill our hearts. The picture we get in the Bible is of a God who loves to hear from His people. Everything we read about His heart is that He doesn't need to be begged or badgered into answering. He loves us and acts accordingly!

This instead is to be viewed as a lesson in contrast. This friend is bothered because his friendship is not strong enough to survive the inconvenience. God is not at all like that. God's love for us overwhelms any demands we might have of Him. It is His goodness to us and His love for us that will respond when we call. He is not put out. He is always available. Not one time in the Bible do we see God say, "This is a bad time right now. Could you come back at nine?" No, He welcomes us with open arms. We can't walk through His door enough. He's quick to respond. He's eager to respond. He loves to be asked. He wants us to come and know Him.

So although our worldly attitude could convince us that sometimes when friendship doesn't work, persistence will—the Lord says just the opposite. But that doesn't mean we shouldn't be persistent in our prayers. In fact, Jesus goes on to explain both the need and reason for persistence in prayer:

"So I say to you, ask, and it will be given to you; seek, and you will find; knock, and it will be opened to you. For everyone who asks receives, and he who seeks finds, and to him who knocks it will be opened."

—Luke 11:9–10

Notice He gives three injunctions here: ask, seek, and knock—all of them in the present perfect tense, which speaks of action in the past that continues in the present. In other words, we're to keep asking, keep seeking, and keep knocking. We're to persist in prayer—but not for the reason you might think. God isn't like that friend in bed. We don't have to beat Him over the head before He acts on our behalf. He knows what we need before we ask. It isn't our persistence that will move Him. It is His love for us that will. Our persistence is for our benefit because sometimes it takes us a little while to get to where He can give us His best. We need forming, changing, ministering to. Just check that truth as God dealt with Hannah and prepared her to have a son in 1 Sam. 1.

"Pray without ceasing," Paul wrote in 1 Thessalonians 5:17. "Be instant—or steadfast—in prayer," he told the Romans (12:12). But he never attached "so God will hear you" to these commands. God is not like this friend who isn't really much of a friend. God is for us. He is with us. He wants to be part of our lives. We should be shameless in prayer because when we seek God He will bless us, teach us, and keep us close.

"Ask" means to do just that. Asking is not informing God. Asking is not convincing God. Asking is kneeling at God's feet. The word *seek* implies action, because so often we ask the Lord and then do nothing. Seeking is the action that follows asking. For example, if we pray, "Lord, I want to be a stronger believer," we can be part of the answer by going to church, studying the Scriptures, and spending time with other believers.

When Nehemiah heard about the condition of his beloved city Jerusalem, which the Babylonians had leveled many years earlier, he was so heartbroken that he began to pray that he would be able to help repair it. But since he worked for the king in Babylon and was not likely to get excused from his job, it seemed impossible. Nevertheless, he made a list of the things he would need if he ever was given the opportunity to go. Several months later when the king gave him permission to return to Jerusalem, Nehemiah knew what supplies to request. Following his arrival, enemies began to threaten the workers, saying, "While you're working on the wall, we're going to shoot arrows through your backs." Again Nehemiah prayed. And again, he didn't stop there. The Bible says he also set a watch to protect the workers.

Ask first. Then seek to do what you can. *Knocking* is a word that speaks of persevering. God sometimes answers right away. In Isaiah 65:24, He said to the people, "It will come to pass that before you call, I'll answer. And while you're speaking, I'll hear." That's my favorite verse. I just wish I would experience more of it! In Psalm 13:1, after a particularly frustrating period, David wrote, "How long will You forget me, Lord?" That seems to be more my kind of prayer.

What causes delays in answer to prayer? In Psalm 66:18, David said if we hide sin in our heart, God doesn't hear us. In Proverbs 21:13, Solomon wrote that if we shut our ears to the cries of the poor, we will not be heard when we cry. But some delays are simply meant to bring us to a place of understanding that God's ways are best.

When Paul was given a "thorn in the flesh" because God had shown him so much, he prayed three times for the Lord to get rid of it.

"My strength is made perfect in weakness," God answered.

So Paul said, "I will rejoice in my infirmity" (2 Cor. 12).

Did God change? No, Paul did. And through his asking, seeking, and knocking, he was brought to a place where he could receive from God the things God most wanted to give him. God will delays answers to our prayers for many different reasons—but every one of them is for our good. His hand will not be moved by our persistence. We, however, will be moved through our persistence with God to where He wants us to be.

> "If a son asks for bread from any father among you, will he give him a stone? Or if he asks for a fish, will he give him a serpent instead of a fish? Or if he asks for an egg, will he offer him a scorpion? If you then being evil know how to give good gifts to your children, how much more will your heavenly Father give the Holy Spirit to those who ask Him!"
>
> —Luke 11:11–13

Jesus concludes by comparing and contrasting earthly fathers with our heavenly Father. A father's treatment of his child shows his care. If you, as a sinful person, can be good to your children, how much more would you expect to find that kind of love and care from our heavenly Father who is perfect?

So keep praying—but know this: God is only going to give you the best. No matter how much you pray for the wrong thing, He's going to say no. You can say, "In Jesus' name," but if it's not the best, He'll say no. You can say, "I'm going to quit tithing," but if what you ask for is not the best, He'll still say no. You can threaten to quit going to church. Still, it will be no.

We don't always know how we should pray. We don't always understand what's best. But as we seek the Lord daily, as we seek God's face, and as we persist in prayer, we can do so with great anticipation, knowing we're eventually going to receive the answer we're looking for. It may not be the answer we think we want. But it will be the right one. The old adage to "be careful what you ask for because God may give it to you" is baloney. God never will give us what can't be useful to us, for He loves us as our Father. He's going to give us His best as we wait on Him.

Our good Father, through prayer, will get us to where He wants us to be. Prayer, and persistence in it, is always worth the effort. Pray, pray, pray!

Chapter 73

JESUS' AND SATAN'S KINGDOMS

Luke 11:14–28
(Matthew 12:24–30; Mark 3:22–27)

Afterteaching His disciples about prayer—both in an outline for prayer and the attitude they were to have in prayer, Jesus had an opportunity to teach them about the difference between His kingdom and Satan's.

> And He was casting out a demon, and it was mute. So it was, when the demon had gone out, that the mute spoke; and the multitudes marveled. But some of them said, "He casts out demons by Beelzebub, the ruler of the demons." Others, testing Him, sought from Him a sign from heaven.
>
> —Luke 11:14–16

Matthew's record (Matt. 12:22–30) of this event tells us this man who was possessed by the Devil was not only unable to speak but was blind as well. As Jesus always does, with great authority and in a moment's time, He delivered this man from both. Every place in the Bible where Jesus and the Devil ran into each other in the form of demon possession, it was always the demons who hit the ground. It was hardly a fair fight. The demons fell because Jesus is Lord.

The miracle divided the crowd into two groups. The first group, the religious leaders, said, "Just to explain to you all why this Jesus shows such great power, we happen to know by personal insight that He's made a deal with Beelzebub." As seen in 2 Kings 1:2, Beelzebub was a Philistine god but the name literally means "Lord of the flies." Therefore, the religious leaders were accusing Jesus of being in league with Satan himself. The other group, not quite so outspoken in their doubt, said they needed more proof of who Jesus was—as if the complete deliverance of a blind and mute man wasn't proof enough.

One group was very blasphemous in its unwillingness to believe. The other group was less blasphemous but no less unbelieving. I would think that anyone who raised his or her voice in opposition to Jesus at this point might have had to deal with the man who had just been delivered. It's one thing to argue doctrine with people. It's quite another to have a guy who was blind and unable to speak standing in front of you, saying, "I can see. Jesus did this." Yet no matter how obvious the miracle, the religious leaders of Jesus' day who wanted Him dead were not moved by His absolute authority and instead responded with very illogical arguments and the blindness that only sin and unbelief could produce.

People still do that today. They come up with silly arguments to justify their unbelief. The idea of evolution is a classic example of, "My mind is made up. Don't confuse me with the facts." The idea of uniformitarianism—that nothing has changed, that there is no movement from God to upset the apple cart—doesn't explain the changes in the geological strata, the fossils found there, or the fact that we don't have any transitional life forms. Yet when your mind is made up and you sit in darkness, it's hard to be objective.

In this last year of ministry, Jesus gave more proof than was necessary—indisputable evidence of who He was. But as crowds marveled, the religious folks regrouped. And when they broke out of their huddle, they said, "We can explain this," as they offered the slanderous explanation they'd been giving since Mark 3:22–27 when they said, "He's got the Devil in Him."

As ludicrous as their argument was, Jesus didn't walk away from them, saying, "Have it your way, you are now on your own" Instead, seeing them on the precipice of eternal judgment, He offered them three things to help bring them to Himself and to their senses: merciful logic, a merciful warning, and a merciful invitation:

> But He, knowing their thoughts, said to them, "Every kingdom divided against itself is brought to desolation, and a house divided against a house falls. If Satan also is divided against himself, how will his kingdom stand? Because you say I cast out demons by Beelzebub. And if I cast out demons by Beelzebub, by whom do your sons cast them out? Therefore they will be your judges. But if I cast out demons with the finger of God, surely the kingdom of God has come upon you."
>
> —Luke 11:17–20

Logic and experience both attest to the fact that anything divided against itself won't stand. Get together a team that's at each other's throats and they'll lose. A company whose people are working against each other will fall apart. The same is true of a kingdom. For the Devil to take people into his kingdom through the front door, only to allow Jesus to let them out the back, doesn't make much sense.

We might have just walked away from these religious leaders, saying, "Forget it." Not Jesus. He said to them, "Let's talk about this. Do you really believe what you're saying? Subtraction doesn't help. It weakens."

Jesus then went on to ask about their own religious community. In first century Jewish culture, the religious communities had all kinds of groups seeking to perform exorcisms of those they felt were possessed. We see a group of them in Acts 19.

So Jesus said, "Your own community casts out demons. Are they also demonically moved and empowered—or are you only accusing Me?" Then in verse 20 He drew the logical conclusion when He asked, "What if My power over the Devil is an indication to you that the finger of God is at work and the kingdom of God is among you—that I'm the Messiah?"

This isn't the first time we see the term *the finger of God*. When Moses and Aaron went to Pharaoh at God's direction and demanded that His people be let go, Pharaoh refused. So the plagues began to come. For a while, Pharaoh's magicians were able to recreate them. "That can't be God," they said. "We can do that." Although they were only making matters worse, they thought they were at least keeping up—until the plague of lice. When they couldn't copy that plague, they said to Pharaoh, "This is the finger of God" (Exod. 8:19)—the very term Jesus used.

> "When a strong man, fully armed, guards his own palace, his goods are in peace. But when a stronger than he comes upon him and overcomes him, he takes from him all his armor in which he trusted, and divides his spoils."
>
> —Luke 11:21–22

"What if I am the finger of God?" Jesus had asked. Then He went on to illustrate His position. Satan is a strong man. The man standing before them had been blinded and rendered unable to speak through his power. The man was miserable, bound, and unable to free himself. But when Jesus, the stronger Man, came, He disarmed the strong man and delivered the blind and mute man from Satan's victimization.

"What if I'm the finger of God?" Jesus asked. "What if I'm the stronger Man who is able to defeat the strong man?" In Paul's second letter to the Corinthians, he talked about the god of this world who blinds potential believers' minds so the glorious light of the Gospel of Jesus cannot shine on them and let them believe (2 Cor. 4:3–4). That's Satan's work. He's a strong man—but Jesus is stronger. Jesus came to destroy the works of the Devil, to set people free from the power of darkness.

> "He who is not with Me is against Me, and he who does not gather with Me scatters."
>
> —Luke 11:23

In light of Jesus' merciful logic, He said to the crowd, "You must either stand with Me or you'll have to stand in defiance of Me. But you can't waffle in the middle."

The Bible teaches that compromising our belief system will always fail us. Saul tried to serve the Lord halfway and lost his kingdom. Jeroboam tried to use religion only to the point where it would gain him something—and he lost everything. The people who were moved by the Assyrians to the Samaritan area after the fall of the northern kingdom tried to fear the Lord and serve their own gods, only to be destroyed. We never can juggle our assessment and subsequent decisions about God. The proof is in. He's the stronger Man. We must submit ourselves to His delivering power!

> "When an unclean spirit goes out of a man, he goes through dry places, seeking rest; and finding one, he says, 'I will return to my house from which I came.' And when he comes, he finds it swept and put in order. Then he goes and takes with him seven other spirits more wicked than himself, and they enter and dwell there; and the last state of that man is worse than the first."
>
> —Luke 11:24–26

No doubt the man who had just been delivered was now going to be swayed either by the crowd or by the Lord Himself. So Jesus gave the very chilling warning that if the Lord delivers you from the Devil's grasp, the Devil is not going to be satisfied running around in the wilderness but will try to come back and take over. In other words, if the Lord has delivered your life but you don't let in the Lord—the stronger Man—to protect you, eventually the strong man will come back with his friends. And although you may have cleaned up in one area, you'll find yourself falling in eight others. This means there is no solution in self-help, self-reform, or merely sweeping the place out. Your only solution is to give your life to Jesus, who will move in. Then you'll be protected because He doesn't rent out rooms. He takes over the whole house.

If the one delivered doesn't receive the Deliverer into his life, he will find himself in worse straits down the road. "I quit smoking," he'll say, "but now I drink like a fish," or, "I quit drinking, but now I lose my temper." There's always a way for the enemy to get you unless Jesus changes your heart. You don't want a vacuumed house that just sucks in the latest thing, whatever that next thing may be. So Jesus said, "You've been delivered. But now you've got to be filled."

> And it happened, as He spoke these things, that a certain woman from the crowd raised her voice and said to Him, "Blessed is the womb that bore You, and the breasts which nursed You!" But He said, "More than that, blessed are those who hear the word of God and keep it!"
>
> —Luke 11:27–28

I suspect this woman in the crowd was closer to faith in Jesus than anyone else in the story. She seemed to be saying, "How blessed Your mother must be to have a Son like You, to have raised One with such wisdom and kindness, insight and power." In her own way, she confessed she saw God's power in His life.

But her focus was certainly wrong. So without being unkind, Jesus said, "No, blessed is the man who obeys God's Word. He'll find life."

Unfortunately, the enthusiasm to bless Mary has grown for centuries. It certainly didn't come from the Bible. It wasn't until 431 A.D., at the Council of Ephesus, that Mary was referred to as the mother of God. It was almost two hundred years later that the Catholic Church instituted the practice of praying to Mary. And not until 1854 did the pope float the idea that Mary was immaculately conceived. In 1950, the Catholic doctrine of the Assumption of Mary was established—that not only was she born without sin, but she was raised into heaven without dying. The development of those belief systems continued until 1965 when Mary was declared to be the mother of the church and, therefore, should be sought in prayer for help.

Being an ex-Catholic, I'm pretty sure that most of the folks who believe these things have very good intentions. I'm sure none of them say, "We need to find a different God than Jesus." These are understandings and sentiments that are passed down—much like that of the woman in the crowd who, with zeal and excitement, unknowingly declared something that was absolutely wrong.

When the angel of the Lord came to Mary in Luke 1:38 and told her she would bear the Son of God, Mary said, "Whatever the Lord wants to do." It was her faith that brought blessing and she was honored for her trust in the Lord. She is found for the last time in Acts 1 where, along with her family who would come to believe Jesus was God, she waited with the other disciples for the outpouring of God's Spirit. Neither the record of the early church in the book of Acts nor that of the epistles that carry us forward many years after the resurrection ever mentions the exaltation of Mary. There's only one name by which we can be saved—and that name is Jesus.

I don't see Jesus chastising this woman. I just see her being corrected with great kindness. "Follow the Word of God and keep it," Jesus said—which was not only great advice, but the only way to go. Jesus is God, and Mary, like us, needed Him to save her as well.

Chapter 74

FOLLOW THE AVAILABLE LIGHT

Luke 11:29–36
(Matthew 12:38–42)

After Jesus healed a man possessed by the Devil, the religious leaders wanted to discredit Him. "Of course He can do that," they said. "He's in league with the Devil himself." This wasn't only foolish but blasphemous. But Jesus very kindly reasoned with them and invited them to follow Him. Others in the crowd, although they weren't quite as blasphemous, asked for a sign—for more proof He was who He said He was.

It is to that group that Jesus now turns to speak and His words to them essentially were, "More proof is not what you need. You have enough evidence, you need to act upon it."

> And while the crowds were thickly gathered together, He began to say, "This is an evil generation. It seeks a sign, and no sign will be given to it except the sign of Jonah the prophet."
>
> —Luke 11:29

To the many in this large crowd looking for a sign, Jesus said, "It's a wicked thing you're doing." Why? Because, according to Luke 11:16, they weren't really looking for signs to be convinced of who Jesus was. They were instead looking for reasons to feel comfortable rejecting Him. No amount of proof could convince them. Their minds were made up. Jesus never turned from honest seekers, but these were anything but honest.

In a generation that had lost faith, Gideon was a man with great potential for faith (Judg. 6–7). When the Midianites had so overrun the nation of Israel that they barely could move, God said to Gideon, "Gideon, you mighty man of valor, I want to deliver My people through you."

"Mighty man of valor?" Gideon said. "It's me, Gideon, the least of my family's house. And our house is the smallest tribe in the group. You'd better pick someone else."

"No, I want to use you," God said.

"Then I'm going to need a few signs," Gideon said. But his request was not based on hatefulness or rejection. It came from a heart of doubt that desired to believe. So he put out a fleece and said, "I'd like the fleece wet and the ground dry."

"Done," said the Lord.

When Gideon got up the next morning, he said, "That could have been a fluke. Tomorrow, I'd like to reverse the conditions."

"Done," said the Lord.

When Gideon woke up to find the fleece dry and the ground wet, he said, "OK," and gathered thousands of men to fight.

"That's too many," the Lord said, and by the time He was done, Gideon was left with only three hundred men.

Again, Gideon said, "I'm going to need a sign"—not because he didn't want to believe but because he couldn't see how such a small army could defeat 135,000 Midianites.

So the Lord told him to sneak into the enemy camp and listen to what they were saying around their campfire. Gideon did so and this is what he heard: "I hear Gideon, the sword of the Lord, is coming to destroy us." That was enough for Gideon. The signs the Lord gave had strengthened a heart already willing to believe.

But that wasn't the case with the folks in the crowd here in Luke 11. The problem for sign-seekers is that since their hearts are closed to the Lord, any sign following will eventually lead them astray. In fact, in the last days it will be through lying signs and wonders that the Antichrist will wield his great power. Removed from the Lord Himself, signs are pretty poor guides to the truth.

So Jesus turned to the sign-seekers and virtually said, "What more could I have done? I changed water into wine. I've healed every manner of disease. I've delivered from the power of Satan everyone who has come to Me. I've opened the eyes of the blind. The lame can walk. Even the dead are raised." But none of those were good enough for people who refused to believe.

Whenever Jesus ran into these sign-seekers in the Gospels, He always brought up the issue of the resurrection and used Jonah as an illustration. The resurrection became the final sign, the trump card, the closing argument. This would carry over into the Early Church—where the resurrection was foundational to the message they preached. In Acts 2, never having preached before, Peter stood and said, "The One you killed is now alive." He stood before the Sanhedrin in Acts 5 and in Antioch in Acts 13 with the same message: Jesus is alive.

So here as the cross approached, Jesus spoke clearly of the proof He already had given and reminded the people of their obligation to respond. It's all right to ask questions, all right to have doubts, and all right to wonder. But if the evidence is there, once we have the answer, we must act accordingly.

> "For as Jonah became a sign to the Ninevites, so also the Son of Man will be to this generation. The queen of the South will rise up in the judgment with the men of this generation and condemn them, for she came from the ends of the earth to hear the wisdom of Solomon; and indeed a greater than Solomon is here. The men of Nineveh will rise up in the judgment with this generation and

condemn it, for they repented at the preaching of Jonah; and indeed a greater than Jonah is here."

—Luke 11:30–32

Jesus gave the sign-seekers two examples of people who had less information to go on than they did and yet made the right decision about God. Jonah lived during the days when the Assyrians ruled the world. So wicked were the Assyrians that they maimed those they conquered into submission. Consequently, people were so afraid of them that entire cities killed themselves rather than being captured by them. So when the Lord said to Jonah, "I want you to preach to Nineveh," Jonah, a Jewish nationalist, ran in the opposite direction. But the Lord's not good about letting His prophets do that, so He caused a storm so fierce that the crew of the boat Jonah was on tossed him overboard to appease his God. For three days Jonah lived in the belly of a fish that swallowed him up before being unceremoniously spit up on Nineveh's shore. Go where God sends you Jonah! He was given his message and begrudgingly began to preach.

"Yet forty days and Nineveh will be overthrown," Jonah declared to the entire city—and you know he couldn't have been happier.

But because he had come from this big fish, the heathen king said to all of his people, "We should listen to this guy, scanty as his information is, and cry out for his God's mercy. Let's all fast and put on sackcloth and ashes—even on the livestock. You never know where this God is going to look." Seeing their repentance, God delayed His judgment on the nation—and Jonah was fit to be tied.

Jonah's message was of inevitable judgment and he delivered it with a smile on His face giving no hope of deliverance as he declared it. He didn't call people to repent. He didn't promise them God's mercy. He didn't assure them of God's forgiveness. He didn't do any miracles. No one was delivered from the Devil. He showed no willingness to help them out of their situation. Yet the people turned to God.

Now set Jesus next to Jonah. Jesus came as a loving Messenger, saying, "Come unto Me all you that are heavy laden and I will give you rest" (Matt. 11:28). He had sinless perfection, an inviting tone, a perfect way of life, and miracle-working power. He gave assurance with great promise. He was the fulfillment of Scripture. He embraced everyone who turned to Him. And yet all of those qualities turned a generation in His day away, whereas Jonah, in all of his wickedness, saw an entire generation repent.

"It's going to be a tough day for you when you and those folks from Nineveh stand before God," Jesus said to the sign-seekers. "When God asks the Ninevites why they repented, they'll say, 'We saw a guy come floating out of this big fish's mouth. He told us in forty days we'd be in trouble. So we started crying out to whoever it was who sent him.'

'How about you guys?' God will say to the sign-seekers.

'We saw the blind receive their sight, the lame walk, and the dead raised,' you'll say.

'And you didn't believe?' God will ask.

'No, we wanted more signs,' you'll say. Therefore, you'll be in bigger trouble than anyone else. You had the evidence; you had Jesus right in your midst all along."

The second example Jesus used was the queen of the south, or the queen of Sheba—a very powerful woman who ruled in a kingdom that today is modern-day Yemen. One thousand miles away from the kingdom of Solomon, she was hungry to know the truth when merchants came to her, saying, "We've been to Jerusalem. There's a ruler there you wouldn't believe. He's writing books on zoology, ornithology, and botany. He'll tell you things no one else knows. He understands things no one else gets. And he told us it was because God had blessed him" (2 Chron. 9).

Hearing this, she packed up her donkeys and lots of gifts in case Solomon's information would cost her something and climbed on the back of a camel to ride a thousand miles across the desert—driven only by second-hand information and a heart for the truth. When she finally arrived in Jerusalem, Solomon welcomed her, showed her around, and told her about God's wisdom.

"I heard about you, but they didn't tell me half of it," she said. "Blessed by the Lord your God who has delighted in you and set you on Israel's throne because He loves Israel and His people." And she went home, believing in Solomon's God.

Solomon didn't invite this woman to come. She came on her own. Solomon didn't make it easy for her. He was a thousand miles away. She only had heard reports of him. To see him in person required a difficult journey.

Yet here stood Jesus in the midst of the crowd every day, urging them to come, revealing their hearts to them, and asking them to trust Him, to look to Him, and to believe in Him.

One day the queen of Sheba will stand before the Lord, saying, "I could hardly believe what people said about Solomon, so I went to check it out."

On that same day, the sign-seekers will say, "We talked to Jesus Himself—but we didn't believe Him."

And the queen of Sheba will probably say, "What?!"

> "No one, when he has lit a lamp, puts it in a secret place or under a basket, but on a lampstand, that those who come in may see the light. The lamp of the body is the eye. Therefore, when your eye is good, your whole body also is full of light. But when your eye is bad, your body also is full of darkness. Therefore take heed that the light which is in you is not darkness. If then your whole body is full of light, having no part dark, the whole body will be full of light, as when the bright shining of a lamp gives you light."
>
> —Luke 11:33–36

Jesus' point is that spiritual things are clearly seen. When we come to the Lord, we are given great insight. But if we are driven by something other than the light He produces, we're going to end up in darkness. We know this to be true physically. Close your eyes and you'll run into things. Your progress will be hindered. But if your eyes work, you can move freely. The same thing is true spiritually. If we turn to Jesus, everything in our lives will be guided by His hand. We'll walk in the light. We'll have life. But to stand away from Him like these folks in the crowd and demand more, unwilling to listen or look at what He already has revealed, is to eventually walk in darkness for all eternity.

Jesus wants you to see who He is and why He came. He wants you to see how dark life is without Him and then follow Him. You'll never be able to say to the Lord, "I didn't get it. You didn't show me." You'll only be able to say, "I didn't want to follow. I closed my mind and looked the other way." You'll never be able to accuse Jesus of not turning on the light because, to use a popular commercial phrase, He "left the light on" for you.

Chapter 75

WITHIN OR JUST WITHOUT?

Luke 11:37–44

As He talked to a group that sought yet more signs, Jesus was invited to dinner at a Pharisee's home. Although this religious man had only invited Jesus in hopes of setting Him up and disproving what He had been saying, he would find in Jesus the blunt truth about his own life that he would have to answer for.

> And as He spoke, a certain Pharisee asked Him to dine with him.
> —Luke 11:37

Without the hindsight of history, we would think the Pharisees would have been the kind of people who would have been glad to see Jesus and would have wanted to follow Him. There weren't a lot of rich Pharisees. By and large, they were common folks who had devoted themselves to trying to live holy lives by keeping the Old Testament Law, but which at this time had been redefined by men to weaken its convicting work and enable man, with effort to perform it on their own. So Jesus came and spoke to hearts of sin, to attitude and not just action to show us our need for Him. As a result, neither the scribes nor the Pharisees wanted anything to do with Him because He looked right past their behavior to their hearts and uncovered them.

> So He went in and sat down to eat. When the Pharisee saw it, he marveled that He had not first washed before dinner.
> —Luke 11:37–38

Being invited to this Pharisee's home, Jesus walked in, right past the ceremonial washbowl, sat down, tucked a napkin in His shirt, grabbed a fork, and said, "What's for dinner?" As He did, His host marveled. *Marveled* is the closest Greek word to "blowing your mind" that exists. Traditionally, first-century dinners were eaten with one's hands, which would be a good reason to keep them clean. But that wasn't really the situation here. The issue here concerned a part of temple worship, where as an acknowledgment of his own sin the priest was to wash before he stood before God on behalf of the people. God never said people were to perform this cleansing before dinner. It was nothing more than people's creation of more religion. So Jesus skipped it intentionally and set the scene the way He wanted.

By the way, Jesus never turned down a dinner invitation. Throughout the Gospels, if someone said, "Would You like to eat?" He always said yes. It's great to watch Jesus minister over dinner. However, I'm not sure if, in this case, dinner was ever served. It seems the meal may have ended even before the appetizers arrived. They had invited Jesus, I think, so He might have been dinner as they turned on Him. Not so as Jesus speaks up:

> Then the Lord said to him, "Now you Pharisees make the outside of the cup and dish clean, but your inward part is full of greed and wickedness. Foolish ones! Did not He who made the outside make the inside also?"
>
> —Luke 11:39–40

I love the way the Lord gets to it!

"You want to eat?" Jesus said. "I'm ready!" And He sat right down.

Meanwhile, everyone else was drying his or her hands in the air, looking at Jesus.

"You Pharisees are always washing your hands, forgetting all about your heart," He said.

Not two minutes into the evening and Jesus had already brought up the key issue for these Pharisees, external religion—the greatest danger for anyone looking for life. "Wash all you want," He essentially said, "but you're not getting your hearts clean. You're still greedy. You're still wicked"—or, literally, "You're only interested in yourselves. It's dumb to try to fool God because He not only made your hands—He made your heart and sees everything."

Good argument. Religion fools people, but it never fools God.

When Samuel was sent to Jesse's house to find a replacement for King Saul (1 Sam. 16), he asked Jesse, "Where are your boys? I've got to take a look at them because God has chosen one of them to be king."

"Let me get you the best one," Jesse said and came back with his oldest.

"Good looking kid," Samuel said. "Tall. Smart. I think he's the one." It was then that the Lord told Samuel to quit looking at his outward appearance, because although people look at the outward, God looks at the heart.

Religion is based on outward appearance. Its rules and regulations, practices and rituals are designed for outward consumption. But you can't fool God with it. The problem for the Pharisees—and for most religious people as well—is when they fulfill their outward obligations, they're satisfied no different, not changed in heart. I'm thinking these Pharisees with their clean hands suddenly wanted to hide themselves from Jesus.

> "But rather give alms of such things as you have; then indeed all things are clean to you."
>
> —Luke 11:41

The word *alms* can either mean "good deeds" or "sacrifice." Therefore, the point Jesus made to the Pharisees was, "There's no sense washing your hands when you have a wicked heart. The solution for your problem is to give God what you have and then He can cleanse you. Once He gets your heart clean, anything you do after that is also clean."

What do we have to offer the Lord? Ourselves—along with our weaknesses, sins, and rebellion. It's a horrible deal for the Lord but a great deal for us. We hand Him a broken chair and He gives us a sofa. We hand in our broken lives and He takes us just the way we are and makes of us something He can use for His glory.

The Pharisees' problem was their unwillingness to admit their lives were broken. God doesn't have much to offer people who think they can do it on their own. There's no doctor necessary for the person who isn't sick. But the Lord can work in those who realize their true condition. Give God your life. Let Him clean your heart. Then you'll be clean inside and out. And that's the difference between a relationship with God by faith and a religion that never can accomplish much.

If you have a dirty vocabulary, it's going to take more than mouthwash or a toothbrush. Your heart has to be changed. It's the same way for lust, anger, and jealousy. Most people can curb outward displays of sin. Most folks know how to behave when other people are watching. Even bad people can get away with this, it seems. But no one can fool the Lord. Religion can reform, but only God can give a person a heart that overcomes sin and honors the Lord first.

The problem with sin is that most folks will use religion to try to cover it rather than going to God by faith and receiving life and forgiveness of it, and deliverance from it, in Jesus. In Isaiah 1:10–20, God basically said to His people, "I really don't like your church services. I would rather not attend." In chapter 58, He said, "I see you've been fasting. But then you go out and kill people."

Amos came along and, through him, God essentially said in chapter 5:21–24, "I hate your feast days. I don't want any burnt offerings or grain offerings. I don't care if the peace offerings have been fattened—I don't need them. And while you're at it, could you take away your singing from Me? It's nothing but noise. I don't want to hear the instruments either." Amos ended by saying the Lord is interested in letting justice run like water and righteousness like a mighty stream.

Micah 6:1–8 followed and said to the people, "What do you think we can do to come before the Lord? Do you think we can bow ourselves to Him by giving Him a burnt offering? Maybe a calf that's only a year old—or maybe a thousand rams or ten thousand rivers of oil? Maybe we could offer Him our firstborn for our transgression? How can we come before Almighty God?"

Then he stopped and said, "God has shown you what is required of you. He wants you to do justly, to love mercy, and to walk humbly with Him." Those aren't behaviors—they're attitudes. When the heart is changed, everything's fine. Until then, nothing works because religion can't scratch where you itch. It can't get to where you're hurting. It can't relieve you of sin and its power and its eventual condemnation.

The Pharisees constantly were trying to look good outwardly but they never got to the root of the problem: their sinful hearts.

So Jesus gave them three woes to clarify His point. Woes in the Bible are not good. But they drove home the point that religion, at best, cleans the outside, leaving the heart still wicked.

> "But woe to you Pharisees! For you tithe mint and rue and all manner of herbs, and pass by justice and the love of God. These you ought to have done, without leaving the other undone."
>
> —Luke 11:42

Jesus began with the Pharisees' much-ballyhooed idea of giving. On the one hand, they tithed—which would make them welcome in most churches. They even went beyond their own interpretation of the Law. According to the Mishnah, there were certain spice leaves that were exempt from tithing because they were too small. But the Pharisees tithed even those. While they did that, however, their hearts were still devoid of justice and of God's love for others. They would give meticulously but when it came to righting a wrong, standing up for the needy, or helping the oppressed, they looked the other way. They would go through the formality of giving, but not from a heart of caring. Jesus said their tithing was good—but not at the expense of mercy, grace, justice, and the love of God.

There are many spiritual activities that become non-spiritual activities in God's eyes, if your heart is detached. Giving is certainly one. God isn't broke. He's not dependent on you. He doesn't hope you'll come through so He can pay His bills. God doesn't need our help. We need His.

The same is true of communion, baptism, and dedicating our children; without a pure heart they are exercises that do not impress or bless our Lord. The problem with religion is that it produces a false sense of well being. Ask these people if they love God, and you're likely to hear, "I go to church." But James said undefiled religion that's pure before God is visiting widows in their affliction and taking care of the fatherless. It's more than writing a check and counting leaves. It's a matter of the heart.

> "Woe to you Pharisees! For you love the best seats in the synagogues and greetings in the marketplaces."
>
> —Luke 11:43

Jesus wasn't done with these yet. If these guys' hands were dry after being washed, now they were wet from sweaty palms. "Your heart is not only wrong in giving," Jesus said, "but your desires for ministry are driven by your pride." The Pharisees' hearts were revealed in their self-serving behavior. They loved people acknowledging them, greeting them as teachers, and honoring them publicly in the marketplace where everyone could stand in awe of them. They were driven by people's adulation. Even as the people gathered to worship, these made sure they had the best coveted seats in the place.

> "Woe to you, scribes and Pharisees, hypocrites! For you are like graves which are not seen, and the men who walk over them are not aware of them."
>
> —Luke 11:44

The word *hypocrite* referred to the actors in Greek plays who wore masks to convey their emotions. In Leviticus and Numbers are rules for people traveling to Jerusalem for the feast days. If they walked through a cemetery or brushed up against a gravestone, they could not enter God's presence for a week. This was to teach them that sin brought death and would keep them from God. So people would whitewash the graves to make them easy to see and avoid.

Jesus turned this practice around and applied it to the Pharisees to say, "You guys are like unmarked graves. People aren't warned about you because your external practices make you look holy. But in getting close to you, people are defiled rather than blessed. And instead of being brought closer to God, they're actually driven away."

Religion has always kept people from God. It's people-made and people-driven. It doesn't promote the Gospel of Jesus or God's grace whatsoever. The Pharisees represented the religious way of life. Externally, they seemed as right as people could be. Their devotion, however, didn't impress Jesus because His solution is to change people from the inside out. Religion will leave many thinking they're fine. But they're not. They need salvation and until they admit their sin and need, they will continue in their deception.

Chapter 76

How Do I Handle His Word?

Luke 11:45–54

W e now turn to the second half of the discussion that began in verse 39, as one of the scribes, or lawyers, sitting at the table complained that what Jesus had said to the Pharisees didn't really apply to them.

> Then one of the lawyers answered and said to Him, "Teacher, by saying these things You reproach us also."
>
> —Luke 11:45

I think if there was ever a case of leading with your chin, this was it. "Lord, You're using a big brush and You're splashing paint on us reputable men who are experts in the Word of God," the lawyer, or scribe, said. But he would have been better off just to stick a "Kick Me" sign on his back.

If the Pharisees were those who practiced and taught religion to the people, the scribes, the lawyers, the experts of the Law—all interchangeable terms—were a group of men committed to the interpretation of the Scriptures. They were the ones who wrote out the legal code of the Law. And because they unfortunately came from the same place as the Pharisees, they rewrote what God said until it was hardly recognizable. In fact, in the Mishnah there is a line in the Book of Sanhedrin that says the interpretation of the Law supersedes the Law itself.

As Christians, we know God gave the Law to convince people they couldn't keep it. It isn't that the Law is bad. In fact, it's perfect. But it's impossible for sinful people to keep. It reduces us to what we are: sinful, weak, and in need of a Savior. But the scribes had rewritten it in such a way that, if you were really determined to try, you might be able to keep most of it—or at least put on a pretty good show.

As the handlers of God's Word, the scribes here received from Jesus three woes themselves concerning how they handled the Scriptures and the effect they had on the people who looked to them for instruction. And I suspect it didn't take very long for this lawyer's buddies to wish he had never opened his mouth.

> And He said, "Woe to you also, lawyers! For you load men with burdens hard to bear, and you yourselves do not touch the burdens with one of your fingers."
>
> —Luke 11:46

The scribes had burdened the people with many man-made laws, ostensibly designed to clarify the Bible but which, in fact, did not represent God, His will, or His ways at all. If we go through the Bible, we see from the way the Lord dealt with the Law that its purpose was very simple. When Adam and Eve were put in the garden, God gave them only one law: they were not to eat of the Tree of Knowledge of Good and Evil. Why? Because love, to be love, needs a choice. As Adam and Even chose not to obey the one law God gave them, God gave to His people ten commandments. There were also additional ceremonial laws designed to symbolize people's sinfulness and God's holiness and how to draw near Him. Other laws governed the people in their relationship with the world around them, for God desired to keep them separate. Yet the moral law—the Ten Commandments—never changed and is sufficient to convince us of our sin and need for His help.

However, as man would have it, eventually some six thousand laws would be written from the original Ten Commandments. The Torah, the Law of God, became the Mishnah—the oral traditions and explanations of the Law the scribes gave. Finally, there would be the Talmud, a further explanation of the Mishnah.

We love to complicate things, don't we? Our constitution is short—but look at the laws we've written to explain it. The same is true of God's Law. For example, the Law originally said, "Remember the Sabbath day to keep it holy. Do all of your work in six days and rest on the seventh." That wasn't very complicated—until someone came along and asked, "What is work?" At that point, the simplicity of spending a day worshipping God was changed to, "If you carry a burden heavier than a fig, that's work. And if you put it down and pick it up again, be sure to compute the weight twice."

Religion is man's creation, not the Lord's. So Jesus said to this lawyer, "Woe to you also because you lay burdens on people with your interpretation of the Word of God, yet you don't lift a finger to help them." There is no peace in religion. It always leaves us coming up short. There's no rest in religious people's leadership. There's no hope to be found in a religious philosophy. There's no power in the demands of rules. Even today there are hundreds of thousands of people in churches across our country who are deprived of the salvation God's love has provided through His Son by being told all they need to do is work a little harder, do a little better, and try a little bit more than they did last week.

All men—Christians included—love rules. When people get saved they are so happy to walk in God's grace—but then they eventually start making rules for each other. We are even then still prone to lean toward performance and accomplishments and away from grace. When the Jerusalem Council gathered after the Gentiles started getting saved, they brought in all of the experts to talk about what rules the Gentiles should follow. Paul and Barnabas showed up with Titus, one of their Gentile converts. Peter spoke about his experience at Cornelius' house. By the time everyone's testimony in Acts 15:10 was done, James, the pastor of the Jerusalem Church, said, "It seems to me that we can't put a yoke on the necks of the new believers that we or our fathers were never able to bear. We can't ask them to do things we couldn't do. Instead, we must know and believe that through the grace of Jesus, they can be saved just like we were. It's the grace of God and belief in Jesus that changes a person. So no further rules. Meeting adjourned."

God's Word is to be our delight. It's supposed to bring us life and hope. But the way these lawyers taught it, they left the people feeling burdened and overwhelmed. Loaded down with requirements, they couldn't find help, even from their instructors.

> "Woe to you! For you build the tombs of the prophets, and your fathers killed them. In fact, you bear witness that you approve the deeds of your fathers, for they indeed killed them, and you build their tombs. Therefore the wisdom of God also said, 'I will send them prophets and apostles, and some they will kill and persecute,' that the blood of all the prophets which was shed from the foundation of the world may be required of this generation, from the blood of Abel to the blood of Zechariah who perished between the altar and the temple. Yes, I say to you, it shall be required of this generation."
>
> —Luke 11:47–51

Jesus' second point to the scribes was that they acted just like their fathers before them. In the Kidron Valley in Israel today, just outside the eastern gate, stands Absalom's tomb, along with several others built to honor the prophets. But although the prophets were honored with a monument of stone after their death, when they served the Lord in life, many were killed for bringing God's Word. Jesus charged the scribes with completing what their fathers had begun. They were in partnership to kill Jesus who now had come in fulfillment of the words of the prophets.

For many years, Joash was one of the best kings Judah had ever seen—until his mentor, a high priest named Jehoiada, died. At that point Joash began to listen to the people rather than the Lord and, as he did, the blessings God had brought began to disappear. So God in His love sent Zechariah, the prophet, to Joash with the words, "You're bringing God's judgment upon the people. You're not going to be blessed if you maintain this course. Repent and go back to the way things used to be."

"Who made you a prophet over me?" Joash said. "I'm the king." And he ordered Zechariah's execution. The guards then stoned Zechariah between the temple and the altar (2 Chron. 24:20–21).

Referring to this, Jesus said to the scribes, "You are the same kind of people that made those kinds of decisions. You're religious too—but you hate to hear God's Word."

> "Woe to you lawyers! For you have taken away the key of knowledge. You did not enter in yourselves, and those who were entering in you hindered."
>
> —Luke 11:52

411

Jesus' final word might be the most telling of all. "Woe to you," He said to the lawyers, "because you've taken the key of knowledge—the Word of God, the only way in to the kingdom of heaven—and not only have you rejected it yourselves but you're interfering with those who are seeking to enter heaven through it."

Why don't more people get saved? I think one reason is churches aren't teaching God's Word. The vehicle through which God works—His Word by His Spirit—is set aside for people's religious teachings and cultural or political sermonizing. As a result, people never hear from God. We've got to share the Word of God. It brings life. It's as new, vibrant, and necessary as ever.

> And as He said these things to them, the scribes and the Pharisees began to assail Him vehemently, and to cross-examine Him about many things, lying in wait for Him, and seeking to catch Him in something He might say, that they might accuse Him.
>
> —Luke 11:53–54

Jesus' words were met with anger, challenge, rejection, and plans to destroy Him. The scribes' and Pharisees' hearts were very hard. And yet the Lord was very honest with them. Like I said when we began, I don't think they ever got to dinner. But Jesus sure served up a full plate.

Chapter 77

BEWARE OF HYPOCRISY

Luke 12:1–7

Although Luke 11 ended with the religious as angry with Jesus as they could be, the crowds coming to hear Him continued to grow. It is in this environment that Luke 12 takes place. A classroom was not the setting for these lessons and neither was sitting quietly by the lake. Rather, it was in the pushing and shoving, yelling and screaming of countless people, that Jesus said, "Let Me teach you a few things."

> In the meantime, when an innumerable multitude of people had gathered together, so that they trampled one another, He began to say to His disciples first of all, "Beware of the leaven of the Pharisees, which is hypocrisy."
>
> —Luke 12:1

If you've ever been in a crowd heading somewhere you didn't want to go, you know it's not a good feeling. Imagine being with Jesus—the religious folks are after you, the lawyers don't like you, and the people are questioning you. And now, in the midst of the jostling, pushing, and trampling, Jesus began to teach. I'm sure the disciples thought, *Not here! Not now!* But Jesus wasn't backing down. He continued to set God's truth before them.

The Pharisees had existed as a group for about two hundred years at this point. Between the Old and New Testaments, a Syrian king named Antiochus Epiphanes had overthrown Jerusalem and burned a pig in the temple to say to the Jews, "We'll have it our way," and to defile everything they counted holy.

A young man named Judah Maccabee rose up and miraculously was able to lead a group to get rid of the insurrectionists and reclaim the temple. They cleansed it. The Lord blessed. And out of this new desire for holiness, the Pharisees were born. They were a good group early on. Born out of adversity, they desired to do right before the Lord.

The problem was, in the two hundred years that followed, although their devotion had died, they still looked and acted the part. Paul wrote Titus a letter about these Pharisees, saying, "They profess to know God but in their works they deny Him" (Titus 1:16). Over two hundred years, this very devout group had grown away from the Lord, but was still going through the motions of religious piety and dedication.

It seems that, whether it is we Christians or the Pharisees of old, the outward activity of religion can continue long after the internal fire goes out. These guys were thought to be religious men who loved God—even though they are now found plotting to kill Jesus. So Jesus warned His disciples, saying, "You've got to be careful that what has happened to the Pharisees doesn't happen to you. They used to be faithful, holy men. But look at them now. Beware that you don't fall prey to the leaven that poisoned them, which is hypocrisy."

Hypocrisy is a Greek word that speaks of acting. In Greek plays staged before thousands of people in an amphitheatre, the actors wore big masks to convey the appropriate emotion. Happy faces, sad, worried, fearful, angry and so on. Jesus accused the Pharisees of being like these actors, of wearing masks that covered their hearts that had either lost their fire or never had it in the first place. He had gone to dinner and pulled off some masks, but rather than say, "You're right," those He accused instead determined to kill Him.

The term *leaven* explains how hypocrisy operates. It is used in Scripture in all but two places to speak of the behind the scenes work of sin. Leaven is yeast. It rises because it's a rotting agent. The gasses it gives off cause bread to rise. Jesus used the term to describe various groups of opposition. "Beware of the leaven of the Sadducees," He said in Matthew 16:11. The Sadducees didn't believe in the Devil, angels, heaven, hell, or an afterlife (Matt. 22:23; Mark 12:18). "Beware of guys who live for this life only and have false doctrine to support it," Jesus said. In Mark 8:15, He spoke of Herod's leaven. Herod was a man who, though he knew Jesus was innocent, sold Him out for fear he otherwise would lose his job. Herod was so worldly-minded that he did the wrong thing, even though he knew the right thing to do. Jesus said to beware of the infection that could cause a person to live like that.

Here Jesus spoke of the Pharisees' leaven. Their drive as religious folks was hypocrisy—pretending to be something they weren't. The disciples understood the metaphor of leaven. It was part of daily life. Leaven works slowly and yet, if not guarded against and watched carefully, it eventually will affect every part. So in His spiritual application, Jesus said, "Be careful that you don't begin to cover a wicked walk with supposed outward behavior, because eventually you'll be doing it all the time."

The Bible is filled with God's warnings about hypocrisy. Seven hundred years earlier, in Isaiah 29:13, God said, "The people draw near to Me with their mouths but their hearts are far from Me." I don't know anyone who wants a relationship built on hypocrisy. We would hate it. So does the Lord. Yet when Jesus ran into these Pharisees, that's exactly what He saw. If you don't want to fall into hypocrisy, don't start with it at all. If you're pretending to be something you're not, stop, because the longer you go, the worse it gets and the harder it becomes to be yourself or to be honest with yourself.

> "For there is nothing covered that will not be revealed, nor hidden that will not be known."
>
> —Luke 12:2

At best, hypocrisy is very short-lived because it is dependent on one's ability to conceal things from other people. As long as someone can keep a mask on that no one can see behind, he or she is OK. But Jesus said sooner or later the mask will come off. It's not a matter of "if." It's a matter of "when." Eventually, the truth will come out. And what the Lord knows about each of us, one day everyone will know.

The problem with hypocrisy is the people who are usually the most fooled are the ones wearing the masks. They actually start to think of themselves incorrectly, believing their own lie. They feel secure because God doesn't immediately bring judgment. God is certainly patient—but He's never fooled.

> "Therefore whatever you have spoken in the dark will be heard in the light, and what you have spoken in the ear in inner rooms will be proclaimed on the housetops."
>
> —Luke 12:3

Whispers are meant to be secret. Jesus said they'll turn into shouts. The Pharisees may have thought their plots and plans to kill Him were known only to them—but one day everyone would know the truth. I suspect if we remembered this, we wouldn't say some of the things we might otherwise. Matthew 12:36 says every idle word one day will be brought into judgment. We can get away with a lot—but only for a while.

> "And I say to you, My friends, do not be afraid of those who kill the body, and after that have no more that they can do. But I will show you whom you should fear: Fear Him who, after He has killed, has power to cast into hell; yes, I say to you, fear Him!"
>
> —Luke 12:4–5

Jesus called His disciples "friends"—which may not be such a good title when you're trying to get away from Him in a big crowd! But it is this very friendship with God we have through faith in Jesus that demands we live out our faith in the world rather than wearing the mask of a hypocrite. Here Jesus gave great insight as to why this is a problem. He said we're hypocrites because we're afraid of people. Above all else, we want to make sure they have a good opinion of us. But Jesus said it is God's friendship that gives eternal reward—even if, in the process, we lose our physical lives.

Proverbs 29:25 says the fear of man brings a snare but he who trusts the Lord will be saved. "Don't be afraid of these guys," Jesus said to His disciples. "So they string you up. Big deal. Then they're done with you—but I'm not. You've just begun with Me." People can kill the body but they're unable to inflict eternal injury. I like the fact that Jesus said dying isn't the ultimate disaster. Only dying without fearing God is.

John 12:42 says some of the folks in the Sanhedrin believed in Jesus but they wouldn't confess their faith because they loved men's praises more than God's praises. That's what makes a person a hypocrite. Serve God and don't worry about people's opinions. Don't compromise just so others will be happy. The church certainly could use some saints today who have enough conviction to please the Lord. The Pharisees had a religious exterior designed to bring the honor of men, but their hypocrisy never came close to pleasing God.

> "Are not five sparrows sold for two copper coins? And not one of them is forgotten before God. But the very hairs of your head are all numbered. Do not fear therefore, you are of more value than many sparrows."
>
> —Luke 12:6–7

In Matthew 10:29, Jesus said two sparrows sold for a penny. Here we get five for two pennies, so I think there was a volume discount. In any event, sparrows aren't very valuable. They exist everywhere. Yet God cares about each one. He doesn't forget the sparrows and He knows the number of hairs on your head. That speaks of intimate knowledge, doesn't it? It speaks of constant attention because the number of hairs on a person's head is always changing. God is so intimately concerned about us that He's aware of even the insignificant things in our lives. So we don't need to worry, struggle, or try to get ahead on our own. We just need to please the One who gave His life for us and keeps intimate track of ours. Fear of God brings life; fear of man, hypocrisy, and an outward religion is all you will ever know—then judgment for all of eternity.

Chapter 78

ARE YOU IN JESUS' SECRET SERVICE?

Luke 12:8–12

All of Luke 12 took place in a crowd. It was on-the-job training for the disciples because everything Jesus taught in this chapter had to do with public reception and having to stand one's ground. And it was all taught in the face of some very angry people. It was in these extreme conditions, after having spoken to His own about the hypocrisy of the Pharisees, that Jesus addresses what to do when things seem to turn bad. The subject is dramatic, to the point, and revolutionary—made more so by the fact that the teaching took place in a very unruly mob.

> "Also I say to you, whoever confesses Me before men, him the Son of Man also will confess before the angels of God. But he who denies Me before men will be denied before the angels of God."
>
> —Luke 12:8–9

Because the disciples most likely were feeling at least physically in danger, Jesus spoke to them of the pressure they were going to be under in the days to come, pressure to do what they may have been contemplating: separating themselves a bit from Him. But to these guys with fearful hearts, Jesus said, "Make sure you speak up for Me so I can speak up for you."

The pressure not to follow Jesus had already begun. In John 7:12–13, we read that, although there was much discussion about who Jesus was, no one spoke openly of Him for fear of the Jews. There was great interest in Him but also great pressure to fit in with the crowd and refuse Him. Even among the chief priests and rulers there were many who believed in Jesus. But because they didn't want to be put out of the synagogue and they loved people's praises more than God's praises, they didn't say anything.

According to historical records, in the first three centuries over five million Christians were put to death for their faith by a succession of ten different Caesars, each angry that there would be a group of people who refused to call them "god." I don't suspect any of us ever will be asked to die for our faith—and yet we have the same obligation the disciples faced.

Jesus used the word *confess*, which literally means "to say the same." Therefore, as His followers we're to say what Jesus said. We're to speak for the things of the Lord. Then when we stand before Him, He'll speak for us.

"Come, and I'll tell you what the Lord has done for my soul," the psalmist exclaimed. Likewise, we're to live openly for the Lord even if it's before a hostile crowd. God has placed the church in a hostile world. Whether the hostility is severe or subtle, we still must have an answer for why we believe what we do. The Lord wants us to stand in association with Him—not be ashamed of Him or interested in the opinions of others more than His.

In less than a year Peter would deny Jesus three times in the space of an hour or two. Yet after the resurrection and ascension of our Lord, Peter—now born-again and filled with the Spirit—is brought by the Lord to the very same courtyard he had denied the Lord to stand before the same people and deliver the same message. This time, however, with God's help, Peter didn't fail (Acts 4). He said, "I want to go on record as saying there's only one name given among men whereby we can be saved." Peter moved from the fear of people to the boldness of God by the new birth and the Holy Spirit's work in his life.

It's not always so easy to follow Jesus. There is often a cost to be counted. Right before he was beheaded, Paul wrote to Timothy, "If you want to live a godly life, you're going to suffer persecution" (2 Tim. 3:12). And to all of the churches scattered because of persecution, Peter said, "Don't think this fiery trial is strange. Rejoice. You are being made partakers of Christ's suffering. And if you suffer reproach for His name, you're blessed" (1 Pet. 4:12–14).

> "And anyone who speaks a word against the Son of Man, it will be forgiven him,
> but to him who blasphemes against the Holy Spirit, it will not be forgiven."
> —Luke 12:10

In the pushing crowd, Jesus told the disciples, "Be an example for Me. Stand with Me so I can stand for you. Anyone who speaks out against Me will be forgiven but if they resist or reject the Holy Spirit, nothing can be forgiven."

That there could be an unforgivable sin startles some people. But this blasphemy of the Holy Spirit is it. It's one sin from which you can't retreat. If you're worried about what it might be, I think you can begin by going through the Bible and making a list of what it isn't, because you can find almost every conceivable sin in someone's life which the Lord does forgive. David was a liar and an adulterer and a murderer—yet God offered him forgiveness. The woman in Luke 7:47 said her sins were many, but Jesus said she had been forgiven them all. The prodigal son ran off with an inheritance and lived like the world likes to live (Luke 15). Yet when he came home, broke and without a penny to his name, he was welcomed, clothed, and blessed. Peter denied Jesus three times, yet it was Peter to whom Jesus went specifically to say everything would work out. For years, Paul's took upon himself the task of actually killing Christians. But he was forgiven even of that by God's grace. The list of forgivable sins is extensive indeed.

In John 16:8, Jesus said that when the Holy Spirit came into the world, He convicted the world of sin because they wouldn't believe in Jesus. The Holy Spirit's work is very clear: He goes to the lost and says, "Your sin requires a Savior. You've got to go to Jesus."

Here against a backdrop of rebellious, hard, angry hearts like those in this crowd, one of the things the disciples were to remember was that they had to stand with Jesus. Second, they had to remember that if the folks who were angry with Him did not respond to the Spirit's witness, they eventually would have no place to go. If they denied the Spirit's witness that says, "Go to Jesus," they had nowhere else to turn. Why is ignoring the Holy Spirit the one unforgivable sin? Because it turns people away from their one and only hope: the sacrifice of Jesus Christ at Calvary and His resurrection.

The Bible says as believers we can grieve the Holy Spirit (Eph. 4:30). We can even quench Him (1 Thess. 5:19). But we can't blaspheme Him if we've given Jesus our lives. That part of His work has been accomplished in us. So while we're out there being a witness for the Lord and confessing Him before people, we should remember that the people listening to us are hearing the only answer they'll ever get. It's a serious matter. They can't go anywhere else and if they turn from Jesus they now have no hope at all.

> "Now when they bring you to the synagogues and magistrates and authorities, do not worry about how or what you should answer, or what you should say. For the Holy Spirit will teach you in that very hour what you ought to say."
>
> —Luke 12:11–12

Jesus told His disciples that if they got in trouble for their witness, the Holy Spirit would enable them to speak for Him even in their distress. What a great promise! In fact, He reiterated it in Luke 21:12–15 when He talked about how difficult life would be in the last days. That doesn't mean believers will get off the hook altogether, but that they'll be able to speak properly and boldly in their witness, even under great duress. Stephen did that, yet he was stoned. So did Paul—before he was beheaded.

I don't care about dying here. I just want to hear, "Well done. High five!" when I get to heaven.

Jesus doesn't have any Secret Service agents. We're all here out in the open. "Are you with Me or not?" He asks. I think our culture needs to see Christians who aren't ashamed of Him. I don't want Him to be ashamed of me. He already has plenty of reasons to be—I don't want to add to the list! His grace makes me acceptable and will you as well.

Chapter 79

I WANT IT! I WANT IT!

Luke 12:13–21

As Jesus taught His disciples a number of ministry lessons in the context of the pushing and shoving that surrounded them, He was interrupted by two men in the crowd. But rather than being upset by the interruption, Jesus turned it into a lesson for the disciples as well as those listening to Him.

> Then one from the crowd said to Him, "Teacher, tell my brother to divide the inheritance with me." But He said to him, "Man, who made Me a judge or an arbitrator over you?"
>
> —Luke 12:13–14

There is plenty of evidence to show that first-century rabbis often were called on to settle family disputes. But Jesus didn't want any part of that. In fact, rather than dealing with the argument, He dealt with what motivated it. He used the word *man*—which, in the culture of the day, would have been equivalent to saying, "Who are you?" If the first lesson to His disciples in the crowd was about hypocrisy, and the other was about boldness and being all in, this one was all about covetousness.

> And He said to them, "Take heed and beware of covetousness."
>
> —Luke 12:15

In verse 1, talking about hypocrisy Jesus said, "Beware." Here He added, "Take heed" to the warning—which makes it a more serious injunction, because the translated word means "to be on your guard constantly." Covetousness is a very subtle enemy. We should stand guard against it because it can sneak in and ruin our lives.

The word *covetousness* means "a yearning for more." It is not a good word in the Bible. It is not to be a characteristic of the believer. It isn't something we should want. But being born sinful, it is invariably something we all have. The yearning for more, the "I have to have that as well," is something found in every person's heart.

In the Ten Commandments are the words: "You shall not covet your neighbor's house, wife, servant, possessions, or anything that belongs to your neighbor." One would suspect that wouldn't need to be there if it wasn't a problem, that the Lord wouldn't need to say to any of us, "Quit wanting that," if it wasn't something that often takes place in our hearts.

A disciplined and devoted Jewish man, Paul thought he was safe with God. As he went through the Law, he found himself saying, "I've done that. I can do that. I'm there. I'm fine"—until he got to the part about coveting. Then he realized even he was unable to keep the Law. He was able to control his actions, but coveting, being an attitude, was a different story altogether.

Advertising in our culture is done with a knowledge of covetousness, implying that your life will not be full until you have a certain product, that it is the missing link between you and total bliss. And even as believers we justify coveting by saying, "We're not buying anything. We're just looking." But coveting is an attitude—so "just looking" is actually coveting without the behavior.

The problem with stuff is the more you have, the more time it takes because if you buy it, you've got to use it. After all, it's ridiculous to pay for that boat if it just sits in the driveway.

Don't have time? You always can skip church. That's why Jesus says, "Knock it off! Be careful! Look out! Duck!"

When Israel was about to go into captivity, one of the indicators of their sinfulness was their lives were dominated by covetousness. Jeremiah spoke to the people in chapter 6 and said, "From the least to the greatest, from the priest on down to the prophet, everyone is driven by covetousness." Ezekiel came along and God said, "You see the people. They come and sit before you as if they're My people. They hear your words but they won't do them. Their mouths will show much love but their hearts are just pursuing their own gain. They are driven by covetousness."

There never has been a time when a generation has had more possessions than we do. In fact, the abundance of our possessions has spawned a new industry: the storage unit. Storage units didn't exist in the 1920s. People didn't need them in the 1930s. Everyone just put his or her stuff in a garage or closet.

But now we have too much stuff to fit in our garages or closets. Now we have to pay someone else to watch it—as well as assure us we'll have access to it twenty-four hours a day, seven days a week, in case we want to get to Grandma's lamp out of storage at three A.M. Coveting hordes what it has, while reaching out for more. Jesus said to the crowd and to His disciples, "Be careful of this. Be on guard against this. Watch out for this because it's a characteristic of your old life and it's going to seek to take out your new life."

"For one's life does not consist in the abundance of the things he possesses."

—Luke 12:15

Jesus gave us the definitive principle on coveting when He said, "Your life doesn't consist in the abundance of the things you possess." The big lie of the flesh and the world system is that it tells you your life does indeed consist of what you own, what you have, or what you're working to get. People such as Bill Gates and Oprah Winfrey are the success stories. Regardless of what their spiritual outlooks might be, their bank accounts say they are "successful." We also have TV shows about wealth and lifestyles, cars and stars' homes. These programs capture people's hearts and imaginations because they can't seem to get enough information—wishing they had it, coveting.

When the children of Israel entered the Promised Land, they saw the awesome power of the God they served when the walls of Jericho imploded. Even though they were told they couldn't take any of the spoil because it belonged to the Lord, a man named Achan so coveted a designer garment and some gold that he stole and hid them. Twenty verses later, Achan was dead. So was his family—and a bunch of soldiers who went out to fight the next battle without God's blessing because they weren't aware of the sinfulness in their camp. The new life in the new land came at a price. And what Achan thought was his gain was actually his ruin (Josh. 6–7).

We've gone so far in trying to protect our covetous hearts that some churches have developed doctrines that teach if you have a lot and demand of God a lot, you're more faithful than others. You just need to name it and then claim it, these churches say—believe it and receive it. But this is nothing more than a lie designed to make covetousness seem spiritual. Jesus cleared up all the confusion when He said, "Your life doesn't consist of what you have."

According to the Bible, Solomon had more possessions than anyone who ever lived (Eccles. 2). There wasn't one thing he couldn't afford—and yet by the time he wrote the book of Ecclesiastes, looking at life from God's perspective, he said, "I know God will give wisdom and the knowledge and joy of the Lord to someone who is good in His sight, while to the sinner He will give the job of working to gather and collect so someone else may have it" (Eccles. 2:26). The frustration of the lost is their lives consist of coveting, or getting more and more without satisfaction. But those who love the Lord get joy, wisdom, and peace and are truly satisfied, for their lives do not consist of what they own but of Who they know.

It's relatively easy to read Jesus' words. Living them out, however, is an entirely different matter because we constantly are faced with the lust for gain. Through the illustration that follows, Jesus told us the reason we fall for covetousness is we forget our lives are spiritual, not temporal. The world's philosophy is, "If only . . . if only I had a new house, a new car, a new wife, or new kids, then I'd be happy. Then I'd be satisfied. Then I'd be content." But you never will be content in those things. You never will be satisfied with those things because Jesus said, "Drink of this water and you will thirst again."

After thirty years as a Christian, Paul said in Philippians 4:11, "I've learned in everything to be content. I've learned to be abased. I know how to abound. I can do all things through Christ who strengthens me." Paul's contentment had nothing to do with what he had or didn't have. His peace came from his relationship with God and God's promises to him.

So the writer to the Hebrews wrote in chapter 13:5, "Let your conduct be without covetousness. Be content with the things you have." And the very next part of the verse says, "Know this: He'll never leave you or forsake you." In other words, we can rest because the Lord isn't going anywhere, He will always be with us. Now that's living!

Jesus was interrupted—but He used the interruption to give the disciples a revolutionary principle and warning about life. He then gave an illustration to drive home the principle.

> Then He spoke a parable to them, saying: "The ground of a certain rich man yielded plentifully."
>
> —Luke 12:16

Notice that the man in the story was already rich. His barns were already full. But he had to have more—one more year, one more crop, one more endeavor.

> "And he thought within himself, saying, 'What shall I do, since I have no room to store my crops?' So he said, 'I will do this: I will pull down my barns and build greater, and there I will store all my crops and my goods. And I will say to my soul, "Soul, you have many goods laid up for many years; take your ease; eat, drink, and be merry."'"
>
> —Luke 12:17–19

Along with the cares and anxiety of how to handle all he had, this man also had a false sense of security. He thought he'd retire with ease and enjoy his latter years. He thought he was set for life. But that's a far cry from Jesus' instruction to pray. "Give us this day our daily bread," isn't it? In Greek, the rich man used the word *I* eighteen times and the word *my* four times. This man was all about himself. But he was out of touch with reality because although he had enough to last for years, what he didn't have was the assurance that he would last another day.

James wrote in chapter 4:13, "Come now those of you who say, 'Today or tomorrow we're going to do such and such a thing.' How do you know you're going to make it to tomorrow? What is life? It's like a vapor. It vanishes away. You ought to be saying, 'If the Lord wills.'" But the rich man had no time for that. There were barns to tear down and rebuild, and crops to sow and reap.

Notice that this fellow never acknowledged God's blessings or sought His will. As a result, Jesus called him a fool:

"But God said to him, 'Fool! This night your soul will be required of you; then whose will those things be which you have provided?'"

—Luke 12:20

"Tonight you're going to die," God said. "Then who will get what you've gathered together?" Doubtless it would be someone like the man in the crowd who had interrupted him, fighting over the inheritance who had asked the question in the first place. On the same day this man planned his comfort, God planned his demise because our destiny isn't in our hands—it's in God's.

In Psalm 39:4, David wrote, "Lord, make me to know my end. Make me to measure my days that I might know how frail I am, that my age is as nothing before You, that my life is at best a vapor and a shadow."

"So is he who lays up treasure for himself and is not rich toward God."

—Luke 12:21

There is a deception about covetousness and a foolishness that is bound in all people's hearts—but from which we, as believers, can be delivered. Life must be rich toward God. If we value Him more than anything else, we'll spend our labor on that which truly will satisfy. We'll put first things first. We'll store up treasures in heaven where the Lord will hold them.

Don't be rich toward yourself. Be rich toward God. Beware of covetousness. Take heed. It lurks in the dark, looking for victims. Your life isn't defined by what you own but by Who owns you. It's a warning well worth your attention in these covetous last days.

Chapter 80

DISCIPLES DON'T WORRY

Luke 12:22–34

When Jesus was interrupted with a question about the division of an inheritance, He told the story of a foolish rich man whose only concern was his wealth. Attached to that teaching came the other side of the coin. That is, if riches and a need for bigger barns aren't a problem, then maybe worry about the lack of them is. But I think if we look at what Jesus said to the disciples in this big crowd and write out the four or five principles He presents, we can pursue Him in faith, and as believers live worry-free. That kind of living is God's desire for us just as much as parents don't want their kids worrying, for they will take care of them.

> Then He said to His disciples, "Therefore, I say to you, do not worry about your life, what you will eat, nor about the body, what you will put on. Life is more than food, and the body is more than clothing."
>
> —Luke 12:22–23

The word *therefore* attaches this teaching to the study on covetousness that preceded it. The word *worry* is an Anglo-Saxon word that originally meant "to strangle." The word itself tells us worry can have a stranglehold on our lives. So the first principle Jesus gave was that worry is destructive. For the disciples, a constant concern about this life would have slowed them down in their service to Him. That is why Jesus began by saying, "Don't let worry about the day-to-day events of life strangle you."

Within the context of first-century life, most of the disciples came from agrarian societies where a lot of time was devoted simply to existing. If you didn't plant the seed and water and weed it, you wouldn't have much to eat in the year to come. If you didn't shear the sheep and spin the wool and make clothing, you would be cold come winter. That's not the case today. We go to the market and our greatest concern is the expiration date. As for clothes, we just wait for a sale.

Food and clothing constantly would have been on these disciples' minds—yet Jesus said to them what He says to us: "Worry strangles your life." Worry is interesting, because while it's easy for us to trust the Lord with all of eternity, it seems harder for us to trust Him with tomorrow's needs. Worry, as we discover, is not only destructive but deceptive for, as Psalm 127:2 tells us, it is worthless to get up early and go to bed late just to eat the bread of sorrows—going through life worrying from one day to the next how things are going to go.

To substantiate His point, Jesus illustrated God's provision of both food and clothing with nature itself:

> "Consider the ravens . . . ."
>
> —Luke 12:24

The word *consider* in Greek means to stop and examine closely, to study very carefully, and to meditate on for a while. So stop and consider . . .

> ". . . for they neither sow nor reap, which have neither storehouse nor barn; and God feeds them. Of how much more value are you than the birds?"
>
> —Luke 12:24

Worry is destructive because it chokes those who engage in it. It's deceptive because it begins to replace what real life is all about. Also, it blinds us to the fact that we have a God who cares for us and values us. Ravens, or crows, are everywhere. These squawking birds don't know anything about farming. They don't make plans. They don't sow. They don't reap. They don't store things. Their existence is dependent solely on God's care. And because they can't carry the next meal with them, they spend most of their time concerned about food. They're much harder to feed than we are because we can stock the refrigerator or pack a lunch. But these ravens have to eat every three hours. Anything but a blessing, they're noisy and, because they are scavengers, they are even on the list of unclean animals in Leviticus 11. Yet the Lord takes care of them.

Jesus isn't suggesting we don't work—only that we don't worry. The birds have to go out and look for food, but they're not concerned. They're able to rest in God's provision. Jesus said, "Consider the birds. Now consider yourselves. You're much more valuable than the raven. So do your part—but rest. Work hard—but quit fretting and worrying. God is faithful."

The next time you start worrying, look out the window for a bird and see if any of those noisy black crows have gray feathers.

> "And which of you by worrying can add one cubit to his stature? If you then are not able to do the least, why are you anxious for the rest?"
>
> —Luke 12:25–26

Worry is destructive and deceptive. It blinds us—and it is powerless. Have you ever heard people say, "I'm not worrying. I'm just concerned" as they try to give worry a good spin? The problem is, there's no good spin for worry in the Bible. We cannot accomplish anything through worry. Jesus used the Greek word here for *stature*, which means "to increase in measure." It could apply to age or height. In other words, Jesus asked His disciples how many had added a day to his life or an inch to his height through worry—the implication being that if we can't, then worry is a powerless worthless practice.

> "Consider the lilies, how they grow; they neither toil nor spin; and yet I say to you, even Solomon in all his glory was not arrayed like one of these. If then God so clothes the grass, which today is in the field and tomorrow is thrown into the oven, how much more will He clothe you, O you of little faith?"
> —Luke 12:27–28

The lilies are the little anemone flowers found all over Israel in the spring. When they're in bloom, it's like the hills are covered with beautiful blankets. But they only last about two weeks. Jesus told His disciples to consider how these flowers grow. They don't work hard. In fact, they don't do anything. They grow because God's hand is on the fields. And without worry or concern, they become the fields' ornament. By comparison, Solomon, the wealthiest man who ever lived and could have designed anything he desired, didn't look nearly as good as the temporary lilies.

Consider the flowers. Then consider yourself. The flowers last a few days. We last for eternity. As He did with the birds, Jesus again argued from the lesser to the greater. And we are greater in both cases.

Worry is a self-declared lack of trust in God. Lacking trust in His Word, in His promises, in His provision, and in His capacity, we worry. "I believe, but help my unbelief," said the father in Mark 9:24 who brought his son to the disciples to be healed. He was willing to admit he had great doubts, although he had great desire to see God work. We excuse our worry by calling it wisdom, love, or prudence. Here Jesus called it a lack of faith. Therefore, next time you're tempted to say you're worried about something, say instead that you're faithless and see if it doesn't change the way you look at things.

> "And do not seek what you should eat or what you should drink, nor have an anxious mind. For all these things the nations of the world seek after, and your Father knows that you need these things."
> —Luke 12:29–30

The Lord doesn't want us worrying. He doesn't want us struggling. We have to confront the worry lie with the truth of God's care. Worry is absolutely inconsistent for us as Christians. It's a characteristic only of unbelievers because their lives are only about this life and have nothing to do with God.

In verses 24 and 28, Jesus said God provides for the birds and the flowers. But He said it is our Father in heaven who provides for us. We have a heavenly Father who knows our needs. How can we be a witness to the world about God's care if we're always torn apart with concern, fear, and worry? Worry makes us act like unbelievers. But we're different, aren't we?

Every time you begin to worry, say to yourself, "It's destructive. It's deceptive. It's a lack of faith. It doesn't accomplish anything. God knows my needs. He takes care of the flowers, and that crow's still alive. So I'll be all right. I'm not like the world. I have a Father in heaven." If you have to tell yourself that five hundred times a day, start there. Maybe next year, it will only be two hundred times a day. Learn it well!

> "But seek the kingdom of God, and all these things shall be added to you."
> —Luke 12:31

When the Jews went from Babylon to Jerusalem to rebuild the temple, they had barely began before opposition and lack of interest stopped the project. For twenty years, although they were back in the land, they had no place to worship. So God sent Zechariah and Haggai to say to the people, "Do you guys think it's time for you to be living in your paneled houses while the temple of the Lord lies in ruin? You should consider your ways. Think about how your life has been going since that's been your priority. You've sown much but only a little crop comes up. You eat but you're never full. You drink but you're not satisfied. You clothe yourself but you're never warm. You earn wages but they seem to go into pockets with holes in them. Here's what you should do: go to the mountains, get some wood, and come and build the temple, the place of fellowship. Rather than running to your own house, run to glorify Me. You're having problems because I've blown on the things you've brought home. I've told the field not to grow, I've kept the rain from falling, and I've kept you from being blessed, because you've kept yourself from Me. So come and serve Me and eat your bread and labor in peace with joy" (Hag. 1:3–11).

Seek the kingdom first. This doesn't mean quit working—it means quit worrying. It's impossible to quit worrying if we're not convinced God is telling us the truth. But if we know He is, it's just a matter of being reminded.

> "Do not fear, little flock, for it is your Father's good pleasure to give you the kingdom."
> —Luke 12:32

The words *do not fear* indicate to me that trying to live without worry is hard. But we need to remember God's heart—His joy and His pleasure are to give us the kingdom and bless our lives. To convince us of this, Jesus used every comparison possible to paint the picture: a flock with a shepherd, a father with a child, and a king with his kingdom. Most parents' greatest joy is to bless their kids. That's God's heart. So for us to worry is to deny He loves us.

"Sell what you have and give alms; provide yourselves money bags which do not grow old, a treasure in the heavens that does not fail, where no thief approaches nor moth destroys."

—Luke 12:33

If we really believe God will meet our needs, we can divest ourselves of that which usually grips people's hearts and invest in eternal things because the greatest investment we'll ever make is in God's work. In verse 32, Jesus said God delights in giving to us. In verse 33, He said God delights in our giving to those in need and to the work of the Lord. The fruit of that kind of life is moth-proof and burglar-proof. The dividends are postponed—but the investment is sure. It's the best interest rate we'll ever find. Yet it's a matter of faith.

"For where your treasure is, there your heart will be also."

—Luke 12:34

Heart and treasure always go together. Your energy, pursuits, care, and thoughts always will follow your heart. If your treasure is in the cares of the world, peace will get choked out of your life. But if your treasure is in the Lord, His Word, and His pursuits, that's where your heart will be as well. If you're preoccupied with God's Word, you can't be preoccupied with worldly existence. Your heart is either set on perishables or on that which doesn't perish. It's either in heaven or the bank. It's either in the retirement fund or on the mission field.

Worry and faith both have fruit: don't reap the fruit that worry brings.

Chapter 81

SPIRITUALLY PREOCCUPIED

Luke 12:35–48

In the last year of Jesus' ministry, the crowds of followers had grown enormous. The religious leaders however, had never been so angry. No longer was there only talk of killing Jesus, but specific plans were being made as to how and when. Therefore, along with discovering His plans were different from theirs, the disciples were learning that to follow Him would require tremendous trust and a conviction He was right, for their could be a price to pay for associating with Him.

So Jesus here taught them about where their eyes should be focused. Christians should be spiritually preoccupied with the coming of the Lord, for that will keep us in line!

> "Let your waist be girded and your lamps burning . . . ."
>
> —Luke 12:35

In Jesus' day, and still in the Middle East today, many men wore long, flowing white robes. While this is good for keeping cool, it's not so good for working or moving about in a hurry. So men wore belts or sashes to pull up their robes for greater mobility. *Girding your waist* meant you were ready to move out. It was an act of being prepared. After warning them about hypocrisy, covetousness, and worry, Jesus said to His disciples, "Here's how you should live: be ready to go."

In light of all of the previous verses about wealth and daily cares, Jesus said to His disciples, to the church, and to you and me, "You should have an eye that is looking up and a heart that's ready to go." Not only that, but your lamp should be burning. The lamp in Scripture speaks both of God's Word as a light to our path and of our witness to the world. "Let your light so shine that men will glorify God," Jesus said to His disciples. Follow the light of God's Word. Be an example in the world. And be ready to take off when the Lord is ready to take you home.

> ". . . and you yourselves be like men who wait for their master, when he will return from the wedding, that when he comes and knocks they may open to him immediately."
>
> —Luke 12:36

In the first century, Hebrew weddings lasted many days. So the time of the master's return from the festivities was uncertain. Yet these were faithful servants who waited for him. They didn't know when he would be coming but they were ready when he did. If it was late, they were clothed for action. The house lights were on. And that's the way the church ought to be living its life in the world. We ought to be caught up not with the cares of this world, the gathering of riches, or worrying about what we don't have. We ought to be caught up with waiting to be caught up by our Master Jesus.

These are remarkable servants. They don't give in to fatigue and say, "It's two A.M. He's not here. I'm beat. He can make his own food." No. They weren't discouraged. They weren't in despair. They just wanted to be ready to serve him. Jesus said to His disciples, "This is how you should wait—not passively trying to survive, but actively and continually waiting upon God."

Thirty years down the road, Paul wrote in Philippians 3:20, "Our citizenship is in heaven. That's where we're looking with great joy for the coming of our Lord Jesus." That's what we as Christians do. And notice that when He comes, we're immediately going to respond. When the rapture of the church takes place and the trumpet sounds, we've got to go. There's no fifteen-minute warning. The stars of the universe are not going to blink on and off like houselights at the end of intermission. We're going to have to be ready, or we're not ready. We'll either go in—or be left out.

> "Blessed are those servants whom the master, when he comes, will find watching. Assuredly, I say to you that he will gird himself and have them sit down to eat, and will come and serve them."
>
> —Luke 12:37

If we want to have blessed lives, we should be watching for the Lord. And the great surprise is, when the Lord comes, we're going to sit down and He's going to serve us. In Luke 22:27, Jesus said to the disciples, "Whom do you think is greater—the one who sits at the table or the one who serves? Of course he who sits at the table. But I didn't come to be served. I came to serve. You do the same."

Eight or nine months later, in John 13, Jesus will take a bucket and begin to wash His disciples' feet. "I have given you an example," He will declare. "Now serve as I have served you." But the promise is that one day in heaven we ourselves will be served and blessed.

> "And if he should come in the second watch, or come in the third watch, and find them so, blessed are those servants."
>
> —Luke 12:38

The Lord doesn't come when we expect Him, does He? I thought I'd never see thirty before His return. Now I can't remember thirty! We've got to be ever-ready, like the battery. Hebrew time was broken into three watches: six P.M. to ten P.M., ten P.M. to two A.M., and the third watch from two A.M. to six A.M. Jesus' point was we can watch for a little while, but it's easy to get tired of waiting. I get tired of waiting for just about everything, don't you?

Second watch, third watch—it seems to get later and later. I've seen Christians lose hope, and their excitement for the Lord's return fading. The perspective to get out there and share their faith is gone. They settle in, or sometimes go back to the ways of the world, and give up altogether.

Paul wrote in Galatians 6:9, "Don't grow weary in well doing. In the end, you're going to reap if you don't faint." We do grow weary—but the blessed ones are those who stick with it.

In verse 37, Jesus said we're blessed if we're watching. Here in verse 38, He said we're blessed if we stick with it no matter how long it takes.

> "But know this, that if the master of the house had known what hour the thief would come, he would have watched and not allowed his house to be broken into. Therefore you also be ready, for the Son of Man is coming at an hour you do not expect."
>
> —Luke 12:39–40

In verses 39 and 40, Jesus used an example found in several places in the Gospel: the comparison of a bad situation with a good one. The bad situation is that of being robbed. Crooks never call ahead. They don't make an appointment. They just steal your stuff when you least expect them. Thieves prey on surprise and unpreparedness—and it works for them. But the one who is robbed suffers loss.

By comparing this to His coming, Jesus said, "I don't want you to be caught by surprise, so be ready." Those who look for the Lord are blessed; those who aren't watching for Him will suffer loss—and the loss will be eternal.

Jesus' point in verse 40 is that since we cannot know in which watch He will come, our only recourse is always to be ready. Are you ready today? How many loose ends do you have to tie up? How many calls would you have to make to share quickly with those you love but haven't spoken to? How many things should you have taken care of, but you put off because the Lord wasn't coming? It's been thirty years—be ready!

People do countless things to prepare for the future. They eat right to live longer, exercise to feel better, and put money away to retire sooner. We do a hundred things for temporary gain but very little for eternity. And yet that's where our investment should be.

We ought to get up in the morning, saying, "I wonder if it's today." That's the way the Lord wants us to live, because the tendency is to forget and lose sight, to grow weary and quit serving, and to let the light grow dim.

> Then Peter said to Him, "Lord, do You speak this parable only to us, or to all people?" And the Lord said, "Who then is that faithful and wise steward, whom

his master will make ruler over his household, to give them their portion of food in due season? Blessed is that servant whom his master will find so doing when he comes. Truly, I say to you that he will make him ruler over all that he has."

—Luke 12:41–44

When Peter asked if this instruction was specific to the disciples or if it applied to everyone, Jesus said, "It applies to you—and to everyone else." Blessed are those who watch. Blessed are those who continue to watch, even though the hour is late and He seems delayed. And blessed are those who do. Who is the faithful servant? It's the one who takes care of things in the master's house until the master returns.

For Peter, his calling was to be a pastor and an evangelist. He would do that faithfully for years to come. I don't know what your calling from the Lord might be. But wherever God calls you, go serve Him faithfully, for then you will find blessing as you wait. No one is called to sit and wait. There is no such thing as the ministry of doing nothing.

Who is the faithful servant? The one who ministers to God's people, the one who takes care of the household, and the one who serves from his heart—all because he loves the Lord as He waits for Him to return.

The problem for many employers is their employees only work when they're being watched. When the cat's away, the mice play. Yet the unexpected coming of the master of the house will verify which servants are faithful. As faithful servants our reward will be that we'll be given even more to do to serve our God in the Kingdom Age. That is, God will entrust us even more in the future because we were faithful with what He gave us here and now as we waited, not knowing when He would come for us.

Years later, Peter wrote two rather long letters to the church at large, which was scattered by persecution. One of the things he wrote in the fifth chapter of his first letter was, "I want to exhort you, elders. I also am an elder. I've been a witness for Jesus' suffering. I've been a partaker of the glory that's coming. You have to be sure you shepherd the flock of God, but do it as overseers, not out of compulsion. Do it willingly because the chief Shepherd is coming and He's bringing a crown of glory with Him for you that won't fade away." After asking Jesus whether His parable applied only to the apostles, Peter obviously understood it was meant for everyone.

As you're waiting, are you serving the Lord? Are you using the gifts God has given you? Are you plugged in somewhere, offering benefit to God's people and bringing God's Word to the world? None of us are called to stagnate. Waiting is doing. Serving and watching go together. In fact, serving will enhance our vision and outlook.

"But if that servant says in his heart, 'My master is delaying his coming,' and begins to beat the male and female servants, and to eat and drink and be drunk, the master of that servant will come on a day when he is not looking for him, and at an hour when he is not aware, and will cut him in two and appoint him his portion with the unbelievers. And that servant who knew his master's will, and did not prepare himself or do according to his will, shall be beaten with many stripes. But he who did not know, yet committed things deserving of stripes, shall be beaten with few. For everyone to whom much is given, from him much will be required; and to whom much has been committed, of him they will ask the more."

—Luke 12:45–48

The last principle concerning waiting, watching, and doing is that the time delay between our looking for the Lord and His coming ultimately will expose the position of our heart. There will be those who hypocritically go along with the program, seeming to be devoted to the Master. But at some point, they will decide it is all for nothing, that He's not coming and that they can't wait any longer. And they will return to the life they said they had left. The godly lifestyle is set aside. They start being wicked toward people and abusive toward the saints. They fill their lives with the cares of the world and deal with their cares the way the world does. Their relationship with God and their hope in the Lord wanes and then is lost all together. For them, the immediacy of Jesus' return is gone, as is their preoccupation with the things of the Lord.

If we read Hebrews 11, where the Lord defines saving faith, we find a list of men and women from the Old Testament about whom the Lord says, "That's the kind of faith I'm looking for." After giving several examples from many loves, Paul says, "The people who speak like these are those who declare they are looking for a homeland. If they had been aware of the country they left, they might have been mindful to go back there. But they're looking for a new home and a new country. Therefore, God is not ashamed to be called their God and is preparing a city for them." True faith doesn't retreat. It goes forward. Those who continue in the walk and continue to press on are evidence of saving faith. Where else can I go once I've gone to Jesus? I can't go anywhere else. He's the only way, the only truth, and the only life. So the old apostle John wrote in (1 John 2:18–19).

Time will weed out those who are pretending to be something they're not. And Jesus said the servant who begins to discount the master's coming and move away from his waiting finds himself packaged together with the unbelievers, because true believers will wait. Peter said so in (John 6:67–6) when asked by Jesus if he and the disciples would be leaving the Lord as others had began to do.

When is Jesus coming? I don't know. But I do know we're to be waiting and looking day in and day out—and to be working as we wait. John wrote in 1 John 3, "What a blessing God has given us that we can be called God's children. It doesn't yet appear what we're going to be like, but we know when He comes, we'll be like Him because we'll see Him as He is. If you have this hope in you, you purify yourself even as the Lord is pure." If the Lord is coming, my life changes. I don't procrastinate. I don't wait to forgive someone. I witness to those who need to hear. I read my Bible. I have my lamp lit.

I want to be burning in my heart for the Lord each and every day. I want to keep my eyes upon Him, look up to Him and be found doing those things He desires of me. I want to be looking up, doing what God has called me to do. I want to be ready when He comes, don't you? He's coming for those who are ready. The believer will be ready; the unbeliever cannot be. One will find a blessed hope in the Lord's coming. The other will feel like a thief has just broken into his house. Only what has been stolen is of eternal value.

Are you ready?

Chapter 82

GOD'S HEART AND YOURS

Luke 12:49–59

We come to the last in the series of lessons Jesus taught His disciples in the crowd. Here, at the end of Luke 12, the cross is little more than six months away. In reading the chapters that follow, it seems that the cross loomed larger in Jesus' eyes with each passing day. I think I can understand that.

> "I came to send fire on the earth, and how I wish it were already kindled!"
> —Luke 12:49

Whenever the Lord's coming is mentioned, fire is representative of God's saving work and the Holy Spirit's anointing. For the lost, God's fire speaks of His judgment to come. Therefore, whenever Jesus' coming is discussed, there is both a blessing and a judgment, salvation and loss, depending on how a person responds.

Centuries earlier, Jeremiah had become so frustrated with teaching God's Word to people who didn't listen that he determined he wouldn't say another word. In chapter 20:9, he wrote of himself, "I said I wouldn't make any more mention of God or speak any more in His name—but His Word was in my heart like a burning fire and I couldn't hold it back." Jesus came to send His fire into the world—both in judgment and salvation. But God's will certainly is that His fire might come upon lives to change them and draw them to Himself. He takes no delight in the death of the wicked.

Just six months from this point we will find 120 very new believers with tongues of fire floating over their heads sitting in Jerusalem—a one-time event but one that spoke of the very thing the Lord desired to do (Acts 2). Jesus said to these born-again saints, "Go out now to all the world and start fires. Take the Holy Spirit. Tell people who I am."

But here, looking at this large crowd, Jesus said, "I've come to make sure you might have life. I just wish it could start now."

> "But I have a baptism to be baptized with, and how distressed I am till it is accomplished!"
> —Luke 12:50

Before the fire could be poured out however, the cross would come first. And Jesus said, "Though I wish it was over, I realize what I still have to go through for it to be accomplished." I don't doubt that the agony of the cross and the price for the fire Jesus longed to have poured out was a constant thought on His mind. It wasn't an easy road to walk. But it was the reason He came. Verse 49 was the reason. Verse 50 was the price. It was inevitable. It was expected and planned for. It would be accomplished. People would be saved. Fire would be sent. The Holy Spirit would be poured out. But the cost was enormous and the suffering was extremely personal.

"I am distressed," Jesus said. That word in Greek means "to be pressed from both sides." When Paul wrote to the Philippians in chapter 1, he said, "I don't know whether I'd rather be here or with the Lord. I'm hard-pressed between the two. I have a desire to leave here and be with Christ. That would be far better for me. But for me to stay here would be better for you. I'm pressed in two directions." So was Jesus. He wanted the Holy Spirit's fire to be poured out into the world. But to come to that would require His sacrifice and death upon the cross.

In chapter 12:2, the writer of Hebrews said it was for the joy set before Him that Jesus endured the cross, even though He despised the shame. What drove Jesus? According to Hebrews, it was His love for us. That is, whenever *Maybe this isn't such a good idea* crossed His mind, it was of us that He was reminded—and then the cross became a great idea. Hard? Yes. Horrible? Certainly. But that's why He came. At noon on the day of Jesus' crucifixion, darkness covered the earth as God turned His back on His Son. That's what our sin would have done to us permanently—it would have kept us from God forever. Jesus came to keep us from that fate worse than death.

> "Do you suppose I came to give peace on earth?"
>
> —Luke 12:51

I'm sure my answer to Jesus' question would have been yes. In fact, I think the shepherds and angels sang about it in Luke 2:10. And seven hundred years earlier, didn't Isaiah 9:6 call Jesus the Prince of Peace? Certainly, Jesus did bring peace between people and God as He removed the sin that separated them from God. He even made peace between men. But because of the Gospel's demand, there is also division that can arise as a result. We're either in Christ or we're not. We either believe in Him or we don't. We either follow Him or we refuse. It places all of us in two camps. The cross still separates today, and the division can be as sharp as it was in the crowd as Jesus spoke these words—or six months later as the religious called for His death. There are still people today crying, "Crucify Him!" while some missionaries give their lives so He might be proclaimed.

It cost Jesus everything to give His life. We shouldn't be surprised if it costs us something to follow Him.

> "I tell you, not at all, but rather division. From now on five in one house will
> be divided: three against two, and two against three. Father will be divided
> against son and son against father, mother against daughter and daughter against
> mother, mother-in-law against her daughter-in-law and daughter-in-law against
> her mother-in-law."
>
> —Luke 12:51–53

Jesus' name brings persecution. If you go to China today and preach in the street, you won't last very long. The same is true in Saudi Arabia, United Arab Emirates, Egypt, or even Jerusalem. But the area of greatest division is amongst those for whom you care the most: your family. Husbands are lost while their wives are in church praying for them. Kids who aren't walking with God break their parents' hearts. Yet this division is the very thing the Lord went through as He was to be separated from His Father.

> Then He also said to the multitudes, "Whenever you see a cloud rising out of
> the west, immediately you say, 'A shower is coming'; and so it is. And when
> you see the south wind blow, you say, 'There will be hot weather'; and there is.
> Hypocrites! You can discern the face of the sky and of the earth, but how is it
> you do not discern this time?"
>
> —Luke 12:54–56

According to what we have read, most of the people in the crowd were not there because they were hungry for the Lord, but because they were attracted to the pushing and shoving, the tumult and excitement. So Jesus contrasted their ability to predict the weather with their inability to recognize Him. In Israel, weather forecasting is relatively easy, because if the wind is westerly from the Mediterranean it always means rain, and if it's from the Sinai or out of the desert, it always will be hot. "You're good at figuring out the weather, but you're not at all aware of the days in which you live," Jesus said to the crowd, because they had failed to understand the many signs and prophecies God had given them about His coming for generations past.

Now redemption stood knocking at the door and they missed it. Jesus called them hypocrites because they were pretending to be spiritual when, in reality, their hearts were spiritually dull and blind to the obvious.

Who else had spoken like Jesus? Who else had been so powerful? Who else had been so decisive? Even the Romans acknowledged that He spoke with authority. Who else had opened the eyes of the blind? And hadn't Isaiah 61:1–2 said that's what the Messiah would do? Jesus had healed the sick, raised the dead, and delivered people from the clutches of hell. Daniel had written an extensive prophecy in chapter 9:23–27 that said the Messiah would appear in Jerusalem just a few months to the day from when Jesus spoke these words. Micah 5:2 said He would be born in Bethlehem. Zechariah 9:9 said He would ride into Jerusalem on a donkey. As far back as Genesis 49:10, a prophecy was given that the scepter, or power of government, would not depart from Judah's hand until the Messiah came. It had only been a few years earlier that the Romans had taken the right of self-determination away from the Jews. At that point, the rabbis began to weep that God's promise through Jacob had failed. But the only failure was their failure to realize that standing in their midst was the Messiah Himself.

More than three hundred prophecies would be fulfilled—yet the people in the crowds weren't putting two and two together.

"Why are you missing it?" Jesus asked. And I suspect He would say the same thing to our generation. We can track asteroids and split atoms, we can put humans in space and use a telescope to see Neptune, but we can't see the days in which we live. We can see the stars—we just can't get to heaven. We have scholars meeting to determine which parts of the Bible are inspired and which are not. We have legislators meeting in city government to be sure we remove any representation of the God of the universe from our public life. Jesus expected those in His generation to heed the signs of the times. I think He expects the same from ours.

> "Yes, and why, even of yourselves, do you not judge what is right? When you go with your adversary to the magistrate, make every effort along the way to settle with him, lest he drag you to the judge, the judge deliver you to the officer, and the officer throw you into prison. I tell you, you shall not depart from there till you have paid the very last mite."
>
> —Luke 12:57–59

To illustrate the necessity and urgency of making a decision for Him based on the evidence, Jesus told the story of two people going to court, one who knew he was guilty. His advice was: Settle out of court before the evidence is heard, because once it's heard, you're cooked. You have no chance. So be honest with yourself. Fix it before it's too late. It will cost you—but not nearly as much as if you saw your case through to the end, knowing you are guilty.

The same thing holds true with Jesus in a spiritual sense. Realize you are guilty and that your case is hopeless. Get right with God through faith in His Son before it's too late, because if you wait, you'll have a price to pay you can't afford.

The Roman army was set to march into Jerusalem soon after this and destroy it so completely that there would not be one stone left upon another. But as Jesus spoke these words, there was still hope. "Are you ready? Can you read the signs? Will you judge for yourself—and then follow Me?" For us, the weather forecast says He's coming soon—but it's not too late.

Chapter 83

ETERNAL CAUSE AND EFFECT

Luke 13:1–9

Jesus had talked recently with religious leaders, fledgling disciples, and an unruly crowd. To the religious leaders, He had said, "Your hearts are filthy even though your hands clean." To the disciples, He had said, "Don't be hypocrites like these religious folks. Don't be driven by the fear of man. Determine to please God rather than man." To the crowd He had said, "Think for yourselves because if you're going to arrive in eternity without Me, you're going to have to pay what you owe. And that is a price you can't afford."

Here, in an effort to get the spotlight off of themselves, some in the crowd attempted to change the subject. Yet as always, Jesus was able to turn back to His subject: the needs for all men to be saved for all have sinned so take care of it now before it is too late (Luke 12:56–59), which is what he had been saying before He was interrupted.

> There were present at that season some who told Him about the Galileans whose blood Pilate had mingled with their sacrifices.
>
> —Luke 13:1

We don't have a biblical account of this situation other than what we read here. Therefore, without Jesus' response, we might have been hard-pressed to figure out the point these men were trying to make. But, because of all we are told in the four verses that follow, we can put two and two together fairly easily.

The Galileans were Jews who lived in the north, above Samaria. To the southern-dwelling Jews, they were seen as rural hicks, uneducated fishermen, and backward farmers. Jews in the north never got along well with the intellectual, industrial communities to the south. In this particular incident, northern Jews, or Galileans, had come to offer sacrifice in Jerusalem. As they did, Pilate's soldiers killed them, their blood mingling with the sacrifices they were making. We aren't told whether this was due to some kind of rebellion or disturbance, or simply the wickedness of Rome. But Jesus' answer tells us the implication of the question was that some there believed that because they were Galileans, their deaths were probably justified.

And Jesus answered and said to them, "Do you suppose that these Galileans were worse sinners than all other Galileans, because they suffered such things? I tell you, no; but unless you repent you will all likewise perish."

—Luke 13:2–3

There is a common fallacy among people that somehow God has a way of getting even and He does it through tragedy. In this way, man attempts to connect personal suffering with personal sin. One of the best examples of this might be the question the disciples asked in John 9 concerning the fellow who was born blind. "Who sinned?" they asked. "This man or his parents?"

It is the same line of reasoning Job's buddies used to try to explain to him why he was suffering so much, why his children had been killed, why he had a disease he couldn't get rid of, and why his wife had turned on him. Yet if we read through the book of Job, about the only thing we can link to Job's suffering is his godliness, because hadn't it all began with God asking Satan if he ever had seen a man as faithful as Job?

So here Jesus asked, "Is that really what you think? Do you really suppose that those men died as evidence of God's displeasure with them, that He summoned them all so He summarily could slay them?"

The Bible does say that tragedy and suffering can be the result of sin. To the paralytic Jesus healed, He said, "Don't sin anymore," which seemed to imply that his suffering might very well have been sin-related. There are certainly things we can do to make life difficult. If we violate spiritual laws and continue to set them aside, we can suffer greatly by the choices we make. But tragedy and personal sin do not always have a link. So Jesus redirected attention to the one link that always can be made: that of rejecting Him and spending eternity without Him.

People mistakenly think God is a vindictive taskmaster waiting to see who will sin so He can bring down the proverbial hammer on them. Yet as we go through Scripture, we discover that the folks who seemed to suffer the most were oftentimes the godliest. In Psalm 73:1–2, Asaph said, "I'm quitting. I see how the wicked prosper. They curse God and yet they're blessed. They mistreat others and yet they're blessed. When they get old, they're not sick a day in their lives and they die in their sleep. Nothing ever goes wrong for them. This isn't fair. My feet almost slipped until I considered where they were headed. Then I realized life is short compared to forever."

Good fortune is no proof of God's favor. Faith in Jesus is. I read of the example of a couple sent to Papua New Guinea many years ago. They were committed to translating the New Testament into a tribal language and had been working for months along with their two daughters. At three in the afternoon one day, they sat down to rest next to a river where they were camping when the side of a mountain broke loose and killed them all in about thirty seconds. In a world full of vacant hillsides, in a world full of people whom we might have liked to see under the mountain instead, and in a world with far too few missionaries, God took some really good people that afternoon. Was it because of their sin? Jesus said it wasn't. But if God based it on who was ready, He took the right people. They were ready indeed.

According to what Jesus said at the end of Luke 12:58–59, personal sin has a court date. So settle out of court. Get to Jesus before the Judge metes out judgment against you. Here the crowd, lacking understanding, tried to divert personal responsibility and passed judgment on those who had suffered greatly. Jesus, however, told these opponents of His message that direct links cannot be made between suffering in this life and personal sin. There is, however, a direct link between what we choose to do with Jesus and where we'll spend eternity.

> "Or those eighteen on whom the tower in Siloam fell and killed them, do you think that they were worse sinners than all other men who dwelt in Jerusalem? I tell you, no . . . ."
>
> —Luke 13:4–5

Jesus strengthened the impact of His point by picking something from the headlines they all knew about. Siloam was just outside Jerusalem. There, a tower had toppled over and killed eighteen people who were in the wrong place at the wrong time. The problem was, these weren't Galileans. These were Jews—southern-dwelling, Jerusalem Jews. They weren't killed by violence but by an accident. "Does your same theory apply to them?" Jesus asked. "Did they deserve what they got?"

In verse 2, He had used a word for sinner that meant "to miss the mark." Here in verse 4, He used a word for sinner that spoke of someone who was in debt and hadn't made payments. His point was, "Do you think God gathered them all together under that tower to receive His payment for their wickedness?" And His answer is the same: No.

> ". . . but unless you repent, you will all likewise perish."
>
> —Luke 13:5

I believe repentance is one of the missing links in what is passed off as preaching today. Repentance is comprised of many things—but it is primarily known by what it is not. Repentance is not penitence or sorrow. It may be accompanied by sorrow but isn't defined by it. Most people who get caught are penitent. Most people in jail tell you they're sorry. But they're sorry mostly for getting caught.

Repentance isn't penitence. Neither is it penance. Some teach that there needs to be suffering for the Lord to forgive and that self-loathing is an appropriate response. But the Bible doesn't ask for that. In fact, the wages of sin being death, self-loathing doesn't go nearly far enough. Neither is repentance reformation. Many people want to turn over a new leaf and promise to change. They make resolutions and set self-imposed standards. But plenty of people seeking to reform their lives never repent.

The word *repentance* simply means "to turn around." When it is applied to our sin and the Lord, it requires me to stop going my way and start going God's way. I stop trusting myself and start trusting Him. I stop doing what I want and start doing what He wants. I stop being the lord of my life and let Him become the Lord of my life instead.

In verse 3, the word *repent* is a present imperative tense verb. That means it is to be done all the time. In verse 5, it is an aorist tense verb, which means it is a one-time action with ongoing consequence. Put the two together and we can conclude that we ought to know the day we initially repented and turned to the Lord—but we also must make repentance part of each day because there's always a tendency to want to "unrepent" or return to our old way of life where we sat upon the throne.

> He also spoke this parable: "A certain man had a fig tree planted in his vineyard, and he came seeking fruit on it and found none. Then he said to the keeper of his vineyard, 'Look, for three years I have come seeking fruit on this fig tree and find none. Cut it down; why does it use up the ground?' But he answered and said to him, 'Sir, let it alone this year also, until I dig around it and fertilize it. And if it bears fruit, well. But if not, after that you can cut it down.'"
>
> —Luke 13:6–9

No doubt the primary application of this parable was to the nation of Israel, because throughout prophecy Israel was represented both as a fig tree and as a vineyard. For three years Jesus had been coming to His own people, but they hadn't received Him. Yet God's grace is to wait, to be patient.

I think this parable can't be limited to Israel alone, however, because God wants fruit from every life. "Herein is My Father glorified," Jesus said in John 15:8, "that you bear much fruit."

The crowd had thought God dealt with sinners through tragedy, violence, and bad luck. "Not so," Jesus said. God is patient and longsuffering—but when judgment falls, it will be final. Therefore, while you have the chance, turn and come to Him for life!

Chapter 84

STRAIGHTENED ON THE SABBATH

Luke 13:10–21

Jesus had been teaching His disciples many lessons in the crowd—lessons about hypocrisy, the fear of people, and worry; about watching and waiting; and about repentance. Here we move away from the crowd and back to the road as Jesus continued to minister to His disciples. The day of His death was a mere 6 months away.

Some of these events took place in the area of Perea, or present-day Jordan. In Jesus' day, Perea consisted of the villages on the east side of the Jordan River, made up of both Jewish and Gentile communities. When you find Jesus being confronted in Perea, it's usually by religious leaders who had traveled from Jerusalem, fifty or sixty miles away.

In Jesus' first appearance in a Jewish synagogue during His public ministry, He had read the promise from Isaiah 61:1–2 that the Messiah would open the eyes of the blind and set the captives free. Here, in His last appearance in a synagogue in the Gospel accounts, He does the very thing He said He had come to do: set free one who had been held captive by her infirmity for nearly two decades.

> Now He was teaching in one of the synagogues on the Sabbath. And behold,
> there was a woman who had a spirit of infirmity eighteen years, and was bent
> over and could in no way raise herself up.
>
> —Luke 13:10–11

I love the Greek word for "behold." It means, "Stop whatever you're doing and look at this!" As Jesus was teaching in the synagogue, a woman walked in late to the service who was so bent over that she was unable to straighten up. The medical terms Luke used to describe her condition indicate that, along with being outwardly deformed, she was in tremendous pain. Yet here she was, coming to worship God nonetheless.

Verse11 tells us her condition was the result of a spirit of infirmity. In other words, it was caused by a demon. In verse 16, Jesus confirmed this by saying she was bound by the Devil. There are times when the enemy's influence brings sickness to bear on a life. Most sickness, however, is simply the result of sin in general.

There are very few things that get better with time—and our bodies aren't one of them. Sickness happens. It's part of dying. As a doctor, Luke differentiated between sickness that is the result of demonic influence and that which is the result of sin in general, when he wrote of Jesus in chapter 6:18, "All who came to Him, He healed them of their diseases as well as those who were tormented by evil spirits."

As we develop our understanding of God, the question usually comes up as to why God would allow people to suffer at all—especially those who belongs to Him. Why wouldn't He just heal us? Why wouldn't He deliver us? Why would the Devil even have a part in any of these things?

As the book of Job opens, Satan has come to present himself to God. "Have you considered my servant, Job?" God asks. "He's blameless in all of his ways."

"Of course he is," Satan said. "You give him everything he wants. Quit doing that and he'll curse You to Your face."

So God said to Satan, "Take away his stuff." And, with great enthusiasm, Satan went off to destroy, because that's what he desires to do. Job's children died and he lost his wealth. Yet in the midst of this, Job blessed God.

In Job 2, when Satan showed up again, the Lord said, "Have you checked out My servant, Job? Though you turned My hand against him, look at him."

"Sure," Satan said. "He's still healthy. If you took away his health, he'd curse you to Your face."

So God said, "Lay your hand on him but do not take his life." To the degree that he's allowed to destroy, Satan will do so immediately. Satan's goal is to harm and eventually destroy us. God, on the other hand, has in His heart only good and wants to bring us to an anticipated end, as Jeremiah 29:11 declares. Sometimes He allows the enemy to bring suffering to bear—but always with the heart of benefiting and blessing our lives. Satan in that way is but a pawn in God's hands.

But God's ways are something we don't always understand. Whenever people say, "Pastor, why does God—" I interrupt them and say, "Sorry. I've got to stop you there. I don't know. But I do know God is good. And I don't find one place in Scripture where God allows things that aren't, in the end, good for me as I seek Him."

By the time we come to Romans 8, we will hear Paul say, "All things work together for good to those who love God, who are called according to His purpose." And if we read a little farther and get to Revelation 21:4, it will say, "In that day, the Lord will wipe every tear from their eyes and there will be no more death, no more sorrow, no more crying, no more pain." That's the place we're headed, but we're not there yet.

If there was ever someone who had a reason not to come to church, I think it would have been this woman. She had a debilitating illness that brought her undue attention from others. She was slow moving and would have held up the crowd. Sitting would have been nearly impossible. To top it all off, she had been praying for eighteen years for the Lord to heal her—and not a single prayer had been answered.

Eighteen years is a long time to be bent over to the point that you can't look up. We might have understood if she had said, "I'm tired of going to church. I'm disappointed. I'm embarrassed. I'm resentful." But not this woman. She came to worship. She came to give her life to the Lord week after week.

I wonder what would have happened if she had just skipped that week? That was the week Jesus was there. That was the week God would meet with her. Had she just slept in, given up, or quit trying that week, she would have missed all God wanted to do. I think blessedness is always found in the path of those who seek God no matter what. She was not going to be deterred by anything she may have used as an excuse not to come. And I truly believe if we seek the Lord with everything we have, even when things are difficult, we'll find from God much more than we expect, because it isn't that God is unwilling to work—it's more often we're unwilling to come and wait upon Him.

This woman came worshipping, even though she had plenty of reasons not to. And she came adoring God even though she very well may have been disappointed in His dealing with her life.

> But when Jesus saw her, He called her to Him and said to her, "Woman, you are loosed from your infirmity." And He laid His hands on her, and immediately she was made straight, and glorified God.
>
> —Luke 13:12–13

As the woman came in late, no doubt she attracted attention. After all, her condition would have prevented her from sneaking in quickly. When Jesus called her to the front, I don't know how long it took her to get there, but the minute she did, Jesus said, "Woman, you have been loosed," using a present imperative term meaning "for once and for all." With a word Jesus set her free from the demonic activity that had held her captive for eighteen years.

Now one would think that, at this point, everyone in the congregation would rise to their feet cheering. I mean, this was the woman's home fellowship! Many of them would have seen her struggle every Sabbath for eighteen years. Held the door for her, made room for her. And now, here she was, standing upright! Time for a JESUS cheer.

> But the ruler of the synagogue answered with indignation, because Jesus had healed on the Sabbath, and he said to the crowd, "There are six days on which men ought to work, therefore come and be healed on them, and not on the Sabbath day."
>
> —Luke 13:14

Is it just me or does it seem to you that this ruler is slow on the uptake? Luke said he was indignant—a word for furious. He was angry at Jesus for healing on the Sabbath and angry at the woman for coming to be healed on the Sabbath and he wanted to be sure the crowd knew it . How foolish! For one thing, the woman hadn't come to be healed. She had come to worship. Healing was Jesus' idea. And what if she had come back the next day? Who would have touched her life then? Certainly not this rabbi. He had no heart for the Lord, no faith whatsoever, no compassion or proper understanding of God's heart. What a strained environment Jesus stepped into to share God's Word.

But this would-be spiritual ruler here equated healing with work. It might have been work for him to heal—but it wasn't for Jesus. He enjoyed it plenty. It seems to me such a strange state of mind if, in one breath, you can acknowledge the absolute deliverance of a woman so severely infirmed for such a long time—and yet not be able to see it as a work of God and cry foul according to your religious traditions. It angered Jesus and He spoke up clearly to the ruler and before the crowds.

> The Lord then answered him and said, "Hypocrite! Does not each one of you on the Sabbath loose his ox or donkey from the stall, and lead it away to water it?"
> —Luke 13:15

"You're a two-faced man," Jesus cried. "You make exceptions for far less important things. You untie your animal, walk him over to get a drink, and tie him back up on the Sabbath. Somehow that's all OK. But this woman, hearing four words, is able to stand up—and that's a big problem for you?" It interests me that legalists always have a way to find a loophole for themselves. For them, there's always an escape clause—but not for anyone else.

> "So ought not this woman, being a daughter of Abraham, whom Satan has bound—think of it—for eighteen years, be loosed from this bond on the Sabbath?"
> —Luke 13:16

I believe the term *daughter of Abraham* is more than a reference to this woman's ethnicity, because that would have been obvious. Rather, I think it's a reference to the fact that her heart was right with God by faith, as was Abraham. After calling Zacchaeus out of the tree to have lunch with Him, Jesus said in people gathered outside the house, "Today, salvation has come to this house. Here is a son of Abraham"—a reference to Zacchaeus' new-found faith. (Luke 19:9) Later, Paul said in Galatians 3:6, "Abraham believed God and his belief was counted as righteousness. Only those of you who are of faith can really be called sons of Abraham." Faith is what drew this woman to the synagogue Sabbath after Sabbath. And faith was the open door through which Jesus healed her. Only a blinded religious system would find fault with and miss His wonderful work.

> And when He said these things, all His adversaries were put to shame; and all the multitude rejoiced for all the glorious things that were done by Him.
> —Luke 13:17

Initially the ruler and his cohorts were ashamed of their words and the crowds rejoiced. But both shame and joy were temporary. In fact, this event—because He healed on the Sabbath—would become a cornerstone of the campaign to kill Jesus. Yet in every place of worship we will find the faithful, like this woman, touched by God and the absolutely unfaithful, like this ruler, in his complaint. Which leads to our next verses and the parable Jesus told.

> Then He said, "What is the kingdom of God like? And to what shall I compare it? It is like a mustard seed, which a man took and put in his garden, and it grew and became a large tree, and the birds of the air nested in its branches." And again He said, "To what shall I liken the kingdom of God? It is like leaven, which a woman took and hid in three measures of meal till it was all leavened."
> —Luke 13:18–21

Both Matthew 13 and Mark 4 record Jesus sharing these stories in different settings to illustrate the same point. Here on the heels of the confrontation between an unbelieving ruler and a very humble, believing lady, Jesus told the story to a synagogue full of folks— some who believed, some who didn't. And His point was that the number of true believers is far smaller than the total number of those appearing in fellowship might lead you to conclude. You might see a church full of people, but that doesn't mean they all belong to God.

There are people in churches all over the country—but that doesn't mean they're saved and following Jesus. It just means they're in church. They look like believers, but only God knows the heart. One day He will judge in anger the religious person with his religious rules and welcome those like the believing, once-bent-over woman, standing straight, glorifying Him, who had come each week out of love to worship her God!

Chapter 85

JESUS DECLARES
HIS DEITY

John 10:22–42
(John 5:26–27, 14:9, 20:28–29)

W e now turn in our chronology to the Gospel of John and join Jesus in Jerusalem at the winter feast of dedication.

> Now it was the Feast of Dedication in Jerusalem, and it was winter. And Jesus walked in the temple, in Solomon's porch.
>
> —John 10:22–23

This Feast of Dedication, or the Festival of Lights (also known as Chanukah), is certainly a joyous Jewish occasions. Although this wasn't one of the feast days God laid out in the Old Testament, Jesus came to the temple to celebrate this feast commemorating God's miraculous cleansing of the temple, the deliverance of it from Antiochus Epiphanes, and the restoration of fellowship with God by His people. That John notes it was winter may very well be a comment on the fact that time was running out. Winter had come—and soon, Jesus will be giving His life.

Solomon's porch in the temple area was like a big foyer or lobby. Although it was outdoors, it was the place people gathered for fellowship and discussion. When the disciples began to minister to the early church, Acts 5:12 says they gathered in Solomon's porch. Here we find Jesus there amongst the people.

> Then the Jews surrounded Him and said to Him, "How long do You keep us in doubt? If You are the Christ, tell us plainly."
>
> —John 10:24

Maybe it's just me, but after three-plus years of public ministry, it seems that anyone who would say to Jesus, "So, are You the One?" would have had to have been living under a rock, because everything He had done and said would have convinced anyone carefully observing that He was the promised "Messiah."

Throughout the Gospels, Jesus avoided the term *Messiah* because of the military and political connotations it carried. That is, the Jews of Jesus' day were certain the coming Messiah would get rid of the Romans, return the land to the Jews, and allow them to freely govern themselves once again. But the people—the disciples included—had to learn differently. So Jesus didn't talk much about being the Messiah in the big group. But to individuals, His disciples, and those wanting to hear and follow, He was more than direct about who He was:

When Andrew first met Jesus, he said, "We found the Messiah, the Christ" (John 1:41). After listening to Jesus, Nathanael said, "You are the Son of God, the King of Israel" (John 1:49).

When the woman at the well told Jesus she knew the Messiah was coming, and when He did He would tell people all things, Jesus said, "I who speak to you am He" (John 4:26).

After the woman shared with her village that she had met Jesus, and after they came and heard Him themselves, they said to her, "We believe in Him—not because of what you told us but because we have heard Him ourselves. This is indeed the Messiah" (John 4:42).

After Jesus healed the blind man in John 9:24–39, the religious folks said, "He can't be the Messiah because He healed on the Sabbath Day."

The ex-blind man, not knowing about any of that, replied, "I don't know about that, but I know I was blind and now I see. So, whoever He is, He's a Man from God."

After he was thrown out of the synagogue, Jesus hunted him down and asked, "Do you believe in the Son of God?"

"Who is He, Lord," the man said, "that I might believe in Him?"

And Jesus said, "You've seen Him and I who speak to you am He."

Jesus had told many hungry in heart who He was, and His works, as well, would have been enough to convince anyone. These folks at the feast had been given sufficient information and proof over the past three years. It wasn't a lack of information but of blame shifting, making excuses for their unwillingness to turn to Him. So they say instead, "Come on, Jesus, How long are You going to make us doubt?"—as if their unbelief was really His fault and He had been less than clear so they could decide about Him. Yet our Lord God had given them more than they needed to know. He doesn't want blind faith—but an intelligent response to the truth given. If we're not going to get saved, it's not going to be God's fault. It will be ours.

> Jesus answered them, "I told you, and you do not believe. The works that I do in My Father's name, they bear witness of Me. But you do not believe, because you are not of My sheep, as I said to you, My sheep hear My voice, and I know them, and they follow Me."
>
> —John 10:25–27

I love Jesus' answer because it's so direct. "Why don't You tell us if You're the Messiah?" the religious leaders said.

"I have told you and I've shown you," Jesus said. "Both what you've heard and what you've seen verify who I am."

When Isaiah wrote about the Messiah in 700 B.C., he said in chapter 35:5, "When the Messiah comes, the eyes of the blind will be opened and the ears of the deaf will be unbound." Therefore, just reading the prophets and comparing it to what they saw Jesus do should have been enough to cause the religious leaders to say, "That might be Him." After all, no one else had an eye-opening, dead-raising ministry.

Believers in Jesus follow Him—follow His voice and His direction. God knows them and their lives are different. If you're walking your own way, living your own life, it's probably because you're not one of God's sheep. God's sheep act differently. They follow Him.

> "And I give them eternal life, and they shall never perish; neither shall anyone snatch them out of My hand. My Father, who has given them to Me, is greater than all; and no one is able to snatch them out of My Father's hand."
>
> —John 10:28–29

I love the benefits of being one of Jesus' sheep. We are given eternal life. We don't earn it. We don't deserve it. It's not a reward. We just look to Jesus in faith as our Savior and Lord. And no one can take us out of God's hand. I like that picture, don't you? God saved me and then promises to finish what He started. God saved me and promises to deliver me at the end of the line. God saved me and assures me I never will be taken out of His hand.

In Philippians 1:6, Paul said, "I have confidence in this very thing—that He who began a good work in you will complete it until the day of Christ." Whew! I'm glad God's hanging on to me, because I've let go of Him plenty of times.

To the Corinthians—not exactly a mature church—Paul said, "God is going to present you blameless one day before His coming" (1 Cor. 1:8).

Jude 24 added, "Unto Him who is able to keep you from stumbling and present you faultless before His glory with great joy."

If you're saved, you should never worry about losing your salvation. In fact, Jesus said in John 6:37–40, "This is the will of the Father who has sent Me that I should lose none but that I should raise them up on the last day." That's very plain talk, isn't it?

> "I and My Father are one."
>
> —John 10:30

Verse 30 is in a neuter tense which speaks not of person but of essence. It refers to the biblical doctrine of three Persons but one God—the "tri-unity," the Trinity. The word *trinity* is not in the Bible. But the description of God the Father, God the Son, and God the Holy Spirit being one God can be found from cover to cover.

A couple of hours before Jesus gave His life, Philip said to Him, "Lord, could You show us the Father? That's all I need."

And Jesus said, "I've been with you so long—don't you believe I'm in the Father and the Father is in Me, that the words I speak I don't speak of My own authority but the Father gives them to Me? If you believe that I am in the Father and the Father in Me, you'll be fine. But if you don't believe the words, believe the works I do for they will tell you who I am" (John 14:7–11).

These religious, hard-hearted men who tried to cover their lack of faith and unwillingness to believe the facts by challenging Jesus publicly heard Jesus say that He and the Father were one. And if you don't believe they understood what He was implying, was claiming, all you need to do is read the next few verses.

> Then the Jews took up stones again to stone Him.
>
> —John 10:31

If Jesus isn't God, they should have stoned Him, because His claim would have been blasphemous. But if He is, they were wrong and their unbelief knew no bounds. Notice the word *again*. This wasn't the first time this group had tried to kill Him. They had tried before. They would try again.

> Jesus answered them, "Many good works I have shown you from My Father. For which of those works do you stone Me?"
>
> —John 10:32

"Which of My Father's works are you killing Me for?" Jesus asked. "Opening the eyes of the blind—you didn't like that? The lame walking—upset about that? Cleansed lepers—you didn't appreciate that?" His question brought them back to the argument that the very works He did should have told them who He was because only God could accomplish those things.

> The Jews answered Him, saying, "For a good work we do not stone You, but for blasphemy, and because You, being a Man, make Yourself God."
>
> —John 10:33

Isn't this amazing? "We're not contesting Your works," the religious leaders said. "It is Your words that offend us." Jesus' words very well might have been offensive if His works hadn't backed them up. But His works ought to have allowed Him to claim who He was, because no one else could do them but God.

People today say Jesus was a good man, a nice man, and maybe even a prophet. But that's it. No, He's more than that. He's God. And if He isn't God, He can't be Savior.

Jesus answered them, "Is it not written in your law, 'I said, You are gods'? If He called them gods, to whom the word of God came (and the Scripture cannot be broken), do you say of Him whom the Father sanctified and sent into the world, 'You are blaspheming,' because I said, 'I am the Son of God'?"

—John 10:34–36

Jesus quoted a well-known verse from Psalm 82:6. The Hebrew word for *gods* is *Elohim*—which was used to refer to the Old Testament judges God placed over His people to represent His will, provide kindness to the poor, and support the weak. They were called gods because they stood in God's place. Yet even though the position was sacred, the judges themselves sometimes were wicked.

Jesus' position was that since wicked judges were called gods, how much more right did He have to claim to be the Son of God when everything He had said and done was absolutely untainted by sin and tremendously powerful?

"Scripture cannot be broken," Jesus said. I love how He constantly went back to the Bible as a place to stand.

> "If I do not do the works of My Father, do not believe Me, but if I do, though you do not believe Me, believe the works, that you may know and believe that the Father is in Me, and I in Him."
>
> —John 10:37–38

For some people, simply hearing the truth is sufficient. Others, like Thomas, need to see it first, it seems. "If you have trouble with My words," Jesus said, "look at the works I do because they'll convince you."

I am so moved by how Jesus loved these men enough to plead with them to look at the evidence. I came to know Jesus seeing the lives of my friends changed by Him. I didn't know the Gospel, but I knew something had happened to my drug dealer buddy and I wanted to know more. Words preached without a corresponding lifestyle are often powerless. But no one can deny the power of a life changed. No one should have denied the words of Jesus, which were backed in full force by His awesome works. Yet as Jesus appealed to them, their flesh and anger overwhelmed their senses. Truly, sin blinds! So we read:

> Therefore they sought again to seize Him, but He escaped out of their hand. And He went away again beyond the Jordan to the place where John was baptizing at first, and there He stayed. Then many came to Him, and said, "John performed no sign, but all the things that John spoke about this Man were true." And many believed in Him there.
>
> —John 10:39–42

Jesus left Jerusalem in December. He was to die in April. Except for coming back to town for Lazarus, we don't find Him in Jerusalem in our scriptural accounts until the week before the cross. He left town here and dwelt in the wilderness—where people flocked to Him in droves. What the religious community in Jerusalem was unwilling to grab hold of, the common person was hungry for more of.

They believed in Him because of what they had heard and seen. Don't write off Jesus because you do not fully understand everything His every word. Look at the evidence behind His claims. He's the only One who can give you life—and there's an empty tomb that proclaims He's God and can be trusted to save you!

Chapter 86

DOES GOD KNOW YOU?

Luke 13:22–35

Here in the thirteenth chapter of Luke, Jesus is back on the road, encountering individuals who believed their salvation was based on their nationality, or their works or even their birthright. Like many who claim they know God, the real question might better be, "Does God know you?" That is the subject of our study here.

> And He went through the cities and villages, teaching, and journeying toward Jerusalem. Then one said to Him, "Lord, are there few who are saved?"
> —Luke 13:22–23

I think the question from this unnamed person in this unnamed city shows Jesus had been talking specifically about salvation as He traveled from city to city teaching, ministering, and reaching out. "Are there only a few folks getting saved?" this person asked. Both from the context and the answer Jesus gave, we can conclude rather quickly that the questioner believed that, because he was a Jew, he would be fine with God. Jesus increasingly had been speaking about sin and our need to repent—and yet the general understanding among the Jews was they were OK with God because of whom they were. Even the Mishnah says all Jews will be right and glorified with the Lord unless they have done something horrendous. Men like Korah and Absalom in the Old Testament, who had betrayed the people and turned from God, would be set aside. But otherwise, because of their background, ethnicity, and religion, the Jews would be fine, at least according to the Mishnah.

On the other hand, the Jews were sure that the Gentiles, for the most part, wouldn't make it. Oh, there would be some exceptions such as Rahab and Ruth, who wised up and came to their senses, but it was only the nation of Israel—to whom God had spoken, to whom He had sent the prophets, and to whom He would send the Messiah—who had the inside track on everything having to do with the future before God.

So when this person said, "So there's just a few of us, right?" the audience would have expected Jesus to say, "Of course! I know you. You'll make it. Due to your nationality, lineage, and four thousand years of history with God as a nation, you're in." But that's not what Jesus said. In fact, His answer was that the line between being "in" with God or not—between being saved and unsaved—was not nationalistic at all. It was spiritual and personal. Salvation requires personal choice. There is no wholesale entering in as a nation or people simply because of God's historical dealing with you. You must come alone; you must enter in by faith in Jesus Christ.

> And He said to them, "Strive to enter through the narrow gate . . . ."
> —Luke 13:23–24

Well aware of the crowd's wrong assumptions about salvation, Jesus said, "You shouldn't worry so much about how other people are trying to get in. You just want to be sure you make it." In Greek, the word for *strive* means to "agonize" and is used to describe athletes who will do anything necessary in training to seek to win. Jesus didn't suggest here, or anywhere else, that people have to work their way into heaven. But He was saying to the individual who is comfortable in his or her background, "While the door is open, you should be sure you have done everything to believe so you know where you stand. You better put all your efforts into knowing and then following that which will bring you life."

People today often spend a great deal of time being sure that what they buy will last. Before buying a new dryer, we will first buy the latest edition of *Consumer Reports* so we can check its history. Will it last eleven years? We certainly don't want one that will last only nine. "Do you have one of those?" we ask our friends. Then we go online and check with people we don't even know, to see what they're saying about it.

Yet when asked if they're going to make it to heaven, people very glibly say God will be happy to see them. Asked how they know this to be so, they say it's just what they believe.

We seem to have less of a concern to be sure about eternal things than about that new dryer.

"Are you going to heaven?"

"Oh, yeah, I go to church all the time."

"Is that enough?"

"I know Hymn Fifty-seven."

"Is that enough?"

"I know a priest."

"Good. But does God know you?"

The word *strive* that Jesus uses here is in the present tense. He tells us to not delay but to enter in today! Do it now! Don't put it off.

You can't make heaven by sitting back confident only in your earthly citizenship, lineage, or your in-laws' faith. Jesus said there's a narrow gate through which you must enter and that salvation requires a response from every individual heart to His claim that He's the only door. There's no inside track. There aren't many roads that lead to heaven, just faith in Jesus the narrow road.

">. . . For many, I say to you, will seek to enter and will not be able."

—Luke 13:24

The implication is the majority of the audience wouldn't make it because they were resting in some kind of settled complacency about their eternal future.

"Is this important?" they might have asked one another.

"I don't know. I don't think it's that big a deal. I think God will sort it all out. I've got more important things to think about. I need new tires for the car. Eternity? I'll get to it on Sunday."

The nation of Israel had the prophets, Law, and the temple. Yet Paul wrote in Romans 2:25–29, "Don't think your circumcision will get you in. That won't do it. You need to be saved. You need your heart changed."

The way to heaven is not some grand entrance through which everyone comes skipping nonchalantly. It's a narrow door where people must enter only one at a time. There is no "group meeting" with God. To the big crowds in John 6, Jesus had said, "You shouldn't work so hard for food that's perishing. If you want to work hard, labor for those things that lead to eternal life, which the Son of Man will give to those who believe in Him."

Have we made sure that the road we're on, the convictions we hold, and the door we're using is the right one? It's a question much more important than anything else we'll consider. Jesus came and died and rose so we might come to Him and enter.

> "When once the Master of the house has risen up and shut the door, and you
> begin to stand outside and knock at the door, saying, 'Lord, Lord, open for us,'
> and He will answer and say to you, 'I do not know you, where you are from,'
> then you will begin to say, 'We ate and drank in Your presence, and You taught
> in our streets.' But He will say, 'I tell you I do not know you, where you are from.
> Depart from Me, all you workers of iniquity.'"
>
> —Luke 13:25–27

Not only is it important to strive to enter in at the narrow gate, but it's important to know time is running out, and there is limited opportunity to make that right choice. When the door shuts, whatever choice we've made we have to live with for all eternity. Paul said to the Hebrews in chapter 4:7, "Today if you won't harden your hearts like they did in the wilderness, then come." *Today.* Eventually this opportunity slams shut. We die and we're ushered in—and for those on the wide road, it will be an eternal tragedy.

Notice that in both verses 25 and 27, Jesus said to the fellow standing in front of Him, "I don't know you." That individual was kept out of God's kingdom not because he didn't believe he knew God. He thought he did. He was kept out because God didn't know him.

No, no, no. Of course You know me, he must have thought. *I sit in row 8, seat 4 every Sunday;* or *I taught Sunday School;* or *I was a deacon for eleven years. I have a plaque on my wall to prove it. What do You mean You don't know me? I know You.*

But you see, it's not a question of our knowing God. It's a question of His knowing us. And He only knows us when we come to His Son and place our faith in His work and our sins at the cross and the Holy Spirit moves into our hearts and we are born again. You see how narrow is the way. You might declare, "I know God in my own way; it is personal between Him and me." The important question is, "Does He know you." Not in the sense that God knows all, but have you come to Him through the only Door?

Superficial encounters with Jesus don't establish a relationship. That requires a life commitment, a step of faith, a right dividing of the Scriptures, and a hanging on to Jesus as we go down this narrow road. But saying to Him one day, "You know me; we've hung out; I prayed that time I had to go to the doctors, I know lots of verses," won't cut it. You have to ask yourself if your relationship with the Lord is authentic. When you say, "Lord," does He answer?

Jesus said in John 10:27, "My sheep hear My voice and I know them." In 1 Corinthians 8:3, Paul wrote that "if anyone loves God, he will be known by Him." To the Galatians in chapter 4:9, he said, "After you came to know God, you became known by God." In each case, the emphasis is on God knowing us. Familiarity with Him isn't nearly enough. He must be the Lord of our lives.

Depart from Me has to be the worst words anyone could ever hear, because if God is done with us, we're done.

> "There will be weeping and gnashing of teeth, when you see Abraham and Isaac and Jacob and all the prophets in the kingdom of God, and yourselves thrust out. They will come from the east and the west, from the north and the south, and sit down in the kingdom of God. And indeed there are last who will be first, and there are first who will be last."
>
> —Luke 13:28–30

Weeping in the Bible speaks of helplessness. "Gnashing of teeth" is only used in two contexts: bitter pain and/or tremendous rage. The crowd now found itself separated from the very folks to which they had assumed to be linked. Why? Because Abraham, Isaac, and Jacob were men of faith. Their relationships with God were personal. They had developed over time through trust, stepping out, and self-denial.

"Abraham is our father," the crowd had argued in John 8:39–40.

"If Abraham was your father, you would do the works of Abraham," Jesus answered. "You're trying to kill Me. Abraham wouldn't do that."

The Jews had been the first called. Now they were last. The Gentiles were the last called, but now they could be first as they came from every corner of the globe. Even those not part of the covenant people could now come to the Lord, because all must come through the narrow gate and all are invited to come.

Why do many miss out? Why do many wait so long? I think it's because most people assume early on that their familiarity with religious things and their token devotion to God in whatever way they see fit is good enough. Religious pride and confidence in denomination or nationality begins to hinder people from seeing they personally need a Savior because they are themselves sinful and need help and must one day stand before God alone. Pride interferes, sin blinds, and people settle in, never considering where the road they're on is going.

> On that very day some Pharisees came, saying to Him, "Get out and depart from here, for Herod wants to kill You." And He said to them, "Go, tell that fox, 'Behold, I cast out demons and perform cures today and tomorrow, and the third day I shall be perfected.' Nevertheless I must journey today, tomorrow, and the day following; for it cannot be that a prophet should perish outside of Jerusalem."
>
> —Luke 13:31–33

The Pharisees were certainly no friends of Jesus. Therefore, rather than sincerely warning Him of Herod's intentions, they used the threat to seek to push Him towards Jerusalem where the Sanhedrin lay in wait. Jesus' answer, however, was, "I'll work My own schedule, if that's all right with you. I've got things to do today and tomorrow and then I'm going to be perfected"—a veiled reference to the resurrection. He continued, "And then I'm going to go to Jerusalem because no prophet will be killed outside Jerusalem." In other words, "You're saying Herod wants to kill Me, but I know who really wants to kill Me: the religious community in Jerusalem."

> "O Jerusalem, Jerusalem, the one who kills the prophets and stones those who are sent to her! How often I wanted to gather your children together, as a hen gathers her brood under her wings, but you were not willing! See! Your house is left to you desolate; and assuredly, I say to you, you shall not see Me until the time comes when you say, 'Blessed is He who comes in the name of the Lord!'"
>
> —Luke 13:34–35

Jesus used these words again when He overlooked the city of Jerusalem during Passion Week. Then it was in reference to the Romans who would soon follow to destroy Jerusalem. Here it was in reference to those who didn't want to exchange their national trust for personal faith in Him. He had given them all they needed. But they were not willing to accept it. And one day it would be too late.

Does the Lord know you? It's not your labor—it's His that can save. But you've got to be sure. Your argument that you know God won't hold water with Him. But His knowledge of you opens the door, and His sheep know His voice, and He knows them.

Chapter 87

Guess Who's Coming to Dinner?

Luke 14:1–14
(Matthew 12:9–13)

From all we can gather, it would seem Luke 14–17:10 all took place on one Sabbath day. In these chapters we find a series of sermons to various groups of people—all of them designed to invite them to come and be saved.

Here we take a look at another dinner to which Jesus was invited. The dinners Jesus attended, given by the Pharisees, didn't go very well for they only invited Jesus to dinner in order to get even with Him or ahead of Him, and He always turned the tables to show them their heart and His. The account before us is no exception, as Jesus used the lifestyles of the scribes and Pharisees to prove their religion didn't work and their need for Him still remained.

> Now it happened, as He went into the house of one of the rulers of the Pharisees
> to eat bread on the Sabbath, that they watched Him closely.
> —Luke 14:1

The last dinner like this was back in Luke 11:37–54 where Jesus told the religious men there that, even though they looked good outwardly, their hearts were wicked.

According to what we will read, the Pharisees had invited everyone who was anyone to this dinner. Their plan was to bring the big shots to watch Jesus, so there wouldn't be any doubt as to what had to be done with Him when He once again broke their rules, as they were sure He would. To prompt that action these heartless religious men had invited a sick man to be among them, knowing if they positioned him in front of Jesus, regardless of the fact that it was the Sabbath, Jesus would heal him, giving them all the ammunition they would need to make their case to take Him out.

Walking into this dinner, with everyone pretending nothing was up, one would sense something was going on by the coldness in the air, the forced smiles, and the phony courtesy. John had written earlier that Jesus never committed Himself to man because He knew what was in man. Jesus knew exactly what was happening—which is very interesting to me—because He willingly walked into this trap, into a place I think you and I, if given the choice, would not have gone. Jesus was willing to go because His heart was to reach all men and give even the worst—and these deceivers of the people were the worst—plenty of opportunities to turn and live.

And behold, there was a certain man before Him who had dropsy.

—Luke 14:2

We have seen the word *behold* before, which is the translation of a Greek word that means "check this out carefully" or "take particular note." The focus is on the trap that mercilessly had been set as the Pharisees maneuvered this man to a place where Jesus couldn't miss him. The Greek description of his disease speaks of fluid retention often caused by organ failure. This man was certainly gravely ill and there was very little hope of seeing him recover. The Pharisees put this fellow right in front of Jesus, using him in all of his suffering for such wickedness. According to what follows, it would seem he was the only one in the room not involved in the scheme. Without any love for God or their neighbor, these religious leaders were going to great lengths to carry out their plans.

It is remarkable to me that the Pharisees' opinion of Jesus was right, in the sense that they believed if He saw someone suffering, He would help him. Yet their hearts were so blind and cold that they could use such a sick plan to seek to discredit Jesus while remaining unmoved by His ability to heal.

And Jesus, answering, spoke to the lawyers and Pharisees, saying, "Is it lawful to heal on the Sabbath?"

—Luke 14:3

Jesus answered. Answered what? No one had asked a question—but He answered the Pharisees' plot and cruel intention. He addressed their hearts and wicked thoughts. "I'm so glad to have a room full of wise religious men," He essentially said. "What do we do about this man who's so sick and in obvious pain on the Sabbath? Anyone?" I love the question because no matter how the Pharisees had answered it, it ruined their plot. If they had said, "Yes, You can heal on the Sabbath. It's good to be good to people," their plan would have fallen apart. But if they had said, "No, You can't really help this guy who is hurting so, sorry, but it's the Sabbath," they then would have shown themselves to be as inhumane as they truly were. What can they reply?

"What do we do with this guy?" Jesus asked. The Pharisees already had condemned Him for ministering on the Sabbath. But they didn't want to take the responsibility for prolonging the suffering of someone Jesus could help. The consequences of their own religion had now trapped them. Only one thing to do.

But they kept silent . . . .

—Luke 14:4

Ask people what they think about any given topic and they usually will tell you. In fact, talk shows are driven by the understanding that people love to talk. And these were self-proclaimed experts in the field of religious rules.

461

"I just need a little ruling on the healing," Jesus had said. Silence. "Anyone?" Silence. Why? Because they didn't have a leg to stand on. Their religious ways were harsh and hateful. Everyone there believed Jesus could heal—but none of them wanted to follow Him or surrender their ways to Him as the Lord.

There are seven other places in the Gospels where Jesus is confronted about His "wrongful" actions on the Sabbath. As such, these confrontations between religious people and Jesus—their Law vs. His grace—take center stage, as they do in the hearts of men hearing the Gospel. Law or grace, works or grace . . . This had been going on for three years. And each time there was a confrontation, the religious leaders ended up silent. They had been down this road before. Therefore, someone should have said, "We've tried this, like, six times. He asks a question. We all look dumb. And then He does what He wants. This isn't working for us. Maybe He is right!" How God longs to hear that come from the heart of one depending on his works who meets Jesus and His power and the Cross.

> And He took him and healed him, and let him go.
> —Luke 14:4

There is not one word here about the man's faith. Maybe he had been paid to be there. Everyone else was rich and powerful in the room, but not him. Whatever the reason he was there, there is no evidence he had come out of great faith. But Jesus is Jesus. He'll do as He pleases. He had authority over the sickness and the situation. The sick man didn't go away thanking the Lord or honoring Him. But the focus wasn't on the man. The focus was on Jesus and the religious men and how their wicked blindness, even in the face of Jesus' power and compassion and the fulfillment of prophecy, continued to hold them in unbelief. Jesus asked a single question they couldn't answer. The man was healed. Their plot had failed.

At this point, the Pharisees might have been done with Jesus—but He wasn't done with them. So in the next twenty verses, He hammers home the point that their lives showed they weren't right with God, their ways proved their hearts were wrong, and it was only by coming to Him that they could find life, because if they stayed where they were, they'd never make it. So we read:

> Then He answered them, saying, "Which of you, having a donkey or an ox that has fallen into a pit, will not immediately pull him out on the Sabbath day?" And they could not answer Him regarding these things.
> —Luke 14:5–6

These proud and selfish men who had used the sick for their own devices were now on the hot seat. Not only had they lost face, but they were being told they weren't walking in love and that they were foolish in their position and selfish in their outlook. Jesus had a whole room full of them. And He had the floor. Again a question; again silence was all they offered as a response.

So He told a parable to those who were invited, when He noted how they chose the best places, saying to them: "When you are invited by anyone to a wedding feast, do not sit down in the best place, lest one more honorable than you be invited by him; and he who invited you and him come and say to you, 'Give place to this man,' and then you begin with shame to take the lowest place."

—Luke 14:7–9

Verse 1 says the Pharisees had been watching Jesus. Verse 7 tells us He had been watching them as well. And although He observed their behavior, His advice was intended to show them their hearts. Out of love and concern for them, He said to the big shots who were acting like big shots as they looked for the preferred seats and the best tables in the front, "Look at the way you came to dinner—elbows out, jacket in the chair, saving it for someone more important."

In Luke 11:43, Jesus had said to them, "Woe to you, Pharisees, who are always looking for the best seats in the synagogue." This wasn't the synagogue. This was a party. Yet status and position were what drove them in both cases. The truth was there for anyone watching to see: a free meal was fine. But an honored seat was a must.

The writer of Proverbs 25:6 said, "Put not yourself forth in the presence of the king. Don't try to stand in a place with great men. It is better that they would say to you, 'Come up here,' than that you should be lowered in the presence of the prince whom your eyes have seen." Jesus' advice wasn't new. It was written in the Old Testament, a book the Pharisees should have known well. He spoke to men who were supposed to be teaching God's Word—yet in reality were doing nothing but ignoring it. Watching them vying for position, He said, "That's not a good way to live." That's the way of the ungodly!

To these religious rule-makers dominated by their flesh, Jesus said, "It's more honorable to be humble." It's true in life, but it's even truer in spiritual life because humility is the place you must arrive before you can be saved. It is at the end of ourselves, at the end of self-confidence, that God-confidence can begin. These men were yet far from the life Jesus came to bring to those who humbly repented before Him.

"But when you are invited, go and sit down in the lowest place, so that when he who invited you comes he may say to you, 'Friend, go up higher.' Then you will have glory in the presence of those who sit at the table with you. For whoever exalts himself will be humbled, and he who humbles himself will be exalted."

—Luke 14:10–11

The way of life God honors and faith brings is the life that denies itself. Religion does just the opposite. It consists of elitism and the snobbery of who's the wisest, best, and most honorable. The whole room was filled with them, none of them humble, but all of them rulers.

463

When Mary heard from the angel that she would be the Messiah's mother, she said, "The Lord has noticed the low estate of His handmaiden." She was humbled by it—and God was able to use her.

Jesus said to this room of religious, powerful men, "The very way you set yourselves at the table shows your hearts aren't right with God." We hate haughtiness in others, yet we're prone to it ourselves because that's the way sin works.

"Humble yourself in the sight of the Lord and He will lift you up" (James 4:10).

To the Corinthians, Paul wrote, "Be careful that you don't go around comparing yourselves with others because you'll come up with a foolish conclusion. If you want to measure yourself, stand up next to the Lord, then you'll be humble. If you want to glory, glory in Him" (2 Cor. 10:2).

These folks at the table had religion, but it was betrayed by their lifestyle. They had a practice and a belief system, but they couldn't live it themselves. Jesus said, "You've got to come to know who I am first. Then, in your humility, you'll find life."

> Then He also said to him who invited Him, "When you give a dinner or a supper, do not ask your friends, your brothers, your relatives, nor rich neighbors, lest they also invite you back, and you be repaid. But when you give a feast, invite the poor, the maimed, the lame, the blind. And you will be blessed, because they cannot repay you; for you shall be repaid at the resurrection of the just."
>
> —Luke 14:12–14

Continuing with the same issue and the same topic, Jesus looked at the guest list and said to the host, "Your social behavior reflects your lack of interest in the Lord because everyone on this list is part of your mutual admiration society. Rewrite the guest list. Invite those who are hurting, lost, and suffering. Bless them and God will bless you."

Verse 14 is the first mention of the resurrection in the book of Luke. This verse is saying that people of faith receive their reward for goodness later. It will come after this life. That's good enough for them. Yet you religious people want it now.

I love how Jesus is able at every place we find Him to turn the circumstances into a lesson and message about salvation and eternal life. He only asked those in attendance two straightforward questions: "What do we do about this sick man?" and "What would you do about your faltering animal on the Sabbath?" Yet not one word would come out of their mouths. The first step toward salvation is humility. The hearts of these status-seekers were revealed in their unwillingness to serve others. Jesus said the way we live reveals either the authenticity or absence of our faith, because true members of the kingdom are like the Lord they serve. They've died to self. They promote others. They don't look for great places for themselves but instead look to honor Him.

Chapter 88

EXCUSES TO COVER
OUR REAL REASONS

Luke 14:15–24
(Matthew 22:1–14)

The story Jesus will tell in the passage before us was precipitated by a comment from a guest at the dinner set up to trap Jesus, which we looked at in our last study.

> Now when one of those who sat at the table with Him heard these things, he said to Him, "Blessed is he who shall eat bread in the kingdom of God!"
>
> —Luke 14:15

In verse 13, Jesus had told the Pharisees that instead of inviting only those who could repay their invitation to dinner, they should invite the poor and maimed, the blind and lame, for then they would be blessed. In response, one of the guests dismissively commented, "Well, we will all be blessed when we get to heaven," but might as well have added, "Could someone pass the mustard?" Like the rest of the folks in attendance, he was religious but had very little appetite for the things of the Lord. So he presumed that because he was a Jewish religious man, when the heavenly dinner came, he'd be there.

Jesus, ever seeking to reach those trusting in their religious ways, challenged him and the group to look in their hearts through the parable of the great supper, a parable told here which is repeated later in Matthew 22.

> Then He said to him, "A certain man gave a great supper and invited many, and sent his servant at supper time to say to those who were invited, 'Come, for all things are now ready.'"
>
> —Luke 14:16–17

Both here and in Matthew 22:1–14, Jesus' story concerns the feast a king gave in honor of his son's marriage. The picture culminates in Revelation 19:9, where we read, "Blessed are those who are called to the marriage supper of the Lamb." It is a picture the Lord used to describe the church, the true believers, and their union to Christ.

The Lord gives us bits and pieces in the Scriptures about what heaven will be like. And the picture given makes me want to be there! It's more than eating, it's banqueting. It's more than singing, it's joyful singing. It's more than happiness, it's rejoicing. The most important wedding feast in the history of humanity is the marriage supper of the Lamb. And we hold in our hands an invitation, as we will be the bride of Christ.

In the first century, wedding invitations to potential guests were customarily sent as two distinct invitations, though arriving together. Guests would be invited three to six months early. They would first respond as to whether or not they would be able to attend. Then on the day itself, when all the food was ready and the tables set, someone would come to the guests' homes and escort them to the wedding. This served a couple of purposes. Not only did it allow the host to figure out how much food had to be prepared, but the guests did not have to wait for everything to be ready.

To accept the first invitation and refuse the second was the ultimate insult. But that's exactly the picture Jesus painted of these religious men who said they wanted to be with the Lord, as the comment in our text about the blessedness of being in heaven one day, but in their daily lives refused to follow Him.

Jesus spoke to the religious Pharisees individually, to the nation of Israel as a whole, and to us as Gentiles as well, saying the same thing: we can come and find life. The problem is not the invitation, which has been given. The problem is, are we coming when called?

> "But they all with one accord began to make excuses."
>
> —Luke 14:18

In the parable, Jesus will speak of three men who first had said they would come, but would now beg off when all was ready. Each of them has an excuse. Had they verbalized their real reason for not coming, it might have sounded like this; "I have more important things to do. I know I said I was coming, but you don't realize how full my schedule has become."

Benjamin Franklin once said that a fellow who's good at making excuses is rarely good at anything else. And Billy Sunday once said, "An excuse is a skin of a reason stuffed with lies." Excuses can sure fool us. In fact, we can begin to believe our own excuses. The Lord, however, sees through them all.

> "The first said to him, 'I have bought a piece of ground, and I must go and see it. I ask you to have me excused.' And another said, 'I have bought five yoke of oxen, and I am going to test them. I ask you to have me excused.' Still another said, 'I have married a wife, and therefore I cannot come.'"
>
> —Luke 14:18–20

"I bought a piece of real estate. I should really go look at it," the first man said. I think anyone in any kind of business would agree that buying a piece of property sight unseen and then choosing to look at it when another commitment already had been made is a weak excuse at best. Throwing in the words *I must*, this man tried to cloak his excuse with duty and urgency. "Oh, I would like to come, meant to come, want to come, but I must . . . ."

The second one sending excuse was a little less courteous. He didn't argue duty. He didn't say he had a pressing need. He just said, "I'm heading out the door. I can't be bothered. This is a bad time. I made plans. I know I made a commitment. But you know how life goes. I bought five yoke of oxen. I'm on my way to test them." What a flimsy excuse! Who's going to buy ten oxen—about 20,000 lbs. of livestock—for the express purpose of pulling a plow through a field without first checking to see if they can walk straight or even have four legs? Weak excuses all for the sake of getting this earthly life to move forward at the expense of the life to come.

The third man's excuse was terse and rude. He simply blamed his wife. Maybe he was referring to Deuteronomy 24:5, where there was a military exemption for a time for new husbands. But this wasn't military service. It was a wedding, an invitation from people who loved you—a great place to come and introduce his lovely new wife, and for her to have shown off her handsome new husband. Excuses!

So Jesus offers the kingdom, His rule, a feast, blessing, mercy, rest, victory, friendship, salvation, and life forevermore. Yet many filled with excuses turn their backs on His invitation to come to Him and be saved so they might spend more time with their possessions and obligations.

Jesus doesn't devalue any of these responsibilities. The Lord wants us to be good stewards. The problem is that when you neglect your relationship with Him for those things, you lose everything.

I think the closer you walk with the Lord, the better husband and father you'll be and the better businessman and friend you'll be. Why do we allow possessions and affections to become our excuse for not following Jesus and feasting with Him? The excuses in the parable begin to cloud the true reasons. And really, the only one who believes the excuses we make is us. We convince ourselves that tending other things is so important that it becomes an acceptable reason. God doesn't see it that way however.

The bottom line to all three of these people is, "I really don't want to come." We can couch it in terms like "I must," "I'm on my way," or "I can't." But we really can just fill in the blank with "I really don't want to come. I have no desire to be there. I have no appetite for those things. I have other things that are more important to me than You."

I personally think the excuses would have evaporated if these men had really wanted to attend. The same guy who will say, "I can't make church on Wednesday night because I'm so busy," somehow finds time to take those free tickets to the Lakers playoff game and go. I am convinced we always will find the time to do what is an absolute necessity to us. We will do what we must—whatever "must" is in our eyes. And that is the issue isn't it?

I firmly believe we should be in church, learning the Bible as often as we can be. It's the thing we lack the most, the thing we need the most, and the only thing we take with us when we go. God's Word is His love for us—and we should know it. But how do we convince people to make that a "must" in their lives?

The religious leaders in Jesus' day acted as if they wanted the kingdom. In fact, the fellow in verse 15 presumed he'd be there. But his life didn't say he wanted that. His "must" wasn't the Lord first. The hardest people to reach are those who talk like this man and yet live like him.

In Matthew 22, where this same parable is told, Jesus added a couple of things we aren't given here. One of them is that the master sent the servants back to these people making excuses and gave them another chance to respond. This is what Matthew writes:

> And Jesus spoke to them again by parables and said, "The kingdom of heaven is like a certain king who arranged a marriage feast for his son, and sent out his servants to call those who were invited to the wedding; and they were not willing to come. Again, he sent out other servants, saying, 'Tell those who are invited, "See, I have prepared my dinner; my oxen and fatted cattle are killed, and all things are ready. Come to the wedding."'" But they made light of it and went their ways, one to his own farm, another to his business. And the rest seized his servants, treated them spitefully, and killed them. But when the king heard about it, he was furious. And he sent out his armies, destroyed those murderers, and burned up their city."
>
> —Matthew 22:1–7

The invitation came again, but they made light of it and went their own way, even becoming violent with those bearing the message from the master. Ultimately, judgment came—and the end was tragic.

> "So that servant came and reported these things to his master. Then the master of the house, being angry, said to his servant, 'Go out quickly into the streets and lanes of the city, and bring in here the poor and the maimed and the lame and the blind.'"
>
> —Luke 14:21

"Go invite the less fortunate," the master said—the ones Jesus had mentioned to them in verse 13. "Go invite those with less privilege and less understanding, those who are more cognizant of their needs and less encumbered by their schedules, those who would find the opportunity a blessing rather than a responsibility."

The invitation had gone to the religious man, but he had refused. So the poor, the hungry, and those who were aware of their need were invited and eagerly began to come.

"Not many wise or noble will enter into the kingdom of heaven," Paul wrote to the Corinthians. "It's the foolish of the world that shame the wise."

> "And the servant said, 'Master, it is done as you commanded, and still there is room.' Then the master said to the servant, 'Go out into the highways and hedges, and compel them to come in, that my house may be filled. For I say to you that none of those men who were invited shall taste my supper.'"
> —Luke 14:22–24

The next instruction from the master was to go outside the city along the highways, compelling as many as could come so the house would be full. At the end of Matthew 21, Jesus told two parables to the religious leaders about how the nation of Israel had been called first and had been given great privilege, and how they were the holders of God's Word, the stewards of God's promises, and the bearer of the Messiah. Yet even with all of those benefits and privileges, the nation itself—at least the religious leaders—had turned against the One who had come to save them. In both parables, Jesus said, "I'm going to take the good news, the Gospel, and give it to a nation that will follow it."

When Paul spoke in Acts 13:46–49 about the salvation God would bring, he said to the group listening, "It was necessary that the Word of God should be spoken to you first. But since you reject it and judge yourself unworthy of eternal life, we're going to turn to the Gentiles; for the Lord has commanded us that we should be a light to the Gentiles and that there would be salvation to the ends of the earth."

When Paul was under house arrest in Rome in Acts 28:23–31, the Jews gathered to listen to him. He told them again how the prophets and the Law of Moses pointed to Jesus. Some were persuaded; others wouldn't believe. Finally, he said, "Isaiah was right about you. He said you would hear but not understand, that you would see but wouldn't perceive, that your heart is dull and your ears hard of hearing. So the Lord sent me to the Gentiles."

That's the Lord's way. The invitation came first to the Jews. In the end times, it will come again to the nation of Israel. Today, it comes to individuals—to Jew and Gentile alike, to whoever wants to come. The poor, lame, blind, those in the city or without the city all are welcome.

"Compel them to come in," the master said to the servant. We read the word *compel* and think "force." But *compel* simply means to do all one can not to take no for an answer. It's an invitation from the heart to bring people to the place where they might know, love, follow, and want to serve the Lord. The feast must be full. We must go out and compel people to come, to convince them of God's love, and to show them and help them to see that Jesus is Lord.

When was the last time you invited someone to church or called them with your Bible open and said, "I just believe God wants me to share this with you"? How much "compelling" is in your life? How much "compelling" drives your actions?

We are invited to come and then sent out to call others. The Jews had received two invitations. One came from the Law and the prophets, the other from the Messiah

Himself. But it was clear what they loved most. The question is, do we really long for Jesus and His feast or are there so many more important things in our lives that our excuse is if we can get to church on Sunday, that ought to be more than enough?

If you find yourself driven by other things, think about what it cost Jesus to put on the feast. Nothing is left to do but for us to come. One day the last will come, the dinner will begin, and the door will be shut. Until then, whoever will may come.

We should come with great joy and then go out with great responsibility, because the Lord's house needs to be filled. He died so His table could be full. And no excuse is good enough to keep you from His love. Won't you come, the feast is ready!

Chapter 89

COUNTING THE COST

Luke 14:25–35
(Matthew 10:37–39)

Jesus left the dinner of Luke 14:1–24 with a huge crowd following His every movement. With the cross just around the corner, He here turned to warn these people about the cost they would incur by following Him and the difference between being in the crowd and being a disciple who would serve God no matter the cost. On the heels of the three excuses for why people hadn't followed, Jesus would say to the crowd, "Are you going to follow? If you will, here's how."

> Now great multitudes went with Him. And He turned and said to them . . . .
> —Luke 14:25

Jesus had spoken about wanting His banquet table full. But to walk with the Lord requires more than simple allegiance. At some point, our commitment to God is tested and we have to decide one way or the other.

My wife died at twenty-five years old of leukemia, leaving me with two small children after 6 years of marriage. I was so angry with God that I picked up my Bible when I returned from the hospital that day and threw it across the street into the ivy. I then went out drinking with my dad. I had been saved for six years—it's not hard to get drunk when you haven't had a drink in six years. I came home that night and got very sick.

When I woke up laying next to the toilet, I said, "Lord, I don't feel good."

And I remember the Lord saying so clearly, "I thought we were through."

"No, we're not," I said. I went out that very night, crawling across the street, found my Bible in the ivy and said to the Lord, "I'm going to follow You no matter what."

It was one of those defining moments in life where I had to be all in or all out, because I couldn't rationalize being in the middle. At some point, everyone is pushed to that point, aren't we? Faith is easy when everything's going our way and God's doing exactly what we want Him to do. But then we run into that place where God's decisions conflict with ours, then our true allegiance is uncovered.

In this crowd with Jesus were a lot of hangers-on. They were allured not by who He was, but only by the miracles He did. They just wanted to be where the action was.

So Jesus now turns to speak to this large crowd. What He said to them was on the one hand very stern but on the other very merciful, because He never called anyone to follow Him without giving them the full picture. He wanted to tell them of the cost. He wanted to discourage light-hearted commitments or following under false pretenses. He looked ahead and told them what they could expect. Though this definitely would thin out the crowd at some point, it also would strengthen the work.

Twelve hundred years earlier, in Judges 6–7, the Midianites had all but overthrown Israel and were threatening to put them out of their misery when God spoke to a young man named Gideon, saying, "I want to use you to deliver your people." Gideon thought this was a horrible idea. He didn't feel up to the job. He didn't feel qualified. He tried to get out of it. But the Lord put His hand on Gideon and finally got him to call together an army to fight the Midianites, who were lying in the mountains seemingly as numerous as stars without number. Gideon's army numbered 32,000 people.

"That's too many," the Lord said. "When I give you victory you will be prone to take credit yourselves." I'm sure Gideon thought he needed ten times that many! However, the Lord told him to send home those who were afraid and immediately 22,000 left, leaving Gideon with 10,000.

Not enough, Gideon must have thought.

"Still too many," the Lord said. Fascinating how quickly pride and self would be tempted to take and seek glory for God's work. So still too many!

Then He told Gideon to have the men drink from the brook. Of those remaining, 9,700 lay on their bellies, stuck their faces in the water, and drank. Only three hundred bent a knee, put in their hands, drank out of a cupped hand, and kept their heads up watching for the enemy, alert and prepared.

"Let's use the three hundred," the Lord said. "They're more prepared. I'll do this great work with them."

He thinned the crowd but He perfected the work. And He used these three hundred to bring great deliverance. So Jesus speaks to the large crowd about commitment and cost. He continued:

> "If anyone comes to Me and does not hate his father and mother, wife and chil-
> dren, brothers and sisters, yes, and his own life also, he cannot be My disciple."
> —Luke 14:26

The word *disciple* is the word most often used in the Bible for a follower of Jesus, and speaks of someone who sits to learn, one in training, an apprentice. Verses 26, 27, and 33 all end with the words *cannot be My disciple*. Therefore, we would do well to consider what Jesus said lest we become disqualified. I think these verses should have us conclude that discipleship is lost when our devotion is lost, when our priority is misplaced, and when our willingness to follow is absent. Can't learn anything like that!

The first declaration is shocking. And I think it was intended to be so to draw attention. "What do You mean I'm supposed to hate my father and mother, my sister and brother and wife?" we ask. "I thought I was supposed to love them." We have to be careful when we isolate verses, because in so doing we can come to the wrong conclusions rather quickly. The Bible indeed teaches us that we're to honor our mother and father, love our wives as Christ loved the church, and raise our children in the admonition of the Lord. Therefore, it doesn't take much study to conclude that this word *hate* must mean something other than what we immediately presume.

As Jesus used it, *hate* is a comparative word in the context of what needs to go first. In other words, as this multitude followed Him for all kinds of reasons, Jesus wanted them to evaluate where He fit into their lives. "If you're going to be My disciples," He said, "you must love Me in such a way that every other relationship pales by comparison." Even our own lives must fall into this category. We should be more interested in what the Lord wants than what we want to the point that we would lay down our lives to follow Him. If He's first and everything else follows, then everything works. Only a husband who loves the Lord can love his wife as Christ loves the church. Only a parent who loves the Lord can be an example of the Father's love for them. The person who loves the Lord is fit for everything. The person who doesn't is out of balance.

So Jesus' word to the crowd was, "I've got to be first. If you have to make a decision between what I want and what you want, I want you to choose what I want." But that isn't always so easy. After reading and listening to three or four different studies on this verse, I'm amazed at how we want to water it down or redefine it to fit our ways. Yet Jesus said it pretty clearly. It's hard to misunderstand the words *I have to be first*. And in this large crowd, I suspect there were many who thought of Jesus as a novel individual: bold, brash, powerful, fun to listen to, exciting to be around. But He wasn't first.

> "And whoever does not bear his cross and come after Me cannot be My disciple."
> —Luke 14:27

If the first requirement of discipleship is "first things first," the second one is there's a cross to bear for following Jesus. I have heard this concept absolutely butchered. People will say, "We have this rowdy, loud neighbor. He's just our cross to bear"—as if everything difficult in life becomes their cross to bear. An unruly neighbor isn't a cross to bear. A difficult spouse isn't a cross to bear. A hard job isn't a cross to bear. Economic distress isn't a cross to bear. Those might be difficulties. But that's not what Jesus was speaking about here.

Jesus went to the cross to take our sins and declare a message that cost Him His life. If we're going to give Him first place in our lives and surrender ourselves to Him and His cause, there inevitably will be suffering that will come our way for identifying with Him in this world. That is the cross of which He speaks.

In John 15:20, Jesus said, "A servant is not greater than his master. If they persecuted Me, they will persecute you." That is the cost that comes from walking with Jesus in this world.

To the second-generation Christians, Peter wrote, "Don't think it strange concerning the fiery trial that is to try you. Rejoice to the extent that you have become a partaker of Christ's suffering, so that when His glory is revealed, you can also be glad with exceeding joy." To breeze through life and have an easy time of it won't happen as a Christian—not if you are living openly for Jesus in this world.

To the crowd Jesus said, "If you want to be My disciple, I have to be first. And you have to be willing to pay the price for hanging around Me." His disciples certainly did. Except for John, all of them met violent deaths for their faith and testimony. By comparison, we have an easy time of it. Maybe it is because we are not too outspoken, not to concerned to put Him first, not to willing to stir the pot so to speak.

Jesus followed these words with two short parables designed for one purpose: have the crowd determine whether or not this is what they wanted.

> "For which of you, intending to build a tower, does not sit down first and count the cost, whether he has enough to finish it—lest, after he has laid the foundation, and is not able to finish, all who see it begin to mock him, saying, 'This man began to build and was not able to finish.' Or what king, going to make war against another king, does not sit down first and consider whether he is able with ten thousand to meet him who comes against him with twenty thousand? Or else, while the other is still a great way off, he sends a delegation and asks conditions of peace. So likewise, whoever of you does not forsake all that he has cannot be My disciple."
>
> —Luke 14:28–33

These two illustrations are similar with only a slightly different emphasis. The builder has plenty of time to evaluate the cost, while the king has only a limited amount of time before the enemy overruns his capital. In both parables, the goal is a careful calculation because the downside of not thinking it through is either to quit somewhere in the middle and become a laughingstock or to be defeated altogether. In other words, Jesus' application is that a commitment to Him should be one that is well-thought and well-considered, a decision made with all the facts in mind.

In addition to putting Jesus first and taking up the cross, the third requirement of discipleship is to count the cost and to be willing to give up everything to follow Him. Even when the cost is high and difficult, even when it appears it's the losing way to go, I have to be willing to go Jesus' way.

Your faith in Jesus and your life in the world intersects hundreds of times each year. You might go days and everything seems fine—but then there are times you have to make a choice concerning your friends, your job, or an opportunity before you.

I do what I want most of the time. I do it on my own terms so often. And as long as it costs me nothing, walking with the Lord is easy. But when my life intersects with God's will, I have to make a decision. When someone wrongs me, I could either sue him and take him to court for all he's worth or I can let the Lord handle it, suffer loss, and be a witness. If I choose the latter, instead of getting even, I'll find rest. When I'm not thanked for my efforts, I can say, "I'm not going to do this anymore" or I can keep serving the Lord. These are the intersections between how we live and our commitment to Jesus.

> "Salt is good; but if the salt has lost its flavor, how shall it be seasoned? It is neither fit for the land nor for the dunghill, but men throw it out. He who has ears to hear, let him hear!"
>
> —Luke 14:34–35

In Jesus' day, salt was used for more than seasoning. It was used as a preservative, for while salt can't kill bacteria it can retard its growth. And it is this application Jesus made for the believers. They are to be the salt of the earth—to slow the effects of sin. Jesus sends out disciples who have counted the cost, are bearing the cross, and putting Him first. As they do, they're salt. But if they don't, they become like salt that has lost its saltiness and is good for nothing—too briny to put in the fields, too caustic to put in the fertilizer.

Joseph was salt in Egypt. Daniel and the boys were salt in Babylon. Esther was salt in Persia. Are we being salt in our culture today?

According to the next two verses in Luke, although the scribes and Pharisees complained, the tax collectors and sinners said, "We want life." The results that follow in chapter 15 show that many chose to follow Him. Those who did brought such great joy to Jesus that He told them three stories about the kind of joy He finds in His heart when, out of the crowd, someone comes who truly wants to be His disciple. Keep reading!

Chapter 90

GOD'S REJOICING OVER YOU

Luke 15:1–10

Beginning in chapter 14, Luke gives us three and a half chapters that took place on one Sabbath day. Here in Luke 15–16, Jesus gives us four parables that have one lesson: God's heart of rejoicing over those who come to Him.

> Then all the tax collectors and the sinners drew near to Him to hear Him.
>
> —Luke 15:1

Most of the people in the crowd had heard Jesus give some pretty tough messages about getting rid of pride, refusing to serve self, seeking the lowest place, and taking up the cross—not necessarily messages that would cause people to say, "Yeah, I think I'll follow Him." But the sinners in the crowd didn't run away from Jesus. They ran toward Him. They couldn't wait to hear what He had to say next. Their hearts He had touched.

If you have ever felt the need to water down the Gospel message because you wanted to make it more palatable to people, I hope this verse convinces you there is no need to do that. There are few harsher words than those found in chapter 14—but rather than chasing people off, they drew those who were hungry to hear even closer. Jesus didn't sugarcoat the Gospel. People took it on the chin, but at the same time, His message got through to the hearts of the hungry. He was able to speak about judgment and still come across letting people know they could be forgiven. He spoke seriously and sternly—and yet the lost knew He loved them. Lord, help us share in that way as well!

> And the Pharisees and scribes complained, saying, "This Man receives sinners and eats with them."
>
> —Luke 15:2

For all that Jesus had taught and said over the past three years, the scribes and Pharisees still didn't understand how He could spend five minutes with the likes of tax collectors and sinners and not seek out respectable people like themselves. But as Jesus had shared in the parable of the great supper, respectable people always have excuses for not walking by faith, whereas needy people come with great joy. "You're going to forgive me, restore me, and give me life? I'm in!" they say. And He does!

I love the compliment Jesus receives from His critics here in verse 2. Jesus welcomes sinners? Good! That means I can come! *Receives* is not a word that means He'll make an appointment with us. It means He'll gladly welcome us with open arms and embrace us with a joyful heart. We never find God approving sin—but He welcomes sinners all day long so He might change them and make them His own.

In Jewish culture, one of the most intimate things one can do with friends is to eat with them, to derive life from the same source they do and partake from the same sustenance. The Pharisees ate only with other Pharisees. But Jesus loved to eat with sinners. If you have any doubt that Jesus would accept you the way you are, just read what His enemies said about Him, because their accusation against Him was that He was accessible to and even ate with sinners. We read in Hebrews 2:11, "He that sanctifies and he that is sanctified is one. Therefore, the Lord is not ashamed to call them brethren." Nine chapters later, talking about Old Testament saints, we read, "They're looking for a heavenly country. They desire a better place. Therefore God is not ashamed to be called their God" (Heb. 11:16). The Lord loves to be identified with anyone who comes to be identified with Him.

I am to this day amazed that God loves me so much considering He knows all about me. The fact that you might love me is more understandable because you only see me at my best. But if you go home with me and still love me, we've got something going. Beyond that, the Lord knows my every intent and thought—and He still loves me. Oh, my goodness! He never quits. He eagerly welcomes fellowship. He's the Good Shepherd.

Years earlier, when the Lord sent Ezekiel to speak to the nation, the religious leaders in Judah had become so corrupt that rather than lead the people in the Lord's ways, they were instead using them for their own gain. God spoke to them in Ezekiel 34, "Woe to the shepherds who feed themselves. You don't strengthen the weak. You don't heal the sick. You don't bind up the broken. You don't bring back those who have been driven away. You don't look for those who are lost. You just rule with force and cruelty. I'm going to be the Shepherd. I'm going to look for My flock. I'm going to seek them out and deliver them from every place I find them even on dark and cloudy days."

I've always been convinced that if the world could see God's love through His Son, a lot more people would get saved. The problem is, all they usually see is religion—and that drives them away. But if they could see Jesus in us, they might come running!

> So He spoke this parable to them, saying: "What man of you, having a hundred sheep, if he loses one of them, does not leave the ninety-nine in the wilderness, and go after the one which is lost until he finds it? And when he has found it, he lays it up on his shoulders, rejoicing. And when he comes home, he calls together his friends and neighbors, saying to them, 'Rejoice with me, for I have found my sheep which was lost!' I say to you that likewise there will be more joy in heaven over one sinner who repents than over ninety-nine just persons who need no repentance. Or what woman, having ten silver coins, if she loses one coin,

does not light a lamp, sweep the house, and search carefully until she finds it? And when she has found it, she calls her friends and neighbors together, saying, 'Rejoice with me, for I have found the piece which I lost!' Likewise, I say to you, there is joy in the presence of the angels of God over one sinner who repents."

—Luke 15:3–10

I believe in verse 3 Jesus uses the word *parable* in a singular form, although it is followed by four parables, because the lesson is singular. Each is designed to show us God's heart and joy over those who respond to His invitation. As seen in verses 4 and 8, both parables began on a note of loss. The shepherd lost one sheep out of a hundred. The woman lost one coin of ten. From a business standpoint, the shepherd lost 1 percent of his livelihood—a bad break, but probably not something that would have put him out of business. Therefore, his motivation was not financial. His motivation was love. But because first-century women were not allowed to work, the loss of even a single coin could have had significant impact. So the woman's motivation was driven far more by value than by love. She needed that coin to make it through.

Both the shepherd and the woman immediately began their search. The shepherd put all of his energy into finding this pitifully defenseless animal he called his own. And that's the picture the Lord paints of Himself and His relationship to us. He said in Isaiah 40:11 that He would feed the flock like a shepherd, that He would gather the lambs in His arms and carry them in His bosom, and that He would gently lead those with young. Speaking through Ezekiel, He said, "I will seek out what is lost and bring back what is driven away. I will bind up the brokenhearted, strengthen the sick, and take care of those in need."

Poor ancient homes traditionally did not have windows, which made them very dark. They also had straw covering the floor, which would have made the woman's lost coin even more difficult to find. She would have had to get on her hands and knees to make a diligent search and that's exactly what she did.

Both the woman and the shepherd show us the same thing: that the Lord loves sinners and that they are of such value to Him that He would go to any length, even the sending of His Son to find them. When I came to the Lord, it wasn't because I was looking for Him but because He was searching for me. In the same way, Jesus had been searching for the people by preaching the truth to them, expounding the Scriptures, pointing to Himself, and differentiating between religion and relationship with God. And as God's Word was preached and presented to the people, some came.

How has the Lord been searching for you? In the same manner: turning on the light where there was darkness and bringing you His Word when you didn't know or understand it. Salvation always begins with God. If you come, it's only because He's been longing for you and seeking to bring you to Himself.

I love the picture of the shepherd spying the lost sheep, running over to it, picking it up, cleaning it off, checking it out, and throwing it on his shoulder. We don't hear any cross words for the sheep—no "Hey, you stupid sheep. What have I told you about wandering off." It was just, "Welcome, so glad I have found you!"

The oldest statue ever recovered from a western church is a third-century statue of the Good Shepherd with a lamb on His shoulders and the greatest smile you've ever seen. It thrills my heart to think that when I came to the Lord, it made Him smile. Psalm 28:9 says, "Lord, save Your people. Bless Your inheritance. Shepherd over them. Bear them up forever." And He does. Isaiah, as he was speaking for the Lord in 46:4, said, "Even to your gray hairs, I'll carry you for I have made you. I will bear you, carry you, and deliver you."

The result of the found sheep and the found coin is the same: such joy that neither the shepherd nor the woman could keep it to themselves. The same is true when it comes to God. In fact, the initial joy over the newest addition to the family seems momentarily to outshine the settled joy of those who already have come.

The Pharisees hated sinners. They saw themselves above them. They saw no need to spend five minutes with them. But God is just the opposite. He saves sinners. He's a friend to sinners. He has an answer for their sin. And while the Pharisees stood back in judgment, God actively hands out mercy and grace to all who will receive Him.

It's a good thing God is looking for you, isn't it? You wouldn't seek Him, but He has sought after you. And if you decide to be found and receive His grace and follow His love, you'll not only put a smile on His face but on those of His angels as well. Come!

Chapter 91

THE PRODIGAL SON

Luke 15:11–32

The first two verses of chapter 15 show the sinners and tax collectors gathered around Jesus and the religious leaders mocking Him for associating with people like that. Jesus tells three parables in chapter 15, each designed to reveal God's heart. In the first two parables, God was the seeker—the shepherd who looked for the sheep and the woman who searched for the coin. In this third parable, however, the Lord is the One who is sought. And it is an explanation and application set into the context of verses 1–2. The setting is important because Jesus wanted the people in the crowd to know that God's heart was far different from those of the religious men who looked down on them. This parable adds to our understanding of God's heart: "No matter where you've been, you can come looking for God and find Him."

> Then He said, "A certain man had two sons. And the younger of them said to his father, 'Father, give me the portion of goods that falls to me.' So he divided to them his livelihood. And not many days after, the younger son gathered all together, journeyed to a far country, and there wasted his possessions with prodigal living."
>
> —Luke 15:11–13

If you've had children grow up with you, you understand there comes a time when every one of them at some point wants to break away from the nest, test his wings, and make a life for himself. It's usually heart wrenching for parents to watch because they wish they could keep their kids home forever.

I don't doubt this father said, "You're not going to find what you're looking for out in the world, my boy; you don't know how good you have it." I'm sure he raised his objections in his love for his son. But choice is something God give us. This son was of age and, despite his father's objections, as soon as his money cleared the bank, he was gone.

We aren't told much about the life the son chose other than that it was in a faraway country, a life he thought would suit him just fine. But there is no lasting satisfaction to be found in the world, because the wages of sin are bound to come. Jesus' description of this young man is that he wasted his life in prodigal living. We've defined the word *prodigal* by the story. We think *prodigal* refers to someone who has left and comes back, but in reality *prodigal* means "lavish" or "without bottom." In other words, this young man went out and lived as if he'd always have plenty, indulging himself with what he thought was an endless supply. He was the prodigal son in the sense that he was living it up as if he had it all. In that sense *prodigal* can also apply to the father because the father was at home with a boundless love, a bottomless love, an endless love for his son. And, ultimately, the mercy and forgiveness this boy would return to, he would find for himself only coming from His God.

The word *wasted* is an interesting word because Jesus very clearly said he wasted what he had searching for something else. He had been rich by the world's standards but eventually was left with nothing, and he still hadn't found it. The world can satisfy for a while, but ultimately it leaves all who look to it bankrupt.

> "But when he had spent all, there arose a severe famine in that land, and he began to be in want. Then he went and joined himself to a citizen of that country and he sent him into his fields to feed swine. And he would gladly have filled his stomach with the pods that the swine ate, and no one gave him anything."
> —Luke 15:14–16

It is always about the time when our resources in the world run out that our real need becomes clear. We then also realize that there are a lot of things the world can't satisfy. Everything this son had bought and everything he had owned was absolutely insufficient for the life he now had to live. We can buy much, but we can't buy joy. We can't buy peace either. Nor is there a way to purchase hope. And we can't find rest with a credit card. We can fake it for awhile. But when the true need comes, worldly confidences and possessions are the very things that leave us wanting the most. Worldly coveting is not only unsatisfying in the present, it leaves us ill-prepared for the future.

So here's a young man who, however long his money had lasted while he lived the prodigal life, now had nothing in a time of famine. The idea that sinful living brings freedom is a lie. It actually brings slow death. He had gone out to find himself, but found nothing. Why? The Bible says we were created to please God. We were made to worship Him. We are ill fit to do anything else. In fact, the harder we try, the more frustrated we become. You wouldn't put bread on your lawnmower to toast it, or mow the lawn with your couch. They're not suited for those things. Neither are we suited to live out our lives in the pleasure of the world without ever considering God. We won't function well there. This young guy discovered he didn't fit. He thought of going home. But that's a hard turn, isn't it? Pride would tell him he could make it on his own, that he could get back on top. He became a slave to the very life he had chosen.

I imagine those in this mostly-Jewish audience winced when Jesus said, "And the young man joined himself to someone from that country," because it literally meant he joined himself to a Gentile. He was in the wrong land. He was far away from God. And now he was a pig farmer—not exactly a fit task for a Jewish son. He had found rock bottom. Verse 16 adds that the people who once seemed to care for him before now cared no longer. Just a few months earlier, everyone loved him and had answered his call on the first ring. Now no one called, and neither did anyone answer his calls for help.

> "But when he came to himself, he said, 'How many of my father's hired servants have bread enough and to spare, and I perish with hunger! I will arise and go to my father, and will say to him, "Father, I have sinned against heaven and before you and I am no longer worthy to be called your son. Make me like one of your hired servants."'"
>
> —Luke 15:17–19

If you want to remember this story in order with just a few words, try these: *sick of home, sick, homesick, home.*

I wonder what would have happened if some of the son's friends had rallied around him and paid his rent for a few months. He very well might have decided he could make it and put off going home at all. But sitting in the slop, he had little other choice.

It isn't wise to hinder God's work in alleviating for people the consequences of their choices when they are still living smack dab in the middle of them. The fact that no one gave him anything put the son in a position where all he could do was make a decision about what the rest of his life was going to mean.

There is a darkness about sin that keeps people blind to the problems they will create. They don't see them. There's no awareness as to how deep they've gotten or how far they've fallen. "How could I have been such a fool?" they finally say when they come to their senses—but that can take quite some time.

According to what God's word tells us, sinners are not in their right spiritual minds, and can't be, until God reveals to them what their lives are like. He often uses life's circumstances to wake us up. It wasn't until the prodigal son finally came to his senses that he saw the great benefit home could bring. He was tired of suffering. He wanted to alleviate some of the problems sin had caused. I mention this because there is a movement among many pastors today to remove words like *sin, hell*, and *judgment* from their messages because they find them harsh and they don't want to turn away people. I choose to leave them in because it isn't our concern to make you happy. It is our concern to let you know who God is. Only He can make you happy. Only He can provide rest.

"I'm going to say this to my father," the prodigal son declared. "Father, I've sinned against heaven and before you." That's ultimately the place God wants to bring us, isn't it? Without knowing it, this young man was quoting the first couple verses of the Sermon on the Mount. He was poor in spirit. He was mourning over his sin. He was spiritually hungry for the things of God. He wanted what God had to offer and saw himself as unable to achieve that on his own. It's hard to come to that point and admit you've sinned, isn't it? Yet the moment you confess, salvation is not far behind because when you are broken, your ambition and outlook on life changes—along with your view of God and His ways.

After coming to his senses, the son's plan was to offer an apology and a request to be a servant. He wasn't coming home and demanding anything. He wasn't coming home, saying, "I'm your son. You owe me a break." No, he was going to say, "I'm not your son. I don't act that way. I haven't responded that way. I just want to have a place where I can work. I want you to put me in the position of a servant."

There are a lot of people who never come to the point of realizing, as they sit in the pigsty, that this isn't the way to live. Sometimes they are stuck there because no one will tell them of God's heart and His willingness to deliver and bring life. What the prodigal found, however, he never could have imagined: that God's grace watches the hills for a son to return.

If you don't know the Lord, this is how God watches for you. Like the shepherd, He goes to find the lost sheep. Like the woman, He greatly values your life and sends the Holy Spirit—but it has to be your decision to come.

> "And he arose and came to his father."
>
> —Luke 15:20

Once we come to our senses, we have to act in repentance and return to the Lord. Nothing happens until we arise and go to the Father.

> "But when he was still a great way off, his father saw him and had compassion, and ran and fell on his neck and kissed him. And the son said to him, 'Father, I have sinned against heaven and in your sight, and am no longer worthy to be called your son.' But the father said to his servants, 'Bring out the best robe and put it on him, and put a ring on his hand and sandals on his feet. And bring the fatted calf here and kill it, and let us eat and be merry; for this my son was dead and is alive again; he was lost and is found.' And they began to be merry."
>
> —Luke 15:20–24

"Why does He hang around with sinners?" the Pharisees said of Jesus in verse 2. The answer is that God loves sinners and His desire is that they would come home. What the young son soon would learn was that his father's love was such that he daily strained his eyes across the horizon, looking for a silhouette that looked like his son's. When the son was still a great way off, this prodigal father, with great love, ran toward his son. It's the only place in the Bible you'll find God doing a sprint. Far away, moved with love, this father ran out to meet his son, smothering him with kisses. The verb used is a present-perfect tense, meaning he didn't stop kissing his son. And this dirty, rejected one who smelled of pigs was embraced by the father he once had longed to leave behind. Maybe you don't have to hit rock bottom to come home, but even if you have, there's still time.

Through his tears, the son began to say what he had rehearsed in verse 21. But he only was able to get out his confession of sin before he was stopped. "I don't deserve to be your son anymore. I'll just be one of the farm workers," he was going to say. He had a solution—but his father had a better one.

That's usually the case when people repent of their sin. They go to God oftentimes with a solution. "Look, here's the deal," they say. "I know I haven't done so well, but here's what I want to do from this time forward."

What we must understand right away is that God has a far better idea. He'd just like to adopt us as His own and pour out His mercy and grace upon us. God's not looking for you to pay. He's already paid. He's looking for you to come. The son wanted to pay for his sin by becoming a slave. The father just wanted his son back. And that's the difference. The religious person is driven by payment rather than by love.

God doesn't want payment—He wants you. And He will run and receive you if you'll just come to your senses and arise and go to Him. You might have a deal to offer, a plan you've devised, or an idea you want to run by Him. I guarantee He's heard it already. "Oh, is this the one where you . . .? I've heard that one before," He'll say. "See if you don't like My idea better: Let's get you a new robe, kill the fatted calf, and let all of heaven rejoice."

> "Now his older son was in the field. And as he came and drew near to the house, he heard music and dancing. So he called one of the servants and asked what these things meant. And he said to him, 'Your brother has come, and because he has received him safe and sound, your father has killed the fatted calf.' But he was angry and would not go in. Therefore his father came out and pleaded with him."
>
> —Luke 15:25–28

Yet the good news was anything but good to the elder son, representative of the scribes and Pharisees. He didn't want to join in the joy and didn't want to come to the celebration of his brother's return. He was angry. The Greek word used here for *anger* speaks of smoldering resentment. In other words, he had been mad for a long time at his father's concern for his younger brother. And although his father pleaded with him—from an imperfect tense verb that means he constantly and continually said, "Come on in. Look, he was lost but now he's found. You gotta join us."—the elder son refused. Why? Because his relationship with his father had nothing to do with faith but everything to do with duty, performance, and accomplishment.

"So he answered and said to the father, 'Lo, these many years I have been serving
you; I never transgressed your commandment at any time; and yet you never
gave me a young goat, that I might make merry with my friends.'"

—Luke 15:29

Notice that the elder son's testimony has nothing to do with grace, mercy, love, or repentance of sin. It has everything to do with "You know what I've been doing for you all this time? I've never once talked back. I've never once refused your demands. You owe me a lot. And yet you've never even given me money to throw a party with my friends." That's not a relationship with the father. This religious guy just wanted his reward. And this young Pharisee saw himself as far better than the son outside who had failed so miserably.

"But as soon as this son of yours came, who has devoured your livelihood with
harlots, you killed the fatted calf for him."

—Luke 15:30

The elder son wasn't thrilled with grace either, nor was he excited about mercy. He presumed all of his younger brother's money went to prostitutes. In many ways this elder son seemed further removed in heart from his father than the brother who had squandered all he had in the world and returned in humility and sorrow. It shows us it is possible to leave the father while never leaving the farm. You can be in church all your life and not know God. You can be as religious as a person can be and never know God.

"And he said to him, 'Son, you are always with me, and all that I have is yours.
It was right that we should make merry and be glad, for your brother was dead
and is alive again, and was lost and is found.'"

—Luke 15:31–32

Still the father loved the elder son and continued to beg him to come in. Do you know how hard it is for legalists to find comfort in enjoying God's mercy? How hard it is for the self-righteous to accept God's way of receiving people by faith and repentance? And yet the father said to his oldest son, "I know you don't agree with it. I know you don't like it. But it's right. We should rejoice. We have reason to celebrate. My son was dead. And now he's alive by his faith."

The scribes and Pharisees should have been rejoicing that the tax collectors and sinners were coming to Jesus. But they were not. Having grown up in Calvary Chapel, over the years I have heard tremendous criticism about the kinds of people who go to church there. "You're nothing but a bunch of drug addicts and losers," some say. That's right. Proud of it. Couldn't be happier. I think God rejoices. And so do we when people come to their senses and arise and go to the Father.

The prodigal son story certainly explains verses 1 and 2 and is still the answer for legalists who expect God to reward and acknowledge their goodness. He will not. He cannot. But if we'll come out of the world and look to Him, we'll find Him looking for us and running in our direction, grace in hand and the blood of His Son to make us clean.

Chapter 92

A Lesson from the Worldly Wise

Luke 16:1–13

We continue in one Sabbath day of Jesus' ministry as reported to us by Luke in Luke 14–17:10. Here in chapter 16 Jesus speaks to both His disciples and the Pharisees about how the love of money will betray the heart of the ungodly and the need for His people to use their money for His honor. The Pharisees taught that wealth was a sign of God's blessing—which sounds very much like the faith teachers of today who, incessantly focusing on money, rarely get to the subject of true riches.

> He also said to His disciples: "There was a certain rich man who had a steward, and an accusation was brought to him that this man was wasting his goods. So he called him and said to him, 'What is this I hear about you? Give an account of your stewardship, for you can no longer be steward.' Then the steward said within himself, 'What shall I do? For my master is taking the stewardship away from me. I cannot dig; I am ashamed to beg. I have resolved what to do, that when I am put out of the stewardship, they may receive me into their homes.' So he called every one of his master's debtors to him, and said to the first, 'How much do you owe my master?' And he said, 'A hundred measures of oil.' So he said to him, 'Take your bill, and sit down quickly and write fifty.' Then he said to another, 'And how much do you owe?' So he said, 'A hundred measures of wheat.' And he said to him, 'Take your bill, and write eighty.' So the master commended the unjust steward because he had dealt shrewdly."
>
> —Luke 16:1–8

The office of steward was a highly-entrusted position, for a steward controlled his master's money—paying the bills and collecting debts. When Paul wrote to the Corinthians about being a steward of the things of God, he said, "It is required that a steward be found faithful." Here in our story Jesus tells us of a man who was not faithful. He had mismanaged or probably embezzled funds from his master. When this was brought to the master's attention, he said to the steward, "What have you done? Let's open the books and if you're found to be a crook, you won't have your job anymore."

Knowing he was indeed a crook, the steward also knew that when the audit was completed, he'd be out of a job. No one would give him a good recommendation. He was too old to go back to manual labor and too proud to beg. There had to be another way. As he contemplated what he could do, he came up with a plan, one he could carry out in the two or three weeks he'd still have access to the files before the evidence was fully gathered.

Verse 4 says his goal was that *they* would receive him when he lost his job. Who is "they"? His master's debtors. He would try to endear himself to the folks who owed his master lots of money so that when he was out of a job, they would owe him. We are given two examples of how he carried forth his plan, although I'm sure there were probably many more.

One fellow owed the master a hundred measures of oil, perhaps olive oil. A measure of oil was about nine gallons. "Just write down that you owe 450 gallons instead of the 900 and I'll sign it," the steward said.

He then went to the next fellow and asked, "How much do you owe my master?" The answer was a hundred measures of wheat. A measure of wheat is about ten bushels. So the steward cut it by 20 percent and said, "You only owe eighty bushels."

This went on down the line and eventually, when the audit was completed and all came to light, the master found out what had been taking place. In verse 8, he commends his unjust representative for his shrewd dealings. He didn't commend him for cheating, nor was he was happy about the loss he suffered as a result. But he commended his steward, as crooked as he was, for the foresight to feather his own nest before losing his job. You have to hand it to this steward. He had some shrewd ideas and was going to make sure they worked for him.

Jesus now makes the comparison between this man's behavior and what He wanted His disciples and us to learn from it when it came to our spiritual service.

> "For the sons of this world are more shrewd in their generation than the sons of light. And I say to you, make friends for yourselves by unrighteous mammon, that when you fail, they may receive you into an everlasting home."
> —Luke 16:8b–9

The original word for *mammon* is the word for the Canaanite god of wealth. It is unrighteous in the sense that it is only good for this world. Jesus said of this man feathering his nest, only a few weeks before he was to lose his job, "Those in the world are far sharper when it comes to their future planning and outlook than are the sons of light. Here's what you should do: if you use the money with which God has entrusted you to bring spiritual life to others, when you die, that very fruit will meet you at the door."

Jesus said in the Sermon on the Mount it is foolish to lay up for ourselves treasures on earth because everything around us ruins it—the rust, the moth, the thief. Rather, we are to store up for ourselves treasure in heaven where none of those things affect it. Spiritual fruit is the only thing we can send ahead—and that's exactly what Jesus encourages us to do here—be wise in our generation with great spiritual foresight.

To the world, money is the end. It's the having, purchasing, and owning that matter. To the believer, however, it ought to be only a tool—something by which we can reach the world for Christ. The children of the world are experts at seizing opportunities for making money and getting ahead. They are good at investments that move them forward. Here Jesus says God's kids don't do nearly as well in investing in spiritual things that will bring heavenly rewards and eternal benefits.

The minute you "fail," or die, your money—no matter how little or how much you have—will mean nothing to you anymore. You won't make one more purchase or return one more item. And no matter what the percentage you're getting on your investment, it will be meaningless. Yet if you take advantage of the time you're here to invest in reaching the lost, when you die, waiting at the door to meet you will be all of those who came to know the Lord through your investments in spiritual things. On earth, you may never know how well you have done—but you will know one day when you arrive in glory.

So to the disciples, Jesus said, "You ought to use the money with which God entrusts you for eternal dividends." And that is the challenge for each of us as well. How are you planning to use what you have been given? How shrewd are you in investing that with which God has blessed you? When you die, you'll find out it didn't belong to you, but to Him all along.

One day we'll give an account for our stewardship—and then we will see what we've done and if we've been wiser than this wicked employee in the story.

> "He who is faithful in what is least is faithful also in much; and he who is unjust in what is least is unjust also in much. Therefore if you have not been faithful in the unrighteous mammon, who will commit to your trust the true riches? And if you have not been faithful in what is another man's, who will give you what is your own?"
>
> —Luke 16:10–12

The next lesson is that being trustworthy with what God has given us will prove we can be entrusted with spiritual oversight. The argument is easy to understand but hard to put into practice. If we can't handle what is the least—and to the Lord, money is the least because it only lasts for this life—how can God give us any kind of spiritual responsibility, true riches, or things that last forever? You can't separate the way you steward the money God has given you from the way you would oversee spiritual things. Therefore, the use of money by the saints is an accurate reflection of their spiritual stewardship potential and their assessment of true eternal values. The use of the "least" is the acid test of how much you value true riches.

When David gathered together the people to give to the building of the temple, he said, "But who are we, Lord, and who are this Your people that we can stand and offer so willingly these things? Everything we have has come from You. And of Your own, we have given it back to You."

"No servant can serve two masters; for either he will hate the one and love the other, or else he will be loyal to the one and despise the other. You cannot serve God and mammon."

—Luke 16:13

The last lesson here is straightforward as well: you can't play in the middle. Many folks think they can do both—they are mistaken. We either love God or love the world's gain. You cannot do both, for each requires a full devotion. So you can't serve God and love money any more than you can walk in two different directions at the same time.

As Christians, there's nothing wrong in shopping for the best deal, saving for a rainy day, managing our investments wisely, or seeking the best rates on our loans. But having said that, Jesus wants us to know we can't balance a love of money with love for Him.

Some people give sparingly because they think the church has enough money. Other people give inconsistently because they only give when they have something left over. A lot of people give sorrowfully and out of fear, with great foreboding and a sense of obligation. But if God is your Master, then money is your servant. As a steward, you can use it for a lot of good things and you can make the sacrifices necessary to invest in places that will bear eternal fruit. If, on the other hand, money becomes your master, you'll constantly be under great stress, because not only is it never satisfying, but it will only buy things that perish and have no future attached to them.

In 2008, nearly five hundred people got saved at our weekly services. Every week we get calls from those who came to know the Lord while listening to our radio program. We have a church in the Philippines that we were privileged to plant, attended now by nearly 1000 people. (I suspect when we get to heaven, there will be Filipino faces welcoming you who have invested in the works of God there!) There is a church in Oregon and one in the north of England in which we have invested, as well as one on the west side of Wales. There are folks who come to our church every Tuesday morning to get food and clothing because they can't afford them on their own. They hear about Jesus—some get saved. It will be awesome one day to go to heaven and see who's waiting for us and what God did with the investments we made!

Who's your Master? One day, at the gates of heaven, your stewardship will answer this question very clearly. Don't love money so much that you refuse to invest it in the things that actually will bear fruit. Show better foresight, and send it ahead in lives God wants to touch.

Chapter 93

RICH MAN,
POOR MAN

Luke 16:14–31

In Chapter 16 Luke focuses on riches or money. In verse 1, we read, "There was a certain rich man . . . ." In verse 14, we read, "Now the Pharisees, who were lovers of money . . . ." In verse 19, we read, "There was a certain rich man . . . ." In seeking to reach these religious carnal people, Jesus leaves no stone unturned in addressing their lifestyles and loves so He might yet again offer them life.

After speaking to the disciples in the beginning of the chapter, from verse 14 to the end of the chapter Jesus deals specifically with the Pharisees—first about their outlook and then about the consequences of living the kind of life that loves money.

> Now the Pharisees, who were lovers of money, also heard all these things, and they derided Him.
>
> —Luke 16:14

The word *derided* speaks not of a verbal response as much as an expression, like an eye roll that showed disagreement. The Pharisees' smirks were evident often. Jesus felt their behavior invited comment:

> And He said to them, "You are those who justify yourselves before men, but God knows your hearts. For what is highly esteemed among men is an abomination in the sight of God."
>
> —Luke 16:15

Because He loved these religious folks who were so caught up in their religion, Jesus both challenged and warned them about the road they were on, saying, "You find your reward or justification in people's approval, yet what they approve God does not, for He values other things." A religious man seeks the applause and admiration of others. He wants to be known and acknowledged for his great religious devotion. Here, as the Pharisees turned up their noses at Jesus, they did so to look good to others without any concern whatsoever about what God had been teaching them; words of life missed because the focus was on what others thought, not upon what He said!

491

In the Sermon on the Mount, Jesus taught, "Be careful about being people-pleasers in your spiritual pursuits because if that's your goal, you already have your reward." That's the problem with religion. Religion is interested in man's opinions. Faith is interested only in God's honor. God sees beyond the smirk to the heart.

I think about the Lord sending Samuel to Jesse's house to find a new king. When Jesse marched out his best-looking, oldest, and apparently wisest son, Eliab, Samuel said, "Bingo. That was easy. He's the one."

But before he had a chance to bless him, the Lord said, "He is not the one."

What do You mean he's not the guy? Samuel must have thought. *Have You taken a good look at him? He looks kingly!*

"Not him," God said again. "People look at the outward appearances but I look at the heart."

"Then who's the guy?" Samuel asked.

"It's that little red-headed, smelly kid out in the back. If you smell sheep on him, you'll know he's the one" (1 Sam. 16).

Like everyone else, Samuel looked at Eliab's height and stature. People tend to do that. What we forget is God looks at our heart. Over the years, I have found I can be easily fooled. But that's not true of God. You can't pull the wool over His eyes. And it's certainly a mistake to be more concerned with your reputation with man than with your standing before God. God sees what we do not. When Jesus wrote the seven letters to the Revelation churches, He began each one with, "I know your works." And then He told them what was in their hearts, to say, "I know what you're doing—but I also see why you're doing it."

Here was a whole group of religiously confident men shaking their heads while Jesus was teaching. "I know all about you," Jesus said. "In fact, what you highly esteem is an abomination with God. You guys are pleasing each other—but what you think is so great, He doesn't."

> "The law and the prophets were until John. Since that time the kingdom of God has been preached, and everyone is pressing into it. And it is easier for heaven and earth to pass away than for one tittle of the law to fail."
>
> —Luke 16:16–17

The Pharisees had developed an understanding of the Law that was quite different from God's Word. God's purpose for the Law had always been to convict people so that when they read it, they'd realize they couldn't keep it and would turn to Him for help.

With John the Baptist's arrival, the last Old Testament prophet in the sense that he was the last prophet to appear before Jesus, all of the evidence was in. Every prophecy and picture found in the Old Testament of the coming Messiah had been given. But these religious men did not believe or embrace the Scriptures. They were unprepared for Jesus.

The word *pressing* here is very interesting because it's a word that connotes violence. Here it speaks of an intense internal struggle. When Jesus showed up on the scene, the people were caught in a great dilemma. The religious leaders had taught them to earn their way to heaven and trust in their hard work. Yet as Jesus offered, "I have come with grace. Just believe in Me. Have faith," it produced a tremendous struggle within their hearts, just as it does for us today. We grow up thinking we can work our way to heaven, and then we meet Jesus and we find out that won't work.

Jesus said that since the kingdom of God had been preached, everyone was pressing into it except those who ought to have known the best. They were not willing to enter into the conflict. They just wrote off His truth as if it were a lie. Yet Jesus said no matter how much they sought to ignore it or set it aside, God's Word would be fulfilled. And heaven and earth will pass away before it will.

> "Whoever divorces his wife and marries another commits adultery; and whoever marries her who is divorced from her husband commits adultery."
>
> —Luke 16:18

Although this verse seems to enter the discussion from seemingly out of nowhere, in reality, Jesus used the scribes and Pharisees' position on divorce as an example of one of their teachings that, like most of their positions, ran absolutely contradictory to God's Word. There was a school of thought among some of the scribes and Pharisees that said divorce for any reason or dissatisfaction was acceptable to God.

In Deuteronomy 24:1–4, Moses had said that although divorce could be allowed for reasons of uncleanness, the man who divorced his wife couldn't take her back. The word for *uncleanness* spoke of adulterous behavior. But some of the scribes and Pharisees interpreted it to mean anything from a bad hair day, to burnt toast in the morning, or pajamas past noon. So Jesus used that one passage, a hot-button topic of the day, to say, "Look what you have done with My Word."

Often, beginning in verse 19, He gave what appears to be a true account to show the Pharisees where their decisions would lead them.

> "There was a certain rich man who was clothed in purple and fine linen and fared sumptuously every day."
>
> —Luke 16:19

There are approximately forty parables in the Scriptures, but none with personal names. Most parables are introduced with, "He spoke a parable to them." This account does not begin that way. Therefore, it would appear this is a true story that can be taken literally and not as the parables, by simile or metaphor

There are a lot of rich men in the Bible who did well with the Lord—among them Abraham, David, and Joseph of Arimathea. I think this man, however, represented the Pharisee's life. He lived richly. He wore purple—dye made from shellfish that was so expensive only kings could afford it. He ate the kind of meals that only those who could pay the price could eat each day. He lived the high life. He put it on display. To these lovers of money, Jesus said, "Let me tell you of a rich man who so loved his riches."

> "But there was a certain beggar named Lazarus, full of sores, who was laid at his gate, desiring to be fed with the crumbs which fell from the rich man's table. Moreover the dogs came and licked his sores."
>
> —Luke 16:20–21

What a contrast between the rich man and this poor man named Lazarus! Although, as we will see, the rich man knew Lazarus' name, he ignored the needy around him. Rather than doing what verse 9 said to do, he spent his money on himself.

> "So it was that the beggar died, and was carried by the angels to Abraham's bosom. The rich man also died and was buried. And being in torment, in Hades, he lifted up his eyes and saw Abraham afar off, and Lazarus in his bosom."
>
> —Luke 16:22–23

When this life ends for both the beggar and the rich man, they both go to judgment. There are no second chances. There is no soul sleep. As Hebrews 9:27 says, it is appointed unto men once to die, then the judgment.

When the beggar died, the angels met him and carried him to Abraham's bosom—a place where the dead who believed waited for Messiah to come and open heaven's doors by His blood. The poor man's funeral would have been uneventful. Being a beggar, his body would have been placed in the garbage heap outside of town to be burned with the daily trash of the city.

The rich man's funeral, on the other hand, would have been quite a social event. But I doubt anyone on that side of the casket knew where he had gone. *Hades* in Greek, *sheol* in Hebrew, had another other compartment where the wicked are kept until one day, at the final judgment, the grave will give up its dead and they will be sent to a place called "Gehenna," to a future of eternal suffering.

From Matthew 12:40, we know this place was located in the center of the earth because Jesus said just as Jonah was three days and three nights in the belly of the great fish, so He would be three days and three nights in the heart of the earth. When Paul wrote to the Ephesians, he said in chapter 4:8 that Jesus, who ascended on high to lead captivity captive and to give gifts to people, first descended into the lower parts of the earth. Peter wrote that Jesus went preaching to the captives in prison. Therefore, it would appear that when Jesus died, He descended into hell—into sheol—to bring those who were waiting in Abraham's bosom into heaven as the firstfruits of His work on the cross while those in the other compartment saw they were wrong, learned of their fate, and heard of His victory.

The picture is given here in Luke and substantiated in many verses. Death certainly is not the end. It's only the beginning.

> "Then he cried and said, 'Father Abraham, have mercy on me, and send Lazarus that he may dip the tip of his finger in the water and cool my tongue; for I am tormented in this flame.' But Abraham said, 'Son, remember that in your lifetime you received your good things, and likewise Lazarus evil things; but now he is comforted and you are tormented. And besides all this, between us and you there is a great gulf fixed, so that those who want to pass from here to you cannot, nor can those from there pass to us.'"
>
> —Luke 16:24–26

Notice that the rich man's faculties were still intact. He could see. He could cry. He could remember. If you're saved, this life is as bad as it gets for you. But if you're not saved, this life is as good as it will ever be. The rich man cried out for help, but it was too late. Between Lazarus and him was a huge chasm that even human sympathy couldn't cross.

Notice also that Abraham drew the rich man's attention to how he had lived and the choices he had made. In the context, to the scribes and Pharisees Jesus said, "Look at this rich man. Look at the end of his life."

People ask how a good God can send people to hell. The answer is that God doesn't send anyone to hell. He invites us to heaven. Yet there stood the religious men who refused His Word and taught it in a twisted way, ignoring guys like Lazarus and despising Jesus for hanging out with them.

> "Then he said, 'I beg you therefore, father, that you would send him to my father's house, for I have five brothers, that he may testify to them, lest they also come to this place of torment.' Abraham said to him, 'They have Moses and the prophets; let them hear them.'"
>
> —Luke 16:27–29

The rich man's fate was not due to his riches. It was due to his love of them and his lack of love for God. If the rich man had read the Word, obeyed the Word, and taken heed of the Word, he could have lived. When he said, "Go save my family," Abraham answered that they had all they needed because they had the Word.

> "And he said, 'No, father Abraham; but if one goes to them from the dead, they will repent.' But he said to him, 'If they do not hear Moses and the prophets. Neither will they be persuaded though one rise from the dead.'"
>
> —Luke 16:30–31

When Lazarus, Mary and Martha's brother, was later raised from the dead, some believed while others did not. Four months later, Jesus died and rose. Did the scribes and Pharisees repent? No. Instead, they paid off the Roman guards sent to watch over the grave, to tell a story about how someone had stolen His body.

If you're determined not to believe, even overwhelming evidence won't help you. You've got to check out the Word, see what God says, and respond. You only have this life. Don't wait until five minutes after you're dead to decide you were wrong, for by then it will be five minutes too late.

Chapter 94

DISCIPLESHIP DUTIES

Luke 17:1–10
(Matthew 18:1–7; 18–35)

B eginning in chapter 14 and continuing through 17:10, Luke spends three and a half chapters giving us one Sabbath day in Jesus' life that had begun at a dinner to which He had been invited for the sole purpose of accusing Him of breaking the Sabbath law. Jesus had been speaking to His disciples and the crowds as well, offering them a life far more valuable than the one offered to them by the religious leaders, who had been misrepresenting God for a long time.

These first ten verses of chapter 17 were meant specifically for the disciples—those who had become convinced of who Jesus was and were learning to walk with Him in the midst of these very difficult times.

> Then He said to the disciples, "It is impossible that no offenses should come, but woe to him through whom they do come! It would be better for him if a millstone were hung around his neck, and he were thrown into the sea, then that he should offend one of these little ones. Take heed to yourselves."
> —Luke 17:1–3

Because of the human condition, sin makes stumbling inevitable. There isn't a place we can turn that there isn't the opportunity or temptation to do the wrong thing. We can't hide from sin. We only can come to know the Lord so we can turn away from it. Although stumbling is inevitable, Jesus told His disciples here to be sure they weren't the cause.

The word *offense* is the Greek word *skandalon*, from which we get our word *scandal*. It is the word most often used by Jesus to talk about anything that can trip us up. In Corinthians 1:23, Paul said, "We preach Christ crucified. To the Jews, a stumbling block (*skandalon*) to their works-oriented relationship with God. To the Greeks, to the idolaters, the Gospel was simply foolishness. But to those who are being saved, it's the power of God to salvation."

"Don't be like the ones with their robes of self-righteousness wrapped tightly around them," Jesus said to His disciples. "Don't cause My little ones to stumble." Jesus said to His disciples, "Don't mess with God's kids." And His warning is so serious that He said if you trip one them up in their pursuit of God, it would be preferable for you to go swimming with cement floatees. That's spoken like a true father, isn't it?

497

We don't want to be like those religious leaders. We want to help people come to the Lord, not be driven away from Him.

When Paul wrote his letter to the Romans, he spent an entire chapter on one issue: a person's liberty and how it affects others. He said in chapter 14 that because we will give an account of ourselves to God, we must quit judging one another and instead resolve never to put a stumbling block in front of our brother or sister.

In 1 John 2:10, John said a believer is someone who abides in the light and that there should be no occasion in a believers' life for stumbling another. A true believer is one who is careful about the way he or she lives. As God's people, we must be kind to others, so as never to stumble them in their walks with God.

> "If your brother sins against you, rebuke him; and if he repents, forgive him. And if he sins against you seven times in a day, and seven times in a day returns to you, saying, 'I repent,' you shall forgive him."
>
> —Luke 17:3–4

The Greek word for *sin against you* is the same as the word for *stumble*. So after a warning not to be a stumbling block, Jesus told His disciples that if someone else caused you to stumble, tell them. If they repented, they were to be forgiven—even if it happened seven times in one day.

So important is this issue of stumbling that Jesus said, "Don't cry, 'Foul!' if you're offended. Don't get even. Don't try to take matters into your own hands, don't grumble, or complain. If you belong to the Lord and someone's behavior trips you up, share that with them. Give the person the opportunity to make it right."

That's a great way to remove stumbling in our midst, isn't it? We tell each other. We repent. We forgive. The slate is clean. Seven times in one day would suggest *sorry* is a word without much meaning. But we're to forgive anyway. God's job is to judge sincerity. Our job is to respond properly. The believer can forgive because he knows he has himself been forgiven.

Again, this looks good on paper, but is difficult to carry forth into behavior. For one thing, we never want to confront anyone. We'd like someone else to do that. Secondly, we hate repenting, or being told we are offensive or we are wrong. And finally, the natural man would rather keep account of wrongs than forgive them. Yet that's exactly what we must do if we're going to discover God's best.

We have to confront when we don't want to. We have to look to restore when we don't want to. We have to forgive when we don't want to. No wonder the disciples asked for more faith.

And the apostles said to the Lord, "Increase our faith." So the Lord said, "If you have faith as a mustard seed, you can say to this mulberry tree, 'Be pulled up by the roots and be planted in the sea,' and it would obey you."

—Luke 17:5–6

To be able to confront, restore, and forgive, the disciples realized they'd need more faith. But Jesus said, "Just a little bit of faith can get a lot done. It's not the amount of faith. It's the using or exercising of it." There's an interesting attachment in the Bible between God and us, in the sense that what attaches us to God is our faith in Him and our dependence on His ability to do in us what He requires. And according to the Bible, the only thing that makes this bond of faith stronger is our coming to know God better.

Romans 10:17 says faith comes by hearing and hearing comes by God's Word. This means that as I get to know God better, I am in a better position to walk with Him by faith. Why? I'm able to prove that what He says is true. I'm able to know His heart is for me and not against me. I become confident in His ability and willingness to stand with me. I become aware of His mercy and grace—if I fall, He'll pick me up. As I come to know God better, my faith grows, and so does my willingness to do what He says.

Abraham started off with a little faith. "Leave home and come with Me," God said. Years later, when he knew God better and there was not enough land for both his and Lot's flocks, Abraham said to Lot, "Pick a side and I'll take the other." Seeing the desert on one side and the rich, fertile ground of Sodom on the other, Lot chose Sodom. Abraham was content with the desert. Because Abraham had come to know the Lord better, he could trust Him more—even to the point where, twenty-five years later, he was willing to sacrifice his own son, believing God could raise him from the dead, for God had promised that through his son Isaac would his seed be called. Even death, could not thwart the sureness of God's Word and promise.

Joseph was but a teenager when his brothers sold him into slavery because they hated him. Years later he became Vice-Pharaoh, second in command of the known world. When his brothers came to beg for food, they didn't recognize him. But because Joseph had come to know God better, he was able to say to them, "What you meant for evil, God meant for good. He sent me ahead to keep you alive."

David stood over a sleeping Saul, who for seven years had chased him over every mountain and through every desert in all of Sinai. But David couldn't slit his throat because he knew God too well. He knew God had made Saul king.

Faith in God allows us to do what He wants. Hearing what the Lord wanted—the forgiveness, confrontation, and repentance—the disciples said, "We're going to need more faith for that." But Jesus' answer was the issue isn't volume. It's use. It's not how much faith we have but how much by faith we're willing to step out and do. Am I going to die to myself, forgive, and be merciful because I've been blessed—or not?

"And which of you, having a servant plowing or tending sheep, will say to him when he has come in from the field, 'Come at once and sit down to eat'? But will he not rather say to him, 'Prepare something for my supper, and gird yourself and serve me till I have eaten and drunk, and afterward you will eat and drink'? Does he thank that servant because he did the things that were commanded him? I think not. So likewise you, when you have done all those things which you are commanded, say, 'We are unprofitable servants. We have done what was our duty to do.'"

—Luke 17:7–10

"Don't think too highly of yourself when you're beginning to obey God by faith." Unprofitable servants are those that don't profit. I've yet to hear Christians call themselves unprofitable. We usually brag about our great faith and of what God has done through us. In reality, however, if God hired based on talent, we'd all be out of a job! Don't come bragging to the Lord. Just believe Him. Act on what He has taught you, but realize that's only what you're supposed to do.

We don't want to be stumbling blocks. We want people to come to know Jesus. For them to do that, they're going to have to see His love in us.

Chapter 95

ONE SLATED FOR LIFE—
THE OTHER FOR DEATH

John 11:1–54

After three and a half chapters of Luke's account of one Sabbath in Jesus' life—His run-in with the religious leaders and His offer to the crowds of who He was and what He could do, in John 11 He heads back into Jerusalem at a very dangerous time, with the religious leaders looking to have Him killed. He returned specifically to minister to Lazarus, Mary, and Martha.

In his gospel, John used seven miracles to build his case that Jesus is God. The first was set at a family wedding feast in Cana. The last happened also to a family—Mary and Martha were suffering their brother's death in Bethany, a little town just outside of Jerusalem, on the back side of the Mount of Olives. In the first miracle, Jesus showed Himself to be Lord over creation when He made wine from water. Here in the last one, He shows Himself to be Lord over life itself.

Bethany is only on the map today because it was there that Jesus raised Lazarus from the dead. If you've been to Bethany, you know that if you take three steps in any direction, you've left town. However, because of what the Lord did there, everyone knows about Bethany. Likewise, I hope everyone will know what your town is about because of what Jesus did in your life.

Mary, Martha, and Lazarus loved Jesus. And at a time when it was very dangerous to believe in Him or follow Him, they did. Although they publicly declared their faith, they did not find themselves insulated from the tragedy life can bring. Yet when tragedy struck, they had someone to turn to—and so do we. So here we see Jesus, the One slated for death, so Lazarus could be slated for life.

> Now a certain man was sick, Lazarus of Bethany, the town of Mary and her sister Martha. It was that Mary who anointed the Lord with fragrant oil and wiped His feet with her hair, whose brother Lazarus was sick. Therefore the sisters sent to Him, saying, "Lord, behold, he whom You love is sick."
> —John 11:1–3

There are six different Marys in the Gospels, so John identified this Mary as the one who, in the next chapter, pours ointment on Jesus' feet and wipes them with her hair.

501

Bethany is on the east side of Jerusalem. At the base of the Mount of Olives is Gethsemane, where Jesus would be buried. But just over the top of the hill, you will enter Bethany. And although from Bethany you can't see the East Gate, if you walk 1,000 feet, you can. So Mary, Martha, and Lazarus lived within earshot of the constant sacrifices and worship, as well as the trouble and difficulty, that religion had brought to the people as they gathered often on the temple mount, just across the Kidron Valley.

This is where Jesus often stayed when He was in town. As a result, Mary, Martha, and Lazarus had come to know and love Him. And they were sure of His love for them. It was bad enough that Lazarus was sick—but worse that Jesus was over thirty miles away in Perea on the other side of the Jordan, where He had been for quite some time. No doubt choosing the fastest runner they could find, Mary and Martha sent the message to Jesus that the one He loved was sick, using the word *phileo*, a family love.

When I argue with God that He ought to do something for me because of how much I love Him, I run out of arguments very quickly because my love for Him is fickle and weak. But if, like Mary and Martha, I go to the Lord dependent on His love for me, I'm in great shape because His love for me is always the same.

It would nearly have been a two-day trip to Perea from Bethany to where Jesus was, no matter how fast one went. When Jesus received the message, He waited two days to come into town, only to find that Lazarus had been buried for four. So it appears that when the runner got to Jesus, even if He had come immediately, Lazarus would have been dead two days already. Yet God gives us some insight as to what was going on that Mary and Martha couldn't see.

> When Jesus heard that, He said, "This sickness is not unto death, but for the glory of God, that the Son of God may be glorified through it." Now Jesus loved Martha and her sister and Lazarus.
>
> —John 11:4–5

Jesus heard the news of Lazarus' illness but didn't immediately come running. He simply said to the messenger, "This is not a sickness to death. God is going to be glorified." Whenever the words *glory of God* are applied to Jesus, it is always in relationship to showing who He is so people would know He wasn't just a man, prophet, or nice person, but that He was God who had come in the flesh. Jesus knew what no one else knew—that God the Father had a plan through which the people around Him were going to better understand who He was. The sisters and their brother were going to be aware of Jesus in a new way—but for this to happen, He would have to delay His coming.

We are told much the same thing in the story of Job. We get the inside story Job never gets: that the Lord was setting him on display, proving his faith, making solid his hope.

Meanwhile, back in Bethany, Lazarus had died. According to Jewish practice—still the same today—the burial took place on the same day as the death. Friends and family gathered at Mary and Martha's house after the funeral and were still there four days later when Jesus arrived. They had been praying for a miracle. God apparently had decided not to deliver, they thought. They had seen Jesus heal the sick and open the blind eyes of others, but He didn't do it for them, even though they put Him up and thought they were family.

So here we find a very frustrated and conflicted family, a dead brother—and the will of God thirty miles away, saying, "This isn't unto death. This is so the glory of God can be seen."

> So when He heard that he was sick, He stayed two more days in the place where He was. Then after this He said to the disciples, "Let us go to Judea again." The disciples said to Him, "Rabbi, lately the Jews sought to stone You, and are You going there again?" Jesus answered, "Are there not twelve hours in the day? If anyone walks in the day, he does not stumble, because he sees the light of this world. But if one walks in the night, he stumbles, because the light is not in him." These things He said, and after that He said to them, "Our friend Lazarus sleeps, but I go that I may wake him up."
>
> —John 11:6–11

The disciples were fairly practical when it came to their own safety. Knowing the Jews in Jerusalem were trying to kill Jesus, they told Him they didn't think it was such a good idea for Him to go there at this time. Yet in the face of danger, Jesus said, "I'm doing My Father's will, walking in the light. If I'm doing My Father's will, no amount of danger needs to worry Me. If I was living on My own, that's when trouble would come. But because I'm doing My Father's will, there's no problem."

The disciples said, "It's dangerous."

Jesus said, "I'm in the light. I'll be all right."

> Then His disciples said, "Lord, if he sleeps he will get well." However, Jesus spoke of his death, but they thought that He was speaking about taking rest in sleep. Then Jesus said to them plainly, "Lazarus is dead. And I am glad for your sakes that I was not there, that you may believe. Nevertheless let us go to him."
>
> —John 11:12–15

Even though Lazarus was dead, Jesus still called him His friend because death doesn't end your life. I love that He used the word *sleep* to refer to death. For the believer, rather than fear or turmoil, there is rest to be found in the grave. It was a word the disciples didn't immediately understand even though back in Luke 8, when Jesus was called to Jairus' house after his daughter died, He said, "She's not dead. She's sleeping." Instead, the disciples were worried about risking their necks to go into town simply to wake up a friend of Jesus just because he was oversleeping.

By the way, no one ever died in Jesus' presence. Death just doesn't work when He's around. If He'd have been there, death wouldn't have stood a chance. But because He wasn't there, Lazarus was allowed to die physically and Jesus was about to put His glory on display. He told the disciples very clearly that Lazarus was dead—but that their faith would grow as a result. Jesus didn't do this very often, but when He did, it was always so powerful no one should have missed who He was.

> Then Thomas, who is called the Twin, said to his fellow disciples, "Let us also go, that we may die with Him."
>
> —John 11:16

This is classic "glass-half-empty Thomas." Thomas loved Jesus but he was a fatalist. He was called "the twin," but we never meet his brother. Maybe that's because as prone to doubt as each of us is, we're all his twin by nature.

> So when Jesus came, He found that he had already been in the tomb four days. Now Bethany was near Jerusalem, about two miles away. And many of the Jews had joined the women around Martha and Mary, to comfort them concerning their brother. Then Martha, as soon as she heard that Jesus was coming, went and met Him, but Mary was sitting in the house. Now Martha said to Jesus, "Lord, if You had been here, my brother would not have died. But even now I know that whatever You ask of God, God will give You."
>
> —John 11:17–22

The burial was over. The grieving had begun. Most of the week had passed—and only Jesus was aware of the reason for the delay. The sisters were increasingly angry as well as brokenhearted. Breaking cultural rules, Martha ran across town, got right in Jesus' face, and said, "Thanks a lot. If You had shown up earlier, this wouldn't have happened." Yet, in despair, she also added, "I know even now what You ask God to do, He'll do." You might assume from her words that she believed in the resurrection, but in verse 39, she protests at the thought of the stone being rolled from the tomb. Yet she wanted so much to believe.

> Jesus said to her, "Your brother will rise again."
>
> —John 11:23

To those suffering the loss of someone they love, Jesus said, "This isn't the end of the story. This isn't where life ends. This isn't all there is." When Job had such a hard time figuring out how God could allow his children to die and how he was supposed to bear up under the grief, after he and his buddies put their heads together for fourteen chapters, he finally came out with this: "If I knew man could live again, I could bear the grief. I would spend my days longing for that day."

All Job wanted to know was whether or not this life was the end of the line. And that's the first thing Jesus said to Martha to comfort her. "This isn't the end," He said. "Your brother's going to live again."

> Martha said to Him, "I know that he will rise again in the resurrection at the last day."
>
> —John 11:24

Martha knew about the resurrection in a far-removed kind of way, but it held very little comfort for her at this time.

> Jesus said to her, "I am the resurrection and the life. He who believes in Me, though he may die, he shall live. And whoever lives and believes in Me shall never die. Do you believe this?"
>
> —John 11:25–26

Jesus' comfort to someone facing death without many answers and with anger at God was simply this: "I'm your hope." He tied all the future outlook of those standing beside a grave to a Person—Himself. "If you die believing in Me, you're going to live," He said. "And if you live believing in Me, your view of death will not be the same as the world's. You'll never die."

"I am the resurrection," Jesus said. He is the great I AM. And in a minute, He will prove that He was indeed. But did Martha believe? That's the key.

> She said to Him, "Yes, Lord, I believe that You are the Christ, the Son of God, who is to come into the world."
>
> —John 11:27

Martha's response fell a bit short. "I believe you're the Savior that was promised," she said. But in the next verse, she leaves without responding to Jesus' claim to be Lord over both the living and the dead.

> And when she had said these things, she went her way and secretly called Mary her sister, saying, "The Teacher has come and is calling for you." As soon as she heard that, she arose quickly and came to Him. Now Jesus had not yet come into the town, but was in the place where Martha met Him.
>
> —John 11:28–30

I don't know if Jesus was calling for Mary. I suspect Martha was pushing Mary out there to see if she could get something out of Him. After all, she was the one always sitting at His feet.

505

> Then the Jews who were with her in the house, and comforting her when they
> saw that Mary rose up quickly and went out, followed her, saying, "She is going
> to the tomb to weep there." Then, when Mary came where Jesus was, and saw
> Him, she fell down at His feet, saying to Him, "Lord, if You had been here, my
> brother would not have died."
>
> —John 11:31–32

Like Martha, Mary didn't understand Jesus' plans. Like Martha, she was disappointed
He hadn't shown up earlier. Mary had the same emotions as Martha. But she had a different posture. She fell at His feet.

> Therefore, when Jesus saw her weeping, and the Jews who came with her weep-
> ing, He groaned in the spirit and was troubled.
>
> —John 11:33

The Greek word for *groaned* literally means "to snort like a horse." It's the word for being
unable to keep your emotional response inside. A deep breath escapes. It overwhelmed
Jesus to see this poor woman in such grief. The Greek word for *troubled* is the word for
"trembling" or "a shaking of the body."

> And He said, "Where have you laid him?" They said to Him, "Lord, come and
> see." Jesus wept.
>
> —John 11:34–35

Verse 35 is the shortest verse in the Bible but uses the strongest word for *wept* in all of
Scripture—one that means "to burst into tears." Why would Jesus cry, especially considering in five minutes He would make everything fine? He had the solution, the power, the
capacity. He knew why He was there and what He would do. Why, then, would He cry?
The Bible gives us all the answers. He looked at this woman He loved and the sorrowful
people all around her and wept over the fact that sin produces sorrow—and that if people
have no hope, this is about as far as they go. Seeing the despair of the people He loved
because they didn't yet know who He truly was, Jesus burst into tears.

> Then the Jews said, "See how He loved him!" And some of them said, "Could
> not this Man, who opened the eyes of the blind, also have kept this man from
> dying?" Then Jesus, again groaning in Himself, came to the tomb. It was a cave
> and a stone lay against it.
>
> —John 11:36–38

As He walked toward Lazarus' tomb, an above-ground cave with a stone rolled against
it, Jesus groaned within Himself, but not as loudly as He had previously. And I suspect the
Lord groans a lot when He hears us sneer in unbelief at the promises He's made.

"All things work together for good to those who love God," He says.

Yet we say in our hearts, "No, they don't."

"I'll provide your every need," He says.

And we say, "No, You won't."

We will stand in unbelief against the very things God has promised because He has delayed His coming, He didn't come through like we thought, or He didn't do it the way we asked. Every generation says of God, "If He's so good, can't He prevent pain, sorrow, sickness, and death? Couldn't He have prevented this?" Sin brought pain, sorrow, sickness, and death. God didn't. God brought life through His Son.

> Jesus said, "Take away the stone." Martha, the sister of him who was dead, said to Him, "Lord, by this time there is a stench, for he has been dead four days." Jesus said to her, "Did I not say to you that if you would believe you would see the glory of God?"
>
> —John 11:39–40

Belief in Jesus is the only criterion for you to see God's glory. It's not very complicated to understand—just believe.

> Then they took away the stone from the place where the dead man was lying. And Jesus lifted up His eyes and said, "Father, I thank You that You have heard Me. And I know that You always hear Me, but because of the people who are standing by I said this, that they may believe that You sent me."
>
> —John 11:41–42

We don't find Jesus praying publicly much in the Bible—we usually find the Pharisees doing it to be admired. Here Jesus' prayer was thankfulness that the Father would now again powerfully show these He loved who Jesus truly was.

> Now when He had said these things, He cried with a loud voice, "Lazarus, come forth!" And he who had died came out, bound hand and foot with graveclothes, and his face was wrapped with a cloth. Jesus said to them, "Loose him, and let him go."
>
> —John 11:43–44

It's a good thing Jesus said, "Lazarus, come forth" and not just, "Come forth," because that would have been the end of the whole graveyard!

I wish we had more of the story. I'm thinking Mary and Martha passed out. I know I would have! And you know Lazarus probably wasn't very happy being awakened from his restful sleep and time with Abraham.

As was the custom, Lazarus was completely wrapped from head to toe—even as Jesus soon would be. But Jesus ordered him to be loosed and set free. He still does that for all who are dead in sin who come to Him: loosed and set free!

> Then many of the Jews who had come to Mary, and had seen the things Jesus did, believed in Him. But some of them went away to the Pharisees and told them the things Jesus did.
>
> —John 11:45–46

Verse 45 seems like the only normal response. Verse 46 makes no sense to me at all. Jesus ordered someone to return from the dead, and he did. This alone ought to have convinced anyone that His Word was true.

God sometimes delays His coming to bring us to a better understanding of who He is. I suspect none of us would pray, read our Bibles, or go to church much if life was just a breeze. It is the pressure of life that keeps us spiritually honest and the difficulties of life that keep us praying and seeking God. God wants us to surrender—but that doesn't come easily.

Samson was one whose life God blessed. He could have surrendered at any time—but he didn't. Finally, at the end of himself and all but forgotten, he prayed one last prayer and said, "I want to give You my life to take Your enemies out"—and God gave him the strength to do it. Sometimes, as was literally the case with Samson, it's when the roof falls in and the grief comes down that God is most real and we're able to know Him all the better. At last some of the folks mourning with Mary and Martha made a decision to follow Jesus. I'm sure Mary and Martha eventually thought their four days of suffering were worth it. God has a way of working—so we might see His glory.

> Then the chief priests and the Pharisees gathered a council and said, "What shall we do? For this Man works many signs. If we let Him alone like this, everyone will believe in Him, and the Romans will come and take away both our place and nation."
>
> —John 11:47–48

Comprised of both Sadducees and Pharisees, the Sanhedrin had seventy-one members and was the ruling party in Israel. The political arm of the Sanhedrin was the Sadducees— primarily chief priests and religious rulers—who didn't believe in life after death. The Pharisees, on the other hand, believed in life after death but thought they could earn their way to heaven and so they covered their wickedness with external holiness. The Pharisees and Sadducees joined together only when it came to Jesus, because they both hated Him for exposing their hearts.

> And one of them, Caiaphas, being high priest that year, said to them, "You know nothing at all, nor do you consider that it is expedient for us that one man should die for the people, and not that the whole nation should perish." Now this he did not say on his own authority, but being high priest that year he prophesied that Jesus would die for the nation, and not for that nation only but also that He would gather together in one the children of God who were scattered abroad.
>
> —John 11:49–52

Caiaphas was a wicked priest who ruled from 18–36 A.D. Put in power by the Romans because they didn't like his father-in-law, Annas, Caiaphas served as a puppet of Rome. As this particular discussion unfolded, Caiaphas stood up and said, "Here's the deal: We kill this one man, Jesus, and everyone lives. One dead and the nation is secure, our money is safe, and our position remains intact. It's just one man. He's got to go."

Although Caiaphas was wicked, he held the position of high priest, a position God had established and used for centuries. And just as God had spoken through Balaam's donkey, so He spoke through this wicked life. One Man would indeed die—not only for the nation but for everyone everywhere who would believe in Him.

From a human perspective, this would be a brutal murder designed only to serve self-interest. From God's viewpoint, however, it was the sacrifice of His Son for the salvation of all.

> Then, from that day on, they plotted to put Him to death. Therefore Jesus no longer walked openly among the Jews, but went from there into the country near the wilderness, to a city called Ephraim, and there remained with His disciples.
>
> —John 11:53–54

Eight weeks later, Jesus came into Jericho and headed up to Jerusalem to the cross. "You'll see My glory," Jesus said. Those who believed followed Him. Those who refused were left to plot a murder without a trial and judge a man guilty of death before ever speaking to Him.

We can't really be neutral about Jesus. We either make Him Lord or try to crucify Him. We can't have it both ways because He won't let us live in complacency. We have to make a decision about who He is.

"I am the resurrection and the life," Jesus said to Martha. "Do you believe this?" If I do, even the worst of times are filled with hope in Him. Even in the darkest of days, He rules and will bring victory. If I don't, I really have nowhere to turn and I have no answers for life. Just weeping and frustration and then the judgment of God.

Two thousand years ago, Jesus came so we could have hope. Today, He sometimes delays His coming because He wants us to know Him better. But He is coming again. Are you ready?

Chapter 96

LESSONS FROM THE TENTH LEPER

Luke 17:11–19

Here in Luke 17, Jesus was called upon by ten men suffering with leprosy. One of the lessons the Lord gives us through them is that there is a huge difference between receiving a temporal miracle from God or having our lives changed eternally.

> Now it happened as He went to Jerusalem that He passed through the midst of Samaria and Galilee. Then as He entered a certain village, there met Him ten men who were lepers, who stood afar off. And they lifted up their voices and said, "Jesus, Master, have mercy on us!" So when He saw them, He said to them, "Go, show yourselves to the priests."
>
> —Luke 17:11–14

Heading toward Jerusalem, Jesus came to an unnamed town where He was met by the distant cry of several men. Verse 14 tells us He heard them long before He saw them. Both in the Old and New Testaments, leprosy is one of the most horrible diseases we find. Because it originates from within and its effects aren't seen until it has done great damage, it is often used symbolically as a picture of sin in our lives.

In Leviticus 13–14, the Lord gave direction and insight regarding this disease. The priests were given the responsibility of diagnosing a person with leprosy. If they weren't sure, the person in question was to be quarantined. If, upon re-examination, the person did indeed have leprosy, he was to shave his head, cover his mouth, and leave town. He no longer was welcome in the city, his home, or the place of worship. Lepers lived out their lives only in the company of other lepers, living isolated from all others they loved.

Called Hansen's disease today, leprosy still cannot be cured but it can be treated and curbed. Yet in Jesus' day, it led only to a horrible death. So when we read of ten lepers standing at a distance crying out, we can be sure that they not only were crying loudly but they were a sight to see—frightening groups of the walking dead. Their cry was more than simply, "Hey, Jesus, got a minute?" No, they would have cried with everything they had. And that's how we got saved, isn't it? We came to the end of ourselves and, with everything we had, we cried out for God's help.

No doubt these lepers had heard of Jesus and His power. When He sent out the twelve apostles in Matthew 10:8, part of their instruction was that they were to cleanse the lepers.

When John the Baptist wondered if Jesus was truly the Messiah, he sent a couple of his disciples to ask. "Tell John how the blind receive their sight, how the lame walk, and how the lepers are cleansed," Jesus responded (Luke 7:22). Healing became the proof that God was around because only He could do the impossible. So by the time three and a half years had passed, we have to believe that every leper in every place Jesus might have visited would have been lining up to see if they could get His attention. And if we were in these lepers' sandals, I think we'd have been screaming too.

"Go show yourselves to the priest," Jesus said, because the Lord is always willing to heal anyone who is willing to come. Want to be saved? He'll save you. Want to be forgiven? He'll forgive. Nothing remains to be done but your coming and being convinced He can do it. If you see your sin and lack, He will give you life.

The command to show themselves to the priest was, according to Leviticus 14:1–2, what any leper who believed he was cured was to do in order to get a clean bill of health, a certificate allowing him back into society. The problem was, this was rarely, if ever, granted. Leprosy was, after all, incurable. I suspect that up until Jesus' time, the priests who came out of the schools never learned that page of the Law: what offering to offer for a cured leper—because no one was ever healed of leprosy. But now, with increasing regularity, these folks whom Jesus had touched and wanted a clean bill of health were rolling into the priests' offices. What a ministry these lepers were having to the priests!

When these ten lepers heard Jesus tell them to go show themselves to the priests, I wonder if some in the group said, "We traveled all night for, 'Go show yourselves to the priest?' I can't show myself to the priest like this. Look at me! He's going to throw me out. I look horrible!" But faith requires obedience and not always full understanding.

There's an interesting difference in the Bible between feelings and faith, because so often if we don't feel something, we think it can't be faith. By definition, however, faith is a belief in God, period, and that may or may not be undergirded with feeling.

I got saved in a home Bible study. Of the 100 people there, maybe ten or twelve of us got saved that night. But I was the only one who wasn't crying. My neighbor was a Christian guy—so I went home, knocked on his door, and said, "I think I got saved, but I'm not sure I did it right."

"Why?" he asked.

"Because I'm not crying or anything. I don't feel any different. No goose bumps. No shaking. I think I missed it. What did I do wrong?" I even told him the prayer I had prayed and asked him if it was the right one.

It frustrated me that I didn't have the feelings the others seemed to have. But faith is, first of all, conviction and action. Sometimes feelings come sooner. Other times they come later. Here were ten lepers who, in desperation, needed Jesus to come and heal them. But in the midst of all of that, they had nothing to go on other than His Word. It's the same way we live our Christian lives. Sometimes our feelings support our walk. Other times they tend to hinder them. You come to church and you don't feel like worshipping. You've had a hard day. You just want to close your eyes and rest, yet you know God inhabits the praises of His people. So you sing. You don't want to. You don't even feel like it. But you do it because that's what the Lord asks of us. And by the time you're done, you're at rest and God has blessed you. He inhabited you and you're strengthened. It was the right thing to do—but you didn't feel like that when you began.

Faith and feelings don't always respond together. Sometimes our bodies just take awhile to catch up. "I'm too busy to pray. I'm too mad to forgive. I'm too hurt to respond. I'm too fearful to step out. I'm too self-conscious to think God could use me for five minutes," we tell ourselves. But by faith we do it anyway. Then the feelings roll in, don't they? But faith even without feeling is still faith.

So on blistered feet, with bent bodies and bleeding hands, the lepers had no other choice but to go.

In 2 Kings we are given a story that goes along with this issue of faith and not always seeing God's promise fulfilled immediately. Naaman was a great man who was blessed by God in many ways. God had used him to overthrow the Jews in their idolatry so they could learn to walk with Him. From all we read, he was an honest, powerful, and very successful individual. But, like all of us, he was a leper—a sinner who would have given everything he had to be whole and delivered. In his house was a Jewish servant girl, a captive from one of his raids. You would think this girl would have said of him, "I hope he rots and dies." Instead, she did something entirely different: she trusted the Lord and told Naaman's wife that there was a prophet in Samaria who could heal him.

You have to love this young girl's attitude. Isaiah 24:15 says we are to glorify God even in the fire. She was certainly an example of that. She showed great compassion and was a powerful witness to her captors. You can imagine how Naaman and his wife would have grabbed on to this as their last straw of hope.

"There's a cure across the border," Naaman said to his boss, the king. "I gotta go. Whatever it takes, I'll do. I'll take all the money I have, the rewards I can offer, the fine clothes I can gather, and a letter of endorsement." Unfortunately, he hadn't listened very well to his servant, who said he should go to the prophet in Samaria. Rather than going to Elisha, as she had said, however, he went to the king, a wicked man.

"I can't kill and make alive," the king said after reading the king of Syria's letter. "He's just trying to find another reason to invade our country again."

I love Elisha's response in 2 Kings 5:8 when he heard of it and sent word, "If this man's looking for God here in Israel, he won't be disappointed, send him to me." So for you today. If you're looking for the Lord, you'll not be disappointed.

So Naaman went with all of his goods and stood at the door of Elisha's house. It paints a picture for me of one arriving at a church service. Stricken with an incurable disease called sin, he shows up with everything he has, hoping to strike a deal with God.

I read of a sculptor who paid a tramp on the streets of London in advance to pose for him because he thought he would make an interesting picture of humanity. But when the tramp showed up the next day clean-shaven and dressed in new clothes, the picture in the sculptor's mind was ruined. That's the way people often come to church. If we still think we've got what it takes with God, we're not going to hear much. We'll have ruined His work. But if we realize we have nothing to offer, then we've got something because then God can begin to work. Naaman was ready to pay whatever a cure might cost. He just wasn't ready to humble himself.

When Elisha sent a messenger to tell him to dip in the Jordan seven times, Naaman was furious. First, in sending a messenger, rather than coming himself for Elisha hadn't shown him the respect he was accustomed to being shown. The same is true of the sinner. If you want to get right with God, you don't come expecting respect. You come on your face. Salvation begins with humility, saying, "God, I have nothing to offer and nothing with which to bargain. I'm just coming for mercy." Elisha knew the message was more important than the messenger and that this ruler had better look to God instead.

Second, notice that, like most people who head for church looking for help, Naaman thought he knew how God should work. It's interesting how we expect God to work according to our ways. And yet we read in His Word, "Let the wicked man forsake his ways. Let the unrighteous man forsake his thoughts. Let him return to the Lord, seek the Lord, and He'll be found." Naaman came with his idea of how God should save and deliver, and his pride was so much in the way that he initially refused Elisha's command.

I would think people in their desperate situations would be more compliant, not less. Look how sin works. You want to say to him, "Hey, pal. You're the one who is so sick. Why argue? What do you have to lose? Give it a go." That's basically what his servants said, and Naaman was convinced to dip seven times in the Jordan—but I suspect that every time he came out of the water, he gave them a dirty look that said, "Just wait till I get out. You're all dead!"

We read in 2 Kings 5:15 that after Naaman's flesh was restored like the flesh of a little child, he said, "Indeed, now I know that there is no God in all the earth, except in Israel." Here was a man who had his heart, mind, and testimony changed in front of his entire entourage because God answered his prayer. It took a little while to break though his self-confidence and self-worth—but then God worked.

And so it was that as they went, they were cleansed.

—Luke 17:14

Just as Naaman dipped in the Jordan and his flesh was restored, so as the lepers began to walk, their skin began to clear, their sores began to heal, their feet began to feel better, and they were aware something was going on. God was doing something—and all of their physical changes represent what God will do spiritually in any life given to Him. As we seek Him, follow Him, and do as He says, we too will find His deliverance from sin.

> And one of them, when he saw that he was healed, returned, and with a loud voice glorified God, and fell down on his face at His feet, giving Him thanks. And he was a Samaritan.
>
> —Luke 17:15–16

It was at this point that one of the ten turned around and left the obligation of the Law, overwhelmed by a greater obligation to worship. Why didn't all ten lepers come back? The distinction Luke makes that he was a Samaritan is really the distinction between a religious person and one who has come to know that Jesus is God. Religion can't change your heart. God alone can do that. It can remove a lot of stuff out of your life, but it can't make you right with God. So the Samaritan fell at Jesus' feet and worshipped with a loud voice. The Greek phrase used here is the one from which we get our word *megaphone*. In other words, this guy was not singing, "Just As I Am" quietly under his breath. He was screaming at the top of his lungs, "YOU ARE GOD! I'M HEALED! LOOK AT ME!" And why wouldn't he? Can you imagine the life he used to live changed by God's grace and mercy?

We read in the book of Nehemiah that as God's people rebuilt the wall around Jerusalem, they sang so loudly that people in the next county could hear them. Why wouldn't we do this, considering all God has done for us?

> So Jesus answered and said, "Were there not ten cleansed? But where are the nine? Were there not any found who returned to give glory to God except this foreigner?"
>
> —Luke 17:17–18

When most people read this story, they become frustrated with the nine who didn't show up. But how many times has God blessed us and we just run out the door, forgetting about Him until the next time we need something from Him? What we need is that "megaphone mentality" where we want to sing God's praises for all He has done.

The only honest response of a person's heart to God's goodness is faith and thanksgiving. You find that in the tenth leper, but not in the hearts of the religious nine. They were well and healthy physically—but if they didn't come around to the place where they were going to be right with God, things were not going to get better for them. In fact, they would get a whole lot worse because they had a leprosy of even greater import that would damn their souls, a sickness they couldn't shake—apart from coming to God by faith in His Son Jesus Christ.

> And He said to him, "Arise, go your way. Your faith has made you well."
>
> —Luke 17:19

The word Jesus used for *well* means "complete" or "whole"—not just physically but spiritually. The other nine did their religious duty, checked in with the priest, and went back home. But this man recognized Jesus for who He was. Even greater than his physical cure was his spiritual awareness of the One who had just touched his life.

That's the difference between being touched by God and being touched by God in your heart. The difference between "well" and "whole" is your faith in Him. God will do a lot of things for you. He'll bless you tremendously. But you don't only want to experience His blessings. You want to know Him.

Chapter 97

THE KINGDOM NOW AND THEN

Luke 17:20–37

As Jesus headed for Jerusalem, He was accosted by the Pharisees with a question about the kingdom of God. Because they had all grown up with the same understanding, the Messiah and His hope held the same promise: deliverance for Israel from her political foes. By the time we get to Luke 19, as Jesus heads for Jerusalem through Jericho, the disciples were getting so excited about what they believed was waiting for them there that Jesus stopped and told them a parable to explain that the kingdom of heaven wouldn't immediately appear.

In this last year of His public ministry, Jesus spoke often about death and dying, about being arrested and killed. He always added, "On the third day, I'll rise"—but the disciples never seemed to hear that part because once they heard the word *die* they appeared to stop listening all together. After all, they had the sequence of events all worked out in their own minds—and death wasn't part of it. They needed to learn that there was more to God's plan than their plan.

The kingdom of God was one of Jesus' favorite subjects. Mentioned eighty-five different places, it was the good news of His coming, both to save and then one day to rule. At the heart of His teaching, the kingdom of God was also the primary subject of many of His parables. Yet the disciples, along with the Jewish people as a whole, were hanging on to the idea that when the Messiah came, their problems would be over.

If you've studied the Bible, you know it teaches that the Messiah would come twice. First, to give His life for our sins so that we might be saved. As he arose and ascended into heaven the Holy Spirit was sent and took up residence in the hearts of believers, and the kingdom of God was established within them. The second time the Messiah comes will be at the end of the Church Age and seven years of great tribulation—not to suffer and die but to rule and bring judgment. The people of Jesus' day were unable to distinguish between the two comings of our Lord. That is why, in His last months, Jesus spent so much time addressing these gaps in their understanding.

As we read about the Messiah's rule, we can see why the people were eager for it to begin. Isaiah talks about the kingdom of God as a time without end, when the government will be placed on God's shoulders, when He will judge in righteousness forever. But because the people overlooked the role of His first coming, Jesus began to teach His disciples how the timeline would unfold. It wasn't an easy concept. If you look ahead to the resurrection and beyond you will see that one of the last things the disciples say to Jesus is, "Is it now?" It was difficult for them to grasp even then. The scribes and Pharisees used the conflict between what they thought they knew and what Jesus had been telling them as points of confrontation and argument.

> Now when He was asked by the Pharisees when the kingdom of God would come, He answered them and said, "The kingdom of God does not come with observation; nor will they say, 'See here!' or 'See there!' For indeed, the kingdom of God is within you."
>
> —Luke 17:20–21

Because these religious enemies of Jesus came only to stir up strife, He answered them only briefly before He moved on to answer the disciples. When does the kingdom of heaven show up? Not with observation, or literally, not with an outward, visible show. The prophets were correct—one day the kingdom age will come and the Lord will indeed rule. But before that were His death, resurrection, and the Church Age. People aren't going to be able to point and say, "It's over here and here are the lines and borders of the kingdom." No, it will be established "without observation"—out of sight, within people's hearts.

When Jesus talked to Nicodemus about heaven, He said, "Unless you're born again, you can't even see the kingdom of God." Two verses later, He said, "Unless you're born of the Spirit, you cannot enter the kingdom of God." Wherever we read of the kingdom of God or the kingdom of heaven, it's a designation of a place where the Lord is King, where people subject themselves to Him, where they bow their knee, follow His rules, ascribe to His plans, and join His cause. If you're saved, you're in God's kingdom. He's your King. You're His subject. One day, He's going to rule openly and visibly. But for now, He rules in your hearts. It's "without observation." There's no country—but there is a people.

If you're saved, you've already begun to experience what it means to have Jesus as King. You have peace and hope, direction and strength. To be sure, it's all mixed in with sin, weakness, and failure. But one day, when that's all removed, you'll see the fullness of the kingdom.

> Then He said to the disciples, "The days will come when you will desire to see one of the days of the Son of Man, and you will not see it. And they will say to you, 'Look here!' or 'Look there!' Do not go after them, or follow them. For as the lightning that flashes out of one part under heaven shines to the other part under heaven, so also the Son of Man will be in His day."
>
> —Luke 17:22–24

To His disciples, Jesus said, "You're going to have to live your life looking for My return, waiting for it, as the kingdom of God is established within you. And although there will be counterfeit Messiahs and false claims, when I return, everyone will know. There won't be any doubt."

The "without observation" of Jesus' first coming in verse 20 becomes complete observation in verse 22 regarding His second coming when, as Revelation 1:7 says, every eye shall see Him coming in the clouds with power and with great glory.

In the meantime, the kingdom of God is within the hearts of believers as the church waits.

> "But first He must suffer many things and be rejected by this generation."
> —Luke 17:25

This is the key verse no one figured into the equation—that God would send His Son first to die and to save. In fact, there are plenty of Old Testament prophecies about the suffering Messiah. But if you go to the Bible with your mind made up, either you change your mind or you change the Scriptures. Psalm 22, Isaiah 53, and Daniel 9 give very clear descriptions of suffering, crucifixion, beatings, bloodshed, and substitutionary death. But if you read them with the idea that the Messiah is only to rule, you have to spiritualize them or set them aside altogether.

Jesus said, "Before we get to glory, there will be suffering and humiliation." Then He continued to instruct His disciples concerning the days in which He would be revealed.

> "And as it was in the days of Noah, so it will be also in the days of the Son of Man: They ate, they drank, they married wives, they were given in marriage, until the day that Noah entered the ark, and the flood came and destroyed them all. Likewise as it was also in the days of Lot: They ate, they drank, they bought, they sold, they planted, they built; but on the day that Lot went out of Sodom it rained fire and brimstone from heaven and destroyed them all. Even so will it be in the day when the Son of Man is revealed."
> —Luke 17:26–30

Jesus compared the days prior to His return with past times seen in Scripture. In the days of both Noah and Lot, people were completely unaware that the Lord was about to act in judgment. They were drinking, eating, marrying. It was life as usual. Even though Noah took 120 years to build a boat 150 miles from water and preached righteousness, no one cared. As a result, no one was ready. The same day Noah entered the ark, there were plans for marriage, eating, and drinking, all carefree. And then judgment fell—but no one was ready except Noah and his family.

"And as it was . . . so it will be" when Jesus comes again. Neither Noah nor Lot was sinless. But both of them found deliverance because they waited on the Lord and had spiritual eyes to see.

> "In that day, he who is on the housetop, and his goods are in the house, let him not come down to take them away. And likewise the one who is in the field, let him not turn back. Remember Lot's wife. Whoever seeks to save his life will lose it, and whoever loses his life will preserve it."
>
> —Luke 17:31–33

From Daniel 9, Matthew 24, and Revelation 12, we know that the period between the rapture of the church and Jesus' second coming is seven years. We're told that in the first three and a half years, the antichrist will come as a peacemaker and rebuild the temple. But then on the day of its dedication, he'll demand to be worshipped as god and his true colors will be revealed. From that point, the great Tribulation will roll forward, and for three and a half years, God's judgment will fall. To those living in that time, Jesus said, "If you see that happen, don't even bother going in your house to get your stuff. Just get out of Dodge. Don't look back. Don't turn around. Remember Lot's wife. She looked back. She thought she had a few more minutes with the world, a few more minutes with her stuff, a few more minutes with her old life. But it led to her demise."

> "I tell you, in that night there will be two men in one bed: the one will be taken and the other will be left. Two women will be grinding together: the one will be taken and the other left. Two men will be in the field: the one will be taken and the other left." And they answered and said to Him, "Where, Lord?" So He said to them, "Wherever the body is, there the eagles will be gathered together."
>
> —Luke 17:34–37

In Revelation 19:18, at the final battle, we read of the Lord sending an angel to call for the birds, saying, "Gather together to eat the flesh of kings and the flesh of all men who have defied God." Here the verse reads, "Wherever the body is, there the vultures will be gathered." It is a word from the Lord that, ultimately, those who look for His second coming better be ready for Him or else His coming won't be so sweet.

We don't know when Jesus is coming. It could be today; it could be ten years from now. But we do know that when He comes we're going with Him because we belong to Him. When we are taken, however, those who are left behind will face a future of judgment and, unless they turn to Jesus, it is that separation of which He spoke here.

Today, the kingdom of God dwells within the hearts of men. It's still the Church Age. But when Jesus comes, the rapture will take place and the clock will begin the countdown to His return. We must be ready. And we must help others see that He came the first time to suffer, but when He comes the second time, it will be to rule.

Chapter 98

Prayerful Waiting

Luke 18:1–8

In response to a question posed by the Pharisees about the kingdom of God, Jesus told His disciples there would be a length of time in which they would need to wait, watch, and hope. Here in Luke 18, He speaks to them about how they should wait. And in so doing, He gives us some words that can totally change the way we pray. In verse 1 and again in verse 9, Jesus tells two parables about prayer. These are two of only a few parables in the entire Gospel accounts where, before He told them, Jesus gave us the reason for them.

When Paul wrote to Titus as the overseer of the churches on the isle of Crete, he said, "Teach the church to watch and wait, to be in tune and ready, to be expecting that which God will do." Here in Luke 18, Jesus gives us one way that we as His saints can continue to minister in these last days and not give up or lose heart.

> Then He spoke a parable to them, that men always ought to pray and not lose heart . . . .
>
> —Luke 18:1

Instead of panic and discouragement that may accompany difficulties in ministry and outreach, the body of Christ must find their confidence in their Lord and know that God has good reason for delaying His coming. In the situation that the church finds itself today, we have to understand that as we pray and seek the Lord in the midst of waiting, we can learn a wonderful lesson about God's timing and sovereignty in our lives.

In a time when few believe the Lord is coming again, when persecution for declared faith in Jesus is on the rise and men's hearts are growing colder, the church can still have great hope as they go to serve Him. So the parable:

> . . . saying: "There was in a certain city a judge who did not fear God nor regard man. Now there was a widow in that city . . . ."
>
> —Luke 18:2–3

Luke talks about widows more than all of the other Gospel writers combined. Jesus often used widows as pictures of helplessness because, without a welfare system to support them, they were defenseless in the culture of the day. Unless their family stepped in to help, they had no one. God makes great promises to widows as representative of all who trust Him. Like the widow, on our own we're helpless, but with God's promise and care, we can have hope. So here, a helpless widow and a powerful heartless judge.

> ". . . and she came to him . . . ."
>
> —Luke 18:3

The word for *came* is in the imperfect tense in Greek, which at least leaves open the possibility that the widow came often in her desperation. And she may not have just shown up at his courtroom, but approached the judge in the marketplace, on the street, at the gates of the city, and even out with his friends. Wherever she found him, she tried to talk to him. She came not to badger him, but because she had no other options. Hers was a persistence born of necessity. There weren't ten ways to attack her problem. There was only one. She had to keep asking for help until she got it. With nothing to lose and everything to gain, she wasn't going to back down.

> ". . . saying, 'Get justice for me from my adversary.'"
>
> —Luke 18:3

This widow didn't come for vengeance. She didn't want to make a killing. She wasn't looking to get ahead. She just wanted justice. So she went to the man in the position to make it right. Unfortunately, she found the worst judge imaginable.

> "And he would not for a while . . . ."
>
> —Luke 18:4

The judge's response was typical of what we have read of him. He simply wouldn't help her. Using the imperfect tense again, this implies that every time she came, he refused her case, pleas, tears, and argument. He didn't see any benefit to himself and, therefore, saw no need to be bothered by her. Yet the widow continued to cry out to him, for her need was too great and her options too few. Eventually, even this cynical judge was pushed to the point where he finally helped her.

> ". . . but afterward he said within himself, 'Though I do not fear God nor regard man, yet because this widow troubles me I will avenge her, lest by her continual coming she weary me.'"
>
> —Luke 18:4–5

Notice it wasn't compassion that drove this judge. Nor was it a concern for justice. It was simply selfish frustration. The Greek word for *troubling* speaks of being punched in the eye. In other words, the widow had beaten him down with her constant pleas. Badgering had done its work and the squeaky wheel was about to get some grease.

> Then the Lord said, "Hear what the unjust judge said."
>
> —Luke 18:6

From verse 1, we know that the purpose of this parable was to convince the disciples that, while they were waiting for the Lord in a hostile world, they should not lose heart but should continue to pray with great hope. Unfortunately, many have taken this parable out of context, removed the explanation found in verse 1, and not bothered to stop at verse 6. As a result, they come to the conclusion that the purpose of the parable and the lesson it seeks to convey is that feverish prayer is a virtue God seeks to develop in us, and if we will frantically knock on His door, it's just a matter of time and our ability to keep badgering Him that will bring His answer to our lives.

The Bible, however, says just the opposite. Feverish prayers do not move God. Nor is He moved by constant requests. Because He's God, He's going to do what's right. Prayer is for our benefit, not for His. He doesn't take notes while we pray. He doesn't say, "Oh, is that right? I didn't know that. Thanks for filling Me in." He doesn't leave prayer saying, "That was really helpful." How could He? He already knows everything.

There are two kinds of parables: parables of comparison and those of contrast. In the former, Jesus paints a picture and says, "I am just like this." In the parables of contrast, He says, "I'm not at all like that." And wherever you find parables of contrast in the Bible, the distance between the spiritual truth and the physical setting is set as far apart as possible so the lesson is most easily identifiable. Here Jesus paints a picture of a horrendous judge in order to say, "Although you are indeed like the widow, I am not at all like the judge."

If this were a lesson in comparison, we would have to conclude that God is unloving and unjust, selfish, ungracious, and merciless. We would have to conclude that we have to get, plead, and put ourselves in His face every moment of the day to even open the possibility that He might eventually hear us. But nothing could be further from the truth about God. God is the exact opposite of the unjust judge. In fact, in verse 7, Jesus explains the contrast further.

> "And shall God not avenge His own elect who cry out day and night to Him, though He bears long with them? I tell you that He will avenge them speedily. Nevertheless, when the Son of Man comes, will He really find faith on the earth?"
>
> —Luke 18:7–8

"If the unjust judge finally answered the widow, how much more shall God answer His own?" Jesus asked. One of the things the Bible teaches about God is that He loves to hear

His people's prayers. Psalm 34:15 says the Lord's eyes are on the righteous and His ears are open to their cry, that He hears and delivers them out of all of their troubles. Is that the God you know? That's the God He wants you to know. God loves it when we pray. He desires that we should come. And unlike the judge of this parable, He doesn't need badgering or begging to move on our behalf.

The world looks at prayer as making a deal with God. If they give a little, He should give a lot. If they do a little for Him, He should do a lot for them.

When Elijah confronted the prophets of Baal in 1 Kings 18:21–40, he said, "Let's ask our gods to send fire from heaven and then we'll know who the real God is. You go first." They cried out for their god to come, but nothing happened. Finally he said to them, mockingly, "Yell a little louder. It could be he's talking to someone else. Or maybe he's on a journey. Or asleep. Maybe you should wake him up." Still nothing.

Yet our calling never finds God put out by our coming, for He invites us constantly to come and longs to have fellowship with us and meet our needs. If there is a delay, it has nothing to do with God somehow waiting for us to fill up our volume of praying so He can give us something. It is a delay that goes far beyond what we're asking. He has a bigger purpose. And when the time is right, He will answer speedily.

I can find a handful of places in the Bible that say, "While they were praying, God answered." I love those. But that usually doesn't happen. It's usually pray and pray some more and, "Hey, Lord, what's the deal? We've been praying for a long time." Then at some point, God does what He wants—and we say, "What a perfect answer!"

Basic to our outlook on prayer, we must factor in the understanding that God is for us. In his second letter to the scattered saints, Peter said in chapter 3:8–9, "Don't be ignorant of this: to the Lord, a day is like a thousand years and thousand years like a day." In other words, God's time is so different than ours. Then Peter added, "The Lord isn't slack concerning His promises as some of us would count slackness. But He's longsuffering toward us. He's not willing that any should perish but that all should come to repentance."

We have to change our understanding of God and prayer. "Come, Lord Jesus," we pray. He wants to come in the worst way but He has things to do before He can.

Mary and Martha said, "Lord, if You'd have just been here, our brother wouldn't have had to die. Way to go. You let us down." But did He? If you know the story, you know it turned out exactly the way God intended. In God's economy, prayers are answered the moment they're able to be answered. There won't be a ten-minute delay. God's willing, desiring so much to move on our behalf.

The word for *speedily* means *swiftly*. It doesn't mean *immediately*. It means when the time is right, God will move without delay and act accordingly. He'll act the moment He can. Any delay is not God dragging His feet. It is Him doing things in proper order of importance. He's not wasting time. He's not angry. He's not put out. You don't need to browbeat Him into doing something. He wants to help—speedily.

How do we survive the rough days without turning back? And how do we make a difference in our world as we wait for His return? We pray. And we trust that God's delays are wise. We're to pray all the time—not to badger God into doing something, but so we can learn to depend on Him and become convinced that His ways and timing are perfect. I don't know how often I've been angry God didn't answer my prayer, only to look back and see His timing was absolutely perfect. He answered exactly how and when I would have—had I known everything.

The church's ability to live and do well in the last days depends on knowing God's heart when it comes to our prayer life and to know that there won't be five minutes that pass beyond what is necessary to accomplish His will and your cry to Him for those things. When the Lord comes, will He find faith on the earth? That's the question. We must not lose sight of His love or promises. If He can't come this year, great. He'll come next year. I'm not quitting. He's good at what He does. He just wants us to trust Him. Come He will the moment He can. Until then, if you're not saved, and hearing this, would you please come to Jesus for life? You may be the last one He's waiting for.

Chapter 99

Two Ways to Pray

Luke 18:9–17

After giving a parable that contrasted a judge unwilling to help a widow in need with a God who longs to answer our prayers speedily, Jesus gave a second parable with prayer as the backdrop and again the parable is defined before it is taught.

> Also He spoke this parable to some who trusted in themselves that they were righteous, and despised others.
>
> —Luke 18:9

This parable focuses on the religious person who, trusting in his own works, thinks he has earned an answer from God for his religion and his obvious superiority over another he sees as spiritually inferior both in will and action. One of the greatest deterrents to accepting Jesus and being saved is the confidence we usually hold that we can do it ourselves. In fact, when we share our faith with the others, the first thing we often hear are these words: "I'm good enough. I've tried hard enough. I'm sincere enough. Therefore, God will certainly accept me when that time arrives." But Jesus continually addressed the false notion that heaven can be had as a reward for performance.

In Matthew 7:21–23 He said in the day of judgment many will list their spiritual accomplishments—prophesying, casting out demons, and doing wonderful works. But as they do He will say to them, "Depart from Me. I never knew you." In so doing He places the idea of accomplishment in a box labeled "Not Good Enough, Insufficient."

When Paul wrote to his trainee, Titus, he said in chapter 3, "It isn't works of righteousness we have done that save us, but it is God's mercy and grace."

If we could do it on our own—if we could work it out by ourselves—the Bible would be filled with "Do this" and "Do that." Instead, Jesus said, "I am the door into the sheepfold. If anyone tries to enter in but doesn't use the door, he is a thief and a robber." There aren't four hundred ways to heaven, three hundred ways to God, or twelve ways you can go. There's only one. It's Jesus.

Yet this parable addresses those who mistakenly assume they're right with God by their religious works and that pride makes them condescending of others. One of the inevitable consequences of self-righteousness is despising others, for if we want to make ourselves look good, we will have to find others we consider in worse shape than ourselves. Unfortunately, this self-righteous attitude can find its way even into the hearts of saints who begin to look down their noses at the lost. But think again, for as believers, we're no better than anyone else. We're just saved. Yet read of this religious man:

> "Two men went up to the temple to pray, one a Pharisee and the other a tax collector. The Pharisee stood and prayed thus with himself, 'God, I thank You that I am not like other men—extortioners, unjust, adulterers, or even as this tax collector. I fast twice a week; I give tithes of all that I possess.' And the tax collector, standing afar off, would not so much as raise his eyes to heaven, but beat his breast, saying, 'God, be merciful to me a sinner!' I tell you, this man went down to his house justified rather than the other; for everyone who exalts himself will be humbled, and he who humbles himself will be exalted."
> —Luke 18:10–14

The Pharisee and the tax collector represent the extremes of the society in which Jesus lived. The Pharisee was held in the highest reputation of piety and religion. If you talked religion, you talked Pharisee. Pharisees were the best at outward shows of holiness. They wrapped their robes around them tightly so sinners wouldn't brush up against them, and they stopped in the middle of the street to pray whenever the call for prayer went out.

Tax collectors, on the other hand, were the dregs of society. Not only did the Romans hire them to collect taxes from their fellow Jews, but they made their living by tacking their own fee on top of the already exorbitant taxes. Because they sold out their own people, everyone despised them. In Luke 3:12–13, tax collectors came to John the Baptist, wanting to prepare their hearts for the coming Messiah. John's advice to them was to exact from people nothing more than what was fair—evidently a foreign concept to them.

So in Jesus' parable here were the two extremes—both at the temple, both seeking to approach God, and both looking to be heard from on high. And God, hearing in secret, recorded their prayers openly so we might better understand how we are to come to Him.

The fact that the Pharisee prayed with himself ought to tell us how that was going. He went to talk to God and ended up talking only to himself. In contrast to the tax collector's approach in verse 13, it would seem the Pharisee moved as close to the curtain into the holy place as possible. He approached God with great confidence because he was used to being honored. Although he used the word *God* at the beginning of his prayer, he never referred to Him again.

Notice also that he didn't compare himself to Joseph, Daniel, or Samuel, but with what he considered to be the worst guy possible, saying, "I'm glad I'm not like him," pointing or nodding or simply referencing the tax collector over there in the distance.

I suspect if we're really looking to make a case for ourselves before God, it wouldn't be hard to find people to whom we can feel superior. There always will be someone whose sins look a whole lot worse than ours do. Even our own sins look a lot worse in others. So up to the front of the temple walked this confident Pharisee, completely oblivious to the fact that the man he despised would be acceptable in God's sight, while he himself would be refused.

It is only as we look at God's standard found in His Son that we find ourselves falling short, just like everyone else. If you go down to the Huntington Beach pier here in Southern California, run with all your might, and jump off, you might get eight feet out while someone else might only get six—but neither of you will hit Catalina Island out in the Pacific some 26 miles. All will fall short of her shores. In like manner, we only have to compare ourselves to Jesus. And once we do, we start to be a lot kinder to other people because we realize we've missed the same boat they have.

After pointing out others' weaknesses, the Pharisee then called attention to his own strengths. By Jewish Law, he would have been obligated to fast once a year on the Day of Atonement. Beyond that, fasting was an exercise of religious devotion that was supposed to be done in secret. He had been fasting twice a week. The Pharisees fasted on Mondays and Tuesdays—market days—when people were shopping for food, the bazaars were open, and they could walk around and show off their piety. In addition to this, we read in Luke 11 that the Pharisees actually tithed their seeds—one for the Lord, nine for them. "If you want to be that exact, fine," Jesus had said. "But don't neglect the more important things like mercy, justice, and the love of God."

The Pharisees were proud of their external behavior but God was interested in their hearts. "To obey is better than sacrifice," Samuel said to Saul. We can't buy off God with our tithes. He wants our lives. He doesn't need our money. He wants us.

Five times in two verses the Pharisee used *I*. He never mentioned that he was a sinner or that he needed God's mercy. He came with full hands and a heart overflowing with himself. No wonder Jesus said he was one who prayed with himself. His prayers hit the ceiling but they didn't make it to God because God doesn't listen to people who try to impress Him with their religious accomplishments.

We then turn to look at the other fellow. Unlike the Pharisee who expected God to accept him because of his religion, he came humbly and fearfully, hoping only in God's mercy. One man would go home with his sins blotted out. The other would go home worse than when he had walked in, because he missed God completely, yet thought all was well.

What does God look for? He looks for humility. He looks for repentance. He looks for honesty about our sin. He looks for those who come as the tax collector. Isaiah said, "Thus saith the high and the lofty One who inhabits eternity, whose name is holy: 'I dwell in a high and holy place with those who are of a contrite spirit to revive the spirit of the humble and to revive the spirit of the contrite.'" God brings life to those who realize they don't have it on their own.

The tax collector found himself far from the entrance to the holy place, fearful and ashamed of being there, desperate to know God yet acutely aware that his whole life had hindered him from coming. Unsure of his place and aware of his guilt, in fear and trembling, he stood near the back door. Like that of the Pharisee, his prayer also began with the word *God*. But what followed was far different. "Be merciful to me, a sinner," he prayed. His estimation of himself was that he had been a failure before God. He humbled himself—and the Lord responded.

Two men. One expected God to receive him. The other didn't but hoped anyway. The lesson is obvious: If you come to God with your hands full, you're going to be sent away empty. But if you come empty, you'll be sent home full.

> Then they also brought infants to Him that He might touch them; but when the disciples saw it, they rebuked them. But Jesus called them to Him and said, "Let the little children come to Me, and do not forbid them; for of such is the kingdom of God. Assuredly, I say to you, whoever does not receive the kingdom of God as a little child will by no means enter it."
>
> —Luke 18:15–17

Trying to protect Jesus, the disciples were acting like Pharisees by keeping some moms and their children away from Him. Jesus corrected the disciples, invited the little kids to come, and using them as examples of the kind of faith that allows people into the kingdom.

Kids are an interesting example because not only are they utterly dependent for every need but they are simple and easily satisfied. If you buy them expensive gifts, chances are they'll like the boxes better. If you offer them a dime or a nickel, they'll take the nickel because it's bigger. On the heels of His story about the Pharisee and the tax collector, Jesus said, "It's the dependent, simple faith of a child that brings you in."

We have to come to God by faith. And we have to come relying only on His mercy because whatever we've done for God is certainly not enough to get us into heaven. For that, we need a Savior. Only one here in Jesus' parable went home in peace.

Chapter 100

ONE THING IS MISSING

Luke 18:18–30
(Matthew 19:16–30; Mark 10:17–31)

Into the context of Jesus' parable about the self-righteous prayer of a Pharisee and the repentant prayer of a tax collector comes the story of the rich young ruler. Big on accomplishments, great on goal setting, and a very nice man by the world's standards, he seemed to have everything. What he didn't have, however, was a child's faith nor the assurance of the forgiven tax collector who had come empty handed and left forgiven and full.

> Now a certain ruler asked Him, saying, "Good Teacher, what shall I do to inherit eternal life?"
>
> —Luke 18:18

Mark tells us this young ruler actually came running after Jesus as He was leaving town. Falling on his knees in the dust of the road, he asked Jesus the one question he had been hoping to ask, the one to which he needed an answer, and the one he had given his all to try and answer himself, yet without success. "Good Teacher," he said, "what can I do to inherit eternal life?" The question in Greek is in the aorist tense which means he expected the Lord would give him something to do—a checklist or formula, or something to difficult to accomplish. He hoped he had the ability. He knew he had the will.

What is interesting about this man is that although he had so much going for him, he would have been the first to admit he hadn't yet found what he was looking for. He still longed to have eternal life. Eternal speaking both of extent, forever and of quality, the kind he obviously saw in Jesus but did not yet find in his own life.

> So Jesus said to him, "Why do you call Me good? No one is good but One, that is, God."
>
> —Luke 18:19

From what we continue to read, it would seem that Jesus' response was designed to wake up this young man to the fact that he had stumbled onto something very significant. The words *Master* or *Teacher* were commonly used for rabbis. But *good* was reserved only for God. Therefore, in asking the young man why he had called Him "good," I think Jesus was bringing him to the place of seeing that He was God. "What attracted you to Me," He said, "is that I'm God."

> "You know the commandments: 'Do not commit adultery,' 'Do not murder,' 'Do not steal,' 'Do not bear false witness,' 'Honor your father and your mother.'"
> —Luke 18:20

In Matthew's account of this story, we are told Jesus first said, "To find eternal life, keep the commandments."

"Which ones?" the young ruler asked.

All of the commandments on the first tablet have to do with our relationship with God. The commandments on the second tablet have to do with our relationship with others. This fellow had found his great hope in the second tablet of the Law. So Jesus purposefully highlighted the things this young man considered his strengths and finest accomplishments.

"Which commandments?" the rich young ruler asked.

"You know them," Jesus answered. "Not stealing, not cheating on your wife, being a good guy."

Oh, those are the ones I was hoping You'd say, the young ruler must have thought. And I'm sure hearing them brought a smile to his face.

> And he said, "All these things I have kept from my youth."
> —Luke 18:21

Mark 10:21 then records the following awesome words: "Jesus beholding him, loved him." To this hopeful young man who came with his best foot forward, Jesus said, "I know you've been trying. I know you've been working hard at it. I know you've given it all you've got. But you still don't have it, do you?" With all his eagerness to report his good works, the young ruler knew eternal life had eluded him and he readily admitted it by asking Jesus the question.

It takes more than being a good man to get to heaven. It takes more than being a moral man, a nice guy, a fair guy, or an honest guy. The rich young ruler was all of those things. He was good. But he wasn't good enough.

When we talk to people who aren't saved and ask them how they're going to be right with God one day, they invariably turn to the second tablet of the Law. "I'm a fair guy," they say. "I'm an honest guy. I don't drink too much, smoke too much, lie too much, cheat too much." They've been pretty good to others, but God is far from being first in their lives and their goodness is ammunition for their argument that they can do it.

So when Jesus heard these things, He said to him, "You still lack one thing. Sell all that you have and distribute to the poor, and you will have treasure in heaven; and come follow Me."

—Luke 18:22

In Matthew 19:20, as the young man said, "All these things I have kept from my youth," he added the words, "what do I still lack?"

In the Matthew account, Jesus' answer begins with, "If you want to be perfect, you still lack one thing." In other words, "If you really want to do it all on your own and make this thing work for yourself, if you want to be perfect, you lack one thing."

I suspect when this man heard Jesus say, "You've just got one more thing to do on your list," his eyes lit up.

I knew I was close. I've almost got it! he must have thought.

"If you want to be perfect, get rid of your stuff," Jesus said.

And the rich young ruler must have said, "Huh?"

It was one step, but a big step. Jesus put His finger on the one thing this young ruler wasn't willing to do: give up on his false gods. If you're ever going to have eternal life, one thing is for sure: Jesus doesn't want to share the limelight. He wants to have it all. You cannot have trust or confidence in anything or anyone else.

Riches can be used for great things. But they are worthless when it comes to eternal life. They can't buy peace or joy, rest or hope. Those items aren't for sale—God transfers them to us by faith. "Want eternal life?" Jesus asked. "Get rid of that which is keeping you from Me."

In His love for this young man, Jesus pointed out what was hindering him. This man believed in God. He sought to keep a part of the Law diligently. And yet he stood guilty of idolatry. He fell into the trap that most folks do by thinking performance and diligence would prevail over a commitment of the heart. They won't. You can do good all of your life, but if you don't love God, it will profit you nothing.

"One thing you lack." It was a big thing. It was a life-changing thing. The only way this young man would find real life was by leaving what he had and hanging on to Jesus.

That's still true. Sometimes there's one big thing that keeps people from making a commitment to the Lord and one big thing that keeps them from enjoying the eternal life He alone can give. A quest for success, a demand for power, or putting friends, lifestyle, or habits before the Lord; all those little gods that keep people from the one true God who can give them the quantity and quality of life they so want.

"What can I do? What do I lack?" asked the rich young ruler.

"Get rid of your false hopes and come follow Me," Jesus said. "I'm God. I'm to be first. Let's go."

But when he heard this, he became very sorrowful, for he was very rich.

—Luke 18:23

Hearing Jesus' answer, the rich young ruler got up off his knees, dusted himself off, turned his back, and walked away. He had wanted to know what to do. But when he found out, he couldn't do it. It's such a poignant picture because he came to the right Person, asked the right question, got the right answer—and then did the wrong thing. He was perfectly positioned to be saved but in the end he wasn't, because there was a god ruling his heart greater than the God who offered him life. He wanted eternal life but he wanted one thing more. He couldn't let go of the comforts with which he had surrounded himself because he didn't agree with God about his sin.

> And when Jesus saw that he became very sorrowful, He said, "How hard it is for those who have riches to enter the kingdom of God. For it is easier for a camel to go through the eye of a needle than for a rich man to enter the kingdom of God."
>
> —Luke 18:24–25

Matthew 19:25 wrote that the disciples were astonished, because to them this man met the criteria and qualified for heaven. Yet Jesus had been teaching—especially in this last year—that we can't get to heaven with a Pharisee's heart. We have to come with a broken heart and a child's faith.

For the rich young ruler the problem was riches. Riches tend to be a problem for a lot of people. If you have them, you tend to rely on them. That is why one distinct advantage of being poor is you have to trust God. "Give us this day our daily bread" means far more to the person whose only hope is God's provision than it means to those who have more than an ample supply. People satisfied with what they have don't see their need for God. Jesus said we can't serve two masters. The rich young ruler thought he could.

To His flabbergasted disciples, Jesus then said, "It's easier for a camel to go through the eye of a needle than for a rich man to enter the kingdom of God." It is possible to get a camel through the eye of a needle—but it will destroy the camel. And I think that's the point. Salvation is beyond our capacity. The only way you're going to find eternal life is if God takes your life from you and gives you one in return. Trusting in riches renders us unreachable because God doesn't want second place. He won't be a "silver medal" God.

> And those who heard it said, "Who then can be saved?" But He said, "The things which are impossible with men are possible with God."
>
> —Luke 18:26–27

Jewish thought in the first century and beyond was that if you were rich, it meant God approved of you. Blessing was directly tied to riches. Therefore, in the disciples' eyes here was a man whose riches told them God was pleased with him, a man who had a perfect record of goodness. No wonder it was hard for them to comprehend that he wasn't bound for heaven.

If you're still trying to save yourself with your accomplishments, take note. You should underline this verse and quote it to yourself every time you think you've got life figured out. Eternal life can only be found in the work God came to accomplish at Calvary for each of us! How do you get to heaven? Trust Him to save you and He will.

> Then Peter said, "See, we have left all and followed You."
>
> —Luke 18:28

Hearing the conditions, Peter was thrilled. "We've left everything to follow You," he said. Indeed, for the last couple of years Peter had left behind a business, a wife, a reputation, comfort, and his home to trek around the country and be marked as a follower of Jesus. "Will that get us eternal life?" he asked.

> So He said to them, "Assuredly, I say to you, there is no one who has left house or parents or brothers or wife or children, for the sake of the kingdom of God, who shall not receive many times more in this present time, and in the age to come eternal life."
>
> —Luke 18:29–30

Although anything Peter gave up to follow Jesus paled in comparison to what Peter would receive, with the word *assuredly* Jesus made it clear that serving is never to be for gain but for the desire to live by faith.

We don't know what happened to this young ruler. I'm hoping he went a hundred yards down the road and, realizing Jesus was his only hope, turned around and came back. That would have been good. The Lord certainly would have given him life.

Jesus is the only One who can give peace the world doesn't know anything about, joy in the midst of tragedy, and hope in a world that seems to grow more hopeless by the year. Lay everything down and go to Him. Don't be like the rich young ruler. Don't let one thing keep you from God.

Chapter 101

Jesus Knew What Lay Ahead

Luke 18:31–43
(Matthew 20:17–19; 20:29–34;
Mark 10:32–34; 10:46–52)

After the rich young ruler went away sad because the Lord had put His finger on what he trusted most, Peter said, "Unlike the rich young ruler, we've left everything to follow You"—the insinuation being, "What will we get in return?" Here Jesus uses Peter's question to speak to His disciples about a sacrifice He would make that would be far greater than any they had made and about a faith that saved, as opposed to the rich young ruler's faith, which had come up short.

> Then He took the twelve aside and said to them, "Behold, we are going up to Jerusalem, and all things that are written by the prophets concerning the Son of Man will be accomplished."
>
> —Luke 18:31

Ten days before the cross, Jesus arrived at Jericho. As He did, He took the disciples aside and said to them, "This is it. This is the final chapter. Now we are close. The end is near." What He had been telling them for a year about His arrest and suffering, and the death He would face, He now told them again.

Mark tells us that as the disciples followed Jesus toward Jerusalem, they were afraid. One lesson to learn from what the Gospels give us about this time is that Jesus knew what lie ahead. He went to the cross willingly and His determination to do so frightened His disciples.

So we read here Jesus saying, "All of the things the prophets wrote concerning the Son of Man are going to be accomplished." The term *Son of Man* was a title Jesus used to describe Himself more than any other name. It is a direct reference to Daniel 7:13–14, where we read about the Son of Man being given a kingdom that would end. It's a prophetic picture of the coming Messiah, a title that was given solely to Him. Whenever we study Jesus' suffering, we certainly must understand that none of these things transpired without His knowledge. This is God in control. This is what God intended. This is God fulfilling His Word. This was His idea!

Jesus knew what was waiting for Him seventeen miles down the road. Imagine the kind of pressure this must have placed on Him.

When I started working as a chaplain with the Los Angeles County Sheriff's Department, I remember the first time I rode along on a "shots fired" call. *We should be going away from them*, I thought. But as deputies, they are trained to run to the problem. For our benefit they are willing to stand in harm's way, and I so enjoyed my time serving them as they served us.

"We have to go," Jesus said. But I'm sure everything in His body was screaming, "No, we don't"—everything, that is, except His heart of love for us.

> "For He will be delivered to the Gentiles and will be mocked and insulted and spit upon. They will scourge Him and kill Him."
>
> —Luke 18:32–33

Seven hundred years earlier, Isaiah had written, "The Lord has opened My ear. I was not rebellious. I didn't turn away. I gave My back to those who struck Me, My cheek to those who would pluck out My beard. I didn't hide My face from their shame and from their spitting. The Lord will help Me so I will not be disgraced. And I have set My face like a flint" (Isa. 50:5–7). Jesus knew it was time for this prophecy concerning Him to be fulfilled.

Jesus' crucifixion and death were foreordained by God. The disciples didn't understand this yet—but by the time you come to Acts 2:23, Peter will stand up and speak about Jesus' death, describing Him as being taken by God's determined purpose and foreknowledge. In Hebrews 12:2, we read it was for the joy set before Him that Jesus endured the cross, although He despised the shame. Jesus' motivation was us and the glory of the Father. Our motivation should be Him and His glory!

> "And the third day He will rise again."
>
> —Luke 18:33

Each time Jesus spoke of His death, He added the wonderful promise and hope, "On the third day, I'll rise." Yet the disciples never once caught it or even so much as responded to it. Jesus laid out for them the next week and a half: trial, crucifixion, resurrection. But I think they stopped listening somewhere around "suffering and death."

> But they understood none of these things, this saying was hidden from them, and they did not know the things which were spoken.
>
> —Luke 18:34

For at least three years or more, these men had been with Jesus every step of the way. Yet His words about suffering, death, and resurrection still didn't seem to register. In fact, three times in this verse alone we read that they were spiritually dull. To make matters worse, it is written in the imperfect active tense, which means they weren't getting any better at understanding, at least, not yet.

Why? There are a couple of good reasons we must consider. First, although the Holy Spirit was with them, He did not yet indwell them. When we were saved, we opened the Bible and it immediately began to make sense, for the Holy Spirit came to dwell within us the moment we believed. The light came on. God began to speak. This would not happen for the disciples until after the Resurrection. In John 2:22, John wrote, "When He had risen from the dead, the disciples remembered what He had said and they believed the Scriptures and the word which Jesus had spoken." It was all being stored away, but there was no way to interpret or understand it yet without the Holy Spirit teaching them, reminding them, making spiritual truths understandable.

A second issue was that the disciples had made up their minds that Jesus wasn't going to die. He was going to rule. And the Scriptures weren't going to change their opinion a bit. At least not for now. Even though Jesus told them very directly, "On the third day, I'm going to rise," they never heard it. Who heard it? His enemies. That's why they set a guard in front of the tomb.

Rather than listening to Jesus talk about His death and resurrection, the disciples actually were planning their careers and hopeful advancements that they believed were headed their way over the next few weeks. They believed Jesus would soon overthrow the Roman government. In fact, it was immediately following this discussion that Mark tells us in chapter 10:37 that James and John asked if they would be able to sit at His right and left in His kingdom.

In some ways, things haven't changed much. We're living on the edge of the Lord's second coming today. Everything He has said would happen has—yet most people still aren't ready and worse, are oblivious to the signs of the times.

> Then it happened, as He was coming near Jericho, that a certain blind man sat by the road begging. And hearing a multitude passing by, he asked what it meant.
>
> —Luke 18:35–36

Matthew 20 and Mark 10 tell us it was as Jesus was leaving Jericho that He came upon this blind man they identify as Bartimaeus. Luke says it was as He was coming near Jericho. For years, skeptics pointed to this discrepancy as proof that the Bible contained errors. Until archeology discovered their had been two Jericho cities in that day. There was an old city that had existed for more than a thousand years. And then there was the new city Herod had built as his winter retreat. So as Jesus left one Jericho, He entered another.

To be blind in Jesus' day meant that you were often reduced to begging, for there was no welfare system. With maybe a million people coming through on their way to Passover, the streets would at this season would have been loud and busy. But this blind man noticed something different was going on and asked about it.

> So they told him that Jesus of Nazareth was passing by. And he cried out, saying, "Jesus, Son of David, have mercy on me!"
>
> —Luke 18:37–38

Having heard of the healings Jesus had brought to other blind men during the last three years, Bartimaeus, I suspect, had been hoping to meet Him for quite some time. His use of the term *Son of David* as he cried out immediately identified him as someone who believed Jesus was the Savior, the Messiah to come. He may have been blind physically—but spiritually he saw what most of the crowd did not.

> Then those who went before warned him that he should be quiet, but he cried out all the more, "Son of David, have mercy on me!"
>
> —Luke 18:39

The crowd warned him to be quiet. But if you were blind and needed help, you'd cry out too. A good way to come to the Lord is not to care what others think, especially when you have learned only the Lord can meet your needs.

> So Jesus stood still and commanded him to be brought to Him.
>
> —Luke 18:40

I love this picture because, above the din of the traveling crowd and the religious parade, Jesus heard a voice crying out—and He stopped. At a time when His heart was filled with pressure, ten days from death, He very well might have been oblivious to everything around Him. But when He heard a cry for help, He stopped.

We're told in Mark 10:49 that the crowd said to Bartimaeus, "Be of good cheer. The Lord is calling for you," and that as he stood up with their help to go to Jesus, he threw away his outer garment. This was quite an act of faith, tossing aside the one thing that would have given a beggar like him, living on the street, warmth and comfort. It was as if he declares, I won't be needing that anymore.

> And when he had come near, He asked him, saying, "What do you want Me to do for you?"
>
> —Luke 18:40–41

"What do you want?" That's a good question, isn't it? What if the Lord asked you that? What would you say? Jesus knew what Bartimaeus wanted. He always knows. But that's how prayer works. He knows, but He still wants us to bring our needs to Him.

He said, "Lord, that I may receive my sight." Then Jesus said to him, "Receive your sight; your faith has made you well." And immediately he received his sight, and followed Him, glorifying God. And all the people, when they saw it, gave praise to God.

—Luke 18:41–43

When Bartimaeus started speaking, he was blind. By the time he finished speaking, he could see. That's how God honors faith, isn't it? We cry out for salvation and by the time we're done speaking, we're saved. But we've got to ignore the crowds and just follow Jesus to discover His wonderful plans for us.

I think the fact that Mark mentions Bartimaeus by name suggests Jesus did a great work in his life and he became an influence in the early church.

So here, ten days from the cross, we see Jesus' heart. Just around the corner, Jerusalem and Golgotha awaited. But He wanted us to know that He knew. And if, like Bartimaeus, we can respond by faith despite the passing crowd's advice, God will open our eyes so we'll be able to see Him too. Everywhere in the Gospels, whoever turned to Jesus found life. And that's still true today.

Chapter 102

JESUS SEEKS THE LOST

Luke 19:1–10

From Luke 9–19, we learn more about the final year of Jesus' ministry than from any of the other Gospel accounts. Luke especially focuses on the personal relationships Jesus had with those He encountered—the Lord always available to whoever is willing. Which brings us to this wonderful story of Zacchaeus.

> Then Jesus entered and passed through Jericho.
>
> —Luke 19:1

In the first century, Jericho was a major city. Coming from the north to Judea, the Jews crossed the Jordan River, went south on the eastern side of the Jordan, and then crossed back at Jericho in order to avoid Samaria. As a result, Jericho became the crossroad between Galilee and Jerusalem. In addition, it was one of the only stops before hitting the desert for those heading out of Jerusalem into Egypt, making Jericho a very cosmopolitan and influential city.

> Now behold, there was a man named Zacchaeus who was a chief tax collector, and he was rich.
>
> —Luke 19:2

Zacchaeus means "righteous one." Evidently, his parents had great hopes for their son. Unfortunately, he turned out to be anything but righteous. The Romans offered the job of tax collector by region to the highest bidder. This made tax collectors dishonest, uncaring, harsh people who everyone in the nation saw as traitors. They were so hated by the general populace that the religious leaders often pointed to the time Jesus spent with them as proof that He couldn't possibly be the Messiah.

We are told here that Zacchaeus was not just a tax collector but a *chief* tax collector. This indicates he was the regional director, the head crook, the Godfather. Josephus, the Jewish historian, wrote that first-century Jericho made great money from balsa wood and the extract that came from it. So Zacchaeus collected taxes in one of the wealthier cities and, through gouging and exorbitant rates, was able to make himself all the wealthier.

Zacchaeus to his neighbors and city was the lost cause. For him all hope was gone. I like the picture the Lord gives us because He sees much more than we do. Zacchaeus' story is a picture of God knowing what's in our hearts and responding the minute we look to find Him. It's a beautiful picture, because inside this wicked man beat a heart that was breaking. And although everyone hated Zacchaeus, Jesus did not. Less than two weeks away from the Cross, where He would give His life for people like Zacchaeus, Jesus would reach out to a broken man. Everyone else saw a wicked, mean-spirited, dishonest man. But He saw a breaking heart.

> And he sought to see who Jesus was, but could not because of the crowd, for he was of short stature. So he ran ahead and climbed up into a sycamore tree to see Him, for He was going to pass that way.
>
> —Luke 19:3–4

Zacchaeus wanted to see Jesus, but he was a short guy and the crowd was large. So he showed up an hour late for the Rose Parade and couldn't get near the curb. If he was only curious, he'd have gone home, thinking he'd catch Jesus another day. But there was more going on for Zacchaeus than that. So he ran ahead and climbed a tree to see if he could get a look at Jesus.

I find that interesting because it seems to me that before we got saved, a lot of us wouldn't admit readily that we were having trouble. We're good at concealing what God sees. He's aware of our needs even when we're unwilling to admit them. But any action on our part toward Him will find Him running to us.

In first-century Jewish culture, men didn't run in public. And they certainly didn't climb trees. But Zacchaeus wouldn't have cared less what anyone else thought. His abandonment of pride tells you this was a fellow ready to be delivered from his sinful life. In John 12:42 we read that among the chief rulers of the synagogue many believed in Jesus but because they didn't want to be put out of the synagogue, they remained closet believers. Zacchaeus was past that. Throwing dignity to the wind, he climbed a tree, immune to the judgment of others and in hopes of finding a solution in Jesus for his hurt.

> And when Jesus came to the place, He looked up and saw him, and said to him, "Zacchaeus, make haste and come down, for today I must stay at your house." So he made haste and came down, and received Him joyfully.
>
> —Luke 19:5–6

You have to believe Zacchaeus thought, *He knows my name. He's been talking to the people. This can't be good. But that smile can't be bad.* I think this might very well have been the first time Zacchaeus had heard his name yelled in a crowd without some four-letter epithet attached to it. Jesus had led a huge crowd of disinterested people down the street to get to the one guy who was more than interested—he was hungry and ready. There were many around Him, but Zacchaeus was the one on whom He had set his eyes.

The Bible teaches we don't seek God on our own. Romans 3:12 tells us there is none that does right, that all have turned aside. So for the Lord to even bring us to a place where we even want Him in our lives is a huge work of His grace. At the same time, once God opens our eyes, there's still the need to respond to His calling. When Paul wrote to the Philippians, he said, "It is the Lord who works in you both to will and to do of His good pleasure." God will do the work—but we have to respond.

Zacchaeus had had enough of life. He didn't have peace. He couldn't buy joy. He couldn't sleep through the night. Knowing that, Jesus called him. But Zacchaeus, up a tree, still had to decide publicly to follow.

Jesus' words to Him are very interesting. "Hurry up," He said. Was it late? Was He hungry? I don't think so. I think it was now or never for Zacchaeus. Jesus wouldn't be back next week.

In his second sermon, Peter said to the people, "You should repent when these times of refreshing come from the Lord." In other words, "Move while God has your attention. Respond while you're listening because you don't always have that privilege." It's dangerous to put God off when He speaks to you, because if you say no enough times, there are plenty of verses that tell us it becomes easier to say no and harder to say yes.

We're not told either in the Bible or in history what had brought Zacchaeus to this point. We can presume it was his wicked lifestyle, the people's hatred, and the realization that riches can't satisfy. Maybe he knew Matthew, who was also a tax collector before he became a disciple. What we do know is Zacchaeus was hungry for life. So when Jesus said, "Let's go," he was ready.

> But when they saw it, they all complained, saying, "He has gone to be a guest with a man who is a sinner."
>
> —Luke 19:7

When Jesus healed Bartimaeus, the people rejoiced. Here He has lunch with a tax collector and the people couldn't have been more unhappy. *After all,* they must have thought, *if Jesus likes Zacchaeus, how good could He be?* The difference between the crowd and Zacchaeus, however, is Zacchaeus knew he was too short to see Jesus on his own, while the crowd thought they were plenty tall enough.

> Then Zacchaeus stood and said to the Lord, "Look, Lord, I give half of my goods to the poor; and if I have taken anything from anyone by false accusation, I restore fourfold."
>
> —Luke 19:8

By the time Zacchaeus and Jesus emerged from Zacchaeus' house, Zacchaeus was almost unrecognizable. This is not the same man who went in. He had a new countenance. He spoke out in public. He called Jesus "Lord." He wanted to restore the things he had. Our lives can't stay the same once we know the Lord. Days from Calvary, the Good Shepherd had found another lost sheep—and the proof was his changed life.

> And Jesus said to him, "Today salvation has come to this house, because he also is a son of Abraham; for the son of Man has come to seek and to save that which was lost."
>
> —Luke 19:9–10

Every Jew would have seen himself as a son of Abraham. But Jesus said that because Zacchaeus came to know Him as Lord, he truly had come to know the God of his forefathers, the Savior, the Messiah. To the critics in the crowd, Jesus said, "This is why I've come: to seek and then to save the lost." Zacchaeus had been lost. Now he was found.

If you're tired of the way you are living and are willing to humble yourself and trust Jesus to give you life, He's more than willing. In fact, after leaving Zacchaeus, He continued His walk to the cross—just so Zacchaeus' story could be yours.

Chapter 103

How Is
Your Investment Doing?

Luke 19:11–27
(Matthew 25:14–30)

O n the heels of Jesus' words to Zacchaeus that the Son of Man had come to seek and save those who are lost, Jesus gave the following parable to the crowd that had gathered, and again we receive an explanation as to the purpose of the parable.

> Now as they heard these things, He spoke another parable, because He was near Jerusalem and because they thought the kingdom of God would appear immediately.
>
> —Luke 19:11

Here in the crowd—and especially among the disciples—the anticipation was that they were going to Jerusalem so Jesus would take over and rule. Although He had explained several times that before He ruled He would have to die, they still weren't willing to hear. There are a couple of times in the Gospels when the people tried to make Jesus king on their own. So this wasn't new. But because of their proximity to Jerusalem, Jesus told a parable to remind them of what He already had told them, one that had a direct parallel with the headlines of the day.

From a historical standpoint, Rome very rarely handed out the title of "king" to its rulers, especially the regional ones. An exception to this was Herod the Great, who had been called a king by Caesar. When Archalaeus, his son, came to rule in the area, he was frustrated that he was not given the same title as his father. So he went to Rome with the express purpose of appealing to Caesar to give him the title of king. But rather than testifying on his behalf, his family members said, "This guy's a crook. He's a killer." Fifty Jewish and Samaritan men and women were there to meet him as well, all opposed to his being made king. And if that wasn't bad enough, some eight thousand expatriates living in Rome who had been chased out of the area showed up to oppose him. As a result, Caesar's answer to Archalaeus was, "If you ever deserve it, you can have it." And he sent him back home.

Jesus used this hot topic of the day to say that, unlike Archalaeus, He would leave and be successful in His return as King.

Therefore He said: "A certain nobleman went into a far country to receive for himself a kingdom and to return."

—Luke 19:12

Hearing this, I suspect most people immediately would have thought of Archalaeus. Not only that, but Jesus was in Jericho, where Archalaeus' palace was.

"So he called ten of his servants, delivered to them ten minas, and said to them, 'Do business till I come.'"

—Luke 19:13

A mina was a monetary unit equal to one hundred drachmas. A drachma was about a day's wage. So a mina was one hundred days' pay—a valuable trust. There was one other parable the Lord told at this time, which was recorded in Matthew 25:14–30, the parable of the talents. But there are significant differences between the two—the parable in Matthew 25 finds individuals with varying amounts of talents and the parable speaks of using all God gives you for His glory. Here in Luke every servant received the same amount, speaking of opportunity. The sky's the limit. You can serve as much as you like and use all God gives you.

Every one of us has been given the same opportunity and the same responsibility. When Paul wrote to the Thessalonians, he said in 2:4 of his first letter to them, "As we have been approved by God to be entrusted by the Gospel, so we'll speak—not to please men but to please God who tries our hearts." When he wrote his first letter to Timothy, he referred to the glorious Gospel committed to his trust (1 Tim. 1:11). And at the end of that same book, he told Timothy to guard that with which God had entrusted him (1 Tim. 6:20).

Wherever we turn in the Bible, we are reminded that the responsibility of God's servants is to take His Word and deliver it to the world. When Paul wrote to the Ephesians, he said in 5:16 that we should redeem the time because the days are evil. The word *redeem* means to purchase every opportunity. In other words, if you get a chance, use it. Don't miss any open door, because time is running out. Our lives are short. The window of opportunity is narrow. While we're here, we must be busy.

If the Lord called you home today, who would step forward as fruit of what you've done with the trust you've been given? You don't want to come to the end of your life lamenting what you might have done for the Lord.

"But his citizens hated him, and sent a delegation after him, saying, 'We will not have this man to reign over us.'"

—Luke 19:14

Jesus warned of opposition from those who wouldn't want the King of Kings to rule over their lives. Jesus spoke of the conditions in the world while He was gone, in which the church would have to go forth and bear Him witness. In fact, just down the road, in John 19, the crowd will utter these horrible words, "We don't want this Man to rule over us." Archalaeus was rejected for his own wickedness. Jesus was rejected for ours.

> "And so it was that when he returned, having received the kingdom, he then commanded these servants, to whom he had given the money, to be called to him, that he might know how much every man had gained by trading."
>
> —Luke 19:15

Those who are alive on the earth when the Lord returns will give an account. For the believer who has gone ahead, the Bible teaches there is a place called the judgment seat of Christ, or the *bema* seat. It will be a place not to determine if you're saved, but to determine your rewards. In 1 Corinthians 3:13–15, Paul wrote that every person's work will be thrown in the fire and the fire will show what sort of work it was. Gold, silver, and precious stones will endure. Wood, hay, and stubble will be consumed. This isn't a matter of salvation but of rewards, appointments, and the Lord's gifts for faithfulness.

In the verses that follow, Jesus gives the account of three of the ten servants and how they fared when He, the Master, returned.

> "Then came the first, saying, 'Master, your mina has earned ten minas.' And he said to him, 'Well done, good servant; because you were faithful in a very little, have authority over ten cities.' And the second came, saying, 'Master, your mina has earned five minas.' Likewise he said to him, 'You also be over five cities.'"
>
> —Luke 19:16–19

The first and second servants returned with 1,000 percent and 500 percent increases respectively. As a result, they were given positions in the kingdom directly proportional and commensurate to the diligence they had shown while the king was away. Likewise, although our presence in God's kingdom is assured by God's mercy and grace, our position in His kingdom would appear to be related to the faithfulness and diligence we show while Jesus is away.

"Well done," the master said to both the first and second servants. The Lord did not chastise the one who brought 5 minas as not being up to par with the one who had brought 10. The opportunities are out there, and as I said, the sky is the limit. But then came the third example, the fellow from whom we needed to learn.

> "Then another came, saying, 'Master, here is your mina, which I have kept put away in a handkerchief. For I feared you, because you are an austere man. You collect what you did not deposit, and reap what you did not sow.' And he said to him, 'Out of your own mouth I will judge you, you wicked servant. You knew that I was an austere man, collecting what I did not deposit and reaping what

I did not sow. Why then did you not put my money in the bank, that at my coming I might have collected it with interest?'"

—Luke 19:20–23

The third guy simply buried the trust and lived his life. And whatever slanderous excuse he presented about the king's character, the bottom line was, he valued the king's trust very lightly.

The parallel is obvious. There are a lot of ways to get out the Word: We can pray. We can witness. We can go to the mission field—or we can support those who do. We can, through personal evangelism and lifestyle, touch many lives. What we can't do is be passive, do nothing, and expect somehow to have influence. We won't. And we will have to answer for it on the day we arrive in the kingdom.

> "And he said to those who stood by, 'Take the mina from him, and give it to him who has ten minas.' (But they said to him, 'Master, he has ten minas.') 'For I say to you, that to everyone who has will be given; and from him who does not have, even what he has will be taken away from him. But bring here those enemies of mine, who did not want me to reign over them, and slay them before me.'"
>
> —Luke 19:24–27

The servant with ten minas was blessed. The servant with five minas was also blessed. But the third servant's unwillingness brought nothing. So the king took from him that with which he had been entrusted and with which he should have been faithful. The judgment was far more severe, however, for those who, hearing from the servants, refused to believe them. They ended up standing before God and were destroyed for all of eternity.

We live today between verses 14 and 15. Soon the Lord will come. He may come for all of us, or He may just come for you. But in either event, you will have to give an account for the trust God has given you and the deposit He left with you. We have equal opportunities to step out. One day our works will be placed on the scale and God will see what we've done with them. Those who invest in the kingdom, although many will refuse, will receive unthinkable rewards. To those who hide it, there is a certain amount of shame awaiting them. But to those who have rejected Him altogether, there is only judgment.

I would underline the words *Do business until I come* in your mind. If you don't have the time, find the time. If you can't find the time, make the time because it won't be long before people no longer will be able to hear the Gospel message. And who knows when your own days will be finished!

You'll run into a lot of "We don't want this Man ruling over us," but then again, you'll find many who, one day, you'll be able to present to the Lord as the fruit of your faithfulness to His trust.

SECTION 4

THE FINAL WEEK OF MINISTRY

Chapter 104

PASSION WEEK BEGINS

Luke 19:28–44

(Matthew 21:1–11; Mark 11:1–11; John 12:12–19)

After talking to the crowd about the difference between His first coming to die and His second coming to rule, it would appear that Jesus went the last miles to Jerusalem alone.

> When He had said this, He went on ahead, going up to Jerusalem. And it came to pass, when He drew near to Bethphage and Bethany, at the mountain called Olivet, that He sent two of His disciples . . . .
>
> —Luke 19:28–29

It was in Jericho that Jesus had led Zacchaeus to faith and opened Bartimaeus' eyes. Today, the walk from Jericho to Jerusalem is about eighteen miles. Due to the landscape, it is most likely the same route Jesus took. As you head for Jerusalem, you come up the back side of the Mount of Olives before crossing a deep canyon, the Kidron Valley, and passing through Bethphage and Bethany, which are still in existence today but are very small towns, much like in Jesus' day.

In John 12:1–8, we're told Jesus arrived with His disciples at the home of Mary, Martha, and Lazarus on Saturday night and that in celebration of Lazarus' resurrection from the dead the sisters made dinner. Martha was serving and Lazarus, along with Mary, sat at the table. But as they were celebrating, Mary left the table and returned with spikenard. *Nard* means "perfume" and *spike* means "pure" or "genuine." Mary poured this expensive perfume on Jesus' feet and dried His feet with her hair. The whole place smelled absolutely wonderful!

Judas complained that this was a tremendous waste. "We could have sold that for quite a profit and given the money to the poor," he said. But John said Judas said this not because he cared about the poor, but because he was a thief and had his hand in the till.

"Leave her alone," Jesus said. "She has kept this for the day of My burial. The poor you will always have with you. You will not always have the Son of Man with you."

Mary seems to be the one who, more than anyone else, was aware of the fact that Jesus was going to die. So she brought that which was most valuable to her, the most costly, and gave it to Jesus in preparation for His death less than a week away.

John went on to say that there were many at Mary and Martha's house that Saturday night not only to see Jesus but because they wanted to see Lazarus. They probably poked him and asked if he really had died. And as they heard his story, many began to believe in Jesus. So the chief priests decided that when they killed Jesus, they'd kill Lazarus too.

That was Saturday night. Here in Luke, we're given what took place the following morning. After Jesus went ahead to Jerusalem, He called a couple of His disciples together . . .

> . . . saying, "Go into the village opposite you, where as you enter you will find a colt tied, on which no one has ever sat. Loose it and bring it here. And if anyone asks you, 'Why are you loosing it?' thus you shall say to him, 'Because the Lord has need of it.'" So those who were sent went their way and found it just as He had said to them. But as they were loosing the colt, the owners of it said to them, "Why are you loosing the colt?" And they said, "The Lord has need of him."
>
> —Luke 19:30–34

It would appear that Jesus had made deliberate preparations for this day. All four of the Gospels record how the disciples retrieved the colt Jesus would use to ride into Jerusalem. The word *colt* or literally "young donkey" is important, because five hundred years earlier the prophet Zechariah said in Zechariah 9:9 that the King would be coming, bringing salvation with Him, and riding on a colt.

In Bible times, kings rode into the cities they conquered on magnificent horses. Only kings coming in peace rode donkeys. With this mode of transportation carefully chosen, everything was ready for Sunday morning.

> Then they brought him to Jesus. And they threw their own clothes on the colt, and they set Jesus on him. And as He went, many spread their clothes on the road. Then, as He was now drawing near the descent of the Mount of Olives, the whole multitude of the disciples began to rejoice and praise God with a loud voice for all the mighty works they had seen, saying: "Blessed is the King who comes in the name of the Lord! Peace in heaven and glory in the highest!"
>
> —Luke 19:35–38

With tens of thousands of people in town, this must have been quite a sight. Jesus constantly had warned people that before He came to rule, He had come to die. But nothing was going to deter these folks from believing in their hearts what they had always hoped—that as the Messiah, Jesus would win their political freedom.

Gathered for all the wrong reasons, the crowd began to treat Jesus like royalty. They laid their coats on the ground and their tunics in the road. According to the other Gospels, they waved palm branches in the air. As Jesus rode to the summit, they couldn't contain their excitement. They began to sing, shout, and rejoice over all they had hoped was to come.

As He neared the top of the Mount of Olives, they began to sing the Hillel psalms, the psalms of ascent. Every family coming to Jerusalem for feast days sung Psalm 113–118 three times a year. They're songs about the Messiah—His rule and reign, how great He is, and how all the world one day will bow at His feet. The people grabbed hold of the very psalms they had been singing for generations because their expectation was that by the next day they'd be in charge and the Romans would be ousted. Luke tells us they sang with a loud voice. It seems to me that when people are excited, they sing loudly. This wasn't a "have to" but a "want to."

Due to the topography in Israel, if someone speaks loudly on the Temple Mount, he or she can be heard a mile and a half away on the Mount of Olives. On the corner of the Temple Mount the Romans had built the Antonio Fortress where Herod had thought it wise to station soldiers twenty-four hours a day to keep an eye on the religious people who always seemed to be troublemakers. So I'm sure this Roman garrison would have heard the crowd singing, "Here comes our King."

If Herod was at a meeting in the fortress, he might have laughed and said, "Who does this guy think he is?" But he wouldn't be laughing by the end of the week.

> And some of the Pharisees called to Him from the crowd, "Teacher, rebuke Your disciples." But He answered and said to them, "I tell you that if these should keep silent, the stones would immediately cry out."
>
> —Luke 19:39–40

The Pharisees were becoming irate. "Do You hear what they're saying about You, Jesus? They're singing to You like You're some kind of Savior, some kind of Messiah," they said. But Jesus wouldn't stop them. Not today, not this day. This was the day for which He had come.

John 12:19 tells us they said to one another, "See what we've accomplished? Nothing. The whole world is going after Him." And although according to Matthew 26:5 they had planned to kill Jesus after the Passover feast, this day's events convinced them they couldn't wait any longer and they'd do it first chance they had. What they didn't know was that the Lord already had planned the day He would die.

> Now as He drew near, He saw the city and wept over it, saying, "If you had known, even you, especially in this your day, the things that make for your peace! But now they are hidden from your eyes. For days will come upon you when your enemies will build an embankment around you, surround you and close you in on every side, and level you, and your children within you, to the ground; and they will not leave in you one stone upon another, because you did not know the time of your visitation."
>
> —Luke 19:41–44

What a picture to see crowds with false expectations beside themselves with joy and Jesus, well aware of what was going on around Him, broken-hearted. It wouldn't be but a few days from now that the people would be screaming at the tops of their lungs, "Crucify Him! We have no king but Caesar. We don't want this Man to rule over us." But here they were saying, "Hosanna. Save now! Blessed is He that comes in the name of the Lord." Jesus wept for He knew what the people didn't know themselves. He wept because He knew what would come as a result of their rejection.

There is no stronger Greek word for *wept* than this one. As when Jesus wept over the reaction to Lazarus' death earlier, the Greek word describes someone whose chest heaves, who sobs loudly and uncontrollably. Here as Jesus' eyes fell upon the city, as He saw the people around Him with the palm branches and the joy and the singing, He wept. The other Gospels tell us He said, "How often I would have gathered you together as a hen gathers her chicks under her wings. But you wouldn't come." How moving to know that the King who came for us and loves us would weep when we refuse to come to Him.

For generations the prophets had foretold the day Jesus would present Himself publicly to the nation. About five hundred and seventy years earlier, the prophet Daniel was in his eighties when he read Jeremiah's prophecies and realized the captivity of which he had been part for seventy years in Babylon was almost over. "What should I be doing as we get ready to go back home?" he asked the Lord. In answer to his prayer, the Lord sent the angel Gabriel to him. In Daniel 9:24–27 He gave Daniel four verses that explained His dealing with the nation Israel up until the time of His second coming.

One of the things the angel told Daniel was that between the day the command was given to rebuild Jerusalem and the Lord's coming would be sixty-nine blocks of seven years—or 483 years. According to Nehemiah, it was on March 14, 445 B.C., that Artaxerxes gave the command to rebuild Jerusalem. The Sunday before Passover fell on April 6, 32 A.D.—483 years later. Based on the Babylonian calendar of 360 days a year, Jesus entered Jerusalem on the exact day foretold by Daniel.

So when we read *especially in this your day*, it is more than just a declaration that every day belongs to the Lord. It's a declaration that this was the day that the Messiah would come as declared exactly in prophesy by Daniel as the angel of the Lord revealed.

We know from history that thirty-seven years later, after a 1,443-day siege in 70 A.D., Titus and the Roman army's tenth legion climbed over the walls of Jerusalem and destroyed the city. The temple, set on fire by an overzealous soldier shooting a fiery arrow through a window, burned to the ground. But because of the gold inside which had melted, the Romans carefully dismantled the temple one stone at a time to retrieve the gold that had run into the cracks. Not one stone was left on another—just as Jesus had said.

Josephus, the Jewish historian, wrote that when the troops came into the city, the first day alone some 600,000 Jews were killed. As a result, the nation found itself scattered to the four winds. The carnage was horrible.

No wonder Jesus wept.

Chapter 105

MONDAY OF
PASSION WEEK

Mark 11:12–24; John 12:20–50

Following Jesus' entry into Jerusalem and His weeping over the city for what He knew lay ahead, Mark 11:11 tells us that after looking at the temple, Jesus returned to Lazarus' house, the hour being late. This week, He would stay at the home of Lazarus, Mary, and Martha every night before spending Thursday night in the Garden of Gethsemane.

> Now the next day, when they had come out from Bethany, He was hungry. And seeing from afar a fig tree having leaves, He went to see if perhaps He would find something on it. When He came to it, He found nothing but leaves, for it was not the season for figs. In response Jesus said to it, "Let no one eat fruit from you ever again." And His disciples heard it.
>
> —Mark 11:12–14

Four days from the cross, Jesus set out for Jerusalem and the Temple area. Mark tells us He was hungry—but I don't think the issue was physical hunger. During His wilderness temptation, Jesus had gone forty days without food. I think Jesus' desire had been to find spiritual fruit among His people. Here in this last week, when the big confrontation would be between religious people and His offer of salvation, He still was searching with great hunger for those who would look to Him—fruit!

In Israel, spring figs grow on the previous year's fruit shoots. These figs are smaller and blossom in March and April. The larger figs grow on new shoots between August and October. Spring figs always display leaves first. So when Jesus saw a tree with leaves, He expected there would be fruit. When there wasn't, He cursed the tree in the only record of Jesus using His power to destroy something. In the context of prophecy, Jesus' action was the visual portrayal of His dealings with Israel as a nation—how He had come to His own but had been refused by them. He had come to the nation and its spiritual leaders, saying, "Religion isn't good enough. You have to have a relationship with God. To bear fruit, you're going to have to have more than religion."

The nation of Israel is most often portrayed in Old Testament prophecies as either a fig tree or a vineyard. So this Monday as He headed toward Jerusalem, in cursing the fig tree, Jesus spoke of the empty promises of a religious system that cannot save a life.

So they came to Jerusalem. Then Jesus went into the temple and began to drive out those who bought and sold in the temple, and overturned the tables of the money changers and the seats of those who sold doves. And He would not allow anyone to carry wares through the temple. Then He taught, saying to them, "Is it not written, 'My house shall be called a house of prayer for all nations'? But you have made it a den of thieves." And the scribes and chief priests heard it and sought how they might destroy Him; for they feared Him, because all the people were astonished at His teaching.

—Mark 11:15–18

Jesus walked down the little road that goes over the Mount of Olives through the Kidron Valley and back up the other side into the East Gate and the area of the temple. So before Him he saw the temple with its gold and marble pillars shining in the sun. And because it was Passover, it would have been packed with worshippers.

Going up the stairway into the temple, the first place one came to was the court of the Gentiles. Three hundred yards long and 250 yards wide, it was a very large area and the only place a Jew could bring his Gentile friends to share their Lord with them. But even though it was intended to serve as the place where God could be introduced to the pagan, it had become a religious marketplace.

In Exodus 30:13–15, the Lord told the people that when they came for feast days, all men twenty years of age and older were to bring half a shekel. This would cover the operating expenses of tabernacle—and later, temple—worship. In Jesus' day, the high priest had declared that Roman currency was unacceptable, even though in Rome-occupied Israel that was virtually the only type of currency readily available. So people coming to worship had to exchange their Roman denarii into shekels to give it here.

Then there was the issue of the Passover lamb—which was to be a year-old lamb without spot or blemish. The problem was, en route to the temple no matter how spotless the lamb was at the beginning of the journey, it was sure to have cut its foot or rubbed against a thorn by the time it arrived, rendering it unacceptable as an offering. It "just so happened," however, that in the Gentiles' court were stalls of lambs and other animals for sale—each with the rabbinical stamp of approval—available for only two dollars on the dollar. So in the Gentiles' court were livestock, tables of wine and salt, and the tables of the moneychangers charging exorbitant rates to convert your monies to temple coins. What a scam—especially considering that Josephus wrote that in 65 A.D., thirty three years later, 225,000 lambs were sacrificed in Jerusalem during Passover week alone.

The high priests, Annas and Caiaphas, and many others made themselves wealthy under the guise of serving the people who had come by Law to simply serve the Lord. This particular morning, Jesus had had enough. Actually, He had had enough three years earlier when one of the first things He did in His public ministry was cleanse the temple. But little had changed.

The way the temple was positioned, one would have had to go nearly twice as far to get out of the city, down to the Kidron, and up the Mount of Olives without passing through the Gentiles' court. So rather than providing a place of worship and an introduction to the things of God, the Gentiles' court had also become a thoroughfare. The din of the crowd, the cry of the vendors, the smell of the stalls, the push of the worshipper, the selling of the animals, the traffic in the court, the irritation in the lines, the crooks, the frustration—welcome to God's temple.

In His zeal for His Father's house, Jesus came and single-handedly turned over the tables. Half-shekels must have flown everywhere. Booths were knocked down, animals let go, passers-by on the impromptu path must have had their packages knocked from their hands, and great turmoil must have followed. But Jesus could not be stopped.

From Mark we know Jesus cleansed the temple on the Monday of Passion Week. From John we know that although the Gentiles' court had become a den of thieves, there were in it some Gentiles who came seeking God.

> Now there came certain Greeks among those who came up to worship at the feast. Then they came to Philip, who was from Bethsaida of Galilee, and asked him, saying, "Sir, we wish to see Jesus." Philip came and told Andrew, and in turn Andrew and Philip told Jesus.
>
> —John 12:20–22

Maybe it was due to Philip's Gentile name that these Greeks felt comfortable approaching him and asking to see Jesus. Philip lived to the north in Bethsaida, the Galilee area. Bethsaida bordered what was called Syro-Phoenicia, an area comprised of a number of Gentile cities in the northern territories. So maybe these Greeks sought out Philip because he seemed the most like them in dress or appearance. Their request was very simple: they wanted to meet Jesus. I find it interesting that when Jesus was born, Gentile wise men came from the east looking for the King of the Jews. Here, when He was about to die, Greeks came from the west looking for that same King.

Not sure what to do, Philip went to Andrew for advice. And Andrew lived up to his reputation that whenever you see him in the Gospels, he's bringing someone to Jesus. He did it with his brother, Peter. He did it with the little boy with the fish and bread. And here he's doing it again. I think if you're an Andrew, great will be your reward in heaven.

> But Jesus answered them, saying, "The hour has come that the Son of Man should be glorified. Most assuredly, I say to you, unless a grain of wheat falls into the ground and dies, it remains alone; but if it dies, it produces much grain."
>
> —John 12:23–24

This is the first time we hear Jesus say aloud, "My hour is come." A year earlier, knowing His hour had come, He had begun heading toward Jerusalem. Just the day before this, the people had sung, "This is the day the Lord has made." This was the day the prophets had foretold. When He finally allowed public worship the day before, it was because His hour had come. It was time to be glorified.

Whenever you find Jesus using the term *glorified*, it is always in reference to His victory over death and His ability to show you who He is by doing that which only God could do. In answer to the Greeks' request to see Him, Jesus said, "Now is My time to be glorified." In other words, "Now is the time to fully demonstrate who I am." They want to see Jesus—they will indeed see who He truly is!

If the Greeks or anyone else were going to see Jesus, they were going to have to see Him in light of the cross. To highlight this, Jesus used an analogy that wasn't Jewish, but one both Jews and Greeks could readily understand. Using a farming principle—the germination process—Jesus said, "I'm going to be 'planted.' I'm going to die. I'm going to rise. Then you will see My glory."

The reason the first-century church would see so many conversions was that everywhere they went, they preached the cross. And as the cross was preached, people saw God. As the cross was preached, lives were changed. It's Jesus' death and resurrection—the love and glory of God—that brings life.

> "He who loves his life will lose it, and he who hates his life in this world will keep it for eternal life. If anyone serves Me, let him follow Me; and where I am, there My servant will be also. If anyone serves Me, him My Father will honor."
> —John 12:25–26

This was Jesus' final public teaching recorded in the Gospels. From this point on, although He met with confrontational groups and talked to His disciples, He didn't declare anything else publicly. His final public teaching was this: Serving Him means believing in Him. Believing in Him means following Him. Following Him means we're going to be where He is.

> "Now My soul is troubled, and what shall I say? 'Father, save Me from this hour'? But for this purpose I came to this hour. Father, glorify Your name."
> —John 12:27–28

As Jesus spoke of the seed being planted, I'm sure His thoughts turned to what the cost would be. Jesus was fully God—but He was also fully human. So imagine living every day, knowing what was coming: the horrible treatment, the tremendous physical suffering, the agony in the garden, the mocking trial, the scourging, the crown of thorns. But the most horrifying part was being separated from the Father. "What am I supposed to say now that I am anxious over these things?" Jesus prayed. "Let's call it off? No. This is the reason I have come."

For us, so often prayer is a place where we bring a shopping list of things we want, hoping we can cash in on a few. But in the Bible, prayer is the place to find God's will and ask for the strength to follow it. Prayer doesn't change God. Prayer changes us. And here Jesus, as our Example, prays for strength and help—that God might be glorified and His will be accomplished.

> Then a voice came from heaven, saying, "I have both glorified it and will glorify it again." Therefore the people who stood by and heard it said that it had thundered. Others said, "An angel has spoken to Him." Jesus answered and said, "This voice did not come because of Me, but for your sake."
>
> —John 12:28–30

For the third time in the Gospels, God the Father speaks audibly, identifying and encouraging His Son. At Jesus' baptism, which mentioned His death, the Father spoke. On the Mount of Transfiguration as Elijah and Moses came to speak of Jesus' death, the Father spoke. And here, within eyesight of Mount Calvary, as Jesus talked to the people about the life that comes from death, the Father spoke again.

The people weren't sure what they had heard. Was it natural or supernatural? Was it an angel or thunder? But Jesus did, being in the center of His father's will.

> "Now is the judgment of this world, now the ruler of this world will be cast out. And I, if I am lifted up from the earth, will draw all peoples to Myself." This He said, signifying by what death He would die.
>
> —John 12:31–33

Jesus made His purpose clear: Man is bound to sin. There's a god of this world. There's a way of the world. And you can't get out of it on your own. That's why He came. The cross becomes the great divide. People think they can get free from this bondage on their own strength, by their own power, through their own effort. They can't. If they could, Jesus wouldn't have had to die. He just would have had to send a bigger rule book. Instead, He came to save and deliver, because sin has to be dealt with and the Devil destroyed.

> The people answered Him, "We have heard from the law that the Christ remains forever; and how can You say, 'The Son of Man must be lifted up'? Who is this Son of Man?" Then Jesus said to them, "A little while longer the light is with you. Walk while you have the light, lest darkness overtake you; he who walks in darkness does not know where he is going. While you have the light, believe in the light, that you may become sons of light." These things Jesus spoke, and departed, and was hidden from them. But although He had done so many signs before them, they did not believe in Him that the word of Isaiah the prophet might be fulfilled, which he spoke: "Lord, who has believed our report? And to

whom has the arm of the Lord been revealed?" Therefore they could not believe, because Isaiah said again: "He has blinded their eyes and hardened their hearts, lest they should see with their eyes, lest they should understand with their hearts and turn, so that I should heal them." These things Isaiah said when he saw His glory and spoke of Him.

—John 12:34–41

As He spoke about the cross, Jesus was interrupted by some who wanted to argue. "Scriptures say the Messiah will rule forever, so what's this about Him being lifted up to die?"

The Bible is filled with verses declaring that the Messiah is indeed going to rule forever. But that's His second coming. First, He had to die. So Jesus answered their unbelief with a warning: "While the light's on, take advantage of it. While you can see clearly, move toward the Lord because if you stay where you are, darkness eventually will overwhelm you."

There are thirty-six specific miracles of Jesus recorded in the Gospels, miracles of every conceivable variety—over the processes of nature, evil spirits, sickness, and death. And He had done so before numerous witnesses. "If you want life, follow Me," He said.

"We didn't think the Messiah was going to die. Therefore, we don't think You're Him," the people argued. But who other than the Messiah could have done what Jesus did? The light was certainly on—but the people turned away. Unbelief in the face of such proof was deliberately fostered and left them without excuse. They had plenty of reasons to believe—and not a single reason not to.

Unbelief is what will doom us. If you discount and write off God's work long enough, you can come to a place where, instead of being *unwilling* to believe, you are *unable* to believe. Exodus 4–14 is the account of God's dealing with Pharaoh. Did Pharaoh have proof that Moses wasn't kidding and that God was with him? Absolutely. When he opened the cupboard and the frogs jumped out, he probably said, "OK. I get it." But then he played word games and hardened his heart to the point where it was impossible for him to believe. Was that God's will? No. He did everything He could to turn on the light and give proof to Pharaoh. But eventually Pharaoh had come to the end of the line concerning opportunity.

"My Spirit will not always strive with man," God declared in Genesis 6:3.

"Seek the Lord while He may be found," Isaiah said in chapter 55:6.

"How will we be saved if we neglect such great salvation?" the writer to the Hebrews asked in chapter 2:3.

If God is speaking to you about your sin and need for salvation, then come to Jesus and be saved. While the going's good, you should go. While God has your attention, you should respond.

After quoting two prophecies from Isaiah through which God foretold the rejection of His Son, John turned his attention to those who did believe, fearful as they were.

> Nevertheless even among the rulers many believed in Him, but because of the Pharisees they did not confess Him, lest they should be put out of the synagogue; for they loved the praise of men more than the praise of God.
>
> —John 12:42–43

To be put out of the synagogue essentially meant you were cast out of society. The doctor wouldn't see you. The farmer wouldn't sell to you. Your neighbor wouldn't talk to you. The guy down the street wouldn't help you. You were absolutely dead to them. Therefore, although some of the religious folks knew Jesus was the Messiah prophesied in Scripture, they were afraid to follow Him for fear of the ostracism it would bring. After Jesus' death, a couple of these guys came out of the woodwork: Joseph of Arimathea and Nicodemus. The cross forced their hands. At this point, however, fear and compromise replaced sitting at His feet and learning of Him.

> Then Jesus cried out and said, "He who believes in Me, believes not in Me, but in Him who sent Me. And he who sees Me sees Him who sent Me. I have come as a light into the world, that whoever believes in Me should not abide in darkness. And if anyone hears My words and does not believe, I do not judge him; for I did not come to judge the world but to save the world. He who rejects Me, and does not receive My words, has that which judges him—the word that I have spoken will judge him in the last day. For I have not spoken on My own authority; but the Father who sent Me gave Me a command, what I should say and what I should speak. And I know that His command is everlasting life. Therefore, whatever I speak, just as the Father has told Me, so I speak."
>
> —John 12:44–50

Jesus came to offer life. "See Me, see the Father," He said. "Hear Me, hear Him. His words will lead you to life. But if you reject Me"—the word for *reject, atheteo* in Greek, means "to consider worthless"—"you're in trouble."

If you can discount God's love and plan and write off His words and works as nothing, you have deliberately taken a stand for which you will pay. And you will lose.

In Munich, Germany there are literally a million street signs. Yet when I was driving there, I wasn't paying attention and missed one obvious one, turning the wrong way on a one-way street. A police officer immediately stopped me, screaming and blowing his whistle. "You ought to put up a sign," I said in my embarrassment, seeking to make light of my foolishness. Boy did he give me an earful!

When we get to heaven, we're not going to be able to say to God, "You should have put up a sign." He did: the cross. If you'll hear His words, you'll have life. To turn away from them or ignore them is to turn away from the only hope He has provided. So while the light's on, go to Jesus.

Chapter 106

Tuesday Team
Sanhedrin Suffers a Setback

Luke 20:1–19
(Matthew 21:23–27; 21:33–46;
Mark 11:27–33; 12:1–12)

With the exception of Jesus' last hours, beginning with the Last Supper, the Gospel writers give us more information about Tuesday than about any of the other days of Passion Week. It was a day filled with confrontation, as Jesus' enemies did whatever it took to carry out their plot to have Him killed. Yet we see Jesus answer these men graciously and provide an opportunity for life at every turn.

Before He faced these confrontational groups, however, Mark fills us in on what took place as He made His way to the temple:

> Now in the morning, as they passed by, they saw the fig tree dried up from the roots. And Peter, remembering, said to Him, "Rabbi, look! The fig tree which You cursed has withered away." So Jesus answered and said to them, "Have faith in God. For assuredly, I say to you, whoever says to this mountain, 'Be removed and be cast into the sea,' and does not doubt in his heart, but believes that those things he says will be done, he will have whatever he says. Therefore I say to you, whatever things you ask when you pray, believe that you receive them, and you will have them. And whenever you stand praying, if you have anything against anyone, forgive him, that your Father in heaven may also forgive you your trespasses. But if you do not forgive, neither will your Father in heaven forgive your trespasses."
>
> —Mark 11:20–26

On His way to the temple the day before, Jesus had cursed a fruitless fig tree as an illustration of the religious leaders of the nation's failure to bring forth spiritual fruit. Here again passing by this same tree, Peter noticed it had died overnight. It had no nourishment to sustain it, just as religion is incapable of sustaining life.

"Look at the tree. It's dead," Peter said.

Jesus answered, "Have faith in God," using the present-tense imperative. In other words, Jesus said, "Look to God and keep looking to Him. Religion will kill you, but He'll give you life."

It is faith, not ceremony, for which the Lord is looking. Faith in Him and His Word will remove every obstacle and every mountain. Your life was impossible until the Lord moved in. Then He changed you completely. And as your life is submitted to Him, stay close to bear fruit constantly (Ps. 1).

As Jesus arrived at the temple on this Tuesday morning, Luke picks up the story:

> Now it happened on one of those days, as He taught the people in the temple and preached the gospel, that the chief priests and the scribes, together with the elders, confronted Him and spoke to Him, saying, "Tell us, by what authority are You doing these things? Or who is he who gave You this authority?"
>
> —Luke 20:1–2

Here we find Jesus doing what He had always done: preaching the good news of God's plan and teaching God's ways. We find both the words *teaching* and *preaching* throughout the New Testament. "Preaching" is almost always used in reference to the lost. It's a word that means "to stand on the corner and shout," like the herald who used to bring the day's news. Preaching is bringing the good news that God loves us, has a plan for us, and can forgive us through the sacrifice of Jesus. "Teaching," on the other hand, is almost always a reference to the saints' instruction. Churches should be both preaching and teaching. We need to be taught the things of God—and if we're taught well, we should then be preaching and sharing with others.

As Jesus was teaching He was interrupted and confronted by the big guns of the Sanhedrin, the Jewish governing body that were over the people's religious and civil affairs. Among them, the chief priests, Annas and Caiaphas, who were Sadducees, like every other first-century chief priest. As such, they didn't believe in life after death.

Also in this group were the scribes—the students of Scripture who interpreted the Law as they saw fit. Although they didn't represent God, they believed in life after death. When the elders are listed with the chief priests and scribes, it is usually a reference to the heads of the clans and families in Israel who were advisers to the Sanhedrin. The elders were the business community. So this was a pompous yet powerful delegation that approached Jesus. They came to Him with questions—but the word *confront* tells us where their hearts were. They weren't coming to ask questions because they wanted answers. They were coming to ask questions they hoped had no answers so they could put Jesus on the spot. And their first question was, "Who do You think You are? And who gave You permission to do what You're doing?"

> But He answered and said to them, "I also will ask you one thing, and answer Me: the baptism of John—was it from heaven or from men?"
>
> —Luke 20:3–4

Three times in Luke 5, three times in Luke 6, twice in Luke 11, and twice again in Luke 20, Jesus answered a question with a question. It's not that He was unwilling to answer seeking hearts. In fact, spend time in the Word and you can't help but come away with the conclusion that the Lord wants people to know Him. He's a God who reveals. He gives answers. He doesn't hide Himself. He wants us to come and learn of Him. But for the folks not really interested in Him, there was no sense in giving them information they didn't want—information for which they would have to be held responsible in judgment. The Gospel is good news only to people who know they're sinners.

"By whose authority do You act?" the religious leaders asked Jesus.

"Was John's baptism from heaven or from men?" He answered.

John's testimony of Jesus was that He is the Savior. For a long time people came to John and said, "We need to repent. We're sinners. We need help." Of John's baptism, Luke said in 7:29 that when the people heard John, even the tax collectors agreed with God about their condition. In other words, even the worst of the worst recognized their need for a Savior as John spoke his message to them of the coming Messiah. But verse 30 says John would not baptize the Pharisees and lawyers, for they would not receive the message that they too were sinners in need of salvation and a Savior.

From the beginning this group had a hard time with John. So quite a question. If they said his baptism was from heaven, Jesus could have answered their question. But they didn't. They had no intent of changing. They were there only to argue.

> And they reasoned among themselves, saying, "If we say, 'From heaven,' He will say, 'Why then did you not believe him?' But if we say, 'From men,' all the people will stone us, for they are persuaded that John was a prophet." So they answered that they did not know where it was from.
> —Luke 20:5–7

John was so popular that Luke tells us in chapter 3 the whole region went out to see him. This was no easy undertaking. Not only did it require a twenty- to thirty-mile journey, but the Jordan area where he baptized was a favorite hideout of thieves. The people, however, were so pressed in heart that they came—which isn't surprising. The Gospel is always good news to people who know in their hearts that they're sinners. It just doesn't fare so well among religious men who don't want to let go of their religion.

So in their huddle, the scribes and Pharisees said, "If we say John's baptism was from God, we're responsible for his words. But if we say it was of man, we'll lose the crowd and what we hoped to accomplish here will backfire."

So what did they do? They did what cowards always do: they lied. "We don't know," they said. They could have said, "We don't want to answer. Nice move, Jesus. Checkmate." Instead they said, "We can't answer."

When we talk to people about the Word of God and they refuse to hear the message of conviction and yet hope, we often see them turn the conversation to an argument over some obscure point that means nothing to them.

"You need to get saved," we say.

"Well, the Bible is open to interpretation," they answer.

"But Jesus said you need to be born again. What part of those five words don't you get? You're all right with 'you must be,' right? The 'born again' thing is just two more words and you're there! How confusing can it be?"

"Well, you feel one way; I feel another," they say. "I have my own relationship with God."

"You can't have your own relationship with God," we say. "God made the rules. And He says you must be born again!"

We find the same thing here. "Hey, Jesus," they said. "Who do You think You are?"

"Let Me ask you about John," He answered, "because if you believe John, you'll know who I am. But if you don't, whatever I tell you won't matter."

> And Jesus said to them, "Neither will I tell you by what authority I do these things." Then He began to tell the people this parable . . . .
>
> —Luke 20:8–9

With the scribes, priests, and elders still standing by, Jesus turned to the people He was teaching in verse 1 and told them a parable concerning the refusal of Israel's leadership to recognize Him as the fulfillment of Scripture. By the end of the story, in verse 19, Luke writes by the empowering of the Holy Spirit that the chief priests and scribes, knowing Jesus' remarks were directed at them, decided this would be the day they would take Him out.

> "A certain man planted a vineyard, leased it to vinedressers, and went into a far country for a long time. Now at vintage-time he sent a servant to the vinedressers, that they might give him some of the fruit of the vineyard. But the vinedressers beat him and sent him away empty-handed. Again he sent another servant; and they beat him also, treated him shamefully, and sent him away empty-handed. And again he sent a third; and they wounded him also and cast him out. Then the owner of the vineyard said, 'What shall I do? I will send my beloved son. Probably they will respect him when they see him.' But when the vinedressers saw him, they reasoned among themselves, saying, 'This is the heir. Come, let us kill him, that the inheritance may be ours.' So they cast him out of the vineyard and killed him."
>
> —Luke 20:9–15

Through the prophet Jeremiah the Lord had said to the nation, "I have planted you as a noble vine, a seed of the highest quality. How did you become this degenerate plant and this alien vine?" (Jer. 2:21). Israel identified so clearly with the idea that they were God's vineyard that even in the first century on the door leading into the holy place was a 100-foot-high grape cluster with a solid gold vine wrapped around it. Even today, the Israeli travel and tourism logo depicts two men carrying a vine and grapes.

The vine depicted the land and the fruit stood for the faith for which God looked among His people. In His parable, Jesus gave three examples of men who were sent to look for fruit but were beaten instead and sent away empty-handed. Throughout the nation's history, it was always the leadership who took out the prophets. They drove Elijah into the wilderness. They cut Isaiah in half. They stoned Zechariah to death.

"Which of the prophets didn't your fathers persecute?" Stephen asked right before he was stoned in Acts 7:52.

This parable was a word to the leadership, not the people. As the vineyard's owner, you might have said, "I'm going to prosecute, evict, and grab an eye for an eye." But that's not what God said. He said, "I'll send My Son."

I once read these words: "If you reject Jesus, He'll answer with tears. If you wound Him, He'll bleed so you might be cleansed. If you kill Him, He'll redeem you. And if you bury Him, He'll rise."

God's patience is phenomenal, isn't it? He puts up with us and waits for us to come around. God didn't give up on Israel. He sent His only Son. When they killed Him, the leaders thought they finally were through with the threat. But they were very much mistaken.

> "Therefore what will the owner of the vineyard do to them? He will come and destroy those vinedressers and give the vineyard to others."
>
> —Luke 20:15–16

"What will the owner of the vineyard do?" Jesus asked. In Matthew's account, the people answer that the owner should utterly destroy the wicked vinedressers and give the vineyard to vinedressers who would bring forth fruit the way they should (Matt. 21:41). Here Jesus repeated their answer and said the owner would come and destroy them and give the vineyard to others—another nation in Matthew's account. In other words, Gentiles like us would also have an opportunity to be saved.

> And when they heard it they said, "Certainly not!" Then He looked at them and said, "What then is this that is written: 'The stone which the builders rejected has become the chief cornerstone'? Whoever falls on that stone will be broken; but on whomever it falls, it will grind him to powder." And the chief priests and the scribes that very hour sought to lay hands on Him, but they feared the people—for they knew He had spoken this parable against them.
>
> —Luke 20:16–19

The word *stone* was a very familiar Old Testament reference to the Messiah. When Jacob was blessed in Genesis 49:24, he was told from him would come the shepherd, the stone of Israel. So when Jesus quoted Psalm 118:22 here—a psalm they had been singing only two days earlier as He came to the top of the Mount of Olives—it was prophetic of the religious leadership's rejection of the Messiah.

The stone is Jesus. The builders were the leaders. What they were trying to build was in their own power, by their own strength. But it was Jesus who needed to be the cornerstone of the work, for on Him, the church would be built.

The priests and scribes realized Jesus was speaking to them. Yet though they understood this, they didn't change their ways and turn to Him because their religion—the building of their own kingdom—was more important to them. Their hope lay with self.

"If you fall on Me, you'll be broken," Jesus said. "But if I fall on you, you're dust." Either way, we have to deal with Jesus. Either we deal with Him willingly now or wait until He falls on us, which won't be so good. These religious folks chose the latter. But many in the crowd fell on the Lord in faith.

God is not finished with Israel as a nation. After the rapture of the church, there will be seven years of tribulation where He will deal specifically through Israel to the world. And then in the millennial kingdom that follows He will rule and reign from Jerusalem. But for now, in this present age of grace, there is no national dealing with Israel, but rather every individual heart is invited to come to Jesus and be saved.

Chapter 107

GIVING GOD WHAT IS HIS

Luke 20:20–26
(Matthew 22:15–22; Mark 12:13–17)

Here in Luke 20:20, we read of the second group of challengers who came to Jesus on this long Tuesday of Passion Week. Matthew and Mark tell us these challengers consisted of Pharisees and Herodians—a religious group and a political group of men who traditionally hated each other but were united in their greater hatred of Jesus.

Although the Pharisees' religion wasn't heartfelt, it did give them great power over the people. Nationalistic to a fault, they cautiously led the resistance against Rome. The Herodians, on the other hand, were those without any religious conviction who had defected to Rome's side simply to profit from Rome's power. As such, they were traitors in the people's eyes. Neither of these groups wanted to see Jesus do well—the Pharisees because they felt He eroded their base, the Herodians because He posed a threat to their way of life. So here came the religious men with the government men in tow, thinking if they asked Jesus questions about government issues, they might be able to accuse Him of being an insurrectionist.

> So they watched Him, and sent spies who pretended to be righteous, that they might seize on His words, in order to deliver Him to the power and the authority of the governor. Then they asked Him, saying, "Teacher, we know that You say and teach rightly, and You do not show personal favoritism, but teach the way of God in truth."
>
> —Luke 20:20– 21

In Mark 12 we're told the Sanhedrin actually sent this group. Headquarters made this plan. The new tactic was different from the first challenge in that this wasn't confrontation—this was flattery. Rather than fighting against Jesus, they were going to pretend to be *with* Him. This second group came pretending to have the right motives, talking to Jesus as if they couldn't wait to hear what He had to say. They came laying a trap, "You're so great. You're so awesome. You're so honest. We know You tell it like it is. We know You don't play favorites. Your words are God's truth."

Flattery is the mirror image of gossip. Gossip is something we say behind someone's back that we never would say to their face. Flattery is something we will say to someone's face that we never would say behind their back. They're both deceitful and Jesus smelled the deceit a mile away.

"Is it lawful for us to pay taxes to Caesar or not?"

—Luke 20:22

The Pharisees and Herodians' strategy is fairly obvious. If they could hang Jesus on the horns of a dilemma in front of the people, they could get Him no matter what He said. In Jesus' day, the Jews absolutely hated paying taxes. I don't know that that has changed much—but it is worse when you're paying taxes to an occupying nation and have no rights to self-determination or representation. The zealots, who had risen in power fifty years before this event, had been leading the charge to rebel and not pay taxes at all. Josephus tells us that twenty-five years earlier, they had led a tremendous rally against the Romans that brought a harsh response. Their next big move was in 66 A.D., which not only left many dead but led to the city's destruction four years later.

But He perceived their craftiness, and said to them, "Why do You test Me?"

—Luke 20:23

Proverbs says people who flatter their neighbors spread a net for their own feet. These guys were about to discover the truth of that. It's a mistake to try to fool God. When David handed power to his son, Solomon, in 1 Chronicles 28:9, he said, "My son, know the God of your father. Serve Him with a loyal heart and a willing mind because He searches the heart and understands its thoughts and intents." God knows you. You can't put one over on Him. He'll "perceive your craftiness" every time.

"Show me a denarius. Whose image and inscription does it have?"

—Luke 20:24

A denarius, the day's wage of a laborer, was a very small coin. Made of four grams of silver, it pictured Caesar's head on one side with the inscription, "Tiberius Caesar the son of the divine Augustus Caesar." The other side portrayed him sitting on a throne with a diadem on his head over the inscription "Pontiface Maximus" ("The Highest Priest") because these wicked men actually thought they were gods. In fact, for several years Tiberius told the people if they confessed their sins to him, he could forgive them. Therefore, when Jesus asked whose picture was on the coin, so hated was Caesar that I bet the crowd had a hard time even saying his name.

And He said to them, "Render therefore to Caesar the things that are Caesar's, and to God the things that are God's."

—Luke 20:25

"Give that which bears Caesar's imprint to him and that which bears God's imprint to Him," Jesus said. This simple answer not only simultaneously stole the thunder from His accusers and maintained His standing with the crowds, but it also became the cornerstone for what the New Testament teaches about a believer's relationship with the government, no matter how good or evil it might be.

Paul spent eleven chapters in the book of Romans developing the idea of the doctrine of salvation by faith. In chapter 12:1, he said we should present our bodies as living sacrifices to God and serve Him only. Then in chapter 13 he spent most of the chapter saying, "Here is the Christian's responsibility to his government: you're to submit to it as one that God has established, because even if it's an evil government, it's there for your good."

Throughout the Bible, government is seen as established by God. "By Me the kings reign and the rulers declare justice," God declares in Proverbs 8:15. And in Proverbs 21:1, the writer says the king's heart is in the Lord's hand and He can turn it wherever He wants.

In Daniel 2:20–23, Daniel was sent to Nebuchadnezzar to tell him the Lord not only changes the seasons but sets up and removes kings and that Nebuchadnezzar in his pride and resistance to God was walking on thin ice. But Nebuchadnezzar was a cocky man. By the time we get to chapter 4:30–37, some time had passed and we see him walking around the hanging gardens of Babylon saying, "Look at this beautiful city I have built, this nation I have led, this world I rule." Daniel gave him another word from the Lord at this time—that he would be driven from men and be forced to live among the beasts of the field until he recognized that the Most High rules in the kingdom of men. Nebuchadnezzar eventually came to his senses and acknowledged the only true God of Israel—but he got there the hard way, having lost his mind and his pride along the way.

Because God is in control, we're to submit to governments whether good or bad. I think that's hard sometimes for us Christians. We'd much rather think of ourselves as politically savvy. But look at the government to which Jesus was calling these folks to submit. Read anything on the Roman Empire and you'll see there was tremendous abuse. Under Roman rule, one-third of the population was made slaves. People were massacred by the thousands without any reparation, and taxation left others virtually unable to survive, while the rulers lived in excess, thinking they were gods. The people had no voice, no representation, no recourse—yet Jesus said, "Give to Caesar that which is his."

A lot of times Christians complain about how their tax money is spent. But that's not our responsibility. Our responsibility is to pay it. What the leaders do with it is their problem. In the two thousand or so pages of the Bible, there are only two or three examples of civil disobedience. Told he could no longer pray, Daniel was thrown to the lions when he didn't comply. Told they had to bow to a statue, his friends were thrown in a fiery furnace when they refused. In the few instances when believers defied the law of the land, they willfully and cheerfully went to their deaths rather than defy God. The rule of thumb is to give to the government what the government demands. It becomes the standard for all that follows in the New Testament.

But the instruction to "render" in verse 25 is different from "pay" in verse 22. The word *pay* does not have any further obligation attached to it. It simply means to hand over funds. The word *render,* on the other hand, has responsibility attached to it. In other words, "to render" means "to owe."

What do you owe God? For starters, you owe Him your very breath because He holds it in His hands. The last night Belshazzar ruled in Babylon before he was overthrown, Daniel 5:23–31 said to him, "You've lifted yourself up against the Lord of heaven. You've worshipped gods of silver and gold, iron and bronze. You've resisted the very God who holds your breath in His hands." Belshazzar owed God his life but he hadn't responded.

"Whose inscription is on you?" Jesus asked the schemers, addressing the real issue. "You can pay your debt as you owe it to this wicked government—but then you better turn and render your life to a God that is very good, a God who holds your next breath in His hands. And if you're about to tell Me you've done that, then why are you here to try to trap Me?"

> But they could not catch Him in His words in the presence of the people. And they marveled at His answer and kept silent.
>
> —Luke 20:26

The Greek word for "marvel" means "to leave one as stone" or "to astonish." In other words, it stops us dead in our tracks but also carries with it the idea of wonder and admiration. In the confrontation with these Pharisees and Herodians, Jesus had offended neither the government nor the people. They admired Him—unfortunately for many, not enough to submit their lives to Him. They stopped short of salvation and turned away with only admiration. They left in silence. How extremely sad.

How important it is to realize we owe God our lives. We owe Him for all He has given us. And because Jesus gave His life for us, our debt is sky high. Everything I have belongs to Him. Everything He had He gave for me. What does God want from us? "What shall I render to the Lord for all His benefits toward me?" the psalmist asked in Psalm 116:12—and the word *render* in the Septuagint, the Greek translation of the Old Testament, is exactly the same as the one here in Luke.

What do I owe the Lord for all He has blessed me with? Psalm 116:13 says, "I will take the cup of salvation."

What does God want from you? Faith in Him that receives His offer of life in His Son, Jesus Christ. He wants you to come and be saved!

Chapter 108

SAD YOU SEE

Luke 20:27–40
(Matthew 22:23–33; Mark 12:18–27)

On Tuesday as He ministered to the people, Jesus found one religious group after another lying in wait for Him with questions they hoped would make Him look bad, diminish His popularity, and have Him arrested—hopefully with charges that could have Him executed. They all had one goal in mind: to get rid of Jesus because He cramped their style and threatened their way of life.

The first group had consisted of scribes and Pharisees who asked Him on what authority He had upset their temple business the day before. The second was a mixed group of Pharisees and Herodians. The Pharisees asked about taxes while the Herodians judged His answer. Here we find the final group coming to Jesus before the huge throngs to whom He was ministering.

> Then some of the Sadducees, who deny that there is a resurrection, came to Him . . . .
>
> —Luke 20:27

The Sadducees didn't believe in life after death. But it wasn't always that way. Five hundred and fifty years earlier, when the nation of Israel had left Babylonian captivity and reestablished the temple, there was a high priest named Zadok who gathered around him counselors and Bible students who later would become the Sadducees. At that point, they were faithful. They loved the Lord and the Scriptures. But as time passed, they drew further and further away from God. According to Jewish historian Josephus, the Sadducees were very wealthy, powerful humanists whose only interest in religion was how much money they could make from it.

There were far fewer Sadducees than Pharisees, but because of their money and relationship with Rome, they had a much greater influence over the people's lives. Knowing the leadership in Israel at that time was absolutely against life after death, we can understand why in Acts 4, when Peter preached the resurrection, that they wanted to arrest him and why preaching the Gospel at that time was extremely dangerous. It is this group that now comes to Jesus, sure of themselves that where everyone else had failed they could succeed, for they knew this belief in an afterlife was pure nonsense. So the set-up question to address that very issue:

570

. . . And asked Him, saying, "Teacher, Moses wrote to us that if a man's brother dies, having a wife, and he dies without children, his brother should take his wife and raise up offspring for his brother. Now there were seven brothers. And the first took a wife, and died without children. And the second took her as wife, and he died childless. Then the third took her, and in like manner the seven also; and they left no children, and died. Last of all the woman died also. Therefore, in the resurrection, whose wife does she become? For all seven had her as wife."

—Luke 20:27–33

In the Law, God stipulated that if a married man died without having had children, his oldest brother was obligated to take his brother's widow as his wife, to name the firstborn son after his brother, and to give that son all of the inheritance that would have been due him had his father lived. In this way, the correct land distribution was preserved. In Genesis 38, we see this principle practiced in the story of Judah and his three sons—even before the Law was given. But although the question the Sadducees posed to Jesus was based on a principle the people would have understood readily, they presented it in the form of a convoluted riddle.

Often I find that people who are unwilling to believe the obvious take similar approaches to disprove the Bible. They usually come with what they call common sense, as if somehow the whole universe revolves around their ability to get it and if they don't understand it, it can't be right. "My ways are higher than your ways. They're beyond your finding out," the Lord declared in Isaiah 55. That's good, isn't it? I think we should have a God who is smarter than we are. I'm glad when I don't know what to do He still has an idea, and when I run out of strength He still has some left over. But these guys had reduced God to some fool they—with their common sense—thought they could put in His place. After all, if their argument truly had merit, wouldn't two husbands have sufficed? Did they really need seven? Hyperbole and unbelief combined!

The first part of Jesus' answer to them is found in Matthew 22:29 where He said, "You've made a mistake. You don't know the Scriptures and you don't know the power of God." In other words, they were wrong on two counts. First, they didn't know the Bible, and second, they didn't know God and what He's able to do—which has to be the key to answering virtually every hypothetical question people pose to try to attack God or His Word with their "common sense" complaints.

How we get in trouble when we exalt our human logic and understanding above God's wisdom, making what we understand the sole parameter for truth. That's dangerous, especially since it is God's truth that sets people free. It is His wisdom, not ours, that is needed. Overcome evil with good. Turn the other cheek. Don't worry about tomorrow. Love your enemies. To save your life, lose it. None of those things is good common sense—unless you know the Lord and discover it is far more than that, it is the power of God working in us who have come to know Him as our Lord.

571

The problem with the Sadducees' assumption is they limited God because they didn't know Him, and they didn't go to His Word to understand what was coming.

> Jesus answered and said to them, "The sons of this age marry and are given in marriage. But those who are counted worthy to attain that age, and the resurrection from the dead, neither marry nor are given in marriage; nor can they die anymore, for they are equal to the angels and are sons of God, being sons of the resurrection."
>
> —Luke 20:34–36

Notice Jesus makes a distinction between "this age"—the one in which they were living—and "that age"—the one to come, in essence saying human existence doesn't stop with this age. It continues on. When Paul stood before Agrippa in Acts 26:8, he said, "Why does it seem like such an incredible thing to you that God could raise the dead? He's God. Of course He can do that!" Jesus said the same thing here.

In this age, one of the primary reasons people get married is to perpetuate the human race. In heaven, however, there's no need for marriage because no one is going to die. Therefore, marriage is for this life but not for the next. If you're in a bad marriage, you might be saying, "Amen!" But if, like me, you're in a good marriage, it's hard to imagine anything better. Heaven being heaven, however, our joy will be full. God doesn't have worse things in mind. He's got better things.

"Counted worthy" means to be made worthy apart from one's own merit. "I am the resurrection and the life," Jesus told Martha. "If you believe in Me, even if you die, you'll live" (John 11:25). At ninety years of age, the apostle John wrote that he who has the Son has life and without Him, there is no life (John 3:36). It is Jesus who makes us worthy—and one day, we'll be like angels in the sense that we'll never die.

> "But even Moses showed in the burning bush passage that the dead are raised, when he called the Lord 'the God of Abraham, the God of Isaac, and the God of Jacob.' For He is not the God of the dead but of the living, for all live to Him."
>
> —Luke 20:37–38

But because the Sadducees believed the Torah, the first five books of the Bible, Jesus drew their attention to Moses, to whom God identified Himself as the God of Abraham, Isaac, and Jacob—even though Jacob had been dead four hundred years by then. If you say to me, "I was your father's friend," the assumption is either you're no longer his friend or my father is no longer around. If, however, you say, "I am your father's friend," the assumption is both you and my father are alive. So to these guys reading the books of Moses, Jesus said even then Moses, Abraham, Isaac, and Jacob still had a vital relationship with God and were, therefore, still very much alive.

Then some of the scribes answered and said, "Teacher, You have spoken well." But after that they dared not question Him anymore.

—Luke 20:39–40

Like the two groups before them, the Sadducees were silenced. But the fact that they were done questioning Jesus didn't mean He was done questioning them. So He continued to reach out to them—even in these last few hours before the cross.

Chapter 109

WHO'S YOUR DADDY?

Luke 20:41–47
(Matthew 22:41–23:36; Mark 12:35–40)

On Tuesday of Passion Week, Jesus was waylaid by three groups trying to trap Him. The scribes and elders questioned Him about what kind of authority He had to cleanse the temple. The Herodians asked Him about taxes. The Sadducees posed a riddle about the resurrection. But each group swung and missed—until, as Luke wrote, "They dared not question Him anymore." They had come to make Jesus look bad. Instead, they made Him look even better and exposed themselves and their wicked hearts.

> But when the Pharisees heard that He had silenced the Sadducees, they gathered together. Then one of them, a lawyer, asked Him a question, testing Him, and saying, "Teacher, which is the great commandment in the law?" Jesus said to him, "You shall love the Lord your God with all your heart, with all your soul, and with all your mind. This is the first and great commandment. And the second is like it: You shall love your neighbor as yourself. On these two commandments hang all the Law and the Prophets."
>
> —Matthew 22:34–40

In Luke 10:25–28, a lawyer in a similar situation had asked Jesus a similar question to tempt Him. And Jesus had given the same answer. Here, after answering the question of the lawyer, Jesus had a question for him and his friends.

> While the Pharisees were gathered together, Jesus asked them, saying, "What do you think about the Christ? Whose Son is He?" They said to Him, "The Son of David."
>
> —Matthew 22:41–42

What do you think about the Christ? That's a hugely important question. In fact, it's the only question that has an answer with eternal consequences. In Matthew, the pronoun is plural: "What do you all think about the Christ?" Jesus wasn't so much asking their personal opinion as their professional opinion. It was as if He was saying, "You scribes and Pharisees who are so happy that I just put the Sadducees in their place—what do you think about the Christ? As Bible students, what is your concept of the Savior?"

The word *Christ* is the Greek word for the Hebrew *Meshiach* or *Messiah* and spoke of the One who was coming. The traditional or popular belief was the Messiah would be a descendant of King David, that He would be a man much like Moses, and that when He came, He would establish a world order that would put Israel and the Jews in control.

Without any hesitation, the Pharisees said, "He is the Son of David." And they were right. At the time of their captivity in Babylon, God sent Jeremiah with a message of hope. In Jeremiah 23:5, He said, "The days are coming when I will raise up unto David a righteous Branch and a King. He will prosper and reign and execute judgment and justice upon the earth." Jesus never refused the title "Son of David." But He wanted to show that the Bible teachers' concept of the Messiah was too small. He was more than the Son of David—He was almighty God. Although the Pharisees were plotting to destroy Him, He was hoping to save them. His heart was merciful and kind to those who had so misused the Scriptures. They needed the entire counsel of God's Word and they didn't have it. They had heads filled with Bible verses but hearts that were empty.

Thirty years earlier, when the wise men had come to Herod, saying, "Where is He that is born King of the Jews?" Herod asked the scribes where the Messiah was to be born.

"Bethlehem," they immediately answered. They knew the answers to the questions about Scripture. But if their knowledge didn't move them two miles down the road to see for themselves, what good was it?

Luke picks up the story from there.

> And He said to them, "How can they say that the Christ is the Son of David? Now David himself said in the book of Psalms: 'The Lord said to my Lord, "Sit at My right hand, till I make Your enemies Your footstool."' Therefore David calls Him, 'Lord'; how is He then his Son?"
>
> —Luke 20:41–44

David lived in a very patriarchal age where the father was the absolute ruler of his home. It was the father who decided who would get the birthright, who would be blessed and who would not, and who would go forward and who wouldn't. Even on his deathbed, unable to see and propped up on his arm, the father was joined by his family, who would gather to hear what he had to say because it would determine their future.

Jesus' point to these men was very simple: If David is writing about the Messiah to come, how can He also be his son? Why did they suppose David called the Messiah his Lord if he's only his son? Maybe He's more. Maybe He's God Himself.

Jesus invited these men to rethink their convictions based solely on the Scripture—which, by the way, is a wise thing to do. You can say you believe a million things, but what does God have to say? How do you substantiate your hope? You not only want to know what you believe but why you believe it. The facts are there about who Jesus is, what He has done, and why He came. Study them. Have an answer for the hope that lies within you. In

His love, Jesus challenged these scribes who claimed to know Scripture. They could have said, "We've never seen that. Could You explain it to us?" But they didn't.

In Revelation 22:16, Jesus said, "I am both the root and the offspring of David, the bright and morning star." He declared Himself to be both the Creator and the son of David. That's what the scribes had missed and the nation had failed to see. That's why their understanding of the Messiah needed to be reevaluated. He is God and man!

When Peter stood up on Pentecost forty-three days later, he ended his sermon with a quotation from Psalm 110, the same Psalm Jesus quoted to the Pharisees—and three thousand people were saved. To them, it made sense. But not to these Pharisees. Matthew tells us they said nothing. They weren't moved at all to consider, rethink, or confess they were wrong, or to ask for more time or more explanation. Their minds were made up and nothing—not even Scripture—was going to change them.

So rather than discuss it with them further, Jesus turned to His disciples.

> Then, in the hearing of all the people, He said to His disciples, "Beware of the scribes, who desire to go around in long robes, love greetings in the market-places, the best seats in the synagogues, and the best places at feasts, who devour widows' houses, and for a pretense make long prayers. These will receive greater condemnation."
>
> —Luke 20:45–47

"Be careful of these guys," Jesus said to His disciples. "They're dishonest and self-serving, ungodly and hypocritical. I know you have great reverence for them but you don't need to because they are far from what they appear to be."

The nation had been defiled by the scribes' unwillingness to teach the Bible. People's souls had been destroyed by their unwillingness to teach the truth—even to those hungry to hear it. They never applied the Word to themselves and didn't teach it to others. So Jesus gave strong warnings about them because even in these last moments, when He reached out to them, they refused to listen.

"They desire to go around in long robes." In other words, they loved clothes that identified them as holier than everyone around them. They loved the impressive title, the best seats, the upward climb on the social ladder. And although they were snatching the homes of widows unable to make their payments, they were praying long, pretentious prayers for them. Long prayers are OK, but not pretense. These prayed to impress people with their non-existent relationship with God. And Jesus spoke to them, saying greater condemnation awaited them as a result.

Masquerading as religiously committed to God but driven by a love of what profited them, they wanted the benefits of holiness without paying the price for it. The tragedy was that the Bible never touched them, though they held it in their hands every day of their lives.

More than having a Bible, you want to be sure the Bible has you. Don't go to it looking to support what you've already decided must be the truth. That was the scribes' failure. The mark of a true believer is God can teach him, and the Bible is the truth on which he stands.

Chapter 110

WOE TO YOU, SCRIBES AND PHARISEES

Matthew 23:1–39
(Mark 12:38–40; Luke 20:45–47)

J esus had arrived in Bethany at Mary and Martha's house from Jericho on Saturday night. On Sunday morning, He had presented Himself to the people, riding into the city on a donkey, as was the custom of kings coming in peace. The people had thrown down their coats and sung songs foretelling of the Messiah.

On Monday morning, He had cursed a fig tree that should have already borne fruit, cleansed the temple, and met with some Greeks who came to worship God. On Tuesday, He had had a discussion about the fig tree and talked to a lawyer about loving God with all one had. He had then endured the interruptions and confrontations with three groups that had come with varying arguments designed to discredit Jesus or hope He incriminated Himself in some manner so that He might have been arrested. We have looked at each of these and now come to His meeting with the scribes and Pharisees.

If you ever wanted to know what God thinks of religion, you will find it here. Religion wants to meet God on its own terms. It wants to twist God's words to people's benefit. It is a charade, pretending to be something it isn't. Blunt and to the point, I'm sure Jesus' words were shared with anger, yet also a sadness concerning these leaders of the nation who had led the people astray.

The scribes began in Ezra's day. They were the Bible teachers, righteous men who loved the Lord. Yet it hadn't taken but a couple hundred years for them to become those who would rewrite the rulebook. The Pharisees were their advocates, the synagogue leaders, and a religious, powerful group. It is both to them and to the crowds that Jesus spoke in the first twelve verses of Matthew 23 as He drew their attention to five characteristics of religion.

> Then Jesus spoke to the multitudes and to His disciples, saying, "The scribes and the Pharisees sit in Moses' seat. Therefore whatever they tell you to observe, that observe and do, but do not do according to their works; for they say, and do not do. For they bind heavy burdens, hard to bear, and lay them on men's shoulders; but they themselves will not move them with one of their fingers."
>
> —Matthew 23:1–4

Moses' seat was the lawgiver's seat, a position that demanded respect. But while exalting the Law of Moses, what the Pharisees taught and what they did were two entirely different things. That's always the problem with religion and His first point: religion talks but cannot accomplish. It says but doesn't do. Many people use Jesus' name but few follow His ways. God's not at all interested in lip service. He wants our lives.

Second, religion lays heavy burdens on people but offers no help.

"Stop lying," religion says.

"How?" people ask.

"Just stop it," is the only answer religion has to offer—which would be great if it worked. But I found myself to be a self-driven man. Sin dominated my life. Religion could point out my failures but it couldn't bring me to a solution. When I came to Jesus, however, I found rest in Him and His power working in me to overcome sin.

"If you're laboring, if you're heavy-laden, come to Me," Jesus said, "and you'll find rest." The scribes and Pharisees were adding ever-increasing burdens to the people's lives with no solution as to how they could be accomplished. When we come to Jesus, however, we look to Him, believe in Him, and depend on Him to do the work. He cleanses our lives and enables us to live for Him. It is so different from the work of religion, which places the burden solely on our shoulders.

> "But all their works they do to be seen by men. They make their phylacteries broad and enlarge the borders of their garments."
>
> —Matthew 23:5

The third characteristic of religion is it is motivated by the opinion of others. From here to verse 12, Jesus point outs the insatiable fleshly drive to be noticed, acknowledged, and glorified. On the contrary, we want to be sure that when we serve the Lord, we serve only the Lord. And if He's the only One who sees it, that's just fine.

Phylacteries are the little leather boxes containing Scripture passages that Orthodox Jews wear on their hands and foreheads even today in obedience to the Lord's command in Deuteronomy to bind His Word on their arms and foreheads. The practice was intended to be a reminder that the Lord should govern our thoughts and actions. But over time, these were wearing phylacteries the size of refrigerator boxes for people to notice them. We do that sometimes too, don't we? We think if one bumper sticker on the car is good, imagine what 840 will do!

In Numbers 15:38–40, the Lord told His people to put fringes of blue, the color of the sky, on the border of their garments as a reminder that they were to be a heavenly-minded people. But if the tassels on the common man were two inches long, those of the scribes and Pharisees were long enough to trip over so people would notice. For the Pharisees, spiritual success was measured by the people's recognition and praise.

"They love the best places at feasts, the best seats in the synagogues, greetings in the marketplaces, and to be called by men, 'Rabbi, Rabbi.'"

—Matthew 23:6–7

The fourth characteristic of religion is its love of position and recognition. The chief seats of the feast were those to the right and left of the host, facing the crowds. What the Pharisees didn't understand was it is not the degree a person has received but to what degree he or she is submitted to the Lord that matters. Only God's work in our lives will determine our effectiveness. It's not what we do for Him, but what He does through us that counts.

"But you do not be called 'Rabbi'; for One is your Teacher, the Christ, and you are all brethren. Do not call anyone on earth your father, for One is your Father, He who is in heaven. And do not be called teachers; for One is your Teacher, the Christ."

—Matthew 23:8–10

Finally, Jesus warned the disciples about the title-taking and honor-seeking so prevalent in religion. As believers, we're brothers and sisters. We're family. It's such a good comparison because whatever God has called you to do in the church is as important as what anyone else is doing. It's the Lord's church. He's the Head. Therefore, anything good that comes from the church is all due to Him. Yet in religious circles, like the world, status, position and power are all honored and exalted. So we read:

"But he who is greatest among you shall be your servant. And whoever exalts himself will be humbled, and he who humbles himself will be exalted."

—Matthew 23:11–12

Jesus came to establish an upside-down kingdom wherein the greatest is the servant and the humble one is exalted. Religion does just the opposite.

After speaking to the crowd, Jesus turned directly to the scribes and Pharisees and gave them eight woes. If we contrast them with the beatitudes of Matthew 5, we see they represent the difference between religion and the life God wants for the believer.

"But woe to you, scribes and Pharisees, hypocrites! For you shut up the kingdom of heaven against men, for you neither go in yourselves nor do you allow those who are entering to go in."

—Matthew 23:13

The first woe adds the word *hypocrites*. This Greek word speaks of an actor who wears a mask to communicate the emotion he is portraying. Jesus saw these religious men as actors, pretending to be something they weren't, falsely interpreting what God had said and, in so doing, making others' pursuit of God almost untenable. Religion always gets in the way of people coming to God. That is why the world needs to see genuine believers walking with God by faith.

> "Woe to you, scribes and Pharisees, hypocrites! For you devour widows' houses and for a pretense make long prayers. Therefore you will receive greater condemnation."
>
> —Matthew 23:14

The Pharisees used their position for their own personal gain, taking advantage of even those with the most need. By doing that, they brought greater condemnation on themselves.

> "Woe to you, scribes and Pharisees, hypocrites! For you travel land and sea to win one proselyte, and when he is won, you make him twice as much a son of hell as yourselves."
>
> —Matthew 23:15

Religious men pride themselves in going the extra mile to persuade others to their way of thinking. But that way of thinking doesn't lead to the Lord—it only leads to that way of thinking. Converts are left without the truth because the only truth they know is a lie. There's more to life than sincerity. You've got to have truth—otherwise you leave people stranded.

> "Woe to you, blind guides, who say, 'Whoever swears by the temple, it is nothing; but whoever swears by the gold of the temple, he is obliged to perform it.' Fools and blind! For which is greater, the gold or the temple that sanctifies the gold? And, 'Whoever swears by the altar, it is nothing; but whoever swears by the gift that is on it, he is obliged to perform it.' Fools and blind! For which is greater, the gift or the altar that sanctifies the gift? Therefore he who swears by the altar, swears by it and by all things on it. He who swears by the temple, swears by it and by Him who dwells in it. And he who swears by heaven, swears by the throne of God and by Him who sits on it."
>
> —Matthew 23:16–22

The Bible teaches that it is better not to promise anything than to promise to do something and not do it. That is why, on the Sermon on the Mount, Jesus said, "Don't swear by the earth because that's where God puts His feet. And don't swear by heaven because that's where He keeps His throne. Don't swear by Jerusalem because that's the city of the great King. And don't swear by your own head because you can't even change the color of your hair. Just let your nay be nay and your yea be yea" (Matt. 5:33–37).

The scribes and Pharisees rewrote the rules, making a way where people could actually lie to God and think they would get away with it. Their religion became word games and semantics to alleviate accountability for sin. True faith has nothing to do with wording and everything to do with the heart.

> "Woe to you, scribes and Pharisees, hypocrites! For you pay tithe of mint and anise and cummin, and have neglected the weightier matters of the law: justice and mercy and faith. These you ought to have done, without leaving the others undone."
>
> —Matthew 23:23

Religion loves external obedience but isn't interested in internal attitude. Here, in the area of tithing, the Pharisees went to the extreme. Driven by showmanship rather than a love of the Lord, they counted out even their spice seeds, making sure God got one of every ten. But that's external behavior. The weightier matters of the Law have to do with mercy and faith—qualities not so easy to put on display and, therefore, things the Pharisees didn't care about.

God is not interested in spiritual activity if your heart is disengaged. Your going to church on Sunday morning doesn't cover the rest of the week if you're not walking with Him. He wants your life. These guys majored on the minors and replaced faith with counting out spice seeds. Legalism always does that. It will become a stickler for details and leave you blind to God's great truths.

> "Blind guides, who strain out a gnat and swallow a camel!"
>
> —Matthew 23:24

Following Jesus' arrest in John 18:28, the Pharisees refused to enter Pilate's palace on the grounds that doing so would defile and prohibit them from keeping Passover. They were worried about religious defilement while they were plotting an innocent Man's murder. Maybe that's the best description of straining at a gnat and swallowing a camel. If a bug fell in their wine or water and was ingested, because they weren't to eat blood the Pharisees would cough up a lung to get it out. But as far as their practices, they ate the whole camel. That's the way religion works.

> "Woe to you, scribes and Pharisees, hypocrites! For you cleanse the outside of the cup and dish, but inside they are full of extortion and self-indulgence. Blind Pharisee, first cleanse the inside of the cup and dish, that the outside of them may be clean also."
>
> —Matthew 23:25–26

Appearance means everything to a religious person. But God's advice is if you get your inside clean, your outside will do fine. So we preach Jesus who alone can cleanse our hearts. He alone can give new life, a new spirit, and new hope. Politics won't solve the problem. Good morals won't do it, either. Whatever law you hope to get passed or candidate you hope to elect is external. They can't change a life. Only Jesus can.

> "Woe to you, scribes and Pharisees, hypocrites! For you are like whitewashed tombs which indeed appear beautiful outwardly, but inside are full of dead men's bones and all uncleanness. Even so you also outwardly appear righteous to men, but inside you are full of hypocrisy and lawlessness."
>
> —Matthew 23:27–28

In Israel, tombstones were marked clearly so people traveling to Jerusalem for the feasts wouldn't accidentally brush up against them and thus be prohibited from participating in worship. Jesus compared the religious man to these graves. They looked good on the outside, but because of their hypocrisy, anyone who got close to them became defiled by them. Inside their flowing robes were hearts still dead in sin.

> "Woe to you, scribes and Pharisees, hypocrites! Because you build the tombs of the prophets and adorn the monuments of the righteous, and say, 'If we had lived in the days of our fathers, we would not have been partakers with them in the blood of the prophets.' Therefore you are witnesses against yourselves that you are sons of those who murdered the prophets. Fill up, then, the measure of your fathers' guilt. Serpents, brood of vipers! How can you escape the condemnation of hell? Therefore, indeed, I send you prophets, wise men, and scribes: some of them you will kill and crucify, and some of them you will scourge in your synagogues and persecute from city to city, that on you may come all the righteous blood shed on the earth, from the blood of righteous Abel to the blood of Zechariah, son of Berechiah, whom you murdered between the temple and the altar. Assuredly, I say to you, all these things will come upon this generation."
>
> —Matthew 23:29–36

Jesus' last woe referred to the Pharisees' practice of building beautiful graves to honor the prophets. If you go to Israel today, outside the eastern gate and down the Kidron Valley you still will find Zechariah's and Absalom's tombs. Beautifully carved and very ornate, they are visible from miles away. But Jesus said had the Pharisees been living in the prophets' day, they would have killed those prophets just as surely as their forefathers had killed the prophets who foretold the Messiah's coming. The Pharisees were plotting to kill the Messiah Himself. From beginning to end, the culpability fell on them because they had the advantage of seeing the Lord Himself.

"O Jerusalem, Jerusalem, the one who kills the prophets and stones those who are sent to her! How often I wanted to gather your children together as a hen gathers her chicks under her wings, but you were not willing! See! Your house is left to you desolate; for I say to you, you shall see Me no more till you say, 'Blessed is He who comes in the name of the Lord!'"

—Matthew 23:37–39

Jesus spoke similar words on Palm Sunday, looking over the city. Here He spoke to them as He left the temple area for good. Jesus gave His life for the people. The wickedness, hatefulness, deceitfulness, and hardness of their hearts did not diminish His love for them—but He couldn't force His love on them. It won't be until His second coming that national Israel will recognize Jesus as their Messiah. Then they will loudly declare, "Blessed is He who comes in the name of the Lord."

Chapter III

UNLIKE THE SCRIBES AND PHARISEES

Luke 21:1–4
(Mark 12:41–44)

Tuesday was an extremely rough day for Jesus. The leaders had been nothing but combative and spiritual fruit was hard to find. On His way out of Jerusalem, down the Kidron Valley and up to the Mount of Olives, He would have had to pass through the women's court in the temple—a place that easily could hold fifteen thousand people. It also housed the treasury, which consisted of thirteen brass trumpets into which people would drop their offering. It was in this treasury that Jesus stopped and, as Mark records, watched how the people came to give.

> And He looked up and saw the rich putting their gifts into the treasury, and He saw also a certain poor widow putting in two mites.
>
> —Luke 21:1–2

If you've ever sat in a busy place—a shopping mall at Christmas or an airport in the summer—and watched people go by, imagine yourself in a crowd and Jesus sitting on a chair watching you go by. It's sobering to realize that the Lord watches—and He sees much more than anyone else. Of Him, David said in Psalm 139:2, "You know my sitting down. You know my rising up. You understand my thoughts afar off. You comprehend my path. You're acquainted with all of my ways. You know me very well."

In this prominent place during this busy week, there was great opportunity for the religious man to draw attention to his generous giving. That is certainly not new. I once saw a man on a telethon come to the microphone and say, "I'd like to give five hundred dollars anonymously." He didn't give his name—but his face was certainly there for all to see! I wonder how many charities would survive without celebrity benefits, published subscription lists, and bronze plaques or pictures of donors. This is unfortunately what so often drives our giving, for until Jesus is Lord, we sit on the throne of our lives and self is our only concern. Sin focuses on self, not God.

Historical records tell us the rich brought their offerings to the temple in bags so heavy that the servants' help was required to carry them. The procession of giver and servants wound through the gathered crowds heading for the treasury. When these bags of money were emptied into the brass trumpets, you can imagine the noise they made. And the giver left with a "top that" attitude because when we have the ability to do a good deed on a scale impossible for others, we can create for ourselves a delusion of superiority. God, however, is hardly impressed.

In the midst of the fanfare and self-glory, a woman dressed in widow's clothes made her way to the front. After all the charades and confrontations with the scribes and Pharisees that had taken place that day, and after the self-promotion of the rich, here came someone who would bring joy to Jesus' heart. Here came the hero of the story, dressed in the poverty of her widowhood. Forbidden to work, widows were dependent on others to care for them. And those whose families didn't care could be reduced to begging to survive.

We don't know how hard it had been for this woman, but we do know she had virtually nothing to her name. In her hands were two lepta, or mites, worth a quarter of a cent. *Lepta* means "to peel or shave"—like the thinnest possible slice of meat. That was all she had. I suspect that when she walked toward this treasury area, she hoped to go unnoticed. If God saw her, that was sufficient. She didn't come to gain any glory. Two mites hardly would have been enough for that, because we know two thin wafers of coins wouldn't make much noise landing on the piles of shekels the wealthy had thrown in. And the fact that she had two coins afforded her the choice to keep one of them. But she did not.

There were no oohs and aahs, no crowd stopping to listen. But across the way sat Jesus, watching with great joy. It hadn't been a great day—but it was now. In fact, Mark tells us in 12:43 that Jesus called to His disciples, "Come here and see!" Luke continues:

> So He said, "Truly I say to you that this poor widow has put in more than all; for all these out of their abundance have put in offerings for God, but she out of her poverty put in all the livelihood that she had."
>
> —Luke 21:3–4

The rich had been giving much. The noise had been deafening. But in God's economy, this woman had given more than all of them put together. Jesus' reasoning is straightforward, revealing, and hard to miss. The rich gave out of their abundance, overflow, and extra—that which required no sacrifice, while the widow had given out of her poverty—that which she needed to survive. Mark used the term *whole livelihood*. Luke wrote "all the livelihood that she had." She needed to live off what she had given away. She had to choose between food for the body and satisfaction for the soul. She needed food, but longed for worship. And there, unnoticed by anyone but the Lord, she chose the latter and caused God's heart to rejoice.

No one had to tell her to do this. No one had to pressure her into it. This was between her and God, which gives us our second lesson about giving. That is, not only is God interested in how we give, but He measures our giving by what it costs us. It's proportion, not portion, in which God is interested. The amount doesn't matter because He doesn't need our help. But what it costs us matters greatly to Him.

David understood this. By numbering the people, he had brought God's judgment upon them. Needing to build an altar so the plague could be stopped, he went to Mount Moriah and offered to buy a piece of land from a man named Araunah on which to build it.

"Take it!" said Araunah. "Hurry up! I don't want to die. Neither do my kids!"

But David refused, saying, "I'll pay you what it's worth because I cannot give to God that which costs me nothing" (1 Chron. 21:24).

For a rich man, a great amount may be too little. For the poor, the smallest will never go unnoticed in heaven. God is interested in giving that costs us something. When Paul wrote his second letter to the Corinthians, he said to them in chapter 8, "I want you to know how much grace God has bestowed on the Macedonian churches, that in all of their great affliction of trials and their deep poverty, they have been giving to you with great liberality."

The widow certainly revealed that kind of heart—the kind for which God is looking. She gave all she had and Jesus honored her giving.

The only reason we should ever give is because we love Jesus. We shouldn't give because there's a need. We shouldn't give because there's pressure put upon us. We shouldn't give because someone else does. None of those things moves God's heart or pleases Him. But I truly believe that once we come to know the Lord and fall in love with Him, we want to give because that's what love does—it gives. The church's focus ought not to be raising funds. It ought to be raising disciples who love Jesus. If we do that well, God will, through the hearts of those who have fallen in love with Him, meet the church's needs.

In Exodus 25, the people were called on to provide funds and materials to build the tabernacle so God's presence could travel with them through the wilderness. Eleven chapters later, the workers building the tabernacle told Moses the people were giving too much. So Moses went back to the people and said, "Stop. We've got more than we need." When was the last time you were anywhere where you were told to quit giving? If a ministry doesn't rely on the Lord, it's going to rely on pitches, fund-raisers, and teary-eyed pleas that never end and never should have begun. That's not the way God works.

So how are we to give? The IRS doesn't care with what attitude you pay them. But God does. Why? Because He doesn't need anything from us. He's not dependent on our money. He's not waiting for our resources. He looks only for our love—and love sacrifices. All of the rich people's money thrown in the brass trumpets while Jesus was watching has long ago come and gone. But the widow's investment of two mites still bears fruit today. Two thousand years later, in every church that teaches the Gospel they're saying, "There was this widow. She was awesome!"

Not having much doesn't diminish your ability to serve God. It all comes down to how you give, with what heart, and what it costs you. Those are the questions we should ask ourselves every time the offering plate goes by. And if either of the answers isn't suitable, we should go home and work it out with the Lord. He's not interested in our money after all; He's interested in us.

Chapter 112

THE OLIVET DISCOURSE

Mark 13:1–37; Matthew 25:1–46
(Matthew 24–25)

On Tuesday, His last day in Jerusalem, Jesus had spent the better part of the day preaching and teaching. Although He was interrupted constantly by one group after another who came to try to trip Him up, He always came out on top and the people loved Him all the more.

Now it was late Tuesday afternoon and Jesus was leaving for good. Out the East Gate, down the slopes of the Kidron Valley, and up the other side on the Mount of Olives, He was ready to go. He had come to do a work and it had been accomplished. So He headed back to Bethany for the night.

As they walked, maybe it was their sense of Jesus' heaviness that caused the disciples to say, "Look how beautiful the temple looks!"

But Jesus' response, that one day soon not one stone would be left on another rendered them almost speechless. They couldn't help but ask Him, "When will these things be? What will be the signs of Your coming and the end of the age?"

So Jesus sat down on the Mount of Olives, overlooking the city, and gave His disciples one of the longer sermons recorded in the Gospels. The Olivet Discourse, so named because it was given on the Mount of Olives, is found in Mark 13, Luke 21, and Matthew 25, and is Jesus' response to His disciples questions concerning the temple's destruction, the signs of His coming, and the things that will take place at the end of the age. It is His word to Jewish people about Jewish hopes. He gave them general signs of the times through Mark 13:9 and specified about what would take place before the fall of the temple from verses 10 through 13. Then, beginning in verse 14, He switched gears and move forward past the Church Age, past the Rapture, and past the first half of the Tribulation to talk about the coming of the antichrist and His own return.

> Then as He went out of the temple, one of His disciples said to Him, "Teacher, see what manner of stones and what buildings are here!"
>
> —Mark 13:1

The temple must have been magnificent. According to John 2:20, Herod had been restoring it for forty-six years with all of the slave labor and money available to him. It is no wonder it was considered one of the great wonders of the Roman world and that the people were as proud of it as they could be. There were nine massive gates around the Temple Mount, one of which was solid brass. Every dome had a gold plate. You could see it for miles. In his *History of the Jewish Wars,* Josephus wrote in Book V that some of the stones in the temple were thirty-five feet long, twelve feet thick, and twelve feet high. Weighing 120 tons, they were the size of a boxcar. It is phenomenal that these stones, cut out of bedrock and taken from Solomon's quarries, were moved by slave labor alone.

We're not told why the disciples mentioned the temple. But after the day's confrontations and His scathing words to the scribes and Pharisees, I don't know that they weren't saying, "Lord, look how beautiful this place is. It'll be all right."

> And Jesus answered and said to him, "Do you see these great buildings? Not one stone shall be left upon another, that shall not be thrown down."
> —Mark 13:2

Jesus' response to the mention of the temple's beauty had to be the most startling thing the disciples could hear. But His words would come to pass with absolute accuracy. In A.D. 70, after surrounding Jerusalem for over a year, Caesar finally ordered Titus to take the city—but to save the temple for his own use. Due to the flaming arrow of an overly-ambitious soldier, however, the temple burned to the ground and Caesar ordered every rock removed in order to extricate the gold that had melted and run down the cracks.

On this Tuesday of Passion Week, however, the disciples certainly didn't understand what Jesus meant, so they asked Him.

> Now as He sat on the Mount of Olives opposite the temple, Peter, James, John, and Andrew asked Him privately, "Tell us, when will these things be? And what will be the sign when all these things will be fulfilled?"
> —Mark 13:3–4

Matthew 24:3 recorded the disciples saying, "When will these things be? What will be the sign of Your coming and of the end of the age?"

I suspect that, for the disciples, all three of those questions had the same answer. After all, these were the same disciples who saw Jesus' going to Jerusalem as a sign He was about to take over. They didn't distinguish between a Messiah who came to die and the One who would come to rule. They didn't see two kingdoms. So they associated the temple's destruction with a takeover by Jesus. As a result, they had to learn that the Messiah would come twice and that there would be a space of time wherein they would have to wait and serve Him in great difficulty. So don't lose sight of the context. Removed from Jesus speaking to Jewish men about the future of their city, the temple, and His coming, this passage can be easily misunderstood.

And Jesus, answering them, began to say, "Take heed that no one deceives you. For many will come in My name, saying, 'I am He,' and will deceive many."
—Mark 13:5–6

The Greek word *deceive* is where we get our English word *planet* because in the days before orbits were understood, planets, or "wandering stars," seemed to be going nowhere. "Be careful you don't start wandering after someone who claims to be God's representative but isn't," Jesus said. Underlying this is the issue of time. It would take time for false teachers to arise and develop a following.

When Paul left the Ephesians prior to the destruction of Jerusalem in 70 A.D., he told them, "I know when I leave that devouring men are going to come and seek to draw others after themselves. They're going to be like wolves and speak perverse things. Be careful of these guys" (Acts 20:29–30).

During the Tribulation, Satan will fill the heart of the antichrist, the last false prophet, and thousands upon thousands will follow him.

"But when you hear of wars and rumors of wars, do not be troubled; for such things must happen, but the end is not yet."
—Mark 13:7

Again, this speaks of length of time. In Jesus' day, the Roman government had enjoyed a tremendously long era of peace. Because they controlled the world, there was little uprising. But that didn't last. In fact, history shows the world has had only one year of peace for every thirteen years of war. War is part of the world's sinful condition. As such, wars are not signs of the Lord's imminent return as much as they are signs of the times of waiting. And as we wait, we have to deal with the sin that surrounds us.

"For nation will rise against nation and kingdom against kingdom. And there will be earthquakes in various places, and there will be famines and troubles. These are the beginnings of sorrows."
—Mark 13:8

The word *sorrows* is a word that speaks of birth pains. Wars and rumors of them, regional conflicts, even racial conflicts—which the phrase *nation against nation* might very well speak of—will continue along with natural disasters like earthquakes and famine. They will all be birth pains, a part of life as we wait for the Lord to come. But birth pains pick up speed. They go from ten minutes apart to five minutes apart to three minutes apart. And at some point, you say, "That baby's pretty close now!" So as we see conflicts and disasters increase, we realize the Lord's coming is drawing ever nearer.

To trouble and sorrows, earthquakes and famine, Luke added the word *pestilence*, from which we get our word *virus*. All of these are precursors to the Lord's coming—"birth pains" that should remind us He can come at any time.

In verse 9, there is a change of tone. Luke 21:12 introduces these verses with "And even before all of this . . . ." In verses 9–13, there is a primary application of prophecy to the disciples. There is also application to the church. And there will be a greater application to the Tribulation saints who will die for their faith. But the primary application is to the disciples, whose questions Jesus was answering.

> "But watch out for yourselves, for they will deliver you up to councils, and you will be beaten in the synagogues. You will be brought before rulers and kings for My sake, for a testimony to them."
>
> —Mark 13:9

"Be careful," Jesus said. "You're going to suffer greatly for My name and as a testimony to the world for My sake."

The history of the first-century church certainly bears this out. As we read through the accounts of the early church, we see Peter and John arrested by the Sanhedrin and Stephen killed by the same group. Herod beheaded James. Paul was hunted in every city before finally being killed by Nero. All told, over six million believers died for their faith in the first three hundred years of the church's life.

We hate suffering. But the Lord seems to have used the church's suffering to get out His Word to the world. The way we handle difficulty and how we respond to problems becomes a light to those sitting in darkness. It was but a few years from this night on the Mount of Olives that Roman law changed to make Christianity a capital offense punishable by death. Through the saints' testimonies and blood, many became believers—even in Herod's family, Caesar's household, and the prison guards. But it wasn't an easy road.

Years after Stephen's murder by the Sanhedrin for his message to them concerning Jesus, Paul said in Acts 22:20 that he stood by, consenting to Stephen's death. He went on to share that it was the way Stephen died—the way he gave glory to God—that planted a seed in Paul's heart that would come to fruition later.

When the Lord puts you in difficult spots—maybe you lose your job for your testimony, or your family sets you aside because you're walking with the Lord—who knows if God won't use that very thing to bring many others to Him? Trials come at great cost, but God never wastes the tears of the saints.

> "And the Gospel must first be preached to all the nations."
>
> —Mark 13:10

"Go into all the world and preach the Gospel to every creature," Jesus said in Mark 16:15. And thirty years after the resurrection, Paul was able to write that the Gospel had indeed been preached in all the world (Col. 1:6). Though we don't see it preached in all the world today is not an obstacle to Jesus' return. Revelation 14:6–11 says He'll send an angel across the heavens telling people in every language the way they can be saved. God will not leave people without a witness—but to go into all the world and preach the Gospel is still the church's mandate.

> "But when they arrest you and deliver you up, do not worry beforehand, or premeditate what you will speak. But whatever is given you in that hour, speak that; for it is not you who speak, but the Holy Spirit."
>
> —Mark 13:11

This is the only place in the entire Bible where the Lord says, "Don't study. Don't plan. Don't look ahead." This is not a word to lazy people who refuse to study. This is for those who are on trial for their lives, wondering if they would say the right thing. This is God's promise to those who would walk with Him and risk their necks for the Gospel to go forward. He will give you what to say that very hour! Rest in Him!

> "Now brother will betray brother to death, and a father his child; and children will rise up against parents and cause them to be put to death. And you will be hated by all for My name's sake. But he who endures to the end shall be saved."
>
> —Mark 13:12–13

Hatred for Jesus overcomes even blood ties. It was true in the first century, true in Nazi Germany when those who protected the Jews often were turned in by their own families, and it will be true in the Tribulation when those who refuse the mark of the beast will be betrayed even by those closest to them.

"Hated by all men for My name's sake" applies to the church as it shares the good news of the Gospel. But here's the encouragement: Endure to the end. Persevere. Hang in there even when trials seem hard and long because the Lord is coming—and in the end, you will be blessed.

> "So when you see the 'abomination of desolation,' spoken of by Daniel the prophet, standing where it ought not" (let the reader understand), "then let those who are in Judea flee to the mountains. Let him who is on the housetop not go down into the house, nor enter to take anything out of his house. And let him who is in the field not go back to get his clothes. But woe to those who are pregnant and to those who are nursing babies in those days! And pray that your flight may not be in winter. For in those days there will be tribulation, such as has not been since the beginning of the creation which God created until this time, nor ever shall be."
>
> —Mark 13:14–19

Here an event is introduced that won't take place until the middle of the Tribulation, and it was first prophesied in Daniel 9. After reading the book of Jeremiah and realizing the seventy-year captivity of the Jews was almost over, Daniel prayed, "Lord, I don't know what the future holds, but I'm willing to be a part of it. What's coming next?" In answer to this prayer, Daniel was given the future of the nation of Israel—a very important word that would define what would come later in the book of Revelation. The prophecy said that from the time of his request, there were seventy heptads or seven-year periods determined for the nation of Israel. There would be seven until the city was rebuilt and sixty-two after that until the coming of the Messiah.

Both from the Old Testament and historical writings, we know that Artaxerxes, king of Babylon, issued the command to restore and rebuild Jerusalem on March 14, 445 b.c. Forty-nine years later, the walls, city, and temple were rebuilt. According to the Daniel prophecy, there would be sixty-two more seven-year periods, or 434 more years, until the coming of the Messiah. If we do the math, based on the Babylonian calendar we come to April 6, 32 a.d.—the day Jesus rode into Jerusalem on a donkey, presenting Himself as the Messiah. Daniel was told that after these sixty-two weeks, the Messiah would be cut off, the city would be destroyed, and the people would be displaced—which is exactly what happened when, following the Roman destruction of Jerusalem in 70 a.d., the Jews were driven into every corner of the earth.

Sixty-nine seven-year periods have passed. But the clock of prophecy has stopped. There is only one seven-year period remaining. Called the seventieth week of Daniel, or the time of Jacob's trouble, it is the seven-year period between the church's rapture and the Lord's return—when God again will deal specifically in and through the nation of Israel.

In Daniel 9:27 we read, "Then he shall confirm a covenant with many for one week. But in the middle of the week he shall bring an end to sacrifice and offering. And on the wing of abominations shall be one who makes desolate, even until the consummation, which is determined, is poured out on the desolate." The "he" in this verse refers to the antichrist, also foretold in Daniel's prophecy. The antichrist will sign a treaty with Israel, most likely by coming up with a solution for the temple's rebuilding without compromising the Muslims' Dome of the Rock, also on the Temple Mount. But exactly at the three-and-a-half-year mark, rather than being the magnanimous man everyone thinks he is, the antichrist will demand that he be exalted as god, that no one buy or sell without his mark, and that anyone who refuses to bow to him will be killed. And his demand for worship and sacrifice will be the abomination that will make the temple a place of desolation.

The *abomination of desolation* is an important phrase. "Abomination" in the Old Testament refers not only to things God detests but is almost always related to idolatry or sacrilege. Matthew wrote in chapter 24:15 of the abomination of desolation standing in the holy place. In 2 Thessalonians 2:3, Paul referred to the son of perdition sitting as god in the temple as an abomination. It is this abomination that will usher in tribulation like the world has never seen. So Jesus' warning to the Jews is to flee to the mountains.

In Isaiah 16:1, we read of a place called Sela in the rock city of Edom, which is today the city of Petra in Jordan. Built into the rock cliffs, with but one very narrow entrance that barely a horse can pass through, it is totally defensible. And from all we read in Bible prophecy, it seems this is the place the Lord has prepared to hide His people during the three-and-a-half-year period when the antichrist's sole desire will be to destroy them.

Did the disciples understand this? I suspect they understood none of it. But they must have been taking notes because it appears later in all the Gospels.

> "And unless the Lord had shortened those days, no flesh would be saved; but for the elect's sake, whom He chose, He shortened the days."
>
> —Mark 13:20

So severe will the Tribulation be that, were it to go longer, no one would survive. Who are the elect? Remember the context. Although the church will be referred to as "the elect of God," as in Colossians 3:12, Jesus was talking to Jewish men about Israel's future. So in that context, the elect here spoke of the nation to whom God was giving warning and for whom He promises protection. In Isaiah 45:4, Israel is called God's elect and the same is true here.

> "Then if anyone says to you, 'Look, here is the Christ!' or 'Look, He is there!' do not believe it. For false christs and false prophets will rise and show signs and wonders to deceive, if possible, even the elect. But take heed; see, I have told you all things beforehand."
>
> —Mark 13:21–23

Jesus warned again of the antichrist, his false prophet, and the demons' work. "Don't be fooled," He said. "I'm telling you ahead of time."

> "But in those days, after that tribulation, the sun will be darkened, and the moon will not give its light; the stars of heaven will fall, and the powers in the heavens will be shaken. Then they will see the Son of Man coming in the clouds with great power and glory. And then He will send His angels, and gather together His elect from the four winds, from the farthest part of earth to the farthest part of heaven."
>
> —Mark 13:24–27

Following the Tribulation—Matthew added *immediately*—the sun will be dark, the moon will not give its light, the Son of Man will appear in heaven, and all the Jews will be gathered together to the Lord. Paul wrote to the Romans that all of Israel will be saved at this time when the deliverer comes out of Zion. From the book of Revelation in chapter 16:16 we know that right before the Lord comes, all of the nations of the earth will gather together in the Valley of Megiddo, where the Battle of Armageddon will take place—which really won't be much of a battle, because when the Lord shows up with the word of His mouth and the brightness of His coming, His victory will be a foregone conclusion.

After laying out for the disciples what will take place in the Tribulation when God again deals with Israel, everything beyond verse 27 says, "Watch. Take heed. Be ready."

> "Now learn this parable from the fig tree: When its branch has already become tender, and puts forth leaves, you know that summer is near. So you also, when you see these things happening, know that it is near—at the doors!"
>
> —Mark 13:28–29

Although throughout prophecy Israel is represented as a vineyard or a fig tree, but I don't believe the fig tree represents Israel here. Luke recorded Jesus beginning this parable by saying, "Look at the fig tree; look at *all the trees*." The fig tree being the most predominant tree in the Judean landscape, I think its use here was more agricultural than prophetic. This being early April, they would have been almost in bloom—something the disciples certainly would have recognized. So using the fig tree as an example, Jesus said to them, "You ought to be able to recognize the nearness of the days in which you live by the signs that precede them."

The term *these things* applies both to the near and the far term, both to 70 A.D. and the time of the Tribulation.

"What are the signs of the end?" the disciples had asked.

"When you see these things, it's getting close," was Jesus' answer.

Taken together, all of the signs, times, and seasons the Lord laid out paint a clear picture of our own days. For the Lord's return to be sure, Israel will have to be back in the land. She is. There will have to be a huge power base in Europe from which the antichrist will spring. There is, as seen in the fact that the Euro trumps every other currency in the world. There will have to be conflict over land in the Middle East driven by a hatred of Israel. There is. There will have to be a radicalization of terror to explain the destruction that will come. There is. Add to this the general signs of famine, war, rumors of war, earthquakes, pestilence, riots, and viruses, and it doesn't take long before you begin to say, "This could be it."

Everything is adding up. Everything is in place. Nothing remains to be accomplished for the Lord to come. And because those things are close, the rapture of the church which precedes them is closer still—even at the door.

> "Assuredly, I say to you, this generation will by no means pass away till all these things take place."
>
> —Mark 13:30

The word *genea*, or *generation*, is a word most often translated as *race* or *nationality* in the Bible. If that is the way Jesus used this word, the promise to which He referred is a tremendous miracle because He said of Israel, "This nation will not pass until everything takes place." Within forty years of Jesus speaking these words, Titus and the tenth Roman legion destroyed Jerusalem, killed millions, and set in motion the Diaspora in which the Jews who survived ran in fear to all corners of the earth, where they remained for nearly two thousand years.

Historically, no ethnic group without a homeland has ever been able to maintain its identity for more than five generations. They are instead absorbed into the ethnic background of whatever culture in which they find themselves. That's why we don't know any Babylonians or Assyrians. The Jews, however, are the exception to this rule because although they had no place to call home from 70 A.D. to 1948, they remained a separate people, surviving even the attempt to exterminate them less than seventy years ago.

Today, more than 50 percent of all Jews live in Israel. They have ambassadors in every major country of the world seeking to bring people home. God has maintained Israel's identity all along. They are His people, and His care cannot go unnoticed.

If Jesus used the word *generation* in reference to time, however, then by definition a biblical generation is anywhere between thirty-eight and one hundred years. Although there is no way to define the term clearly in this context, both meanings address the same issue: Our readiness. Are you ready?

> "Heaven and earth will pass away, but My words will by no means pass away."
> —Mark 13:31

Everything we see is rotting. Our bodies won't last. The earth won't last. The sun won't last. In fact, the sun loses 1.3 million tons of mass every second, coming to us in the form of energy and light from 93 million miles away. Peter asked, seeing these things were going to be dissolved, what kind of people we ought to be. If we know this is the end, we better hang on to God's Word because it is the only eternal, permanent thing we possess.

> "But of that day and hour no one knows, not even the angels in heaven, nor the Son, but only the Father. Take heed, watch and pray; for you do not know when the time is."
> —Mark 13:32–33

If we can differentiate between the seasons in which we live, we ought to be able to understand the signs in which we live as well and live in readiness to stand before the Lord. Jesus' final words to His disciples here and in Matthew 25 were all designed to say, "Look around. See the days in which you live and be ready for what's ahead."

"It is like a man going to a far country, who left his house and gave authority to his servants, and to each his work, and commanded the doorkeeper to watch. Watch therefore, for you do not know when the master of the house is coming—in the evening, at midnight, at the crowing of the rooster, or in the morning—lest, coming suddenly, he find you sleeping. And what I say to you, I say to all: Watch!"

—Mark 13:34–37

The word *watch* is in the present tense because the only way to be ready is to keep watching. In Luke's account, Jesus said, "Take heed to yourself lest your heart be weighed down with carousing, drunkenness, and the cares of this life; lest the day comes upon you unexpectedly as a snare for all of those who dwell upon the face of the earth."

The term *carousing* is a medical term in Greek referring to headache and nausea that come from too much eating or drinking. Drunkenness is a state in which one is out of touch, unaware of what's going on around them. As for the cares of this life—food, clothing, rent, children, husband, wife—we're to seek first God's kingdom and His righteousness and He'll take care of all of them.

We live in a time where the last days are upon us. Israel has been brought back into the land. As you watch the days and signs of the times, I think you will see that the Lord could come in our generation. And wouldn't that be awesome? When I got saved in the early seventies, I knew the Lord was coming by the eighties—'85 for sure, '90 at the very latest. Turn of the century? Look out below! Yet here we are still. But it doesn't change the promise. Jesus said heaven and earth will pass away, but His Word never will. Are you ready?

At the end of this long sermon Jesus gave to His disciples three parables that fit together concerning His judgment of the nations at His return.

"Then the kingdom of heaven shall be likened to ten virgins who took their lamps and went out to meet the bridegroom. Now five of them were wise, and five were foolish. Those who were foolish took their lamps and took no oil with them, but the wise took oil in their vessels with their lamps. But while the bridegroom was delayed, they all slumbered and slept. And at midnight a cry was heard: 'Behold, the bridegroom is coming; go out to meet him!' Then all those virgins arose and trimmed their lamps. And the foolish said to the wise, 'Give us some of your oil, for our lamps are going out.' But the wise answered, saying, 'No, lest there should not be enough for us and you; but go rather to those who sell, and buy for yourselves.' And while they went to buy, the bridegroom came, and those who were ready went in with him to the wedding; and the door was shut. Afterward the other virgins came also, saying, 'Lord, Lord, open to us!' But he answered and said, 'Assuredly, I say to you, I do not know you.' Watch therefore, for you know neither the day nor the hour in which the Son of Man is coming."

—Matthew 25:1–13

The parable's lesson is obviously that we need to be ready for Jesus' return. The ten virgins, or maidens, have a lot of similarities. They all went out to meet the bridegroom, they all had lamps, they all slumbered, and they all ran out to meet him when He arrived. But only five were received.

The difference between the maidens was significant however: the wise five had oil and the foolish five did not. Throughout the Bible, oil is representative of the work of God's Spirit—that which He pours out on our lives when we come to know Him and are saved. So as He has continued to do in this lesson of the Olivet Discourse, Jesus made the distinction between those who are *in* church and those who are *the* church, between those who sit in the pews and those who sit in the heavenlies. There were many religious folks in Jesus' day who had a religion without a relationship with God—the scribes and Pharisees not the least among them. They had the light of the Word to lead them but they had refused to walk in that light. They had refused Jesus for three and a half years. His warning to them was that one day their opportunity would be gone. While the temptation would be to borrow from others, a relationship with God can't be borrowed from someone else. In other words, you won't get to heaven because your father was a pastor.

In the letters to the seven churches in Revelation 2–3, we see over and over again that not everyone in the church is saved. In our own day, there are a lot of people across the country who go to church—but how many know the Lord? How many expect God to be glad when He comes to find them? We want to be sure we know the Lord and that we're willing to risk everything we have to be ready for His coming.

The prophet Zechariah 4:1–6 had a dream in which he saw oil flowing into bowls connected to the lampstand in the temple through tubes connected to three olive trees. The Lord then sent an angel to explain his dream—that it wasn't by our might or power, not by anything we could ever do, but by His Spirit that we're saved, molded, shaped, and made ready to stand before Him.

"For the kingdom of heaven is like a man traveling to a far country, who called his own servants and delivered his goods to them. And to one he gave five talents, to another two, and to another one, to each according to his own ability; and immediately he went on a journey. Then he who had received the five talents went and traded with them, and made another five talents. And likewise he who had received two gained two more also. But he who had received one went and dug in the ground, and hid his lord's money. After a long time the lord of those servants came and settled accounts with them. So he who had received five talents came and brought five other talents, saying, 'Lord, you delivered to me five talents; look, I have gained five more talents besides them.' His lord said to him, 'Well done, good and faithful servant; you were faithful over a few things, I will make you ruler over many things. Enter into the joy of your lord.' He also who had received two talents came and said, 'Lord, you delivered to me two talents; look, I have gained two more talents besides them.' His lord said to him, 'Well done, good and faithful servant; you have been faithful over a few things. I will make you ruler over many things. Enter into the joy of your lord.' Then he who had received the one talent came and said, 'Lord, I knew you to be a hard man, reaping where you have not sown, and gathering where you have not scattered seed. And I was afraid, and went and hid your talent in the ground. Look, there you have what is yours.' But his lord answered and said to him, 'You wicked and lazy servant, you knew that I reap where I have not sown, and gather where I have not scattered seed. So you ought to have deposited my money with the bankers, and at my coming I would have received back my own with interest. Therefore take the talent from him, and give it to him who has ten talents. For to everyone who has, more will be given, and he will have abundance; but from him who does not have, even what he has will be taken away. And cast the unprofitable servant into the outer darkness. There will be weeping and gnashing of teeth.'"

—Matthew 25:14–30

As with the previous parable, this parable speaks of the waiting time. A talent was a weight measurement that in the parables represented assets the Lord entrusted to us, gifts of talents that can be used for His glory or misused just to serve ourselves. To two of the three servants, the master gave five and two talents, respectively. And both of them brought to him a 100 percent return on his investment. In both cases, there was faithfulness to the trust given. The third fellow, however, buried his one talent and did nothing.

As believers, our salvation is sure—but the Bible says that after the Lord gathers us to heaven, our works will be thrown in the fire to determine whether they were done for God's glory or our own. Because God gives different resources to different people, we don't have to be something we're not to serve Him. We only have to use that which God gives us.

The first two servants heard words that must have been music to their ears when the master said, "Well done." The third servant, however, did not. His was the same fate as the maidens without oil, as he became another example of someone who was in the church but not in the Lord.

Notice that his excuses highlight his misconception about his master. "You're a hard man," he said. Lots of people say the same thing about God, but they've got it all wrong because Jesus said His yoke is easy and His burden light. "You're the reason for my faithlessness," the third servant said to the master. "I didn't want to take any chances. You're so tough I decided doing nothing was better than risking everything."

His argument reminds me of the Proverbs 26:13–14 passage declaring a lazy man will cry out there's a lion in the streets to keep from working and that, as the door swings on its hinges, so a lazy man swings on his bed. "If you thought I was wicked and harsh, it should have been even more incentive for you to do something," the master said to the third servant. "You could have at least brought back interest."

The lesson is clear: Be ready. Be filled with oil. And as you wait, serve the Lord with the talents and gifts He's given you because you don't want to have to give a reason one day for why you could teach, act, or sing so well, yet failed to use those abilities for God's glory.

> "When the Son of Man comes in His glory, and all the holy angels with Him, then He will sit on the throne of His glory. All the nations will be gathered then He will separate them one from another, as a shepherd divides his sheep from the goats. And He will set the sheep on His right hand, but the goats on the left. Then the King will say to those on His right hand, 'Come, you blessed of My Father, inherit the kingdom prepared for you from the Foundation of the world: for I was hungry and you gave Me food; I was thirsty and you gave Me drink; I was a stranger and you took Me in; I was naked and you clothed Me; I was sick and you visited Me; I was in prison and you came to Me.' Then the righteous will answer Him, saying, 'Lord, when did we see You hungry and feed You, or thirsty and give You drink? When did we see You a stranger and take You in, or naked and clothe You? Or when did we see You sick, or in prison, and come to You?' And the King will answer and say to them, 'Assuredly, I say to you, inasmuch as you did it to one of the least of these My brethren, you did it to Me.' Then He will also say to those on the left hand, 'Depart from Me, you cursed, into the everlasting fire prepared for the Devil and his angels: for I was hungry and you game Me no food; I was thirsty and you gave Me no drink; I was a stranger and you did not take Me in, naked and you did not clothe Me, sick and in prison and you did not visit Me.' Then they also will answer Him, saying, 'Lord, when did we see You hungry or thirsty or a stranger or naked or sick or in prison, and did not minister to You?' Then He will answer them, saying, 'Assuredly, I say to you, inasmuch as you did not do it to one of the least of these, you did not do it to Me.' And these will go away into everlasting punishment, but the righteous into eternal life."
>
> —Matthew 25:31–46

In the final parable, we move past the waiting and past the serving to the time of Jesus' return to the earth and the gathering together of all of the nations for His judgment. Following this judgment, some will be allowed to enter the Kingdom Age—the thousand-year reign of Christ on the earth. Others will not. According to Daniel 12:11–12, this judgment of the Lord will take forty-five days.

Although the term *My brethren* in verse 40 most likely refers to the nation of Israel because they are the ones the antichrist will go after specifically, the overriding lesson remains the same. That is, that true saints serve the Lord by serving others in need of His love.

More than anything else, the Lord wants to give life. So while there is time, go to Him and be filled so you'll be ready when He comes. And then you can begin to use the gifts

He has given you to serve Him instead of yourself. The fruit you bear as a result will cause His heart to rejoice.

These are the last words of instruction Jesus gave His disciples as they watched the sun set from the Mount of Olives, now only hours before the cross.

Chapter 113

WEDNESDAY/THURSDAY
PLOTS AND PLANS

Luke 22:1–13
(Matthew 26:1–5; 14–16;
Mark 14:1–2, 10–11; John 11:45–53)

None of the four Gospels gives us any information about what happened between sundown on Tuesday and sundown on Wednesday of Passion Week. Instead, they take us immediately to Thursday—the day of preparation for the Passover.

I think maybe the best lesson we can draw from this portion of the story is that God was in control every step of the way. It is easy to read this account and think He was overwhelmed, that He got out-plotted, that there were some things that didn't go well. But none of that's true. In every detail of the trial, betrayal, arrest, and crucifixion, it is Jesus' plans that were carried out fully. Regardless of Judas and his buddies' plots, Jesus gave His life only when He was ready. He rose as He had said. All things were accomplished according to His purpose.

That's always the case. You may find yourself frustrated with people, situations, or circumstances. But if you know the Lord, you should know He is in charge of all of those things and that nothing yet has been created that can throw Him off His plans for your life. The enemy may plot, but only the Lord's plans will succeed.

> Now the Feast of Unleavened Bread drew near, which is called Passover.
>
> —Luke 22:1

Passover was the annual commemoration of God's deliverance of the nation of Israel from 430 years of bondage in Egypt. Following Pharaoh's refusal to let God's people go, a series of plagues came, culminating in the death of the firstborn of every house unmarked by the blood of a lamb. The death angel would pass over the houses marked by blood, thus providing a prophetic picture of the Lamb of God who would come to take away the sins of the world.

Two weeks after Passover was a weeklong feast called the Feast of Unleavened Bread. Because leaven in the Bible is a picture or illustration of sin, in preparation for this feast every house was scoured to remove even the smallest peace of leaven. Passover and the Feast of Unleavened Bread paint a beautiful picture—that Jesus' blood cleanses not only the penalty of sin but its power as God delivers our lives!

Thursday was a very busy day for this preparation. For one, the city of Jerusalem was overrun with people. It is estimated that as many as 256,000 animals were slain during Passover. With one animal sacrificed for every family, and families averaging ten in number, there could have been more than two million people in town getting ready for Passover. And that's not even counting the vendors and beggars who lined every street. As we read verse 1, we should imagine a town overrun with people.

Not only were there many people, but everyone would have been very busy. According to Jewish Law, one division of twenty-four priests would have been at the temple at any one time leading worship, offering sacrifices, and interceding for Himself people. But during Passover, all twenty-four divisions reported for work to cleanse the temple of leaven, slaughter the animals, and take the blood of the offering and throw it on the altar before returning the animal to the one who offered it to roast and eat with his family. It was twenty-four hours a day of tremendous labor.

> And the chief priests and the scribes sought how they might kill Him, for they feared the people.
>
> —Luke 22:2

As the Lord's plans went forward, the wicked men's plots continued. They had been wanting to kill Jesus for a long time. As far back as Mark 3:1–6, after He had healed the man with the withered hand in the temple, the religious leaders had been plotting His overthrow and murder.

The week thus far hadn't gone well for the religious leaders. Jesus had cleansed the temple on Monday, saying they were nothing more than a money-hungry bunch of religious hypocrites who couldn't care less about God. They hadn't done very well in the Tuesday debates either, as Jesus had denunciated them in front of the people time and again exposing them and their wicked hearts. Therefore, it was long past a question of whether or not to kill Him, but simply a matter of when. After all, they didn't want an uproar from the crowds.

> Then Satan entered Judas, surnamed Iscariot, who was numbered among the twelve.
>
> —Luke 22:3

Here on Thursday morning, Satan had entered Judas' heart. This man's life had been surrendered to the wrong spirit and his way of life had been invaded by hell. We know from Mark 14:3–9 that as Jesus and the disciples had dinner at Simon the leper's house, Mary had come with expensive ointment and had begun to pour it on Jesus.

"What a waste," Judas had protested, "That money could have been given to the poor."

"Leave her alone," Jesus said. "She has anointed Me for My burial."

Directly following this, we read that, almost as if this was the last straw for him, Judas left to make a deal with the chief priests (Mark 14:10). The price was set at thirty pieces of silver, according to Matthew 26:15—about a month's income in those days. In Zechariah 11:12–13, we read, "So they weighed out for my wages thirty pieces of silver. And the Lord said to me, 'Throw it to the potter'—that princely price they set on me. So I took the thirty pieces of silver and threw them into the house of the Lord for the potter." Why was this written? So you might know that God was well aware of this plot! He knew the price. He knew what they would do with the money. He knew Satan was working. But He was in charge. Never forget that.

Whenever you're frustrated as a believer because things get in the way, if you can remind yourself that God's in control, you'll find His rest. If you start blaming your wife, your kids, your neighbors, the barking dog, or your boss, you'll go nuts. But if you let God be God and submit yourself to Him, you'll be at peace.

If you meet the Lord and get saved, He'll bring out the best in you and your life will change for good. But if you meet Him and choose to walk away, you'll become the worst of people because you'll have turned away from the only hope you had. You see this in Judas and others in Scripture who, coming into contact with God, decided they didn't want to follow Him. Like King Saul, they heard, they saw, they experienced—but they didn't receive. And unparalleled wickedness beyond all natural reason was the result. After walking over three years with Jesus, watching every miracle and listening to every sermon, would you really be able to turn away? Judas could and did.

> So he went his way and conferred with the chief priests and captains, how he might betray Him to them. And they were glad, and agreed to give him money. So he promised and sought opportunity to betray Him to them in the absence of the multitude.
>
> —Luke 22:4–6

Thank the Lord for His grace! How we might be otherwise!

> Then came the Day of Unleavened Bread, when the Passover must be killed. And He sent Peter and John, saying, "Go and prepare the Passover for us, that we may eat." So they said to Him, "Where do You want us to prepare?" And He said to them, "Behold, when you have entered the city, a man will meet you carrying a pitcher of water; follow him into the house which he enters. Then you shall say to the master of the house, 'The Teacher says to you, "Where is the guest room where I may eat the Passover with My disciples?"'" Then he will show you a large, furnished upper room; there make ready." So they went and found it just as He had said to them, and they prepared the Passover.
>
> —Luke 22:7–13

Thursday was a tremendously busy day for everyone who had come to worship. There was the purchasing of the lamb for those who didn't live close enough to bring their own. There was the slaughter of the lamb, the buying of the spices, the securing of a place to celebrate the Passover meal. The Law dictated that Passover be eaten within the city walls. Jesus was staying in Bethany on the other side of the Mount of Olives. Therefore, along with the thousands of others, He too had to find a place for Himself and His disciples to partake of the meal together. To do this, He sent two trusted disciples ahead, giving them directions that were at the same time specific and vague.

A man carrying water on his head would have been an unusual sight in first-century culture. Women carried water on their heads in earthenware pitchers. Men carried water in animal skins. So Jesus' direction was specific because this sight would have been hard to miss. But it was vague in the sense that He didn't say anything about where the place was. I suggest that He did this knowing Judas was looking for an opportunity to betray Him out of the public eye, and the Passover meal would have been a great place to do that. But no one *took* Jesus' life. He laid it down willingly. Judas found out the location too late for him to run to those waiting to hear where Jesus was.

Jesus wanted to spend His last few hours with His own. He had a lot to teach them and encourage them about. It is most Bible scholars' guess that this dinner probably took place at John Mark's family home, where we find the church meeting early on in the book of Acts. If so, it would explain a twelve-year-old John Mark out in the garden later that night, spying from the bushes—the same John Mark who went on to write the Gospel of Mark years later.

Much like our Thanksgiving, Passover usually was eaten with family. But Jesus' family thought He was crazy. So He ate with His disciples. After this day, there was no need to celebrate Passover in the original sense because Jesus' death gave Passover a new meaning and opened the door for the celebration of Communion.

So the disciples went off to make ready, finding everything just as Jesus had said. They purchased the lamb. They stood in the long lines to have the blood placed at the altar. They saw the meat roasted. They picked up the bitter herbs. They stewed the fruit in the wine. They ritually cleansed the room. All day long, they were busy. Soon all was ready.

Chapter 114

THE LAST SUPPER

John 13:1–38

Beginning here with the Last Supper, we find one of the lengthiest discussions Jesus had with His own. While He might have focused on His agony, He didn't. Instead, He focused on God's love for mankind. There is so much to learn. God help us hear from You!

> Now before the feast of the Passover, when Jesus knew that His hour had come that He should depart this world to the Father, having loved His own who were in the world, He loved them to the end.
>
> —John 13:1

In Luke 12:50, we see Jesus saying to His disciples as they headed for Jerusalem, "I have a baptism to be baptized with and I'm in great distress until it is accomplished." In other words, Jesus was fully aware that He had come to die.

I think there's great benefit to us not knowing what's coming down the pike. It's good to know who holds tomorrow—but I'm not sure I want to know what tomorrow holds. Jesus, however, lived in constant awareness that He had come to die—yet His thoughts were not for Himself, but for those whom He had been given. That is why He spent much time telling them He would depart—or literally that He would be transferred from one place to another. He was going back to the Father, but to get there He would have to go through the cross. He would do so with great love.

He used the word *agapao*, a selfless love that made Him more concerned about His disciples than His own suffering. The fact that He loved them to the end, to the fullest extent, is not a time reference. It's a reach reference. In every place they had need, He would prepare them for what they would face.

Jesus knew Philip would be confused. He knew three of His inner circle would fall asleep when He asked them to pray. He knew Thomas would be so distraught that He wouldn't even bother coming to the meeting after His death. He knew all would forsake Him—yet He also knew they were His. And He loved them to the end. His hour had come, but it was His love for them that was foremost on His mind.

And supper being ended . . . .

—John 13:2

This literally reads, "The preparation for supper being ended . . . ."

> . . . The Devil having already put it into the heart of Judas Iscariot, Simon's son, to betray Him, Jesus, knowing that the Father had given all things into His hands, and that He had come from God and was going to God, rose from supper and laid aside His garments, took a towel and girded Himself. After that, He poured water into a basin and began to wash the disciples' feet, and to wipe them with the towel with which He was girded.
>
> —John 13:2–5

Verse 3 is extremely important because it explains the heart behind the behavior of verses 4 and 5. Knowing the Father had put everything in His hands, knowing He had come from God and was going to God, Jesus knew His origin, position, future, and destiny. And in all of that knowledge, He grabbed a towel and began to wash feet.

The lesson is this: If you know where you stand with God, you are free to serve. You have no agenda because you no longer live for man's approval. You don't need to make a name for yourself. You don't need to be noticed. If you know where you stand with God as a believer, you can serve without being noticed or applauded because all you're interested in is pleasing the Lord. Jesus—God Himself, the Ruler of the universe, the One to whom one day every knee will bow—was so secure in His position that He was able to get on His knees and do a slave's work.

In Jesus' day, whenever you came into someone's home after walking the dusty roads, a slave immediately would wash your feet in order to make you feel comfortable and welcome. But no one at this table was willing to do that—not for each other, not for their Master. Instead, we read again and again about the disciples' argument concerning who the greatest would be. For them, serving was out of the question because they had an agenda. Jesus didn't. He knew where He stood.

The key for us to serve selflessly lies in knowing where we stand with God. If I know my sins are forgiven, and if I know God will fill me with His Spirit and that when I die I'll go to be with Him, I really shouldn't have much of an agenda other than to please Him. So I'm free to serve those who can't thank me, reward me, or repay me.

I can imagine the embarrassed looks on the faces of the disciples gathered around that U-shaped table. "Oh, man, we should have thought of that," they must have whispered as Jesus began to wash their feet. It's a beautiful picture of what He came to do for people: He left the banquet table of heaven, wrapped Himself in flesh, poured the water of the Word into our lives, and cleansed us from sin.

> Then He came to Simon Peter. And Peter said to Him, "Lord, are You washing my feet?"
>
> —John 13:6

Watching Jesus wash the other disciples' feet, Peter felt it was not right. So with supposed spiritual insight and as much humility as he could muster, he said to Him, "There is no way in the world that this is the way it should be." Yet although his argument was driven by affection and love for the Lord, Peter missed the entire lesson.

> Jesus answered and said to him, "What I am doing you do not understand now, but you will know after this."
>
> —John 13:7

"I know it doesn't make sense now. Just let it go. You'll get it later," Jesus said—which is often the way the Lord works. Flood season was not a good time for a couple million people to cross a river overflowing its banks. Yet it was then He said to Joshua, "Tell the priests to walk out into the Jordan, and when they get up to their knees, I'll part the water for the people to cross into the Promised Land." Although the priests probably didn't get it, they obeyed. And as they did, the Lord rolled back the river thirty miles upstream. As a result, not only did the priests and people know God was with them, but so did everyone who lived along the river. Word got out very quickly that the God of the Hebrews was God indeed.

It was when Philip was preaching in Samaria and packing the stadium every night that the Lord told him to go to the middle of nowhere. Philip could have said, "I'm not leaving the work of the ministry. I'm as popular as can be. We're getting huge altar calls. This is certainly what You want to do." Instead, rather than argue with God, he obeyed. And it wasn't until he got there that the Lord showed him a man in a chariot who had questions that needed answers (Acts 8).

The same thing happens with us. The Lord directs us and we don't get it. But we're not asked to get it. We're only asked to obey. And it is as we do that we'll see God work.

> Peter said to Him, "You shall never wash my feet!" Jesus answered him, "If I do not wash you, you have no part with Me." Simon Peter said to Him, "Lord, not my feet only, but also my hands and my head!"
>
> —John 13:8–9

Instead of just listening, Peter went from bad to worse. But Jesus' words stopped him in his tracks. "All right, Peter," He said. "If I don't wash you, we part company"—which was the last thing Peter wanted to hear because, with all of his impulsiveness, Peter loved the Lord. So when he heard that if Jesus didn't wash him he wouldn't be part of Him, Peter was willing to be washed, from head to toe! So if we're going to come to Jesus, we've got to be washed in His blood because there's no way we can make ourselves presentable.

The word *part* is the word for something held in common. If we want to have something in common with the Lord, we have to be washed by Him. He's the One to whom we have to turn in repentance and confession.

> Jesus said to him, "He who is bathed needs only to wash his feet, but is completely clean; and you are clean; but not all of you." For He knew who would betray Him; therefore He said, "You are not all clean."
>
> —John 13:10–11

Peter had a relationship with the Lord. He already had been a man of faith who had come to receive. But here we see the issue of maintaining a relationship with God that sin otherwise can interrupt. Initially, we need to be bathed, washed, and saved. But once we're saved, we need to come to the Lord often, saying, "Lord, forgive me, wash me, and cleanse me that I might maintain my relationship with You." Otherwise, sin steals our joy, redirects our priorities, and robs us of our knowledge of God and His Word. Sin can cut you off—not from life but from living the kind of life God makes available. Sin won't take away your salvation, but you'll be living as if you had little of it.

To maintain a healthy walk with the Lord, I think it should be an imperative part of one's daily prayer life to say, "Lord, here are the things in my life I need You to cleanse." When Aaron and his sons were called to the priesthood in Exodus 29, they were washed from head to toe. But in Exodus 30, when they began their service, only their hands and feet were washed because God already had cleansed and anointed them. They simply needed to wash away those things that would defile.

John wrote in his first epistle that if we confess our sins, God is faithful and just to forgive them (1 John 1:9). The Greek word for *confess* is *homologeo*, which means "to say the same thing." When we agree with God about our sins, bring Him our weaknesses, and ask Him to change us, Jesus' blood shed for us cleanses us and maintains our relationship with Him. That's why Jesus taught on the Sermon on the Mount that a part of our prayer life should be a daily seeking of God's forgiveness.

Many Christians suffer spiritually and fall out of fellowship because they don't confess their sins. On the other hand, lots of good things happen through daily confession. For one thing, we quickly begin to appreciate God's mercy. The fiftieth time we come with the same sin and hear the Lord forgive us, we say, "It is amazing that God would meet me here fifty times." We don't have that kind of patience. But God does.

Not only does confession cause me to remember God's goodness, but it causes me to depend on His power. A lot of Christians begin on their knees but live the rest of their lives defiantly standing on their own two feet. We can't. Confession brings me to the place where I am kept dependent on the Lord, which is why I think Communion is so helpful.

Communion brings us back to the beginning, where we realize the only hope we have for life is Jesus' sacrifice.

Third, confessing our sins every day insulates us from the enemy. In 2 Corinthians 10:4, Paul said the weapons of our warfare are mighty for pulling down the strongholds and what exalts itself against the knowledge of God. Satan would love to get us to feel guilty and condemned about our sins. He would love to convince us that God can't forgive us. He would love to isolate us from God's grace and keep us from thinking He can use us. In other words, if he can get us to look to ourselves rather than to God, he's got you. Confession pulls down that stronghold. It keeps Satan from being able to entrap us with our sins.

> So when He had washed their feet, taken His garments, and sat down again, He said to them, "Do you know what I have done to you? You call Me Teacher and Lord, and you say well, for so I am. If I then, your Lord and Teacher, have washed your feet, you also ought to wash one another's feet. For I have given you an example, that you should do as I have done to you. Most assuredly, I say to you, a servant is not greater than his master; nor is he who is sent greater than he who sent him."
>
> —John 13:12–16

Jesus contrasted the lowly task He had performed with the high titles His disciples called Him. The word *master* means "teacher"—one in whom you would trust and believe. The word *Lord* or *Kurios* speaks of absolute authority. "I am indeed what you call Me," Jesus said. "It is in that position of authority that I have humbled Myself to wash your feet. And I want you to follow My example." On the heels of the disciples' argument about being the greatest, Jesus said, "If you want to be great, you ought to have been washing feet. No task should be too menial, no service too demanding. If I, your Lord, can empty Myself and be a servant, then you must follow My example and serve each other."

In Peter's first letter, he told a young church beleaguered by Nero's persecution to clothe themselves with humility (1 Pet. 5:5). The word he chose for *humility* was one that spoke of a slave who put a knot in his garment and bent down to serve. All of those years later, the picture of Jesus serving and teaching the night before He was crucified was still fresh in Peter's mind and now at the forefront of Peter's sermon.

> "If you know these things, blessed are you if you do them."
>
> —John 13:17

A head full of knowledge gets us nowhere. Joy comes by serving, Jesus said. And on this night when He wanted to teach them so much, He began by giving His disciples a lesson they would never forget as, with clean feet, they sat down to eat.

"I do not speak concerning all of you. I know whom I have chosen; but that the Scripture may be fulfilled, 'He who eats bread with Me has lifted up his heel against Me.'"

—John 13:18

It was David in Psalm 41:9 who said, "He who eats bread with me has lifted up his heel against me," referring to his trusted friend, Ahithophel, who sided with David's son, Absalom, in an attempt to take the kingdom from David. Here Jesus quoted that Old Testament passage in reference to Judas—one who, for over three years, had witnessed every miracle and listened to every sermon, and had seen God's mercy and grace poured out through His Son. Ahithophel was the grandfather of Bathsheba, the woman whose husband David ordered killed so he could make her his wife. Therefore, Ahithophel must have felt he had just cause to betray David. Judas, on the other hand, had not a single reason to betray Jesus.

In Jesus there was no sin, no betrayal, no unfaithfulness, and no ill word spoken. Jesus never had let down Judas and never had given him wrong information. Jesus always had been perfect in every way. But Judas was sure he knew better than God what needed to be done. Around the Last Supper table sat eleven other men with very misconceived ideas of what the Messiah should do. Yet every one of them made it just fine. They learned. They grew. And God blessed them, helped them, and used them mightily. But Judas had a different agenda. He wasn't a child of God—which ought to give us ample warning that simply hanging around church isn't sufficient. Each of us needs a personal relationship with God.

"Now I tell you before it comes, that when it does come to pass, you may believe that I am He."

—John 13:19

After telling His disciples there was a betrayer in their midst, Jesus said, "I'm telling you this so when Judas does what he will do, you'll know I didn't get caught off guard, but rather that I was in charge, and in complete control"—which would be wonderful comfort for them in the days ahead as they, too, faced great difficulty.

"Most assuredly, I say to you, he who receives whomever I send receives Me; and he who receives Me receives Him who sent Me."

—John 13:20

To soften the blow, Jesus told His disciples that although one would defect, they could expect to see others who would believe. In this, Judas became a good example of how ministry works: some people listen and follow while others only pretend and eventually disappear.

I think of all of the difficulties in ministry, the hardest one is to see people you think are saved walk away from God. I would think that after three years this group of eleven would have been amazed to see Judas walk away from Jesus.

> When Jesus had said these things, He was troubled in spirit, and testified and said, "Most assuredly, I say to you, one of you will betray Me."
> —John 13:21

Notice that Jesus was troubled in spirit before He told His disciples one of them would betray Him. I don't find Jesus a stoic in the Scriptures. He didn't have a stiff upper lip where nothing seemed to bother Him. He traveled a road of suffering rejection and did so knowing better than anyone else the consequences of the rejection He faced. So when He knew Judas was about to head out the door to have that meeting, collect the dough, and betray Him, it broke His heart. Jesus was a "Man of sorrows, acquainted with grief." And although the time of Judas' defection had come, it caused Jesus a lot of grief to know he was about to take his final steps into eternity. Did Jesus know Judas would turn? Sure He did. Yet the responsibility of the choice Judas made was his alone. And the choice he made broke Jesus' heart.

> Then the disciples looked at one another, perplexed about whom He spoke.
> —John 13:22

Matthew records that the disciples were extremely sorrowful. After hanging around each other for three years, they must have known each other well. Yet no one suspected the betrayer. Not a one. To their credit, each of them was tenderhearted enough to think that maybe it was himself. The fact that no one said, "I bet it's Judas" shows that Jesus never singled out Judas. Instead, He loved him just as He loved the other eleven.

> Now there was leaning on Jesus' bosom one of His disciples, whom Jesus loved.
> —John 13:23

When you read John's gospel you notice John always refers to himself as the one Jesus loved. That's a great way to see yourself, isn't it? John was a fighter. He was called the "son of thunder." His only question early on was, "Shall we take them out?" But eventually, it was this son of thunder who was most enthralled with the love God had for him. If you ever have a problem with your self-esteem, just go back and read about how much God loves you and you'll feel just fine! At this U-shaped table, everyone reclined on his left arm on a pillow, leaving his right hand free for eating. Sitting next to Jesus' was John, who could lean back into Jesus' chest. To Jesus' right, in the place of honor, was Judas.

> Simon Peter therefore motioned to him to ask who it was of whom He spoke. Then, leaning back on Jesus' breast, he said to Him, "Lord, who is it?" Jesus answered, "It is he to whom I shall give a piece of bread when I have dipped it." And having dipped the bread, He gave it to Judas Iscariot, the son of Simon.
>
> —John 13:24–26

John asked Jesus bluntly but apparently very quietly of whom He spoke. Jesus' answer must have been very quiet as well because we read in verse 28 that no one really knew what was going on. Offering Judas this morsel dipped in the spices was like giving a toast. His action said, "Are you with Me?" And to take it would say, "I am." So the disciples out of earshot must have thought that Judas, being the honored guest at the table, certainly could not have been the betrayer. But Judas' last chance, with eternity swinging in the balance, found him with his heart far away.

> Now after the piece of bread, Satan entered him. Then Jesus said to him, "What you do, do quickly." But no one at the table knew for what reason He said this to him. For some thought, because Judas had the money box, that Jesus had said to him, "Buy those things we need for the feast," or that he should give something to the poor. Having received the piece of bread, he then went out immediately. And it was night.
>
> —John 13:27–30

God marked the exact moment Judas crossed the final frontier, when his doom was sealed with no return. As Jesus looked deep into Judas' eyes, it was as if he spoke to the Devil himself when He said, "Get it done now." So Judas left the Light of the World to do his deeds in the dark of the night, making a name for himself that no one ever would use again either in this life or the next.

> So, when he had gone out, Jesus said, "Now the Son of Man is glorified, and God is glorified in Him. If God is glorified in Him, God will also glorify Him in Himself, and glorify Him immediately."
>
> —John 13:31–32

After Jesus sent out Judas, events began to move quickly toward the cross. But as Jesus thought about the cross, He didn't think about tragedy, defeat, martyrdom, or disgrace. All He could see was the glory that would come from it. For although the road was dark, the home stretch was at hand. And although the road was steep, with a cross standing at the top, all Jesus could think about was the glory that would come from it: people would be redeemed. Hebrews tells us it was for the joy set before Him that Jesus endured the cross. "Ah, I've been looking forward to this"—knowing His Father would be glorified and Satan would be put out of business.

"Little children, I shall be with you a little while longer. You will seek Me; and as I said to the Jews, 'Where I am going, you cannot come,' so now I say to you. A new commandment I give to you, that you love one another; as I have loved you, that you also love one another. By this all will know that you are My disciples, if you have love for one another."

—John 13:33–35

Knowing His disciples were in for some tough times, Jesus called them "little children." It is the first time we see this term—one of great parental love—used in the Gospels. One of the things Jesus' death accomplished was a change in relationship to the Father. No longer only friends of God, believers were adopted into His family.

"I'm not going to be around, but My love will dwell in you. And as the world sees that love, they will know that you belong to Me," Jesus said to His disciples. The ultimate sign of God's presence is love—the kind of love religion can't produce and people can't imitate for long; the kind of love Jesus had and has for us.

How does Jesus love us? Over and over again, the ultimate demonstration of His love sees Him going to the cross for those who hated Him, forgiving our sins and giving us life. And that's the kind of love the disciples were to have for one another. But that took some doing—for in this group of eleven guys sat Simon the zealot, who led the march against taxation, and Matthew, who collected taxes. In this group sat Simon, the daring guy who would jump out a window before asking how many stories up he was, and Thomas, who had to have proof at every turn. In Acts we read that the disciples were all of one accord. But that wouldn't be possible until the Holy Spirit moved into each heart through the new birth and brought in them the love of God!

Simon Peter said to Him, "Lord, where are You going?"

—John 13:36

From the book of Leviticus 19:18 on, people were commanded to love one another as they loved themselves. In verses 34 and 35, Jesus gave a radically new commandment: that we are to love each other as He loves us. Yet apparently Peter and the disciples heard only verse 33, where the Lord said He would be going to a place they couldn't come. "Where?" asks Peter.

Jesus answered him, "Where I am going you cannot follow Me now, but you shall follow Me afterward." Peter said to Him, "Lord, why can I not follow You now? I will lay down my life for Your sake." Jesus answered him, "Will you lay down your life for My sake? Most assuredly, I say to you, the rooster shall not crow till you have denied Me three times."

—John 13:36–38

"If it's a matter of fighting against those who are coming to get You, You can count on me," Peter said. And the fact that He later drew a sword against a thousand Roman soldiers indicates to me he believed what he said. But Jesus, who knew Peter better than Peter knew himself, was certain what Peter was all about. Therefore, unlike Judas, Peter was not asked to leave the room. And unlike Judas, we find Peter in John 18 and 21 being restored.

So we see these two very interesting men: Judas, who had fooled people for three years but couldn't fool God, and Peter, who although he was pretty sure he was a little stronger and more faithful than the rest, was still in a place where God would use him greatly.

Chapter 115

THE LAST PASSOVER

Luke 22:14–23

The first Passover took place in Egypt, where God's people had been enslaved by one pharaoh after another for over four hundred years. After Pharaoh's refusal to let His people go, God unleashed ten plagues upon the nation, the last one being the death of the firstborn of every home. To spare His people, God directed them to put the blood of a lamb on the sides and tops of their doors so when the death angel came, he would pass over them. The people were to eat their last meal with their shoes on and belts buckled, ready to move. And as the families gathered that night, with screams ringing out from the homes of the Egyptians whose firstborn had been taken, God led His people into the wilderness and toward the Promised Land.

Now, 1400 years later, Jesus met with His disciples to observe the Passover with them:

> When the hour had come, He sat down and the twelve apostles with Him. Then He said to them, "With fervent desire I have desired to eat this Passover with you before I suffer . . . ."
>
> —Luke 22:14–15

In Hebrews 12:2 we are told that it was for the joy set before Him that Jesus endured the cross. What joy could there have been in the cross? The scourging, the crown of thorns, the spitting and rejection? Of course not. The suffering, the pain, the separation from the Father? No way. What came from the cross? You did. And because of you, Jesus endured. Because of you, He fervently desired to eat this last Passover meal. Jesus had sat through thirty Passover meals before this one. And at each, there had been the promise of the One to come—except for this year. This year was the one that would bring salvation to all people and open the doors of heaven. This was the Passover that would end all Passovers. The next year, they wouldn't need one. The type would by then have been fulfilled.

> ". . . For I say to you, I will no longer eat of it until it is fulfilled in the kingdom of God."
>
> —Luke 22:16

The next time we will see Jesus eating with the saints is at the Marriage Supper of the Lamb during His millennial reign after He returns to set up His kingdom. But until then the Communion He established from this Passover meal sustains the church as it looks back to the Cross and forward to His return.

> Then He took the cup, and gave thanks, and said, "Take this and divide it among yourselves; for I say to you, I will not drink of the fruit of the vine until the kingdom of God comes."
>
> —Luke 22:17–18

The Passover meal had four different cups of wine used at various times throughout the service, signifying the verses in Exodus 6:1–8 where the Lord declared He would rescue His people from bondage, redeem them with an outstretched arm, take them as His people, and be their God. In this, the cups spoke of what God would do for people who could not do for themselves.

As Jesus passed one of these cups to His disciples, He said, "I'm not going to drink this anymore until the kingdom of God is established." If we read ahead in the Gospel accounts, we know the next time Jesus tastes wine is immediately before He dismisses His spirit when the soldiers offer Him wine on a sponge at the end of a spear as He hangs on the cross. At that point, the kingdom of God had indeed come. The door was open to all who would believe.

> And He took bread, gave thanks and broke it, and gave it to them, saying, "This is My body which is given for you; do this in remembrance of Me." Likewise He also took the cup after supper, saying, "This cup is the new covenant in My blood, which is shed for you."
>
> —Luke 22:19–20

Up until this moment, it was the eating of the Passover lamb that identified those who were alive because of the blood shed. From this point on, Jesus wanted His disciples to identify Him with the Passover lamb, to see that He was the deliverer God had sent.

After supper, Jesus took the cup, which spoke of redemption, and said, "This is My blood." Don't miss the association. It's a new covenant.

The old covenant depended on people's obedience. But even as the writer to the Hebrews pointed out, although the people told Moses they would do whatever God wanted, it only took only a short time thereafter before they turned to the worship of idols. The Law never could change people's hearts. The sacrifices could cover sins as it looked ahead to the One who would someday come to cleanse sin completely. In this celebration of the Passover, Jesus said, "This is the blood of the new covenant. From now on, people's lives will not depend on their faithfulness, but upon God's."

Passover looked forward to the cross. Communion looks back to it. If you were raised Catholic, as I was, you probably were taught that at some point in the Mass, the bread and wine actually become Christ's body and blood. But in John 6:63 Jesus, having spoken of eating His body and drinking His blood, declared, "The flesh doesn't profit you anything. The words I speak are spirit and life." Any truth in the Bible taught metaphorically can't be turned into a physical reality because it removes the metaphor. The Passover meal was spiritually significant. It spoke of the bondage from which God's people were delivered and of the redemption God would bring. The bitter herbs spoke of the harshness and suffering God's people would endure in the wilderness. But none of it was intended to be material or literal. Neither can the elements of communion be made such. But what they represent is the sacrifice of our Savior, His life for ours, poured out!

God can bring us out of Egypt, through the wilderness, and away from the bondage of sin into a Spirit-filled life. But we have to remember where our lives started, because we didn't save ourselves. Jesus came to redeem us by His broken body and shed blood.

> "But behold, the hand of My betrayer is with Me on the table. And truly the Son of Man goes as it has been determined, but woe to that man by whom He is betrayed!" Then they began to question among themselves, which of them it was who would do this thing.
>
> —Luke 22:21–23

If Luke is accurate in his chronology, then Judas had Communion with the disciples. If John is correct, Judas was dismissed prior to this portion of the Passover meal. How can we know who's right? We can't. My personal conviction is that Luke's timeline is more topical because in verses 24 through 27 he talked about an argument over greatness that broke out at the table. John's timeline, on the other hand, is more sequential because his intent was to show God's sovereignty over people's affairs.

Verse 22, however, says something indisputable. That is, it was Jesus who determined how these events should play out. I love the balance the Bible teaches between God's sovereignty and people's responsibility. So often one is taught at the expense of the other. Certainly, God is the One who has to move toward us if we're dead in sin and lost in darkness. But because He has moved toward us, it is our responsibility to choose, when given the Light, to see.

Chapter 116

WHO IS THE GREATEST?

Luke 22:24–27

O n this night before Jesus was arrested and eventually murdered following a series of illegal trials—and before He would make the ultimate sacrifice for our sins—the disciples were gathered around a table, arguing about greatness in hushed tones. If you thought the disciples discussed deep theological issues or how to apply Old Testament prophecy as they sat around at night, you'd be wrong. It was:

"I'm better than you are."

"No, you're not."

"Yes, I am."

In fact, throughout the Gospels every argument about greatness followed on the heels of Jesus having told them, "I'm going to suffer and die."

In Luke 9:44 Jesus said, "I want these words to sink into your ears: the Son of Man is about to be betrayed into the hands of men." Two verses later, we read of a dispute among the disciples over who would be the greatest. In Matthew 20:18–19, on the way to Jerusalem, Jesus said, "The Son of Man will be betrayed into the hands of the chief priests and scribes. They will deliver Him into the hands of Gentiles who will mock, scourge, and crucify Him. And on the third day, He will rise again." In the very next verse, we read of the mother of the sons of Zebedee asking Jesus if her boys could sit on His right and left when He took over. In Mark 9:31, on the way to Capernaum, Jesus said, "The Son of Man is about to be betrayed into the hands of men. They're going to kill Him. But He will rise on the third day." When Jesus later asked His disciples what they were discussing on the road, Mark tells us they kept silent because as they were walking they were arguing about who should be the greatest (Mark 9:33–34).

In every place you find Jesus talking about dying, you find the disciples talking about living the high life. And because they had, up to this time, missed the cross and Jesus' heart as a servant, they found themselves at the Last Supper doing what most folks in the world do: struggling for greatness, power, and control.

Two hours from this point, Jesus was on His face in the Garden of Gethsemane, sweating great drops of blood as He faced the inevitable for our sins. And there were eleven guys—at least three we know of—sleeping like babies and dreaming about their glory days to come, so detached from servanthood and yet so locked into the world's ways. So we amazingly read here:

> Now there was also a dispute among them, as to which of them should be considered the greatest. And He said to them, "The kings of the Gentiles exercise lordship over them, and those who exercise authority over them are called 'benefactors.'"
>
> —Luke 22:24–25

Jesus made a comparison between His kingdom and the kingdom of the world and how greatness is measured: "In the Gentile world—the unbelieving world—greatness is displayed through authority." That is the way the world measures greatness. It gives titles to people to identify their positions. It honors those who have many under them. It notes staff size or income level. It uses power and might as yardsticks to measure greatness. It is all about the impression we make among people—and has nothing to do with God.

Jesus could have come into the world using worldly standards of greatness. If you were planning the introduction of Jesus to the world, you probably would not have chosen some out of the way place like Bethlehem, and you certainly wouldn't have put Him in a feeding trough in a barn. You would have called the newspapers and television stations. You would have run bulletins and made announcements. And by the time Jesus came, the whole world would have been waiting because that's the way we do P.R. But that's not God's way.

Although Jesus could have demanded respect, by the time He was in His third year of ministry most people had abandoned Him. And when He died, there were only 120 people waiting in an upper room for word they thought would be all bad. There weren't millions. There weren't tens of thousands. I would think that if you raised the dead, healed the sick, and opened the eyes of the blind, there would be more than 120 waiting for you at home. But not Jesus. The world loves honor. But God's not interested. That's not the way it works in His kingdom. It's only the way it works in the world.

I think if Jesus had wanted to put an end to the disciples' arguments about greatness, He could have said, "The next time any of you bring up the subject of greatness, you're dead." And by the time there were five apostles left, there would have been no more discussion about it. But He didn't do it that way. Jesus doesn't demand allegiance. He calls us to faith.

> "But not so among you; on the contrary, he who is greatest among you, let him be as the younger, and he who governs as he who serves. For who is greater, he who sits at the table, or he who serves? Is it not he who sits at the table? Yet I am among you as the One who serves."
>
> —Luke 22:26–27

In Hebrew culture, the oldest child didn't have to share his inheritance with his younger brothers and sisters. That was his legal right. The younger could depend on his father's love to care for him, but he didn't have a legal leg to stand on. But in God's kingdom, the greatest will be the younger, the servant, the slave, the child. In other words, in His kingdom, things are absolutely backwards from the world and its ways.

It is in fact so contrary that it requires constant training. It did for the disciples, and I suspect it does for us. We love being masters, and yet the Lord says if you want to be great, be a slave. Humble yourself as a servant. Jesus wants to give us His image and then put us out in the world so the world sees the difference. The world operates on glory and power, on position and influence. The church, on the other hand, operates from the point of servanthood, following our Lord who became a servant to all. The church that truly follows the Lord doesn't have to tell people about their changed lives. People will see it for themselves, because it is so different from what they know.

In Philippians 2:5, Paul wrote, "Let this mind be in you that was also in Christ Jesus." Let this motive, intent, and nature characterize our lives: Jesus was God, yet He made Himself of no reputation, emptied Himself of all of His status, set aside all of the image and power and honor the world would say He could use to get something done, and became a slave.

A lot of politicians and movie stars spend lots of money on image consultants because perception is a big deal. Nobody drives a Rolls Royce for transportation. People buy them to make a statement of who they are in the world. Jesus did just the opposite. He made Himself of no reputation. He emptied Himself and became obedient, even to death on the cross. Then He told us to follow Him.

How much have you died to you? How much time are you taking to make sure others are blessed? How much are you serving? If you're willing to be God's servant, He's more than willing to use you as such.

Chapter 117

THE KINGDOM NOW AND THEN

Luke 22:28–30

On the heels of their argument about greatness, Jesus overlooked His disciples' weakness to say to them with great love, "You have a future and a hope because you're sticking it out with Me." The disciples had stayed with Jesus over the last three and a half years while everyone else had packed up and left. As far back as John 6, as Jesus began to talk about commitment and involvement, we read, "After that day, many left and walked with Him no more."

"Are you leaving also?" Jesus had asked His disciples.

"Where would we go?" Peter had answered. "We know You have the words of eternal life. We've come to believe that You are the Christ, the Son of the living God."

It was that conviction in their hearts that kept them close. They understood little, had lots to learn, and were as immature as could be—yet they hadn't gone anywhere. And when everyone else had packed up, they still were determined to walk with Jesus. They loved Jesus They stayed put. They were faithful to Him.

I love Jesus' heart because at a time when He was facing the greatest difficulty He would ever know, He told His disciples that even their smallest display of loyalty would one day be greatly rewarded. And even though within hours the disciples would run for their lives to save their own necks, He knew their hearts—just as He knows ours.

> "But you are those who have continued with Me in My trials."
>
> —Luke 22:28

The word *trial* is the typical Greek word for *trial*—one that is impossible to define apart from the context. It can speak of the Devil's allurements to your flesh to get you to do something God would hate, or that would cause you to stumble and fall. But it is also the same word used to test something for its genuineness. The Lord often will test our faith to prove how genuine it is. He does this to show us how far along we've come. He puts us in situations to help us apply what we've learned. But He never tempts us to do evil. Only the Devil does that.

Following Jesus' temptation in the wilderness, Luke wrote that the Devil departed for a while—but only until he could find another opportunity to attack. The temptations were horrendous and they worked themselves out in persecution, bitterness, attacks, lying in wait, and attempts on His life. The disciples had stuck with it for three and a half years, during which time they had learned that to follow Jesus' footsteps did not mean things would go easily or smoothly. Yet they had stayed with Him. They hadn't turned away.

Up to this point, Jesus was able to deflect any flak that came the disciples' way. For them it was kind of like hanging out with your dad. If anyone was going to mess with you, you'd just say, "Dad," and that would be the end of it.

The religious leaders came to the disciples to question them about eating on the Sabbath. But before they could say a word, Jesus stepped up and said, "Do you have a problem?"

"Yeah, they're eating on the Sabbath."

"Well, it's you guys who aren't following the Word of God by following your traditions," Jesus said (Matt. 15).

Jesus was the One the disciples could hide behind, make faces, and then hide again. But now He was leaving. Now they would have to stand on their own. For them, God's work was just beginning because the Lord was about to leave them. He would send His Spirit to help them, but they would have to finish the race. They would have to pay a price. They would learn what true greatness was all about.

> "And I bestow upon you a kingdom, just as My Father bestowed one upon Me, that you may eat and drink at My table in My kingdom, and sit on thrones judging the twelve tribes of Israel."
>
> —Luke 22:29–30

In this life, as the church, we're going to stand where Jesus stood and in many ways receive the same kind of rejection He did, which is why He said to His disciples, "I'm going to bestow upon you a kingdom." The word *bestow* is a legal term that means, "I'm going to appoint you to be in charge of these things." And so they were. "Here, you take the ball and run with it," Jesus said. "Bring the Gospel. Preach the good news. Tell folks about Me."

When Paul went door-to-door and church-to-church in Acts 14:22, he strengthened the souls of all the disciples, exhorting them that they should continue in the faith and saying to them, "Through much tribulation, you must enter into the kingdom of God. You're going to get in, but it won't be an easy road." One day, we will rule and reign and have fellowship with Jesus forever. But in this life, in the meantime, we have to stand fast, gain victory over temptation, pass the test of our faith with flying colors, and proclaim that God's kingdom is at hand.

In Deuteronomy 8:2, when Moses was speaking to the people about their past, he said, "You remember how the Lord led you these forty years through the wilderness to humble you and test you so you might know what was in your heart." God knew what was in their hearts, but they needed to see it more clearly. We can be easy on ourselves. We talk a lot about faith—but until we're put in the place where we have to make a choice, we really don't know how strong it is.

God called Abraham away from family and friends, security and hope, to go to a place he had never been. He shared his faith with his wife and convinced his children of God's hope and promises. And although he died not having received the promise, he saw it far off and embraced it.

Moses was forty years old when, according to Hebrews 11:23–26, he looked around Pharaoh's palace at all the prosperity and security that was his, and seeing the Jews making bricks out of mud and spit, he said, "I've got to go down there." And although from the outside it appeared he was getting a raw deal by becoming a slave, in reality he saw God's long-term promises and said he would rather suffer reproach with God's people than have the pleasures of sin for a little while. He applied the faith he had in the God of eternity to the circumstances of the present. He valued the things of God far more than himself, his benefit, or what he might have to forfeit in the process. He compared the best the world had to offer with the worst he might face as a believer, and he made the right choice.

How do we live our lives as Christians? Most people approach Christianity in terms of what God can do for them. Yet while there's plenty to get, if God's going to use us it's going to be because we're willing to die to ourselves and to go out in the world and be His representatives. What will come your way? The same things Jesus faced. It won't be any easier for you than it was for Him. You might wish it were. You might avoid it by saying nothing and doing nothing. But if you're going to live a godly life, persecution awaits.

On the eve of Jesus' death, although greatness waited for the disciples, it meant death for them. It meant putting Jesus first and denying themselves. It meant sharing in His suffering and triumphing over difficulty. It's not easy as a Christian to live in this world. Everything around us is at odds with our Lord. It's an uphill climb, an upstream swim. The tide isn't with us. Neither is the current. But if, like Abraham, you realize you're passing through, or if, like Moses, you're willing to grab hold of the fact that what is coming is far more valuable than what you're holding on to now, you're liable to be willing to pay the price and find true greatness.

It won't always be easy to see the value in it—especially when you're on the suffering end—but the cost compared to the glory is far more than worth the wait.

Chapter 118

JESUS PRAYING FOR US

Luke 22:31–34
(Matthew 26:31–35; Mark 14:27–31; John 13:36–38)

In this section before us we are given some great insights into how God prepares to use us, how the Devil works to oppose us, and what the Lord does about it—lessons that will serve us well as we walk with Him and seek to serve Him, especially in these last days.

> And the Lord said, "Simon, Simon! Indeed, Satan has asked for you, that he may sift you as wheat. But I have prayed for you, that your faith should not fail; and when you have returned to Me, strengthen your brethren." But he said to Him, "Lord, I am ready to go with You, both to prison and to death." Then He said, "I tell you, Peter, the rooster shall not crow this day before you will deny three times that you know Me."
>
> —Luke 22:31–34

Although all four of the Gospels record Peter's denial of Jesus in the garden outside the high priest's house, only Luke gives us this additional information about Satan's involvement, Jesus' awareness of what Peter was facing, and the intercession He promised Peter before it ever took place. Since there aren't any indications in any of the Gospels as to what prompted this discussion, it's safe to assume that the argument about greatness that had begun in verse 24 had continued. Peter had made some bold claims that basically put the other guys on the defensive when he so much as said, "I don't know about these guys, but I'll be faithful."

In whatever context these words of Jesus were presented, it is no surprise that Peter, being the most vocal, would be the one who would now hear from Him.

We know that the Devil's greatest plan for the world is to hide the truth of God's love from us. In fact, when Paul wrote to the Corinthians, he said, "If the Gospel we have is hidden, it is hidden from those who are perishing, in whom the god of this world has blinded their minds lest, seeing the light of the Gospel, it would shine upon them and they would believe" (2 Cor. 4:3–4). The Devil's desire is to keep people from salvation. He doesn't want us to know that Jesus died for us and that without Him we're not going to make it to heaven. He doesn't want us considering putting our faith in Him. He wants to keep us from the only door that leads to life.

But when we get saved, the Devil's tactics change because he effectively has lost us to the Lord. His desire then turns to keeping us from finding the Lord's joy and from being used by Him. That's what he tried to do to Peter. Put him on the shelf.

Notice that Jesus had to use Peter's name twice. He used his old name because this is the old guy. This wasn't the Peter who would build his life on the rock. This was Simon, the one who thought he knew everything. When the Lord says things twice, it's usually for emphasis. In fact, throughout the Bible, the Lord repeats men's names five times more often than He does women's. (I believe I initially heard this statistic from my wife!) This might tell you how sensitive women are to the Lord's voice and how men are much more like Peter. If Peter was in the midst of an argument with the disciples, he probably hadn't heard his name spoken by Jesus the first time.

Then Jesus said, "Indeed"—or "pay attention, check this out, listen carefully"—"Satan has asked for you." That's pretty chilling news, isn't it? From what Peter says in verse 33, he absolutely was unaware of the battle that was going on for his soul. He was filled with Peter. Looking down his nose at the rest of the guys, he essentially was saying, "No, no, Lord. You've got me all wrong." But we had better be careful when we tell the Lord He's wrong.

We should be aware of the battle and the wicked desire of the enemy, whose hopes and plans are to destroy us. If you know you have an enemy who is seeking to keep you from the things of God, you'll find yourself more willing to trust God than to complain about your circumstances and more willing to hang onto Him than to be moved by what's going on around you.

The book of Job, like many of the poetic, or wisdom, books of the Old Testament, deals with the big issues of God's goodness, God's ways, the place of tragedy, and the purpose of life. In them, we find that God never does anything without bringing us to the place where we can be believers who find His strength even in the worst of times. As a result of God's permission, Job's children are killed. He loses much of his wealth. And he is covered with boils from head to foot. Yet we read that Job never sinned or charged God foolishly.

Like Job, Peter was about to have a run-in with Satan. Thirty minutes earlier, Jesus had said, "Peter, you're not what you think you are." But Peter wasn't learning the lesson very quickly. He would learn it the hard way—but he would learn it nonetheless. Peter needed to learn that his strength was not in himself. His strength was in the Lord. That's a hard lesson to learn. It would be good if we could just read it in a book and then do it. But like Peter, we're pretty slow, and it often takes a more persuasive experience to convince us of that.

Something very apparent in Greek but not in English is that the word *you* in verse 31 is plural. This means Jesus said, "Simon, Satan has asked for you all." When Peter said he was willing to die for Jesus, the other disciples said the same thing (Matt. 26:35). Satan was not only Peter's enemy, but every disciple's enemy. Yet when we get to verse 32, the word *you* is singular because Jesus' prayer is specific. We're all the focus of Satan's hatred, but we are each the focus of God's personal intercession through His Son.

Jesus knew what Peter was about to face in the next few hours and the defeat that would make him bitter and disappointed with himself. Peter thought he was very loyal. To find out otherwise would be horrible. So Jesus warned him and yet assured him that he ultimately would be all right.

I think we do ourselves a great disservice if we picture the Lord angry every time we fail. If nothing else, know from this lesson that God is never surprised when we don't come through. He doesn't once say, "I thought this time he was going to make it." He knows we're not going to make it! He knows us better than we know ourselves. So because He's our Savior, He stands in the gap between us and the Father to bring us through it and learn from it, so He might use us to reach others who need to know Him.

Notice in verse 31 that not only was Peter called by his old name, and told that Satan wanted him, but he was also told the purpose—that Satan wanted to sift him like wheat. Sifting wheat is productive work. If you beat wheat, the husks fall off and are blown away, leaving the grain to eat. However, when it comes to Satan, he's not looking for fruit. He's just looking for the beating part. He wants to beat your head against the rocks. He wants to destroy your life. Jesus wanted Peter to know He had prayed for him.

If you stop and think about God in heaven, seated on the throne, and Jesus the Savior, the Lord of all, interceding on your behalf, it ought to take a lot of pressure off you. People say, "My life is so difficult. Everything is against me." But wait a minute. Jesus is praying for you. And I think if anyone will have His prayers answered, it's Jesus!

Jesus doesn't pray that Peter be delivered from the trouble coming around the corner. He just wants him to come out better, stronger, and more available to serve. "I'm praying that your faith doesn't fail," He said. Jesus didn't see Peter's denial as a cancellation of his faith but simply as a lapse. Peter didn't forsake his faith. He just needed to learn he was weak. Once he learned that lesson, he would be very useful to the Lord.

One of our greatest areas of stumbling is self-confidence. We always seem to fall in our strengths.

Abraham was known as the father of those who have faith. Yet if we go back and read about his life, we see the places he fell were a demonstration of a lack of faith.

The Lord said, "Leave your home and follow Me."

Abraham said, "I'm bringing my dad."

The Lord said "Leave your family."

Abraham said, "I'm bringing my nephew."

When he arrived in the Promised Land, a famine arose and he departed to Egypt, telling the Pharaoh his wife was his sister in order to save his own skin.

Moses was the meekest man who ever lived, which means he was able to leave his anger with God and let God work out his problems. Every time Moses failed, however, it was in the area of meekness. He killed an Egyptian rather than trust the Lord. He got mad at the people and beat the rock in the wilderness rather than leave his anger with God and simply speak to the rock as God had commanded.

Peter was loyal—a guy you would love to have as a friend. But he failed when it came to standing firm under pressure, because his confidence was not in the Lord but rather in himself. But that all changed. If you want God to use you, learn from Peter that He only can do so once you die to yourself. Peter had great intentions and an emotional commitment that was as honest as the day is long. He just had to learn that God's strength would keep him, but that his own would fail him.

We can be spared a lot of disappointment simply by trusting God rather than ourselves. We have to learn to live between John 15:5, where Jesus says, "Without Me you can do nothing" and Philippians 4:13, where Paul says, "I can do all things through Christ." The balance between those two verses is where your life is. I can't do it without Him so I shouldn't even try. On the other hand, I shouldn't limit God simply because I'm weak because, with Him, I can do anything. And if He's in it, I want to be in it.

I know I'm ready to be used by the Lord when I realize His Word is better than mine, His ability is stronger than mine, His insights are clearer than mine, and His will is right and mine is not. If I can appropriate that truth, I'll be dead to self and very much alive to the things of God. And like Peter, I can go out and strengthen the brethren because I will have something to give them: hope in the Lord I serve.

Chapter 119

FROM CARRIED TO WALKING

Luke 22:35–38

For three and a half years the disciples had been cared for completely. What they ate, where they went, and where they stayed was all up to Jesus. But now with the cross only hours away, they needed to learn to be responsible in a way they hadn't yet known.

> And He said to them, "When I sent you without money bag, knapsack, and sandals, did you lack anything?" So they said, "Nothing."
>
> —Luke 22:35

Back in Luke 9, right before Jesus left the northern part of the country to go toward Jerusalem, He put His twelve disciples in groups of two and gave them authority to cure all diseases and deliver people from demons. "I want you to go and preach that the kingdom of God is here," He said. "Don't take anything with you. Don't take money, a staff, an extra pair of shoes, bread, or an extra jacket. Just go." In Luke 10, Jesus put seventy others in groups of two and gave them basically the same instructions.

The first time Jesus sent out both the disciples and apostles with His power, they went without any kind of natural resource beyond what God said He would provide. They went out to learn to walk by faith—which always has to be the first lesson we learn as a Christian.

> Then He said to them, "But now, he who has a money bag, let him take it, and likewise a knapsack; and he who has no sword, let him sell his garment and buy one. For I say to you that this which is written must still be accomplished in Me: 'And He was numbered with the transgressors.' For the things concerning Me have an end." So they said, "Lord, look, here are two swords." And He said to them, "It is enough."
>
> —Luke 22:36–38

If walking by faith is the first lesson we have to learn, adding common-sense responsibility to our faith is the second. Isaiah 40:11 says like a shepherd, the Lord carries His young. But to minister to others in His name, there comes a time when we have to walk. And it isn't such an easy thing to do. When I was first saved, it seemed everything I prayed for came to pass in about eight minutes. But somewhere along the line, the feelings kind of dwindled. I didn't feel saved all the time. I knew God's Word was right, but somehow the feelings didn't support the conviction. God would make me wait days, weeks, or even longer before He answered. And eventually, I realized the time to walk had come.

If anything of any significance is going to get done, God has to work. But we have to be responsible to do our best and give it our all. And that is so often where the problem begins. People define faith as doing nothing. But that's like being in a boat tied to the dock and saying, "Come on, Lord, direct my path." You won't go anywhere. There is nothing unbiblical about planning and nothing wrong with being responsible.

I think Jesus' suggestion that the disciples ought to buy a sword tells us how tough the times were. The first century was not a time to mill around. The wild animals were not in the zoo and most of the criminals were not in jail. People lived in walled cities for a reason.

While there are some folks who use these verses to teach that the church should be active in its advocacy and take the kingdom by force, the Bible teaches nothing of the sort. In fact, throughout Scripture we see the Lord saying just the opposite—that it's not by might, nor by power, but by His Spirit. When you see the early church facing difficulty, you see them face it through prayer, not fighting.

There is a balance between being responsible and being faithful. The early church was both. Sending out people to plant churches and elders in every city required great planning. Paul's strategy of going to the major cities first so word might get out to the surrounding areas was highly effective. The plans and strategies were carried out with great faith. So the disciples were told that with faith in God should come careful planning and common sense, for faith is not defined by irresponsibility and barring God's specific instructions to take nothing along, making plans as you go.

I don't know what God wants to do with you—but I know it isn't to have you just sit. Do your best—and watch God work.

Chapter 120

On the Road to Gethsemane

John 14:1–31

Having finished the Last Supper, Jesus took a forty-five-minute walk from the Upper Room, out the East Gate, down into the Kidron Valley, over the brook, and then halfway up the western slope of the Mount of Olives to the Garden of Gethsemane. John is the only one of the Gospel writers to record the words Jesus gave His disciples during that walk. I don't know if they understood all He said at this time, but I do know John recorded Jesus' words, and in the days and weeks that followed the disciples certainly would take great comfort in them.

The last few hours had been pretty difficult for the disciples. For the last year, Jesus had been telling them about His death and what was waiting in Jerusalem. In addition, they must have sensed an increase in the tension between Jesus and the religious leaders. Yet they had written all of this off because they believed Jesus was the Messiah and they knew the Messiah had come to reign. Therefore, suffering wasn't part of the equation.

Sometimes, like the disciples, we can be so sure of something that when the Lord speaks to us through His Word we just don't hear it because we've got our minds made up already.

Within the hour, Jesus would be sweating great drops of blood under the pressure of taking the world's sins on His shoulders and the Father's turning away from Him. And yet in His great love for the disciples, He wasn't absorbed with His own conflict but instead was concerned about theirs. He saw their faces. He knew their disillusionment. He needed to get them through these next few days.

Reading Jesus' words in this context, we find great hope in the things He promised them. We can summarize His words as: "You're going to get saved and you're going to know Me for who I am. The Holy Spirit is going to work in you and lead you. You're going to continue the work I started. Then you're going to come and be with Me. And at some point, I'm going to come back for the church and gather it to Myself."

"Let not your heart be troubled . . . ."

—John 14:1

Jesus didn't minimize the disciples' concerns. There were some hard issues they would have to face—like angry religious people out to get them. But it wouldn't be good enough

631

for them not to worry. They had to have a reason not to worry. So Jesus said, "Don't worry. Here's why."

> ". . . you believe in God, believe also in Me."
>
> —John 14:1

Or literally, "you can believe in Me as being God." Unfortunately, the disciples hadn't made that leap yet. They believed Jesus was like Moses—a Man who would deliver them. But peace comes only when Jesus is God in your heart, when you see Him for who He is.

The word Jesus used for *believe* is in the present tense here and throughout this discussion, because what is needed is an ongoing, living dependence on Him as God. That is what we need to preach because people have confidence in many things—their codes, their creeds, and their works. But the only hope for heaven is that Jesus is God, the only One in whom we can trust.

The disciples' expectations required some radical adjustment because they all were hoping for rule and conquest, position and power. During the next few days, these disciples did not walk by faith. They ran in fear. They hid in disillusionment. They were brokenhearted in despair. But a few days later, when Jesus rose and they recognized who He was, with the Holy Spirit poured out on them, their peace returned along with a determination to go out into the world to live—and even die—for Him.

> "In My Father's house are many mansions; if it were not so, I would have told you. I go to prepare a place for you."
>
> —John 14:2

If we had to develop an understanding of heaven based solely on the Old Testament, we wouldn't have much to go on. The New Testament shines much greater light on the place of God's presence where we are headed. It calls heaven a city, a country, a kingdom, and a paradise. There are many insights about heaven in the New Testament—and the longer we live, we come to know of friends and relatives waiting for us there who have gone before. One of the most appealing descriptions of heaven in the New Testament is what Jesus calls it here: the Father's house.

Many folks are so fearful of death and chilled about the thought of dying that they don't want to talk about it. For them, death is scary—a door that is shut, through which no one returns. But that's not the case for believers. We're not going to some unknown place but to our Father's house. The disciples needed to understand that to get there, however, Jesus was going to have to go first and prepare a place for them.

The word *mansion* speaks of a permanent residence. I don't think the Lord is overseeing a crew using two-by-fours to build you a physical house. In fact, the house waiting for you is not made with hands. It's eternal in the heavens. It's a residing place, custom made for you, where you can dwell in a body suitable for heaven's environment.

After being stoned and left for dead outside of Lystra, Paul later wrote of being taken to heaven. "I don't know if I was dead or alive," he said, "but I can't even begin to put into words what I saw. It was so good, I'd come up short no matter what I said. But I tell you this: I'd rather be there than here" (2 Cor. 12:2–4). Having visited and returned, Paul said, "That's the place for me!"

> "And if I go and prepare a place for you, I will come again and receive you to Myself; that where I am, there you may be also. And where I go you know, and the way you know."
>
> —John 14:3–4

"I'm leaving, but don't panic," Jesus said. "Don't be troubled. Don't be worried. I'm going to prepare a place for you. This has to be the way it is because I'm the only way in. But I will return. You can count on it." In the second chapter of the letter to his protégé Titus, Paul called this the blessed hope of the church.

> Thomas said to Him, "Lord, we do not know where You are going, and how can we know the way?"
>
> —John 14:5

To Thomas' credit, he never pretended to have faith he didn't have. So he said to Jesus, "You're wrong on both counts. I don't know where You're going and I don't know how to get there."

> Jesus said to him, "I am the way, the truth, and the life. No one comes to the Father except through Me."
>
> —John 14:6

"I'm the way—singular. I'm the truth—singular. I'm the life—singular," Jesus said to Thomas. There is no multiple choice here. There aren't five ways to go.

I remember seeing a Christian film about a missionary in Africa who had a tough time getting through some of the jungles to the villages. So he hired a local guide, who showed up with a big machete. After they'd gone two or three miles, the missionary realized his guide was cut up everywhere. His arms were cut. His face was cut. His back was scarred. So he asked, "Do you know where we're going?"

"Do I know where we're going?" the guide answered. "Before I got here, there was no way to this village. Now I am the way."

That's what Jesus did. He came, took upon Himself a body that became bruised for us, and then became the way. Want to go to heaven? You've got to go to Jesus, because if you think you can get there any other way, you're on the wrong path. Jesus will have scars in heaven to attest to the price He paid to get us there. We arrive in heaven with His name on our lips and our name in His book.

Outside of London is Hampton Court Palace, which boasts the world's largest maze of hedges. With hedges fifteen feet tall, you go in and five minutes later you don't know where you are. The good news is there are phones everywhere with a guide on the other end to give you directions. But unless you say, "I'm lost," he won't help you. This is a pretty good picture of getting to heaven. If you tell God you're lost, He'll point you to His Son.

Jesus is the full revelation of God's plan for man. It's very narrow—very much like math. Two plus two is four. There are a lot of wrong answers, but only four is right. "Truth is very subjective," people say. No, it's not. Truth is objective. It comes from God. Jesus is the only way, truth, and life. How do you get to the Father? You've got to go through Jesus. You can't get there through hard work, good intentions, charitable deeds, or comparing yourself with people worse than you. You only can get there through Jesus Christ.

> "If you had known Me, you would have known My Father also; and from now on you know Him and have seen Him."
>
> —John 14:7

The Old Testament had lots of names for God. Jehovah means "God of covenants, the Becoming One." It taught us that God keeps His Word. Adonai, or "the sovereign Lord who commands and rules," seems pretty distant, as does Elohim, the "God of all creation." But here in the New Testament, Jesus said, "God can be your Father."

You may have had a horrible father on earth, but that's not true of our Father in heaven. He's all that you would want and more.

> Philip said to Him, "Lord, show us the Father, and it is sufficient for us." Jesus said to him, "Have I been with you so long, and yet you have known Me, Philip? He who has seen Me has seen the Father; so how can you say, 'Show us the Father'? Do you not believe that I am in the Father, and the Father in me? The words that I speak to you I do not speak on My own authority; but the Father who dwells in Me does the works. Believe Me that I am in the Father and the Father in Me, or else believe Me for the sake of the works themselves."
>
> —John 14:8–11

Philip said, "Make the Father visible to our eyes and we'll be satisfied."

In verse 7 and again in verse 9, Jesus said, "You have to look with understanding. You have to see beyond the physical to the spiritual reality of who I am. And once you see who I am, you'll know the Father." Jesus is God in focus, but Philip hadn't yet made that connection.

"Don't you believe that the Father dwells in Me, that I'm speaking His words, that I'm doing His work?" Jesus asked Philip. "If you don't believe the words I speak in His name, then look at the works I'm doing. Men don't open the eyes of the blind, make the lame walk and the dead rise. God alone does! Put it together, Philip. See with understanding."

> "Most assuredly, I say to you, he who believes in Me, the works that I do he will do also; and greater works than these he will do, because I go to My Father. And whatever you ask in My name, that I will do, that the Father may be glorified in the Son. If you ask anything in My name, I will do it. If you love Me, keep My commandments."
>
> —John 14:12–15

Jesus took His disciples from who He is and what His plan is to what He wanted to do with them. "Your belief in Me is now going to put you in the position I was in: the Father working in you. Now it's your turn. I'm going to come and dwell with you. But you're not going to stop at healing the sick. You're going to do a greater work."

What could be greater than healing the sick, raising the dead, and giving sight to the blind? Salvation is greater. No one could be assured of getting into heaven before Jesus died. But within six weeks, Peter would preach a six-minute sermon and three thousand people would be saved—a greater work. Hearts would be changed, lives would be touched, and God's Spirit would move into people's hearts. What's greater than opening the eyes of the blind? Opening the eyes of a blind heart. What's better than raising the dead so they can die again? Seeing the spiritually dead brought to life, never to die.

Verses 13–15 are tied to the narrowness of the verses that precede them so we don't get caught up with those who seek to manipulate them to say God has to answer every prayer we make in faith. That's ridiculous. The words *in Jesus' name* are not a formula. They are a privilege. They are not the exclamation point behind our prayer to get what we want. They are a recognition that we're not asking for ourselves but for Jesus' sake, that He is the One we serve.

Sixty years later in his first epistle, John wrote, "Whatever we ask, we receive from Him because we keep His commandments and do those things that are pleasing in His sight." In verse 16, Jesus told the disciples how that will happen.

> "And I will pray the Father, and He will give you another Helper, that He may abide with you forever—. . . ."
>
> —John 14:16

In the following two and a half chapters of John, we are given so much information about the personality, deity, and work of the Holy Spirit. Up to this point, Jesus had been the Hero, the Champion of every story. If you were low on food, He could make food out of nothing. If there was a storm at sea, He could calm the waves. If a Pharisee snuck up on

Him, He could see through their plans. So how would the disciples survive without Him? They wouldn't need to worry. They wouldn't need to be upset. Their hearts wouldn't need to be troubled because even though He was leaving, Jesus wasn't leaving them alone. The Father would send another Helper, a Comforter to see them all the way through.

People often view the Holy Spirit as a power rather than as a Person. Simon the sorcerer was like that. Seeing people get saved under Philip's preaching and filled with the Spirit through Peter and John's prayers, he said to Peter, "I'll give you good money for that trick."

But Peter put him in his place, saying, "You're offensive to God and in danger of His judgment."

If you think of the Holy Spirit as a power, your only question will be, "How can I get more of the Holy Spirit?" But if the Holy Spirit is God Himself, your only question will be, "How can the Holy Spirit get more of me?" And you'll find yourself submitting to His work.

Jesus made it very clear here what kind of Comforter the Holy Spirit is by using the word *another*, or *allos* in Greek, meaning "another of the same kind." In other words, Jesus said, "I will send you another Helper of the same nature as I, God the Holy Spirit."

Comforter or *parakletos* is a word that means "one who pulls alongside to give support." It's the same word used for Jesus in 1 John 2:1.

Jesus was our first Helper. The disciples certainly had learned to depend on Him. But with His earthly work about to end at the cross, He said, "I'll send you another Comforter, the same kind as Me, who will *meno*, abide, and make His home with you forever." The disciples were not left alone. God continued with them—not in the Person of Jesus but in the Person of the Holy Spirit.

> ". . . the Spirit of truth, whom the world cannot receive, because it neither sees Him nor knows Him; but you know Him, for He dwells with you and will be in you."
>
> —John 14:17

The idea that the Holy Spirit would dwell within men was an absolutely unknown concept because there was no Old Testament basis on which to understand this. Throughout the Old Testament, we see the Holy Spirit coming upon people for a period of time to fight a battle or to give insight into what to do next. But He came and went. That is why David's greatest fear after his sin with Bathsheba was that God would take the Holy Spirit from him (Ps. 51:11). The concept of the new birth and the need to have the Lord dwell in us by His Spirit was unknown to the disciples or anyone else.

> "I will not leave you orphans; I will come to you."
>
> —John 14:18

Jesus wouldn't leave His disciples as sheep without a Shepherd, or as children without a parent, forsaken and unable to care for themselves. Although He would leave them physically, He would be with them spiritually in the Person of the Holy Spirit. In fact, the last thing He said to them when He ascended into heaven in Matthew 28:19–20 was, "Go into all the world. Teach them to observe everything I've commanded and I will be with you always, even to the end of the age."

> "A little while longer and the world will see Me no more, but you will see Me. Because I live, you will live also."
>
> —John 14:19

The last time the world saw Jesus was when He was carried to a tomb. The believers, however, saw Him for six weeks after the resurrection—sometimes by ones, twos, and tens; sometimes by as many as five hundred. They saw Him because they believed in Him—today as well only the saints see God at work, see His hand, see His Word and look forward to His coming again.

> "At that day you will know that I am in My Father, and you in Me, and I in you."
>
> —John 14:20

The Sunday evening of resurrection weekend, Jesus appeared in the Upper Room, startling the disciples. Among other things, He breathed on them and said, "Receive the Holy Spirit." As a result, they began to understand the relationship of this new birth that is so vital. Luke described the experience in 24:45, where he wrote, "And He opened their understanding, that they might comprehend the Scriptures." Remember when you got saved and the Bible made sense? The Gideon Bible you never could understand in the hotel room came alive. The same thing took place in the Upper Room.

> "He who has My commandments and keeps them, it is he who loves Me. And he who loves Me will be loved by My Father, and I will love him and manifest Myself to him."
>
> —John 14:21

Having come to know and believe in Jesus, if you want to know Him more fully, here's how: Obey His Word. If you want to know the Lord more, do what He says. Don't just listen, act on it—because as you do, the Holy Spirit will move you, the Father will love you, and the result will be that Jesus will make Himself known to you.

The word *manifest* means "to clear up what is hidden." Do you want the Lord to work in you more? Do you want Him to use you more? Do you want to have more peace? Obey Him. Do what He's already taught you and asked of you.

> Judas (not Iscariot) said to Him, "Lord, how is it that You will manifest Yourself to us, and not to the world?" Jesus answered and said to Him, "If anyone loves Me, he will keep My word; and My Father will love him, and We will come to him and make Our home with him. He who does not love Me does not keep My words; and the word which you hear is not Mine but the Father's who sent Me."
>
> —John 14:22–24

In light of verse 17, where Jesus said the world wouldn't know Him but the disciples would, Judas said, "How?"

"By the Spirit," Jesus answered. Imagine God, the Creator of the universe, coming to dwell in you. That has great potential, doesn't it?

"I wonder how I can serve the Lord?" we ask.

Well, the God of the universe will move in.

"I know. But I wonder if I can do it."

No, He'll move in.

"But I'm not very strong."

Listen, knucklehead! The Lord Himself is moving into your life!

"We will make our home in your life," Jesus said. And when Jesus says, "Will," you can count on it. It doesn't matter if you're rich or poor, smart or not so bright. If you open your heart, Jesus will move in and begin to work in you.

On the other hand, if men reject His words of life, if they don't want to be born again, and if they are determined to make it on their own, they'll have no relationship with God. Jesus is the Father's only way to life. You can claim all day long that you love God, but you can't meet God without Jesus.

The faithful want to walk with God and seek to do what He says. We don't always succeed, but the Lord knows our hearts. In fact, He inspects hearts far more than labor. If we're going to learn anything, God's going to have to teach us. If anything's going to stick, God's going to have to help us. If we're going to have victory, God's going to have to enable us. Another Helper has come.

> "These things I have spoken to you while being present with you. But the Helper, the Holy Spirit, whom the Father will send in My name, He will teach you all things, and bring to your remembrance all things that I said to you."
>
> —John 14:25–26

"I know a lot of this is over your heads right now," Jesus said, "but I'm telling you now so that when you are reminded of it later, it will make sense." We read in John 2:22 that it was when Jesus had risen from the dead that the disciples remembered what He had said to them and believed the Word He spoke. We read the same thing in John 12. The disciples understood none of these things at first—but when Jesus was glorified, they remembered the things He had done and said and they believed in Him. It required an outpouring of the Spirit for them to put it all together. So we are taught by the indwelling Holy Spirit.

As you read through the Gospels and into the book of Acts, you see that as the Holy Spirit is given to the disciples, they begin to learn extremely quickly. Peter preached his first sermon only fifty days after the resurrection. And if you read his sermon in Acts 2, check out how many Scriptures he pulled from the Old Testament and how he put them together perfectly. This was the guy who had been shooting off his mouth for three and a half years, the guy who, only six weeks earlier, was as confused as could be. It's phenomenal to watch God's Spirit leading and guiding into all truth. We still rely on Him today.

> "Peace I leave with you. My peace I give to you; not as the world gives do I give to you. Let not your heart be troubled, neither let it be afraid. You have heard Me say to you, 'I am going away and coming back to you.' If you loved Me, you would rejoice because I said, 'I am going to the Father,' for My Father is greater than I."
>
> —John 14:27–28

"I have good plans for you," Jesus said. "Don't worry, I'm not going to leave you like orphans. You're not going to be lost. I'm going to send the Spirit from My Father to you. He's going to dwell with you. We're going to come and live in you. If I told you I'm coming back, you ought to be glad I'm getting out of this body because I get to be reunited with My Father, who is greater than I. Yet one day I will return for you!"

> "And now I have told you before it comes, that when it does come to pass, you may believe. I will no longer talk much with you, for the ruler of this world is coming, and he has nothing in Me. But that the world may know that I love the Father, and as the Father gave Me commandment, so I do. Arise, let us go from here."
>
> —John 14:29–31

"You won't see Me much longer face to face," Jesus said. Satan was already at work in Judas, the Sanhedrin, the priests, Herod, and Pilate. But Jesus would defeat the enemy once and for all because Satan had nothing on Him. Satan has plenty on us—and if it weren't for Jesus, that list would destroy us. But in Jesus, that list was destroyed.

The disciples saw Jesus after His resurrection enough to be assured He was alive, but they still had to learn to walk by faith, relying on the work of God's Spirit to lead and guide them. Now it would be a life of faith, no more by sight but by the Spirit's work.

I'm sure looking back that John was thrilled. But that night, walking through the valley in the dark, I'm not sure Jesus' words meant anything to him. The Holy Spirit brought them to his memory later—and because of John's faithfulness in recording them, they mean the world to us today.

Chapter 121

ABIDING IN THE VINE

John 15:1–11

In John 14, Jesus told the disciples what He was going to do for them. In John 15, He told them what they needed to do in response. I believe the first eleven verses of John 15 are the most crucial verses in Scripture for believers because they introduce a concept that, if missed, can cause one's spiritual life to be very frustrating, but if understood brings great rest. It is the issue of abiding and bearing fruit.

The word *fruit* appears six times in these eleven verses. The word *abide* appears ten times. God wants to use our lives. He wants to pour Himself in and through us. He wants our lives to matter, to count, to be fruitful. And so, as they walked toward Gethsemane, Jesus talked to His disciples about abiding and fruit bearing.

> "I am the true vine and My Father is the vinedresser."
>
> —John 15:1

One of the symbols for Israel seen throughout the Old Testament is that of a vine or a vineyard. In Psalm 80:9, the psalmist wrote, "You caused us to take deep root so that we might fill the land." In Jeremiah 2, when the nation wasn't doing very well, speaking for the Lord, Jeremiah 2:21 said, "I've planted you as a noble vine of the highest quality. I don't know what has happened to you that you have turned into a degenerate plant, an alien vine." In Isaiah 5:1–18, we see the same picture.

When the Lord called him by the burning bush to go to Pharaoh and tell him to let His people go, Moses said to the Lord, "Who shall I tell them sent me?"

"Tell them I AM that I AM sent you," the Lord answered (Exod. 3).

Here we find Jesus using that very name for Himself. In fact, John revolves much of His teaching around Jesus' seven "I AM" declarations: I am the bread of life, I am the light of the world, I am the door, I am the good shepherd, I am the resurrection and the life, I am the way, the truth, and the life, and I am the vine.

As a whole, Israel had turned away from God. But a personal relationship with Jesus is what He wanted for them and for us. We might be put off by religion, but God has true life to offer. Notice that it is the Father Himself who walks through the vineyard to cultivate it and to make sure it is watched over faithfully. He doesn't assign the care of it to another.

"Every branch in Me that does not bear fruit He takes away; and every branch that bears fruit He prunes, that it may bear more fruit."

—John 15:2

The phrase *in Me* indicates Jesus was speaking exclusively to believers. The phrase *bears not fruit* is in the present tense because there is a danger that believers can become unfruitful, no longer bringing forth fruit for the Lord.

When Paul wrote to Titus, overseer of the churches on the island of Crete, he said, "Make sure the people maintain their good works and meet urgent needs. Be sure they don't find themselves unfruitful." Maybe the prime example of unfruitfulness in the Bible is Lot. From the Old Testament account, we never would know Lot ended up in heaven, because we don't see him accomplish anything for the Lord. Yet in his second letter, Peter called him righteous. This tells us a person can be unfruitful and still make it to heaven. But God's desire is certainly far more than that. He wants to use our lives to affect others and turn them to the Lord.

So every branch that isn't bearing fruit, He takes away. And that is where people sometimes get tripped up. The Greek word for "take away" is *airo*, which means "to lift up, to raise up, or to take up." After Lazarus died, when Jesus told the disciples to take away the stone, the word used is *airo*. When the ten lepers lifted up their voices, saying, "Jesus, Master, have mercy on us," the word was *airo*. In Acts 4, after the young church had been threatened with physical punishment if they continued preaching about Jesus, they raised their voices to God—and the word again was *airo*. Even in Revelation 10, John used the *airo* in speaking of the angel whose hand was raised to heaven.

What was Jesus saying to His disciples? "I am the vine. My Father trims the branches. If you're one of the branches attached to the vine and you're not bearing fruit at the present time, My Father will lift you up." It isn't a statement of condemnation. It isn't one that should strike terror in our hearts. It is, rather, a promise from the Lord that the Father will seek to support us, build us up, and bring us back to a place of fruitfulness.

Every branch that isn't bearing fruit the Lord will lift up. And every one that is bearing fruit He will prune so it will bring forth more fruit. The whole idea of pruning is one of preparing us to bear more fruit. But be careful when you say you want to bear a lot of fruit, because the Lord just may start working!

The word for *prune* in Greek is *kathairo*, from which we get our word *catharsis*. It is most often translated in the Bible as "to cleanse" or "to purify." Although it can certainly mean "to cut," of the fifteen times we find it in the New Testament, thirteen times it is translated "to clean, to wash, or to make pure." When we read of Jesus washing the disciples' feet, it is the word *kathairo* that is used.

So this verse shouldn't strike terror in our hearts. On the contrary, it is a word of encouragement.

In the vineyard, branches often became weighed down and buried in the dirt. That's why often you will see the branches in vineyards strung up on wooden posts. They have to be off the ground to bear fruit. So when the insects come and the overgrowth shades them from the sun and its nutrients, it is the vinedresser's responsibility to cut them back so they may bear fruit more easily.

"I'm the true vine," Jesus said, "and My Father keeps all of the branches trimmed and fruitful. If you're not currently bearing fruit, He'll pick you up. And if you are, He'll cut you back and cleanse you so you can bear more fruit."

It's not enough to be saved. God wants to work in us so He can work through us. The end result of our faith is not so we can sit in church and smile about our lives but so we can go out of church and reach out to those who can't smile at all.

> "You are already clean because of the word which I have spoken to you."
> —John 15:3

The water God uses to clean us is His Word. Commit yourself to His Word and you can be fruitful. "How can a young man cleanse his way?" the psalmist asked. "By taking heed to the Word of God," He answered. How can I be fruitful? By paying attention to God's Word. Especially in our day when the Bible is being set aside more often, it's important that we know God's method of preparing us to be fruit bearers is to save us and then to continue to cleanse and build us up through His Word.

> "Abide in Me, and I in you. As the branch cannot bear fruit of itself, unless it abides in the vine, neither can you, unless you abide in Me. I am the vine, you are the branches. He who abides in Me, and I in him, bears much fruit, for without Me you can do nothing."
> —John 15:4–5

In all the disciples had heard the last few hours about their responsibility and about being sent out into the world as sheep among wolves, I'm sure their fear level rose significantly. But Jesus' advice was simple—and it hasn't changed in all these years. As a believer, if you want to be fruitful, your one job is defined in one word: *abide*. And it is about as easy, and yet as difficult, as it can be.

The word *abide* in Greek is *meno*. Meno is translated "remain, dwell, continue, tarry, or endure." In the Bible when it is used in reference to a place it means "don't depart." When it is used in reference to time, it means "continue without end or without interruption."

So here's your part: Stay close to Jesus in fellowship. Be diligent with Him in Communion. Let Him make Himself at home in your life. Make your decisions guided by His Word. Let His Spirit be your strength. The result will be that your life will be fruitful because, just like separating a branch from the vine brings death to the branch, so trying to separate yourself from Jesus and still serve Him brings fruitlessness. Yet abiding is the secret to fruit-bearing.

It isn't a very difficult comparison to understand. We can bear fruit as branches only as we abide in the vine, because a branch on its own is useless, fruitless, and lifeless.

What kind of fruit is the Lord looking for? He is looking for fruit both in your life and through your life. And you really can't separate one from the other. When Paul wrote to the Romans, he said, "I can't wait to come and see you so I can have fruit among you as I've had among other Gentiles." People who get saved by watching your life and listening to your words God calls "fruit." He would like you to be fruitful so many folks get saved. Romans 6 tells us that walking with the Lord in holiness is the fruit of a life that has been dedicated to Him.

Fruit can also be giving—as in Romans 15:28, when Paul wrote, "As soon as I drop off the fruit you gave me, I'm headed for Spain." As seen in Galatians 5:22–23, fruit is the work of the Holy Spirit producing love, peace, and longsuffering in your heart. Hebrews 13:15 says the fruit of your life with God is praise and worship.

So depending on the context, all of those things are fruit. If you walk in God's love, worship from the heart, do good works, help those in need, reach out to those who need to know the Lord, and live a life that draws other people to Jesus. That's the fruitful kind of life God wants you to live. How can you be that kind of person? The only requirement is that you abide in Christ—just hang out with Jesus. Let Him do the work He longs to do in and through you. Listen to what He says. Let His Word be the light of your life. Make sure that what you do and desire line up with what He wants and has revealed. Fruitlessness usually can be traced to a meager communion with God, where a relationship with Him is virtually non-existent, or very poor at best.

In Psalm 92:13, we read that if we are planted in the Lord's house we will flourish in our God's courts. Verse 14 says we'll bear fruit in our old age that will be both fresh and flourishing. So it doesn't matter how old you are, how long you've known the Lord, or how much you've learned. The key is hanging out with Jesus. Once you abide, fruit bearing takes care of itself.

Some people make fruit their goal. "OK, I'm going to start loving people," they say. But that's impossible because you'll run into somebody you simply cannot love on your own in about eight minutes! Fruit can't be a goal. Fruit is a byproduct of abiding. Whenever you substitute activity for abiding, not only are you fooling yourself, but you're not going to be very fruitful. If you're busy for the Lord but have no time for fellowship with Him, no time to study His Word, or no time for worship, you're really going down the wrong road.

Jesus didn't say, "Go out and do your best and then ask God to bless it." He said fruit comes to those who, like a branch to a vine, abide in Him. If I brought a branch from an apple tree and said, "This is from the best apple tree I've ever had. The fruit is juicy and big. When an apple grows on it, help yourself," you wouldn't bother waiting in line. Because it's separated from the tree, the branch is dead. It can't grow fruit on its own.

There is no such thing as "freelance Christianity." God blesses those who hang out with Him. And the further the distance between you and the Lord, the less fruit you can expect in your life. It's just that simple. To the degree that you abide, you either become a dead branch or a very fruitful one. It's an irrefutable fact of the spiritual life.

You are as close to the Lord today as you have chosen to be. If you lack fruit, it's also by your choice. He's available. His door is always open. The illustration of the vine and the branches is not only obvious, but one that demands a response.

If you simply wrap yourself around Jesus, you'll find that fruit won't come from struggling or striving, from planning or even from trying. God's love will come forth. God's joy will rule your heart. God's peace will be the measure of the day. The things you see won't move you. Because you're hanging out with Jesus, you'll have great hope when the world says there isn't any.

How easy God makes it for us! Don't worry about pruning yourself or watching over other branches. It's not your job to be the vinedresser for them. Fruit comes by just hanging in there with Jesus. And in due season, blossoms will appear, fruit will follow, and you'll be amazed by what God has done in your life.

In chapter 14:8, Hosea said, "I'm like a green cypress tree, Lord, and now Your fruit is found in me." That's what we want, isn't it?

So to these disciples who were wondering what was to become of their lives, Jesus said simply, "Don't worry. Just hang in there with Me."

> "If anyone does not abide in Me, he is cast out as a branch and is withered; and they gather them and throw them into the fire, and they are burned."
> —John 15:6

Those who would like to terrify others often have used verse 6. "Be fruitful! Hurry up or you'll be cast aside!" they say. But I think the analogy doesn't change. What happens to a saint who doesn't abide and becomes that lonely branch? Any opportunity for bearing fruit is gone. And although he'll still be saved, he won't bear fruit. He'll be the Lot of the New Testament. It is equivalent to salt losing its savor or John writing in his second epistle, "Don't lose the things you've worked for. Be sure you receive a full reward."

Paul wrote in 1 Corinthians 3:9–15 that one day in heaven our works will be tested as to what sort they are. If they make it through the fire, we'll be rewarded. If they don't, although we will be saved our works will be burned. The problem with vine branches is the wood is good for nothing other than either bearing fruit or burning. You can't make furniture from it because it's too soft. You can't make kitchen utensils out of it because it burns too quickly. You can't even make a peg to hang your hat on because it can't bear weight. It's worthless unless it's being used for fruit bearing or firewood. So either my life is in communion with Jesus and I bear much fruit and glorify the Father—or, by neglecting Him, I dry up, am set aside as a witness, and don't produce fruit that will make it through the fire. Oh, I'll make it to heaven—but I won't have accomplished anything else of lasting value.

"If you abide in Me, and My words abide in you, you will ask what you desire, and it shall be done for you."

—John 15:7

Yet if I abide in Jesus, stay close, and make Him my life, and if His Word guides my steps, I can ask what I want and it will be done for me. That's a great promise, isn't it? But notice there are two conditions attached. First, it is made to someone whose heart is occupied with Jesus. Second, it is made to a life that is being regulated by God's Word. Abiding is not some fitful kind of spasmodic on-again-off-again, every-Sunday-for-half-an-hour relationship. God wants constant, habitual, daily fellowship with us. And if He has that, our prayers will reflect His will. They will reflect our relationship with Him. This is a promise to believers who abide in the Lord and whose lives God's Word directs.

James wrote that we have not because we ask not, and we ask amiss. If you're not in the Word much, you won't have Christ's mind or God's heart. And your prayers will reflect it. The key to getting what we want is to want what God wants—which is the best for us anyway.

In 1 John 5:14, John wrote, "This is the confidence we can have in Him, that if we ask anything according to His will, He hears us. And if He hears us, we know we have the petition we desire of Him." What a great promise! Why do we have so little power in prayer? It could be that for many, there's little communion with God. He's not a machine where you put in a dollar and pull a lever. He wants to form your heart and change your life so you might become a vessel He can use.

"By this My Father is glorified, that you bear much fruit, so you will be My disciples. As the Father loved Me, I also have loved you; abide in My love. If you keep My commandments, you will abide in My love, just as I have kept My Father's commandments and abide in His love. These things I have spoken to you, that My joy may remain in you, and that your joy may be full."

—John 15:8–11

"Follow My example," Jesus said. "I'm about to give My life in obedience to the Father because I love you. Now you abide in Me by obeying My Word and following My ways. And the result will be not only that your fruitfulness will be great but that your joy will be full."

How can you have the joy of the Lord? Hang around Jesus. Let His ways be yours. Most folks try to incorporate Jesus as a part of their life in the areas they think they need help. But for the rest, God is set aside. What God wants is that your life might be wrapped around His, that you might be attached like a branch is to a vine, because all the life you need comes from Him. Abiding in fellowship provides joy like nothing else can and fruit that is eternal.

It's all about abiding.

Chapter 122

Thursday/Friday
His Love Reaching the World

John 15:12–27

It was late Thursday night/early Friday morning on the Jewish calendar as, on their way to the Garden of Gethsemane, Jesus continued talking to His disciples about the work they would do once He ascended into heaven.

> "This is My commandment, that you love one another as I have loved you."
> —John 15:12

Here Jesus gave His disciples the commandment that always comes up first: the idea of loving one another. But it isn't like the Old Testament commandment to love one another as you'd like others to love you. This one has an entirely new standard—a love that is based on Jesus' love for us. And it is not only the cornerstone of the church but God's miraculous work in our hearts that actually could bring us to love people the way God loves us.

In John 13:34–35, Jesus said it was by this love that all men would know we are His disciples. In other words, this love is so distinctive that no one could mistake it for anything else. This love is the Greek word—*agape*—that is almost unique to the Bible. In fact, we find it only very rarely in classical Greek before Jesus came. It was He who gave the word meaning. It is God's love in believer's hearts and it is different from any kind of love man will be able to produce on his own. It is a love that is self-sacrificing and that seeks the benefit of others before benefit for itself. It is laid out before us in the life Jesus lived, the words He spoke to His enemies, and the prayers He offered even on behalf of those who drove nails through His hands. And it comes to the believer through the indwelling of the Holy Spirit.

Agape is not defined in the Bible as an emotional feeling. Rather, it has everything to do with decision and action. People at their best can feel *phileo*, or reciprocal love. That's about as good as it gets for us. We love people who are nice to us. But if you love your enemies, suddenly you stick out like a sore thumb, especially in a world driven by selfishness and self-interest.

Jesus' command was that the church walk in God's love toward the world and one another in such a way that, rather than an emotional response, love becomes a decision and commitment to act. That is why John wrote in 1 John 3:18, "Let us not love in word or in tongue but in deed and in truth." Jesus' command can't be obeyed if it is only a call for a different emotional response. We can't love our enemies by feeling. If, however, we bless them, pray for them, and overcome evil with good, not only is that a sign of God's work in us but it's a great sign to the world that something is different about us, because that isn't the way the world works.

> "Greater love has no one than this, than to lay down one's life for his friends."
> —John 15:13

I remember reading of John Knox and how the Lord had called him to Scotland. Seeing the people not walking with God, he had arisen one night to pray and cried out to the Lord, "Give me Scotland or I die." An hour later, he said, the Lord spoke to him as clearly as he ever remembered, saying, "Die, and I'll give you Scotland." Ultimately this is how the church has to go out into the world. We have to die to ourselves and walk in God's love.

> "You are My friends if you do whatever I command you."
> —John 15:14

Isn't it awesome that God would call you His friend? I understand your calling God your friend, but the fact that God would want to hang around with us is amazing. Up until this point, God only had called two people His friend: Abraham and Moses. Most people choose friends very carefully. They choose people with common interests and compatible personalities. They choose friends who are loyal and faithful and kind—which is why people usually have very few good friends. Yet the Lord looks at us and says, "Here's My friend—the one who trusts in Me."

> "No longer do I call you servants, for a servant does not know what his master is doing; but I have called you friends, for all things that I heard from My Father I have made known to you."
> —John 15:15

Servants are not friends in a relationship sense because servants are not given insights or revelations. Servants get instructions. The employee can't say to his boss, "Why?" He can only say, "OK." Psalm 25:14 says the secret of the Lord is with those who fear Him and that to them He will reveal His covenant. As God's people, we've been let in on the family secrets—the how, what, when, where, and who. We know where we're going, what's coming up, what God wants to do, and what He's promised. Because we've been brought into the family, we have the unspeakable privilege of knowing God's heart. People in the world don't know God's will. But the church does. And to those who love Him, God constantly reveals His plans. Oh, He may not give us explanations for every one of His actions, but we know His heart.

As believers, we see the days in which we live. The world doesn't. We see the struggles that go on in people's lives and the spiritual forces behind them. We see how sin and its fruit abound. We see how we are close to the Lord's coming, what the future holds for Israel, and what life is going to be in eternity to come. Paul wrote to the Thessalonians, "You know the day of the Lord is coming like a thief in the night and when people say, 'peace and safety,' sudden destruction will come upon them as a woman in travail. But you, brethren, are not in darkness that the day should overtake you like a thief." Why? Because we're part of God's family. We've been brought in by faith in Jesus.

> "You did not choose Me, but I chose you and appointed you that you should go and bear fruit, and that your fruit should remain, that whatever you ask the Father in My name, He may give you. These things I command you, that you love one another."
>
> —John 15:16–17

Jesus' friendship with us was established by Him, not by us. That God would choose me amazes me. Sometimes people love us because they don't know us—yet if they knew us, they wouldn't love us. The Lord knows everything about us and loves us anyway—which to me is a marvelous love. And that's the love God wants to put in us.

God chooses us, enables us, fills us with His love, and then asks us to obediently go out in the world, and by His Spirit, bear fruit. That's the work of the church. You should learn from this verse that God's end work in your life is not that you sit in a pew with a head full of knowledge. God's end work in your life is that He sends you out to tell others about His love and bear fruit that will remain. None of us is called to a ministry of sitting. We're called to go out into fields that are white and where laborers are few.

> "If the world hates you, you know that it hated Me before it hated you. If you were of the world, the world would love its own. Yet because you are not of the world, but I chose you out of the world, therefore the world hates you."
>
> —John 15:18–19

The word *hate* appears seven times in the next ten verses. Instead of sugar-coating the conflict, Jesus wanted to prepare the disciples for what they would face. Following the resurrection, the disciples were free to go fishing. But get to Acts 2, where the preaching begins, the power of God falls, and lives begin to be touched, and the opposition immediately grows. By chapter 4, saints were arrested and thrown in prison for nothing more than laying their hands on the sick and praying for them.

This is a far different message than today's "health and wealth" message. Jesus said very straightforwardly, "There are tremendous advantages to being saved—but don't think for a minute that the world is a cakewalk. It's not."

When the apostles in Acts 5 were arrested and beaten for their faith, we read that they left the presence of the council rejoicing that they had been counted worthy to suffer shame for Jesus' name. "We're in the right place!" they said.

When people hate you for your faith and for standing with Jesus, there's no need to feel guilty or take it personally. Sometimes I hear Christians say, "I shared the Lord with them and now they won't talk to me. If I'd only been a little kinder." But how much kinder can you be than saying, "Look out! Cliff ahead! Bridge Out! Eternal life at stake!"? Jesus did everything perfectly. He said the right thing at the right time with the right heart—and they killed Him. So I wouldn't feel too bad if it seems like you're failing. If you walk with God in His love, fruit will come—but it will come in the midst of a culture and a worldly attitude toward believers that makes life difficult.

Paul said to Timothy in the last letter he wrote, "If you want to live a godly life in this world, you're going to suffer persecution." If you're walking with Jesus, you probably won't make the "Who's Who List" here on earth. The world hates God, so don't expect better from His enemies than Jesus got.

This was a lot to consider for these disciples walking with Jesus. In the following fifty years, all but one of them was murdered for their faith and the willingness they had to preach. In the next three hundred years—from Nero to Diocletian—over six million saints were thrown to the lions, burned at the stake, and tortured in all manner in an effort to quiet them. But instead of dying, the church continued to grow. You and I have it so easy by comparison! Some cross words, some rejection and alienation is often the worst we in the West see for our faith. Yet Jesus said:

> "Remember the word that I said to you. 'A servant is not greater than his master.'"
>
> —John 15:20

Jesus had made this same declaration as He washed the disciples' feet in John 13.

> "If they persecuted Me, they will also persecute you. If they kept My word, they will keep yours also. But all these things they will do to you for My name's sake, because they do not know Him who sent Me."
>
> —John 15:20–21

Why are we going to suffer? Because we're identifying with Jesus. Why does the world persecute the believer? Because it doesn't know God. For years, Paul was convinced that sending Christians to prison was doing God service. Today, most persecution still arises from religious people who have no relationship with God at all.

> "If I had not come and spoken to them, they would have no sin, but now they have no excuse for their sin. He who hates Me hates My Father also. If I had not done

among them the works which no one else did, they would have no sin; but now they have seen and also hated both Me and My Father."

—John 15:22–24

Response is an individual responsibility. Jesus said, "I've come and spoken the words and done the work so that man has heard and seen and can conclude I can only be God. They can't say, 'We didn't get it' because who else was raising the dead, opening the eyes of the blind, commanding demons to come out of people, or multiplying loaves of bread and fish? They were works of God that can't be denied."

"I don't believe the Bible," people say. Great. But what are you going to do with changed lives?

"But this happened that the word might be fulfilled which is written in their law, 'They hated Me without a cause.'"

—John 15:25

Jesus did everything right. He never failed one place along the way. What provoked people's hatred? The wickedness of hearts that love darkness rather than light. Jesus spent His life blessing and He was given the cross. So He said, "Don't be too surprised when this comes your way. I know it will—but I also know that the work of the Spirit through your life will bring forth fruit that will remain."

"But when the Helper comes, whom I shall send to you from the Father, the Spirit of truth who proceeds from the Father, He will testify of Me. And you also will bear witness, because you have been with Me from the beginning."

—John 15:26–27

Having been warned of the trials, the disciples very well may have wondered how they would do this. Jesus said, "You're going to walk in My love and be filled with the indwelling Spirit, who will testify of Me through the witness you'll be." The church becomes that dwelling place for God the Holy Spirit. It will not be our power, wisdom, or strength, but the presence of the Holy Spirit who will do Jesus' work and confirm the words we speak. What the world does with the information is up to them. Your responsibility is to be a witness.

The apostles went out and began to bear witness to such a degree that by the time we get to Acts 17:6, the accusation against them is that they had turned the whole world upside down. I think if we rely on the Lord, love people, and are obedient witnesses no matter the cost, our world will be turned upside down as well. Will it be easy? No. But what else are you going to do—the Lord came to save those who are lost!

Chapter 123

HOW CAN I REACH THE LOST?

John 16:1–11

With all that the disciples had heard on their walk with Jesus from the Upper Room to the Garden of Gethsemane, fear and doubt must have filled their hearts. And sorrow would soon enough. As we come to chapter 16, Jesus continues the discussion of suffering in the ministry and what lay ahead for these His disciples.

> "These things I have spoken to you, that you should not be made to stumble. They will put you out of the synagogues; yes, the time is coming that whoever kills you will think that he offers God service. And these things they will do to you because they have not known the Father nor Me. But these things I have told you, that when the time comes, you may remember that I told you of them."
> —John 16:1–4

In laying out what would appear to be a very somber future, Jesus said, "I want to let you know this ahead of time, so when life gets difficult in serving Me, you won't stumble."

"Lord, we've left everything to follow You. What are we going to get?" Peter had asked in Matthew 19:27. Here in John 16, Jesus answered, "Here's what you're going to get—a tough time as you go out to serve Me." Ready to depart, Jesus told His disciples what to expect to give them a clear view of what lay ahead.

From the catalog of suffering the Gospels lay out for the church, Jesus picked up two examples that the disciples would face: excommunication and execution. "Excommunication?" you say. "That's not so bad." That's because in America, to be denied membership in a church or even to be put out of one seems rather insignificant. You'll run out of time before you'll run out of churches you could attend in its place. But that was not the case in Jesus' day. In Jewish society, the synagogue was not only the place of worship, it was the social hub of the society and where you went to find a job, get medical help, find a husband or a wife, and even to be mourned after you died. So this threat of expulsion was a very big issue.

In John 9 the parents of the blind man Jesus healed backed off their confession of faith rather than risk losing the synagogue's support. And in John 12, we read that many among the rulers believed in Jesus but wouldn't confess, because they would be put out of the synagogue had they done so.

Going from city to city preaching the Gospel, Paul always went to the synagogue first. But it often was the synagogue that rallied to be sure he was driven out of town. The Gospel's message even elicited murder plots, arrests, and beatings. That was the kind of opposition waiting for the church right around the corner.

Jesus warned that the reason people would act this way is because they didn't know the God they said they served.

> "And these things I did not say to you in the beginning, because I was with you."
>
> —John 16:4

One of the things we discover throughout the Bible is God only gradually reveals His plans. When Israel came out of Egypt, the Lord said, "I'm going to take you to a land flowing with milk and honey." What He didn't mention were the giants in the land, the walled cities they would have to conquer, or the armies of well-trained soldiers that would outnumber them by thousands. In fact, when the people left Egypt, God didn't lead them directly to the Promised Land, because He knew if they saw the Philistines, they would want to go back to Egypt. Instead, they needed to see the Lord part the Red Sea, provide food for them from heaven, and defeat the Amalekites. God wanted to prove Himself so that by the time they arrived a year later on the edge of the Promised Land, they would be able to look at the enemies and the walled cities and say, "That's nothing for God. He can handle this."

Unfortunately, they didn't learn the lesson. They shrank in their unbelief and rather than their problems becoming small in comparison to their God, they took their eyes off God altogether, and their problems became insurmountable.

God has a way of not telling us everything that's coming. But He does tell us what we need to know at the time. I appreciate that. Here Jesus said to His disciples, "I'm telling you these things now because I'm leaving. I didn't tell you before, because I was with you."

> "But now I go away to Him who sent Me, and none of you asks Me, 'Where are You going?' But because I have said these things to you, sorrow has filled your heart."
>
> —John 16:5–6

To be fair, in chapter 13, Peter had said, "Where are You going?" And in chapter 14, Thomas had said the same thing. But no one had asked Jesus where He was going in a positive sense. All of the disciples' questions came out of desperation. They didn't focus on God's good plans but on their loss. Because they saw no blessing for them in Jesus' leaving, none of them had asked, "What's going to happen next? This is going to be exciting." They all instead simply panicked.

Reckoning loss for Jesus' sake as gain is something we find great difficulty doing. When the disciples heard Jesus was leaving, they didn't say, "Good plan." They said, "Oh, no." They were not able to see the glory that would come out of loss. And yet we're called to do the same thing, aren't we?

You lose a job, the girl you like doesn't like you, you wreck your car, you don't qualify to buy the house—what good can possibly come out of any of that? We know for certain that Jesus' death, resurrection, ascension, and the sending of the Spirit were the greatest things that every happened to mankind. Our sins are forgiven. Our names are in heaven. The Holy Spirit dwells within us. He's going to see us through. The Lord is coming again. Everything worked out just great—but try convincing these guys, who were seeing everything they hoped to accomplish falling apart before their eyes, of that.

After the resurrection and six additional weeks of seeing Jesus come and go, the disciples' fears were dispelled and their doubts gone. But up to this point, they were struggling.

> "Nevertheless I tell you the truth. It is to your advantage that I go away; for if I do not go away, the Helper will not come to you; but if I depart, I will send Him to you."
>
> —John 16:7

"Though you haven't considered or asked in that context, let Me tell you the truth," Jesus said. "You think My staying is best. I assure you it is not. In fact, your greatest advantage is if I go and the Holy Spirit comes."

None of the disciples had given that a thought. They just wanted Jesus beside them every step of the way because that's all they knew, and that was to them as good as it got. If things could get better—they didn't see it. If Jesus had died, risen, and said, "I'm not leaving. I'm going to make the Upper Room My headquarters. You can all make appointments. First come, first served. Fifteen minutes, max. Call ahead."—the line would have stretched into eternity. "I'm just waiting to talk to Jesus," people would sigh. "I just hope I see Him before I die."

But that was not the Lord's plan. His plan was to give His life for the sins of the world and then send the Holy Spirit to come and dwell in individual hearts. When Moses said he needed help, the Lord chose seventy faithful proven men upon whom to put the same Spirit that was upon Moses. Moses said, "I wish everyone would be filled with the Spirit." That's God's desire too.

> "And when He has come, He will convict the world of sin, and of righteousness, and of judgment: of sin, because they do not believe in Me; of righteousness, because I go to My Father and you see Me no more; of judgment, because the ruler of this world is judged."
>
> —John 16:8–11

The first work of the Holy Spirit is to convict people's hearts of sin because unless they believe they are sinners, the idea of needing a Savior is useless. To further clarify matters, this word *sin* is singular because at the root of all sin is self. Self declares it has no need for help. That's the base of people's problem. They are self-centered, self-dependent, and self-confident. But the Holy Spirit has come to convince people otherwise.

Trying to convince people they are sinners usually meets with a lot of opposition because that isn't really part of our nature to embrace news like that. In fact, sometimes the quickest ways to get people to justify themselves is to simply tell them they are sinful. We can't convince someone they are sinful. That kind of spiritual understanding comes only through God's Spirit working in a heart.

Look how righteous Paul thought he was when he was killing Christians. Had anyone tried to argue with him, it would have done no good. Yet as he watched Stephen dying and forgiving the men throwing the rocks, the Spirit was able to speak to him. And when Paul finally relinquished control of his life, the Lord said, "It's been hard for you, hasn't it, Paul, to kick against the goads of My Spirit?"

What an awesome help it is to us to realize that, as we share God's Word, people will be influenced far more by the work of God's Spirit than we ever can hope to accomplish by our arguments. All we are required to do is share what God has taught us and we will see God do great things.

The second work of the Holy Spirit is to convict the world of righteousness. The word *righteousness* means "that which God accepts" or "that which pleases God." When Jesus died and rose, He was accepted into heaven. He didn't get to the clouds and say, "Hey, it's locked." No, heaven's doors flew open to Him. He was perfect in every way.

Most people like to measure themselves against their neighbor. We can always find goofs that are worse than us, but they're not the standard. Jesus is. And we're either going to have to be as holy as Him or hope that He shares some of His righteousness with us. It's either going to have to be your perfection or your trust and faith in Jesus and His perfection that provides you access into heaven.

The third work of the Holy Spirit is to convict people of judgment. The judgment that has come has destroyed the ruler of this world. Therefore, you can't use the argument, "That's just the way I'm made," or, "This is just the way our family is," or, "I'm Irish," or, "I'm tall." Although the ruler of this world would like to destroy you, the Lord has destroyed his work and given you freedom to do the right thing. There isn't hopelessness in life. There is freedom in Christ.

Every conversion in the book of Acts took place through a person who was saved. The key to being a witness like that is to be filled with the Spirit and share God's Word. Will it be difficult? Sure. Will you run into resistance? A lot of it! But if you're a vessel filled with the Spirit, God can work mightily in your life.

Jesus said, "If I go, the Holy Spirit will come. When He comes, He'll go after those in the world who are lost."

And He'll do it through your life.

Chapter 124

IN HIM WE OVERCOME THE WORLD

John 16:12–33

Beginning at the Passover meal, the disciples had seen the conversation with Jesus continually turn towards death, suffering, and being scattered. It had no doubt left them wondering and worried. What they had been hearing certainly didn't fit with their expectations of the coming Messiah. And every passing hour seemed to bring even greater doubt, fear, or despair. Not only had they heard about a betrayer in their midst after all these years, but Jesus' washing their feet just didn't seem right. Peter had tried to make sense of it all, and promised that no one would be as faithful as he. But Jesus said, "Before morning, you'll have denied Me not once or twice but three times." And then He started talking about leaving them behind—and it just didn't sit well. Oh, they wanted to learn. They loved Jesus and certainly wanted to listen. But the rapid-fire topics all pointed to something they did not even want to consider. Soon the Holy Spirit would come to dwell within them and teach them God's ways, and they would see the blessing of His sacrifice. But not before the cross, and so the disciples listening were having a difficult time reconciling all Jesus was talking about. Here in our verses Jesus addresses that:

> "I still have many things to say to you, but you cannot bear them now. However, when He, the Spirit of truth, has come, He will guide you into all truth: for He will not speak on His own authority, but whatever He hears He will speak; and He will tell you things to come. He will glorify Me, for He will take of what is Mine and declare it to you."
>
> —John 16:12–14

Jesus began by saying, "There's a lot I'd like to teach you, but you're not ready." I would think not! I would think by the time the disciples got to chapter 16, what they didn't want was any more information. What they already heard had overwhelmed their hearts.

Growth takes time, doesn't it? We have five grandchildren now, and one of our granddaughters is interested in how "tall" she has grown. Every time she comes for a visit, she goes to the wall where we measure their heights and says, "Am I taller? Am I taller?"

"No," we say.

"Are you sure?" she says.

"Yes," we say. "We measured you just last week."

How do we grow? We eat and wait. The same thing is true spiritually. We just hang around and let the Lord teach us and minister to us. And although we don't get it all at once, we get it eventually. In Isaiah 28:10, the Lord said to the people, "Here's how I'm going to teach you: Precept upon precept, line upon line, here a little, there a little." There are no shortcuts to spiritual maturity. We've just got to hang around and eat—and as we do, the fruit will come and the progress will show. You've probably read a passage in the Bible you've read previously, when all of a sudden you see something you've never seen before. You wonder how it got there—but it was there the last time you read it. It just wasn't time for you to learn that part yet.

The disciples were not yet born again. They didn't have the Holy Spirit dwelling within them. But in a few days, their eyes would be opened, the fog would be lifted, things would become clear, and they would begin to understand.

"I have a lot of things to tell you now but you're not ready," Jesus said. "But when the Spirit comes, He will guide you into all truth and will glorify Me."

It amazes me how much we know of the future plans God has for the church, of the Rapture, and of the time of the Tribulation. Every generation is given more insight. It was as an old man that Daniel began to write down the prophecies God gave him. By the time he got to chapter 12:8–10, he basically said to the Lord, "So, what does this all mean? I don't get it."

"Just put it away," the Lord answered. "Seal up the book until the end. It's for those in the last days."

And today being the last days, God makes the book of Daniel clear to us.

There's much to learn of God's will and ways. The disciples needed to know that the Lord wasn't just going to abandon them. He was going to come and be with them through His Spirit. If you're ever in a position to teach others, verse 13 should give you great comfort, especially if you feel the pressure is on you. It's not. As a pastor, I don't for five minutes think anyone comes to hear from me. But if the Lord can use me to teach you, and we can hear from Him, I rejoice in the opportunity to be His vessel.

> "A little while, and you will not see Me; and again a little while, and you will see Me, because I go to the Father." Then some of His disciples said among themselves, "What is this that He says to us, 'A little while, and you will not see Me; and again a little while, and you will see Me'; and, 'because I go to the Father'?" They said therefore, "What is this that He says, 'A little while'? We do not know what He is saying." Now Jesus knew that they desired to ask Him, and He said to them, "Are you inquiring among yourselves about what I said, 'A little while, and you will not see Me; and again a little while, and you will see Me'? Most assuredly, I say to you that you will weep and lament, but the world will rejoice; and you will be sorrowful, but your sorrow will be turned into joy.

A woman, when she is in labor, has sorrow because her hour has come; but as soon as she has given birth to the child, she no longer remembers the anguish, for joy that a human being has been born into the world. Therefore you now have sorrow; but I will see you again and your heart will rejoice, and your joy no one will take from you."

—John 16:16–22

Can't you hear the disciples saying, "Do you get that? I don't get it either. Go ask Peter. He always seems to figure stuff out. Don't ask Thomas. He doesn't know anything." All of them wanted to ask Jesus about what He was saying, but none of them dared.

So Jesus made it easy on them. "You're talking about what I said, aren't you?" He asked. Then He went on to liken what He was talking about to a child's birth—how short the time of pain is compared to how great the blessing that results from it. Pointing to the example of a mother giving birth, He said, "The birth of a child will swallow up the pain of the delivery." That certainly is true. If it weren't, there would be a lot more single-child families! The mother sees the cute little baby and forgets how hard it was. Only as she finds herself pregnant again do those memories stir.

The same would be true of Jesus' death. It would be devastating to the disciples but in a few days—a little while—He would be back, alive, overcoming the grave. And the very thing that broke their hearts would bring them overwhelming joy. The world would think it had won, the enemies of Jesus thrilled He was dead and buried. But just you wait He says.

"And in that day you will ask Me nothing. Most assuredly, I say to you, whatever you ask the Father in My name He will give you. Until now you have asked nothing in My name. Ask, and you will receive, that your joy may be full."

—John 16:23–24

Jesus said, "Soon, along with settled joy of Me being alive, will be the glory of you having access to the Father in My name." The ultimate subject of the book of Hebrews is a sinful people's access to a holy God. Jesus accomplished that. In giving us His name, Jesus made it possible for us to come to the Father with His authority.

You might have a hard time cashing an out-of-state check at a bank—unless your dad's the president of the bank. Then you can simply mention his name and you'll be fine. The same thing is true of the heavenly Father. Though I cannot come to Him on the basis of who I am or what I've done, yet in the name of His Son Jesus I am welcomed and accepted. There is, however, one aspect of "in Jesus' name" that people often lay aside. That is, Jesus' name also demands conformity to His will, because in every place you read of Jesus' name, you also read of His will. If you were to go to the same bank where your father is the president, with a machine gun in hand to take what you wanted, your name affiliation would no longer serve you well. The access you had would be forfeited by your behavior because it wouldn't conform to your father's will.

It's the same thing when you pray in Jesus' name. Some in the church think Jesus' name is magic, that if you say it loud enough and long enough you can get whatever you want. But that is not conforming to His will. If you come to do the Father's will, if you've died to yourself, and if you want what He wants and follow Him, then you can ask what you will.

> "These things I have spoken to you in figurative language; but the time is coming when I will no longer speak to you in figurative language, but I will tell you plainly about the Father."
>
> —John 16:25

Throughout the Gospels, we see Jesus employing "figurative language," or stories, to teach spiritual truths by comparison to what is understood. When we come to the Epistles, there are far fewer stories and far more direct doctrinal teaching because with the Holy Spirit poured into our hearts, we can understand things in spiritual terms.

> "In that day you will ask in My name, and I do not say to you that I shall pray the Father for you; for the Father Himself loves you, because you have loved Me, and have believed that I came forth from God."
>
> —John 16:26–27

Throughout the New Testament we read that Jesus is at the right hand of the Father making intercession for us. Yet here Jesus highlights the fact that because we have believed in Him and loved Him, we can come directly by His name to the Father who loves us and who will hear us and care for us. Jesus will continue to be our reason for access, our Intercessor, but we can come in Him at anytime and be welcome in the presence of the Father.

> "I came forth from the Father and have come into the world. Again, I leave the world and go to the Father." His disciples said to Him, "See, now You are speaking plainly, and using no figure of speech! Now we are sure that You know all things, and have no need that anyone should question You. By this we believe that You came forth from God." Jesus answered them, "Do you now believe? Indeed the hour is coming, yea, has now come, that you will be scattered, each to his own, and will leave Me alone. And yet I am not alone because the Father is with Me. These things I have spoken to you that in Me you may have peace. In the world you will have tribulation; but be of good cheer, I have overcome the world."
>
> —John 16:28–33

I'm sure the disciples wanted to put a good face on their confusion. They didn't want to disappoint Jesus by having to say yet again they didn't understand and so they tell the Lord, "Oh, now we get it, that's clear!" But Jesus knew the truth and calls them on their words with great tenderness.

"You're going to scatter," He said. "But you'll find your peace in Me." They would abandon Him for a few days in fear, but He wouldn't abandon them, and neither would the Father abandon His Son. Because He overcame the world, they would triumph. And soon, the Holy Spirit would make these up-and-comers overcomers as well.

Chapter 125

JESUS PRAYS FOR US

John 17:1–26

From what we learn from John 18:1, it appears Jesus stopped by the brook at the bottom of the Kidron Valley on His way to the Garden of Gethsemane, where He would pray not only for the disciples, but for those who would believe in Him through their testimony. Having listened to Jesus' final words of instruction and encouragement, we now get this rare chance to listen to Him pray in a time of tremendous crisis during the final hours before the cross.

In His prayer, we see Jesus' estimation of the last three and a half years—how He viewed His life and ministry. We are also given a glimpse of the Father's will and His plans for each of us, as well as an understanding of the principles necessary to live the Christian life successfully. How can we come to the end of our life knowing we have done what God desired for us? We find that here in Jesus' prayer.

> Jesus spoke these words, lifted up His eyes to heaven, and said, "Father, the hour has come. Glorify Your Son, that Your Son also may glorify You, as You have given Him authority over all flesh, that He should give eternal life to as many as You have given to Him. And this is eternal life, that they may know You, the only true God, and Jesus Christ whom You have sent."
>
> —John 17:1–3

On a dark night with confused disciples, Jesus began His prayer by saying, "The hour is here, Father. It's time for You to be glorified."

I think most of us pray, "Here, Lord. I have a shopping list. Maybe You'd like to read it for Yourself. I'm a little busy."

But prayer, from a scriptural standpoint, is not a place to have our will done in heaven. It's a place to have God's will done on earth. So as Jesus came to the last moments before the cross, He said, "Father, it's time to go through with these things we planned. Be honored in My life and in My death." Even at the end, Jesus came to submit Himself to the Father.

In a few minutes, as Man, Jesus would struggle over the cost of our salvation. It wasn't the physical pain that put Him off. It was rather the separation from the Father that sin would bring that He had never experienced. But the cross, with all of its humiliation and indignity as our sins were heaped on Jesus, ultimately would bring life to any who turn to depend upon Him. At the cross the unbelievable love of God for us would be set on display. Jesus prayed, "Father, I want to bring You glory. I want to do this well. I want to honor You."

"I have glorified You on the earth."

—John 17:4

Who is getting the glory for your life—for how smart you are, how faithful you've been, and the good works you do? Jesus had such a way of doing good things that when He left, people worshipped God. Ultimately, a successful Christian life is one that brings glory and honor to the Lord, gives Him credit, puts Him first, and draws all attention to Him. You'll know you're on the right track if people leave your presence talking about how good God is.

Paul said to the church at Corinth, "There aren't many wise, noble, smart, or powerful among you. But it's the weak and the foolish that confound the wise, because God alone could take that kind of life and make it useful" (1 Cor. 1:26–27).

He went on to say, "We have this treasure in earthen vessels so that the excellency of the power might belong to God, not to us." In other words, it is the Holy Spirit's work in the lives of the weak that brings others to declare, "Isn't God something?!"

"I have finished the work which You have given Me to do."

—John 17:4

God has a work for you that is particular to you—no one else has been chosen to do it but you. You can be faithless and God will use another, but you're the one to whom He gives first opportunity. Notice that concerning His work, Jesus used the word *finished* and the phrase "You have given Me." It is one thing to start a good work. It's another to finish it. The road away from most Bible studies is crowded with people who wanted to obey and swore that one day they would, but for now are just too busy. The problem is, the end of life will sneak up on them and they will realize they didn't use it to serve God at all. They had the opportunity; they just didn't use it.

People constantly find reasons not to finish the work God has given them. They'll tell you other good works they're involved in, and as soon as those are finished they'll be right there. But it seems their list never gets done.

I don't know what God has called you to do, but I would say to you to do it well and give it your all, because when you die you want to say, "I have finished."

In a couple of hours from now, Jesus will shout, "It is finished" from the cross. At the end of His life He was able to say, "I have accomplished what My Father wanted." But notice what He finished was that which the Father had given Him to do. That is an important distinction because we never will be finished meeting people's expectations. There always will be someone who expects more of us than we can deliver. So if we spend our lives trying to please people, boy, are we going to be tired! That isn't God's calling. Although we're to love one another, we're to serve the Lord first.

Over and over we find Jesus pressed to meet people's expectations. In Mark 1:35–39, after ministering all evening, Jesus got up before daybreak the next morning to pray. When the disciples found Him, they said, "Everyone is looking for You."

"Let's go to another town," He answered, "because I have been called to preach." He left people's expectations to serve the Father instead. He was always busy, but always at rest. His schedule was full—but only with doing what He had been called to do. That is why He is able to say to us, "Come to Me if you're heavy laden. I'll give you rest." People's burdens will give you ulcers. God will give you peace.

> "And now, O Father, glorify Me together with Yourself, with the glory which I had with You before the world was. I have manifested Your name to the men whom You have given Me out of the world. They were Yours. You gave them to Me, and they have kept Your word."
>
> —John 17:5–6

The word *manifest*—*phaneroo* in Greek—means "to make visible either through declaration or illustration." Jesus had preached to the disciples and lived His life in their sight in such a way that watching Him, they met God. "I've lived out Your nature so that seeing Me, they have seen You," He prayed.

Over fifty years later the apostle John would write in his first epistle (1 John 1:2–3), "We have seen and bear witness and declare to you that eternal life which was with the Father and was manifested to us—that which we have seen and heard, we declare to you." In other words, he remembered looking at Jesus and seeing God.

Another attribute of a successful Christian life is that others should learn about God simply by watching and listening to you. What are you making visible about the Lord to those around you? You want to come to the end of your life and be able to say, "Lord, I have shown them who You are. I'm weak, but You're strong. I can't, but You have." Paul said we are living epistles read by all men. What are they reading about Him from your life?

When Moses went up to Mount Sinai to get the Law, he came down with God's glory reflected on his face. He wasn't aware of it, but others saw his face and knew he had been in God's presence (Exod. 34:29). Following their arrest for the healing of a lame man in Acts 4, the Sanhedrin took note that although Peter and John were uneducated, their boldness came as a result of being with Jesus (Acts 4:13).

That's a great legacy to have, isn't it? When our time is up, it would be great to say, "I want to come home, Father. But while I've been here, folks have learned about You through my life and know You better for knowing me."

"Now they have known that all things which You have given Me are from You. For I have given to them the words which You have given Me; and they have received them, and have known surely that I came forth from You; and they have believed that You sent Me."

—John 17:7–8

Another attribute of a successful Christian life is seen in Jesus' statement, "I have given them the words which You have given Me." Back in verse 6 Jesus said they had *kept your word*: where *word* is logos and speaks of the scriptures in their entirety. Here in verse 7 *words* is *rhema*, a Greek word that speaks of a particular scripture or portion of scripture applied to a particular situation. How vital it is that we be those through whom God can share His Word and apply His word to every life with whom we come in contact.

Are people hearing from you what God has to say? When asked for counsel, do you share what God has spoken? Are you a vessel to whom and through whom God will speak? At the end of your life, it won't matter how much your estate is worth, if there's a building with your name on it, or how big your house is. God doesn't judge by any of that. His question is, "Have you given My Word to people?" Jesus, in review, saw that as an important accomplishment as He finished His Work.

"I pray for them. I do not pray for the world but for those whom You have given Me, for they are Yours. And all Mine are Yours, and Yours are Mine, and I am glorified in them. Now I am no longer in the world, but these are in the world, and I come to you. Holy Father, keep through Your name those whom You have given Me, that they may be one as We are."

—John 17:9–11

Of all the things Jesus might have prayed for that night, He prayed that the disciples would be one. He had begun His prayer saying, "Father, the time has come for You to be glorified in Me." Here He adds, "I'm glorified in those You have given Me."

I read that and say to myself, "You've got to be kidding. Peter will deny You. Thomas will doubt You. Three will sleep while You're suffering. And everyone will head for the hills in a few hours." Those were His guys. Yet Jesus didn't see them as half-listening, confused, resistant hearts upon which you could not depend. He saw them soon filled with the Spirit.

"While I was with them in the world, I kept them in Your name. Those whom You gave Me I have kept; and none of them is lost except the son of perdition, that the Scripture might be fulfilled. But now I come to You, and these things I speak in the world, that they may have My joy fulfilled in themselves."

—John 17:12–13

664

The next attribute of a successful Christian life Jesus highlights in His prayer is found in verse 12. Of the disciples, Jesus said, "I have kept them in Your name." In fact, seven times in this prayer Jesus referred to the disciples as a gift from the Father. He used the word *kept* twice here in verse 12. The first use means "to watch over" as a shepherd might watch over his sheep, to see what the needs might be. The second use of *kept* is more along the lines of guarding or providing security. "These are the ones You have given Me," Jesus said. "And I have kept them. I have fed them, protected them, and watched over them."

Every place in the Gospels when the world tried to get to the disciples, Jesus got in the way. Whether it was the Pharisees in Matthew 9, who asked why they weren't fasting, or the boy at the base of the Mount of Transfiguration who, possessed of the Devil, the disciples were unable to deliver, Jesus always intervened and stood up for His own. If there were taxes to be paid, Jesus not only paid His but Peter's as well. In a few minutes after this prayer, nearly a thousand soldiers will show up at the Garden of Gethsemane with swords and clubs. But by the time Jesus is done with the mob, the disciples will get away scot-free because He kept them. The only one He loses is the one who was hopelessly doomed, Judas, the son of perdition, not one of Jesus' own—an imposter.

Because the church is where God has placed us to get from here to Him, one of the keys to living a successful Christian life is being in a position where He can use you to encourage others in their walks. Whom are you helping get through the day, encouraging, and being an example to? For whom are you praying? So often people view the church only as a place of being served and come wanting to know what the church can do for them. But that's not the way the Lord sees the church. He sees it as a place where we come to help and to be helped, so we make it together and are kept.

The disciples weren't easy to keep. They were tough guys to have around and yet Jesus was able to say, "I've kept them. I've hung on to each one. I've brought them to this point." How much we need that as a body! In every letter he wrote, Paul spoke about the church's function and purpose and how there is strength to be found in the body of Christ. The church is the vehicle God has ordained to enable the saints to make it together through this world. You might think that's a bad idea, that the church is full of weak, selfish, sinful losers. Yep, that's all we've got. But that's who the Lord keeps.

> "I have given them Your word; and the world has hated them because they are not of the world, just as I am not of the world. I do not pray that You should take them out of the world, but that You should keep them from the evil one. They are not of the world, just as I am not of the world."
>
> —John 17:14–16

Once we receive God's Word, we no longer have a worldly outlook. As a result, the world begins to hate us just as it hated Jesus, who also was not of the world. The hatred is not personal. It's because the believer lives a life contrary to what the world says is the right way to live. Knowing this ought to drive us to more fellowship.

The Lord had prepared and kept His disciples. They now needed to care for one another.

It is interesting to me that Jesus prayed, "There's trouble in the world, but leave them there." I think most Christians believe deliverance means God taking the problem away. But it isn't God's plan to remove you from hostility or difficulty. He doesn't insulate you so you have no touch with the world. He wants you in the world, just not of it. The Good Samaritan got his hands dirty. But he left an impression—and so should we. When Elijah was being opposed, he said, "Lord, I just want to die now." But the Lord told him He had much work left for him to do.

God protects the saints in many ways, but they can be summarized in two: internally through His Word and His Spirit, and externally through the fellowship of the church. The church is the place we can be encouraged and blessed, taught and kept. Go to the world to minister and reach out; then return often to the church for fellowship and strength. Jesus had done so for His own; we are to do so for one another.

> "Sanctify them by Your truth. Your word is truth."
>
> —John 17:17

Sanctify means "to set apart for a specific purpose." If you're the Lord's He wants you set apart for Him. And although that puts you at odds with the world, it also gives you the opportunity to be a light in a dark place. He doesn't want you hidden; He wants you on display. Like a light on a tabletop that can't be hidden, He wants to show you off as a work of His Spirit. As the truth of God, His Word penetrates our hearts and lives. We will be set apart from the world and set apart for His glory.

> "As You sent Me into the world, I also have sent them into the world."
>
> —John 17:18

A successful Christian's life is lived out in the world. We're not of the world, but yet the Spirit sends us out in it. Our mission in this resistant environment is to continue the work Jesus began.

"As You sent Me, I send them," Jesus prayed. We are sent with the same purpose, power, and reliance on God that Jesus had to reach the lost and to take answers to those looking for hope. Many will refuse. But some will hear. It's a rescue mission and as we were rescued by the knowledge of His love, so others wait to hear and be saved as well.

Are you stepping out and taking advantage of the opportunities you have to reach out to others? Jesus said the fields are white. It's the laborers that are few. Too often we think just the opposite. But if you want a successful Christian life, go into the world and offer Jesus' hope to those trapped in sin. Rather than letting the refusals turn you away, let the accepting hearts encourage you to continue.

"And for their sakes I sanctify Myself, that they also may be sanctified by the truth. I do not pray for these alone, but also for those who will believe in Me through their word; that they all may be one, as You, Father, are in Me, and I in You; that they also may be one in Us, that the world may believe that You sent Me. And the glory which You gave Me I have given them, that they may be one just as We are one: I in them, and You in Me; that they may be made perfect in one, and that the world may know that You have sent Me, and have loved them as You have loved Me."

—John 17:19–23

Jesus hadn't even sent out the disciples yet, but He knew they were ready and so prayed for the fruit they would bear. He prayed for the second generation of believers, the third generation—all the way to you and me. This is the Lord's prayer for us. And here we are today in the twenty-first century, still with the same task at hand, carrying forth Jesus' message to the world. The Lord's prayer for every generation consists of two things: a love that reflects God's love for the world, and that through that love the world would see that Jesus is the Messiah.

"Father, I desire that they also whom You gave Me may be with Me where I am, that they may behold My glory which You have given Me; for You loved Me before the foundation of the world. O righteous Father! The world has not known You, but I have known You; and these have known that You sent Me."

—John 17:24–25

"Father, I want these where I am," Jesus prayed. The only request He made in the entire prayer was that the saints one day be where He is, so they could see Him in all of His glory—which assures me I'm going to heaven because Jesus never prayed a prayer that wasn't answered.

To the Thessalonians, Paul wrote, "God hasn't appointed you to wrath but to obtain salvation through our Lord Jesus Christ who died for you so that, whether you're alive or dead, you're going to be with Him."

"And I have declared to them Your name, and will declare it, that the love with which You loved Me may be in them, and I in them."

—John 17:26

The word *declared* means "to bring into focus" or "to be made known." Ultimately, the responsibility and call of God's people is to present to the world a clear picture of who God is. "You've seen Me, you've seen the Father," Jesus said to Philip.

Paul later said, "Follow me like I follow the Lord."

People should learn from us what we have learned. We should bear witness to God's name in a lost and dying world.

What makes a successful Christian life? Consider the following questions:

Who gets the glory in the way you live—you or God? "I went to school. I worked hard. I spent a lot of sleepless nights." Big deal. Who gets the glory? "If you knew the sacrifices I've had to make." I don't care. Who gets glorified? Jesus is the One who made the ultimate sacrifice for *you*.

Are you working toward finishing the work God has given you? Do you even know what He's called you to do? If so, are you doing it, or are you finding reasons to do other things?

Will you be able to say to the Lord at the end of your life, "I have made clear to those You gave me Your character and Your name"? Are people drawn closer to the God of the Bible by your life?

What do people hear coming out of your mouth? A successful Christian speaks God's words, which are powerful and able to change hearts.

Are you more concerned about meeting the needs of others in the church than about making sure your own needs are met?

Are you living your life as a light in a dark place?

The answers to those questions will tell you how you are doing. Die without money, without property, and without gain. But don't die spiritually unsuccessful. Jesus in His prayer here shows us what is of value, so we might live accordingly for Him!

Chapter 126

AGONY IN THE GARDEN FOR US

Luke 22:39–46
(Matthew 26:36–46; Mark 14:32–42)

Luke's purpose in writing his Gospel was specific: he focused on Jesus' humanity. As a result, he often tells us what we don't find in the other Gospels about Jesus; that He was tired, resting, or weeping—those things that relate to our humanity. In the passage before us, Luke tells us what took place in the Garden of Gethsemane over a period of about three hours, focusing on the torment Jesus faced knowing He would have to relinquish His relationship with His Father, which He had enjoyed for all of eternity. He who knew no sin would become sin for us so we could be made right with God through Him.

The Bible is very reserved when it talks about Jesus' physical suffering. Information about the beatings He endured isn't given to us in chapters, but in very small bits and pieces. It is as if the Lord wanted us to see that He gave His life, but not to highlight the physical aspect of what that meant.

Here Luke goes out of his way to be sure we understand a portion of that suffering and the depths to which Jesus would go for us. It is certainly one of the most moving portions of the Bible you will read. And as you consider the price the Lord paid so you could live, it should deepen your appreciation and love for Him.

> Coming out, He went to the Mount of Olives, as He was accustomed, and His disciples also followed Him. When He came to the place . . . .
> —Luke 22:39–40

From the other Gospels we know this place was the Garden of Gethsemane. *Gethsemane* is a Chaldean word that means "wine press." And to this day, there still are olive trees and winepresses at the base of the Mount of Olives. In John 18:2, we read that Judas knew of this place because Jesus often went there with His disciples. So now that the time had come, Jesus went to the place where Judas knew He would be.

In their meeting, the chief priests had said to Judas in Matthew 26:5, "We'd like to wait until the Passover is over. Jesus is liked by a lot of people. This could cause us great trouble." But the fact that He was now in a location far removed from the crowds gave Judas what he thought was the perfect opportunity to corner Jesus. In actuality, it was the

Father who sent His Son to be the Passover Lamb and He wouldn't be denied. It would be His plan that was carried out.

> . . . He said to them, "Pray that you may not enter into temptation."
>
> —Luke 22:40

"Now's a good time to pray," Jesus said to His disciples. The Sanhedrin weren't going to be satisfied with getting Jesus. They would get rid of Him, or so they thought, and then turn on His followers, who soon enough would feel the heat themselves. Good time for prayer, says Jesus. *Proseuchomai*, the Greek word for *pray*, is in the aorist tense, meaning "start now and don't stop."

Jesus would practice what He preached for the next three hours. He would pray by Himself as His disciples slept. Jesus knew what was coming. In a couple of hours, they all would run for their lives. Peter would deny Him at the top of his lungs. And all of them would be brokenhearted over the events that would take place. But they didn't pray. They went to sleep.

"You're going to forsake Me," Jesus said. They said they wouldn't.

"Pray," He said. And they slept.

No wonder these days were so hard on them. They hardly listened at all.

> And He was withdrawn from them about a stone's throw, and He knelt down and prayed. . . .
>
> —Luke 22:41

Matthew 26:36–37 tells us Jesus left eight of His disciples at the entrance to the garden. He then took Peter, James, and John into the garden and began to pray. Matthew 26:38–39 also records Jesus taking the three aside and saying, "My soul is exceedingly sorrowful even unto death. Could you stay with Me and watch with Me?" Luke says He knelt. Matthew says He fell on His face. The words Matthew used to describe Jesus' suffering are the most extreme Greek words you'll find. "To be sorrowful unto death" means to feel as if the pressure you're under could kill you. This was quite a time of prayer and battle for our souls! So Jesus began to pray:

> . . . saying, "Father, if it is Your will, take this cup away from Me; nevertheless not My will, but Yours, be done."
>
> —Luke 22:42

The cup Jesus spoke of is a reference to the death He would have to die—the suffering, the slander, the abuse, and the separation that He would have to endure. "Are they able to drink the cup that I have to drink?" He had asked John and James' mom. A couple of hours earlier at dinner, He had picked up the redemption cup of the Passover and, handing it to the disciples, had said, "Here is the cup of My blood shed for you, a new covenant between God and man."

It was that very cup that brought this tremendous struggle to His flesh. And Jesus was so anguished by it that His prayer recorded was simple and straightforward, "Father, if there's another way, let's set aside the cup. If man can be made right with You in some other manner, let's put aside the cup."

Why the terror? Jesus had told the disciples at dinner a couple of hours earlier, "I'm looking forward to this. I can't wait till it is accomplished." He had prayed, "Father, I can't wait to come home." Yet now as Jesus came to the garden, the full brunt of His work faced Him and, at least from a fleshly standpoint, it overwhelmed His body, emotions, and outlook. The issue for Jesus wasn't the physical suffering, but what sin does to people and what sin would do to Him. The consequence of His becoming sin was that the Father would break His fellowship with His Son and turn His back on Him. Jesus would be alienated and set apart. And He couldn't bear to think about that. To be rejected by His Father as He died in our place was unthinkable to Him. Yet He would do it for us.

As Isaiah wrote, our iniquities have separated us from God; our sins have hidden His face from us. The thought of this horrified Jesus. In fact, it was almost too much for Him to bear. So He struggled hour after hour in prayer. But He kept closing the discussion with, "Nevertheless, not My will but Yours be done."

I have found over the years that when we don't care about something most of us will pray, "Lord, whatever You want." But when things begin to matter, rather than saying, "Father, I want what You want," we start to tell Him what to do. If you have a child in the hospital do you say, "Lord, whatever You want," or do you say, "Please, Lord, You've got to make him well"? If you're out of a job, do you say, "Lord, whatever You want," or do you say, "Lord, let's get some money in here. What's the deal?" When we think something important is at stake, we start to direct God. Not Jesus. At His time of greatest anxiety, when the pressure was such that He sweat blood, He said, "Father, I want what You want."

> Then an angel appeared to Him from heaven, strengthening Him. And being in agony, He prayed more earnestly. Then His sweat became like great drops of blood falling down to the ground.
>
> —Luke 22:43–44

Only Luke mentions the angel coming to minister to Jesus. We're not told what he said or did. We are told in the Bible that the Lord sends angels to minister to us as the heirs of salvation, that we can entertain angels unaware, and that they always behold the face of our Father in heaven. In His humanity, Jesus needed strengthening and care. And so do we. I suspect when we get to heaven we're going to be surprised by how often the angels stepped in on our behalf that we were totally unaware of.

Paul wrote in Hebrews 5:7 that Jesus "offered up prayers and supplications, with vehement cries and tears to Him who was able to save Him from death." The term *vehement cries* in the Greek means "to scream" and the word for *tears* means "to sob uncontrollably." I can't begin to try to explain or understand what Jesus went through. But I know that He did. With heavy sobbing and much wailing, He began to sweat great drops of blood.

If you are under enough pressure, there is a medical condition where the capillaries in your sweat glands can explode. It's very rare and can be fatal. Jesus faced that type of pressure and His flesh could barely endure it.

I suggest you take this portion of scripture and meditate on it and let the Lord show you how much He loves you. Hebrews 12:2 says it was for the joy set before Him that He endured the cross. You're the joy set before Him. The Bible says we love Him because He first loved us. As Jesus saw you in the future—cleansed, forgiven, and adopted into His family, He was encouraged to see it through.

In Lamentations 1:12, Jeremiah wrote prophetically about Jesus' suffering, saying, "Is it nothing to you all who pass by, behold and see if there is any sorrow like my sorrow which has been brought upon me." No one had to do this. Although the thought was horrifying to Him, only Jesus was willing to be cut off from the Father so you and I never would have to be.

> When He rose up from prayer, and had come to His disciples, He found them sleeping from sorrow. Then He said to them, "Why do you sleep? Rise and pray, lest you enter into temptation."
>
> —Luke 22:45–46

Mark tells us in chapter 14:37 that, as Jesus finished the first hour of prayer, He went back to find the disciples sleeping and woke up Peter, saying, "Simon, what are you doing sleeping? Couldn't you watch with Me one hour? You should watch and pray lest you enter into temptation. Your spirit is willing but your flesh is weak." And He went back to pray again while Peter went back to sleep.

In the second hour, Mark tells us Jesus returned again and woke them all up. "Can't you watch with Me for an hour? Be careful to pray," He said. But Mark says their eyes were heavy and they didn't know how to answer Him.

He went off again for a third hour to pray and it was only when He came back the third time that, finding them asleep, He said, "Just rest." He wouldn't wake them until the betrayer was at hand and the noise across the valley was such that He knew it was time. But by then He had resolved in prayer that the Father's will for Him was to go this route. There was no other way.

I think if you stop and spend some time with Jesus in the garden, you'll be moved to love Him. If you can just pass by, I feel sorry for you that your heart would be so hard. It's a pretty awesome place to spend an hour or more. Don't sleep through it.

Chapter 127

THE KISS, THE SWORD, OR THE CUP

Luke 22:47–53
(Matthew 26:47–54; Mark 14:43–47; John 18:2–11)

And while He was still speaking, behold, a multitude; and he who was called Judas, one of the twelve, went before them and drew near to Jesus to kiss Him. But Jesus said to him, "Judas, are you betraying the Son of Man with a kiss?"
—Luke 22:47–48

As Jesus had finished His time of agony in prayer and resolved to rest in the Father's care, the disciples slept as Jesus waited for Judas and his men to arrive. He could hear them coming, crossing the Kidron Valley in the middle of the night. There is really no way to sneak up on Him, especially when you're bringing lanterns and swords with you and there are so many men. I suspect they thought Jesus would try to run.

John 18:3 tells us Judas had received a detachment of troops. The word for *detachment* in Greek is the word for *band*. It constituted one-tenth of a legion. A legion was six thousand men. So Judas was given some six hundred armed men plus the chief priests' soldiers, the folks from the Sanhedrin, and the high priest and his men. There easily could have been eight hundred to nine hundred men coming for Jesus in the middle of the night, armed to the teeth.

Matthew 26:47 tells us these men were armed with swords and clubs. John tells us they came with lanterns, torches, and weapons. On top of all of that, at Passover there would have been a full moon. The light was on these doing their work in the dark. And no one was taking any chances. Judas had even established a sign for his posse: by a kiss, he would signal who Jesus was and whom they were to take into custody.

After three and a half years of healing the sick and opening the eyes of the blind, Jesus should have been easy for the soldiers to pick out of a crowd. But although people had heard of Him, they hadn't necessarily seen Him. So Judas made a plan to identify Him. Two words for *kiss* are used here in our Luke passage. The one in verse 47 uses the Greek word *phileo*, which is the strongest human love or emotion we can find apart from God. It speaks of a kiss driven by love and concern for another. Judas came to give Jesus that kind of kiss. But the word Jesus used in verse 48 is the *philema* and denotes a customary greeting you would give someone you didn't know. In other words, He literally said to Judas, "You pretend to know Me and love Me but there is no affection in your greeting. It is as if we have never met." If nothing else, Jesus let Judas know He knew what Judas was up to. Isn't it amazing how low people can go when they turn away from God?

I don't know what inflection Jesus' voice took in verse 48. But we have to believe with all we know about Him that His tone wasn't condemning as much as it was sorrowful. Describing this situation, Luke refers to Judas as one of the twelve. No one ever had had greater access to seeing Jesus heal, deliver, teach, explain, and love man for three and a half years than Judas. No one had had greater opportunity to experience the tenderness He showed than Judas. Yet because he had a different agenda and a heart determined to go his own way, even thirty pieces of silver was enough to turn him away.

If someone has ever betrayed you, you know how difficult that is. I know it hurt Jesus deeply. It wasn't a surprise to Him, but that didn't make it any easier.

David had a friend named Ahithophel. They prayed together. They worshipped together. They were inseparable friends. And yet when Absalom, David's son, decided it was time to overthrow his father, Ahithophel joined Absalom's cause, leaving David high and dry. "It's not an enemy who reproaches me or I could have borne it," David wrote in Psalm 55:12–14, "And it isn't someone who hates me who has exalted himself over me. Then I could hide myself from him. But he was a man who was my equal. He was my companion. We took sweet counsel together. We walked to the house of God among the people."

Knowing this was coming didn't lessen the hurt for Jesus. I'm sure the betrayal broke His heart.

In John 18, we see what happened next:

> And Judas, who betrayed Him, also knew the place; for Jesus often met there with His disciples. Then Judas, having received a detachment of troops, and officers from the chief priests and Pharisees, came there with lanterns, torches, and weapons. Jesus therefore, knowing all things that would come upon Him, went forward and said to them, "Whom are you seeking?" They answered Him, "Jesus of Nazareth." Jesus said to them, "I am He."
>
> —John 18:2–5

"I AM" was the name God took in the Old Testament to define who He was.

> And Judas, who betrayed Him, also stood with them. Now when He said to them, "I am He," they drew back and fell to the ground.
>
> —John 18:5–6

Judas gave Jesus a kiss. Jesus let Judas know He knew what he was up to and then turned to confront the nearly one thousand armed men. "Whom are you looking for?" He asked. "We're looking for Jesus of Nazareth," they answered. "I AM," Jesus said. And as He said it, this army of men with lanterns, clubs, and swords fell down backward.

Can you imagine this picture? So many tough soldiers lying on their backsides, lanterns extinguished, swords flying.

"I AM."

Boom!

Awesome! That's the way we like it, isn't it? The soldiers might have been saying, "We really should have brought more guys." But how many more did they want to fall down?

At this point, Jesus could have said, "OK, got to go," and taken off. But He knew why He was there. He had resolved this issue in prayer. He was going to the cross—not because Judas had come with a thousand men but because He wanted to. He would go willingly. Every soldier lying on his back should have been convinced that the group's show of force meant nothing to the Lord. The only way they arrest Him now is if He chooses to co-operate.

> Then He asked them again, "Whom are you seeking?" And they said, "Jesus of Nazareth." Jesus answered, "I have told you that I am He. Therefore, if you seek Me, let these go their way," that the saying might be fulfilled which He spoke, "Of those whom You gave Me I have lost none."
>
> —John 18:7–9

After being asked again, Jesus said, "I've told you, I AM. So let My disciples go." He not only showed who was in charge, that He would go willingly, and that a thousand soldiers meant nothing to Him, but He also showed He was watching out for His disciples because it wasn't their time to die yet. I wouldn't doubt that the religious leaders had more intentions than just grabbing Jesus. They wanted everybody. They were going to shut down the whole movement. But the Lord would have His way.

Which brings us back to Luke's account:

> When those around Him saw what was going to happen, they said to Him, "Lord, shall we strike with the sword?" And one of them struck the servant of the high priest and cut off his right ear.
>
> —Luke 22:49–50

The disciples had been asleep for three hours. They were sorrowful and had only roused when the group, led by Judas, walked in on them in the garden. They watched everyone fall down and it must have appeared that the soldiers were going to grab Jesus. The first thing out of their mouths was, "Lord, do You want us to fight?"

Men are indeed this way most of the time. I mean, there were eleven disciples with two swords between them against nearly a thousand armed men. On the one hand, it was very courageous. From a fleshly standpoint, we might admire them. But I suspect they were emboldened by the fact that Jesus already had knocked down a thousand men with just two words. So it was as if the disciples were saying, "If You're going to knock them down again, Lord, we can stab them before they get up."

We know from John's gospel (John 18:10) that it was Peter who didn't wait for an answer. He had one of the two swords and began swinging at the closest one to him—who just happened to be a man named Malchus, an aide to the high priest. Even if you're a fisherman, there's nothing like a sword to give you confidence! We're told he cut off this servant's right ear. I don't doubt Peter was aiming for his neck and Malchus ducked. As the ear went flying, it looked like there would be a showdown.

Peter, the man full of promises who earlier had said to Jesus, "These guys might forsake You but I'll die for You," thought he could prove his allegiance. What he would discover however was that it is much harder to live for Jesus than die for Him. I'm sure Peter would have given his life right there, but to live for Jesus would prove more difficult.

We can learn a lot from Peter about what not to do. He slept when he should have been praying. He talked when he should have been listening. He boasted when he should have been paying attention to what the Lord was saying. And he fought when he should have been surrendering as God's plans were being carried out. Here he fought the wrong enemy with the wrong weapon. The enemy was not the high priest's servant, the soldiers, or even Judas. The enemy was the Devil. This was spiritual warfare.

In Ephesians 6:10–20, Paul went to great lengths to teach us that the weapons of our warfare are not carnal. A fleshly fight can't accomplish what God wants, which is why James wrote that "the wrath of man does not accomplish the righteousness of God." A lot of times we forget who our enemy is. Your boss gives you a hard time and right away you think he's the enemy. Your husband or wife gives you a bad time and he or she is the enemy. Your kids don't call back and they're the enemy. Your neighbor has a party that is way too loud, and now they are the enemy. Peter not only fought the wrong enemy, but he fought with the wrong weapon. Jesus fought with God's Word, the Sword of the Spirit. Not Peter.

Later, Jesus will say to Pilate, "If My kingdom was of this world, My servants would fight. But it's not of this world" (John 18:36). The kingdom of God is not taken by force, but entered into by faith. And the work is done by the preaching of the Word and the Holy Spirit's outpouring. It's important we know that, because it's easy to fall back on what we once thought was our strength.

I love the description of Jesus in Matthew 12:18–21, where we read, "Behold My servant whom I have chosen, My beloved in whom My soul is well pleased. I will put My Spirit upon Him. He will declare justice to the Gentiles. He will not quarrel or cry in the streets. A bruised reed He will not break. A smoking flax He will not extinguish until He sends forth justice and mercy." God's method is one of gentleness, kindness, mercy, and the power He brings to bear as people follow His will. Peter still had the old mentality that force works. But force doesn't work to accomplish God's will. We have to let the Lord work. Peter would learn that. For now he was out there on his own and in trouble.

> But Jesus answered and said, "Permit even this." And He touched his ear and healed him.
>
> —Luke 22:51

Matthew fills in the other part of this conversation in chapter 26:52–53, as Jesus said to Peter, "Peter, put away your sword because if you take up the sword, you'll perish by the sword." There's always a bigger sword, isn't there? If you want to live by the flesh, there's always a bigger, badder, meaner enemy waiting for you. Then He told him, "Don't you think I could pray to the Father and He would provide Me with twelve legions of angels? But then how could the Scriptures be fulfilled?"

A legion is six thousand men. If there were eleven apostles and Jesus, He was assigning six thousand angels to each one of them. If push came to shove, they'd win. But Jesus wasn't there to win that way. He came to serve. He came to follow His Father's will. So, instead of calling 72,000 angels, He turned to love His enemy and reattached Malchus' ear.

This is Jesus' last miracle before the cross and it was done to correct a blundering disciple's mistake. I think the Lord has performed miracles like that over the centuries, to cover our tracks as we foolishly sought to defend His name in our own strength and caused nothing but trouble instead. It is amazing to me that no one in the crowd was moved by this healing work. I hope we at least see Malchus in heaven.

> Then Jesus said to the chief priests, captains of the temple, and the elders who had come to Him, "Have you come out, as against a robber, with swords and clubs? When I was with you daily in the temple, you did not try to seize Me. But this is your hour, and the power of darkness."
>
> —Luke 22:52–53

The presence of so many showed that Judas knew Jesus very little. He expected resistance, a fight, or a flight. He didn't realize that if Jesus didn't want to go, He wasn't going. The Pharisees and religious leaders had foregone their Passover meal, waiting to hear from Judas that it was time to move. In fact, they will say to Pilate in John 18, "We can't come into the Praetorium because we haven't eaten the Passover yet." In other words, they would be ready to eat their religious meal just as soon as they committed murder. This is a portrait of far more than simply men who are hateful. These were men driven by Satan himself. And Jesus pointed out how cowardly they had been, that all week when He had been in the temple, no one had bothered to try to grab Him, because they knew that wouldn't work. They did their best work at night. So does the Devil.

We know from other verses that Jesus looked at this time as His hour. He saw it as heaven's greatest hour, the time of people's salvation. But it was also the hour of the Devil's greatest attempt to destroy. He was throwing everything he had at Jesus, thinking if he could get rid of Him, that would be the end of it. But what Satan thought was his greatest hour would turn out to be his complete downfall. He was done to begin with, but this made certain his plans to keep men in bondage were now undone—Jesus came to save!

As Jesus looked at the crowd, He didn't see hateful individuals. He saw Satan stirring people's hearts. He saw the right enemy and challenged the men, hoping to reach those who were there. They came with lanterns looking for the Light of the World. It's an amazing picture, isn't it?

In 2 Corinthians 4:3–4, Paul wrote, "If our gospel is veiled, it is veiled to those who are perishing, whose minds the god of this age has blinded, who do not believe, lest the light of the gospel of the glory of Christ . . . should shine on them."

Today, Satan still roams around free to be the god of this world and offer darkness. He still does his best work in the dark. But Jesus wants to expose darkness, call people to the Light, and change their hearts. One day He'll come to rule and the enemy will be His footstool. One day Satan will be seen for who he is. But today we either live in Jesus' light or the Devil's darkness.

In the next couple of hours, Jesus will be subjected to six trials: three religious, three civil, none legal. He will be brought to Caiaphas, taken to Annas, brought before the entire Sanhedrin, then taken to Pilate, to Herod, and finally back to Pilate. But before that, here in the garden, we learn three lessons:

- You can pretend to love Jesus as Judas did, when in reality your heart is in an entirely different place. You can live by the kiss—but it's the kiss of death.
- You can try, like Peter, to serve the Lord with your flesh—with good intentions and people admiring your courage and devotion. But your flesh will save neither you nor anyone around you. It only will provide disasters for God to fix. You can live by the sword, but you'll probably die by it as well.
- Or, like Jesus, you can drink the cup. You can pray, "Father, what is Your will?" and then do what He says.

The kiss, the sword, or the cup—the choice is yours. But only one leads to life.

Chapter 128

HAD A GREAT FALL

Luke 22:54–62
(Matthew 26:55–58; 26:69–75;
Mark 14:48–54, 66–72; John 18:15–18, 25–27)

In John 18:12, John tells us that the detachment of troops and Jewish officers that had come to arrest Jesus *bound Him* as they led Him away. I find this absolutely ridiculous! He had just knocked them all down with an "I AM." Now they were going to put ropes on Him? Yeah, that would hold Him. How blind we are when we refuse His love. Those ropes would do no good, for it was something much stronger that held Jesus. It was His love for the Father and His love for us. Luke continues:

> Having arrested Him, they led Him and brought Him into the high priest's house. But Peter followed at a distance.
>
> —Luke 22:54

Over the next few hours, Jesus will face six mini-trials, all illegal and driven by hatred rather than a hunger for the truth. John tells us He was first led to Annas.

Annas and Caiaphas were relatives and lived in the same palace, according to Matthew 26:55–58. They were both members of the Sanhedrin. The Jews at this time were in a very difficult spot because they now had two high priests. The one by descendancy was Annas. But he had fallen into disfavor with Rome, so Rome had replaced him with his son-in-law, Caiaphas. The people, wanting the opposite of whatever Rome wanted, took Annas' side. Caiaphas was the figurehead in the eyes of the occupying Romans. Jesus was taken to Annas first, and Peter followed at a distance.

So here we have Judas with the betrayers, nine disciples running for their lives the minute they got the opportunity, and John and Peter at the high priest's home. We know from John 18 that John knew them and was allowed entrance. What kind of relationship he had with them we don't know. It wasn't necessarily antagonistic. In fact, John went in with Jesus and then went down to speak with the girl at the gate to let in Peter, according to John 18:15–16.

The Gospels tell us more about Peter than most of the other apostles, and I find most Christians identify with him—not because he's the most spiritual but because he's the most like us. There is no disciple who speaks as much in the Gospel account as Peter, and there is no disciple to whom Jesus speaks more than Peter. From boldly confessing the Lord to speaking from emotion without any kind of understanding, I think we love him because we can relate to him. He was as honest as he was confused, as dedicated as he was slow to listen. Peter was always talking. Sometimes he opened his mouth just to change feet. Other times what came out of his mouth were God's immortal words that we recognize as those of the Holy Spirit Himself.

In Luke 5:1–10, Peter had taken Jesus fishing and, after a night of catching nothing, as the Lord filled the nets Peter realized that in his boat was none other than God Himself. It was Peter's first true revelation of who Jesus was. He said to Him, "Get out of the boat. I'm a sinful man."

"Follow Me," Jesus said, "and I'll make you a fisher of men."

In Matthew 16:15–19, it was Peter who delivered God's supernaturally endowed wisdom in declaring who Jesus was. Yet a few verses later, it was Peter who was delivering a message from Satan and the pit of hell (Matt. 16:23).

Back in Matthew 14:28–32, it was Peter who, seeing Jesus walking on the water after he had been rowing the better part of the night, said, "Is that You, Lord? Can I come out there with You?" It was Peter taking steps on the water and, a few verses later, it was Peter crying out for help.

On the Mount of Transfiguration, it was Peter wanting to become a condo builder. "I can build one for Moses, one for Elijah, and one for You, Jesus," he said. "It's going to be a great community" (Matt. 17:4). God, however, just ignored Peter and kept the attention on His beloved Son.

At the Last Supper, it was Peter who had said to Jesus very emphatically, "You shall never wash my feet" (John 13.8–9). Thirty seconds later, it was Peter who said, "Lord, I'd like a bath."

Every time I want to pick on Peter, I remember I've never walked on water. And to his credit, when most ran, he did not. This story about Peter's fall, which is given to us in nine verses, is certainly for us the most instructive of his life but no doubt for him was the most difficult. It brought him eventually into a closer walk with God, so close that he would give his life for the sake of the Gospel. Peter would have unparalleled fellowship with God—but to get to that point he had to go through these nine verses to die to himself. Dying to yourself is the worst death of all. Peter would go down in flames so he could rise out of the ashes. By the time we reach John 21, the Lord allows him full restoration.

Here we read that Peter followed Jesus and the mob at a distance and, in so doing, became the example of what a lot of people like to do—follow the Lord from afar off. Maybe you're like that. You follow Jesus at arm's length. You want the blessings but you don't want to pay the price. You want the gain that comes from knowing Him without the cost that comes from following Him in a world that doesn't know Him. You want whatever you can get as far as advantage without hearing Him say, "If they hate Me, they're going to hate you." Peter tried so hard in his own strength to fulfill the words of promise he had made. He wasn't Jesus' enemy, but I think at this point Peter only would have voted for Jesus on a secret ballot.

"Far off" never works. It leads to denial and isolation. No matter how hard you try, if your relationship with God is far off it will benefit you nothing, because there's no blessing far off. You only end up right where Peter did.

> Now when they had kindled a fire in the midst of the courtyard and sat down together, Peter sat among them. And a certain servant girl, seeing him as he sat by the fire, looked intently at him and said, "This man was also with Him." But he denied Him, saying, "Woman, I do not know Him."
>
> —Luke 22:55–57

In the dreary damp and cold of the middle of the night, in a courtyard filled with soldiers and Jesus haters, Peter sat at the fire to get warm. Those who follow Jesus from afar are pretty comfortable at the world's fires. Peter had forgotten Jesus' words about being hated by those who hated Him, even though Jesus had said them only days earlier.

At the gate was a servant girl. Luke tells us she intently studied Peter's face. Before she said anything, she wanted to be sure she was right, that this was the guy she thought he was. No doubt around the fire that evening Passover was the big subject—all of the people in town, all of the overtime hours for the soldiers, all of the stir that this Jesus had caused, this odd assignment to get up in the middle of the night and march across the Kidron just to grab one person, and all of them falling down in what must have seemed to them to be a very localized earthquake.

Although he had assaulted the high priest's servant, Peter believed everything was all right, that he had blended in successfully—until this girl said, "You're one of them. You're with Him."

Peter's response was nothing more than a bold-faced lie. "No way," he said.

Peter, the guy who had said to Jesus at dinner, "Even though they all stumble, I never will. I'll die for You," nearly had a coronary when a young girl by the gate who had been staring at him for a while said she thought he had been with Jesus. He couldn't hurry fast enough to his own defense.

Mark adds in chapter 14:68 that as Peter was denying Jesus, the rooster crowed for the first time. I don't know if Peter remembered Jesus' words earlier that evening, when He said, "Before this night is over, before the rooster will have crowed a second time, you will have denied Me three times." Here was the first.

> "And after a little while . . . ."
>
> —Luke 22:58

Verse 58 says, "After a little while . . . ." And then verse 59 says, "After about an hour had passed . . . ." You get the feeling each time that Peter thought he was getting away with it, that everything was fine, and that things were settling down. But each time things get worse.

Why was Peter there? I suspect he was there because he swore he would be, and that he was sure that in his strength he could make it through this. One of the best lessons of Peter's denial is no matter how much you promise, or how determined you are, you can't serve God on your own.

> . . . Another saw him and said, "You also are of them." But Peter said, "Man, I
> am not!"
> —Luke 22:58

The Gospel accounts give us very good insights into this portion of the story. Mark says the second accusation came from the same servant girl who made the first one. Luke tells us it was a man. John says, "They began to say . . . ." So we get the impression that if it was the girl by herself the first time, she was getting some encouragement from others the second time. The crowd started to stir. Peter might have thought he was getting away with things but he wasn't. Suspicions were growing and the heat was rising. Mark tells us in chapter 14 that Peter had walked away from the fire to stand under the porch, maybe to where he couldn't so easily be seen in the dark. This second challenge put even greater pressure on Peter, and he didn't seem prepared to acknowledge that Jesus had said, "Peter, Satan wants to sift you like wheat."

It is extremely difficult to find strength from the Lord when you're following from far off. If you're standing at the world's fire, sitting with His enemies, or hiding under the porch, there is no way you're going to find God's strength for your life. Later, the Sanhedrin will associate Peter's boldness with his having been with Jesus. But not now. All Peter had now was a distant relationship with God. The Holy Spirit will be poured out. Peter will be filled and saved. Then he'll have the strength. But not now.

Notice that one denial led to another. The Bible is pretty clear that one sin, if not dealt with, becomes many. There's an old saying that the Devil's hounds hunt in packs. It is that way with sin. Sin slowly can erode all our resistance. That is why usually the first time we sin is the hardest. Sweaty palms, racing heart, and difficulty swallowing usually precede our fall. The next time is far easier. Sin will work through your life in such a way that it will wear you down.

In 2 Chronicles 25 we see the story of a young man named Amaziah for whom God had great intentions. Amaziah had battled an enemy stronger than he, and God had given him victory. But Amaziah was stupid enough to bring home the gods of the people he had defeated. He later challenged the powerful king Jehoash to battle.

"Leave me alone," Jehoash said. "Yes, you've had victory, but you meddle with me to your own hurt."

Yet although Jehoash warned him time and again, Amaziah would not be stopped. So the battle began and Amaziah's soldiers were killed. Others were shackled and dragged away from the city. Treasure was stolen from the temple and the walls of the city were partially broken down. Protection, riches, and freedom were all lost—which is always the result of sin. Amaziah was told to quit meddling. But one sin always leads to another.

When Lot saw the city of Sodom, the Bible says he moved near it, then moved into it, and finally was swallowed up by it. He never did show the fruit of his walk with God.

I suspect Peter's second denial was easier than his first. Matthew adds in chapter 26:72 that as Peter said, "I don't know Him," he added an oath: "I swear to God. May He strike me dead if I'm lying to you." The pressure was on.

> Then after about an hour had passed, another confidently affirmed, saying, "Surely this fellow also was with Him, for he is a Galilean."
>
> —Luke 22:59

Another hour passes. Peter calms down again, thinking he had made it through the would-be identification. The other Gospels say he returned to the fire. How was he feeling? He probably was making vows to do better, kicking himself for being such a chicken. "I won't let that happen again," he must have said to himself. "I'll be OK. I have an allegiance to the Lord. I don't see any of the other guys around. See, I knew I'd be the only one."

But he was unaware that the news was spreading. And the third challenge was far more serious than the first two. This time there was confident affirmation—it wasn't just a guess or suggestion. The verb tense says it was insistent and sure: "You're the one. I don't care what you say. You're the guy."

According to Mark, they even argued from the point of accent. "Listen to the way you're speaking," they said. "You're a Galilean."

Here had come a whole group of folks who wouldn't be quieted. John 18 adds that one of the main accusers was a relative of Malchus, the guy whose ear Peter had cut off just a few hours earlier in an attempt to kill him.

Things were getting out of hand and far more dangerous. The first two charges might have been tentative and questioning. The last was accusatory and sure. Angry men, mob sentiment—I think it must have seemed to Peter that the courtyard was closing in on him.

Matthew records that Peter began to curse and swear. "I don't know the Man." And immediately a rooster crowed.

> But Peter said, "Man, I do not know what you are saying!" Immediately, while he was still speaking, the rooster crowed.
>
> —Luke 22:60

What had happened to Peter, the man who loved Jesus so much, the one who had been so confident he could stand for Him? Matthew 26 tell us that while this was going on below, above in the portico, Jesus was being questioned about who He was. He had kept silent. Then Annas said to Jesus, "I want to put You under oath by the living God. Now You tell us if You're the Christ, the son of God."

"It is as you have said," Jesus answered. "Nevertheless, I say to you that, hereafter, you're going to see the Son of Man sitting at the right hand of power and coming with the clouds of heaven"—all of the things the Messiah had been prophesied to do in the Old Testament.

Hearing this, Annas tore his clothes and turned to the others, saying, "He's spoken blasphemy. What further need do we have of witnesses?"

While Jesus was up above on trial, affirming who He was, Peter was in the courtyard below, denying he knew Him. What a picture. But what a lesson to us about our own strength. Self-confidence was Peter's claim to fame. But Paul wrote to the Corinthians, "Be careful when you think you stand lest you fall."

Jesus had shared His secret for standing when He said in John 15, "If you abide in Me, if My words abide in you, then you can bear much fruit. But without Me, you can do nothing." Our strength to stand in the world for the Lord, to affect fruit for Him in His name by His Spirit, has nothing to do with self-confidence and everything to do with abiding.

Here's how we find strength: abide in Christ. It doesn't matter how strong we think we are. We have to come to the place where we say, "I can't. But He can."

Peter had worked hard at becoming this vulnerable. I don't know why he stayed by the fire so long except for his self-confidence. And for the third time, he screamed, "No way"—this time punctuated by swearing! He denied the Lord, the rooster crowed, and Peter realized what had happened.

> And the Lord turned and looked at Peter. Then Peter remembered the word of the Lord, how He had said to Him, "Before the rooster crows, you will deny Me three times." So Peter went out and wept bitterly.
>
> —Luke 22:61–62

Notice the order here. Once he had fallen, Peter remembered the Lord's words. Unfortunately, that's how it usually is for us as well. We remember what God had said only when it's too late. Peter had argued with Jesus, disobeyed Jesus, sought to fight for Jesus, and now he was failing Jesus. All of this must have rushed through his head as the rooster crowed. Yet there, from the balcony overhead, Jesus—on trial—was looking directly at Peter.

Their eyes met and I believe Jesus' look said, "Peter, remember I told you I've been praying for you. You're going to make it." I'm sure it was a look of tremendous mercy at a time when Jesus was getting none. God knows our frame. He sees our sin, knows our hearts, and loves us anyway. We often expect more of ourselves than He does. We think we can. He knows we can't. Jesus wasn't disappointed. He already had told Peter this would happen. It was only Peter who was disappointed.

Peter wept bitterly, kept by Jesus' prayers. But notice that when Peter fell, he did something very wise: he looked up. Jesus' look at Peter would have done him no good if he hadn't made eye contact. The first thing to do if you've fallen is look up. Quit trying to hide or run. Look up and find God's face welcoming you home.

Peter's story doesn't end here. On resurrection morning, Peter will be singled out by the angel of the Lord to be told of Jesus' resurrection. The angel will tell the ladies who had come early to the gravesite, "Go back and tell the disciples and Peter that He's alive" (Mark 16:7). Peter had had a horrible few days. But he was about to be restored.

In John 21, there is the public restoration of Peter as Jesus brings him to the point where his self-confidence is no longer an issue. And His promise to Peter is that He will use his life.

Maybe the highlight is in Acts 4, where the Lord brings Peter back to this same courtyard to stand before these same people, this time filled with the Spirit. Prevailing by God's strength, he lets them know exactly who Jesus is. He succeeded with God's help where he had failed on his own. Same Peter? Yes and no. It was Peter devoid of self-confidence and filled with the Spirit. Same man, different standing with God.

Our strength is not sufficient to serve the Lord. Our abilities aren't capable of keeping us from sin or helping us accomplish great things. We can't do anything for God by our own might or power, but He can accomplish great things though us by His Spirit. It's the lesson we learn from Peter's failure.

Chapter 129

FRIDAY:
GOD'S WILL AND MAN'S SINFUL HATRED

Luke 22:63–71
(Matthew 26:59–68; 27:1;
Mark 14:55–65; 15:1; John 18:19–24)

I n Luke 18, Jesus said to His disciples, "We're going up to Jerusalem, where everything the prophets have written concerning the Son of Man will be accomplished. He will be delivered to the Gentiles and mocked."

Everything Jesus had spoken about—this awful story with a glorious ending—now would begin in earnest.

Later, in his first sermon, Peter would tell the crowd that it was by God's determinate purpose and foreknowledge that they had put Jesus to death. As we read through Jesus' trials and crucifixion, I think it's important not to forget that He came to give His life willingly and that this was the Father's will so we might have life. There was no mistake. Things didn't get out of control. Jesus was not the victim of some bad set of circumstances. He wasn't lost because He lacked the support He thought He had. He knew what was awaiting Him. In fact, in the next few hours many Old Testament prophecies of the suffering of our Messiah would come to pass, one right after another. The mocking, scourging, beating, crucifixion among the thieves, His burial tomb and resurrection—even the disciples' running away are all found in prophecy.

Throughout the Bible, the payment required for our sin is clearly laid out so no one would have the impression that Jesus got a bad deal. He went because He wanted to go. He went because that was the only way we could be saved.

The first of Jesus' six trials was before Annas, the Jewish high priest. It was during this trial that Peter denied Jesus. Although biblical coverage of the trials Jesus faced is relatively brief, John gives us a few details:

> Then the detachment of troops and the captain and the officers of the Jews arrested Jesus and bound Him. And they led Him away to Annas first, for he was the father-in-law of Caiaphas who was high priest that year. Now it was Caiaphas who advised the Jews that it was expedient that one man should die for the people.
>
> —John 18:12–14

The high priest then asked Jesus about His disciples and His doctrine. Jesus answered him, "I spoke openly to the world. I always taught in synagogues and in the temple, where the Jews always meet, and in secret I have said nothing. Why do you ask Me? Ask those who have heard Me what I said to them. Indeed they know what I said." And when He had said these things, one of the officers who stood by struck Jesus with the palm of his hand, saying, "Do You answer the high priest like that?" Jesus answered him, "If I have spoken evil, bear witness of the evil; but if well, why do you strike Me?" Then Annas sent Him bound to Caiaphas the high priest.

—John 18:19–24

The response to Jesus' request for witnesses was to slap Him in the face. His enemies wanted respect for the high priest—but they had none for the King of Kings and Lord of Lords.

Now the men who held Jesus mocked Him and beat Him.

—Luke 22:63

Imagine an innocent Man being grabbed without anything to even charge Him with, slapped in the face by one soldier of the high priest and now beaten by the soldiers of another, all while being commanded to justify His position.

And having blindfolded Him, they struck Him on the face and asked Him, saying, "Prophesy! Who is the one who struck You?" And many other things they blasphemously spoke against Him.

—Luke 22:64–65

God made our bodies in such a way that they're pretty good at handling things. You breathe and you usually don't think much about it. Your heart beats without your asking it to. Your eyes blink automatically. If something comes too close to your eye, you close it. If someone swings at your head, you duck. And if you see something coming at you too close to duck, your natural inclination is to roll with the punch. But if a quarterback is looking down field and someone hits him from behind, we say he was blindsided. He couldn't see it coming. Get hit hard enough that way and you end up with a concussion or worse.

With this in mind, look at Jesus. It was after blindfolding Him that the soldiers began to hit Him. This meant He had no ability to anticipate the force, to "roll with the punches." Isaiah wrote in chapter 52:14 that His face was so marred He was unrecognizable. It was a beating from heartless people who showed no restraint or natural compassion. But by His stripes, He would be sure we were healed. He would absorb the judgment that should have been ours.

We seek to avoid persecution because we don't like the price. Even for the church, compromise often seems better than a beating; denial, or even striking back, preferable to allowing the Lord to have His way. But Peter wrote in 1 Peter 2:21 that "Jesus suffered for us and left us an example that we should follow. He committed no sin. No deceit was found in His mouth. When He was reviled, He didn't revile in return. When He suffered, He didn't make threats. Instead, He committed Himself to the One who judges righteously, bearing our sins in His own body and dying for our sins that we might live for righteousness' sake."

As unfair as it was, Jesus willingly took this treatment because there was a purpose attached to it. He didn't deserve it. We did. Paul wrote to the Philippians that Jesus didn't think of the position He held as God to be something He needed to grasp or protect. He left it all behind to suffer for our sakes. He did it willingly so He might give us life.

> As soon as it was day, the elders of the people, both chief priests and scribes, came together and led Him into their council, saying, "If You are the Christ, tell us."
>
> —Luke 22:66–67

After being questioned both by Annas and Caiaphas, the entire Sanhedrin of seventy men—lawmakers, lawyers, decision-makers, and the nation's representatives—were called together. They met right after dawn (not a normal time to meet) to come up with charges against Jesus they could use in an appeal to Pilate. They knew the charges would require some kind of legal flavor in order for this charade to be called justice.

Mark tells us of their renewed efforts to find witnesses against Jesus:

> Now the chief priests and all the council sought testimony against Jesus to put Him to death, but found none. For many bore false witness against Him, but their testimonies did not agree. Then some rose up and bore false witness against Him, saying, "We heard Him say, 'I will destroy this temple made with hands, and within three days I will build another made without hands.'" But not even then did their testimony agree. And the high priest stood up in the midst and asked Jesus, saying, "Do You answer nothing? What is it these men testify against You?" But He kept silent and answered nothing. Again the high priest asked Him, saying to Him, "Are You the Christ, the Son of the Blessed?"
>
> —Mark 14:55–61

During this parade of false testimony, Jesus just stood by. As His nose bled and His eyes swelled shut, no one could agree as to His having done anything wrong. Finally, it was the high priest who took over the Sanhedrin meeting and asked Jesus two questions: "Are You the Christ, the Messiah?" and "Are You the Son of God?"

Back in Luke 20, Jesus had sought to engage some of these same men as they tried to trip Him up in a public debate. Jesus had spent the entire day answering them, saying, "Look at the facts. Check out the evidence. Follow it." And each time they walked away angry. Although the facts were there, their hearts were hard.

Is Jesus God? That's always the question, isn't it? If He's not, then we ought to run as hard as we can in the opposite direction and write Him off as a fraud. But if He is, we have a great responsibility to listen and follow.

> But He said to them, "If I tell you, you will by no means believe. And if I also ask you, you will by no means answer Me or let Me go. Hereafter the Son of Man will sit on the right hand of the power of God."
>
> —Luke 22:67–69

"If I tell you, you won't believe Me," Jesus said. "You've made up your minds. You're not after the truth. You're only asking Me this question to use My answers against Me."

> Then they all said, "Are You then the Son of God?" So He said to them, "You rightly say that I am."
>
> —Luke 22:70

According to Mark 14, Matthew 26, and John 18, at this point, the high priest tore his clothes, signifying he had heard blasphemy. In fact, Matthew records him saying, "He has spoken blasphemy. What need do we have of further witnesses?" Further witnesses? There had yet to be one witness, but facts aren't needed when your mind is made up.

> And they said, "What further testimony do we need? For we have heard it ourselves from His own mouth."
>
> —Luke 22:71

John records the Sanhedrin saying, "We have a law and according to our law, this Man must die because He makes Himself out to be the Son of God."

Some people today say Jesus never claimed to be God. Only people who don't read the Bible can say that. Jesus claimed to be God constantly, the One who was promised, the One who would save us. The Sanhedrin had heard all they needed to hear. Now all that remained for them to do was press their case with the Romans who, save for the political pressure, couldn't have cared less.

Ultimately, the questions for every person are always the same:

Is Jesus the Savior?

Is He God?

If He's not God, His dying for you meant nothing. If He is not God, we can dismiss the entire Bible.

But if He is God, then we have to listen to every word He says, bow in worship, believe, and follow Him with all that we have. What say you?

Chapter 130

WHO'S ON TRIAL?

Luke 23:1–12
(Matthew 27:2; 11–14; Mark 15:1–5; John 18:28–38)

Jesus had been taken under arrest from the Garden of Gethsemane to the house of Annas, the high priest. Then He was taken to the side of the palace that belonged to Caiaphas, the Roman-appointed high priest. When dawn broke, He was taken to the full council of the Sanhedrin. Here in Luke 23, we begin the civil trials that followed—first before Pilate and then before Herod and finally back to Pilate again.

> Then the whole multitude of them arose and led Him to Pilate.
>
> —Luke 23:1

John tells us that once at Pilate's judgment hall, many members of the Sanhedrin refused to enter the Roman palace's courtyard because doing so would have defiled them religiously, and they hadn't yet eaten the Passover. I would think seeking to murder an innocent Man would have been more than enough to qualify for defilement.

The Romans had put Pilate in power in approximately 26 A.D. According to Josephus, when Pilate arrived in town, he had the soldiers walk before him, bearing Caesar's image on the standards they carried—which, to the Jews, was a violation of the second commandment. When the Jews rioted in the streets, Pilate threatened to kill them. Their response was to lay down in the street, bare their necks, and say, "Go ahead." Whether bluff or defiance, he didn't call them on it, but was humiliated publicly, and the rift became greater as time passed. Josephus also tells us that to build an aqueduct outside of town, Pilate had raided the Jewish temple funds to pay for its construction. Luke 13:1 records Pilate mingling Galilean blood with the sacrifice—perhaps a reference to Josephus' account of his sending his cavalry to the town of Gerazim to slaughter people there as a show of force.

Pilate was a very wicked, hard-hearted man with a number of complaints against him lodged in Rome. In 36 A.D., eleven years after he took office, he was recalled to Rome and, according to early church father Eusebius, took his own life en route.

From what the Gospels tell us, it appears Pilate's only hesitation in letting Jesus go was what might happen to him as a result. Would there be another report? Another riot? Another challenge to his position? His jeopardy was far more important to him than the truth. Many today still act with those same priorities: self, self, self!

In John 18, when this group came to present Jesus to Herod, we read in verse 29 that Pilate asked, "What accusation do you bring against this man?"

The chief priests and others responded by saying, "If He hadn't done something wrong, we wouldn't have brought Him to you." In other words, "Don't worry about that. Just do what we tell you."

"You go judge Him according to your own law," Pilate retorted.

"It's not lawful for us to put anyone to death," they argued. And that was true. They had lost that right when they lost their sovereignty as a nation.

Jewish death would have come by stoning. Only the Romans crucified. Later on, the Jews stoned Stephen and tried to stone Paul. But prophecy had foretold that Jesus would die on a cross (Ps. 22). "If I be lifted up," He had said, "I will draw all men to Me."

Again we get an insight into who was actually in charge.

> And they began to accuse Him, saying, "We found this fellow perverting the nation, and forbidding to pay taxes to Caesar, saying that He Himself is Christ, a King."
>
> —Luke 23:2

The Jews left off the blasphemy charge because to the Romans everyone was a god of some kind. Instead, they focused on that which would have concerned Rome more, political sedition, of undermining the government's power.

In Luke 20, earlier that week in the temple area, they had tried to get Jesus to talk about taxes. But Jesus saw through it masterfully. "Whose picture is on the coin?" He had asked.

"Caesar's," they had answered.

"Then give it to him but make sure you give to God what belongs to God," Jesus had said. He hadn't forbidden the paying of taxes. In fact, He had paid taxes Himself and had told Peter to do the same.

The discrepancy of this argument was that because the Jews hated the Romans, anyone who would have led people against Rome in a revolt would normally have been welcomed, not refused by them. Pilate saw that himself and Matthew 27:18 tells us Pilate knew jealousy was the real reason the religious leaders brought Jesus to him.

> Then Pilate asked Him, saying, "Are You the King of the Jews?" He answered him and said, "It is as you say." So Pilate said to the chief priests and the crowd, "I find no fault in this Man."
>
> —Luke 23:3–4

John gives us a little more insight:

> Then Pilate entered the Praetorium again, called Jesus, and said to Him, "Are You the King of the Jews?" Jesus answered him, "Are you speaking for yourself about this, or did others tell you this concerning Me?" Pilate answered, "Am I a Jew? Your own nation and the chief priests have delivered You to me. What have You done?" Jesus answered, "My kingdom is not of this world. If My kingdom were of this world, My servants would fight, so that I should not be delivered to the Jews; but now My kingdom is not from here." Pilate therefore said to Him, "Are You a king then?" Jesus answered, "You say rightly that I am a king. For this cause I was born, and for this cause I have come into the world, that I should bear witness to the truth. Everyone who is of the truth hears My voice." Pilate said to Him, "What is truth?" And when he had said this, he went out again to the Jews, and said to them, "I find no fault in Him at all."
>
> —John 18:33–38

Keep in mind that Jesus had been beaten. He didn't look much like a king. And Pilate said so. But Pilate found himself in a pressure cooker, standing between a calm Jesus and the angry crowd at the door.

> But they were the more fierce, saying, "He stirs up the people, teaching throughout all Judea, beginning from Galilee to this place."
>
> —Luke 23:5

Pilate's conscience was working overtime. He knew Jesus was innocent. He knew the crowd's motivation outside was envy and jealousy. But he also had lots of complaints in Rome and was on unsteady ground in the political arena in Judea. About this time, Matthew tells us in 27:19 that Pilate's wife sent him a note that said, "Have nothing to do with this innocent Man. I've suffered greatly tonight in a dream because of Him."

Pilate was feeling pressure from every direction—from home, from conscience, from political expediency, and from the crowd. Wondering what to do, he thought he had a break when he heard, "This all got started in Galilee." You can almost see the light go on in his mind: *Galilee is outside my jurisdiction. This isn't my problem. It's Herod's!*

> When Pilate heard of Galilee, he asked if the Man were a Galilean. And as soon as he knew that He belonged to Herod's jurisdiction, he sent Him to Herod, who was also in Jerusalem at that time. Now when Herod saw Jesus, he was exceedingly glad; for he had desired for a long time to see Him, because he had heard many things about Him, and he hoped to see some miracle done by Him. Then he questioned Him with many words, but He answered him nothing. And the chief priests and scribes stood and vehemently accused Him. Then Herod, with his men of war, treated Him with contempt and mocked Him, arrayed Him in a gorgeous robe, and sent Him back to Pilate. That very day Pilate and

Herod became friends with each other, for previously they had been at enmity with each other.

—Luke 23:6–12

Herod is an interesting study because for years he had an opportunity to know Jesus. One of the sons of Herod the Great, he was assigned the Galilee area to rule when his father died in 4 B.C. His marriage to a woman named Herodias came under fire from John the Baptist because Herodias was not only the daughter of Herod's half-brother, Aristobulus, but also the wife of Philip, another half-brother. This made her both his niece and his sister-in-law. He had wooed her in Rome and talked her into leaving Philip to marry him. John's speaking out against the marriage made Herodias so angry that she talked her husband into arresting John and throwing him in jail in a place called Machaerus, located above the Dead Sea in the middle of nowhere.

Mark tells us Herod feared John—he knew John was just and holy—and that he heard John gladly. He liked to sit with John in the jail cell and talk to him. What he heard from him started to change the way he behaved. John's ministry was getting through to his heart. I suspect Herod found great refreshment from John with all of the debauchery in Rome.

John's message to the Jews was, "You have to repent." For the first time, the nation itself was called to repent. So the message John gave Herod was that he needed to repent, that he needed a Savior. As John spoke about the kingdom of heaven and Jesus as Messiah, Herod's conscience was stirred. But Herodias hated John and one day at a drunken party Herod had offered to give his daughter up to half his kingdom, whatever she wanted for having danced for him and his drunken friends. Her mother quickly had her ask for the head of John the Baptist. Herod quickly realized he had been duped. Yet he had made an oath, so he gave the order.

Herod's wrong decision set in motion a downward spiral. Following John's death, Jesus' second year of public ministry began and the tens and hundreds who heard Him the first year became thousands during the second. When this news about Jesus reached Herod, he was sure Jesus was John the Baptist come back from the dead. His wickedness came back to haunt him—but rather than repent, he threw himself into politics and power.

At this point, a year and a half has passed and we don't see the same Herod. He is not convicted in his heart. He is not ashamed because of his conscience. He is not moved by fear of Jesus. He only wants to see Him so he might be entertained by Him. We don't find spiritual hunger or conviction of sin in Herod. We just find an appetite for performance. His conscience had been seared. Whatever moved his heart eighteen months earlier no longer moved him now.

So he began to question Jesus. But Jesus stood absolutely quiet and didn't answer a single question.

There are many today who look at Jesus with curiosity or amusement. There's no sense of need, no guilt of sin, and no conscious awareness of failures or even fear of one day appearing before God. It is to the person in that position that the Lord really has nothing to say.

Jesus spoke with tremendous grief to Judas, reasoned with Caiaphas, and gave Pilate some food for thought. But to this man who was once so close to knowing Him, He was silent. Herod stood face to face with the Son of God and saw nothing. So the Son of God said nothing. Some time during the previous eighteen months, Herod's door of opportunity had slammed shut.

"Today if you will hear His voice, don't harden your hearts as in the rebellion," the psalmist wrote. In other words, while God is speaking and you're able to hear, listen because there's no guarantee you'll get another shot at it. In fact, the Bible teaches fairly clearly that if we say no long enough, that position will become an attribute of our lives.

In Genesis 6:3, God said His Spirit wouldn't always strive with people. Herod is proof of that. I don't know how close he got to believing in the God of Israel and the Savior to come, but he had heard John gladly and knew he was just and holy. He was only fooled into killing John because he was more interested in his position before his friends than his standing before God. That is how now he could humiliate and mock the Son of God with no conviction.

Respond when God speaks. Answer the door when He knocks. He'll knock more than once—far longer than we would. But at the same time, Herod tells us that if we ignore His call long enough, we'll go from hearing Him gladly to treating Him with contempt.

Chapter 131

WHAT WILL I DO WITH JESUS?

Luke 23:13–25
(Matthew 27:15–26; Mark 15:6–15; John 18:39–19:16)

The long-standing animosity between the hard-line Roman overlord and the half-Jewish, half-Idumean man would turn to friendship as both men dealt with Jesus. Pilate and Herod became friends with each other, but not with God. Maybe Pilate is best known for his question, "What shall I do with Jesus?" It's a question with eternal ramifications. Unfortunately, he gives the wrong answer.

Luke 23:13 picks up with the return of Jesus from Herod's trial, where, once again, He had been mocked and beaten.

> Then Pilate, when he had called together the chief priests, the rulers, and the people, said to them, "You have brought this Man to me, as one who misleads the people. And indeed, having examined Him in your presence, I have found no fault in this Man concerning those things of which you accuse Him; no, neither did Herod, for I sent you back to him; and indeed nothing deserving of death has been done by Him. I will therefore chastise Him and release Him . . . ."
> —Luke 23:13–16

Pilate was convinced Jesus was innocent. He had declared Him to be so time and again. He first had attempted to send Him to the Jews so they could try Him. He had tried to release Him but the mob had cried out against it. He had tried to defer Him to Herod who had sent Him back. At this point, Pilate was running out of options. But he had to make a decision: What was he going to do with Jesus?

There were a lot of voices screaming in his ear. If it wasn't the religious leaders in verses 1 and 2 or the crowd in verse 5, it was the mob as it gathers in verse 18 or his wife who sends a message about a dream she had. Then there was his conscience crying out for justice and the worry that his job was on the line.

John records Pilate going back and forth between Jesus and the crowd some seven different times, three of those declaring His innocence. But the crowd wasn't going away. So Pilate did something that shows the extremely ugly side of sin: he compromised. In his cowardice, he chose to do something no one should do. He would beat an innocent Man, hoping a beating might satisfy the bloodthirsty crowd. Apparently he thought he could live with a beating on his conscience. But he wasn't so sure about murder.

Scourging was a horrible Roman practice from which Roman citizens were exempt. It was carried out with leather whips that had bone or glass pieces tied to the ends of them. History tells us many people died from scourging. With two-inch chunks of flesh ripped from their backs, it didn't take long for people to become so weak they would confess to things they didn't do just to end the pain. Yet we read in Isaiah 53 that as a lamb before her shearers is dumb, so Jesus didn't open His mouth. He had nothing to confess so He would take it all. Yet as plans were being made for the scourging, another possible out came to Pilate's attention.

> . . . (for it was necessary for him to release one to them at the feast). And they all cried out at once, saying, "Away with this Man, and release to us Barabbas"—who had been thrown into prison for a certain rebellion made in the city, and for murder.
>
> —Luke 23:17–19

Mark 15:5–8 tells us the tradition had been that Pilate would release a prisoner at Passover as a gesture of political tolerance. When he heard someone ask when he would release the prisoner, he thought that would be his chance to let Jesus go.

I suspect Barabbas, an insurrectionist and murderer, was the one initially intended to die with the other two thieves. "Barabbas" is a title, not a name. It means "son of the father." Jesus, the Son of God, would hang on a cross created for the son of the father so we could be called the children of God. It's a beautiful picture.

Matthew gives us further insight as to what was going on with Pilate:

> Now at the feast the governor was accustomed to releasing to the multitude one prisoner whom they wished. And at that time they had a notorious prisoner called Barabbas. Therefore, when they had gathered together, Pilate said to them, "Whom do you want me to release to you? Barabbas, or Jesus who is called Christ?" For he knew that they had handed Him over because of envy.
>
> —Matthew 27:15–18

Knowing it was the religious leaders who were pushing this agenda, Pilate put the question to the crowd, expecting them to say Jesus should be the one released.

> While he was sitting on the judgment seat, his wife sent to him, saying, "Have nothing to do with that just Man, for I have suffered many things today in a dream because of Him." But the chief priests and elders persuaded the multitudes that they should ask for Barabbas and destroy Jesus. The governor answered and said to them, "Which of the two do you want me to release to you?" They said, "Barabbas!"
>
> —Matthew 27:19–21

Barabbas? Pilate must have thought. *This isn't working at all.*

But I believe the interruption from Pilate's wife was a divinely appointed one. Had the religious leaders not had an opportunity to stir them up, I think the crowd would have asked for Jesus to be released. But that wasn't God's will. The crowd called for Barabbas to be released and, although Pilate must have been startled by their answer, God wasn't.

> Pilate said to them, "What then shall I do with Jesus who is called Christ?" They all said to him, "Let Him be crucified!" Then the governor said, "Why, what evil has He done?" But they cried out all the more, saying, "Let Him be crucified!" When Pilate saw that he could not prevail at all, but rather that a tumult was rising, he took water and washed his hands before the multitude, saying, "I am innocent of the blood of this just Person. You see to it."
>
> —Matthew 27:22–24

"What shall I do with Jesus?" Pilate asked, but I think the court is out of control when the judge asks for advice from the crowd. The fellow with the power should be making the decisions. Pilate was not doing that. But it's a significant question because it seems to me from the report in the Gospels that what Pilate had been seeking to do was evade having to answer this question for himself. He wanted to pass it off to someone else. And yet every one of us at some point will have to determine whether Jesus is who He said He was or not.

Jesus' claims are so radical that you really can't stand in the middle in regards to your response to Him. If He stands before you, saying, "I'm the only way to heaven and without Me you're destined for hell," that doesn't leave you a lot of room to be impartial. He either is the Lord, and you do whatever it takes and whatever the cost might be to follow Him, or you reject Him altogether. If you're not for Him, by process of elimination you're against Him. If you're not confessing Him, you're denying Him. If you don't believe in Him, you effectively are rejecting Him regardless of what you might say in defense of yourself and your position.

"What am I supposed to do with Jesus?" Good question, Pilate. What are you going to do with Him? He decided to scourge Jesus and then let Him go, hoping the crowd might find some sympathy. He played his ace in the hole. He beat an innocent Man.

> So then Pilate took Jesus and scourged Him. And the soldiers twisted a crown of thorns and put it on His head, and they put on Him a purple robe. Then they said, "Hail, King of the Jews!" And they struck Him with their hands. Pilate then went out again, and said to them, "Behold, I am bringing Him out to you, that you may know that I find no fault in Him." Then Jesus came out, wearing the crown of thorns and the purple robe. And Pilate said to them, "Behold the Man!" Therefore, when the chief priests and officers saw Him, they cried out, saying, "Crucify Him, crucify Him!" Pilate said to them, "You take Him and crucify Him, for I find no fault in Him."
>
> —John 19:1–6

Jesus' suffering is very understated in the Bible. But we know from historical records that scourging was debilitating and excruciatingly painful, resulting in almost certain death. Jesus would leave this Praetorium carrying a cross for only a few blocks before He needed help—not because He wasn't willing to carry it, but because His body was unable.

As he brought Jesus out, Pilate hoped the bloody mess that was now the Lord would break the people's hearts, and that would be it. Instead, the religious leaders screamed for His death, to which Pilate said, "You take Him."

> The Jews answered him, "We have a law, and according to our law He ought to die, because He made Himself the Son of God." Therefore, when Pilate heard that saying, he was the more afraid, and went into the Praetorium, and said to Jesus, "Where are You from?" But Jesus gave him no answer.
>
> —John 19:7–9

Pilate was a pagan. When he heard the word *God*, he thought of the Roman gods—angry gods not to be messed with. He'd heard a lot of supernatural reports about Jesus. Even his wife had a dream. *Who am I dealing with here?* he must have wondered.

> Then Pilate said to Him, "Are You not speaking to me? Do You not know that I have power to crucify You, and power to release You?" Jesus answered, "You could have no power at all against Me unless it had been given you from above. Therefore the one who delivered Me to you has the greater sin."
>
> —John 19:10–11

The religious leaders knew better. They had the Scriptures. They were raised in the ways of the Lord. They had the promises and the prophecies. Pilate did not have that knowledge. Therefore, their sin was greater than his. To whom much is given . . .

> From then on Pilate sought to release Him, but the Jews cried out, saying, "If you let this Man go, you are not Caesar's friend. Whoever makes himself a king speaks against Caesar." When Pilate therefore heard that saying, he brought Jesus out and sat down in the judgment seat in a place that is called The Pavement, but in Hebrew, Gabbatha. Now it was the Preparation Day of the Passover, and about the sixth hour. And he said to the Jews, "Behold your King!" But they cried out, "Away with Him, away with Him! Crucify Him!" Pilate said to them, "Shall I crucify your King?" The chief priests answered, "We have no king but Caesar!"
>
> —John 19:12–15

Finally, the crowd dropped the other shoe when they said, "You're going to let a king survive? Caesar won't tolerate a threat." It was the one thing Pilate couldn't afford—another report about what he had allowed to happen.

"What kind of threat is this Man?" he asked. "Look at Him standing in a pool of His own blood. Isn't that enough?" But the crowd wouldn't hear it. In fact, Matthew records them saying, "May His blood be upon us and upon our children."

> Pilate, therefore, wishing to release Jesus, again called out to them. But they shouted, saying, "Crucify Him, crucify Him!" Then he said to them the third time, "Why, what evil has He done? I have found no reason for death in Him. I will therefore chastise Him and let Him go." But they were insistent, demanding with loud voices that He be crucified. And the voices of these men and of the chief priests prevailed. So Pilate gave sentence that it should be as they requested. And he released to them the one they requested, who for rebellion and murder had been thrown into prison; but he delivered Jesus to their will.
>
> —Luke 23:20–25

I think one of the saddest verses in all the Bible is the one that tells us people prevailed over Pilate's conscience. How often does the world prevail over our resistance and better judgment? Like Pilate, we face the pressure of self, acceptance, and worldly approval all the time, but when they have victory over our devotion to God's ways, how tragic that day!

I remember my parents lecturing me until they were blue in the face about not running with the crowd. There's something about crowds. You'll do stuff in a crowd that you'd never do alone. Pilate was no different. He gave in to the people's demands. He gave sentence as they requested and delivered Jesus to their will. He might have tried to wash his hands, but that hardly would begin to absolve his sin. Justice did not prevail. Self-preservation prevailed. Peer pressure prevailed. Influence prevailed. Hatred prevailed. The murderer went free and the innocent Man went to death in his place.

Let me encourage you to think about this part of the story the next time you feel like what you're going through isn't fair. I would say *this* isn't fair. Jesus should have been allowed to walk away—no crown of thorns, no purple robe, no punches in the face. He should have walked. Barabbas should have been killed. It wasn't fair—but if it had been, we couldn't have been saved. Sometimes God allows injustices and we see the purpose very clearly. Other times we have no clue as to why. But don't lose sight of the fact that God knows perfectly well what He's doing. And His ways do work out for good—all of them—for those who love Him.

Pilate tried avoiding the consequences of releasing Jesus. He permitted Him to be shuffled around. He allowed Him to be beaten. He ordered Him to be scourged. He sent Him off to be murdered—all the while constantly declaring His innocence.

The Father goes to great lengths to establish Jesus' innocence. Herod and Pilate called Him a just man three times in this chapter alone. Pilate's wife wakes up from a dream, saying, "He's a just Man." Judas, on discovering the chief priests were going to kill Him, said he had betrayed innocent blood. The thief on the cross, and the Roman centurion who stood by. They all declared His innocence.

The world of both religious and irreligious people outside the Praetorium walls could not find a spot or blemish in Jesus. He would indeed be the Lamb of God who would take away the sins of the world. It wasn't Jesus on trial. It was everyone else. And everyone is put to the same test: What will you do with Jesus?

What are your options?

You can hate Him like the religious leaders did because you're envious of Him. For pride's sake, you want nothing to do with Him. He's exposed your heart. He knows you inside out. He warns you of the road you're on and where it will lead. So you want nothing to do with Him.

You can reject Him like the fickle crowd did. The crowd loved Jesus, but the strong words of a powerful few easily influenced them. There were those who, left to themselves, would have cried for Barabbas to be killed and for Jesus to be released. But a few loud and powerful men turned their hearts. You can't follow the crowd and get saved. Salvation is a singular experience. The Lord doesn't save by ZIP Code, or even by family. He comes to you and asks, "What are you going to do with Me?"

You can, like Herod, mock Jesus and send Him away, not finding what you hoped to find.

You can be like Pilate and try to avoid making the choice altogether. You can argue that the pressure and cost of doing the right thing is too high. You can wash your hands—but you'll never find life.

Or you can choose to believe Him, be forgiven by Him, receive Him in His love, and embrace Him as Lord.

What do you do with Jesus? Be sure you have the right answer, because He's the only way to life, and you only get only one life to make the right one!

Chapter 132

THE CRUCIFIXION

Luke 23:26–49
(Matthew 27:31–56; Mark 15:20–41;
John 19:16–22; 28–30)

T he biblical account of the crucifixion is surprisingly very brief. Rather than detailing Jesus' pain and suffering, all of the attention is focused on the people who were there—the soldiers, the religious leaders, the criminals, the disciples, the women. They are the ones whose stories are told: it is the effect of the sacrifice that fills our view.

> Then the soldiers of the governor took Jesus into the Praetorium and gathered the whole garrison around Him. And they stripped Him and put a scarlet robe on Him. When they had twisted a crown of thorns, they put it on His head, and a reed in His right hand. And they bowed the knee before Him and mocked Him, saying, "Hail, King of the Jews!" Then they spat on Him, and took the reed and struck Him on the head. And when they had mocked Him, they took the robe off Him, put His own clothes on Him, and led Him away to be crucified.
>
> —Matthew 27:27–31

At every point, the beating continued. The thorns were a fruit of the ground's curse after man's fall back in the garden. That which the earth brought forth because of sin was now crammed into the head of the Creator.

Luke picks up the story:

> Now as they led Him away, they laid hold of a certain man, Simon a Cyrenian, who was coming from the country, and on him they laid the cross that he might bear it after Jesus.
>
> —Luke 23:26

Jesus was taken from the Praetorium—the meeting hall in the Antonio Fortress that the Romans had built on the Temple Mount to keep an eye on the religious holidays, which were often troublesome. John tells us in chapter 19:17 that as Jesus came out, He bore His own cross. How far He was able to carry it we don't know. Matthew says it was when they came out that they grabbed Simon. This could mean either when they came out of the Praetorium, which meant Jesus would have walked approximately five hundred yards, or it could mean when they came out of the city, which meant He was able to walk farther. We can't be sure. But we are sure that because of the horrific beatings He had endured, Jesus was physically weak. The soldiers who took Jesus to the cross, seeing Him staggering under its weight, enlisted a man to help.

In speaking of Simon's command to carry the cross, Matthew 27:31 uses the word *compel*, which is a political term. Being in a position of power, it was the Romans' legal right to do this. History tells us that when the Romans compelled a man, they put a sword on his shoulder. That was pretty much all they had to do. The man could then either do what they said or he could wear the sword. Had a Roman soldier compelled you, you would have been obligated by law to carry his burden for a mile. The problem was that you could go for a mile, walk two blocks, and then another soldier could begin the process all over again.

In the Sermon on the Mount, (Matt. 5:41), Jesus said, "If they compel you to go one mile, go two. If they want your jacket, give them your coat. Just let the Lord work these things out." But if you were Jewish, you would hate this process, because it was another reminder that the nation was in subjection and under someone else's authority.

Luke 23:26 tells us Simon was a Cyrenian. Cyrene was in the area of present-day Libya, eight hundred miles from Jerusalem. He was no doubt in the city because he had come for the Passover, a devout man coming to seek the Lord. Cyrene at the time was on the trade routes from east to west. It was a big city with a large population of Jews—many of whom would make the eight-hundred-mile trip to Jerusalem three times a year for the feasts. In fact, according to Acts 6:9, there was a synagogue in Jerusalem exclusively for the Cyrenians so they could worship in their own language.

I suspect Simon was humiliated being nabbed. This was the ultimate "Why me?" argument we make to God sometimes.

But in the years following this, we read of the fruit of Simon's conversion—which is certainly what took place this day. In fact, by the time Mark writes his gospel, Simon's sons were well known to the church. As Mark recounted Jesus' death, he identified Simon as the father of Alexander and Rufus. When Paul wrote to the Romans, at the end of chapter 16:13 he told the church to be sure to greet Rufus and his mother, who had been like a mother to him. So the entire family of this man who was forced to carry the cross would become effective tools in the work of the church yet to be born.

I think sometimes we find ourselves resenting what life has done to us. But it is often in the most humiliating circumstances that God can get to us. In Acts 11:19, we read that following Stephen's death, believers left Jerusalem in record numbers. They went to Phoenicia, Cyprus, and Antioch, where they preached to the Jews. But there were some Cyrenian believers who began to speak to the Hellenists—Jews who had grown up in Greek cultures—and for the first time, the preaching of Jesus began to cross the line between Jews and Gentiles. Simon was the catalyst by which an entire country of people removed by eight hundred miles began to have great impact on the world for the Gospel. Simon would go from religion to faith and impact the work God would do in the next generation.

According to first-century practices of crucifixion, a soldier walked in front of the condemned man with a sign stating his charges. Four soldiers surrounded him on either side to keep the crowds away as they walked through the city the long way, so everyone could learn the potential consequence of breaking Roman law. The long way was the deterrent.

After being marched through town, the condemned were taken outside of the city gates and crucified on the highest hill next to the busiest intersection, again so all might see and fear. This particular Passover, with over a million folks in town, Jesus of Nazareth, King of the Jews, was taken to His death with Simon compelled to join Him.

> And a great multitude of the people followed Him, and women who also mourned and lamented Him. But Jesus, turning to them, said, "Daughters of Jerusalem, do not weep for Me, but weep for yourselves and for your children. For indeed the days are coming in which they will say, 'Blessed are the barren, wombs that never bore, and breasts which never nursed!' Then they will begin to say to the mounts, 'Fall on us!' and to the hills, 'Cover us!' For if they do these things in the green wood, what will be done in the dry?"
>
> —Luke 23:27–31

These were not the faithful women who had been following Jesus for years—those who had cooked for Him and cared for Him, those who would get up before dawn on Sunday to prepare His body for burial. These were women from Jerusalem who wept not because they were brokenhearted that Jesus was lost and so was their hope. They probably had very little hope in Him. They wept because Jesus was yet another reminder that their nation was being destroyed by an occupying power.

Turning to them, Jesus said, "Don't cry for Me. My future is secure. I know where I'm headed. But you and your children need prayer. You're the ones without hope."

In Zechariah 9:9, Zechariah prophesied of Jesus that the King would come into Jerusalem riding a donkey. The prophecy is introduced by the words, "Rejoice greatly, O daughter of Zion and shout for joy, O daughters of Jerusalem." There should have been great rejoicing in town over the fact that the Messiah had arrived. Instead, the daughters now weep for themselves and for the future.

In fact, Jesus said something that would have been unfathomable to these women when He said there was coming a time when barrenness would be seen as a blessing. The Jewish culture had always looked upon barrenness as God's judgment, even though it rarely was. So for Jesus to say that not having children would be better than having them must have confused these women greatly. Yet we know from history that a holocaust came approximately forty years later with the arrival of Titus, the Roman general and his tenth, twelfth, and fourteenth legions. They surrounded the city for 143 days—no food in, no people out. Finally, on August 10, 70 A.D., thirty thousand soldiers entered the city gates, and by the end of the day, six hundred thousand Jews were dead. The calamity from which God wanted to spare them they chose for themselves. That is why here, as the women wept over His impending death, Jesus wept for them.

I believe the green wood refers to Jesus. He produced the fruits of healing and forgiveness. But if the Romans did this to Him, what would they do to those whose lives were dry and dead, fruitless and lifeless, when He was gone? Any nation that seeks to live without Jesus only has a limited time. Yet God's will is not to judge. He came to seek and to save.

> There were also two others, criminals led with Him to be put to death.
> —Luke 23:32

In both Matthew and Mark, we're told these two criminals with whom Jesus was crucified didn't spare their words. Like the crowds, the soldiers, and the religious leaders, they spewed mockery, hatred, and blasphemy at Jesus for quite some time. Matthew identified them as robbers and used a term that spoke of violence. But Isaiah 53:12 said Jesus would be numbered with the transgressors, so this is the way it had to be. At each turn, we see fulfillment of Scripture so we never come away from the story of Jesus' death thinking that things got out of hand. God knew exactly what He was doing.

> And when they had come to the place called Calvary, there they crucified Him,
> and the criminals, one on the right hand and the other on the left.
> —Luke 23:33

The word *Calvary* is Latin for the Greek word for *cranium* or *skull*. This place has always looked like a skull—even with all of the erosion, it is still the same today. The Aramaic word for *Calvary* is *Golgotha*. So outside the Damascus gate stood three large crosses on a hilltop that looked like a skull, to be seen by all who passed by.

> Then Jesus said, "Father, forgive them, for they do not know what they do."
> —Luke 23:34

Jesus uttered seven short sentences in the six hours He hung upon the cross, from nine to three. He began with a forgiving heart. "Father, forgive them," He prayed. "They don't know what they're doing." Pilate had known what he was doing. Over and over again, he had said Jesus was not guilty. But here was a group of soldiers who, under obligation to carry out this crucifixion, probably didn't understand the enormity of their crime because they weren't able, as many were, to compare the Old Testament scriptures with Jesus' actions and words. They were raised in Roman culture. There, everyone was a god. So Jesus ascribed them a need for forgiveness with an explanation that their behavior was something they didn't fully understand. They needed forgiveness, but the culpability of their action was less than Pilate's—and Pilate's less than those who had brought Jesus to him.

Throughout Scripture we find that God isn't only right and good but just and fair. We need forgiveness—but with knowledge comes responsibility. So these soldiers, even in ignorance, needed forgiveness. To whom much is given, much is required. To whom little is given, little is required. As brutal as they could be, Jesus saw these soldiers as men who didn't know what they were doing.

Notice again how short the description is of our Lord's suffering. This was a horrific form of capital punishment, yet the focus is not on the pain but on the forgiveness Jesus offered. From Matthew 27:34, we know Jesus was offered some sour wine with gall mixed in to dull the pain. He refused it. He would suffer completely for our sins.

I don't know what your picture is of the cross, but I always think of Jesus' hands. These were hands that had touched deaf ears and blind eyes, hands that had blessed children and fed multitudes. Now they were fastened to a cross. His feet, the ones that the repentant woman of the streets had washed with her tears and Mary just a week earlier had anointed with expensive ointment, now had a stake driven through them. Yet Jesus prayed for the forgiveness of those who drove the stake and the nails because that's what God's love does. Jesus practiced what He preached. He prayed for His enemies.

And they divided His garments and cast lots.

—Luke 23:34

The soldiers tore Jesus' clothes in pieces until they came to His undergarment, a tunic that had been made out of one piece of cloth and was considered to be of value. For that they decided to gamble. Like these soldiers, it seems to me that a lot of people want to talk to Jesus only when they need something they consider to be of value. But when it comes to walking with Him, serving Him, or repenting from their sins, they're not interested. Written a thousand years earlier, Psalm 22:18 foretold these lots would be cast—another reminder that God knew what He was doing and that He was in control.

And the people stood looking on.

—Luke 23:35

The people stood looking on. You can only wonder how they could do that. We know from the other Gospel accounts that although some stood by indifferently, many of them mocked. The fickle crowd that just a week earlier had laid down their coats for Jesus and had said of Him, "Blessed is He that comes in the name of the Lord," now called for His death.

Matthew records the people saying, "You who would destroy the temple and build it in three days, save Yourself. If You're the Son of God, come down from the cross."

But even the rulers with them sneered, saying, "He saved others; let Him save Himself if He is the Christ, the chosen of God."

—Luke 23:35

705

Like the crowd, the religious leaders spewed their hatred toward the cross. But theirs was engendered by Jesus' claim of being the Messiah. He clearly had said to them, "I am God, the Son of God. I and the Father are one." And it was that claim of Jesus that had so enraged these religiously blind folks. They refused to believe He was the Messiah and that He needed to suffer and die for their sins if they were to have hope and a future.

These religious men seemed to possess but little knowledge of the Scriptures. They had Psalm 22:16, which said, "They mocked Me. They shook their heads at Me. They pierced My hands and feet. They cast lots for My garments." They had Isaiah 53, which described the crucifixion in detail, how it pleased the Father to bruise His Son, and how He would be hung between sinners. They had Daniel 9, which spoke of the Messiah coming and yet being cut off for people's sins.

These leaders taught that the Messiah would be a good man with political clout, that He would free the people from the Romans' bondage, and that He would put the nation back on the map. But they set aside everything the Bible teaches about sin and God's redemption. They did something religious people often do: they brought their expectation about God to the Word and sought to make it say what they wanted to hear. But that's a very dangerous approach.

You don't want to come to the Bible with your mind made up, looking for Scriptures to support your ideology. You want to come to the Bible with a clean slate and ask God to speak to you. The Bible is the source of truth, not a tool to support your version of the truth. What the religious leaders didn't realize was that if Jesus saved Himself, He couldn't save them. Jesus, who was without sin, had to die for their sin if they were going to have any hope of standing before a holy God.

"Save Yourself!" the crowds yelled.

"Save Yourself," the rulers mocked.

I'm glad Jesus didn't take them up on it, aren't you?

> The soldiers also mocked Him, coming and offering Him sour wine, and saying, "If You are the King of the Jews, save Yourself."
>
> —Luke 23:36–37

"Save Yourself!" the soldiers said. With their pagan backgrounds, these soldiers most likely saw Jesus as just another troublemaker, railing against the rule and power of the Romans. So from their position of supposed strength, they mocked Him. "King of the Jews?" they jeered. "This is the best they can do for a king?"

> And an inscription also was written over Him in letters of Greek, Latin, and Hebrew: THIS IS THE KING OF THE JEWS.
>
> —Luke 23:38

706

According to John 19:19–22, Pilate had hung an inscription over the cross that read: "Jesus of Nazareth, this is the King of the Jews." Some of those reading it had gone back to him, saying, "Don't write that He is the King of the Jews. Write only that He *said* He was King of the Jews." But Pilate, for the first time in his whole miserable story, stood up for himself and refused to change it.

> Then one of the criminals who were hanged blasphemed Him, saying, "If You are the Christ, save Yourself and us."
>
> —Luke 23:39

The robbers crucified with Jesus also joined in the taunt. Everyone in this story had the same piece of advice: Save Yourself. Save Yourself and we'll believe You. Save Yourself and we'll follow You. Save Yourself and we'll know You're telling the truth.

The idea of saving Himself is the same suggestion Satan had offered Jesus at the beginning of His ministry. In Luke 4 he had taken Jesus to a high mountain, showed Him all of the kingdoms of the world, and promised Him authority over them if He simply would bow down and worship him. The obvious implication of the temptation was that Jesus didn't have to go through the suffering of the cross to gain the world—that He could, in fact, save Himself from it.

The big battle today for the souls of men is to convince people that they cannot save themselves. If you can save yourself, Jesus didn't have to die. But if you can't, the advice to save yourself is a lie that has eternal consequences because the only road that leads to heaven is the cross of Jesus Christ. The suggestion that you can find life apart from the cross is exactly where the battle between the Gospel of Jesus Christ and the world begins.

It is always Satan's plan and goal to keep you from the cross, to keep you from faith, and to convince you that you can save yourself. It is a cry from hell that has taken more than one person there. How do we find life? Paul wrote to the Romans in chapter 6 that our old person has to be crucified with Christ so we no longer become slaves to our flesh's sinfulness. If we have died with Christ, we'll live with Him. Everything that salvation is points to the cross.

Jesus could have delivered Himself. I think if He had jumped off the cross, He'd have made believers of them all. But what did He do instead? What did Jesus do to save us? He did what He asks us to do. He denied Himself so we could live. The nails through Jesus' hands and feet didn't hold Him there. Neither did the powerful religious lobbyists nor the majority of the crowd's perception. He stayed on the cross because He loved His Father and He loved you. His love kept Him there.

> But the other, answering, rebuked him, saying, "Do you not even fear God, seeing you are under the same condemnation? And we indeed justly, for we receive the due reward of our deeds; but this Man has done nothing wrong." Then

he said to Jesus, "Lord, remember me when You come into Your kingdom." And Jesus said to him, "Assuredly, I say to you, today you will be with Me in Paradise."

—Luke 23:40–43

Only Luke gives us this exchange, the second thing Jesus said between nine and noon. It's an interesting picture of two men equidistant from Jesus, both of them there because of their sins, both of them with equal access and equal revelation—and yet look at the difference in response. One is lost; one is saved. One stayed bitter to the end, the other, within only three or four hours of the end of his life, called Jesus his Lord, confessed his sin, and asked for God's mercy. One railed in unbelief, the other saw by faith. It all depends on what you do with Jesus, doesn't it?

We are given another word of Jesus' innocence, this time from one who also hung on a cross. "We're in the same spot, but we deserve to be here. He doesn't," said one thief to the other.

If nothing else, this thief ought to teach us that there's nothing we can offer Jesus to be saved except trust. He cast himself on Jesus' mercy and asked for His grace. This guy never had been to a church service. He didn't have time to be baptized, take Communion, or go on a missions trip. There wasn't any ritual he could follow and no opportunity for outward observation. He was halfway to dead. This was his last stop. But salvation is "not of works, lest any man should boast."

If you question the idea that salvation is solely by faith, I would ask you to look again at this thief because here is a portrait that ought to silence your doubt. Jesus said, "Today you will be with Me in Paradise. Guaranteed." I don't know how much prior exposure this thief had to Jesus. Maybe all he had was the sign hanging over His head and, considering what it said, looked to Jesus and believed it, even though at that point Jesus didn't look much like a king. All the thief had to go on was what the declaration said—and maybe the smile, peace, and rest he saw on our Lord's face. The thief saw by faith what the disciples had missed—that Jesus would have a kingdom beyond this life.

According to verse 40, here's how you get saved: you acknowledge your sin. You turn to Jesus by faith, call on His name, ask Him to be your Lord, and rely on His mercy. In all of the trials, Jesus never once spoke out in His own defense to any of His enemies' accusations or lies. But one voice somewhere off to His right or left, crying out for help, didn't go unheard. Jesus immediately answered and assured Him of His forgiveness and mercy.

No matter what you've done, you can be saved if you'll come. The only thing that will keep you from being saved is you. God's willing. Hebrews tells us it was for the joy set before Him that Jesus endured the cross, although He despised the shame. I think this thief's words gave Jesus a taste of the joy that was ahead. After noon, darkness would fill the earth and Jesus would find Himself forsaken. But here was a foretaste for Him of what was coming, the fruit of His sacrifice.

It's never too late to get saved. While you have breathe you can have life. I don't for a minute think you should use this thief to say to the Lord, "When I'm ready to die, You and I will talk," because there aren't many deathbed conversions in the Bible. This thief was pulled out of the fire with his clothes singed. There are some last-minute reversals found in the Bible, which should encourage us to keep praying and sharing with people to the bitter end. But I wouldn't use it as an argument for stalling because, like Herod, you can stall too long.

"Save yourself," everyone said—except the one who said, "Lord, save me." And it was the one who went looking for grace and mercy who found life. It's still the same for us. We're either saving ourselves or we're being saved. The crowd moves us or the cross does. We're either headed for judgment or paradise. The Devil's lie is that you can save yourself. God's Word says that never can happen.

John tells us that toward noon, Jesus called John over to Him and said to Mary, "Woman, behold your son," and to John, "Son, behold your mother," as He handed the responsibility for Mary's care to John.

The first three hours, Jesus suffered at people's hands. But for the last three hours He suffered at the hands of His own Father, who not only would pour upon Him the sins of the world but would turn away from His Son as He carried those sins. Jesus was separated from God. That's what sin does to us. That is why Paul later wrote to the Corinthians, "He made Him who knew no sin to be sin for us so that we could be made the righteousness of God in Him" (2 Cor. 5:21). That's what took place from noon to three, beginning as darkness covered the earth at midday.

> Now it was about the sixth hour, and there was darkness over all the earth until
> the ninth hour. Then the sun was darkened . . . .
>
> —Luke 23:44–45

The sixth hour is high noon. Jesus had been on the cross for three hours when suddenly darkness covered the entire earth. There are many Bible critics who try to explain this away by saying it was an eclipse. Certainly there are eclipses, but not at Passover, because on Passover there is always a full moon on this side of the sun. The darkness was specific to God's judgment. In fact, in speaking of the Lord's second coming, all of the Old Testament prophets speak of how dark a time it will be. Isaiah wrote in 5:30 that in that day people will roar like the seas and when one looks to the land he will see darkness and sorrow and a light that has been darkened by the clouds.

A couple of days earlier, as Jesus sat down the disciples to explain to them what was soon to come, He spoke of Israel's suffering, the tribulation, and the church's eventual rapture. Of those days, He said the sun will be dark and the moon won't give its light. Stars will fall from heaven. The second coming will be a time of judgment as the world meets the Lord it has rejected.

Writing to a people who were pretending to be religious but weren't faithful to God, Amos said in chapter 5:18, "Woe to you who desire the day of the Lord. What good will the day of the Lord be to you? It will be darkness and not light. Is not the day of the Lord very dark with no brightness in it?"

Jesus came to die for our sins. The visible evidence of God's judgment of our sins is the absolute darkness that filled the noonday sky and remained for three hours. And for nearly all of that time, Jesus suffered in silence. The Gospels give us no words spoken, no description of the crowd, and no record of what took place. Nothing was said as Jesus, silently, hidden from people's eyes, suffered the separation from His Father.

Matthew tells us in chapter 27:46 that toward the end of the ninth hour, as darkness covered the planet, Jesus cried out with a loud voice, "Eli, Eli, lama sabachtani? My God, My God, why have You forsaken Me?" We never will understand the depths of the consequence Jesus faced for our sin. It was God's righteousness that prompted Him to turn away from His own Son and prompted Jesus to cry, "Where are You?" Jesus hung alone. He suffered by Himself.

> . . . and the veil of the temple was torn in two.
>
> —Luke 23:45

The second visible evidence that Jesus' death was working for our deliverance was the tearing of the temple veil that hung between the holy place and the holy of holies. The holy place was the area inside the temple where the priests would come daily to minister before the Lord. The holy of holies was the place of God's presence where the high priest would go once a year with blood to atone for the people's sins. Between these two places hung a veil eighteen inches thick. Matthew says it was as Jesus cried out with a loud voice and yielded up His Spirit that the temple veil was torn from top to bottom. Luke, more interested in the response to and effect of Jesus' work, placed events in a topical rather than chronological order.

The veil was not torn from bottom to top because man did not open the way—God did. In fact, in Hebrews 10:4 we read that it wasn't possible for the blood of bulls and goats to take away our sin. But we now could have boldness to enter into that holiest place of all in a new and living way by Jesus' blood, which He consecrated for us through the veil, that is His flesh. As a result, we can come into God's presence through the body that was broken. We can't come in any other way. We can't sneak in with religious ways or good intentions of doing better. We only can come in through faith. We only can come in through the cross.

In Numbers 21, frustrated with their journey, the Jews coming out of Egypt often blamed both Moses and God. In judgment, the Lord sent snakes into the camp and people began to die as the snakes bit many. It wasn't long before the people in their suffering cried out to Moses, "We've sinned. We've spoken against God and against you. Pray to the Lord that He would take away the serpents." When Moses did this, the Lord told him to make a brass serpent, stick it on a pole, lift it up over the people's heads, and tell them that whoever looked at the serpent would live.

Throughout the Old Testament, brass was associated with judgment for sin. You can just imagine people in Moses' day saying, "I'm not looking at that stupid thing. Just get the snakes out of here!"

"Look at the serpent on the pole. Look at God's judgment," Moses said.

"I'm not looking," some must have said. "That's silly." But their only other alternative was to die.

The serpent, sin, and the Devil were put out of business at the cross. That is why Jesus said, "If I be lifted up, if I'm the One who bears the sin. If man will look at and believe in Me, he'll have eternal life."

What a moment in the darkness it was as the veil was torn and Jesus paid our admission price to heaven!

> And when Jesus had cried out with a loud voice, He said, "Father, into Your hands I commit My spirit." Having said this, He breathed His last.
> —Luke 23:46

If you take a small step back in the chronology, shortly before this point, after nearly three hours of silence John records that, knowing everything had been accomplished and Scripture had been fulfilled, Jesus cried out, "I thirst." Responding to this, the soldiers plunged a sponge into a vessel of sour wine and hyssop, stuck it on a spear, and held it up to Jesus. Jesus had turned down the anesthetic early on. He had suffered completely. But this time He took it to His lips, I suspect so He clearly could be heard when He said, "Tetelestai. It is finished." And here, "Father into Your hands I commit My Spirit."

What was finished? People's redemption, the payment for our sin. And if you hang around long enough to get through the rest of the story, you'll find that as Easter comes rolling around, the firstfruits of that "It is finished" begin to take shape and form.

The next time someone suggests to you that you have to do something besides believe in Jesus' work to be saved, turn them to the words *It is finished*. The Lord doesn't seem to think you need to do any more. His Son's work was sufficient. It was complete.

The first time Jesus spoke in Luke it was to say to His mother and father, "Don't you know I must be about My Father's business?" The last thing He says here in Luke before His death was that He was going home. In John 17 He had prayed that His disciples could have the fellowship with His Father He had. That was the goal—to get people from here to heaven through the cross. And that work was now accomplished.

"Into Your hands, I commit My spirit," Jesus said. For the past many hours, Jesus had been in the hands of sinners. Now He was going back to His Father's loving hands. What better place to go? Jesus didn't just die. He finished. He yielded up His spirit. I love the picture.

Mark 15:44 tells us that when Joseph and Nicodemus came for Jesus' body, Pilate couldn't believe He was already dead. History tells us that death by crucifixion often took three days. So he sent soldiers out to be sure Jesus was dead. The soldiers broke the two thieves' legs, resulting in their deaths. But they didn't have to break Jesus' legs for He was already dead. Prophecy said they wouldn't. Instead, they stuck a sword in His side to be sure He was, and blood and water came out.

> So when the centurion saw what had happened, he glorified God, saying, "Certainly this was a righteous Man!"
> —Luke 23:47

Mark 15:39 records this centurion saying, "Truly, this was the Son of God." It was a confession of faith. This centurion—a Roman soldier, a hardened "crucifixion detail" guy who had a hundred men under him—was moved by all he saw and heard and was at least the second person converted to faith that afternoon.

> And the whole crowd who came together to that sight, seeing what had been done, beat their breasts and returned.
> —Luke 23:48

This was behavior of overwhelming despair, fear, and trauma. But the crowd didn't come to the same conclusion as the centurion. They went away saddened, brokenhearted, and disturbed—but not converted. I believe many of them would be in the crowds forty days from now, listening to Peter tell them Jesus is alive, and becoming part of the three thousand that were saved that day.

> But all His acquaintances, and the women who followed Him from Galilee, stood at a distance, watching these things.
> —Luke 23:49

For the most part, the disciples ran. But the women didn't leave. Their world was falling apart, but love kept them there. They stayed to bury Jesus and were the first up on Sunday morning to finish the job when the Sabbath restrictions were lifted. The last to leave and the first to come, they are in a few days given the reward of being the first to see Jesus alive. Paul wrote to the Hebrews that we can come boldly to the throne of grace and find mercy to help in time of need because the curtain of separation has been removed. Our sin has been dealt with—but only through the cross. I hope that's your message, because people need to hear how they can find their way home.

Chapter 133

WHAT KIND OF DISCIPLE ARE YOU?

Luke 23:50–56
(Matthew 27:57–61; Mark 15:42–47; John 19:38–42)

Concerning the sacrifice of His Son, God says less about the suffering than about the results, what happened to the soldiers, the thieves at His side, and the women standing by. Beginning in verse 50, Luke tells us the story of one other whom Jesus had touched.

> Now behold, there was a man named Joseph, a council member, a good and just man. He had not consented to their decision and deed. He was from Arimathea, a city of the Jews, who himself was also waiting for the kingdom of God. This man went to Pilate and asked for the body of Jesus. Then he took it down, wrapped it in linen, and laid it in a tomb that was hewn out of the rock, where no one had ever lain before.
>
> —Luke 23:50–53

Joseph is an interesting fellow. We know he was a council member, which meant that as a member of the Sanhedrin he was part of the most powerful Jewish court. In fact, Mark tells us in chapter 15:43 that he was one of their prominent members. In chapter 27:57, Matthew adds that he was a wealthy man. His hometown of Arimathea was twenty miles northwest of Jerusalem in the county of Ramah, Samuel's birthplace. Luke adds here that he was a good and a just man, an unusual characteristic for a member of the Sanhedrin. From what we know of them in the Bible, they were, for the most part, wicked men who sought only to serve themselves and who were at the forefront of the movement to kill Jesus.

Yet Joseph was different. A good and just man, he did not consent to the decisions the Sanhedrin had made concerning the plot to kill Jesus or to the meeting they had held earlier that morning to deliver Him to Pilate. Although he was part of the group, he found himself standing alone with a personal faith and a longing hope, waiting for the kingdom of God. As a believer in the Old Testament prophecies, he was convinced Jesus was the One who was promised.

In John 19:38 we read he was a secret disciple of Jesus because he feared the Jews. He certainly wasn't alone in that category. John 12 tells us that among the rulers there were

713

many who believed in Jesus, but because of the Pharisees wouldn't confess Him. They didn't want to be put out of the synagogue and loved men's praises more than God's.

We don't know how many there were—but they weren't able to communicate or stand with one another because they were intimidated by the hardliners. Yet here's Joseph now, coming to the forefront of the Gospel account, willing to risk the very things he had been protecting for so long so he could give Jesus a decent burial, to "make right" all of those years of living in the shadows of secret faith.

This fear is something we find throughout the Gospel accounts. In John 9, when the religious leaders came looking for an explanation for the healing of the man born blind, they asked his parents, "Is this your son?"

"Yes," they said.

"Was he born blind?" they asked.

Now I don't know about you, but if this were my son, at this point, I'd be saying, "Yes! And now he can see! It's a miracle!"

Instead, his parents said, "Yes, he is our son. But as far as what's happened to him, he's of age. Ask him." Later we read that his parents said these things because they feared being put out of the synagogue.

In John 7 we read that as folks were coming to the Feast day in Jerusalem, the talk in town was about Jesus but no one would speak openly of Him out of fear. Yet although there was tremendous pressure on the believers to stifle the very things they believed, Jesus' death was enough to motivate Joseph to reevaluate his fear and take a stand.

Joseph did this at a time when everyone thought whatever hope they had in Jesus had now been buried. He was dead. It was over. But Joseph couldn't stand by idly and do nothing. So he stepped up and identified with Jesus, willing to ruin the life he once hoped hiding his faith would save.

We know from Mark 14 that when the Sanhedrin voted to have Jesus killed, they voted unanimously. In fact, that very morning as they brought Jesus to Pilate, they all accompanied Him with the verdict. But according to verse 51 here in Luke, Joseph had not agreed to any of the Sanhedrin's schemes to get Jesus killed. Therefore, the only conclusion one can draw is that Joseph didn't attend the meeting. And Nicodemus wasn't there, either.

John tells us Nicodemus also showed up to help with the accommodations for Jesus' burial. He was another who had been conspicuously absent from the Sanhedrin's proceedings, another secret disciple and believer in Jesus who John identified throughout his gospel as the one who came to Jesus by night.

Proverbs 29:25 says the fear of people brings a snare, but the person who trusts in the Lord is safe. Joseph and Nicodemus were miserable. It's hard to know the right thing to do and then not do it. It's hard to constantly allow the pressure of others to push you into a lifestyle you don't want. But that's what happened to Joseph and Nicodemus. They were trapped and the pain, misery, shame, and guilt they experienced were far worse than what they might have suffered simply standing up for Jesus. Fear of others keeps the saints silent, keeps our faith hidden, and keeps our lives unfruitful. That's the life Joseph, Nicodemus, and many others lived while Jesus was alive. But now they were willing to come out of the shadows to give it all.

Why wouldn't we be proud to speak of the Lord's love for us? The only conclusion the Bible draws is that the fear of others pushes us away from it. Satan's antidote to living for the Lord is always the same: he wants us to love men's praises more than God's praises. But Jesus said, "If you deny Me before men, I will deny you before My Father in heaven." That's a tough memory verse, isn't it? The words are strong because the temptation is difficult. We want to conform. We want to fit in. We want to be well liked. We don't want to stand out. And yet as Christians in the world, we're going to stand out, because there's really no way to hide in the darkness of the world possessing His light.

There are believers today who justify hiding by the fact that they have to fit in to survive. But Joseph and Nicodemus would disagree because, when Jesus died, suddenly their position and status didn't matter. Now they were willing to risk what before they thought was in jeopardy. Rejection, ridicule, expulsion, or isolation—whatever it was that had kept them from identifying with Jesus no longer mattered.

Yet in the midst of not saying anything for so long, look how much they had lost. They didn't get to talk to their families about their convictions. They didn't get to stand with Jesus in His moment of difficulty. They didn't get to sit in the crowds when He spoke. They weren't part of the seventy who were sent out, anointed by the Spirit to serve others. They didn't get to see the miracles. They weren't part of His life and ministry. In many ways now it was too little too late.

When we talk about peer pressure, we immediately think it's a kid's problem. It's not. It's our problem just as well because when we walk with Jesus, we have to dare to be singular, especially when the pressure is that the fear of others will shut us up and keep us down. We have the answers for eternal life, yet all too often they are bottled up in us due to fear.

Following Jesus' death, Nicodemus brought a hundred pounds of anointing spices to the cross. The average burial required eight ounces—so Nicodemus either was going to take care of the entire city or his guilt drove him to try to make up for what he had let go for so long. I don't know if Joseph and Nicodemus were surprised to see each other. But the cross made them reevaluate everything they had been afraid to admit. Here were men who had spent years denying what they believed to save their careers and gain approval. But when Jesus died, all of that meant nothing. Now they were ready to chuck it all.

Secret discipleship always leads to diminished fellowship with God and we miss out on way too many blessings. But here's the cure for that fear: Jesus' death. It cured Joseph and drew out Nicodemus. I think sitting at the cross long enough to be moved by what Jesus did is the surest cure for a vacillating commitment. "We love Him because He first loved us," John wrote. His love for us has to be the driving force. Guilt won't do it. "I know I should" won't work. "But others aren't faithful" won't help. We need to be driven by the love God displayed for us. It became clear to Joseph and Nicodemus when Jesus died—they could be silent no longer.

So Joseph went to Pilate to ask for Jesus' body. According to Roman law, crucified bodies were to be left on the cross and not allowed a burial, as a gruesome reminder to potential lawbreakers their actions' consequences. But Jesus was already dead. He had already dismissed His spirit.

Mark 15:43 wrote, "And Joseph, taking courage, went to Pilate." It would have taken a great deal of courage to go to a Roman leader who had just been pushed around by the very Sanhedrin of which Joseph was a member. The Sanhedrin had hustled Pilate, demanded of him, threatened him, and pushed him in a corner. And here came one of them asking for the body. Yet although the law was on Pilate's side, prophecy had foretold that Jesus would be buried with the rich—so Joseph was given His body.

Helped by Nicodemus, Joseph took Jesus' body off the cross. And for the first time in the Gospel record, we see Nicodemus in the light.

> That day was the Preparation, and the Sabbath drew near. And the women who had come with Him from Galilee followed after, and they observed the tomb and how His body was laid. Then they returned and prepared spices and fragrant oils. And they rested on the Sabbath according to the commandment.
> —Luke 23:54–56

Between Jesus' death at three and the beginning of the Sabbath at six, the women had only three hours to prepare Jesus' body for burial. According to Matthew 27, Joseph had a personal grave just below the hill on which Jesus had died. Joseph let Jesus use his own grave—but Jesus wouldn't need it for long. He only would "borrow" it for a few days.

In the Gospel account, following Jesus' death we don't read much about the apostles. "Smite the Shepherd and the sheep will scatter," Jesus had said. And they sure did. Men like Nicodemus and Joseph who had lived in the shadows now came to the light. And the disciples who had lived in the light were now back in the shadows, disappointed with Jesus and discouraged by how things had worked out. I find a lot of Christians are like that. They think God lets them down and, rather than waiting on Him and trusting Him, they hit the road, angry and confused.

But then you find these wonderful, faithful women. They had joined Jesus in the north at the beginning of His public ministry. They had identified with Him openly every step of the way. And to the very end, without fear, they stood with Jesus because perfect love casts out fear. Although Jesus' death might have affected their hopes, it didn't diminish their love or their commitment. At the tomb, the men said, "He's dead. Let's leave." But the women said, "We love Him. Let's stay." In two days, when the Sabbath restrictions are lifted, they are the first ones to the tomb. The last ones at the cross, the last ones at the grave, the first ones at the tomb—they will be the first to hear that Jesus is alive.

Secret disciples, timid apostles, faithful women—what does the cross mean to you? Does it bring you out to say to the world, "I believe in Jesus," or does it drive you away? Does it cause you to hide in fear, or does it keep you walking in love with great faithfulness and hope?

What kind of disciple are you?

Chapter 134

SATURDAY/SUNDAY
RESURRECTION MORNING

Luke 24:1–12
(Matthew 28:1–15; Mark 16:1–11; John 20:1–18)

We come now to that which is central to our faith and hope: Jesus' resurrection. Your faith and mine, the whole of Christianity, rests on an empty tomb. If Luke simply had written a biography it would have ended at chapter 23 because in a biography when the subject dies, that's the end. But Jesus' life did not end with His death. He rose. Writing to the Corinthians, Paul said later, "If the Lord isn't risen, our faith is empty and our preaching is vain."

The resurrection does something nothing else could have done. It stamps "Approved," "Verified," and "True" on everything Jesus said and did. Everything He claimed to be—that He was the Way, the Truth, and the Life; that He was God; that there was no other way to heaven but through Him—must be believed and followed because of the resurrection. It is the exclamation point behind the message. It is the proof of our hope.

> Now on the first day of the week, very early in the morning, they, and certain other women with them, came to the tomb bringing the spices which they had prepared.
>
> —Luke 24:1

This first Easter morning brought the believers in Jesus to another day of misery. They trusted He would be the deliverer but woke up again in sorrow. It was the third day now and nothing had changed. But at least for the women, there were some final things that they could attend to before leaving town.

These Galilean women who had been with Jesus since the beginning, and had followed Him from the north, were certainly as brokenhearted as everyone else. But they had a job to do and they took it personally. Immediately following His death, they had tried to prepare Him properly for burial. But they only had had a couple of hours to work before they had to be home and off the streets for Sabbath. So this morning they would go back to finish the task of anointing a decomposing body. Although we are given a few names, we don't know how many went—yet only love could have driven these women to this gruesome task this day.

Having presided over many funerals, I know people often get mad at God when someone they love dies. "Why them?" they ask angrily. "Why now?" You don't find that with these women. You just find sorrow and great love, wanting to be sure they did the right thing by Jesus.

> Now on the first day of the week Mary Magdalene went to the tomb early, while it was still dark, and saw that the stone had been taken away from the tomb. Then she ran and came to Simon Peter, and to the other disciple, whom Jesus loved, and said to them, "They have taken away the Lord out of the tomb, and we do not know where they have laid Him." Peter therefore went out, and the other disciple, and were going to the tomb. So they both ran together, and the other disciple outran Peter and came to the tomb first.
>
> —John 20:1–4

Mary headed out when it was still dark. Putting the accounts together, I believe she didn't leave with the other women, but decided it would take too long to wait for them all and forged on alone. The Bible says a person who has been forgiven much loves much. And if there was anyone among the women who had been forgiven much, it was Mary. In chapter 8:2, Luke said her life had been dominated by seven demons. Yet Jesus had delivered her. Therefore, she would have given anything He would have required.

When Mary arrived at the tomb and saw the stone moved, she assumed someone had moved Jesus' body. So she went to get help from the men. John had a house in town and Peter was staying there with him. Mary woke them to tell them someone had stolen the body. Peter and John ran out and, like most men, John went out of his way to tell us three times in five verses that he won the race to the tomb. We know the end of the story, but they didn't. For all they knew, this could have been a trap. But John's love, and perhaps Peter's guilt, drove them to go anyway.

> And he, stooping down and looking in, saw the linen cloths lying there; yet he did not go in. Then Simon Peter came, following him, and went into the tomb; and he saw the linen cloths lying there, and the handkerchief that had been around His head, not lying with the linen cloths, but folded together in a place by itself. Then the other disciple, who came to the tomb first, went in also; and he saw and believed. For as yet they did not know the Scripture, that He must rise again from the dead. Then the disciples went away again to their own homes.
>
> —John 20:5–10

In this and the other Gospel accounts, several different words for "to look" or "to see" are used. The word for what John did is the word for *faith*. That means, based on the evidence he saw, he concluded that Jesus was alive. The word for *saw* with regard to Peter is *theoreo*.

Rather than come to a conclusion, Peter theorized. Luke tells us Peter marveled—but he couldn't yet put it all together. They then left, leaving Mary alone. Way to go guys!

> But Mary stood outside by the tomb weeping, and as she wept she stooped down and looked into the tomb. And she saw two angels in white sitting, one at the head and the other at the feet, where the body of Jesus had lain. Then they said to her, "Woman, why are you weeping?" She said to them, "Because they have taken away my Lord, and I do not know where they have laid Him." Now when she had said this, she turned around and saw Jesus standing there, and did not know that it was Jesus. Jesus said to her, "Woman, why are you weeping? Whom are you seeking?" She, supposing Him to be the gardener, said to Him, "Sir, if You have carried Him away, tell me where You have laid Him, and I will take Him away."
>
> —John 20:11–15

When the angels asked the reason for Mary's weeping, she wasn't willing to talk, as if to say, "I haven't got time for you. I'm looking for my Lord." But as she turned around, there was another man standing there who asked her the same question. She assumed He was the gardener.

In every place you see Jesus after the resurrection, no one is able to recognize Him on their own. No one. Although He was in many ways the same, He was in every way different. The folks who would have known Him best—like Mary—didn't recognize Him because coming to know God requires a spiritual revelation. He isn't found through observation or intellect. He is seen or discovered by the revelation of God. So it was only as Jesus revealed Himself that they could see who He was.

> Jesus said to her, "Mary!" She turned and said to Him, "Rabboni!" (which is to say, Teacher).
>
> —John 20:16

I think this is where the written word fails and we need an audiotape because Jesus said her name in such a way that Mary recognized Him immediately.

> Jesus said to her, "Do not cling to Me, for I have not yet ascended to My Father . . . ."
>
> —John 20:17

"Do not cling to Me" literally reads, "Don't grab so hard!" Evidently after Mary recognized Jesus, she tackled Him, as if to say, "You're not getting away from me again!"

The relationship the church would have with Jesus would not be one of sight or physical contact, but of faith. Paul later wrote in his second letter to the Corinthians, "We used to know Him after the flesh, but we don't know Him like that anymore." Mary's was the only generation that got to "hang on" physically to Jesus. Every succeeding generation came by faith, not sight.

> ". . . but go to My brethren and say to them, 'I am ascending to My Father and your Father, and to My God and your God.'"
>
> —John 20:17

Jesus' death and resurrection did something nothing else could do. It offered people a relationship with God as Father. "Go tell My brothers I'm going to heaven," Jesus said to Mary. "The door is opened for them to have a Father." Following the resurrection, this was the first commission to preach to others. What a reward Mary got for her love and her diligence! How far removed she was from Thomas, who doesn't even show up when the group gathers later that day and, coerced into coming the following week, argues, "Unless I touch and feel and see, I'm never going to risk myself like that again."

Mark 16:9 tells us Mary did indeed go and tell the disciples who had been mourning and weeping. But when they heard she had seen Him, they thought she was out of her mind.

> But they found the stone rolled away from the tomb. Then they went in and did not find the body of the Lord Jesus.
>
> —Luke 24:2–3

Long after John had outraced Peter to the tomb and long after Mary's encounter with the "gardener," the rest of Mary's entourage arrived. Matthew 16:2 says these women came very early in the morning when the sun had already risen. Mary Magdalene, however, had come while it was yet dark. So group two, the "slowpokes," now arrive. Mark tells us that as they were walking, they asked each other who would roll away the stone so they could get their work done. They didn't know what Matthew tells us—that the Lord already had taken care of this by sending an angel and an earthquake, not so Jesus could get out but so they could get in. Coming to the tomb and seeing the stone already rolled away, they went in. But there was no body to be found.

Matthew tells us they were astonished or, literally, "like those who turned to stone."

> And it happened, as they were greatly perplexed about this, that behold, two men stood by them in shining garments. Then, as they were afraid and bowed their faces to the earth, they said to them, "Why do you seek the living among the dead? He is not here, but is risen! Remember how He spoke to you when He was still in Galilee, saying, 'The Son of Man must be delivered into the hands of sinful men, and be crucified, and the third day rise again.'" And they remembered His words.
>
> —Luke 24:4–8

Matthew 28:5–8 tells us the angels' first words to the women were, "Fear not." Then, according to Matthew, they said, "Jesus is not here. He is risen. Come and see the place where they lay Him." And they took in the women and showed them the empty tomb.

The angels reminded the women of something very important. "Don't you remember what Jesus told you over and over again?" they said. Throughout the Gospel accounts, Jesus had spoken of His death and resurrection, but in their distress these women had set aside God's promises. I think that's a problem for a lot of Christians. We believe God while the going is good but when the pressure is on, suddenly we forget what He said. Rather than being victorious, we're defeated. Rather than being joyful, we're distressed. Rather than being hopeful, we're filled with grief—all because we've forgotten whom we serve and what He had declared!

So as the ladies showed up in such despair, the angels reminded them of what Jesus had said. That's a good thing for us to learn as well. Let God bring His Word back to your memory. May it be the joy of your life, because if you forget what God said, when tragedy comes where else can you turn?

> Then they returned from the tomb and told all these things to the eleven and to all the rest.
>
> —Luke 24:9

Matthew 28:9–10 tells us that as they turned to leave with fear and great joy, the women ran into Jesus. When He told them to rejoice, they bowed at His feet and began to worship Him. "Go tell the disciples I'm risen," He said. "Tell them to go to Galilee where I'll meet with them."

> It was Mary Magdalene, Joanna, Mary the mother of James, and the other women with them, who told these things to the apostles. And their words seemed to them like idle tales, and they did not believe them.
>
> —Luke 24:10–11

When the women told the apostles what they had seen and heard, the apostles thought they were telling idle tales—a medical term used by Dr. Luke to describe someone who babbles incoherently. The apostles couldn't receive their testimony because their grief was so overwhelming that any good news would have been impossible.

God demands faith and trust. And although the resurrection made no sense, it had indeed occurred. I wonder how often we're kept from God's best simply because we can find no logical sense in it.

The resurrection draws a line in the sand. Either we come to Jesus because He was dead and now lives, or we turn from the testimonies of those who have met Him and been changed by Him to take our chances alone. At some point we have to heed God's Word if we're going to find life.

To the rich man in hell who said, "Send me back so I can warn my family there's a place like this," Abraham said, "They have Moses and the prophets. Let them read them."

"But if one would raise from the dead, they would surely believe," the rich man argued.

To which Abraham replied, "If they won't believe the prophets or Moses, neither will they be persuaded even if one would raise from the dead" (Luke 16:24–31).

It all comes back to what God has to say.

Chapter 135

RESURRECTION AFTERNOON

Luke 24:13–32
(Mark 16:12–13)

W e now come to Jesus' appearance to two disciples who had followed Him but were now, like most others, believing they were without hope,

> Now behold, two of them were traveling that same day to a village called Emmaus, which was seven miles from Jerusalem. And they talked together of all these things which had happened.
>
> —Luke 24:13–14

These two disciples—very possibly a husband and wife—were among those who had waited in Jerusalem until the Sabbath restrictions were lifted before they could travel home. They had been with the rest of the group that morning when Mary delivered the message that Jesus was alive, and when Peter and John came to say that the tomb was empty. As much as they may have wanted to believe these reports, however, they apparently could not. I suspect they were walking slowly, glad to get out of Jerusalem and away from the heartbreak.

> So it was, while they conversed and reasoned, that Jesus Himself drew near and went with them. But their eyes were restrained, so that they did not know Him.
>
> —Luke 24:15–16

As they traveled, Jesus caught up with them and began to walk with them. Like everyone else who saw Jesus after His resurrection, they did not recognize Him—and that seems to be the way Jesus wanted it. I think it goes along with the fact that we're saved by faith, not by sight. This generation saw Jesus—but their salvation would not come by seeing Him. It would come by believing in Him. I also suspect that their lack of hope and their unbelief kept the two travelers from seeing Him. Unbelief will do that.

It interests me that Jesus spent the entire afternoon of resurrection day—from lunch until after dinner—with two disciples who, at best, had given up hope. He didn't hunt out the famous apostles. He didn't spend time with the important people. He spent time with these two. Maybe it was so we could know that each of us is as important to Him as everyone else.

And He said to them, "What kind of conversation is this that you have with one another as you walk and are sad?"

—Luke 24:17

Read through the Gospels and you see it never takes long for Jesus to get people to lay their hearts bare and expose their feelings and worries to Him. He knew why this couple was sad—He asked them for their benefit. That's always the case. God already knows all about us, but I think He wants us to share our hearts with Him so we can know He knows.

Then the one whose name was Cleopas answered and said to Him, "Are You the only stranger in Jerusalem, and have You not known the things which happened there in these days?" And He said to them, "What things?" So they said to Him, "The things concerning Jesus of Nazareth, who was a Prophet mighty in deed and word before God and all the people; and how the chief priests and our rulers delivered Him to be condemned to death, and crucified Him."

—Luke 24:18–20

Cleopas is a male name. We are told in John 19:25 that among the women who stood at the cross was Mary, the wife of Cleopas. Therefore, it is possible that these two disciples were Cleopas and his wife, Mary—both headed home, away from their hopes. When Jesus asked why they were sad, Cleopas said, "You must be the only one of the millions who came to Jerusalem who missed the news of what happened this weekend."

"Tell Me about it," Jesus said.

So Cleopas and Mary proceeded to give Him their view of Jesus. "He was a prophet. He was mighty in deed and word before God and all the people," they said. Their conviction about Jesus had come as their understanding grew through His words and deeds.

When John the Baptist sent some of his disciples to Jesus to find out if He was the Messiah, Jesus healed the sick, ministered to the poor, and preached the Gospel. Then He said to the men, "Go back and tell John what you have seen and what you have heard." Jesus' words and deeds became the proof for His claim of who He is. The resurrection would be the ultimate proof.

It's important that we share God's deeds and words. Our changed lives are proof of His work. And His Word is as powerful as it has ever been. It moved the hearts of Cleopas and Mary—and two thousand years later, it's still changing lives.

"But we were hoping that it was He who was going to redeem Israel."

—Luke 24:21

"We were hoping it was He who would redeem us," Mary and Cleopas said. That's past tense. In other words: "Our hope died at the cross. Our hope was buried with Jesus."

"Indeed, besides all this, today is the third day since these things happened. Yes, and certain women of our company, who arrived at the tomb early, astonished us. When they did not find His body, they came saying that they had also seen a vision of angels who said He was alive. And certain of those who were with us went to the tomb and found it just as the women had said; but Him they did not see."

—Luke 24:21–24

"Today is the third day" is a very difficult phrase to understand. Either Cleopas and Mary were saying they were sad because it only had been three days or, like many Jewish believers, they looked to the Old Testament and saw that in many cases the Lord intervened on the third day. Even the reports of the empty tomb, however, didn't stimulate their hopes very much, seeing they were heading home. It just sounded too good to be true. And now it seemed like time was running out. God had passed the deadline. Now it was just too late.

How often do we do that? "All right," we pray, "you've got until Friday, Lord." Friday comes and goes and we give up hope—only to watch Him act gloriously on Saturday. God's never late. We're just in a rush, aren't we?

These two were heading west into the sunset. They should have been looking for the Son rise . . . but fear and unbelief had overwhelmed them.

Then He said to them, "O foolish ones, and slow of heart to believe in all that the prophets have spoken! Ought not the Christ to have suffered these things and to enter into His glory?" And beginning at Moses and all the Prophets, He expounded to them in all the Scriptures the things concerning Himself.

—Luke 24:25–27

After this couple gave Jesus their view of Him, Jesus gave them His view of Himself. To do this, He turned them to the Scriptures. That's always where the answer is. If you're overwhelmed, the best thing you can do is turn back to the truth and hang on to it, because much of our depression, doubt, and confusion is the result of believing the wrong thing. Cleopas and Mary had believed part of the prophecies about the Messiah—the ruling and reigning parts. But they had missed the prophecies concerning His death and resurrection—the reason He came.

"Ought not Scripture to be fulfilled?" Jesus asked. "Let Me teach you what the Bible says." And beginning with the words of Moses, He continued through the Old Testament all the way to the book of Malachi as He gave them an overview of the Messiah's ministry—particularly His suffering and death.

In Genesis He showed them He was the Seed of the woman who would have His heel bruised by the serpent, and the One of whom Abraham spoke when he said, "God will provide Himself a sacrifice."

726

In Exodus, He showed them it was His blood pictured on the doorposts of the homes the death angel passed over.

In Leviticus, He was the Lamb without spot or blemish that the sacrifices foreshadowed.

In Psalms, it was He who was the stone the builders rejected, He whose hands and feet were pierced, and He who was poured out like water with all of His bones out of joint, but none of them broken.

In Isaiah, it was He whose beard was plucked, whose back was given to the smiters, and whose face was marred beyond recognition. It was He who was wounded for our transgressions and bruised for our iniquities, and He who was numbered with the transgressors and whose grave was with the rich.

In Daniel, it was He who would be cut off, but not for Himself.

In Zechariah, it was He who had been betrayed for thirty pieces of silver.

"Search the Scriptures," Jesus had said to His enemies. "In them you think you have eternal life, but they are that which testify of Me." And indeed they did.

"Ought not Scripture be fulfilled?" He asked Cleopas and Mary. "Isn't this the way God declared it would happen?"

Jesus spent the better part of this day with two disciples, sharing His Word for their benefit. I think the lesson is obvious: If you want to learn, God will teach you. If you're hungry to hear, He'll speak.

> Then they drew near to the village where they were going, and He indicated that He would have gone farther. But they constrained Him, saying, "Abide with us, for it is toward evening, and the day is far spent." And He went in to stay with them.
>
> —Luke 24:28–29

No doubt the seven and a half mile trip home flew by as the two disciples hung on Jesus' every word. When it appeared He was going past their town however, they begged Him to stay with them—which is another argument for this being a couple.

> Now it came to pass, as He sat at the table with them, that He took bread, blessed and broke it, and gave it to them. Then their eyes were opened and they knew Him; and He vanished from their sight.
>
> —Luke 24:30–31

Cleopas and Mary recognized Jesus as He broke bread. Did they see the nail prints in His hands? Did they stop for the first time and take a closer look at Him? Or maybe God's Word given to them clearly had begun to rekindle their hope and faith. Maybe it was as their hope began to grow that their eyes began to focus.

For the next forty days, Jesus would come and go as He pleased. People would recognize Him and He'd be gone. People wouldn't be expecting Him and He'd pop in. Only saints saw Him. But the disciples never were sure whether He was there or not which, I guess, is a good thing. We can't see Him physically, but we should be aware of the fact that He's with us.

A week later, Thomas was at the meeting he had refused to attend the week before. When Jesus shows up, He says, "Thomas, put your finger in the holes of My hands and stick your fist in My side." Thomas must have wondered how Jesus knew he had said that. But there was a lot more that Jesus knew.

Here Jesus disappeared from Cleopas and Mary's sight because their relationship with Him would have to change. It wouldn't be by sight but by faith, no longer in the flesh but by the Spirit, as Paul would write in 2 Corinthians 5:7.

> And they said to one another, "Did not our heart burn within us while He talked with us on the road, and while He opened the Scriptures to us?"
>
> —Luke 24:32

Holy heartburn! "Weren't our hearts on fire when He was teaching us the Scriptures?" this couple said to one another.

When the Lord hadn't worked the way Jeremiah thought He would, he said, "I'm not going to mention You anymore or speak of Your name at all." But then he wrote, "His word was in my heart like a burning fire. I could not hold it back."

We need to find more burning hearts in the body of Christ. So often I find Christians' approach to God's Word is very careless—an "I can take it or leave it" mentality, due to the worldliness or compromises in our lives. One thing is for sure: the cure to being lukewarm is to spend time with Jesus and allow His Word to light a fire in your life.

When was the last time your heart truly was moved by God's Word? When was the last time, in private, He began to open up the Word to you in a way that rekindled your love for Him? It wasn't miracles that warmed these disciples' hearts. It wasn't some over-emotional response that caused them to declare things that weren't true. It was as Jesus opened the Scriptures to them that their hearts caught fire. Notice that the fire came not as they talked with Him, but as He talked to them. It was in hearing the Word that the Holy Spirit fanned a fire in their hearts.

Speaking to his students about how imperative it was that they had heard from God before stepping into the pulpit, nineteenth-century preacher Charles Spurgeon encouraged them by saying to them: "Spend enough time with God alone so that your heart catches fire. Then people will gather to watch you burn."

The Lord will do what He has said. Therefore we should sit and listen until our hearts are full. Fear will flee. Discouragement will leave. Hope will take their place, along with a burning desire to know Him better.

Chapter 136

RESURRECTION EVENING

Luke 24:33–53
(Mark 16:14–20; John 20:19–29)

Although the couple on the road to Emmaus had walked nearly eight miles in one direction, they were willing to turn around that moment, even at night on dangerous roads to go back just to tell others that Jesus was alive. That's what happens when you meet the living Lord—you'll do anything to tell others.

> So they rose up that very hour and returned to Jerusalem, and found the eleven and those who were with them gathered together, saying, "The Lord is risen indeed, and has appeared to Simon!" And they told about the things that had happened on the road, and how He was known to them in the breaking of bread.
>
> —Luke 24:33–35

These two, touched by Jesus and overjoyed He was alive, went back, knocked on the door that was locked out of fear, and were let in to hear the discussion among the group that the Lord was alive. In addition to Mary Magdalene, Peter had seen Him as well.

We know from Acts 1:15 that gathered in the Upper Room were about 120 disciples, including Jesus' mother and half-brothers and sisters. When Cleopas and Mary arrived, it was late in the evening and they began to lay out how they had spent the entire afternoon with a stranger they eventually found out was Jesus—how He had hidden Himself from them, how they had invited Him to dinner, how He broke bread, and how their hearts burned when He opened the Scriptures to them.

We're not told anything about Jesus' meeting with Peter. It was absolutely private. But whatever the Lord said to him, I can imagine that, between tears, apologies, and promises, Peter was thrilled to make what had been so wrong at last right. But he also became a great example to us that, despite the promises we make, the Bible says that in our flesh dwells no good thing. The spirit is willing—but the flesh? Peter had to learn that his strength had to be in the Lord. He didn't brag anymore. By the time we see him next, he's a broken man, yet as strong as he'd ever been.

That the Lord visited Peter must have made him the most thrilled of them all. In Luke 22:31, Jesus had said to him, "Satan wants to sift you but I have prayed for you that your faith won't fail. When you're converted, go and strengthen the brethren." This would be Peter's conversion night. Not only that, it would be instrumental in Peter's preparation for going out and preaching the first sermon of the young church.

> Now as they said these things, Jesus Himself stood in the midst of them, and said to them, "Peace to you." But they were terrified and frightened, and supposed they had seen a spirit. And He said to them, "Why are you troubled? And why do doubts arise in your hearts? Behold My hands and My feet, that it is I Myself. Handle Me and see, for a spirit does not have flesh and bones as you see I have." When He had said this, He showed them His hands and His feet.
>
> —Luke 24:36–40

As this couple gave their testimony, Jesus popped in, saying, "Peace," which in this case meant, "Don't jump out the window!" As much as the disciples wanted Jesus to be alive, this would have been a shock. No wonder they thought He was a ghost. But Jesus immediately sought to reassure His own. "Why are you so fearful?" He asked. "Why are those thoughts running through your heads? Come and look at the spike marks in My hands and feet that the nails have left."

In this we're presented with a very interesting picture because in His risen, glorified body, Jesus wasn't subject to the laws of nature that we are. Yet He did carry in His new body the marks of suffering—which means one day when you get to heaven, the only man-made thing you'll find there are the wounds Jesus bears. He'll bear those marks forever, because that's how we'll have gotten in!

In Revelation 5:12, when John is taken to heaven to see the throne and the living creatures, he hears them say with a loud voice, "Worthy is the Lamb that was slain." And John looks and sees One who had been slain. He sees the payment for our sins in Jesus' physical body. Zechariah says when Jesus returns, mankind will look upon Him whom they have pierced.

Jesus invited the disciples to examine Him and to see that He wasn't a ghost. His glorified body is an interesting picture. In 1 Corinthians 15, Paul describes what it must be like and how, like a seed planted, it comes up and is related to the seed in the sense that wheat seeds grow wheat, and tulip bulbs grow tulips, but the crop looks far different than that which was planted. I don't understand all of this—but I'm looking forward to it! In 1 John 3:2, John wrote, "It hasn't yet been revealed what we shall be but we know when He is revealed, we'll be like Him for we'll see Him as He is." In other words, we'll get it later.

The men and women gathered here were really no better off than Thomas. They also needed to see to believe. They needed to touch, handle, and see Him eat. Thomas wasn't there so, Thomas would be singled out for his unbelief—but these had the same problem. Yet Jesus' resurrection left such an impression on the disciples that all of them—including Thomas—eventually went to their deaths for their faith. No one was able to dissuade them of their hope. The resurrection sealed the deal, closed the case, and put an exclamation point behind the sentence.

John opened his first epistle with the words, "That which was from the beginning, which we have heard with our ears, seen with our eyes, which we have looked upon and our hands have handled of the word of life. That we declare to you." Sixty years later, the image of Jesus was still in his mind. "I want you to have fellowship with Him," John wrote. "We were privileged enough to handle Him and look at Him. You're privileged enough to know Him."

> But while they still did not believe for joy, and marveled, He said to them, "Have you any food here?" So they gave Him a piece of a broiled fish and some honeycomb. And He took it and ate in their presence.
> —Luke 24:41–43

I love the fact that the disciples couldn't believe for joy. There's this mixed bag of feelings because they wanted to believe. They saw it with their eyes. Yet it seemed so implausible. It was just too good to be true!

We find that a lot in the Bible when people realize God's goodness. When Jacob, after years, heard Joseph was still alive, he said in Genesis 45:26, "That's too good to be true. I don't know how that's possible." When the children of Israel came out of captivity, we read of them in Psalm 126:1–3, "When the Lord brought us back to Zion, we were like those who dreamed. Our mouths were filled with laughter. Our tongues began to say, 'The Lord has done great things for us.'"

When God begins to bless and we get a clear picture of what He said, our reaction is always the same: "Are You sure?" When you think about the fact that your sins never will be brought up in heaven, that's a glorious thought, isn't it? "Clean slate? Are You sure? That seems too good to be true! I'm going to get to heaven freely welcomed? Are You sure? My name is in the book? Are You sure?" No wonder Peter wrote that we have a joy that is unspeakable and full of glory.

> Then He said to them, "These are the words which I spoke to you while I was still with you, that all things must be fulfilled which were written in the Law of Moses and the Prophets and the Psalms concerning Me." And He opened their understanding, that they might comprehend the Scriptures.
> —Luke 24:44–45

Having taken care of the physical shock, Jesus now turned to the spiritual reality and turned the disciples to that which would have to be their greatest assurance. "This is what the Bible says and what I've been telling you all along," He said. How often in the previous year He had said, "Here's where we're going. Here's what's going to happen to Me," ending with the words, "then they're going to kill Me but I'll rise." This speech didn't happen once—it happened repeatedly. But the disciples' response was always to disregard it because death didn't fit in with their hopes and plans. It didn't register with their idea of what the Messiah would do.

In John 20:22, the companion report in the Gospels about resurrection evening, John says at this point Jesus breathed on the disciples and said, "Receive the Holy Spirit. Whichever sins you remit will be remitted. Whichever sins you retain will be retained." Once the disciples had received the Spirit, they were given the mission of telling people how their sins could be forgiven and that their failure to believe in Jesus was the only sin that couldn't be forgiven.

The Holy Spirit had been with the disciples. Now He would dwell in them. They were born again Easter Sunday evening. And with the coming of the Spirit came the understanding of the Scriptures. The light went on as Jesus began to teach them about Himself through the Word—the Passover Lamb, the suffering Shepherd of Isaiah, the crucifixion that David wrote about in the Psalms. And I'm sure the two on the road to Emmaus, having heard the study for the second time, asked the others if their hearts were burning yet.

> Then He said to them, "Thus it is written, and thus it was necessary . . . ."
> —Luke 24:46

I love that. If God said it, you can count on it. If God declared it, it will take place.

> ". . . for the Christ to suffer and to rise from the dead the third day, and that repentance and remission of sins should be preached in His name to all nations, beginning at Jerusalem. And you are witnesses of these things."
> —Luke 24:46–48

Up until now, the disciples had been confused about the Scriptures and the suffering Messiah. They swung and missed constantly. But as the Holy Spirit took up residence in their hearts, things were beginning to come together.

Because of Jesus' death and resurrection, the disciples now had a message to bear—that repentance would lead to the remission of sins—and that message could be preached in Jesus' name anywhere in the world.

Jesus did come. He did rise. We do have hope. If He hadn't died, there would be no forgiveness. If He hadn't risen, there would be no hope. If he hadn't done both, there would be no good news. But He did. So what do we do now? What do we say to people about salvation? We tell them to repent—*metanoia* in Greek—or literally "turn around." Whenever the word *repent* is used in the Bible, it is used to say to people, "Turn around and come to Jesus. You can't live life on your own. You can't figure it out. You don't have the strength. Your sin will wipe you out. You're headed for darkness. Turn around."

Paul told the Corinthians that godly sorrow produces repentance that leads to salvation. But worldly sorrow over sin just leads to death. Sorrow in itself isn't enough. I have to repent. I have to turn around. I have to do an about-face and go to Jesus (2 Cor. 7:9–10).

Forty days from now, in Matthew 28:18, Jesus will meet with this group and say, "All authority has been given to Me in heaven and in earth so go and make disciples of all nations. Baptize them in the name of the Father, Son, and Holy Spirit and teach them to observe the things I have commanded you. I am with you always, even unto the end of the age." It seemed going to all nations was an impossible task the Lord set before them.

Today we have satellites, computers, TVs, and airplanes. Back then they had sandals, sailboats, sheep, a camel, and a donkey or two. Yet thirty years from this time, Paul says in Colossians 1:5, "You know the hope that has been laid up for you in heaven, which you have heard before when the word of the truth of the Gospel came to you as it has gone out into all the world." In thirty years, filled with the Spirit, the church was able to reach out—and the whole world heard.

The word *witness* is an interesting one because it is the word for *martyr*. More often than not, it is used in the Bible not of those who die for their faith, but of those who give their all to be an example. People think witnessing is throwing a tract out of a moving car or putting a second bumper sticker on the back of your car. But witnessing in the Bible, by definition, is primarily not what you say but who you are. It isn't reformation or good intentions, but a new birth that changes from the inside out. There's a big difference between a sales pitch and a product demonstration. There are a lot of sales pitches out there. We just want to see if it works.

> "Behold, I send the Promise of My Father upon you; but tarry in the city of Jerusalem until you are endued with power from on high."
> —Luke 24:49

Once they were born again, Jesus gave the disciples their commission and message, and the Spirit to teach them—and then He said, "Now don't go anywhere." These men and women were saved back in verse 45. God had opened their understanding. John spells it out in great clarity in chapter 20. But Jesus said, "Don't go out yet. You need power to be a witness." This is repeated in Acts 1 as Jesus prepares to depart from them. In fact, His last words to them are to wait for the empowering that had been promised.

In the Old Testament we see the Holy Spirit with people. We also see Him come upon them as He did with Moses' seventy elders. David, fearful of his sin, prayed that the Holy Spirit wouldn't be taken from him. Here the disciples were told to stay in place, to wait until they received this filling or anointing from on high. Forty days from this point, Jesus takes them to Bethany and they ask Him if that is the time He will restore the kingdom. Jesus answers, "It's not for you to know the times or the seasons which the Father has put into His own power or has under His own authority. But you shall receive power when the

Holy Spirit comes upon you. You'll be witnesses for Me here in Jerusalem, Judea, Samaria, and to the uttermost parts of the earth." Then He ascends out of their sight.

Verse 50 jumps us ahead 40 days:

> And He led them out as far as Bethany, and He lifted up His hands and blessed them. Now it came to pass, while He blessed them, that He was parted from them and carried up into heaven. And they worshiped Him, and returned to Jerusalem with great joy, and were continually in the temple praising and blessing God. Amen.
>
> —Luke 24:50–53

We read in Acts 1:9–12 that as Jesus disappeared from the disciples' sight, two angels showed up and said, "Men of Galilee, why are you standing gazing into heaven? This Jesus who was taken from you into heaven will so come in like manner." So they returned to Jerusalem from the Mount of Olives and entered the Upper Room, 120 in one accord. And the fact that these previously argumentative disciples were of one accord was only the first of many miracles they were yet to see. On Pentecost, 10 days after Jesus' ascension, the Holy Spirit fell upon these saints to empower them to be His witnesses. How we need to be born-again and once saved, be anointed with the power of the Holy Spirit upon our lives as well to be bold witnesses for Jesus in these last days. The disciples were saved but told to wait for power . . . we need not wait any longer. Just ask your heavenly Father to pour out the Holy Spirit upon your life today!

Chapter 137

TODAY
JESUS USES THE LIKES OF US

John 21:1–25

W e very much need to know this last lesson that the Lord puts in the Gospel accounts. It's encouraging. It's wonderful. It's necessary for anyone who, like Peter, has tried to love and serve the Lord in his own strength with good intentions but great failures. We need to know that God has to enable our service and that our love is best displayed not so much by the doing in our own strength, but by believing and trusting Him. God knows our hearts and intentions, and that no matter how good they might seem, we're going to be weak on our own. So He gives us more than one or two chances. He doesn't write us off when others do. It doesn't really matter how far we've fallen. If you're willing, so is the Lord to pick you up and set you back on the path of serving Him.

> After these things . . . .
>
> —John 21:1

After resurrection morning, afternoon, and evening . . .

> . . . Jesus showed Himself again to the disciples at the Sea of Tiberias, and in this way He showed Himself: Simon Peter, Thomas called the Twin, Nathanael of Cana in Galilee, the sons of Zebedee, and two others of His disciples were together. Simon Peter said to them, "I am going fishing." They said to him, "We are going with you also." They went out and immediately got into the boat, and that night they caught nothing.
>
> —John 21:1–3

I think John 20 and the resurrection would have been both a fitting end to John's gospel and a fitting introduction to the book of Acts, which takes the church's work forward. But John was led to write one more chapter, a chapter that focuses on Peter—his great fall, denial, cockiness, and need to be restored. This is Peter's public restoration. The private one had taken place off the record some time on Easter Sunday morning. But Jesus wanted to publicly send out Peter to be a pastor and minister in the eyes of others.

From the rest of the Gospels we know that the Sunday after Easter the disciples were still in Jerusalem gathered together when the Lord met with Thomas. But then the tracking of what took place becomes a little murky. With the Feast of Unleavened Bread over, it would appear the disciples were in Jerusalem another week before they packed their bags and headed home. Most of them lived in the north, around the Sea of Galilee. Jesus had said to them in Matthew 26 that He would meet with them in the hills there.

Of the remaining eleven apostles, seven were on Peter's fishing trip here. We're given five of their names: Simon Peter, Thomas, Nathanael, James, and John. Then we're told two others were there. One could have been Peter's brother, Andrew. The other could have been Nathanael's buddy, Philip. Or it could be that we're to occupy the other two seats and learn with the disciples.

Interestingly enough, Jesus had told them to go up to the mountains in Galilee and wait for Him there. But they didn't stay there. Before the Lord came, Peter said, "Let's go back to fishing" and was able to talk the rest of them into going back to familiar boats and a lake they once worked. We'd almost rather do anything than wait on the Lord, wouldn't we?

But I think Peter was driven by something more than just impatience. He must have felt completely disqualified. The last couple of weeks had been a big bust for him. He had shot off his mouth time and again. He had told the disciples how much more faithful he'd be than they. He had denied the Lord with swearing and cursing. And although he had met with Him, it didn't seem like everything was right. Unable to forgive himself, Peter didn't feel he could serve the Lord in any capacity. What he was good at was fishing. The problem was, the Lord had called him away from that.

It had been three years ago on the same lake—maybe even in the same boat—that Peter had made a commitment to the Lord to forsake everything when Jesus said, "Follow Me and I'll make you a fisher of men." But that was before he had denied Him three times to save his own neck. Peter had expected better of himself even if Jesus hadn't. So now he wanted to go back to his old life since he felt disqualified from anything more. And it wasn't hard to convince everyone else to join him. Just waiting for someone to lead the way, they immediately climbed in the boat. But the Lord had called these men and their calling had been very clear. They were supposed to be meeting on a mountain somewhere around the lake. Instead, they were following Peter in his discouragement, back to their old life.

That night they caught nothing—which is no surprise, because not only is it darkest when you go back to the old life from which God called you, but you always come up empty-handed. Seven professional fishermen in a boat with all of their cumulative experience couldn't coax one fish into the net. They had their favorite spots and had been able to make a living at it for years—but now it wasn't working.

They would have to learn that their fishing life was over, because God had called them to follow Him. And when God calls, going back is of no use. So often we begin following the Lord and then, for whatever reason, we stop and go back to the old way of life as if that would be more comfortable. But fruit comes when we do what God says, no matter how ill equipped, disqualified, or uncomfortable we feel.

> But when the morning had now come, Jesus stood on the shore; yet the disciples did not know that it was Jesus.
>
> —John 21:4

Light dawned on their all-night struggle and Jesus knew exactly where they were. He didn't go up to the mountain and search. He knew right where to find them. But, like every post-resurrection appearance, although He knew where they were and what they were going through, they wouldn't be able to recognize Him until He revealed Himself.

> Then Jesus said to them, "Children, have you any food?" They answered Him, "No."
>
> —John 21:5

Jesus didn't say, "Hey, you backsliding, ex-apostle rebels, catch anything in your pursuit of your old life?" No, He said, "children," *paidion* in Greek, a word a parent would use, meaning "dear little kids." The worst thing you can do to a fisherman is ask him what he's caught when he hasn't caught anything. Maybe for the fishermen it all looked good on paper: seven guys with fishing experience, same boat, same business license, and same lake, vendors, and distribution network. They were sure to do just fine, they thought. Christians do that sometimes. They look back with great longing at the days before they were saved. But three years earlier, Jesus had found these guys ready for new life. It wasn't as great back then as they might have thought now.

Satan often will seek to draw us back with a longing for the old days. Of Abraham and those who went with him, Hebrews says they wandered the land of promise by faith. If they had called to mind the country from which they had come, they might have desired to return—but they desired a better country. It's a good thing to be delivered from the world.

> And He said to them, "Cast the net on the right side of the boat, and you will find some." So they cast, and now they were not able to draw it in because of the multitude of fish.
>
> —John 21:6

Jesus told these fishermen-turned-disciples-turned-fishermen to cast their net on the right side, because whatever the Lord tells you to do is right, isn't it? Success comes when you obey His voice rather than try to do it on your own. And soon they had so many fish in the net, they couldn't get it on board.

> Therefore that disciple whom Jesus loved said to Peter, "It is the Lord!" Now
> when Simon Peter heard that it was the Lord, he put on his outer garment (for
> he had removed it), and plunged into the sea. But the other disciples came in
> the little boat (for they were not far from land, but about two hundred cubits),
> dragging the net with fish. Then, as soon as they had come to land, they saw a
> fire of coals there, and fish laid on it, and bread.
>
> —John 21:7–9

For Peter and John, this whole thing struck a familiar chord. It sounds like that day in
Luke 5 when Jesus had called them to be fishers of men. When John told Peter it was Jesus
on shore, he abandoned the catch, abandoned his friends, and abandoned the purpose for
which he had come because his heart wasn't really in it. His heart was for the Lord. It's just
that he didn't see Jesus as having a place for him.

A hundred yards offshore, six disciples fought to land this huge catch they had been
unsuccessful in finding all night. By the time everyone got to shore, Jesus had plenty of
fish already and was making breakfast. With the same word for *coals* used in both places,
I suspect that the fire of coals on the beach was a painful reminder to Peter of the last
barbeque he had attended—the one where he had denied Jesus.

> Jesus said to them, "Bring some of the fish which you have just caught." Simon
> Peter went up and dragged the net to land, full of large fish, one hundred and
> fifty-three; and although there were so many, the net was not broken.
>
> —John 21:10–11

Hearing Jesus' request to them as a group, Peter went to do the impossible on his own.
What six men couldn't do in getting the net to shore, Peter could. Enabled to do what Jesus
said, he went with great excitement to accomplish God's purpose. John was so impressed
with the catch that he remembered the exact number of fish. And even with so many, the
net didn't break. He'd never seen anything like it.

> Jesus said to them, "Come and eat breakfast." Yet none of the disciples dared ask
> Him, "Who are You?"—knowing that it was the Lord. Jesus then came and took
> the bread and gave it to them, and likewise the fish. This is now the third time
> Jesus showed Himself to His disciples after He was raised from the dead.
>
> —John 21:12–14

After Easter, and the following Sunday with Thomas, this would be Jesus' third recorded
appearance to the disciples. He made them breakfast and, in the midst of eating, cooking,
and fellowship, He spoke to Peter in love.

> So when they had eaten breakfast, Jesus said to Simon Peter, "Simon, son of Jonah, do you love Me more than these?"
>
> —John 21:15

Jesus began by calling Peter by his old name, Simon—the one he had used before Jesus had renamed him Peter. Peter had been told of his fall in the Upper Room before Jesus' death but he hadn't believed it then. He had in anger boasted that even if everyone else in the group denied Him, he would go to his death for Jesus. So Jesus returned to this issue to show Peter that confidence in self is an attribute of the old person, not the new.

I love Jesus' words because there is no help in minimizing the seriousness of sin. "Simon, do you love Me more than these?" Jesus asked, using the word for God's love that the Greeks translated *agapao*. In the Greek construction, the word *these* could refer to the fish. "Do you love Me more than these 153 fish that will get your business off to a running start?" It's a good question. We're supposed to love the Lord more than our jobs and hobbies, more than income and gain. But we can only prove that when we make the choice between the two.

I suspect, however, that *these* referred to the other disciples because that's where Peter had begun his fall, bragging he never would turn away, even if they all stumbled. Peter now is saved with the Holy Spirit dwelling within him. So Jesus asked, "Do you love Me with that selfless, sacrificial, godly love that only the Lord can impart into the hearts of the saints?"

> He said to Him, "Yes, Lord; You know that I love You."
>
> —John 21:15

Peter, in his response, changed the word love to *phileo*. It is the word in the Bible for brotherly affection, or the love of a husband for his wife, or a mother for her children. It is the highest expression of love a person can engender without God's Spirit. Peter was not boasting anymore. It was a different Peter already. He was cautious now. "I love You the best I am able as a son, as a brother, and as a member of Your family," he said. "I'll give You everything I've got. That's all I know to do. I can't use the word *agape*, but I'll do my best."

> He said to him, "Feed My lambs."
>
> —John 21:15

I like the fact that Jesus didn't say, "Is that it?" Instead, it's almost as if He said, "OK, Peter. I can live with that. That's the kind of honesty you need."

The Greek word for *feed* is *bosko*. The word for *lambs* is *arnion*, which is the word for baby sheep. "Take the time, Peter, to bring food to these little sheep of Mine," Jesus said. "That's what I want you to do."

> He said to him again a second time, "Simon, son of Jonah, do you love Me?"
> —John 21:16

Jesus used the same word, *agapao*, but this time left off the words *more than these*.

> "Yes, Lord; You know that I love You."
> —John 21:16

Again, using the word *phileo*, Peter said, "You know I have a deep affection for You."

> He said to him, "Tend My sheep."
> —John 21:16

This time Jesus changed the word from *feed* to *tend*, from *bosko* to *poimaino*, which means "to shepherd." And He changed the word from *lambs* to *sheep*—or *probaton*, a term for grown sheep. "I want you to provide food for the little ones and direction and care to the older ones," Jesus said. "That's your calling."

> He said to him the third time, "Simon, son of Jonah, do you love Me?"
> —John 21:17

"Do you *phileo* Me?" Jesus asked, this time lowering the standard to human best. Twice He had asked, "Do you love Me with God's love?" And twice Peter had said, "I love You with human love." So here Jesus said, "Peter, do you really love Me with human love?"

> Peter was grieved because He said to him the third time, "Do you love Me?"
> —John 21:17

Peter realized what Jesus was saying. He wanted to love Jesus more than anything. But he had no confidence left.

> And he said to Him, "Lord, You know all things; You know that I love You."
> —John 21:17

"To the best that I'm able with what I have to offer," Peter answered. "You know all things." And he used the word *eido*, which means to know with a thorough kind of insight. "You clearly see me. You know exactly what I'm all about. You know my emotional attachment to You. You know I could never love You like You love me." These were words spoken by one with his conscience against the wall, broken before Jesus.

Jesus said to him, "Feed My sheep."

—John 21:17

Jesus used the word *feed* from verse 15 and *sheep* from verse 16 as if to say, "Care for them all, Peter. That's what I want you to do if you love Me."

After His threefold questioning of Peter that corresponded to Peter's three-fold denial of Him, Jesus installed Peter as a pastor to feed and lead what would be a young and growing flock.

Peter had come to the Sea of Galilee thinking he was done. "Let's go fishing," he had said. But he finished breakfast knowing God had other plans, even for a failure like him.

When we read the book of Acts, and Peter's letters written twenty-five or thirty years after this, we find he was able to look back on his life and see all God had done. God certainly would use Peter the next thirty years. He would be a moving force for the church. He would get to preach and see thousands saved. He would catch plenty in the net. And the net wouldn't break.

I think Peter might be one of the best arguments in the New Testament that God is good at making heroes and useful vessels out of those who have fallen and failed. God isn't through because you are, and He isn't unable because you think you are. There's a lot of junk in most of our lives, but God can make of you a vessel for honor if, like Peter, you're broken before Him.

The Gospels end with the story of Peter's restoration because that's why Jesus came—so fallen people could be made whole. What a day this must have been for Peter. I don't think he went back to fishing again.

SCRIPTURE INDEX

John